UNDERSTANDING
Motor Development

———

Infants, Children,
Adolescents, Adults

Third Edition

UNDERSTANDING
Motor Development

---

*Infants, Children,
Adolescents, Adults*

DAVID L. GALLAHUE

Indiana University

JOHN C. OZMUN

Indiana State University

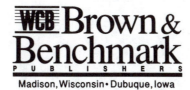

**WGB Brown &
Benchmark**
PUBLISHERS

Madison, Wisconsin • Dubuque, Iowa

11-94

Book Team

Editor *Scott Spoolman*
Production Editor *Jane C. Morgan*
Art Editor *Tina Flanagan*
Photo Editor *Shirley M. Lanners*
Permissions Coordinator *LouAnn K. Wilson*
Visuals/Design Developmental Consultant *Marilyn A. Phelps*
Publishing Services Specialist *Sherry Padden*
Visuals/Design Freelance Specialist *Mary L. Christianson*
Marketing Manager *Pamela S. Cooper*
Advertising Coordinator *Susan J. Butler*

**Brown &
Benchmark**

A Division of Wm. C. Brown Communications, Inc.

Executive Vice President/General Manager *Thomas E. Doran*
Vice President/Editor in Chief *Edgar J. Laube*
Vice President of Marketing and Sales Systems *Eric Ziegler*
Director of Production *Vickie Putman Caughron*
Director of Custom and Electronic Publishing *Chris Rogers*

Wm. C. Brown Communications, Inc.

President and Chief Executive Officer *G. Franklin Lewis*
Corporate Senior Vice President and Chief Financial Officer *Robert Chesterman*
Corporate Senior Vice President and President of Manufacturing *Roger Meyer*

Cover design by Sailer & Cook Creative Services

Cover photos © David Young-Wolff/PhotoEdit, © Myrleen Ferguson
Cate/PhotoEdit, © Tony Freeman/PhotoEdit, © Myrleen Ferguson
Cate/PhotoEdit (Clockwise from upper left).

Interior photos *Section 1:* © Bob Coyle; *Sections 2, 3, 5:* © Jean-Claude Lejeune; *Sections 4, 6:* © James Shaffer; *p. 454:* © Edwin
Reschke.

Copyedited by Kendal Hegamaster Gladish

Copyright © 1982 by John Wiley & Sons, Inc.

Copyright © 1989, 1995 by Wm. C. Brown Communications, Inc. All
rights reserved

A Times Mirror Company

Library of Congress Catalog Card Number: 93–72017

ISBN 0–697–16597–3

Printed in the United States of America

10 9 8 7 6 5 4 3 2 1

As always, To *the Sunshine of My Life:*
Ellie, David Lee, Jennifer and Dan

David L. Gallahue

To *the Treasures of My Heart:*
Ruth, Chet, Gus, and John

John C. Ozmun

Contents

Preface to the Third Edition

Understanding Motor Development is written for students taking a first course in motor development. It is presented in an easy-to-understand and easy-to-use manner to be of significant value to educators from a variety of disciplines including kinesiology (physical education), physical and occupational therapy, special education, early childhood education, and elementary and secondary education. The text attempts to provide both a descriptive and an explanatory profile of the individual from birth through adulthood.

Each chapter begins with a list of **Chapter Competencies** outlining what students should know at the conclusion of the chapter. These are followed by an introduction to the specific topic and an up-to-date research-based discussion. **Chapter Concepts** are highlighted throughout each chapter. These help the reader focus more clearly on the key issues being discussed, and reinforce the importance of obtaining a conceptual grasp of the process of motor development. The **Summary** found at the end of each chapter provides the reader with a condensed overview and delineation of the major points discussed. A list of **Terms to Remember** is presented for readers who desire a quick self-test on important terms used in the chapter. **Critical Readings** conclude each chapter and refer the reader to additional sources of up-to-date information. A comprehensive **Bibliography** is found at the end of the text. Each chapter contains a wealth of tables, figures, and line drawings designed to synthesize information and provide the reader with a clearer understanding of the topic being discussed.

Development is a process that begins at conception and continues throughout life. With the rapidly expanding knowledge base in adult development, this third edition truly takes a life span approach by discussing motor development from conception through adulthood. Also, we have chosen to include primary cognitive and affective factors that affect motor development during each of these periods and have expanded coverage of these topics. Furthermore, this edition now incorporates Dynamical Systems Theory along with the phases and stages of motor development to help provide the reader with an explanatory basis for development as well as a descriptive profile.

Section One, Background, provides the reader with essential introductory information on the study of motor development. Chapter 1, *Understanding Motor Development: An Overview*, examines the history, methods of study, research problems, and terminology used in the study of motor development. Chapter 2, *Models of Human Development,* offers a discussion of developmental models of child development. Particular attention is given to the works of Jean Piaget and Erik Erikson and the implications of their work for motor development. In Chapter 3, *Factors Affecting Motor Development,* there is an important discussion of critical factors within the individual, environment, and movement tasks that influence the process of development throughout life. Section I concludes with Chapter 4, *Motor Development: A Theoretical Model.* It is here that a theoretical framework for studying the process of motor development is presented. The phases and stages of this life span model, as well as the subsystems of the task, the individual, and the environment serve as the organizational framework for the remainder of the text.

Section Two, Infancy, deals with a variety of important developmental topics of infancy. Chapter 5, *Prenatal Factors Affecting Development,* is devoted to discussion of those factors prior to birth that may affect later motor development. *Prenatal and Infant Growth* is the topic of Chapter 6. This chapter provides the reader with a descriptive profile of early growth processes. Chapter 7 examines *Reflexes and Rhythmical Stereotypies* in the neonate and young infant. Particular attention is given to the integration of both into the expanding movement repertoire of the young child. Chapter 8, *Rudimentary Movement Abilities,* discusses the rapidly expanding movement repertoire of infants. The major stability, locomotor, and manipulative tasks of this period are outlined and summarized. An extensive discussion of *Infant Perception* in Chapter 9 concludes the section on infancy. This chapter relates perceptual development to the motor behavior of infants.

Section Three, Childhood, provides the reader with a wealth of important information about childhood motor development. Chapter 10, *Childhood Growth and Motor Development,* offers a general overview of cognitive, affective, and motor characteristics during early and later childhood. This sets the stage for the three chapters that follow. Chapter 11, *Fundamental Movement Abilities,* provides a practical, easy-to-use, three-stage approach (initial, elementary, mature) to observing and assessing the fundamental movement patterns of childhood. Mechanically correct line drawings provide a visual description that coincides with a brief verbal description of each stage, along with frequently encountered developmental difficulties. *Physical Development of Children* is the topic of Chapter 12. A review of the latest information on children's health-related fitness and motor fitness is presented along with information on fitness training for children. *Childhood Perception and Perceptual-Motor Development* is the topic of Chapter 13. Important information on both of these topics is reviewed and synthesized with a view toward their complex interaction with the motor behavior of the individual. Chapter 14 concludes the section on childhood with a discussion of *Childhood Self-Concept Development*. The latest information on self-esteem is reviewed along with the role of movement as an important facilitator of a positive self-concept.

Section Four, Adolescence, examines a number of important topics. Chapter 15, *Adolescent Growth, Puberty, and Reproductive Maturation,* opens this section with a wealth of important and useful information about physical change during this critical developmental period. Chapter 16, *Specialized Movement Abilities,* centers on the topics of specialized movement skill development, fostering improvement, and the developmental sequence of specialized movement skills. This is followed by a discussion of the *Physical Abilities of Adolescents* in Chapter 17 with a view toward their rapidly changing health-related and performance-related fitness. Chapter 18 concludes the section on adolescence with a discussion of *Adolescent Socialization*. Particular attention is given to the role of physical activity in the process of positive socialization.

Section Five, Adulthood, is new to the third edition and provides the latest information available on the rapidly developing area of adult motor development. Chapter 19, *Physiological Changes in Adults,* attempts to answer the question: Why do we age? A lively discussion is offered concerning changes in the adult musculoskeletal system, central nervous system, circulatory and respiratory systems, and sensory systems. Chapter 20, *Motor Performance in Adults,* examines reaction time, balance and postural control, falls, gait, activities for daily living, and the elite performer. Chapter 21, *Psychosocial Development in Adults,* examines a variety of psychological and social factors that influence and are influenced by the motor development and movement abilities of the aging adult.

Section Six, Programming, synthesizes information from the preceding sections. Chapter 22, *Developmental Physical Activity: A Curricular Model,* may be the most important to the field professional. This chapter presents a developmental approach to systematic movement skill acquisition throughout life. Numerous diagrams are used to synthesize the concepts presented in this chapter. This practical application chapter forms the basis for a companion text, *Developmental Physical Education For Today's Children* (Gallahue, 1993), which puts the concepts and principles described here to practical use through the implementation of developmentally appropriate movement programs. Finally, Chapter 23, *Assessing Motor Behavior,* takes a critical look at selected motor assessment instruments for infants and children, adolescents, and adults with a view to their utility in a variety of settings. Although this chapter is last, it is important for the reader to appreciate that all developmentally based programming begins with assessment as a means of ensuring individually appropriate educational experiences.

As with all authors there are numerous people to thank for their many contributions both direct and indirect. With this, the third edition of *Understanding Motor Development*, we would especially like to acknowledge the following:

Our Professional Colleagues: for their diligence and persistence in the pursuit and acquisition of knowledge.

Our Students: for their enthusiasm, inquisitive minds, and dedication to personal as well as professional excellence.

Our Publisher and Editor: for their confidence in our abilities.

Our Families: for their support, acceptance, love, and prayers.

Our God: for His constant presence and the knowledge that in Him and through Him all things are possible.

David L. Gallahue
Bloomington, IN
John C. Ozmun
Terre Haute, IN

Chapter **1**

Understanding Motor Development: An Overview

CHAPTER COMPETENCIES

Upon completion of this chapter you should be able to:

- *Describe the research of several historical and contemporary scholars in motor development*
- *Compare and contrast motor development with other study in human movement (motor learning, exercise physiology, biomechanics)*
- *Demonstrate knowledge of the various forms of analysis that are used in the study of motor development*
- *Discuss advantages and shortcomings of the major methodologies associated with the study of change*
- *Identify key methods of assessing biological maturity*
- *Describe common problems associated with the study of motor development*
- *List the chronological age classifications of human development across the life span*
- *Define terms unique to physical growth and biological maturation*

The study of human development has been of keen interest to scholars and educators for many years. Knowledge of the processes of development lies at the very core of education whether it be in the classroom, the gymnasium, or on the playing field. Without sound knowledge of the developmental aspects of human behavior, educators can only guess at appropriate educational techniques and intervention procedures. Educators who are developmentally based in their instruction incorporate learning experiences that are appropriate not only for the chronological ages, but more importantly, for the developmental levels of the individuals being taught. Developmental educators recognize that, although instruction is an important aspect of the teaching-learning process, instruction does not *explain* learning, development does.

Concept 1.1 Instruction does not *explain* learning, development does.

Considerable research has been conducted and a number of texts have been written on the process of development. The research conducted on the developmental aspects of movement behavior has, until recently, been more limited in scope and magnitude than that conducted on the cognitive and affective processes of development. Historically, developmental psychologists have tended to be only marginally interested in motor development, and then frequently only as a visual indicator of cognitive functioning. Likewise, social psychologists interested in the process of affective development have only given fleeting attention to movement and its influence on the social and emotional development of the individual. Since the primary thrust of motor development research has come from the many branches of psychology, it is natural that motor development has frequently been viewed in terms of its potential influences on other areas of behavior, and as a convenient and readily observable means of studying behavior, rather than a phenomenon worthy of study for its own sake.

Concept 1.2 The study of motor development, until recently, has been overshadowed by interest in the cognitive and affective processes of development.

The study of motor development as a specialized field of scholarly inquiry by kinesiologists (physical educators) did not gain real impetus until the 1970s. Motor development is a legitimate area of study that cuts across the fields of exercise physiology, biomechanics, motor learning, and motor control, as well as the fields of developmental psychology and social psychology. The quest for understanding progressed at a slow but steady pace in the 1960s, and then began to escalate in the 1970s as developmental kinesiologists and psychologists alike shifted their focus away from a normative-descriptive approach back to the study of the underlying developmental processes.

During the 1980s an ever-expanding body of research by a new generation of scholars heightened interest in the study of motor development. An unprecedented amount of theory-based research has been conducted from the 1980s into the 1990s with developmentalists from a variety of fields interfacing with motor development scholars. The study of motor development has taken its place as a legitimate area of scientific inquiry within the fields of kinesiology and developmental psychology. Scholars are currently studying both the underlying processes of development and its many and varied products.

Human development is often studied from a compartmentalized standpoint, which has led to a rather unbalanced view of the developmental process. Development is frequently studied in terms of domains (cognitive, affective, psychomotor) or age-related behaviors (infancy, childhood, adolescence, adulthood, middle age, old age), or from a biological, environmental, or movement task perspective (Figure 1.1). It is crucial that those interested in the study of motor development *not* compound the error of compartmentalization by replicating this model. The study of development must be viewed from the perspective of the totality of humankind. It must recognize that, at the very least, there is an interaction between the individual's biological make-up and his or her own unique environmental circumstances.

Many motor developmentalists are, however, taking this view one step further in recognizing that the specific physical and mechanical demands of a movement task itself actually transact with the individual (biological factors) and the environment (experience or learning factors). See Figure 1.2 for a visual representation of this important concept. Such a transactional model implies that factors within the task, the individual, and the environment are not only influenced by one another (interaction), but also may be modified (transaction) by one another.

The information contained here is not the last word on the process of motor development, but it is an honest attempt to be the latest word. Research and study in this area is expanding rapidly. It is difficult to encompass all that is happening in this unfolding field, and much that you read here is in danger of being obsolete in just a few years. If it is to

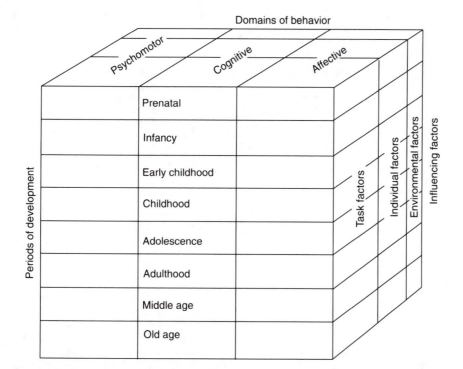

Figure 1.1
The compartmentalized view of human development

(Figure labels: Domains of behavior — Psychomotor, Cognitive, Affective; Periods of development — Prenatal, Infancy, Early childhood, Childhood, Adolescence, Adulthood, Middle age, Old age; Influencing factors — Task factors, Individual factors, Environmental factors)

be of any real value to the field professional, the study of motor development must not focus only on the skilled performer in controlled laboratory settings. It must also analyze and document what individuals of all ages can do under both normal and augmented circumstances. Our knowledge base is constantly growing, and even as this text is being written new hypotheses are being formulated and new conclusions being drawn from the excellent research being conducted throughout North America and the rest of the world.

Life Span Study of the Developmental Process

Development is a continuous process beginning at conception and ceasing only at death. Development encompasses all aspects of human behavior and as a result may only be artificially separated into "domains," "stages," or "age periods." The growing acceptance of the concept of "life span" development is important to keep in mind. Just as study of the skilled athlete during adolescence and adulthood is important, so also is the study of movement during infancy, childhood, and later life. There is much to be gained by learning about motor development at all ages and by viewing it as a lifelong process.

Figure 1.2
A transactional
view of causation in
motor development

Concept 1.3   Development is a lifelong process beginning at conception and ceasing only at death.

A life span perspective does not view development as domain-specific, stagelike, or age-dependent. Instead, the life span perspective suggests that *some* aspects of one's development can be conceptualized into domains, as being stagelike or age-related, while others cannot. Furthermore, the concept of life span development encompasses all developmental change, not just the positive changes generally associated with childhood, but also the changes that take place during adulthood and the aging process.

Motor development is highly specific. The once commonly accepted notion of *general* motor ability has been disproved to the satisfaction of most scholars in the field. Superior ability in one area does not guarantee similar ability in others. The outmoded concept that one either possesses or does not possess ability in movement activities has been replaced by the concept that each person has specific capabilities within each of the many performance areas. Various factors involving movement abilities and physical performance interact in complex ways with cognitive and affective development. Each of these factors is in turn affected by a wide variety of biological, environmental, and specific task-related demands.

The process of development, and more specifically the process of motor development, should constantly remind us of the individuality of the learner. Each individual has a unique timetable for the acquisition and development of movement abilities. Although the "biological clock" is rather specific when it comes to the sequence of movement skill acquisition, the rate and extent of development is individually determined and dramatically influenced by the performance demands of the task itself. Typical age periods of development are just that: typical, and no more. Age periods merely represent approximate time ranges during which certain behaviors may be observed. Overreliance on these time periods would negate the concepts of continuity, specificity, and the individuality of the developmental process.

Concept 1.4   Development is age-related but not age-dependent.

The study of motor development dates back only to the early part of the twentieth century. A number of methods of study have evolved, and a variety of problems have influenced both the quantity and quality of information available. The following sections briefly review the history, methods of study, and problems encountered in the study of motor development.

History of Motor Development

The first serious attempts at the study of motor development were from a maturational perspective, led by Arnold Gesell (1928) and Myrtle McGraw (1935). The maturationalists contended that development is a function of inborn biological processes that result in a universal sequence in infant movement skill acquisition. Since these early pioneering efforts, their names have become legend in motor development research. In fact, much of what we know about the sequence of infant movement skill acquisition is based on the descriptive work of Gesell (1928) and McGraw (1935) as well as that of Mary Shirley (1931) and Nancy Bayley (1935). The surge of research that these scholars brought about was largely motivated by their interest in the relationship of maturation and learning processes to cognitive development. In their separate but remarkably similar studies, these early researchers chronicled the well-known sequences of motor development during infancy. Their naturalistic observations of children provided a great deal of information about the sequential progression of normal development from the acquisition of early rudimentary movements to mature patterns of behavior. Although the rate at which children acquired selected movement abilities varied somewhat, these investigations revealed that the sequence of acquisition was universal and generally invariant.

The studies of Gesell and Thompson (1929, 1934) and McGraw (1935, 1940) are classics in the use of the co-twin control method of studying development. Their research provided considerable insight into the influence of augmented and restricted practice on the acquisition of various movement abilities, and raised numerous questions concerning the effects of early practice. Monica Wild's study of throwing behavior (1938) was the first inquiry into developmental movement patterns in school-aged children. Unfortunately, after her study, which was outstanding in terms of depth and completeness, there was little interest in exploring the various aspects of motor development until the end of the Second World War.

After World War II a new breed of motor developmentalists emerged. Led by Anna Espenschade, Ruth Glassow, and G. Lawrence Rarick (as cited in Rarick 1981), these individuals focused on describing the motor performance capabilities of children. It is important to note that all three were physical educators, and as such were interested in understanding the outcomes of motor development for its own sake. Furthermore, their work focused on movement skill acquisition in school-aged youth rather than on infant motor performance. Although the extent of research during this period was limited and the pace slow, the work of these three early leaders did much to keep motor development alive as a legitimate field of scholarly inquiry. In fact, Clark and Whitall (1989) credit Espenschade, Glassow, and Rarick for motor development's emergence as a separate field of study within the physical education (kinesiology) profession.

Since 1960 the knowledge base in the study of motor development has grown steadily. The work of Lolas Halverson (1966) and several of her graduate students at the University of Wisconsin (Halverson and Roberton, 1966; Halverson, Roberton, and Harper, 1973; Halverson and Williams, 1985) on the acquisition of mature fundamental movement patterns did much to revive interest in children's research because of its emphasis on identifying the mechanisms behind the acquisition of skill rather than the final skill itself. *Fundamental Motor Patterns* (1983) by Ralph Wickstrom and the research conducted by Vern Seefeldt (1972) and his associates (Seefeldt and Haubenstricker, 1982; Branta, Haubenstricker, and Seefeldt, 1984) at Michigan State University on fundamental movement skill acquisition set the stage for the exciting research of the 1980s and beyond.

During the 1980s and 1990s the emphasis of study in motor development has again shifted dramatically. Instead of focusing on the product of development as with the normative/descriptive approaches of the preceding three decades, emphasis shifted back to understanding the underlying processes involved in motor development. Researchers led by the seminal work of Kugler, Kelso, and Turvey (1982), formulated new theoretical frameworks for the control and development of motor behavior. Since then the work of Esther Thelen and her colleagues (1987a, 1987b, 1991), Jane Clark and her colleagues (1988, 1989), and others led to the formulation of a dynamical systems theory of motor development which is guiding much of the research being conducted at the present time.

Concept 1.5   Historically, motor development has gone through periods that have emphasized various explanations of the developmental process.

In summary, the years from about 1930 through World War II could be characterized as the "maturational period" and those from 1946 through the 1970s as the "normative/descriptive period" for the study of motor development. The time from the 1980s to the present may be described as the "process-oriented period" (Clark and Whitall, 1989). In fact, the study of motor development began with a process orientation (i.e., studying the underlying biological processes governing maturation), then shifted to a product orientation (i.e., describing the mechanics of various stages of movement skill acquisition, and developing normative criteria for a variety of motor performance measures), and moved back to a process orientation (i.e., explaining the processes causing change in motor behavior over time). Important research is now being conducted throughout North America and much of the rest of the world on the critically important topic of motor development from infancy through adulthood.

Methods of Studying Development

There are three ways in which motor development is studied: the longitudinal study, the cross-sectional study, and the mixed longitudinal study. Because motor development research involves the study of changes that occur in motor behavior over time, the *longitudinal method* of study is ideal and the only true means of studying development.

The *longitudinal method* of data collection attempts to explain behavior changes over time (i.e., developmental time) and involves charting various aspects of an individual's motor behavior for several years. The longitudinal approach allows one to observe changes in selected variables over time and, although time consuming, treats the study of motor development as a function of developmental time rather than age (i.e., real time). The longitudinal method involves study of a single group of subjects, all at the same age, over several years. The major purpose of the longitudinal study is to measure age-related changes in behavior. It does not, however, permit measurement of age differences in development. In short, the longitudinal method permits study of intraindividual change over time.

The Medford Boys Growth Study conducted by H. Harrison Clarke (1971) from 1956 to 1968 is one of the most complete longitudinal studies of growth ever carried out. The motor development study begun in 1966 by Vern Seefeldt at Michigan State University and carried on today by John Haubenstricker, Crystal Branta, and their colleagues, has collected extensive anthropometric data as well as thousands of feet of film footage on children performing selected fundamental movement skills. Both are fine examples of longitudinal studies of growth and motor development.

It can easily be seen that the longitudinal method of data collection is very time consuming. Additionally, the dropout rate is often great because subjects move or become ill or disabled. Therefore, large numbers of subjects need to be tested to retain a representative sample at the end of the 5- to 10-year study period. Problems in methodology and design are also likely to creep into the longitudinal study. Varying levels of reliability and objectivity in testers over the course of the study period may cause problems in data interpretation. The potential accrued learning effects from repeated performances on the measured items have also proven troublesome. These difficulties have prompted many researchers to opt for the cross-sectional approach.

The *cross-sectional method* of study permits the researcher to collect data on different groups of people at varying age levels at the same point in time. The major purpose of the cross-sectional study is to measure age-related differences in behavior. This method does not permit measurement of age-related change, and has attracted controversy in recent years. Basically, the cross-sectional method yields only average differences in groups across real time and not individual changes across developmental time. The basic assumption behind the cross-sectional study has been that random selection of subjects will provide a representative sample of the population for each age group tested. It is questionable, however, that this assumption can be met in most cases. In reality, cross-sectional studies, while simple and direct, can only describe typical behaviors at the specific ages studied. As a result they are not considered by most authorities to be true developmental studies. The problem is that historically the vast majority of motor development research has used the cross-sectional approach.

To overcome the glaring weakness of the cross-sectional technique, developmental psychologists and motor development researchers have begun to look more closely at combining the cross-sectional and longitudinal research designs in individual research investigations. This sequential method of studying development, or *mixed-longitudinal method,* as it is often termed, combines the best aspects of the cross-sectional and longitudinal methods. It covers all of the possible data points necessary for describing and/or explaining both differences and change over time as functions of development as well as functions of age (Schaie and Baltes, 1975). Basically, subjects are selected and studied cross-sectionally, but also followed longitudinally for several years. This permits comparison of cross-sectional data results with longitudinal results, and serves as a means of validating or refuting age-related changes with true developmental changes. It also gives the researcher an opportunity to analyze and report on preliminary data early in the investigation rather than waiting five or more years.

Table 1.1 Primary Methods of Studying Motor Development

Longitudinal study: The same subjects are studied over a 5- to 10-year period

Cross-sectional study: Different subjects representing a variety of ages are studied at the same point in time

Mixed longitudinal study: A sequential method of studying development that combines essential elements of both the longitudinal and cross-sectional methods.

Experimental method: Random assignment of subjects to treatment conditions. Rigid control of influencing variables

Cross-cultural: May or may not be experimental design. Comparison of various factors across different cultures

Naturalistic observation: Nonobtrusive observation of behavior in the natural environment

Survey: Group or personal interviews on a series of selected topics to reveal attitudes, opinions

Case history: Report on individual subjects providing a variety of detailed background information

---

Concept 1.6 Whereas age-related changes in motor behavior can be studied through cross-sectional research designs, true *developmental* change can only be studied through longitudinal and mixed longitudinal designs.

The longitudinal, cross-sectional, and mixed longitudinal methods of study may be applied to a variety of research formats. Table 1.1 provides a brief overview of these formats for studying development. An investigation may take the form of an experimental study, the most powerful method because of the rigid controls required, or it may be cross-cultural, involving naturalistic observation, surveys, interviews, case history reports, or a combination of these techniques.

As noted earlier, there has been a shift in the study of motor development from process to product and now back to process again. The early researchers emphasized the importance of *process-oriented research*, that is, form and function. H. M. Halverson (Halverson, 1931; Halverson, 1937), Shirley (1931), and Wild (1938) all focused on the sequential acquisition of movement patterns. Their suggestions for studying the process of motor skill development went largely unheeded until the 1980s when interest in such study was revived; it has been a focus of motor development research ever since. The use of cinematography, electrogoniometry, and electromyographic techniques in conjunction with computer analysis has enhanced our knowledge of the process of movement and its underlying motor mechanisms.

Product-oriented research, or research on the performance capabilities of individuals has been conducted for many years. This type of research is concerned typically with the outcome of the individual's performance. The distance a ball travels, the velocity with which it can be kicked, or how far one can jump are examples of motor performance scores. Strength, endurance, power, balance, and flexibility as measured by a particular battery of tests are examples of fitness performance scores.

Concept 1.7   Motor development may be studied from either a *process* or a *product* orientation.

The relationship between process and product, or form ratings and performance scores, is an interesting and largely unresearched area. Wickstrom (1983) indicated, however, that, "There is a positive but not direct causal relationship between form and performance. Mature form enhances performance, but good performance is not totally dependent upon mature form" (p. 6). Factors such as strength, speed of movement, agility, coordination, and reaction time have an impact on performance abilities but may not influence form to any significant degree.

Problems in Studying Motor Development

Data collection, whether it be product- or process-oriented, can be difficult when infants, children, adolescents, and older adults are being studied. Problems in data collection are the chief cause of the scarcity of motor development research information on infants and children.

Infants and preschoolers tend to be challenging subjects unless procedures that accommodate their natural independent natures are adopted. The two primary problems associated with good data collection are inhibited or exaggerated performance and inconsistency in performance. Special precautions must be taken to eliminate, as far as possible, the potential bias of the data caused by these factors. Time-consuming orientation periods and modified data collection procedures that simulate a more naturalistic setting are frequently employed to put a child at ease. This still will not ensure consistency in performance.

For example, when a young child is asked to "throw the ball overhand as far as you can," he or she may throw first with the right hand and then casually begin throwing with the left. Some throws may be overhand, others sidearm or underhand, even after precise instructions on the overhand technique. Some throws may go several yards, others only a few feet. Some throws may closely approximate mature patterns of action while others may look like shot-put attempts or grenade-tossing exercises. The experimenter must exercise considerable patience and work with the child until he or she has demonstrated what the experimenter judges to be a maximum or representative effort using the most

Table 1.2 Conventional Chronological Classifications of Age

Period	Approximate Age Range
I PRENATAL LIFE	(CONCEPTION TO BIRTH)
A. Period of the Zygote	Conception–1 week
B. Embryonic Period	2 weeks–8 weeks
C. Fetal Period	8 weeks–Birth
II INFANCY	(BIRTH TO 24 MONTHS)
A. Neonatal Period	Birth–1 month
B. Early Infancy	1–12 months
C. Later Infancy	12–24 months
III CHILDHOOD	(2 YEARS TO 10 YEARS)
A. Toddler Period	24–36 months
B. Early Childhood	3–5 years
C. Middle/Later Childhood	6–10 years
IV ADOLESCENCE	(10–20 YEARS)
A. Prepubescence	10–12 years (F)
	11–13 years (M)
B. Postpubescence	12–18 years (F)
	14–20 years (M)
V YOUNG ADULTHOOD	(20–40 YEARS)
A. Novice Period	20–30 years
B. Settling Period	30–40 years
VI MIDDLE ADULTHOOD	(40–60 YEARS)
A. Mid Life Transition	40–45 years
B. Middle Age	45–60 years
VII OLDER ADULTHOOD	(60 + YEARS)
A. Young Old	60–70
B. Middle Old	70–80
C. Frail Old	80+

Morphological age is a comparison of one's attained size (height and weight) to normative standards. Normative size has been determined by Wetzel (1948) and others through exhaustive charting of heights and weights of thousands of individuals. The Wetzel Grid (1948) was used for many years by most pediatricians as the primary means of determining the morphological age of their patients. Although not used as frequently today due to secular changes (i.e., generational changes) in height and weight, the Wetzel Grid was at one time the most popular method of determining morphological age.

Skeletal age provides one with a record of the biological age of the developing skeleton. Skeletal age can be very accurately determined by

characteristic pattern of movement. The potential problems are
rious. Learning and fatigue factors may contaminate the data, as m
errors in experimenter judgment.

Concept 1.8 Developmental data collection, for many reasons, often a difficult and time-consuming process.

Another problem that plagues the developmental researcher is i
terrater reliability. It is crucial, for example, that observational asses
ment be systematically analyzed and that observers be carefully train
in how to observe and in what to look for. Still another problem, a:
potentially the most serious one facing the researcher, involves the 1
liability and validity of the measuring instrument itself. A variety
motor development assessment devices are available. Some have be
meticulously designed, while others represent a combination of me
sures of unproven reliability and validity.

The benefits to be gained from motor development research far ou
weigh the problems and pitfalls. As information gradually accumulat
and is replicated, we gain a more accurate picture of the processes i
volved in motor development. Research efforts that employ sound r
search designs and recognize the need for patient, unbiased da
collection are increasing our understanding of motor development acro:
the life span.

Age Classifications of Development

It is interesting to note that developmental levels may be classified in
variety of ways. The most popular method, but often the least accurat
is classification by chronological age. *Chronological age* or one's ag
in months and/or years enjoys universal usage and represents a cor
stant for all. By knowing one's birth date we can easily calculate age i
years, months, and days. Table 1.2 provides a conventional chronolog
ical classification of age from conception through old age. Note that al
though chronological ages are highly specific during the early years, the
become increasingly more general throughout life. As you review thi
table keep in mind that although development is age-related it is no
age-dependent. Chronological age merely provides a rough estimate o
one's developmental level which may be more accurately determine(
through other means.

The *biological age* of an individual provides a record of his or he:
rate of progress toward maturity. It is a variable age that correspond:
only roughly to chronological age, and may be determined by measure:
of: (1) morphological age, (2) skeletal age, (3) dental age, or (4) sexual age

x-ray of the carpal bones of the hand and wrist (Greulich and Pyle, 1959; Tanner and Whitehouse, 1975). Skeletal age is currently used as a laboratory research tool, and in cases where growth is either extremely retarded or accelerated. It is rarely used as a measure of biological age outside laboratory or clinical settings because of cost, inconvenience, and the accumulative effects of radiation.

Dental age is another accurate but infrequently used means of determining biological age. The sequence of tooth development from first appearance of the cups to root closure provides a measure of calcification age. Eruption age may also be determined by charting the progressive emergence of the teeth.

Sexual age is a fourth method of determining biological age. Sexual maturation is determined by the variable attainment of primary and secondary sexual characteristics. The Tanner pubic hair scale (Tanner, 1962) is an accurate means of assessing sexual maturity. It is described in Chapter 15. This method is used infrequently because of social and cultural factors.

A variety of other methods of classifying one's age exists. They include measurements of: (1) emotional age, (2) mental age, (3) self-concept age, and (4) perceptual age. *Emotional age* is a measure of socialization and ability to function within a particular social/cultural milieu. *Mental age* is a complex measure of an individual's mental potential as a function of both learning and of self-perception. It often fluctuates within one's lifetime. *Self-concept age* is a measure of one's personal assessment of his or her value or worth. *Perceptual age* is an assessment of the rate and extent of one's perceptual development.

Concept 1.9 Although chronological age is the most commonly used means of age classification, it is frequently the least valid.

All measures of maturity are variable. They are related to chronological age, but are not dependent upon it. Therefore, anyone who works with human beings, whether they are infants, children, adolescents, or adults must avoid overreliance on a chronological classification of age because of its ease and convenience.

Terminology Used in Motor Development

Gaining a working knowledge of the terms commonly used in any area of study is an important first step. Whether it is medicine or law, special education or economics, there is jargon typical to each field, and motor development is no exception. A variety of terms that have come into common usage are presented in this section. As with the jargon in most areas of study, agreement on the meaning of each term is not universal. We must strive for greater consistency. With this concept in mind, the following definitions are presented.

Concept 1.10 Terms convey critical concepts essential to understanding motor development.

Growth and Development

The terms "growth" and "development" are often used interchangeably, but there is a difference in emphasis implied by each. In its purest sense, *physical growth* refers to an increase in the size of an individual's body or its parts during maturation. In other words, physical growth is an increase in the structure of the body brought about by the multiplication or enlargement of cells. The term growth, however, is often used to refer to the totality of physical change, and as a result it becomes more inclusive and takes on the same meaning as development. In our discussion of growth through this text, we will adopt the former.

Development, in its purest sense, refers to changes in an individual's level of functioning over time. Keogh and Sugden (1985) defined development as "adaptive change toward competence" (p. 6). Such a definition implies that throughout the life span one is required to adjust, compensate, or change in order to gain or maintain competence. For example, the infant learning to walk needs to compensate for changes in his or her base of support and center of gravity. So too, the adult needs to compensate for the diminution and regression in walking competency frequently brought about by arthritis and reduced joint flexibility. We will adopt Keogh and Sugden's definition throughout the text, because it clearly and succinctly states that development is a lifelong process of change.

Although development is most frequently viewed as an emerging and broadening of one's ability to function on a higher level, we must recognize that the concept of development is much broader, and that it is in fact a lifelong process. The study of development is concerned with what occurs and how it occurs in the human organism in its journey from conception through maturity to death. Development is a continuous process encompassing all the interrelated dimensions of our existence, and care must be taken not to consider these dimensions as autonomous or limited to the growing years of childhood. Adults are every bit as involved in the developmental process as are young children.

The interwoven elements of maturation and experience play a key role in the developmental process. *Maturation* refers to qualitative changes that enable one to progress to higher levels of functioning. Maturation, when viewed from a biological perspective, is primarily innate; that is, it is genetically determined and resistant to external or environ-

Figure 1.3
The interrelated
components of
human development

mental influences. Maturation is characterized by a fixed order of progression in which the pace may vary but the sequence of appearance of characteristics generally does not. For example, the progression and approximate ages at which an infant learns to sit, stand, and walk are highly influenced by maturation. The sequence of appearance of these abilities is fixed and resistant to change, with only the rate of appearance being altered by the environmental influences of learning and experience.

Experience refers to factors within the environment that may alter the appearance of various developmental characteristics through the process of learning. A child's experiences may affect the rate of onset of certain patterns of behavior.

The developmental aspects of both maturation and experience are interwoven. Determining the separate contribution of each of these processes is impossible. In fact, a heated debate in the literature over the relative importance of the two has raged for well over a century. As a result, the term *adaptation* has come into vogue and is often used to refer to the complex interplay between forces within the individual and the environment. Figure 1.3 illustrates how the factors of growth, maturation, experience, and adaptation relate directly to the developing individual and to one another.

Domains of Behavior

The classification of human responses into *domains of behavior* was first popularized by Bloom and his associates (1956) and Krathwohl, Bloom, and Masia (1964) in their pioneering attempts to establish a taxonomy of educational objectives. Their separation of behavior into cognitive (intellectual behavior), affective (social-emotional behavior), and psychomotor (motor behavior) has, unfortunately, caused many to deal with each domain as an independent entity of human development. We must not lose sight of the interrelated nature of development and the three domains of human behavior even though we tend to separate them for convenience in our discussion and study of human development.

The *psychomotor domain* includes the processes of change, stabilization, and regression in physical structure and neuromuscular function. In the psychomotor domain, movement may be the result of cognitively mediated processes in higher brain centers (motor cortex), reflexive activity in lower brain centers, or automatic responses in the central nervous system. The psychomotor domain encompasses all physical change throughout the life span. As a result the psychomotor domain may be categorized into the study of motor performance and the study of movement abilities.

Motor performance is the term frequently used to lump together the various components of health-related fitness (muscular strength, muscular endurance, aerobic endurance, joint flexibility, and body composition) and performance-related fitness (speed of movement, agility, coordination, balance, and power) together. Motor performance is associated with the capacity to perform movement tasks, and its study is product-based in terms of how far, how fast, and how many.

Movement abilities is a comprehensive term grouping the three *categories of movement* (locomotion, manipulation, and stability). The study of movement abilities is process-oriented and involves observing the mechanics of movement itself and trying to understand the underlying causes for change. Thus, one may be interested in an aspect of the psychomotor domain as it relates to understanding motor performance, and as it applies to the performance of a variety of movement abilities across age, gender, or social class.

The *cognitive domain* as applied to the study of movement behavior involves the functional relationship between mind and body. The reciprocal interaction of mind and body has been explored by observers ranging from Socrates and Plato to the developmental theorists of the twentieth century. Jean Piaget (1952), known for his theory of cognitive development, is an example of a theorist who recognized the important role of movement, particularly during the early years of life. Piaget's work has done much to spread the notions that perceptual-motor development and academic concept readiness can be enhanced through the medium of movement.

The term *perceptual-motor* came into vogue in the 1960s and 1970s (Kephart, 1960; Williams, 1983) to signify the important influence that sensory cues and the perceptual process have on motor activity. In its broadest sense a perceptual-motor act is any voluntary movement that relies on sensory data to process information used in the performance of that act. In other words, all voluntary movement may be viewed as perceptual-motor in nature. Movements that are subcortically controlled (reflexes) are the only forms of movement of the skeletal muscles that do not require some element of perception.

The *affective domain* as related to the study of human movement involves feelings and emotions as applied to self and others through movement. Movement confidence, self-concept, and cultural socialization are areas of interest to students of motor development. *Movement confidence* is one's belief in his or her ability to satisfy the demands of various movement tasks. *Self-concept* is one's personal assessment of self-worth. It is influenced by a variety of factors, one of which is movement. *Cultural socialization* is the level of social interaction evidenced by an individual. Play behavior has been shown to have a developmental base that manifests itself in changing peer relations and more sophisticated levels of functioning (Ellis, 1973; Coakley, 1987).

Concept 1.11   Human behavior may be classified into three domains: cognitive, affective, and psychomotor.

These definitions of the psychomotor, cognitive, and affective domains as they influence, and are influenced by, developmental processes permit us to clarify a variety of terms that contain the words "motor" or "movement". What follows is not a mere exercise in semantics. Words reflect concepts and convey ideas. It is important that we impose similar meanings on them because even subtle differences in definitions can lead to confusion and lack of clarity.

Motor Development

The term *motor* when used by itself refers to the *underlying* biological and mechanical factors that influence movement. The term, however, is rarely used alone but serves as a suffix or prefix in such terms as: *psychomotor, perceptual-motor, sensorimotor, motor learning, motor control,* and, of course, *motor development.* The terms psychomotor, perceptual-motor, and sensorimotor have gained popularity in the jargon of psychologists and educators. Kinesiologists, on the other hand, have tended to limit use of the prefixes of these words to discussions that focus on specific aspects of the motor process. In other words, the term *motor* is used as a prefix to describe specific areas of study. The following is a brief description of several of these terms as they are commonly used.

Learning is an internal process that results in consistent changes in behavior seen as evidence of its occurrence. Learning is the result of experience, education, and training interacting with biological processes. It is shaped largely by an individual's state of development, and is a function of practice (Piaget, 1952, 1964). Learning is a phenomena in which experience is prerequisite, whereas development is a process that may occur relatively independently of experience. *Motor learning* then is that aspect of learning in which movement plays a major part.

Motor behavior is a generic term defined here as motor learning that embodies learning and performance factors and maturational processes associated with movement performance. Motor behavior research is concerned with the study of motor learning, motor control, and motor development.

Motor control is that aspect of motor learning that deals with the study of isolated tasks under specific conditions. Research in this area looks at the underlying processes involved in the performance of a movement act that are consistent from trial to trial. Much of the current research in motor development, especially that conducted from a *dynamical systems perspective* (see chapter 2, pp. 32–34) approaches it from the standpoint of motor control.

Motor development is progressive change in motor behavior throughout the life cycle. It may be studied both as a process and as a product. As a process, motor development involves the underlying biological, environmental, and task demands influencing both the motor performance and movement abilities of individuals from infancy through old age. As a product, motor development may be regarded as descriptive or normative and is typically viewed in stages (infancy, childhood, adolescence, adulthood, old age) that reflect the particular interest of the investigator.

The terms *motor pattern, fundamental motor pattern, motor skill,* and *perceptual-motor skill* all refer to the underlying sensory, integrative, and decision-making processes that precede the performance of an observable movement. Perception and cognition are important variables because they influence underlying motor processes. Underlying motor processes are involved in the performance of all voluntary movement.

Concept 1.12   ''Motor behavior'' is an umbrella term encompassing the complementary but essentially different areas of study embodied by motor learning, motor control, and motor development.

Movement Forms

The term *movement* refers to actual observable change in the position of any part of the body. Movement is the culminating act of the underlying motor processes. The word movement is often linked with others to broaden or clarify its meaning, but in general it refers to the overt act of moving. The following is a brief description of some movement terms as they are commonly used.

A *movement pattern* as defined by Wickstrom (1983) is ''a combination of movements organized according to a particular time-space sequence'' (p. 5). A movement pattern is an organized series of related movements. More specifically, a movement pattern represents the performance of an isolated movement that in and of itself is too restricted to be classified as a fundamental movement pattern. For example, the sidearm, underarm, or overarm patterns of movement alone do not constitute the fundamental movements of throwing or striking but merely represent an organized series of movements.

A *fundamental movement pattern* refers to the observable performance of basic locomotor, manipulative, and stabilizing movements. Fundamental movement patterns involve the combination of movement patterns of two or more body segments. Running, jumping, striking, throwing, twisting, and turning are examples of fundamental movement patterns.

Although the terms movement pattern and movement skill are often used interchangeably, a *movement skill* is viewed here as a fundamental movement pattern performed with greater accuracy, precision, and control. In a movement skill, accuracy is stressed and extraneous movement is limited; in a fundamental movement pattern, movement is stressed but accuracy is limited and not necessarily seen as the goal.

A *sport skill* is the refinement or combination of fundamental movement patterns or movement skills to perform a sport-related activity. The fundamental movement patterns of twisting the body and striking may be developed to a high degree of precision and applied in a horizontal form to batting in the sport of baseball or in a vertical form to playing golf or serving a tennis ball. The performance of a sport skill requires making increasingly precise alterations in the basic patterns of movement to achieve higher levels of skill.

Movement education is a term that has been defined in a variety of ways, all of which seem somewhat restrictive and shortsighted. It has been defined as a method, as a process, and as an aspect of the physical education program generally limited to children. Logsdon et al. (1984) take a more global view of movement education and define it as follows: "Movement education is a lifelong process of change. This process of motor development and learning has its beginning in the womb and proceeds through a never-ending series of changes until death" (p. 12). For the purpose of our discussion we will view movement education as the lifelong process of changes in motor behavior brought about by opportunities for practice, encouragement, instruction, and the ecology of the environment itself. Input from qualified instructors, positive motivation and reinforcement, and appropriate facilities and equipment facilitate the process of movement education. It is, however, not entirely restricted to these conditions or to specific age ranges.

Concept 1.13   Human movement takes many forms, necessitating use of a variety of terms to help clarify meaning.

Gross and Fine Movements

Movement, whether it takes the form of a movement pattern or a movement skill, may be classified in a variety of ways. There is not a clear delineation between the terms "gross" and "fine", but movements are often classified as one or the other. A *gross motor movement* involves movement of the large muscles of the body. Most sport skills are classified as gross motor movements, with the exception perhaps of target shooting, archery, and a few others. A *fine motor movement* involves limited movements of parts of the body in the performance of precise movements. The manipulative movements of sewing, writing, and typing are generally thought of as fine motor movements.

Discrete, Serial, and Continuous Movements

On the basis of its temporal aspects, movement may also be classified as discrete, serial, or continuous. A *discrete movement* has a very definite beginning and ending. Throwing, jumping, kicking, and striking a ball are examples of discrete movements. *Serial movements* involve the performance of a single, discrete movement several times in rapid succession. Rhythmical hopping, basketball dribbling, and volleying in soccer or volleyball are typical serial tasks. *Continuous movements* are movements that are repeated for a specified period of time. Running, swimming, and cycling are common continuous movements.

Open and Closed Movements

Fundamental movement patterns and movement skills are often referred to as open motor tasks or closed motor tasks (Magill, 1993). An *open movement task* is one that is performed in an environment where the conditions are constantly changing. These changing conditions require the individual to make adjustments or modifications in the actual pattern of movement to suit the demands of the situation. Plasticity or flexibility in movement is required in the performance of an open skill. Most dual and group activities involve open skills that depend on external and internal feedback for their successful execution. For example, the child taking part in a typical game of tag, which requires running and dodging in varying directions, is never using the exact same patterns of movement during the game. The child is required to adapt to the demands of the activity through a variety of similar but different movements. Performance of an open movement task differs markedly from performance of a closed movement task.

A *closed movement task* is "a skill performed in a stable environment where the performer determines when to begin the action" (Magill, 1993, p. 416). A closed movement skill or fundamental movement pattern demands rigidity of performance. It depends on kinesthetic rather than visual and auditory feedback from the execution of the task. The child who is performing a headstand, throwing at a target, or doing a vertical jump is performing a closed movement task.

The reader is cautioned not to be arbitrary in the classification of movement as gross or fine; discrete, serial, or continuous; or open or closed. The vast majority of movement involves some elements of each.

Table 1.3 The Interrelated Nature of Terms Commonly Used in Motor Development

Motor behavior: Study of change in motor learning, motor control, and motor development brought about by the interaction of learning and biological processes

Motor control: Underlying changes in the performance of isolated tasks	*Motor learning:* Underlying changes involved in movement performance

Motor development: Progressive change in motor behavior throughout the life cycle brought about by interaction among the requirements of the task, the biology of the individual, and the conditions of the environment

Motor: Underlying factors affecting movement	*Movement:* The observable act of moving
Motor pattern: Common underlying biological and mechanical processes	*Movement pattern:* An organized series of related movements (e.g., a side-arm pattern)
Fundamental motor pattern: Common underlying process of basic movements	*Fundamental movement pattern:* An organized series of basic movements (e.g., striking)
Motor skill: Common underlying process of control in movement	*Specialized movement skill:* Form, accuracy, and control in performance of a movement (e.g., striking an oncoming object or splitting wood)

Sport skill: The combination of a fundamental movement pattern with form, accuracy, and control in the performance of a sport-related activity (e.g., batting in baseball or softball)

Movement education: The lifelong process of change in movement behavior brought about by the environmental factors of opportunities for practice, encouragement, and instruction (e.g., change in striking abilities over time)

Distinct separation and classification of movements is not always possible or desirable. We are dynamic, moving beings, constantly responding to many subtle environmental factors and the demands of the movement task itself. The arbitrary classification of movement should serve only to focus attention on the specific aspect of movement under consideration. Table 1.3 provides a schematic representation and brief description of terms commonly used in the study of learning and development. The reader will find it useful to carefully review these terms paying particular attention to their interrelatedness. The terms motor and movement, and pattern and skill, which are commonly used interchangeably in the literature, have particularly subtle differences.

Summary

This chapter has focused on a variety of general topics to provide you with a brief overview of the field of motor development. The study of human development may take many forms, one form being the study of motor development. In turn, motor development may be studied in a variety of ways. The field has gone through a rather interesting history in its move from a process-oriented maturational approach, to a product-oriented normative/descriptive approach, and now back to a process approach which is examining underlying mechanisms of motor development.

Research designs and problems in the study of motor development were discussed as they relate to the longitudinal, mixed longitudinal, and the cross-sectional approaches to study. The advantages and limitations of each were discussed, with the caveat that only the longitudinal and mixed longitudinal designs are true studies of development. These research designs look at change in terms of "developmental time" rather than "real time" as in the cross-sectional study.

Various age classifications of development were examined with the intent of conveying the concept that although development is age-related it is not age-dependent. Chronological age is the most frequently used and most convenient indicator of change, but it is the least accurate indicator of development. Age does not generate or cause development; it is merely an indicator of what has transpired because of the developmental process.

The chapter concluded with a discussion of terminology commonly used in the study of development in general and motor development in specific. The intent of this discussion and the ensuing definitions was to help you the reader and us the authors proceed through the text using a common language to maximize understanding of the important topics and concepts to follow.

Terms to Remember

Longitudinal method
Cross-sectional method
Mixed-longitudinal method
Process-oriented research
Product-oriented research
Chronological age
Biological age
Morphological age
Skeletal age
Dental age
Sexual age
Mental age
Emotional age
Self-concept age
Perceptual age
Physical growth
Development
Maturation
Experience
Adaptation
Domains of behavior
Psychomotor domain
Motor performance
Movement abilities
Categories of movement

Cognitive domain
Perceptual-motor
Affective domain
Movement confidence
Self-concept
Cultural socialization
Motor
Learning
Motor learning
Motor behavior
Motor control
Motor development
Movement
Movement pattern
Fundamental movement pattern
Movement skill
Sport skill
Movement education
Gross motor movement
Fine motor movement
Discrete movement
Serial movement
Continuous movement
Open movement task
Closed movement task

Critical Readings

Clark, J. E., & Whitall, J. (1989). What is motor development? The lessons of history. *Quest,* 41, 183–202.

Keogh, J., & Sugden, D. (1985). *Movement Skill Development* (Chapter 1). New York: Macmillan.

Lefrancois, G. (1993). *The Lifespan* (Chapter 1). Belmont, CA: Wadsworth.

Lockhart, A. (1964). What's in a name? *Quest,* 2, 9–13.

Magill, R. A. (1993). *Motor Learning: Concepts and Applications* (Chapter 1). Dubuque, IA: Brown & Benchmark.

Rarick, G. L. (1981). The emergence of the study of human motor development. In G. A. Brooks (Ed.), *Perspectives on the Academic Discipline of Physical Education,* Champaign, IL: Human Kinetics.

Smoll, F. L. (1982). Developmental Kinesiology: Toward a subdiscipline focusing on motor development. In J. A. S. Kelso and J. E. Clark (Eds.), *The Development of Movement Control and Co-ordination* (pp. 319–354). New York: Wiley.

Thomas, J. R. & Thomas, K. T. (1989). What is motor development: Where does it belong? *Quest,* 41, 203–212.

Chapter 2

Models of Human Development

CHAPTER COMPETENCIES

Upon completion of this chapter you should be able to:

- *Compare and contrast maturational, environmental, interactionist, and transactional views of causation in motor development*
- *Demonstrate familiarity with a variety of theoretical models of human development*
- *Discuss changes in cognition as a developing process*
- *Classify theories of development into various conceptual viewpoints*
- *Analyze changes in psychosocial development across the life span*
- *Identify the major developmental tasks across the life span*

KEY CONCEPT: Human development may be studied from a variety of theoretical frameworks, each of which has implications for the motor development and movement education of infants, children, adolescents, and adults.

During the past half century several developmental theorists have closely studied the phenomena of human development. Sigmund Freud, Erik Erikson, Arnold Gesell, Robert Havighurst, and Jean Piaget, among others, have made valuable contributions to our knowledge of human development. Each has constructed theoretical models that depict the many phases and stages one passes through on the journey from childhood to maturity. The models have several similarities, but each reflects its originator's philosophical leanings and particular interests in the study of development.

This chapter will take a brief look at the models of development proposed by these theorists. As a basis for a more detailed study of motor development, we will also examine characteristic ways in which theorists view the phenomena of human development in general and examine three popular theories of development in particular, namely those of Erik Erikson, Jean Piaget, and Robert Havighurst.

Theoretical Models of Human Development

Sigmund Freud's (1927) *psychoanalytic theory* of human behavior may be viewed, in part, as a model of development even though his work centered around personality and abnormal functioning in adults. Freud's famous psychosexual stages of development reflected various zones of the body with which the individual seeks gratification of the "id" (the unconscious source of motives, desires, passions, and pleasure seeking) at certain general age periods. The "ego" mediates between the pleasure-seeking behavior of the id and the "superego" (common sense, reason, and conscience). Freud's "oral," "anal," "phallic," "latency," and "genital" stages of personality development represent the terms applied to the pleasure-seeking zones of the body that come into play at different age periods. Each stage relies heavily on physical sensations and motor activity.

Psychoanalytic theory has received its share of criticism primarily due to the inability to scientifically objectify, quantify, and validate its concepts. It has, however, stimulated considerable research and study and served as the basis for the notable works of Freud's student Erik Erikson (1963), and his daughter Anna Freud (1945).

Erikson (1963, 1980) focused on the influence of society, rather than sex, on development. His *psychosocial theory* describes eight stages of the human life cycle and put them on a continuum, emphasizing factors in the environment, not heredity, as facilitators of change. Erikson's view of human development acknowledges factors within the individual's experiential background as having a primary role in development. His view of the importance of motor development is more implicit than explicit, but he clearly points out the importance of success-oriented movement experiences as a means of reconciling the developmental crises that each individual passes through.

Concept 2.1   There are numerous models of human development, each of which reflects its originator's knowledge, interests, and biases.

Gesell's (1928, 1954) *maturational theory* of growth and development also emphasizes the physical and motor components of human behavior. Gesell documented and described general age periods for the acquisition of a wide variety of rudimentary movement abilities during infancy and viewed these maturation-based tasks as important indicators of social and emotional growth. Gesell also described various ages when children are in "nodal" periods or when they are "out of focus" with their environment. A nodal stage is a maturational period during which the child exhibits a high degree of mastery over situations in the immediate environment, is balanced in behavior, and generally pleasant. Being out of focus is just the opposite; the child exhibits a low degree of mastery over situations in the immediate environment, is unbalanced or troubled in behavior, and generally unpleasant. Maturational theory is not widely accepted today, but it played a significant role in the evolution of child development as an area of study.

A fourth developmental model, that of Robert Havighurst (1972), views development as an interplay between biological, social, and cultural forces through which individuals are continually enhancing their abilities to function effectively in society. Havighurst's *environmental theory* views development as a series of tasks that must be achieved within a certain time frame to ensure the proper developmental progression of the individual. According to Havighurst's model, there are teachable moments when the body is ready and when society requires successful completion of a task. As with the other models discussed, the tasks described by Havighurst rely heavily on movement, play, and physical activity for their development, particularly during infancy and childhood.

Concept 2.2   No one theory is complete or totally accurate in describing or explaining human development, and as a result, all break down at some point.

Another developmental theory currently popular among educators is that of Jean Piaget (1969). Piaget's *cognitive development theory* places primary emphasis on the acquisition of cognitive thought processes. He gained insight into the development of cognitive structures through careful observation of infants and children. The genius in Piaget's work lies in his uncanny ability to pick out subtle clues in children's behavior that give us indications of their cognitive functioning.

Piaget viewed these subtle indicators as milestones in the hierarchy of cognitive development. Movement is emphasized as a primary agent in the acquisition of increased cognitive structures, particularly during infancy and the preschool years. Piaget used chronological age only as a broad and general indicator of cognitive functioning, and relied instead on observed behaviors. These observed behaviors served for Piaget as the primary indicators of the child's ever-increasing complexity in cognitive development. Piaget identified these developmental phases as "sensorimotor" (birth to 2 years), "preoperational" (2 to 7 years), "concrete operations" (7 to 11 years), and "formal operations" (12 years and over). Piaget did not directly concern himself with development beyond about age 15 because he believed that highly sophisticated intellectual capabilities were developed by this time.

All theorists look at the human development from somewhat different points of view, but close inspection reveals remarkable similarities. Each theorist emphasizes movement and play as important facilitators of enhanced functioning. Also, each tends to be more descriptive than explanatory. In other words, they tell us "what" is happening in the normal process of development, rather than "why" it is happening.

The theorists differ, however, in the particular aspects of development they emphasize. The multidimensional facets of development require a comprehensive model to explain behavior. In this regard, all theories have shortcomings, and care must be taken not to subscribe to one at the exclusion of the others. We must be aware of the interrelatedness of human behavior and dispel the notion that the psychomotor, cognitive, and affective domains of human behavior are independent of one another.

Conceptual Viewpoints of Development

Close inspection of the five models of development just outlined, as well as the study of others, reveal a distinct tendency for each model to group around one of four conceptual frameworks. These frameworks are classified here as (1) phase-stage, (2) developmental task, (3) developmental milestone, and (4) dynamical systems theories of human development (Table 2.1).

Concept 2.3 Theories of development may be studied from distinct conceptual viewpoints.

Table 2.1 Conceptual Approaches to the Study of Human Development

Conceptual Approach	Representative Theorists	Research Focus
Phase-Stage Theory	Sigmund Freud	Study of Psychosexual Development from Birth through Childhood
	Erik Erikson	Study of Life Span Psychosocial Development
	Arnold Gesell	Study of Maturational Processes in Central Nervous System Development from Birth through Childhood ("Ontogeny Recapitulates Phylogeny")
Developmental Task Theory	Robert Havighurst	Study of the Interaction of Biology and Society on Developmental Maturity from Infancy through Old Age
Developmental Milestone Theory	Jean Piaget	Study of Cognitive Development as an Interactive Process between Biology and the Environment from Infancy through Childhood
Dynamical Systems Theory	Nicholas Bernstein	Study of Development as a Discontinuous, Self-Organizing, Transactional Process among the Task, Individual and Environment Throughout Life
	Kugler, Kelso, and Turvey	

Phase-Stage Theory

The *phase-stage* approach to developmental theory is the oldest of the conceptual viewpoints, and is sometimes referred to as "classical theory" or simply as "developmental theory" (Lerner, 1986). All classical developmental theorists (i.e., stage theorists), whether they are studying cognitive, moral, personality or motor development, contend that there are universal age periods characterized by certain types of behavior. These behaviors occur in phases or stages, last for arbitrary lengths of time, and are invariant. In other words, stages are sequential and cannot be reordered, but one or more stages may be skipped. Furthermore, stage theory focuses on broad-based changes rather than narrow or isolated behaviors.

Each phase (i.e., typical behavior) generally covers a period of one year or more and may be accompanied by one or more other stages. Some theorists sub-divide particular phases into smaller stages. Others prefer to look at one phase typifying one particular period of time. Most theorists who propose a phase-stage scheme have divided childhood, or even the entire life cycle, into 10 periods or less. The phase-stage concept is probably the most popular among parents and educators and is often reflected in our thinking and speech when we say, "she is just going through a stage" or "I will be happy when he is out of that phase." Freud, Erikson, and Gesell each viewed child development as a phase-stage related process.

Stages have been proposed for several fundamental movement tasks (Wild, 1938; Seefeldt, 1979; McClenaghan and Gallahue, 1978, Gallahue, 1993). Roberton (1977), however, questioned the viability of a rigid stage theory of motor development and has suggested a more flexible stage model based on the components of a movement rather than on the total body configuration. It must be remembered that any phase-stage theory describes only general (i.e., group or normative) developmental characteristics for a generic (average) individual that are postulated to be common to all people. Phase-stage theory gives us a view of the "big picture," but does not accommodate the details.

Developmental Task Theory

A second conceptual viewpoint of development is the *developmental task* approach. A developmental task is an important accomplishment that individuals must achieve by a certain time if they are to function effectively and meet the demands placed on them by society. Proponents of developmental task theory view the accomplishment of particular tasks within a certain time span as prerequisite to smooth progression to higher levels of functioning. This concept of development differs from the phase-stage view in that it is predictive of later success or failure based on the individual's performance at an earlier stage and does not merely attempt to describe typical behavior at a particular age. Havighurst's view of development uses the developmental task concept to both describe and predict behavior from infancy through adolescence. The hemispherical dominance theory and treatment techniques for individuals with learning disorders as proposed by Delacato (1966) also follow a developmental task approach. Although developmental task theories claim predictability, little has been done to test their assertions. Hence, there is considerable question as to their validity.

Developmental Milestone Theory

The *developmental milestone* approach is a third conceptual framework from which development is viewed. Developmental milestones are similar to developmental tasks except for their emphasis. Instead of referring to accomplishments that take place if the individual is to adapt to the environment, this approach refers to strategic indicators of how far development has progressed. The accomplishment of a developmental milestone may or may not in itself be crucial to adjustment in the world as it is with a developmental task. Milestones are merely convenient guidelines by which the rate and extent of development can be gauged. As with phase-stage theory, they are more descriptive than predictive, but unlike stage theories, they view development as a continual unfolding and intertwining of developmental processes, not as a neat transition from one stage to another. Piaget's cognitive development theory is generally considered to be a developmental milestone theory, as is the dynamical systems theory of motor development.

Recognition of the fact that most models of human development tend to fall under one of these three concepts enables us to view the phenomena of growth and development more objectively. Each concept has merit and operates to a certain degree throughout the developmental process. The years of infancy and early childhood do, in fact, require the achievement of certain important tasks such as learning to walk, talk, and take solid foods by a specific age for normal functioning to be established. These years also encompass a variety of stages that children pass through at more or less the same age in addition to a variety of milestones that are achieved as subtle indicators of how far development has progressed.

Dynamical Systems Theory

Developmental theory, to be of practical benefit, must be both descriptive and explanatory. It is important to know about the products of development in terms of what people are typically like during particular phases and stages, developmental milestones and developmental tasks (description). It is equally important, however, to know what causes these changes to occur (explanation). To this end many developmentalists are now looking at explanatory models in an attempt to understand more about the underlying processes that actually govern development. Dynamical Systems Theory is popular among many (Alexander, et al. 1993; Kamm et al., 1990; Caldwell & Clark, 1990; Thelen, 1989). It is based largely on the work of the Russian physiologist Nicholas Bernstein (1967), and expanded by Kugler, Kelso, and Turvey (1982).

The term *dynamical* conveys the concept that developmental change is nonlinear and discontinuous. Because development is viewed as nonlinear, it is seen as a discontinuous process. That is, individual change over time is not necessarily smooth and hierarchial, and does not necessarily involve moving toward ever higher levels of complexity and competence in the motor system. Individuals, particularly those with disabling impairments, are impeded in their motor development. For example, children with spastic cerebral palsy are frequently delayed in learning to walk independently. When independent walking is achieved, their gait patterns will be individualized and achieved when appropriate for each. Although, by definition, development is a continuous process, it is also a discontinuous process when viewed from a dynamical perspective. In other words, development is a "continuous-discontinuous" process.

The dynamics of change occur over time, but in a highly individual manner influenced by a variety of critical factors within the system. These factors are termed "affordances" and "rate limiters." *Affordances* are factors which tend to promote or encourage developmental change. *Rate limiters* are factors that serve to impede or retard development. For children with cerebral palsy, for example, rate limiters are neurological and biomechanical in nature. Affordances may include assisted support, handholds, encouragement and guided instruction.

The term *systems* conveys the concept that the human organism is *self-organizing* and composed of several subsystems. It is self-organizing in that by their very nature humans are inclined to strive for motor control and movement competence. It is the subsystems, namely, the task, the individual and the environment, operating separately and in concert that actually determine the rate, sequence and extent of development. Coordination and control of movement is the end result of several systems working dynamically together in a cooperative manner. No one factor is more important than the other. All subsystems interact in a manner that causes motor behavior to emerge independent of any one subsystem (Alexander, et al. 1993). Children with spastic cerebral palsy, as self-organizing systems, develop individually unique gait patterns in response to their capabilities in terms of meeting the achievement demands of the walking task. Preferred patterns of movement behavior develop in response to unique factors within the individual, the task, and the environment. These movement patterns are the result of the most efficient interaction of the subsystem and the least amount of energy required. Although preferred patterns of movement behavior do exist (chapters 8, 11, and 16), they are altered when the demands of the system dictate change.

Viewed from a systems perspective, there are numerous elements that can change as one grows and develops. Bernstein (1967) referred to these as *degrees of freedom*. The performance of a movement task includes neuromotor as well as biomechanical degrees of freedom. The number of degrees of freedom are, however, constrained through the individual gaining motor control and movement coordination of the movement task, thereby resulting in the formation of movement patterns. The individual develops preferred patterns of movement, but these preferred patterns may be reorganized through control parameters. *Control parameters* are: "those variables that provide a condition for a pattern change. Control parameters do not dictate what change will occur, but when they reach a critical value, they act as an agent for re-organization of the motor pattern'' (Alexander, et al. 1993, p. 3).

Transition from one pattern of movement to another is called a *phase shift*. Phase shifts are plentiful among infants when moving from one form of locomotion (crawling to creeping), to another (creeping to walking). During this time the baby is in a state of instability shifting from one pattern to the other until a new preferred pattern is firmly established.

Dynamical systems theory attempts to answer the "why" or process questions that result in the observable product of motor development. Much of the work to date has centered on infant motor development, but there is an increasing amount of research focusing on dynamical explanations of motor development among children, adolescents and adults in populations of both normal and atypically developing individuals.

For years developmentalists have recognized the interactive role of two primary systems on the developmental process; heredity and environment. Many now, however, have taken this view one step further in recognizing that the specific demands of the movement task itself actually transact with the individual (i.e. hereditary or biological factors) and the environment (i.e. experience or learning factors) in the development of stability, locomotor and manipulative movement abilities. Such a transactional model implies that factors within various subsystems of the task, the individual, and the environment not only interact, but also have the potential for modifying and being modified by the other as one strives to gain motor control and movement competence (Figure 2.1).

Both the processes and the products of motor development should remind us of the individuality of the learner. Each individual has his or her unique timetable for the development of abilities. Although our "biological clock" is rather specific when it comes to the sequence of movement skill acquisition, the rate and extent of development is individually determined and dramatically influenced by the specific performance demands of the individual task itself.

Typical age periods of development are just that: typical, and nothing more. Age periods merely represent approximate time ranges during which certain behaviors may be observed for the mythical "average" individual. Over-reliance on these time periods would negate the concepts of continuity, specificity, and individuality in the developmental process, and are of little practical value when working with individuals from a developmental perspective.

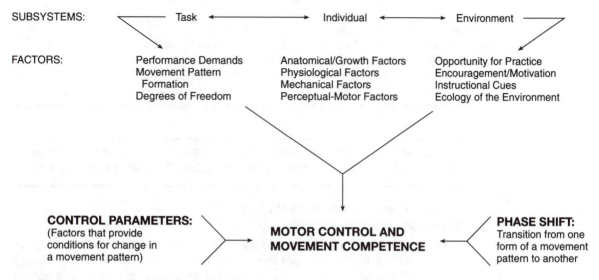

THE DEVELOPMENT OF
MOTOR CONTROL AND MOVEMENT COORDINATION
IS INFLUENCED BY POSITIVE FACTORS
("AFFORDANCES") AND NEGATIVE FACTORS
("RATE LIMITERS") WITHIN THE TASK,
THE INDIVIDUAL AND THE ENVIRONMENT

SUBSYSTEMS: Task ←→ Individual ←→ Environment

FACTORS:

Performance Demands	Anatomical/Growth Factors	Opportunity for Practice
Movement Pattern	Physiological Factors	Encouragement/Motivation
Formation	Mechanical Factors	Instructional Cues
Degrees of Freedom	Perceptual-Motor Factors	Ecology of the Environment

CONTROL PARAMETERS:
(Factors that provide
conditions for change in
a movement pattern)

**MOTOR CONTROL AND
MOVEMENT COMPETENCE**

PHASE SHIFT:
Transition from one
form of a movement
pattern to another

Figure 2.1
Development from a dynamical systems perspective

Three Leading Theories of Human Development

In this section, summaries of three theories, each representing a different conceptual point of view are presented. The phase-stage theory of Erik Erikson, the developmental milestone theory of Jean Piaget, and the developmental task theory of Robert Havighurst have been selected because of their thoroughness, popularity, and important implications for motor development. Dynamical systems theory, based on the work of Bernstein (1967), was discussed in the preceding paragraphs.

Erik Erikson

The psychosocial theory of Erik Erikson (1963, 1980) adheres to the phase-stage approach to studying human development. It is an experience-based theory widely acclaimed by educators and psychologists. The following overview of Erikson's stage theory is presented for clarity and ease of understanding. See Table 2.2 for an outline of Erikson's stages and the approximate age periods when they appear. Note the numerous implications for movement throughout the theory.

Table 2.2 Erik Erikson's Stages of Psychosocial Development

Stage	Approximate Age Period
I Trust vs. Mistrust	Infancy
II Autonomy vs. Doubt and Shame	Toddler
III Initiative vs. Guilt	Preschool
IV Industry vs. Inferiority	School Age
V Identity vs. Role Confusion	Early Adolescence
VI Intimacy vs. Isolation	Late Adolescence
VII Generativity vs. Self-Absorption	Adulthood
VIII Integrity vs. Despair	Old Age

Concept 2.4 One's psychosocial development is influenced by their motor development and movement education throughout the life span.

A. Acquiring a Sense of Basic Trust Versus Mistrust (infancy)

According to Erikson, bodily experiences provide the basis for a psychological state of *trust versus mistrust.* The infant learns to trust "mother," oneself, and the environment through mother's perception of his or her needs and demands. Mutual trust and a willingness to face situations together is established between mother and child. For the neonate, trust requires a feeling of physical comfort and a minimum of fear and uncertainty. A sense of basic trust helps an individual to be receptive to new experiences willingly.

Movement is an essential ingredient of the reciprocal relationship between parent and child. The rhythmical rocking, bathing, and general play behaviors between parent and baby provide a natural means, through movement, for establishing a sense of trust. Mistrust arises out of uncertainty, insecurity and failure to respond to baby's needs for comfort, attention, and mutual play dialogue.

B. Acquiring a Sense of Autonomy Versus Doubt and Shame (toddler)

During the stage in which the toddler is establishing a sense of *autonomy verses doubt and shame,* Erikson believed that continued dependency creates a sense of doubt and shame about one's capabilities. It is therefore critical that the young child assert autonomy as a normal stage of psychosocial development. Children are bombarded by conflicting pulls of asserting their autonomy and of denying themselves the right and capacity to make this assertion. During this period they need guidance and support as they strive for autonomy, lest they find themselves at a loss and are forced to turn against themselves with shame and doubt. At this stage of development, children are typically eager to explore and accomplish new feats. During this period it is essential that proper development of the ego occurs thereby permitting awareness of oneself as an autonomous whole.

Active play is particularly important during this stage because it allows children to develop autonomy within their own boundaries. A child's autonomy emerges from the realization that the environment and the self can be controlled. It is interesting to note that during this stage children frequently violate mutual trust that has been established with others in order to establish autonomy in distinct areas.

C. Acquiring a Sense of Initiative Versus Guilt (preschool)

During this stage in which the child establishes a sense of *initiative versus guilt,* avid curiosity and enthusiasm or feelings of guilt and anxiety develop. According to Erikson, it is during this stage that the conscience is established. Specific tasks are mastered, and children assume responsibility for themselves and their world. They realize that life has a purpose. Children discover that with their greater mobility they are not unlike the adults in their environment. They begin to incorporate into their consciences what their parents really are as people, and not merely what they try to teach them. With improvements in their use of language, children can expand their fields of activity and imagination. Awareness of sex differences also develops at this stage.

During this period children find pleasurable accomplishment in manipulating meaningful toys. Fundamental movement skills are being mastered, influencing children's success in the game activities of their culture. Successful play and game experiences contribute to a sense of initiative. Unsuccessful experiences promote feelings of doubt and shame. In the normal scheme of things a sense of accomplishment in other areas quickly compensates for most guilt and failure. For the child, the future tends to absolve the past.

D. Acquiring a Sense of Industry Versus Inferiority (school age)

Acquiring a sense of *industry versus inferiority* is marked by the development of the skills necessary for life in general and preparation for adulthood. During this phase Erikson believes that children should be finding places among their peers instead of among adults. They need to work on mastering social skills and becoming competent and self-striving. They need feelings of accomplishment for having done well. Failure during this stage is difficult to accept, and there is a distinct tendency by the child to ward off failure at any price. During this period children begin to recognize that they must eventually break with accustomed family life. Dependence on parents begins to shift to reliance on social institutions such as school, the team, or the gang.

During this phase play activities tend to reflect competition through organized games and sports. Boys and girls generally play separately.

Play for its own sake begins to lose importance at the end of this stage. In conjunction with puberty, involvement in play merges into semi-playful and eventually real involvement in work.

E. Acquiring a Sense of Identity Versus Role Confusion (early adolescence)

When acquiring a sense of *identity versus role confusion* there is rapid body growth and sexual maturation. Masculine or feminine identity develops. Feelings of acceptance or rejection by peers are very important. Conflicts frequently arise when peers say one thing and society says another. Identity is essential for making adult decisions about vocation and family life. Youth select people who mean the most to them as significant adults. These role models may be family members, friends, sports heros, or other accomplished individuals in their lives. During this stage of development the individual slowly moves into society as an interdependent and contributing member. A sense of identity assures the individual a definite place within his or her own corner of society.

Organized sports help many youth acquire a sense of identity. Skill proficiency, team membership, and competitive victories all contribute to a sense of identity. Failure and unsuccessful experiences, on the other hand, contribute to a sense of role confusion.

F. Acquiring a Sense of Intimacy Versus Isolation (late adolescence)

Erikson believes that in acquiring a sense of *intimacy versus isolation* that an individual accepts himself or herself and goes on to accept others by fusing his or her personality with others. Childhood and youth are at an end. The individual settles down to the task of full participation in the community, and begins to enjoy life with adult responsibilities, as well as adult liberties. At this stage the individual shows readiness and ability to share mutual trust and to regulate cycles of work, procreation, and recreation.

Play through the games, sports and recreational activities of adulthood serves as one important medium for fostering a sense of intimacy with same sex and opposite sex teammates. Efforts on behalf of a team, whether in a competitive or recreational setting, reflect a level of intimacy due to the need for cooperative behaviors and teamwork. Failure to develop and refine game and sport skills, to at least a recreational level, can lead to a sense of isolation from a team or social group.

G. Acquiring a Sense of Generativity Versus Self-Absorption (adulthood)

Generativity versus self-absorption, according to Erikson, refers to the course an individual pursues in society to provide the next generation with the hope, virtues, and wisdom he or she has accumulated. It also includes parental responsibility to uphold society's interests in child care, education, the arts and sciences, and cultural traditions. This stage is manifested when an individual shows more interest in the next generation than in his or her own problems.

In a movement sense, generativity may be viewed as wanting to pass on the joys and values of play, games, and sport activities to the next generation for their enjoyment and self-fulfillment. Failure during this stage involves self-absorbed disappointment and the inability to accept one's waning capabilities as middle age approaches.

H. Acquiring a Sense of Integrity Versus Despair (mature adult, and old age)

During this final stage in which the mature adult acquires a sense of *integrity versus despair,* Erikson believes that the individual accomplishes the fullest sense of trust as the assured reliance on the integrity of significant others. A different love of one's parents is established. Parents are seen as individuals with weaknesses as well as strengths, and deserving of love for who they are and not what they are. Integrity provides a successful solution to an opposing sense of despair. Fulfillment of this stage involves a sense of wisdom and a philosophy of life which often extends beyond the life cycle of the individual and relates directly to the future of new developmental cycles. Successfully meeting the challenge of this stage enables one to look back on his or her life with all of its successes and failures, good times and bad times, and to do so with integrity. Failure to meet the challenges of this stage causes one to look back with remorse, and to look forward in despair.

Movement in the form of active play, games, recreational sport and general mobility is of real importance during this stage. During this period successful movement, whether it involves walking, driving a car, or swimming laps means independence. Movement at this stage means freedom, and life itself. Looking back upon one's movement accomplishments, and forward at declining capabilities, does not cause despair in the individual who meets the challenges of this stage. Instead, movement helps one to maintain competence and accept physical changes.

Jean Piaget

The developmental milestone theory of Jean Piaget (1952, 1954, 1969, 1974) is currently among the most popular of the theories postulated by experts in the field of child development because of its clarity, insight into, and understanding of the development of cognition. Table 2.3 outlines Piaget's phases of cognitive development. Cognitive development, according to Piaget, occurs through the process of adaptation. *Adaptation* requires one to make adjustments to environmental conditions and intellectualize these adjustments through the complimentary processes of accommodation and assimilation (Figure 2.2).

Table 2.3 Jean Piaget's Phases of Cognitive Development

Phase	Approximate Age-Period
I Sensorimotor	Birth to 2 years
II Preoperational Thought	2 to 7 years
III Concrete Operations	7 to 11 years
IV Formal Operations	11 years onward

Accommodation is adaptation that the child must make to the environment when new and incongruent information is added to his or her repertoire of possible responses. The individual adjusts the response to meet the demands of the specific challenge. Accommodation is a process that reaches outward toward reality and results in a visible change in behavior. For example, when playing in the shallow water of a bathtub or wading pool, a child learns to take into account many of the physical properties and realities of the water. However, when trying to swim in deep water, the child will have to go through a series of new actions (e.g., not being able to touch the bottom, letting go, floating, and breath holding) in order to accommodate to the new reality of deep water.

Assimilation, on the other hand, is Piaget's term for the interpretation of new information based on present interpretations. Assimilation involves taking in information from the environment and incorporating it into the individual's existing cognitive structures. If this information cannot be incorporated into existing structures because of small variations, accommodation can occur. However, if the information is too different from the existing structures, it will not be assimilated or accommodated. For example, giving a toddler a ball to toss may be a new experience, but after a series of accommodations (i.e., adjustments), the child may attempt to play catch. You would not, however, expect the child to challenge you to a game of basketball. Although basketball playing involves various forms of ball tossing, it is too different from playing toss and catch to be assimilated (i.e., incorporated) by the child.

A summary of Piaget's theory follows. Note the numerous implications for movement throughout Piaget's phases of cognitive development.

Concept 2.5 Higher cognitive structures are formulated through the processes of *accommodation* and *assimilation,* both of which rely on self-discovery through play and motor activity.

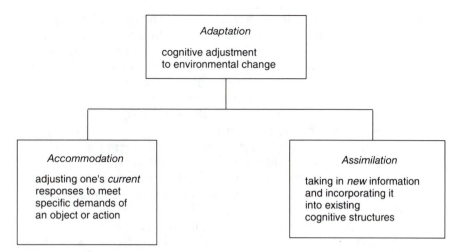

Figure 2.2
Adaptation occurs through the complementary processes of accommodation and assimilation

A. **Sensorimotor Phase (birth to 2 years):**
The *sensorimotor phase* is the period during which the child learns to differentiate itself from objects and others. Motor activity is critical because the child learns through his or her physical interactions with the world. During the sensorimotor phase of development, the major developmental tasks of infancy are coordination of the infant's actions or movement activities and his or her perceptions into a tenuous whole. The sensorimotor phase is composed of several overlapping stages.

1. *Use of reflexes* (birth to 1 month): Piaget believed that there is a continuation of prenatal reflexes for the purpose of enabling the infant to gain additional information about his or her world. Reflexes are spontaneous repetitions caused by internal and external stimulation. Through reflexes and stereotypical behaviors rhythm is established through practice, and habits are formed that later emerge as voluntary movements.

2. *Primary circular reactions* (1 to 3 months): Primary circular reactions refer to the assimilation of a previous experience, and the recognition of the stimulus that triggered the reaction required to generate the experience. At this point in the infant's development, new or past experiences have no meaning unless they become part of the infant's primary circular reaction pattern. During this period reflexive movement is gradually replaced with voluntary movement, but neurological maturity must be reached before sensations can be understood. What previously had been automatic behavior for the infant is now repeated voluntarily, and more than one sensory modality can be used at a time. In fact, accidentally acquired responses become new sensorimotor habits.

3. *Secondary circular reactions* (3 to 9 months): During this stage the infant tries to make events last and tries to make them occur. Secondary circular reactions mean that the focus of the infant is on retention, not repetition as in the previous stage. The infant now tries to create a state of permanency by repeating and prolonging primary circular reactions with secondary reactions. During this stage, two or more sensorimotor experiences are related to one experiential sequence or schema. *Schema* is Piaget's term for a pattern of physical or motor action. For the infant at the secondary circular reactions stage, vision is the prime coordinator of behavior. The other sensory modalities are used to a lesser degree. This is the stage, according to Piaget, where imagination, play, and emotion begin to appear.

4. *Application of the secondary schemata to new situations* (8 to 12 months): Piaget viewed this stage as being characterized by the child's ability to distinguish means from ends; that is, being able to produce the same result in more than one way. During this period children use previous behavioral achievements primarily as the basis for adding new achievements to their expanding repertoire. As a result, there is increased exploration in which ends and means are differentiated through experimentation. Accommodation occurs as the result of experimentation, and the infant can now experience action by observation.

5. *Tertiary circular reactions* (12 to 18 months): Tertiary circular reactions is Piaget's term for the infant's discovery of new means through active experimentation. During this period curiosity and novelty-seeking behavior are developing. Fundamental reasoning comes into play and is developed. As a result, failure to remember is seen as failure to understand. During this period the infant begins to develop spatial relationships upon discovering objects as objects. Imitation develops and play is very important because the child repeats the action phase, linking cognitive processes to movement processes.

6. *Invention of new means through mental combinations* (12 to 24 months): During this stage Piaget recognized a shift from sensorimotor experiences to increased reflection about these experiences. This represents the stepping-stone to the next phase, a more advanced level of intellectual behavior. Children at this stage are capable of discerning themselves as one object among many. Therefore, they tend to perceive and use objects for their own intrinsic qualities. Additionally, they begin to relate objects to new actions without actually perceiving all of the actions themselves. During this stage sensorimotor patterns are slowly replaced by semi-mental

functioning. Imitation copies the action itself or the symbol of the action. Parallel play appears, and identification, as a mental process, becomes evident by the end of this phase depending on the level of the child's intellectual development. Furthermore, this period is characterized by the creation of means and not merely the discovery of means. The rudiments of insight begin to develop.

B. **Preoperational Thought Phase (2 to 7 years).**

During the *preoperational thought phase* the first real beginnings of cognition occur. It is "preoperational" because during this phase the child is not yet capable of mentally manipulating objects, and must rely on physical activity to do so. Additionally, the preoperational thought phase is a period of transition from self-satisfying behavior to rudimentary socialized behavior in the young child. As a result, there is an attempt to adjust new experiences to previous patterns of thinking. Continuous investigation of one's world develops, but the child knows the world only as he or she sees it. Assimilation (i.e., interpreting new information based on present interpretations) is the paramount task of the child. During this phase, emphasis on "why" and "how" becomes a primary tool for adaptation to occur. Conservation of quantity, involving such things as object permanence and conservation of volume, must be mastered before a concept of numbers can be developed.

Language begins to replace sensorimotor activity as a primary facilitator of learning and as the preferred mode of expressing thoughts. Additionally, events are judged by outward appearance regardless of their objective logic. The child responds to either the qualitative aspects of an event or its quantitative aspects, but not both simultaneously. As a result, the child is unable to merge concepts of objects, space, and causality into interrelationships with a concept of time. Time is a nebulous concept that eludes the child in this phase of development.

The child, according to Piaget, is egocentric (i.e., self-centered) in his or her relationship to the world rather than autistic (i.e., non-relating) as in the sensorimotor phase. Play serves as an important means of assimilation and occupies most of the child's waking hours. Imaginary play and parallel play are important tools for learning. Play also serves to enact the rules and values of one's elders. Characteristic of the preoperational thought phase is the child's widening of social interest in his or her world. As a result, egocentricity is reduced and social participation increases. The child begins to exhibit interest in relationships between people. Understanding the social roles of "mother," "father," "sister," and "brother" and their relationship to one another is important to the child at this phase.

C. **Concrete Operations Phase (7 to 11 years)**

During the *concrete operations phase* of development the child becomes aware of alternative solutions, uses rules in thinking, and is able to differentiate between appearance and reality. It is called "concrete" because the child's mental actions (i.e., "operations") are still tied to concrete objects.

The concept of reversibility becomes established during this phase. *Reversibility* refers to the capacity of the child to understand that any change of shape, order, position, number, and so forth can be mentally reversed and returned to its original shape, order, position, or number. Reversibility enables the child to relate an event or thought to a total system of interrelated parts. It enables the child to consider the event or thought from beginning to end, or from end to beginning. This form of operational thought enhances the child's mental capacity to order and relate experiences to an organized whole.

The concrete operational thought level presupposes that mental experimentation still depends on perception. At this phase perceptions are more accurate, and the child applies his or her interpretation of these environmental perceptions knowingly. The child examines the parts in order to gain knowledge of the whole, and establishes means of classification for organizing parts into a hierarchical system.

During this phase play is used by the child to understand his or her physical and social world. Rules and regulations are of interest to the child when applied to play. Play, however, loses its assimilative characteristics and becomes a balanced subordinate process of cognitive thought. As a result, curiosity finds expression in intellectual experimentation instead of active play alone.

D. **Formal Operations Phase (11 onward)**

During the *formal operations phase* childhood ends and youth begins as the individual enters the world of ideas. During this fourth and final phase of cognitive development a systematic approach to problem solving appears. Logical deduction by implication develops, and the individual is capable of thinking vertically; that is, beyond the present. At this level the individual can dream and does not need concrete reality. Deduction by hypothesis and judgment by implication enable one to reason beyond cause and effect.

Robert Havighurst

The theory of Robert Havighurst (1953; 1972; Havighurst and Levine, 1979) is based on the concept that successful achievement of developmental tasks leads to happiness and success with later tasks, whereas failure leads to unhappiness, social disapproval, and difficulty with later tasks. It is interesting to note his disagreement with any theory that proposes an innate basis of growth and development. He believes that living is learning and growing is learning (Havighurst, 1972). Development, then, according to Havighurst, is the process of learning one's way through life. Havighurst conceives of successful development as requiring mastery of a series of tasks. At each level of development the child encounters new social demands. These demands, or tasks, arise out of three sources. First, tasks arise from physical maturation. Such tasks as learning to walk, talk, and get along with one's age-mates are maturation-based. Second, tasks arise out of the cultural pressures of society, such as learning how to read and learning to be a responsible citizen. The third source of tasks is oneself. Tasks arise out of the maturing personality and the individual's values and unique aspirations.

Havighurst's theory has implications for all age levels. His theory is of particular importance to educators because it describes teachable moments in which a person's body and self are ready to achieve a certain task. Educators can better time their efforts at teaching by identifying the tasks that are suitable for a particular level of development, being fully aware that a child's level of readiness is influenced by biological, cultural, and self factors all interacting with one another.

Concept 2.6   There are numerous developmental tasks that must be achieved for the normal process of development to proceed unencumbered.

Havighurst has suggested six major periods of development: infancy and early childhood (birth through 5 years), middle childhood (6 through 12 years), adolescence (13 through 18 years), early adulthood (19 through 29 years), middle adulthood (30 through 60 years), and later maturity (60 years and up). A summary of Havighurst's developmental tasks in outline form follows. The reader is cautioned to be flexible in the interpretation of these tasks with respect to age. Ages are only convenient approximations and should not be viewed as rigid time frames. However, significant delay beyond these age boundaries would, according to Havighurst, represent failure in a developmental task, with resulting unhappiness and great difficulty with future tasks.

A. Infancy and Early Childhood (birth to 5 years)
    1. Learning to walk.
    2. Learning to take solid foods.
    3. Learning to talk.
    4. Learning to control the elimination of bodily wastes.
    5. Learning sex differences and sexual modesty.
    6. Acquiring concepts and language to describe social and physical reality.

7. Readiness for reading.
   8. Learning to distinguish right from wrong and developing a conscience.
B. Middle Childhood (6 to 12 years)
   1. Learning physical skills necessary for ordinary games.
   2. Building a wholesome attitude toward oneself.
   3. Learning to get along with age-mates.
   4. Learning an appropriate sex role.
   5. Developing fundamental skills in reading, writing, and calculating.
   6. Developing concepts necessary for everyday living.
   7. Developing a conscience, morality, and a scale of values.
   8. Achieving personal independence.
   9. Developing acceptable attitudes toward society.
C. Adolescence (13 to 18 years)
   1. Achieving mature relations with both sexes.
   2. Achieving a masculine or feminine social role.
   3. Accepting one's physique.
   4. Achieving emotional independence of adults.
   5. Preparing for marriage and family life.
   6. Preparing for an economic career.
   7. Acquiring values and an ethical system to guide behavior.
   8. Desiring and achieving socially responsible behavior.
D. Early Adulthood (19 to 29 years)
   1. Selecting a mate.
   2. Learning to live with a partner.
   3. Starting a family.
   4. Rearing children.
   5. Managing a home.
   6. Starting an occupation.
   7. Assuming civic responsibility.
E. Middle Adulthood (30 to 60 years)
   1. Helping teenage children to become happy and responsible adults.
   2. Achieving adult social and civic responsibility.
   3. Satisfactory career achievement.
   4. Developing adult leisure-time activities.
   5. Relating to one's spouse as a person.
   6. Accepting the physiological changes of middle age.
   7. Adjusting to aging parents.
F. Later Maturity (60 years and up)
   1. Adjusting to decreasing strength and health.
   2. Adjusting to retirement and reduced income.
   3. Adjusting to death of spouse.
   4. Establishing relations with one's own age group.
   5. Meeting social and civic obligations.
   6. Establishing satisfactory living quarters.

Summary

The process of development is commonly viewed as hierarchical. That is, the individual proceeds from general to specific, and from simple to complex, in gaining mastery and control over his or her environment. Erik Erikson's phase-stage theory, Jean Piaget's developmental milestone theory, and Robert Havighurst's developmental task theory make it obvious that the human organism throughout all aspects of its development is moving from comparatively simple forms of existence to more complex and sophisticated levels of development. Until recently, these levels of development have been expressed primarily in terms of the cognitive and affective behaviors of the individual, with only indirect attention given to motor development. Dynamical systems theory offers new perspectives on development and is particularly relevant to the study of motor behavior.

Although the theoretical formulations of Erikson, Piaget, and Havighurst are of value, none adequately addresses motor development. It is, therefore, appropriate that a theoretical model of motor development that integrates elements from each, plus a dynamical systems perspective be put forth in order that we may describe and explain this important aspect of human development. Chapter 4, Motor Development: A Theoretical Model, is dedicated to this end.

Terms to Remember

Psychoanalytic theory
Psychosocial theory
Maturational theory
Environmental theory
Cognitive development theory
Phase-stage
Developmental task
Developmental milestone
Dynamical systems
Affordances
Rate limiters
Self-organizing
Degrees of freedom
Control parameters
Phase shift
Trust versus mistrust
Autonomy vs. doubt & shame

Initiative versus guilt
Industry versus inferiority
Identity versus role confusion
Intimacy versus isolation
Generativity versus self-
 absorption
Integrity versus despair
Adaptation
Accommodation
Assimilation
Sensorimotor
Preoperational thought
Concrete operations
Formal operations
Schema
Reversibility

Critical Readings

Erikson, E. (1980). *Identity and the Life Cycle*. New York: W. W. Norton.

Kamm, K. et. al. (1990). A dynamical systems approach to motor development. *Physical Therapy*, 70, 763–774.

Kugler, P. N., Kelso, J. A. S., & Turvey, M. T. (1982). On the control and co-ordination of naturally developing systems. In J. A. S. Kelso & J. E. Clark (Eds.), *The Development of Motor Control and Co-ordination*. New York: Wiley (pp. 5–78).

Lefrancois, G. (1993). *The Lifespan* (Chapter 2). Belmont, CA: Wadsworth.

Lerner, R. M. (1986). *Concepts and Theories of Human Development* (Chapter 7). Reading, MA: Addison-Wesley.

Maier, H. W. (1978). *Three Theories of Child Development*. New York: Harper & Row, (Chapters 2–3).

Peterson, R. & Felton-Collins, V. (1986). *The Piaget Handbook for Teachers and Parents: Children in the Age of Discovery, Preschool–Third Grade*. New York: Teachers College Press.

Wadsworth, B. J. (1979). *Piaget's Theory of Cognitive Development*. New York: Longman.

Waldorp, M. M. (1993). *Complexity*. New York: Simon & Schuster.

Chapter 3

Factors Affecting Motor Development

CHAPTER COMPETENCIES

Upon completion of this chapter you should be able to:

- *Identify genetic and environmental factors influencing growth and biological maturation*
- *Derive principles of motor development and apply these principles to teaching/learning situations at various points in the life span*
- *Describe "catch-up" growth, developmental plasticity, and the factors affecting each*
- *Analyze relationships among growth, biological maturation, and physiological changes in motor skill development*
- *Discuss the effects of environmental deprivation on life span motor development*
- *Discuss the effects of enrichment, special practice, and teaching on life span motor development*
- *Define and discuss the concepts of critical and sensitive periods, phylogenetic and ontogenetic skills, and co-twin control*
- *Identify and order from simple to complex the environmental variables that may influence developmental levels*
- *Explain the similarities and differences between bonding and imprinting*
- *Hypothesize about the impact of temperament on the interactive process of development*
- *Describe differences and similarities implied by the terms "low-birthweight" and "young-for-date"*
- *Discuss the long-term effects of prematurity*
- *Analyze the collective impact of eating disorders, fitness levels, and mechanical laws on motor development*

Key Concept: Both the process and product of motor development are influenced by a wide variety of factors operating in isolation *and* in conjunction with one another.

The development and refinement of movement patterns and movement skills are influenced in complex ways. Both the process and product of one's movement are rooted in one's unique genetic and experiential background, coupled with the specific demands of the movement task itself. Any study of motor development would be incomplete without a discussion of several of these influencing factors. This chapter will focus on factors within the individual, the environment, and the task that affect the process of development throughout the life cycle.

Factors within the Individual

The unique genetic inheritance that accounts for individuality can also account for similarity in many ways. One of these similarities is the trend for human development to proceed in an orderly, predictable fashion. A number of biological factors affecting motor development seem to emerge from this predictable pattern.

Developmental Direction

The principle of *developmental direction* was first formulated by Gesell (1954) as a means of explaining increased coordination and motor control as a function of the maturing nervous system. Through observations, Gesell noted that an orderly, predictable sequence of physical development proceeds from the head to the feet (cephalocaudal), and from the center of the body to its periphery (proximodistal). The principle of developmental direction has, however, encountered criticism during the last few years, and should not be viewed as operational at all levels of development or in all individuals. It just may be that the observation of tendencies toward distinct developmental directions is not exclusively a function of the maturing nervous system as originally hypothesized by Gesell, but is due, in part, to the demands of the specific task itself. For example, the task demands of independent walking are considerably greater than those for crawling or creeping. There is less margin for error in independent walking than there is in creeping, and in turn, crawling. In other words, it is mechanically easier to crawl than it is to creep, and to creep than it is to walk. Therefore, the apparent cephalocaudal progression in development may not be simply due to maturation of the nervous system, but also to the performance demands of the task itself. Care, therefore, should be taken when interpreting the concept of developmental direction, particularly during the period of infancy.

Concept 3.1   Neuromotor maturation principles may be used to explain, in part, both the sequence and rate of motor development throughout the life cycle.

The *cephalocaudal* aspect of developmental direction refers specifically to the gradual progression of increased control over the musculature, moving from the head to the feet. It may be witnessed in the prenatal stages of fetal development as well as in later postnatal development. In the developing fetus, for example, the head forms first, and the arms form prior to the legs. Likewise, infants exhibit sequential control over the musculature of the head, neck, and trunk, prior to gaining control over the legs and feet. Young children are often clumsy and exhibit poor motor control over their lower extremities. This may be due to incomplete cephalocaudal development, and to the complexity of the task demands of independent walking.

The second aspect of developmental direction, known as *proximodistal* development, refers specifically to the child's progression in control of the musculature from the center of the body to its most distant parts. As with cephalocaudal development, the proximodistal concept applies to both growth processes and the acquisition of movement skills. For example, with regard to growth, the trunk and shoulder girdle grow prior to arms and legs, which grow prior to the fingers and toes. In terms of skill acquisition the young child is able to control the muscles of the trunk and shoulder girdle prior to the muscles of the wrist, hand, and fingers. This principle of development is frequently utilized in the primary grades when children are taught the less refined elements of manuscript writing before they learn the more complex and refined movements of cursive writing.

The cephalocaudal and proximodistal process is operational throughout life, and has a tendency to reverse itself as one ages. Payne and Isaacs (1991) note that "the most currently acquired movements of the lower body or periphery will be the first to exhibit signs of regression. The process of movement regression slowly evolves in a 'tail to head' and 'outside-in' direction" (p. 11). Certainly, however, older individuals can forestall and reduce such regression by staying active.

Rate of Growth

One's *growth rate* follows a characteristic pattern that is universal for all and resistant to external influence. A minor interruption of the normal pace of growth is compensated for by a still unexplained process of *self-regulatory fluctuation* (Gesell, 1954) that enables a child to catch up to his or her age-mates. For example, a severe illness may retard a child's normal gains in height, weight, and movement ability, but upon recovery there will be a tendency to catch up. The same phenomenon is seen with low-birthweight infants. Despite low weights at birth, most of these babies catch up to the characteristic growth rates of their age-mates in a few years. Conditions surrounding the causes of low-birthweight, such as inadequate nutrition, must not persist. Appropriate intervention must occur early on for this catch-up process to fully manifest itself in the growing infant. Measures of height, weight, and motor development taken prior to age two are generally meaningless for predicting later growth and development.

It should be noted that the self-regulatory process of growth will compensate for minor deviations in the growth pattern, but it is frequently unable to make up for major deviations especially during infancy and childhood. For example, low-birthweight infants under three pounds, and children experiencing severe and prolonged nutritional deficiencies, frequently suffer permanent deficits in height and weight, as well as in their cognitive and motor development.

Concept 3.2   The permanency of growth retardation is particularly devastating during the first two years of life.

Restricted opportunities for movement and deprivation of experience have been shown repeatedly to interfere with children's abilities to perform movement tasks that are characteristic of their age levels. The effects of sensory and motor experience deprivation can sometimes be overcome when nearly optimal conditions are established for a child (McGraw, 1939). The extent to which the child will be able to catch up to his or her peers, however, depends on the duration and severity of deprivation, the age of the child, and the child's individual genetic growth potential.

Reciprocal Interweaving

The coordinated and progressive intricate interweaving of neural mechanisms of opposing muscle systems into an increasingly mature relationship is characteristic of the developing child's motor behavior. Termed *reciprocal interweaving* by Gesell (1954), there are two different but related processes associated with this increase of functional complexity: differentiation and integration.

Concept 3.3   Neuromotor maturation is evidenced through increased ability to differentiate and integrate motor and sensory mechanisms.

Differentiation is associated with the gradual progression from the gross globular (overall) movement patterns of infants to the more refined and functional movements of children and adolescents. For example, the manipulative behaviors of the newborn in terms of reaching, grasping, and releasing objects is quite poor. There is little control of movement, but as the child develops the control improves. The child is able to differentiate among various muscle groups and begins to establish control. Control continues to improve with practice until we see the precise movements of cursive writing, cutting with scissors, block building, and violin playing.

Integration refers to bringing various opposing muscle and sensory systems into coordinated interaction with one another. For example, the young child gradually progresses from ill-defined corralling movements when attempting to grasp an object to more mature and visually guided reaching and grasping behaviors. The differentiation of movements of the arms, hands, and fingers, followed by the integration of the use of the eyes with the movements of the hand to perform eye-hand coordination tasks, is crucial to normal development.

Differentiation and integration tend to be reversible with aging. As one ages and movement abilities begin to regress the coordinated interaction of sensory and motor mechanisms frequently becomes inhibited. The extent to which one's coordinated movement abilities regress is not merely a function of age, but is influenced greatly by activity levels and attitude.

There is little doubt that differentiation and integration operate simultaneously. The complex abilities of the adult cannot be explained merely in terms of a process of integration of simpler responses. What occurs, instead, is a constant interlacing of both differentiation and integration.

Readiness

E. L. Thorndike (1913), the "grandfather" of learning theory, first proposed the principle of readiness primarily in reference to emotional responses to actions or expected actions. According to his concept, readiness was dependent on the biological maturation model, which was popular at the turn of the century. Today's concept of readiness, however, is much broader and refers to readiness for learning. *Readiness* may be defined as conditions within a task, an individual, and the environment that make mastery of a particular task appropriate. The concept of readiness, as used today, extends beyond biological maturation and includes consideration of factors that can be modified or manipulated to encourage or promote learning. Several related factors combine to promote readiness. Physical and mental maturation, interacting with motivation, prerequisite learning, and an enriching environment all influence readiness. At this juncture we simply do not know how to pinpoint exactly when someone is ready to learn a new movement skill. However, research suggests that early experience in a movement activity before the individual is ready is likely to have minimal benefits (Magill, 1993).

Concept 3.4   Readiness for learning is dependent upon convergence of biological, environmental, and physical factors.

In recent years a great deal of attention has been focused on developing reading readiness through appropriate types of preschool and primary grade experiences. Entire educational programs have been built around the notion that children must achieve a certain level of development before they are ready to pursue intellectual tasks such as reading and writing (Bredenkamp, 1987), as well as movement tasks involving locomotion, manipulation, and stability (Gallahue, 1993). Readiness training is a part of many preschool and primary grade educational programs. An integral part of these readiness programs has been the use of movement as a means of enhancing basic perceptual-motor qualities (see Chapter 13). Although it has not been conclusively documented that perceptual-motor experiences have a direct effect on the attainment of specific cognitive readiness skills, it is safe to assume that they have at least an indirect influence because they encourage a child's self-esteem and a positive "Yes I can" approach to learning.

The concept of readiness as it is used today, whether for the learning of cognitive skills or motor skills, is probably best summed up in Bruner's (1965) statement that "the foundation of any subject may be taught to anybody at any age in some form" (p. 12). In other words the burden of being "ready" is as much the instructor's responsibility in recognizing it, as it is the student's. Readiness is a combination of maturational "ripeness," environmental openness, and instructor sensitivity. It has numerous implications for lifelong learning opportunities.

Critical and Sensitive Learning Periods

The concept of *critical and sensitive learning periods* is closely aligned to readiness and revolves around the observation that there are certain time frames in which an individual is more sensitive to certain kinds of stimulation. Normal development in later periods may be hindered if a child fails to receive the proper stimulation during a critical period. For example, inadequate nutrition, prolonged stress, inconsistent mothering, or a lack of appropriate learning experiences may have a more negative impact on development if they occur early in life rather than at a later age. The concept of critical periods also has a positive side. It suggests that appropriate intervention during a specific period tends to facilitate more positive forms of development at later stages than if the same intervention occurs at another time.

One should recognize that the tendency of a child to follow a critical period pattern is closely linked to the theory of developmental tasks and to a lesser degree linked to the milestone and phase-stage views. Havighurst's (1972) theoretical framework of development is actually a critical period hypothesis, applied from the perspective of education.

The notion of critical periods of development has been so pervasive in education that an entire federally funded educational program was established on this premise. Operation Head Start, begun in the 1960s, viewed the age period of three to five years as critical to children's intellectual development. It was hypothesized that if given a "head start" through a carefully structured environment designed to develop school-oriented skills, deprived children would be able to begin school on nearly the same level as their non-deprived counterparts. The results of Head Start programs did not entirely bear out the critical period hypothesis. This was probably due to the existence of more than one critical period for intellectual development. In addition, the age period of three to five years may not be as pivotal as originally assumed. Current views of the critical period hypothesis reject the notion that there are highly specific time frames in which one must develop motor skills (Seefeldt, 1975). There are, however, broad periods during which development of certain skills is more easily accomplished.

Concept 3.5 There are broadly defined sensitive periods during which individuals can learn new tasks most efficiently and effectively.

It is safe to assume that there are *sensitive periods* or broad time frames for development. The point to be made is that critical or sensitive periods should not be too narrowly defined. Failure to account for individual differences and for special environmental circumstances will lead one to conclude that a sensitive period is a universal point in time. Instead, a notion of sensitive periods as broad, general guidelines susceptible to modification should be adopted. Learning is a phenomena that continues throughout life. As scientists learn more about the aging brain and the aging motor system, they continually demonstrate this important concept (Hinton, 1992; Selkoe, 1992). Learning can be a life-long process, and the effects of aging can be slowed and reduced through continual use of the brain and motor system.

Individual Differences

The tendency to exhibit *individual differences* is crucial. Each person is a unique individual with his or her own timetable for development. This timetable is a combination of a particular individual's heredity and environmental influences. Although the sequence of appearance of developmental characteristics is predictable, the rate of appearance may be quite variable. Therefore, strict adherence to a chronological classification of development by age is without support or justification.

Concept 3.6   Interindividual and intraindividual variation are the key concepts upon which developmental education is based.

The "average" ages for the acquisition of all sorts of developmental tasks, ranging from learning how to walk (the major developmental task of infancy), to gaining bowel and bladder control (the first restrictions of a civilized society on the child) have been bandied about in the professional literature and the daily conversation of parents and teachers for years. It must be remembered that these average ages are just that and nothing more. They are mere approximations that serve as convenient indicators of developmentally appropriate behaviors. It is common to see deviations from the mean of as much as six months to one year in the appearance of numerous movement skills. The tendency to exhibit individual differences is closely linked to the concept of readiness and helps to explain why some individuals are ready to learn new skills when others are not.

Phylogeny and Ontogeny

Many of the rudimentary abilities of the infant and the fundamental movement abilities of the young child when viewed from a maturation perspective as proposed by Gesell (1928, 1954) are considered to be phylogenetic; that is, they tend to appear automatically and in a predictable sequence within the maturing child. *Phylogenetic skills* are resistant to external environmental influences. Movement skills such as the rudimentary manipulative tasks of reaching, grasping, and releasing objects, the stability tasks of gaining control of the gross musculature of the body, and the fundamental locomotor abilities of walking, jumping, and running are examples of what may be viewed as phylogenetic skills. *Ontogenetic skills*, on the other hand, depend primarily on learning and environmental opportunities. Such skills as swimming, bicycling, and ice skating are considered ontogenetic because they do not appear automatically within individuals but require a period of practice and experience and are influenced by one's culture. The entire concept of phylogeny and ontogeny needs to be reevaluated in light of the fact that many skills heretofore considered phylogenetic can be influenced by environmental interaction (Bower et al., 1970; Bower, 1974).

Concept 3.7 The acquisition of several types of movement patterns may have their basis in phylogeny (biology), but ontogenetic (environmental) conditions shape the rate and extent to which the patterns are acquired.

Although there may be a biological tendency for the development of certain abilities due to phylogenetic processes, it is simplistic to assume that maturation alone will account for motor development. The extent or level to which any voluntary movement ability is mastered depends, in part, on ontogeny or the environment. In other words, opportunities for practice, encouragement, and instruction, and the ecology, or conditions, of the environment itself, contribute significantly to movement skill development throughout life. There seems to be little solid support for Gesell's (1928, 1954) notion that ''ontogeny recapitulates phylogeny,'' although some phylogenetic behaviors may be present in humankind.

Factors in the Environment

Over the past several years considerable speculation and research has focused on the effects of parenting behaviors during infancy and early childhood as they influence the subsequent functioning of children. Because of the extreme dependence of the human infant on its caregivers and because of the length of this period of dependence, a variety of parental care factors influence later development. Among the most crucial are the effects of environmental stimulation and deprivation, the temperament of the child, and the bonding that occurs between parent and child during the early days following birth.

Bonding

The study of parent-to-infant attachment, or *bonding,* has its roots in the imprinting (i.e. attachment) studies conducted by Lorenz (1966), Hess (1959), and others on birds, ducks, and other animals. Basically, these experiments with animals revealed that the degree to which the newborn imprinted on its mother was directly related to their contact time. This critical period for *imprinting* in animals has been shown to be very short. Klopper et al. (1964), for example, has shown that separation of a mother goat from her kid right after birth for little more than an hour will result in the mother's refusal to accept or nurse. Although human infants do not imprint in the narrow sense of the word as animals do, there is compelling evidence that there is a broad ''sensitive'' period in which parent-to-infant attachment occurs during the early months of post-natal life. If this sensitive period is missed, the parent and child may fail to bond. This may result in later developmental difficulties, particularly in the affective development of the child.

In their review of bonding, Kennell et al. (1979) stated:

> Perhaps the parent's attachment to a child is the strongest bond in the human species. The power of this attachment is so great that it enables the mother and father to make the unusual sacrifices necessary for the care of the infant. Early in life the infant becomes attached to one individual, most often it is the mother. The original mother-infant bond is the wellspring for all the infant's subsequent attachments and is the relationship through which the child develops a sense of himself. (p. 786)

The effects of long-term maternal separation on the motor, cognitive, and emotional aspects of the infant's development have been documented by Spitz (1945), Bolby (1958), and A. Freud (1965) on children evacuated from London during World War II. The results of these investigations, according to Kennell et al. (1979) "have dramatically altered infant care throughout the world" (p. 786).

Concept 3.8   The reciprocal interaction between parent and child impacts on both the rate and extent of development.

Bonding, in essence, is a strong emotional attachment that endures over time, distance, hardship, and desirability. Research has shown that this emotional bond begins developing at birth and can fail to develop or be incompletely established with early separation (Kennell et al., 1974; Leifer et al., 1972; Robson, 1967). The leading factors contributing to initial separation are prematurity and low birthweight, which result in the incubation of the newborn; mild or severe neonatal problems at birth; and standard hospital operating procedures. Fortunately, the trend is now in favor of promoting early parental contact. Fathers are routinely permitted in the labor and delivery rooms and are allowed to take a role in the child-bearing process. Rooming-in is on the increase in many maternity hospitals. Breastfeeding has gained renewed acceptance, and home births are on the rise. Giving birth at home—not always a recommended procedure—is dramatically different from the usual hospital routine. In the home birth, the mother is clearly in command. Instead of being a passive patient, she is an active participant in the birth process, along with significant others and the midwife.

Concept 3.9   Bonding plays an undetermined role in the process of development.

Early attachment between parent and child appears to influence development. One must question, however, if bonding is *essential* to the welfare of the child. Generations of adopted children will attest to the success of their development even though bonding with "mother" was delayed by weeks, months, or even years. The reciprocal interaction between parent and child creates a mutually satisfying and rewarding relationship, the importance of which cannot be minimized. Care must be taken, however, not to define the concept of bonding too narrowly or to overemphasize its importance. Further research is necessary to clearly establish its link to the process of development. The reader is referred to the excellent discussion on infant-mother attachment by Lamb et al. (1985).

Stimulation and Deprivation

A great deal of study has been done over the years to determine the relative effects of *stimulation and deprivation* on the learning of a variety of skills. In fact, there has been considerable controversy among hereditarians and environmentalists over the issue during the past 100 years. Numerous textbooks have recorded the nature versus nurture debates, but little has been settled in the attempt to categorize the effects of each on development. The current trend has been to respect the individual importance of both nature and nurture and to recognize the complexly intertwined influences of maturation *and* experience.

Concept 3.10 Both stimulation and deprivation of experiences have potential for influencing the rate of development.

Students of motor development have recognized the futility of debating the separate merits of maturation and experience and have instead concentrated their research on three major questions. The first of these questions deals with the approximate ages at which various skills can be learned most effectively. The research of Bayley (1935), Shirley (1931), and Wellman (1937) represented the first serious attempts to describe the age at which many of the rudimentary and fundamental movement abilities appear. Each of these researchers reported a somewhat different timetable for the rate of appearance of numerous phylogenetic skills. They did, however, show amazing consistency in the sequential order of appearance of these abilities. This factor illustrates the combined effects of both intrinsic, or maturationally determined, influences on the sequence of development and extrinsic, or environmentally influenced behaviors on the rate of development. Unfortunately, until recently, little has been done to more clearly ascertain the ages at which both phylogenetic and ontogenetic skills can be learned most effectively. The principle of readiness has been viewed as a cornerstone of our educational system, but little more than lip service has been paid to its importance, particularly with regard to developing movement abilities. We know that children can develop many movement abilities early in life, but we still do not know the best time to introduce many skills.

The second question deals with the effects of special training on the learning of motor skills. A number of co-twin control studies have been conducted to ascertain the influence of special practice on early learning. The use of identical twins enables the researcher to ensure identical hereditary backgrounds and characteristics of the subjects. One twin is given advanced opportunities for practice, while the other is restricted from practicing the same skills over a prescribed length of time. The famous studies of Gesell and Thompson (1929), Hilgard (1932), and McGraw (1935) have all demonstrated the inability of early training to hasten development to an appreciable degree. However, it is important to note that follow-up studies of the co-twin control experiments of both Gesell and McGraw showed that the trained subjects exhibited greater confidence and assurance in the activities in which they had received special training. In other words, special attention and training may not influence the quantitative aspects of the movement skills learned as much as the qualitative aspects. Again, we see the complex interrelationship between maturation and experience.

Investigations by Gerber and Dean (1957) recorded the advanced development in Ugandan infants during the first postnatal days and months of life. The investigators concluded that the infants' motor superiority over infants raised in the United States was due, in part, to the enriched environmental stimulation that they received. They were carried on their mothers' backs much of the time, were fed on demand, and were constantly the centers of attention and affection. However, their advanced state at birth (that is, ability to hold head erect, early disappearance of certain reflexes, and so forth) suggests that a genetic factor may also have been the cause of their developmental superiority. Again, we see the interrelatedness of maturation and experience.

With the advent of neonatal and infant intensive care units in the 1970s the survival rate for pre-term and low-birthweight infants has risen dramatically. Parents, physicians, and researchers have wondered about the effects of infant stimulation programs on the subsequent development of these high-risk infants. Ulrich (1984) in her comprehensive review of the research concluded that "Despite difficulties in comparing studies due to the variability of subjects used, and type, intensity, and duration of treatment, the overwhelming evidence indicates beneficial effects" (p. 68).

Such a conclusion is encouraging and leads one to consider the timing and duration of special training or stimulation. Is there a "sensitive period" beyond which the benefits of stimulation are minimally beneficial?

The third question concerns the effect of limited or restricted opportunities for practice on the acquisition of motor skills. Studies of this nature have centered generally on experimentally induced environmental deprivation in animals. Only a few studies have been reported in which children have actually been observed in environments where unusual restrictions of movement or experience have existed.

An investigation conducted by Dennis (1960) examined infants reared at three separate institutions in Iran. The infants in two of the institutions were found to be severely retarded in their motor development. In the third there was little motor retardation. The discrepancy led Dennis to investigate the lifestyles of the children in each institution. The results of his investigation led to the conclusion that lack of handling, blandness of surroundings, and general absence of movement opportunity or experience were causes of motor retardation in the first two institutions. Another investigation, by Dennis and Najarian (1957), revealed similar findings in a smaller number of creche infants reared in Beirut, Lebanon. Both investigations lend support to the hypothesis that behavioral development cannot be fully attributed to the maturation hypothesis. Due to cultural mores, the humanitarian virtues of most investigators, and concerned parents, there are few experiments in which the environmental circumstances of infants or young children have been intentionally altered to determine whether serious malfunctioning or atypical behavior will result. The general consensus of the research that does exist is that severe restrictions and lack of experience can indeed delay normal development.

We need only to look as far as the school playground and observe many girls jumping rope expertly and many boys throwing and catching balls with great skill. When asked to reverse the activities, however, each group tends to revert to less mature patterns of movement. Factors within our culture, unfortunately, often predetermine the types of movement experiences in which boys and girls engage (Gallahue et al., 1994).

Concept 3.11 Extreme conditions of environmental deprivation may disrupt both the sequence and rate of movement skill acquisition.

Dennis (1935) conducted an investigation in which fraternal twin infant girls were reared in a very sterile nursery environment (that is, they were intentionally given a minimal amount of motor and social stimulation). After 14 months in this environment, their movement behavior was compared with normative data and was found to be retarded beyond the normal limits. Social development, however, was well within the limits of the standard norms, a factor that may suggest a greater need for motor stimulation than for social stimulation. This investigation, however, represents the only attempt at intentionally limiting the child's environment to study the possible consequences on development. Care should be taken in drawing any sweeping conclusions from a single investigation without collaborative support.

The child-rearing practices of the Hopi Indians were the subject of another investigation by Dennis (1940). These Indians have traditionally restricted their infants' movement by binding them to cradle boards that mothers carry on their backs. The infants spend nearly all of their first three months bound in the cradle boards. As they grow older, the number and length of freedom periods is gradually increased. Dennis observed that the movement abilities of these children were not retarded as might be expected from the results of the investigations just mentioned. It may be beneficial to consider that perhaps motor activity is not of crucial importance during the first months following birth. Being bound securely to the cradle board and experiencing the rhythmical movements of the mother may, in some ways, have simulated the security of life in the womb. The close physical contact with the mother and an opportunity to begin utilizing perceptual modalities may have been crucial factors in these first months. One may also consider what the infants observed through their developing visual senses while bound to the cradle boards. The infants were generally in positions that permitted viewing of sights going on all around. When not being carried about, the infants were propped up on nearby trees or in corners and able to observe mothers going about their daily chores. The visual and motor stimulation of the Hopi Indian babies was considerably greater than that available in the sterile environments of the Iranian and Lebanese infants and the two girls investigated by Dennis. The Hopi infant study may point to the close identification of the visual modality with the motor dimension of behavior. It leads one to consider the interrelatedness of perceptual and motor functions and the importance of enriching stimulation (Williams, 1983).

It becomes impossible to make a case for either maturation or learning as the sole or even primary influence on development. The literature is overwhelmingly in favor of the interaction of one with the other. This compromise view of development is summed up by Carmichael, who, as early as 1925, recognized that "heredity and environment are not antithetical, nor can they expediently be separated; for in all maturation there is learning; in all learning there is hereditary maturation" (p. 260).

Both maturation and learning play important roles in the acquisition of movement abilities. Although experience seems to have little influence on the sequence of their emergence, it does affect the time of appearance of certain movements and the extent of their development. One of the greatest needs of children is to practice skills at a time when they are developmentally ready to benefit the most from such skills. Special practice prior to maturational readiness is of dubious benefit. The key is to be able to accurately judge the time at which each individual is "ripe" for learning and then to provide a series of educationally sound and effective movement experiences. However, all indications are that young children are generally capable of more than we have suspected, and many of the traditional readiness signposts that we have used may actually be incorrect.

Temperament

Anyone who has been around young children for an extended period is quick to notice the differences in *temperament* (i.e., disposition) that exist. These individual differences in the responsiveness of children are probably caused by their unique environmental and experiential histories. It is interesting to note, however, that differences in temperament are observable even at birth. Persistent differences in newborns have been documented for a variety of physiological and perceptual-motor dimensions in newborns (Eisenberg et al., 1966). Differences in cardiac reactions and response intensity have also been observed, along with varying reactions to environmental conditions (Lipton et al., 1961; Westman, 1973).

The temperaments of children have been classified in a number of ways. The method utilized by Chess and Thomas (1973) is a popular one. They classified children as (1) the "easy child," (2) the "difficult child," and (3) the "slow-to-warm-up child." In a separate investigation Chess and Thomas observed children longitudinally, using a parental report system of data collection. Infants divided into "cuddler" and "noncuddler" classifications exhibited a variety of differences when viewed over time. Noncuddlers were found to sit, stand, and crawl sooner than cuddlers. They were also found to sleep less and to protest more than those identified as cuddlers.

Research by Korner (Korner et al., 1975; Korner, 1981; Korner et al., 1982) highlighted the beneficial effects of rhythmical rocking of babies. Korner's research has shown that premature babies placed on oscillating waterbeds are less irritable, more alert, and more responsive to the human face and voice. Such information may have important implications for premature infants who are routinely placed in incubators and deprived of normal movement and tactile stimulation. The disorganized movements, fragmented sleep patterns, and excessive irritability of premature babies make them difficult to care for, and are likely to affect interaction between parent-child bonding and temperament. Rhythmical rocking may be an effective means to reduce these risks.

Concept 3.12   The temperament of an individual may influence his or her interaction patterns with others, which may enhance or inhibit development.

Although the research on the development of temperament is speculative, it seems safe to assume that because temperament tends to remain consistent from birth, it will have an effect on how parents respond to the child (Osofsky and Conners, 1979). The hyperactive child, the chronic crier, or the fussy child may inadvertently impair the nurturing responses of his or her caregivers. The ill-tempered child may receive less attention than the even-tempered child and, as a consequence, be slower to talk and slower to develop mature movement and socialization skills. The epidemic proportions of child abuse in our culture may be attributable, in part, to the interaction between the ill-tempered child and the parent who in stressful situations is unable to cope with such a child.

Physical Task Factors

A number of additional factors affect motor development. The influence of social class (Malina and Bouchard, 1991), gender (Branta et al., 1987), and ethnic and cultural background (Bril, 1985) all have an impact on growth and motor development. Motor development is not a static process. It is not only the product of biological factors but is also influenced by environmental conditions and physical laws. The interaction of both environmental and biological factors modifies the course of motor development during infancy, childhood, adolescence, and adulthood. Premature birth, eating disorders, fitness levels, and biomechanical factors, as well as the physiological changes associated with aging and lifestyle choice, all impact in important ways on the lifelong process of motor development.

Prematurity

The normal birthweight of an infant is about 3,300 grams (about 7 pounds). Formerly, any infant weighing under 2,500 grams (about 5 1/2 pounds) was classified as *premature*. Today, however, 2,000 grams (4 1/2 pounds) is often used as the standard, unless there is evidence that the gestation period was less than 37 weeks. The practice of labeling a newborn as premature based on gestation period or weight alone is no longer used for two reasons. First, it is often difficult to accurately determine the gestational age of the infant, and second, the highest mortality and morbidity rates are present for infants of the very lowest birthweights (Susser et al., 1972). As a result the terms "low-birthweight" and "young-for-date" have emerged as more accurate indicators of prematurity in the true sense of the word (Kopp and Parmelee, 1979). Prematurity is of major concern because it is closely associated with physical and mental retardation, hyperactivity, and infant death. Prevention is generally considered to be the most important factor in improving infant health and survival rates.

Concept 3.13   Prematurity puts the newborn at risk and frequently undermines the process of motor development.

Low Birthweight. *Low-birthweight* infants weigh less than expected for their gestational age. Two standard deviations below the mean for a given gestational age is the generally accepted criterion for low birthweight (Ounsted and Ounsted, 1973). Therefore, a low-birthweight infant may be one who is born at term (40 weeks) or pre-term (37 weeks or under). Low-birthweight infants have experienced what Warkany et al. (1961) first termed as "intrauterine growth retardation" and are generally called "small-for-date." A variety of prenatal maternal factors have been implicated, including diet, drugs, smoking, infections, and disease (Kopp & Kaler, 1989). Other factors such as social class, multiple births, and geographic locale have been shown to influence birthweight (Ounsted and Ounsted, 1973; Baker & Meonick). The long-term effects of low birthweight are directly related to the degree of intrauterine growth retardation and gestational age of the child. Kopp and Parmelee (1979) stated:

> In summary, it is clear that the infant born with intrauterine growth retardation may have severe medical problems in the neonatal period. Reflexive and behavioral differences may occur in early life, possibly leading to disrupted patterns of parent-infant interaction. The overall outcome for intellectual functioning is relatively positive, even for pre-terms who were small-for-date. Yet, inevitable questions arise. Would the intelligence of this group of children have been higher if they had not been malnourished in utero? (p. 59)

Young-for-Date. Children born at the expected birthweight (less than two standard deviations below the mean) for their gestational age but before full term (37 weeks or less) are called *young-for-date* or *pre-term* infants. There is little agreement on the exact causes of pre-term birth, but a number of factors have been shown to contribute, including drug use, smoking, maternal age, excessive weight gain, and adverse social and economic conditions (Susser et al., 1972). Until recent years the prognosis for young-for-date infants who were either small-for-date or of normal weight for date was bleak. Their morbidity and mortality rates were abnormally high when compared to normal term infants. Drillien (1970) reported that as many as 40 percent showed evidence of neurological and intellectual damage. Recent advances in neonatal intensive care have, however, done much to reduce this.

The pre-term infant is still likely to have more learning difficulties, language and social interaction disadvantages, and motor coordination problems than his or her full-term counterpart (Davies and Stewart, 1975). For some unknown reason, boys seem to be more severely affected than girls. The usual treatment of hospital-born premature infants is to put them in a sterile isolette, where temperature, humidity, and oxygen can be precisely controlled. It has been suggested that the absence of normal stimulation from the mother and the surrounding environment contributes to the retardation (Hasselmeyer, 1964). A study by Solkoff et al. (1969) seems to verify this notion. The results of the two-treatment-group study of premature infants in which one group was given routine care and the other was given five extra minutes of handling per hour seem to support the need for early handling. The extra handling group performed better on two measures. The infants were more active and gained weight faster. Seven months later the handled group still performed better on tests of motor performance and appeared more active and healthier.

Long-term Effects of Prematurity. The data are clear that low-birthweight babies are more likely to die in the first few weeks of life than are normal weight babies. However, tremendous strides have been made in reducing overall infant mortality rate. Figure 3.1 demonstrates a definite positive trend since 1915. Still, statistics such as that presented in Table 3.1 reflect that the United States and several other "developed" countries have a long way to go in the reduction of infant mortality.

The long-term effects of premature birth are not as clear as are the short-term consequences. However, both Lubchenco et al. (1963) and Drillien (1964) found that children who were very small at birth (under 3 1/2 pounds) tended to weigh less and were shorter than their age-mates. Low-birthweight children tend also to be delayed in language development (Crawford, 1982), and have more visual-motor problems in

---

Table 3.1 Worldwide Infant Mortality

A baby born in the United States is nearly twice as likely to die before its first birthday than one born in Finland. Deaths before age 1 per 1,000 live births:

1. Finland	6.0
2. Japan	6.2
3. Sweden	7.0
4. Switzerland	7.7
5. Norway	7.8
6. Denmark	8.2
7. Netherlands	8.4
8. France	9.0
9. Canada	9.1
10. Belgium	9.2
11. Spain	9.6
12. West Germany	10.1
13. United Kingdom	10.1
14. Australia	10.3
15. Ireland	10.5
16. USA	10.5
17. East Germany	10.7

Source: World Population Data Sheet (1985). Population Reference Bureau.

school (Drillien et al., 1980; Rubin et al., 1973); however, no conclusive data are available on the effects of prematurity on later intelligence.

Eating Disorders

We are living in a world far different from that of our ancestors. Vigorous physical exertion is not a necessary part of the daily life pattern of most people. Today, most exercise, if it occurs, is planned and is not an integral part of one's existence. In addition, most of us enjoy, for the present, an abundance of food. It is possible for an individual to consume a large amount of food and use up little of the energy contained in that food. The maintenance of body weight is relatively simple. It requires maintaining a balance between caloric intake and caloric expenditure. If more calories are consumed than are burned over a period of time, obesity is the eventual result. On the other hand, if fewer calories are consumed than expended, weight loss will result over time. Weight loss caused by a long-term aversion to food (anorexia nervosa) or repeated bingeing and purging (bulimia) is of growing concern and must be considered in any discussion of eating disorders.

Concept 3.14 Eating disorders among children, adolescents, and adults dramatically affect their growth and motor development.

Obesity.   Obesity, or any excessive increase in the amount of stored body fat, is considered to be the most prevalent nutritional disease in North America, affecting up to 25 percent of children and adolescents, some 80 percent of whom are in danger of becoming obese adults (Dietz, 1983). Fat has a number of constructive functions. It is a reserve source

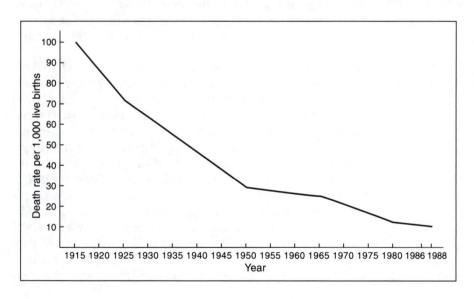

Figure 3.1
Infant mortality changes in the United States, 1915–1988, per 1,000 live births (U.S. Bureau of the Census, 1991)

of energy; it is a vehicle for fat-soluble vitamins; it provides protection and support to the body parts, insulating the body from the cold; and in proper proportion, it enhances the appearance of the body. However, to serve these functions, the proportion of fat desired in adults is about 15 to 18 percent for males and 20 to 25 percent for females (Fomon et al., 1982).

The full-term infant has about 12 to 16 percent fat, much of which develops during the last two months of the gestation period (Documenta, 1970; Fomon et al., 1982). By the sixth month of life body fat percentages have increased to about 25 percent, declining thereafter through childhood to about 15 to 18 percent. During the preadolescent period there is an increase in fat deposits in girls, but not in boys. In fact, there is a small but significant decrease in the percentage of body fat among males (Fomon et al., 1982). Ideally, there is very little change in the percentage of body fat in proportion to total body weight from late adolescence through adulthood. However, the percentage of body fat may range from a low of about 8 percent (typical of the long-distance, ectomorphic runner) to as high as 50 percent (characteristic of the very obese).

It is estimated that more than 70 million Americans are overweight (Wilmore, 1974). The prevalence of obesity in children has been estimated at 13.9 to 22.8 percent in different regions of the United States, and according to National Health Examination Survey statistics, is on the increase (Dietz, 1986; Rosenbaum, 1989). In fact, it is estimated that obese children who have not slimmed down by age 14 have an 85 percent risk of remaining obese as adults (Mossberg, 1989). Kaufman (1975) stated that "there is strong evidence that if an individual is obese as a child, he has a 90 percent chance of being obese as an adult" (p. 78). In North America the percentage of lean body mass tends to decrease with age. The percentage of body fat is the most important determiner of obesity. A person's weight is less crucial than the ratio of fat to lean tissue. Body composition is the only valid criterion for determining obesity.

A growing body of evidence (Stein et al., 1981; Linder et al., 1982) implicates obesity as a factor in the development of atherosclerosis and coronary heart disease. Enos et al. (1955) and McNamera et al. (1971) autopsied teenage soldiers killed in Korea and Vietnam, respectively. Their investigations revealed that coronary and aortic atherosclerosis were present in no less than one third of the soldiers. One of the major suspected risk factors in the development of atherosclerosis and subsequent chronic heart disease is the early development of obesity (Stein et al., 1981). Obesity places additional stress on the circulatory, respiratory, and metabolic systems and may cause, or intensify, disorders in these systems. Obese adults have a well-established increased risk of cardiovascular morbidity and mortality independent of age, cholesterol level, blood pressure, smoking, and glucose intolerance (Pace, Bolton, and Reeves, 1991; Diamond et al., 1991). In addition, obese children and adults frequently suffer ridicule from their peers, poor academic performance, poor self-image, and persistent concern with dieting (Millman, 1980).

The primary environmentally based causes of obesity in individuals with normal hormonal balances are excessive eating and lack of exercise, or a combination of both. Poor eating and exercise habits are formed in childhood and carried on into adult life. The child who is urged to clean the plate at every meal but not encouraged to exercise regularly, has the potential for a serious weight problem.

An area of interest to many who study obesity is the activity levels of obese children. A study by Bruch (1940) examined 160 obese children. It was found that 76 percent of the boys and 88 percent of the girls were rated as inactive when compared to normal youngsters. Further studies by M. L. Johnson and his colleagues (1956) compared the caloric intake and activity of normal and obese girls. The obese girls spent less than half as much time at physical activity as the non-obese girls. Furthermore, Sciafani (1980) demonstrated that physical inactivity appears to contribute to obesity as indicated by studies linking television watching to the prevalence of childhood obesity. Dieting does not appear to be the complete, or even the best, solution to environmentally based obesity in children. In fact, since their food intake may be normal, dieting may cause serious deficiencies in the nutrients required for proper growth and health. Since a major cause of obesity in children is lack of activity, long-term increases in this area may be the best and most healthful solution.

Concept 3.15   Both genetic and environmental factors contribute to the onset and extent of obesity.

The etiology of obesity in most children is unknown, but genetic as well as environmental factors appear to be involved. Obesity appears to be highly familial with either a hereditary or environmental basis or a combination of both (Zonta et al., 1987). Mayer (1968) found the chances of obesity to be 10 percent for children with parents of normal weight, 40 percent with one obese parent, and 70 percent with both parents obese. Twin studies support the concept that genetic factors play a major role in obesity (Stunkard et al., 1986; 1990). Additionally, obesity among children after 10 years of age appears to be strongly genetic with about two-thirds of the variability in body weight attributable to genetic factors. In summary, Malina and Bouchard (1991) reported that:

> The data from a variety of studies suggest that the relative risk of an obese child becoming an obese adult is about 2.0, while the relative risk for an obese adolescent becoming an obese adult may be as high as 5.0 or 6.0 (p. 438).

Although both hereditary and environmental factors play a role, regular, vigorous physical activity may be the most important variable in preventing obesity.

Anorexia Nervosa/Bulimia Nervosa. A problem as perplexing and potentially as dangerous as obesity is *anorexia nervosa,* which is characterized by an aversion to the consumption of food and an obsession with being "too fat" even when the person is clearly underweight. These self-starvers can lose 25 to 50 percent of their normal body weights in the pursuit of thinness. They start dieting and, although emaciated, continue to refuse food because they see themselves as fat. *Bulimia nervosa,* another severe eating disorder, is similar in terms of results to anorexia. The bulimic has the same "need" for thinness but uses a binge-purge process. Bulimics are known to eat enormous quantities of food and then force themselves to vomit. Both disorders have major long-term health consequences, and are related to amenorrhea during the child-bearing years and osteoporosis during the post-menopausal years. The incidence of anorexia nervosa and bulimia is on the rise. Both are particularly prevalent among adolescent girls. Schumer (1983) contends that these disorders are on the rise, increasing so much that probably every family doctor will sooner or later be confronted with an anorexic patient. About 10 percent of all cases of anorexia nervosa are fatal, and many other victims become chronic invalids (Rothenberg, 1976).

Characteristically, in both anorexia nervosa and bulimia, there is no true loss of appetite or awareness of hunger pains corresponding to the body's need for food. Some individuals brainwash themselves into believing that the pain actually feels good. In about 25 percent of the cases, food refusal alternates with eating binges (bulimia). Anorectics become obsessed with food. They think about it, talk about it, collect recipes, and often force their family members to overeat (Bruch, 1979).

In an effort to remove unwanted food from the body, many anorectics resort to self-induced vomiting, or excessive use of enemas, laxatives, and diuretics. All this may result in a serious disturbance of the body's electrolyte balance, which may play a role in cases that end in death (Minuchin et al., 1978).

Concept 3.16 Anorexia Nervosa and Bulimia Nervosa are emotional disorders that culminate in an aversion to food and self-starvation that results in developmental delays and even death.

Anorectics and bulimics usually pursue their goal of thinness not only through food restriction but through exhausting exercise. Many were interested in sports before they became ill. Exercise then became a solitary activity, a way to burn off calories or show endurance. In spite of their weakness due to extreme loss of weight, many anorectics display incredible energy and are hyperactive. Anorectics and bulimics drive themselves to unbelievable feats to demonstrate that they can live up to the ideal of mind over body (Bruch, 1979).

Many female anorectics do not want the curves and roundness associated with the developing adolescent body, and they are often terrified of dealing with sexual matters. By starving themselves, they can remain children forever with no menstrual periods or development of secondary sex characteristics (Bruch, 1979).

Anorectics and bulimics are usually described as having been outstandingly good children. They were the pride and joy of their parents and teachers. Psychiatrists have come to recognize the overwhelming sense of ineffectiveness under which the victims operate. They camouflage their self-doubt with perfect, conforming behavior. The extreme control they exercise over their bodies provides them with a sense of accomplishment. Even a slight weight gain may result in depression and self-hatred (Bruch, 1979).

The anorectic child often grows up in a family with highly enmeshed patterns. Close, interpersonal contact is important to the anorectic child. Loyalty and protection are more valuable to the anorectic than autonomy and self-realization. The individual learns to subordinate the self. The expectation from learning a skill, for example, is not competence, but approval. The reward is love and not knowledge. The family of anorectic children is typically child-oriented. The child grows up protected by parents who dwell on the child's well-being. Because family members focus constantly on the child's actions, an obsessive concern for perfection often develops. The anorectic is both extremely self-conscious and alert to other people's signals. Overinvolvement with the family often hinders the child's ability to deal with the outside world (Minuchin et al., 1978).

Some early warning signals of anorexia nervosa and bulimia nervosa are listed in Table 3.2.

Society is partly to blame for the increase in anorexia nervosa and bulimia nervosa. The lean, slender form is glorified by society, which propagates the idea that being thin symbolizes beauty, desirability, and self-control and is a magic key to a happier life. Educators may be among the first to recognize eating disorders. They should be able to recognize the early stages of either illness while it is still reversible. Once the condition has lasted six months or longer, it becomes exceedingly difficult to treat.

Fitness Levels

It has been stated repeatedly that development does not occur in a vacuum. A wide variety of factors from all three domains of human behavior (cognitive, affective, and psychomotor) influence development, as well as factors within the individual, the environment, and the task itself. Task factors within the psychomotor domain are termed physical

Table 3.2 Early Warning Signs of Anorexia Nervosa and Bulimia Nervosa

Anorexia Nervosa	Bulimia Nervosa
1. Overidentification with a doctor-prescribed weight-control program	1. Eating binges
2. Obsession with dieting and talk of food	2. Irregular weight loss
3. Social isolation accompanying slimness (loner)	3. Long periods in the bathroom after meals
4. No participation in the courting behavior of classmates	4. Variable performance
5. Sudden increased involvement in athletics, usually of a solitary nature	5. Loss of tooth enamel
6. Exaggerated concern with achieving high academic grades	6. Fear of gaining weight
7. Overconcern with weight	7. Prolonged/extreme exercise
8. Failure to consume food	8. Emotional instability and impulsivity
9. Denial of hunger	9. Depression and frequent mood swings
10. Obsessed with exercise	10. Throat, esophagus, stomach or colon problems

and mechanical factors. These factors have a profound impact on the acquisition, maintenance, and diminution of our movement abilities throughout life. Our level of physical fitness coupled with the mechanical requirements of a task greatly influence our ability to move with control, skill, and confidence. Figure 3.2 illustrates this important concept.

Health-related Fitness. The physical development aspects of the motor domain may be divided into *health-related fitness* factors and *performance-related fitness* factors that influence motor development. These terms, however, are difficult to define to the satisfaction of all experts in the field. Health-related fitness is generally defined in broad terms because fitness level requirements vary among individuals. Hence this form of physical fitness encompasses the health-related aspects that influence the ability to perform daily tasks at an acceptable level without undue stress. It also is a state in which ample reserves of energy are available for recreational pursuits and emergency needs. Muscular strength, muscular endurance, aerobic endurance, joint flexibility, and body composition are usually considered the components of health-related fitness. The extent to which each of these factors is possessed will influence an individual's performance capabilities in movement. For example, how far a person can run or ride a bicycle is related to his or her level of muscular strength, muscular endurance, and aerobic endurance.

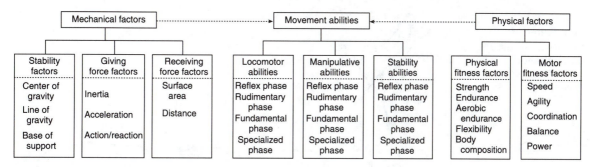

Figure 3.2
Physical and mechanical factors affect the development of movement abilities at all phases of motor development

---

Concept 3.17 One's personal level of health-related and performance-related fitness influences motor development in many ways.

Performance-related Fitness.   Performance-related fitness, also widely known as motor fitness, is the performance aspect of fitness. It is also an elusive concept that has been studied extensively over the past several years and is classified as part of the global concept of fitness. *Motor fitness* is generally thought of as one's current performance level as influenced by factors such as movement, speed, agility, balance, coordination, and power.

The generality and specificity of motor fitness has been debated and researched for years, with the bulk of research evidence in favor of its specificity (Henry, 1960; Henry and Rogers, 1960). For years many physical educators believed that motor fitness was general in nature; as a result, the term general motor ability came into vogue. They assumed if an individual excelled in a certain sport that corresponding ability would automatically carry over to other activities. Although this often occurs, it is probably due to the individual's personal motivation, numerous activity experiences, and several specific sport aptitudes, not to a transfer or carryover of skills from one activity to another. One's motor fitness has a definite effect on the performance of any movement activity that requires quick reactions, speed of movement, agility and coordination of movement, explosive power, and balance.

Biomechanics

Before embarking on a detailed discussion of motor development, it will be useful to review some mechanical principles of movement as they relate to stability, locomotion, and manipulation. There are numerous ways in which the human body is capable of moving. It may appear to

Figure 3.3
The center of
gravity shifts as the
body changes posi-
tion

be an impossible task to learn all of the skills involved in the performance of children's game, sport, and dance activities. Closer inspection
of the total spectrum of movement will reveal, however, that fundamental mechanical laws affect all human movement. Selected mechanical principles are considered here to serve as basic preparation for the
chapters that follow.

Concept 3.18   All movement is governed by fundamental mechanical laws.

Balance.   All masses that are within the gravitational pull of the earth
are subjected to the force of gravity. The three primary factors of concern in the study of balance principles are (1) center of gravity, (2) line
of gravity, and (3) base of support.

A *center of gravity* exists within all objects. In geometric shapes it
is located in the exact center of the object. In asymmetrical objects (e.g.,
human bodies) it is constantly changing during movement. The center
of gravity of our bodies always shifts in the direction of the movement
or the additional weight (Figure 3.3). The center of gravity of a child
standing in an erect position is approximately at the top of the hips between the front and the back of the trunk. Activities in which the center
of gravity remains in a stable position, such as standing on one foot or
performing a headstand, are known as static balance activities. If the
center of gravity is constantly shifting, as in jumping rope, walking, or
doing a forward roll, the activities are dynamic balance movements.

Figure 3.4
The body remains
in balance when
the center of
gravity and line of
gravity fall within
the base of support

The *line of gravity* is an imaginary line that extends vertically through the center of gravity to the center of the earth. The interrelationship of the center of gravity and the line of gravity to the base of support determines the degree of stability of the body (Figure 3.4).

The *base of support* is the part of the body that comes into contact with the supporting surface. If the line of gravity falls within the base of support, the body will be in balance. If it falls outside the base, it is out of balance. The wider the base of support, the greater the stability, as can be seen when one balances on two feet rather than on one foot. The nearer the base of support to the center of gravity, the greater the stability. Someone who is standing erect may be pushed off balance more easily than someone in a lineman's stance with the feet spread and the body slightly forward. The nearer the center of gravity to the center of the base of support the greater the stability. A foot position that allows for a larger base of support in the direction of the movement gives additional stability. This principle is illustrated by the foot position of a runner who is attempting to stop or of a catcher who is trying to receive and control a heavy object.

Giving Force.   Force is one of the basic concepts of movement and body mechanics. Force is the instigator of all movement and may be defined as the effort that one mass exerts on another. The result may be (1) movement, (2) cessation of movement, or (3) resistance of one body against another. There may be force without motion, as is seen in isometric activities, but motion is impossible without the application of some form of force. Three forces relative to the human body are of concern to us: (1) force produced by muscles, (2) force produced by the gravitational pull of the earth, and (3) momentum. The entire science of force is based on Newton's three laws of motion, namely, the law of inertia, the law of acceleration, and the law of action and reaction.

The *law of inertia* states that a body at rest will remain at rest and a body in motion will remain in motion at the same speed in a straight line unless acted upon by an outside force. In order for movement to occur, a force must act upon a body sufficiently to overcome that object's inertia. If the applied force is less than the resistance offered by the object, motion will not occur. Large muscles can produce more force than small muscles. Once an object is in motion, it takes less force to maintain its speed and direction (i.e., momentum) than it does to stop it. This may be readily observed in snow skiing, the glide in swimming, or rolling a ball. The heavier the object and the faster its speed, the more force required to overcome its moving inertia or to absorb its momentum. It is harder to catch a heavy object than it is to catch a light object.

The *law of acceleration* states that the change in the velocity of an object is directly proportional to the force producing the velocity and inversely proportional to the object's mass. The heavier an object, the more force is needed to accelerate or decelerate it. This may be observed when a heavy object (shot put) and a light object (softball) are thrown a given distance. An increase in speed is proportional to the amount of force that is applied. The greater the amount of force imparted to an object, the higher the speed at which the object will travel. If the same amount of force is exerted on two bodies with a different mass, greater acceleration will be produced on the lighter or less massive object. The heavier object, however, will have greater momentum once inertia is overcome and will exert a greater force than the lighter object on something that it contacts.

The *law of action and reaction* states that for every action there is an equal and opposite reaction. This principle of counter-force is the basis for all locomotion and is evident when one leaves footprints in the sand. This principle applies to both linear and angular motion. Its application requires that adjustments be made by an individual to sustain the primary forces in any movement. For example, the use of opposition in the running pattern counters the action of one part of the body with that of another.

Receiving Force. To stop ourselves or a moving object, we absorb force over the greatest distance possible and with the largest surface area possible. The greater the distance over which the force is absorbed, the less the impact on whatever receives the force. This may be demonstrated by catching a ball with the arms straight out in front of the body and then catching again with the arms bent. The same thing may be observed when landing from a jump with the legs bent as opposed to landing with the legs straight. Forces should be absorbed over as large a surface area as possible. The impact is reduced in proportion to the size of the surface area, and the likelihood of injury is diminished. For example, trying to absorb the shock of a fall with the hands and arms extended will probably result in injury because the small surface area of the hand must receive the entire impact. It is far better to let as much of the body as possible absorb the impact.

The final direction of a moving object depends on the magnitude and the direction of all of the forces that have been applied. Therefore, whenever we kick, strike, or throw an object, its accuracy and the distance depend on the forces acting on it. If we are performing a vertical jump, we must work for a summation of forces in a vertical direction, whereas a good performance in the long jump requires a summation of horizontal and vertical forces so that the takeoff is at the appropriate angle.

Separate discussion of the principles of balance, giving force, and receiving forces should not be taken to mean that one is used in the absence of the others. Most of our movements combine all three. An element of balance is involved in almost all of our movements, and we give and receive force whenever we perform any locomotor or manipulative movement. A gymnast, for example, must maintain his or her equilibrium when performing a tumbling trick such as a front flip, and also must absorb force from the body (on the landing). A handball player must move to a position of readiness (giving to and receiving force from the body), contact the ball (giving force to an object), and maintain balance. Although each of the movement patterns and skills discussed in the chapters that follow involve a specific sequence of movements, all incorporate the basic mechanics discussed here because these mechanical principles are common to all movement situations.

Summary

Motor development represents one aspect of the total developmental process. It is intricately interrelated with both the cognitive and affective domains of human behavior and is influenced by a variety of factors. The importance of optimal motor development must not be minimized or regarded as secondary in relation to other developmental areas. Common factors affecting motor development emerge. These factors illustrate the gradual progression from relatively simple levels of functioning to more complex levels. Biological, experiential, and physical factors influence both the process and the product of motor development. Each individual is unique in his or her development and will progress at a rate determined by environmental and biological circumstances in conjunction with the specific requirements of the movement task.

Terms to Remember

Developmental direction
Cephalocaudal
Proximodistal
Growth rate
Differentiation
Integration
Reciprocal interweaving
Readiness
Critical period
Sensitive period
Individual differences
Phylogenetic skills
Ontogenetic skills
Bonding
Imprinting
Stimulation and deprivation

Temperament
Premature
Low-birthweight
Young-for-date
Anorexia nervosa
Bulimia nervosa
Health-related fitness
Performance-related fitness
Motor fitness
Center of gravity
Line of gravity
Base of support
Force
Law of inertia
Law of acceleration
Law of action and reaction

Critical Readings

Bril, B. (1985). Motor development and cultural attitudes. In H. T. A. Whiting & M. G. Wade (Eds.), *Themes in Motor Development*. Dordrecht: The Netherlands: Martinus Nyhoff Publishers.

Lamb, M. E. et al. (1985). *Infant-Mother Attachment*. Hillsdale, NJ: Lawrence Erlbaum Associates.

Malina, R. M., & Bouchard, C. (1991). *Growth, Maturation and Physical Activity* (Chapter 24). Champaign, IL: Human Kinetics.

Payne, G. V., & Isaacs, L. D. (1991). *Human Motor Development: A Lifespan Approach* (Chapter 6). Mountain View, CA: Mayfield.

Ulrich, B. D. (1984). The effects of stimulation programs on the development of high risk infants: A review of research. *Adapted Physical Activity Quarterly, 1,* 68–80.

Chapter **4**

Motor Development:
A Theoretical Model

CHAPTER COMPETENCIES

Upon completion of this chapter you should be able to:

- *Define life span motor development*
- *View an individual's motor behavior as "more" or "less" advanced on a developmental continuum rather than as "good" or "bad"*
- *Demonstrate an understanding of neural, physiological, perceptual, and cognitive changes across the life span*
- *Distinguish between inductive and deductive theory formulation*
- *Describe the phases of motor development*
- *List and describe the stages within the phases of motor development*

KEY CONCEPT: Motor development may be conceptualized, using an hourglass heuristic, as a discontinuous and overlapping phase-stage process.

A major function of theory is to integrate existing facts, to organize them in such a way as to give them meaning. Theories of development take existing facts about the human organism and provide a developmental model congruent with these facts. Therefore, theory formulation serves as a basis for fact testing, and vice versa. Facts are important, but they alone do not constitute a science. The development of a science depends on the advancement of theory as well as on the accumulation of facts. In the study of human behavior, especially in the areas of cognitive and affective development, theory formulation has gained increased importance over the past several years. Theory has played a critical dual role in both of these areas; namely, it has served and continues to serve as an integrator of existing facts and as a basis for the derivation of new facts (Learner, 1986; Bigge & Shermis, 1992).

Until relatively recently, interest in motor development had been concerned primarily with describing and cataloguing data, with little interest in developmental models leading to a theoretical explanation of behavior across the life span. This research was necessary and very important to our knowledge base. But in actuality, it did little to help us answer the critically important questions of what lies underneath the process of motor development, and how the process occurs. Only a limited number of comprehensive models of motor development exist, and there are few comprehensive theories of motor development. Now, however, scholars in motor development are reexamining their work with a view toward more carefully thought out research grounded in sound theoretical frameworks. The intent of this chapter is to present a comprehensive model of motor development, based on specific theoretical viewpoints, in an effort to both describe and explain development and to serve as a basis for generating new facts about this important aspect of human behavior.

Concept 4.1 Few comprehensive theoretical models of motor development exist.

The first function of a theoretical model of motor development should be to integrate the existing facts encompassed by the area of study. The second function should be to serve as a basis for the generation of new facts. One might argue that the facts could be interpreted in more than one way, that is, from different theoretical perspectives. This is entirely possible and, in fact, desirable. Different viewpoints generate theoretical arguments and debates which are the very spark for research to shed new light on differing theoretical interpretations. Even if theoretical differences do not exist, research should be undertaken to determine whether the hypotheses derived from the theory can be both experimentally and ecologically supported (Learner, 1986; Bigge & Shermis, 1992).

Theory should undergird all research and science, and the study of motor development is no exception. Developmental theory must be both *descriptive* and *explanatory*. In other words, the developmentalist is interested in what people are typically like at particular age periods (description), and what makes these characteristics occur (explanation).

Without a theoretical base of operation, research in motor development, or any other area, tends to yield little more than isolated facts. However, without an existing body of knowledge (facts), we cannot formulate theory, and without the formulation and constant testing of theory we cannot hope for a higher level of understanding and awareness of the phenomenon that we call motor development.

Concept 4.2   Theoretical models attempt to describe and explain behavior, and may be inductive or deductive in nature.

A theory is a group of statements, concepts, or principles that integrate existing facts and lead to the generation of new facts. The model of the Phases of Motor Development presented in this chapter is not based solely on the accumulation of facts. Such a model would result from using an inductive method of theory formulation. In the *inductive method* the investigator first starts with a set of facts and then tries to find a conceptual framework around which to organize and explain them. The *deductive method* of theory formulation, as used here, is based on inference and has three primary qualifications. First, the theory should integrate existing facts and account for existing empirical evidence that bears on the content of the theory. Second, the theory should lend itself to the formulation of testable hypotheses in the form of: If _____ , then _____ . Third, the theory should meet the empirical test; that is, hypotheses that are experimentally tested should yield results that lend further support to the theory (Lerner, 1986).

The use of a deductive, rather than an inductive, model enables us to see how well-accumulated facts fit together into a cohesive, understandable whole. It also enables us to identify the information that is needed to fill in gaps in the theory or to clarify or refine it. The Phases of Motor Development outlined here are deductively based and serve as a model for theory formulation. In subsequent sections of the text each phase will be explored in greater detail.

The Phases of Motor Development

The process of motor development reveals itself primarily through changes in movement behavior. All of us, infants, children, adolescents, and adults, are involved in the lifelong process of learning how to move with control and competence in response to challenges we face daily in a constantly changing world. We are able to observe developmental differences in movement behavior, brought about by factors within the individual (biology), the environment (experience), and the task itself (physical/mechanical). We can do this through observation of changes in process (form) and product (performance). Therefore, a primary means by which the process of motor development may be observed is through studying changes in motor behavior throughout the life cycle. In other words, a ''window'' to the process of motor development is provided through an individual's actual observable movement behavior, which provide us with clues to underlying motor processes.

Concept 4.3 The process of motor development may be viewed as phase-like and stage-like.

Observable movement may be grouped into three categories: stabilizing movements, locomotor movements, and manipulative movements, or combinations of the three. In the broadest sense, a stability movement is any movement in which some degree of balance is required (i.e., virtually all gross motor activity). In a narrower sense, a stability movement is one that is both non-locomotor and non-manipulative. The category conveniently encompasses movements such as twisting, turning, pushing, and pulling that cannot be classified as locomotor or manipulative. In this book, stability, as a category of movement, is viewed as more than a convenient catchall term, but as less than a global term applicable to all movement. *Stability* refers to any movement that places a premium on gaining and maintaining one's equilibrium in relation to the force of gravity. Thus, axial movements (another term sometimes used for non-locomotor movements) as well as inverted and body rolling postures are considered here as stability movements.

The *locomotor movement* category refers to movements that involve a change in location of the body relative to a fixed point on the surface. To walk, run, jump, hop, skip, or leap is to perform a locomotor task. In our use of the term, such activities as the forward roll and backward roll may be considered both locomotor and stability movements—locomotor because the body is moving from point to point, stability because of the premium placed on maintaining equilibrium in an unusual balancing situation.

The *manipulative movement* category refers to both gross and fine motor manipulation. Gross motor manipulation involves imparting force to, or receiving force from, objects. The tasks of throwing, catching, kicking, and striking an object as well as trapping, and volleying are gross motor manipulative movements. Fine motor manipulation involves intricate use of the muscles of the hand and wrist. Sewing, cutting with scissors, and typing are fine motor manipulative movements. A large number of movements involve a combination of stability, locomotor, and/or manipulative movements. For example, jumping rope involves locomotion (jumping), manipulation (turning the rope), and

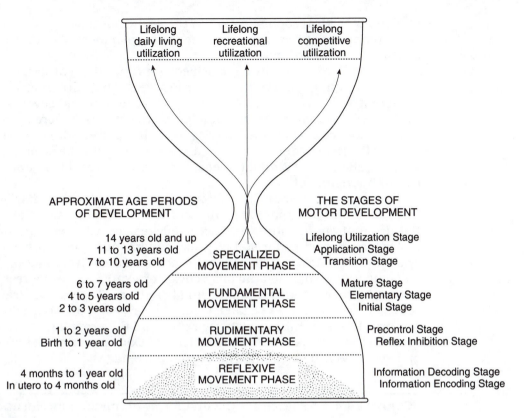

Figure 4.1
The phases of motor development

stability (maintaining balance). Likewise, playing soccer involves lo-comotor skills (running and jumping), manipulative skills (dribbling, passing, kicking, and heading), and stability skills (dodging, reaching, sliding, turning, and twisting).

In summary, if movement serves as a window to the process of motor development, then one way of studying this process is through exam-ining the sequential progression of movement abilities throughout the entire life span. The following Phases of Motor Development and the developmental stages within each phase are designed to serve as a model for this study. (See Figure 4.1 for a visual representation of the four phases and their corresponding stages.)

Reflexive Movement Phase

The very first movements the fetus makes are reflexive. *Reflexes* are involuntary, subcortically controlled movements that form the basis for the phases of motor development. Through reflex activity the infant gains information about the immediate environment. The infant's re-actions to touch, light, sounds, and changes in pressure trigger invol-untary movement activity. These involuntary movements, coupled with increasing cortical sophistication in the early months of postnatal life, play an important role in helping the child learn more about his or her body and the outside world.

Primitive reflexes may be classified as information-gathering, nourishment-seeking, and protective responses. They are information-gathering in that they help stimulate cortical activity and development. They are nourishment-seeking and protective because there is considerable evidence that they are phylogenetic in nature. Primitive reflexes such as the rooting and sucking reflexes are thought to be primitive survival mechanisms. Without them, the newborn would be unable to obtain nourishment.

Postural reflexes are the second form of involuntary movement. They are remarkably similar in appearance to later voluntary behaviors but are entirely involuntary. These reflexes seem to serve as neuromotor testing devices for stability, locomotor, and manipulative mechanisms that will be used later with conscious control. The primary stepping reflex and the crawling reflex, for example, closely resemble later voluntary walking and crawling behaviors. The palmar grasping reflex is closely related to later voluntary grasping and releasing behaviors. The labyrinthine righting reflex and the propping reflexes are related to later balancing abilities. The reflexive phase of motor development may be divided into two overlapping stages.

Concept 4.4   Reflexes are the first forms of human movement.

Information Encoding Stage.   The information encoding (gathering) stage of the reflexive movement phase is characterized by observable involuntary movement activity during the fetal period until about the fourth month of infancy. During this stage lower brain centers are more highly developed than the motor cortex and are essentially in command of fetal and neonatal movement. These brain centers are capable of causing involuntary reactions to a variety of stimuli of varying intensity and duration. During this stage reflexes serve as the primary means by which the infant is able to gather information, seek nourishment, and find protection through movement.

Information Decoding Stage.   The information decoding (processing) stage of the reflex phase begins around the fourth month. During this time there is a gradual inhibition of many reflexes as higher brain centers continue to develop. Lower brain centers gradually relinquish control over skeletal movements and are replaced by voluntary movement activity mediated by the motor area of the cerebral cortex. The decoding stage replaces sensorimotor activity with perceptual-motor ability. That is, the infant's development of voluntary control of skeletal movements involves processing sensory stimuli with stored information, not merely reacting to stimuli.

Chapter 7 focuses on primitive and postural reflexes as they relate to the information encoding and decoding stages. Special attention is given to the relationship between the reflexive phase of development and voluntary movement.

Rudimentary Movement Phase

The first forms of voluntary movement are rudimentary movements. They are seen in the infant beginning at birth to about age two. Rudimentary movements are maturationally determined and are characterized by a highly predictable sequence of appearance. This sequence is resistant to change under normal conditions. The rate at which these abilities appear will, however, vary from child to child and is dependent on biological, environmental, and task factors. The rudimentary movement abilities of the infant represent the basic forms of voluntary movement that are required for survival. They involve stability movements such as gaining control of the head, neck, and trunk muscles; the manipulative tasks of reaching, grasping, and releasing; and the locomotor movements of creeping, crawling, and walking. The rudimentary movement phase of development may be subdivided into two stages that represent progressively higher orders of movement control.

Concept 4.5   The sequence of movement skill acquisition during the rudimentary movement phase is fixed, but the rate is variable.

Reflex Inhibition Stage.   The reflex inhibition stage of the rudimentary movement phase may be thought of as beginning at birth. At birth, reflexes dominate the infant's movement repertoire. From then on, however, the infant's movements are increasingly influenced by the developing cortex. Development of the cortex, and lessening of certain environmental constraints, causes several reflexes to be inhibited and gradually disappear. Primitive and postural reflexes are replaced by voluntary movement behaviors. At the reflex inhibition level, voluntary movement is poorly differentiated and integrated because the neuromotor apparatus of the infant is still at a rudimentary stage of development. Movements, though purposeful, appear uncontrolled and unrefined. If the infant wishes to make contact with an object, there will be global activity of the entire hand, wrist, arm, shoulder, and even trunk. The process of moving the hand into contact with the object, although voluntary, lacks control.

Precontrol Stage.   Around one year of age, children begin to bring greater precision and control to their movements. The process of differentiating between sensory and motor systems and integrating perceptual and motor information into a more meaningful and congruent whole takes place. The rapid development of higher cognitive processes and motor processes encourages rapid gains in rudimentary movement abilities during this stage. During the precontrol stage children learn to gain and maintain their equilibrium, to manipulate objects, and to locomote throughout the environment with an amazing degree of proficiency and control considering the short time they have had to develop these abilities. The maturational process may partially explain the rapidity and extent of development of movement control during this phase, but the growth of motor proficiency is no less amazing.

Chapter 8 provides a detailed explanation of the development of rudimentary movement abilities. Particular attention is paid to the interrelationship between the stages within this phase and the stages within the reflexive phase of development. Attention is also focused on the critical function that the rudimentary movement phase serves in preparing the child for the development of fundamental movement abilities.

Fundamental Movement Phase

The fundamental movement abilities of early childhood are an outgrowth of the rudimentary movement phase of infancy. This phase of motor development represents a time in which young children are actively involved in exploring and experimenting with the movement capabilities of their bodies. It is a time for discovering how to perform a variety of stabilizing, locomotor, and manipulative movements, first in isolation and then in combination with one another. Children who are developing fundamental patterns of movement are learning how to respond with motor control and movement competence to a variety of stimuli. They are gaining increased control in the performance of discrete, serial, and continuous movements as evidenced by their ability to accept changes in the task requirements. Fundamental movement patterns are basic observable patterns of behavior. Locomotor activities such as running and jumping, manipulative activities such as throwing and catching, and stability activities such as the beam walk and one-foot balance are examples of fundamental movements that should be developed during the early childhood years.

A major misconception about the developmental concept of the fundamental movement phase is the notion that these abilities are maturationally determined and are little influenced by task and environmental factors. Some child development experts (not in the motor development area) have written repeatedly about the "natural" unfolding of the child's movement and play skills, and the idea that children develop these abilities merely by growing older (maturation). Although maturation does play a role in the development of fundamental movement patterns, it should not be viewed as the only influence. The conditions of the environment, namely opportunities for practice, encouragement, instruction, and the ecology (setting) of the environment itself, all play important roles in the degree to which fundamental movement patterns develop.

Concept 4.6 Affordances and rate limiters contained in the task, the individual, and the environment have a profound effect on the acquisition of mature fundamental movement skills.

Several researchers and assessment instrument developers have attempted to subdivide fundamental movements into a series of identifiable sequential stages. For the purposes of our model we will view the entire fundamental movement phase as having three separate but often overlapping stages, the initial, elementary, and mature. These stages are described briefly here and in greater detail in Chapter 11.

Initial Stage. The initial stage of a fundamental movement phase represents the child's first goal-oriented attempts at performing a fundamental skill. Movement itself is characterized by missing or improperly sequenced parts, markedly restricted or exaggerated use of the body, and poor rhythmical flow and coordination. The spatial and temporal integration of movement is poor. Typically, the locomotor, manipulative, and stability movements of the two-year-old are at the initial level. Some children may be beyond this level in the performance of some patterns of movement, but most are at the initial stage.

Elementary Stage. The elementary stage involves greater control and better rhythmical coordination of fundamental movements. The synchronization of the temporal and spatial elements of movement are improved, but patterns of movement at this stage are still generally restricted or exaggerated, although better coordinated. Children of normal intelligence and physical functioning tend to advance to the elementary stage primarily through the process of maturation. Observation of the typical three- or four-year-old child reveals a variety of fundamental movements at the elementary stage. Many individuals, adults as well as children, fail to get beyond the elementary stage in many patterns of movement.

Mature Stage. The mature stage within the fundamental movement phase is characterized by mechanically efficient, coordinated, and controlled performances. The majority of available data on the acquisition of fundamental movement skills suggest that children can and should be at the mature stage by age five or six in most fundamental skills. Manipulative skills that require tracking and intercepting moving objects (catching, striking, volleying) develop somewhat later because of the sophisticated visual-motor requirements of these tasks. Even a casual glance at the movements of children and adults reveals that a great many have not developed their fundamental movement skills to the mature level. Although some children may reach this stage primarily through maturation and with a minimum of environmental influences, the vast majority require opportunities for practice, encouragement, and instruction in an environment that fosters learning.

Failure to offer such opportunities makes it virtually impossible for an individual to achieve the mature stage of a skill within this phase, and will inhibit further application and development in the next phase.

Specialized Movement Phase

The specialized phase of motor development is an outgrowth of the fundamental movement phase. During the specialized phase, movement becomes a tool that is applied to a variety of specialized movement activities for daily living, recreation, and sport pursuits. This is a period when fundamental stability, locomotor, and manipulative skills are progressively refined, combined, and elaborated upon for use in increasingly demanding situations. The fundamental movements of hopping and jumping, for example, may now be applied to rope-jumping activities, to performing folk dances, and to performing the triple jump (hop-step-jump) in track and field.

The onset and extent of skill development within the specialized movement phase depends on a variety of task, individual, and environmental factors. Reaction time and movement speed, coordination, body type, height and weight, customs, peer pressure, and emotional makeup are but a few of these factors. There are three stages within the specialized movement phase.

Concept 4.7   Progress through the specialized movement skill phase is dependent on mature fundamental movement skill development.

Transitional Stage.   Somewhere around their seventh or eighth year, children commonly enter a transitional movement skill stage (Haubin-stricker and Seefeldt, 1986). During the transitional period the individual begins to combine and apply fundamental movement skills to the performance of specialized skills in sport and recreational settings. Walking on a rope bridge, jumping rope, and playing kickball are examples of common transitional skills. Transitional movement skills contain the same elements as fundamental movements with greater form, accuracy, and control. Fundamental movement skills that were developed and refined for their own sake during the previous stage are applied to play, game, and daily living situations. Transitional skills are simply applications of fundamental movement patterns in somewhat more complex and specific forms.

The transitional stage is an exciting time for the parent and the teacher as well as for the child. During this stage children are actively involved in discovering and combining numerous movement patterns and are often elated by their rapidly expanding movement abilities. The goal of concerned parents, teachers, and youth sport coaches during this stage should be to help children increase their motor control and movement competence in a wide variety of activities. Care must be taken not to cause the child to specialize or restrict his or her activity involvement. A narrow focus on skills during this stage is likely to have undesirable effects on the last two stages of the specialized movement phase.

Application Stage. From about age 11 to age 13 (the middle school years) interesting changes take place in the skill development of the individual. During the previous stage the child's limited cognitive abilities, affective abilities, and experiences, combined with a natural eagerness to be active, caused the normal focus (without adult interference) on movement to be broad and generalized to "all" activity. During the application stage, increased cognitive sophistication and a broadened experience base enable the individual to make numerous learning and participation decisions based on a variety of task, individual, and environmental factors. For example, the 5-feet, 10-inch 12-year-old who likes team activities and applying strategy to games, who has reasonably good coordination and agility, and who lives in Indiana may choose to specialize in the development of his or her basketball playing abilities. A similarly built child who does not really enjoy team efforts may choose to specialize in a variety of track and field activities. The individual begins to make conscious decisions for or against participation in certain activities. These decisions are based, in large measure, on how he or she perceives the extent to which factors within the task, himself or herself, and the environment either enhance or inhibit chances for enjoyment and success. This self-examination of strengths and weaknesses, opportunities and restrictions, narrow the choices.

During the application stage, individuals begin to seek out or to avoid participation in specific activities. Increased emphasis is placed on form, skill, accuracy, and the quantitative aspects of movement performance. This is a time for more complex skills to be refined and used in advanced games, lead-up activities, and selected sports.

Lifelong Utilization Stage. The lifelong utilization stage of the specialized phase of motor development begins around age 14 and continues through adulthood. The lifelong utilization stage represents the pinnacle of the process of motor development and is characterized by the use of one's acquired movement repertoire throughout life. The interests, competencies, and choices made during the previous stage are carried over, further refined, and applied to a lifetime of daily living, recreational, and sports-related activities. Factors such as available time and money, equipment and facilities, and physical and mental limitations affect this stage. Among other things, one's level of activity participation will depend on talent, opportunities, physical condition, and personal motivation. An individual's lifetime performance level may range anywhere from professional status and the Olympics, to intercollegiate and interscholastic competition, to participation in organized or unorganized, competitive or cooperative, recreational sports and simple daily living skills.

In essence, the lifelong utilization stage represents a culmination of all preceding stages and phases. It should, however, be viewed as a continuation of a lifetime process. One of the primary goals of education is to help individuals to become happy, healthy, contributing members of society. We must not lose sight of this lofty but worthy goal. We must view the hierarchical development of movement abilities as stepping-stones to the specialized movement skill level. We must cease in viewing children as miniature adults who can be programmed to perform in such potentially high-pressure, physiologically and psychologically questionable activities as Little League Baseball and Pee Wee Football. We must view children as developmentally immature individuals, and structure meaningful movement experiences appropriate for their particular developmental levels. When we recognize that the progressive acquisition of movement skills in a developmentally appropriate manner is imperative to the balanced motor development of infants, children, adolescents, and adults, we begin making real contributions to their total development. Specialized skill development can and should play a role in our lives, but it is unfair to require children to specialize in one or two skill areas at the expense of developing their abilities in and appreciation for many other areas.

Concept 4.8   The primary goals of a person's motor development and movement education is to accept the challenge of change in the continuous process of gaining and maintaining motor control and movement competence throughout a lifetime.

The Hourglass: A Life Span Model

The age ranges for each phase of motor development should be viewed as general guidelines, illustrative only of the broad concept of age-appropriateness. Individuals often function at different phases depending on their experiential backgrounds and genetic makeups. For example, it is entirely possible for a 10-year-old to function in the specialized movement phase at the lifelong utilization stage in stability activities involving gymnastic movements, but only at the elementary stage of the fundamental movement phase in manipulative and locomotor skills such as throwing, catching, or running. Although we should encourage this precocious behavior in gymnastics, we should also help the child catch up to his or her age-mates in the other areas and develop acceptable levels of proficiency in them as well.

It is important to gather facts about the process of motor development. Throughout this text we discuss study after study, but if we fail to provide you with a theoretical framework and a conceptual grasp of the process of motor development we will have presented isolated facts that tell you little about their implications for successful developmental teaching, coaching, and parenting. Therefore, we would like to propose a theoretical model for the process of motor development and work through this model with you. This model as presented is *not* a comprehensive theory of motor development. It is an *heuristic* device, that is, a conceptual representation or model of motor development.

Concept 4.9   The Hourglass Model is a helpful heuristic device for conceptualizing and explaining the process of motor development.

In order to understand this model, picture yourself as being an hourglass (Figure 4.2). Into your hourglass we need to place the stuff of life: "sand." Sand gets into your hourglass from two different containers. One is your hereditary container and the other your environmental container. The hereditary container has a lid. At conception our genetic makeup is determined and the amount of sand in the container is fixed. However, the environmental container has no lid. Sand may be added to the container and to your hourglass. We could reach down into the "sand pile" (i.e., the environment) and get more sand to put into your hourglass.

The two buckets of sand signify that the process of development is influenced by both the environment and heredity. The relative contributions of each has been a volatile topic of debate for years. Arguing the importance of each is a meaningless exercise because sand is actually funneled from *both* containers into your hourglass. In the final analysis it does not really matter if your hourglass is filled with hereditary sand or environmental sand. What is important is the fact that somehow sand gets into your hourglass and that this stuff of life is the product of "both" heredity and the environment.

Now, what do we know about motor development during the early phases of life? When we look at the reflexive and rudimentary phases of motor development, we know that sand pours into the hourglass primarily, but not exclusively, from the hereditary container. The sequential progression of motor development during the first few years of life is quite rigid and resistant to change except under environmental extremes. Therefore, we know in the first two phases of motor development that the development sequence is highly predictable. For example, children all over the world learn how to sit before they stand, how to stand before they walk, and how to walk before they run. However, we do see considerable variability in the rates at which the very young acquire their rudimentary movement abilities. This is something in which researchers and program developers have become increasingly interested over the past few years. We have seen a rapid rise in the number

Figure 4.2
Filling the hour-
glass with ''sand''
(i.e., the stuff of
life)

THE
HOURGLASS:

Gallahue's
Life Span Model
of
Motor Development

Motor Control and Movement Competence

Heredity

Environment

SPECIALIZED
MOVEMENT PHASE

FUNDAMENTAL MOVEMENT PHASE

RUDIMENTARY MOVEMENT PHASE

REFLEXIVE MOVEMENT PHASE

INDIVIDUAL

FACTORS

FACTORS

ENVIRONMENTAL

FACTORS
WITHIN THE TASK

of infant stimulation programs, and infant-toddler movement programs. Some make elaborate claims about the worth of these programs
and their ultimate importance to the child. Unfortunately, we have little
hard evidence at this juncture to either support or refute these claims.
The rate of movement skill acquisition is variable from infancy
throughout life. If an infant, child, adolescent, or adult receives additional opportunities for practice, encouragement, and instruction in an
environment conducive to learning, movement skill acquisition will be
promoted. The absence of these environmental affordances (i.e., enabling factors) will inhibit movement skill acquisition. Furthermore, the

acquisition rate will vary depending on the mechanical and physical requirements of each task. If an infant does not have sufficient hand-holds (an affordance) in her environment to enable her to pull herself up to a stand, she will have to wait until sufficient balance (a mechanical task factor) and strength in the legs (a physical task factor) have developed, before she is able to bring herself to a standing position unaided.

In the fundamental movement phase boys and girls are beginning to develop a whole host of basic movement abilities—running, hopping, jumping, throwing, catching, kicking, and trapping. Unfortunately, many professional educators have the notion that children somehow "automatically" learn how to perform these fundamental movements. Many naively think that children at this phase of development will, through the process of maturation, develop mature fundamental movement skills. This simply is not true for the vast majority of children. Most children must have some combination of opportunities for practice, encouragement, and instruction in an ecologically sound environment. These conditions are crucial to helping them through each of the stages within the fundamental movement phase. Furthermore, as the task requirements of a fundamental movement skill change, so too will the process and the product. For example, the perceptual requirements of hitting a pitched ball are considerably more sophisticated than those required to strike a stationary ball or to perform a striking pattern without making contact with another object. Teachers of individuals at the fundamental movement phase must learn to recognize the task requirements of movement skills and analyze them in order to maximize learner success. Teachers who overlook these duties erect proficiency barriers at the specialized movement skill phase.

At the specialized movement skill phase successful performance of the mechanics of movement skills is dependent upon mature fundamental movements. After the transitional stage we progress to the final stages in which specialized movement skills are applied to daily living, recreational, and sport experiences.

Returning to the hourglass, at some point it turns over (Figure 4.3). The timing of this occurrence is quite variable and depends more upon social and cultural factors than upon physical and mechanical factors. For most individuals, the hourglass turns over and the "sand" begins to pour out during the late teens and early 20s. This is a time in which many individuals enter the adult world of work, car payments, mortgages, family responsibilities, and a host of other time-consuming tasks. Time restrictions limit the pursuit of new movement skills and the maintenance of skills mastered during childhood and adolescence.

There are several interesting features in the overturned hourglass that we need to consider. The sand falls through two different filters. One is the *hereditary filter* with which we can do very little. For example, an individual may have inherited a predisposition toward longevity or coronary heart disease. The hereditary filter is going to be either

Figure 4.3
Emptying the over-turned hourglass of life

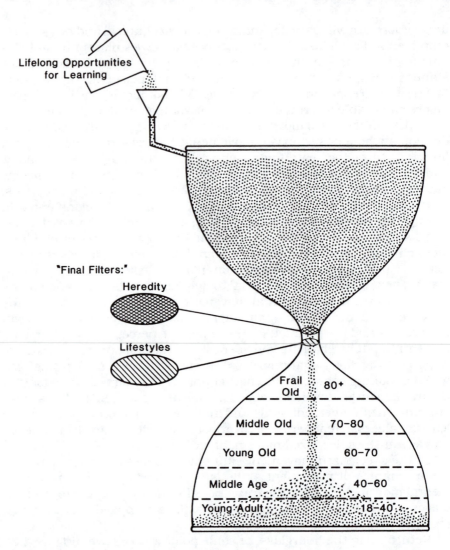

Lifelong Opportunities for Learning

"Final Filters:"

Heredity

Lifestyles

Frail Old	80+
Middle Old	70–80
Young Old	60–70
Middle Age	40–60
Young Adult	18–40

dense, causing the sand to filter through slowly, or easy to penetrate, allowing the sand to flow through more rapidly. Sand that has fallen through the hereditary filter cannot be recovered, but it must pass through a second, or final, filter called the lifestyle filter.

The density of the *lifestyle filter* is determined by such things as physical fitness, nutritional status, diet, exercise, the ability to handle stress and social and spiritual well-being. The lifestyle filter is environmentally based, and we have a good deal of control over the rate at which sand falls through this filter. Although we can never stop sand from flowing to the bottom of the hourglass, we can slow down the rate at which it falls. A former Surgeon General of the United States, Dr. C. Edward Koop, once stated that although we cannot stop the aging process, we can control it by up to 40 percent. We can directly influence how fast sand falls through our hourglasses. As teachers, coaches, and parents we have the wonderful opportunity to shovel "sand" into many "hourglasses." We also have the privilege and the obligation to help others develop "lifestyle filters" that will slow the rates at which sand falls in their hourglasses.

It should be noted that sand can still be added even when hourglasses are overturned and the sand is falling to the bottom. Each of us has *lifelong opportunities for learning.* By taking advantage of the numerous opportunities for continued development and activity, we can add more sand. Obviously, we cannot add sand faster than it is falling and claim immortality. We can, however, extend and improve the quality of life.

It is important to mention that the hourglass heuristic device as described to this point gives the impression that development is an orderly and *continuous* process. Note, however, that the sand at the bottom of the hourglass in both Figures 4.2 and 4.3 is distributed in the manner of a bell-shaped curve. The shape of this curve implies that there is a distribution of movement skills among the categories of movement (locomotion, manipulation, and stability), and within the various movement skills themselves. For example, one may be at the elementary stage in some skills, the mature stage in others, and at a sport skill level in still others. Additionally, one may be at different stages of development within the same skill. For example, when children and adults perform the overhand throw they are often at the initial stage in their trunk action, the elementary stage in their arm action, and at the mature stage in their leg action. Motor development in the hourglass model, therefore, is a *discontinuous process,* that is, a process that although phase-like and stage-like in a general sense, is highly variable in a specific sense. Motor development when viewed as discontinuous, is in effect a *dynamical* (i.e., nonlinear) process occurring within a self-organizing system (i.e., the "hourglass"). See Kamm, Thelen and Jensen, 1990 for an excellent overview of dynamical systems theory.

Concept 4.10 The process of motor development is discontinuous within a self-organizing system.

The hourglass model of motor development is not one-dimensional, that is, unaffected by the cognitive and affective domains of human behavior. Unlike the two-dimensional representation of the hourglass in Figures 4.2 and 4.3, "real" hourglasses are present only in three-dimensional space. As a result real hourglasses have height, width, and depth and must be supported if they are to remain upright. Visualize, if you will, an individual's hourglass as being supported by a cognitive pillar, an affective pillar, and a motor pillar. The hourglass is multidimensional, and as a result there is a triple interaction among the cognitive, affective, and motor domains. In other words, the hourglass model is more than a motor model. It is a model of motor development that influences, and is influenced by, a wide variety of cognitive and affective factors operating within both the individual and the environment.

You may find it helpful to visualize the hourglass heuristic device as you proceed through the following sections dealing with motor development during infancy, childhood, adolescence, and adulthood. Remember, however, that it is not important that you accept this model as proposed. Theoretical models are just that—"models." As such they are incomplete, inexact, and subject to verification and further refinement. What *is* important is that you visualize how the process of motor development occurs. Remember, understanding motor development helps to explain how learning occurs. Both are crucial to the creation of effective, developmentally appropriate instruction.

Concept 4.11   Understanding the process of motor development helps explain how movement skill learning occurs, which is crucial to developmentally appropriate instruction.

Chapter 4

Summary

The acquisition of competency in movement is an extensive process beginning with the early reflexive movements of the newborn and continuing throughout life. The process by which an individual progresses from the reflexive movement phase, through the rudimentary and fundamental movement phases, and finally to the specialized movements skill phase of development is influenced by factors within tasks, the individual, and the environment.

Reflexes and rudimentary movement abilities are largely based on maturation. They appear and disappear in a fairly rigid sequence deviating only in the rate of their appearance. They do, however, form an important base upon which fundamental movement abilities are developed.

Fundamental movement abilities are basic movement patterns that begin developing around the same time that a child is able to walk independently and move freely through his or her environment. These basic locomotor, manipulative, and stability abilities go through a definite, observable, process from immaturity to maturity. Stages within this phase include initial, elementary, and mature. Attainment of the mature stage is influenced greatly by opportunities for practice, encouragement, and instruction in an environment that fosters learning. Under the proper circumstances, children are capable of performing at the mature stage in the vast majority of fundamental movement patterns by age six. The fundamental movement skills of children entering school are too often incompletely developed. Therefore, the primary grades offer an excellent opportunity to develop fundamental movement abilities to their mature levels. These same fundamental skills will be enhanced and refined to form the specialized movement abilities so highly valued for recreational, competitive, and daily living tasks.

The specialized movement skill phase of development is in essence an elaboration of the fundamental phase. Specialized skills are more precise than fundamental skills. They often involve a combination of fundamental movement abilities and require a greater degree of precision. Specialized skills involve three related stages. The transition stage is typically the level of the child in grades three through five. At this level, children are involved in their first real applications of fundamental movements to sport. If the fundamental abilities used in a particular sport activity are not at the mature level, the child will resort to less mature or elementary patterns of movement. It should be obvious that involving children in sport skill refinement before they reach mature levels of ability in prerequisite fundamentals is unwise. When this happens, the immature movements found in the basic patterns are carried over to the related sport skills. The child will in fact regress to his or her characteristic pattern. It is important that sensitive teaching and coaching be incorporated at this point.

When we look at the process of motor development we need to look at it first from a theoretical perspective. Each of us needs to have a theoretical framework to use as the basis for our actions. It is not important that you agree with the theoretical framework presented here. The hourglass model is simply our way of viewing the process of motor development and its implications for life. What is your theoretical framework? How would it influence your teaching, coaching, and parenting, and how does it influence you personally?

Terms to Remember

Descriptive theory	Precontrol stage
Explanatory theory	Fundamental movement phase
Inductive method	Initial stage
Deductive method	Elementary stage
Stability	Mature stage
Locomotor movement	Specialized movement stage
Manipulative movement	Transitional stage
Reflexes	Application stage
Primitive reflexes	Lifelong utilization stage
Postural reflexes	Heuristic device
Information encoding stage	Hereditary filter
Information decoding stage	Lifestyle filter
Rudimentary movement phase	Lifelong opportunities for learning
Reflex inhibition stage	Discontinuous process

Critical Readings

Bigge, M. L., & Shermis, S. S. (1992). *Learning Theories for Teachers* (Chapters 1 and 4). New York: Harper Collins Publishers.

Gallahue, D. L. (1994). Motor Development. In J. Winnick (Ed.), *Adapted Physical Education and Sports.* Champaign, IL: Human Kinetics.

Kamm, K., Thelen, E., & Jensen, J. (1990). A dynamical systems approach to motor development. *Physical Therapy,* 70, 12, 763–775.

Lerner, R. M. (1986). *Concepts and Theories in Human Development* (Chapter 1). New York: Random House.

Roberton, M. A., & Halverson, L. E. (1984). *Developing Children—Their Changing Movement* (pp. 1–16). Philadelphia: Lea & Febiger.

Seefeldt, V., & Haubenstricker, J. (1982). Patterns, phases, or stages: An analytic model for the study of developmental movement. In J. A. S. Kelso, & J. E. Clark (Eds.), *The Development of Movement Control and Coordination* (pp. 309–318). New York: Wiley.

SECTION ▮▮

INFANCY

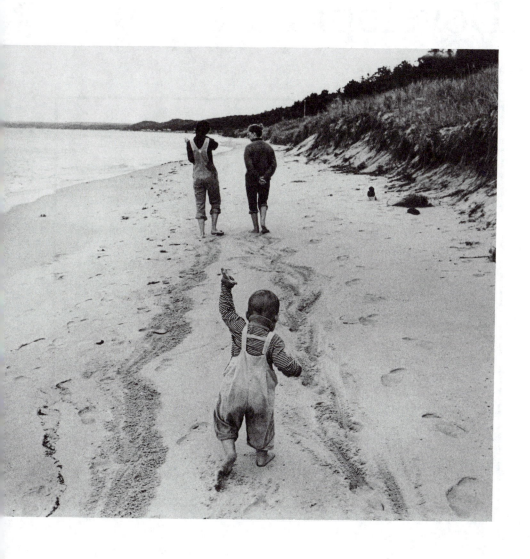

Chapter **5**

Prenatal Factors Affecting Development

CHAPTER COMPETENCIES

Upon completion of this chapter you should be able to:

- *Describe the influence of maternal nutrition on later development*
- *Critically analyze the impact of maternal chemical intake on fetal development*
- *List and discuss factors to be considered when determining the influence of a drug on an unborn child*
- *Distinguish between chromosome-based disorders and gene-based disorders*
- *List and describe the causes and effects of several chromosome- and gene-based disorders*
- *Describe the potential effects of radiation and chemical pollutants on later development*
- *List and discuss several maternal and fetal medical problems that may affect later development*
- *Describe the influence of maternal exercise during pregnancy on fetal development*
- *Demonstrate knowledge of birth process factors that may affect later development*
- *Critically analyze the prenatal period and describe the interrelated nature of a variety of factors that may influence later development*

> **Key Concept:** A number of prenatal factors, many of which can be controlled, affect motor development during infancy and beyond.

Among the most positive contributions of medical technology are advances that have been made in reducing infant mortality. As little as two generations ago prenatal and neonatal illness and death were common in North America. One need, however, only look at less advanced cultures throughout the world, and among the poor, deprived, and neglected in our society, to see that the threat of severely handicapping conditions resulting from a variety of prenatal factors still exists. The current leading cause of severe impairment, among rich and poor, stems from prenatal factors. Birth defects are the most serious child health problem, affecting more than 250,000 babies in the United States each year (March of Dimes, 1988). Although only about 1 percent of the population shows moderate to severe problems in the years before school, Hagberg (1975) estimated that 85 to 90 percent of these intellectual and neurological problems stem from prenatal causes. In a country in which the population will exceed 260 million by the year 2000 (U.S. Bureau of the Census, 1990) it is essential to identify and eliminate prenatal factors that adversely affect later growth and development. It is staggering to contemplate that more than 2 million Americans have severe afflictions because of conditions over which they had absolutely no control. It is doubly staggering when we speculate on the number of individuals who have been only moderately or slightly affected by these conditions.

The number of high-risk pregnancies is estimated to be from 20 to 25 percent, and the number is growing because more women over 35 are becoming pregnant (Freeman and Pescar, 1982). In a *high-risk pregnancy* the expectant mother has a condition before or during pregnancy that increases her unborn child's chances of experiencing either prenatal or postnatal problems. Table 5.1 presents a list of conditions that may put a mother-to-be in the high-risk category. Several of these are described in further detail throughout this chapter.

Nutritional and Chemical Factors

Whatever the expectant mother ingests will affect the unborn child in some way. Whether these effects are harmful and will have lasting consequences depends on a variety of circumstances. The condition of the fetus, degree of nutritional or chemical abuse, amount or dosage, period of pregnancy, and presence of other influencing factors are just a few of the circumstances that influence the probability of teratogenic effects. A *teratogen* is any substance that may cause the unborn child to develop in an abnormal manner. The fetus is "at risk" when any one or more of the following nutritional or chemical factors are present.

Table 5.1 Conditions That May Result in High-risk Pregnancy

Medical Conditions:	Exposure to:	Use of:	History:
Asthma	Certain Medications	Alcohol	Age (<16, >35)
Cancer	Chemical Pollutants	Street Drugs	Bleeding
Diabetes	Cytomegalovirus	Tobacco	Heredity
Hypertension	Excessive Radiation		Nutritional
Heart Disease	Rubella		Inadequacy
Kidney Disease	Toxoplasmosis		Previous Miscarriage
Liver Disease			Seriously overweight
Maternal Stress			or underweight
Thyroid Disorders			Poverty
Sexually Transmitted			
Diseases			

Prenatal Malnutrition

Prenatal malnutrition is a common cause of later developmental diffi-culties throughout the world. *Prenatal malnutrition* may result from one or more of the following three factors: (1) placental factors, (2) fetal factors, and (3) maternal factors.

Placental malnutrition arises out of problems associated with the supply and transport of nutrients from the placenta to the fetus. The fetus depends on the mother's blood supply and the osmotic action of the placenta and umbilical cord for its nutrients.

Fetal malnutrition is associated with the inability on the part of the developing fetus to utilize the nutrients that are available to it. This gen-erally is due to complications in the metabolism of the fetus that inter-rupt or prevent the normal utilization of available nutrients.

Maternal malnutrition is associated with inadequacies in the ex-pectant mother's current nutritional intake as well as her general level of nutrition. Because of this, deficiencies in the mother's diet both prior to and during pregnancy can have a harmful effect on the child. A sound, nutritious diet is absolutely essential for the mother's health and the health of her unborn child.

Concept 5.1   Placental, fetal, and maternal malnutrition negatively influence human development throughout the world.

Malnourishment rather than *undernourishment* is of concern to nutritionists and specialists in child development in the West, where most people enjoy an abundance of food. Literally millions of women of childbearing age are malnourished worldwide. They are not receiving

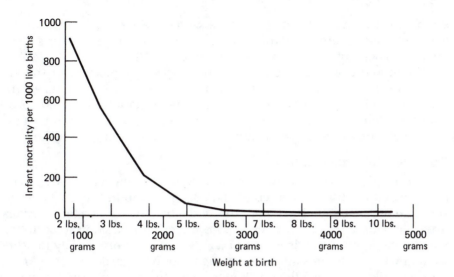

Figure 5.1
The relationship between infant mortality and birthweight (*Source:* White House Conference on Children, 1970)

the proper nutrients through their normal daily intake of food. The reasons for maternal malnourishment range from poor eating habits to poverty, low socioeconomic class, anxiety, stress, and trauma.

The sharpest contrasts in maternal malnutrition and normal nutrition are seen between poor and non-poor mothers. Naeye et al. (1969) studied 252 infants who were stillborn or died within two days of birth. Their survey indicated that infants who were "below the poverty level" were 15 percent smaller than non-poverty infants. Also, a higher percentage of stillborn children were born to impoverished mothers. Maternal malnutrition may account for the fact that low socioeconomic families have a higher percentage of children with birth defects than do higher socioeconomic families with more adequate nutrition (Eichorn, 1979).

Inadequate fetal nutrition is a major factor in low-birthweight infants. Low-birthweight babies are much more susceptible to a variety of developmental abnormalities and have a higher mortality rate than normal birthweight infants (Worthington, 1988). Figure 5.1 demonstrates that the mortality rate for low-birthweight babies is significantly higher than for normal weight infants.

Lack of vitamins C, B-complex, D, K, and E as well as protein deficiencies may result in serious physical and mental damage or even death to the unborn child (Worthington, 1988). McGowan, in 1979, estimated that over 1 million children in the United States suffer from chronic malnutrition to the extent that it interferes with normal brain development. Today estimates of chronic malnutrition in the U.S. are considerably higher. Information about the effects of specific vitamin and mineral deficiencies in the diet of the expectant mother is difficult to gather and verify. It is unethical to study the effects of malnutrition by purposely depriving expectant mothers. It is also difficult to compare mothers with inadequate diets to those who have adequate nutrition because of confounding variables such as extreme anxiety, stress, poverty, and poor nutritional habits (Williams, 1988).

The amount of weight gained by the expectant mother, in the absence of other complications, may serve as a general indicator of the unborn child's nutritional status. Maternal weight gain of 20 to 28 pounds is generally recommended. Table 5.2 lists the proportions of average weight gain during pregnancy (Samuel and Samuels, 1979).

Common Maternal Drugs

The wall of the placenta is porous, and chemicals may penetrate it with tragic results to the unborn child. The drugs found in the average person's medicine cabinet are potentially destructive to the fetus. Every drug has side effects, whether it is a prescription or nonprescription substance. Even if the drug has been given during pregnancy to other women without serious side effects, it cannot be regarded as safe for all unborn children. The following factors need to be considered whenever the influence of a drug on an unborn child is evaluated.

1. The time of pregnancy during which the drug is taken
2. The dosage of the drug
3. The length of time the drug is taken
4. The genetic predisposition of the fetus
5. How these four factors interact

Concept 5.2   Maternal drugs and medications frequently affect the fetus and later motor development.

There are various ways in which a drug may affect the unborn child. Drugs may interfere with organ growth or cell differentiation and result in deviations from normal development. The penetrability of the placenta may be altered and reduce the flow of oxygen and nutrients or

Table 5.2 Distribution of Maternal Weight Gain During Pregnancy

	Weight Averages (in pounds)
Fetus	7.5
Placenta	1.0
Amniotic fluid	2.0
Increase in uterus's weight	2.5
Increase in breasts' weight	3.0
Increase in the mother's fat	4–8
	20–28 pounds

magnify the drug concentration flowing to the fetus. Drugs may impair development and functioning of the fetus's liver, which balances blood waste products called bilirubin. The inability of the biliary ducts to excrete bilirubin efficiently results in *jaundice*. Excessive jaundice results in a condition called *kernicterus*. Kernicterus can result in permanent and devastating brain damage. Table 5.3 provides a few examples of common drugs taken during pregnancy and their associated risk factors.

"Necessary" Maternal Drugs

During pregnancy the expectant mother may be under the care of a physician because of an illness or disease. Good, consistent medical care is doubly important because the developing fetus inside a mother with a special medical condition may also have special needs. The medications prescribed for the mother may have to be modified to protect her unborn child. A mother being treated for epilepsy, for example, should avoid the use of Dilantin and phenobarbital and other drugs used for seizure control. Although she may not be able to discontinue the use of medication completely, the drug should not be taken automatically and the dosage may need modification under medical supervision.

The expectant mother with cancer is at risk when chemotherapy is used to decrease the rate of malignant cell growth, particularly during the first three months of pregnancy. The use of progesterone to correct menstrual cycle abnormalities and to prevent miscarriage should be avoided in expectant mothers because of the potentially harmful effects on the newborn.

Table 5.3 The Effects of Common Drugs on the Unborn Child

Drug	Use	Possible Effects
Coumadin	An anticoagulant used for blood clots	May cause bleeding before or during birth, resulting in brain damage
Diuretics	To treat toxemia, particularly water retention	Water and salt imbalance. An electrolyte imbalance may result in brain damage
Streptomycin	To treat infection in the mother	Impairment of kidneys, hearing, and balance
Aspirin	For aches, pain, fever. Almost 80% of over-the-counter drugs contain aspirin	Death; congenital deformities; bleeding under the skull, causing brain damage; hemorrhaging during birth
Tetracyclines	For acne	Stunts bone and teeth growth

Concept 5.3 Many over-the-counter and prescription medications have the potential to impair fetal development.

The unborn child of a diabetic mother-to-be is particularly vulnerable. The severity of the disease and whether the mother is insulin-dependent has a great deal to do with possible problems. Prior to the development of insulin, diabetic women simply did not have children. After insulin became available (about 1922) more diabetic women were able to give birth. However, the prenatal mortality rate was over 50 percent, and many of the children who survived had serious congenital deformities. Today, with careful management of the diabetes, utilization of special tests to monitor fetal well-being, and excellent medical care the fetal mortality rate has been sharply reduced. Freeman and Pescar (1982) reported that "fetal mortality rates have been dramatically reduced to 3 percent to 4 percent—and nearly all these deaths are due to serious congenital malformations incompatible with survival" (p. 18). A high percentage of babies born to diabetic mothers are, because of their tendency to be larger at birth, delivered by Caesarean section.

Table 5.4 summarizes some common medical conditions, treatments, and possible effects on the fetus.

Table 5.4 Common Drugs for Medical Conditions During Pregnancy and the Possible Effects on the Unborn Child

Maternal Condition	Drug	Possible Effects
Hypertension	Resperine	Choking, gasping, nasal congestion at birth
Thyroid	Thiouracile Iodides Radioactive iodine	Thyroid abnormalities in child: cretinism (hypothyroidism)
Diabetes	Insulin	Excessive birthweight, prematurity, heart defects, jaundice, low blood sugar, convulsions, mental and physical retardation, deformities
Menstrual abnormality	Progesterone	Gross deformities, masculinization of female organs
Allergy or cold	Antihistamines	Deformities (in animal studies)
Epilepsy	Seizure control drugs	Cleft palate and other malformations

Street Drugs

During the past two decades there has been an alarming increase in the habitual use of mind-altering or *street drugs* by women of childbearing age. The use of opiates (opium, heroin), cocaine, amphetamines (speed), lysergic acid diethylamide (LSD), and cannabis (hashish, marijuana) is of great concern to those interested in the well-being of unborn children. Chasnoff et al. (1990) estimated that 10 to 20 percent of all women use street drugs of some form during pregnancy. As a result, approximately 375,000 drug-exposed infants are born each year. Furthermore, the March of Dimes estimates that the number of children exposed to cocaine alone could range from 1 to 4 million by the year 2000.

Legal, moral, and ethical restrictions make it impossible to conduct controlled experiments on the effects of these mind-altering drugs on fetal development. Therefore, our knowledge is limited to laboratory settings with animals and retrospective case studies of users. Although available research is limited to animals and only correlational in nature, it is reasonable to assume that mind-altering drugs are likely to harm the unborn child. With regard to the use of marijuana, Hoyt (1981) said: "The transfer of marijuana's active ingredients through the placenta affects production of testosterone in the fetus, inhibits DNA synthesis in human cells thus increasing the potential for mutation, and is believed to be a contributing factor in certain cases of spontaneous abortion" (p. 31).

Concept 5.4　The use of street drugs by the expectant mother may cause devastating damage to her unborn child.

Fink (1989) reported that cocaine affects the fetus in three ways: as it passes through the placenta, by changing the fetal environment, and by altering the mother's central nervous system which places the fetus at additional risk. Cocaine has the triple properties of being addictive, toxic, and teratogenic. In terms of its teratogenic effects, research data as well as clinical observation clearly indicate that cocaine-exposed infants are at risk of increased mortality, morbidity, and problems in development and long-term behavior. Such problems include low-birthweight, poor infant-state regulation, withdrawal symptoms, hypertension, thermal regulatory difficulties, and learning disabilities (Gittler and McPherson 1990).

Table 5.5 provides an overview of the possible effects of some mind-altering drugs on the newborn child.

Table 5.5 Possible Effects of Street Drugs on Development of the Unborn Child

Drug	Possible Effects
Heroin and morphine	Irritable. Sleeps poorly. High-pitched cry Vomiting and diarrhea Marked physiological withdrawal symptoms Decreased oxygen in the blood tissues Hepatitis from unclean needle Susceptible to infection Complications: 1. Toxemia 2. Breech birth 3. Prematurity 4. Small for date of birth 5. Premature separation of the placenta Complications if not treated: 1. Dehydration 2. Respiratory distress 3. Shock 4. Coma 5. Death
Amphetamines and barbiturates	Miscarriage Birth defects
Tranquilizers	Such drugs as Sominex,® Nytol,® Sleep-Eze® and Compoz® contain two antihistamines that have produced congenital deformities in animals.
LSD (lysergic acid diethylamide)	May cause chromosome damage Sometimes contaminated with quinine or other materials that may harm the unborn child. A few surveys have found a higher incidence of congenital defects in children of LSD users.
Cocaine	Physiological withdrawal Hypertension Poor thermal regulation Low-birthweight Learning disabilities Behavioral problems Increased mortality

Alcohol and Tobacco

Although alcohol and tobacco are considered by many to be mind- or mood-altering drugs, we are treating them separately because of the frequency of their usage and to amplify their potential hazards. It has been variously reported that there are over 1 million alcoholics of child-bearing age. The fetus is affected twice as fast as the mother by her alcohol consumption and at the same level of concentration. Until recently, the widespread myth that the fetus takes what it needs from its mother and is uninfluenced by her consumption of foods and beverages caused expectant mothers to be unconcerned about their alcohol consumption. The potential dangers of alcohol to the unborn child were recognized, however, as far back as the Greek era, when newly married couples were forbidden to consume alcohol in order to prevent conception while intoxicated.

In the 1890s William Sullivan, a physician at a Liverpool, England, prison for women, was the first to carefully document the effects of chronic alcoholism on the offspring of 120 alcoholic inmates. This early study revealed a significantly greater mortality rate among the 600 offspring and a much higher number of developmental difficulties in the infants (Rosett and Sander, 1979). Further research into the effects of maternal alcoholism lagged in the United States and Great Britain after 1920, following the enactment of Prohibition, although some research continued in France and Germany. It was not until 1970 that the actual ''discovery'' and labeling of *Fetal Alcohol Syndrome* (FAS) took place (Witti, 1978).

Concept 5.5   Although completely preventable, alcohol use is the third leading cause of birth defects in the United States.

Alcohol is now recognized as the leading cause of birth defects in the United States, exceeding Down syndrome and spina bifida (Streissguth et al., 1991). About one in every 700 babies born has FAS (Centers for Disease Control). Fetal Alcohol Syndrome and its less dramatic but still preventable counterpart, *Fetal Alcohol Effects* (FAE), are the only birth defects that are completely preventable. Forty to 50 percent of infants born to mothers who are chronic alcohol consumers (i.e., those with a consumption level of two or more average-size drinks per day) or who go on drinking binges are born with FAE (i.e., partial expression of FAS). About 33 percent of the children delivered by mothers who are active alcoholics are born with fully expressed FAS (Malina and Bouchard, 1991). Children with fully expressed FAS are born with mental retardation and marked physical defects. Children with FAE are often at additional risk because they appear to be normal and frequently do not receive the attention they need during the crucial early years to help them reach their full potential. Children with FAE, although lacking in many of the distinct physical features of FAS, have displayed motor development delays, attention deficits, and memory difficulties (Dorris, 1989), all of which frequently lead to a diagnosis of learning disabilities. Table 5.6 summarizes some of the potential characteristics of FAS.

Alcohol in the mother's blood passes directly through the placenta to the fetus. The fetus does not have any ethanol-oxidizing or alcohol dehydrogenasic abilities; therefore, the alcohol is fed directly into its system. Evidence is unclear on the exact amounts of alcohol that are harmful to the fetus and on the critical periods during which it should be avoided. However, a study by Vingen et al. (1986) revealed that consumption of large quantities of alcohol is likely to result in central nervous system damage, growth and mental retardation, and distinct facial

Table 5.6 Characteristics of Fetal Alcohol Syndrome

Growth	Growth failure before birth
	Growth failure after birth
	Small head circumference
	Small in length compared to weight
Eyes	Lesions in the eyelids
	Fold of skin in corner of the eye
	Perceptual problems
	Narrow eyes
Face	Flat mid-face
	Low nasal bridge
	Short, upturned nose
	Minor outer ear deformity
	Underdevelopment of jaw
	Thin upper lip
Other	Heart defects
	Hip dislocation
	Skeletal defects
	Decrease in joint mobility
	Motor development delay
	Abnormal creases in the palm of the hand
	Female genital defects
Behavior	Jittery
	Hyperactive
	Poor coordination
	Poor sucking
	Irregular sleeping
	Self-stimulator
Intelligence	Mental retardation borderline to moderate

abnormalities. Moderate to small doses of alcohol may have the same results, according to the Vingen research. Although social drinking during pregnancy has not been conclusively associated with an increase in risk, the March of Dimes Birth Defects Foundation (1985) maintains that "the best decision is not to have any [alcohol] while you are pregnant." In fact, the Surgeon General of the United States has warned all pregnant women and those planning pregnancies to abstain from drinking any form of alcoholic beverage. Warning labels about the adverse effects of alcohol on fetal development are now required by law on all containers of alcohol consumed in the United States. There is no risk of FAS if alcohol consumption has been stopped prior to pregnancy.

Concept 5.6   Smoking by the expectant mother has been shown to have negative effects on fetal development.

Smoking has been implicated in numerous studies as a cause of low birthweight in infants. The March of Dimes Birth Defects Foundation (1985) further indicated that women who smoke a pack of cigarettes or more a day tend to deliver low-birthweight babies and almost double their chances of miscarriage or stillbirths. Maternal smoking speeds up the fetal heart rate and has an adverse effect on central nervous system integration of the newborn. Furthermore, surveys of children born to nicotine-addicted mothers showed that they tend to rate lower on behavior assessment scales than other children. They tend to be more fretful, less coordinated, less alert, and less responsive to cuddling. There is a higher incidence of respiratory problems in children born of mothers who smoked during their pregnancies. Smoking, according to the March of Dimes Birth Defects Foundation (1985) is most harmful to a baby's growth during the second half of a pregnancy. There may be cause for cautious optimism, in that the effects of smoking may not be cumulative, and their impact on the unborn child may be negligible if smoking ceases early in pregnancy. "The effect of smoking on fetal growth is dramatically shown in cases in which a mother smoked during one pregnancy and not the other. Children born of the smoke-free pregnancy are heavier and longer at birth" Malina & Bouchard, 1991 (p. 34).

Hereditary Factors

Until relatively recently the study of heredity through the science of genetics was only a matter of theory and speculation. Today, however, we have more precise and experimentally verifiable knowledge of heredity. Since it is impossible to discuss it in detail within the confines of this chapter, we will concern ourselves with the potential impact of various hereditary factors on later development.

The union of a sperm with an egg begins the process of development. The sperm carries 23 chromosomes, which contain all of the father's hereditary material. The egg also contains 23 chromosomes, the mother's contribution to the child's heredity. The new fetus, therefore, contains a total of 46 chromosomes (23 pairs). Each chromosome, by the process of cell division (*mitosis*), has a replica in every cell of the body. Genes are found on each chromosome. It has been estimated that each chromosome may contain up to 20,000 genes. The genes determine the vast variety of individual characteristics such as gender, hair and eye color, body size, and physical structure.

Concept 5.7 The genetic inheritance of the fetus will control the upper and the lower limits of its functioning.

Under most conditions the chromosomes and genes remain unaltered throughout the prenatal period. (There is growing speculation that certain chemical substances may contribute to chromosomal damage after conception.) However, a variety of genetic factors prior to conception have been shown to alter the normal process of development.

Chromosome-based Disorders

It has been estimated that between 3 and 6 percent of all conceptions show evidence of *chromosome damage*, and of these about 90 percent will be spontaneously aborted (Ford, 1973). Most chromosome variations are so potent that they are rarely seen in surviving newborns, but fully 1 percent of live infants show evidence of chromosomal damage.

Probably the most common chromosomal alteration is that of *Down syndrome*. Down syndrome is the result of an error in which 47 chromosomes are present rather than the standard 46. This cause of Down syndrome is called trisomy #21 because of the presence of three #21 chromosomes. Trisomy #21 accounts for 95 percent of all Down syndrome cases (March of Dimes, 1984). Down syndrome occurs in approximately 1 out of every 500 to 700 live births. The rate of incidence seems to be age-related and shows dramatic increases in births occurring in women over 45 years of age. In fact, the incidence in women at age 30 is about 1 in 885, while women at 49 years of age have about a 1-in-17 chance of giving birth to a child with Down syndrome (Freeman and Pescar, 1982).

Down syndrome children are often born prematurely. Their rate of growth is slower than normal, often resulting in shorter stature. The nose, chin, and ears tend to be small, the teeth are poorly developed and the eyesight is weak. Poor balance, hypotonus, short arms and legs, and nonelastic skin are other characteristics of the child with Down syndrome. Cardiovascular defects resulting in frequent respiratory ailments are common, along with limited intellectual functioning.

Language and conceptualization skills are generally poor. Motor development appears to proceed in sequence as in the normal infant, but at a substantially slower rate.

The major findings of studies describing the motor development of infants with Down syndrome include: (1) delays in the emergence and inhibition of primitive and postural reflexes, (2) hypotonia and hyperflexia, and (3) substantial delays in the attainment of motor milestones. Elementary school-aged children with Down syndrome display levels of motor development that are consistently behind their non-disabled peers. Furthermore, they tend to fall farther and farther behind as they grow older (Henderson, 1985). This, however, is linked more closely to insufficient environmental stimulation than to identifiable biological factors. In fact, early identification and intervention programs appear to be quite successful in improving the motor functioning of infants and young children with Down syndrome. Activities to improve reflexive behavior and to facilitate the acquisition of rudimentary movement skills such as independent sitting, standing, and walking should be provided during the crucial early years. As Down's children mature, additional opportunities and assistance with fundamental movement skill development should be provided (Gallahue, 1993, 1994). Developmentally appropriate activities should serve as the basis for teaching fundamental movement skills. If and when appropriate, basic sport skills may be introduced.

Chromosome-linked disorders other than Down syndrome sometimes occur. Fortunately, conditions such as Patau's syndrome and Edward's syndrome are rare. Little is known about them other than that they are also associated with an extra chromosome and that they result in severe deformities, retardation, and early mortality. The risk of chromosomal abnormalities increases from 2.5 per 1,000 live births for women at age 30, to 4.5 for women at age 35, and to 3.7 for women at age 40 (Freeman and Pescar, 1982). Certainly age is a factor to consider when a woman wants to become pregnant.

Concept 5.8   Chromosome-based and gene-linked abnormalities will have an impact on later development ranging from mild, to severe, to catastrophic.

Gene-based Disorders

Genetic defects vary widely in their consequences. The severity of the defect is dependent on whether the mutant gene is on an autosomal or on a sex-linked chromosome and whether it is on a single gene or also on its mate. Delay and retardation in motor and cognitive functioning are not usually present in autosomal dominant mutations. Autosomal recessive mutations, however, are often associated with mental retardation and problems in motor development. Nora and Fraser (1974) listed

61 *autosomal syndromes,* one third of which are associated with mental retardation and other developmental abnormalities that interfere with the normal process of motor development. Among the more common autosomal mutations that affect later motor development are clubfoot, sickle cell anemia, Tay-Sachs disease, phenylketonuria (PKU), and spina bifida.

Clubfoot is one of the most common of all birth defects and historically has been one of the major orthopedic problems of children. About one in 400 babies born in the United States each year has clubfoot, and boys are twice as likely to have this condition as girls (March of Dimes, 1984). There are three major forms of clubfoot: equinovarus, calcaneal valgus, and metatarsus varus (Figure 5.2). With *equinovarus* the foot is twisted inward and downward. The Achilles tendon is generally very tight, making it impossible to bring the foot into normal alignment. *Calcaneal valgus* is the most common form of clubfoot. The foot is sharply angled at the heel, with the foot pointing up and outward. This condition is less severe than equinovarus and easier to correct. *Metatarsus varus* is the mildest form of clubfoot. The front part of the foot is turned inward and is often not diagnosed until the baby is a few months old. With all forms of clubfoot, early, persistent treatment will maximize the chances for normal lives. Left untreated until too late in childhood, clubfoot will be a major limiting factor in normal upright locomotion.

Sickle cell anemia is an inherited blood disease. It is a relatively common gene-based disorder occurring in one in every 400 to 600 African-Americans and one in every 1,000 to 1,500 Hispanics. One in 10 blacks carry the sickle cell gene, and there is a 1-in-4 chance that a child of a gene carrier will develop the disease (March of Dimes, 1984). The effects of the disease vary greatly from person to person—anemia, pain, damage to vital organs, and death in childhood or early adulthood are possible. The growth and motor development of individuals with sickle cell disease are often impaired. Also, patients tend to tire easily, and are frequently short of breath. The sickle cell trait or disease can be easily detected through a simple blood test called hemoglobin electrophoresis. A prenatal test to determine if the fetus will carry the trait, be normal, or develop the disease is also available.

Tay-Sachs Disease is a gene-based disorder typical of descendants of Central and Eastern European Jews known as Ashkenazim. Nearly one out of every 25 American Jews carries the Tay-Sachs gene (March of Dimes, 1984). If both parents carry the Tay-Sachs gene there is a 1-in-4 chance that any of their children will develop Tay-Sachs Disease or become carriers. If only one parent carries the gene none of their children can have the disease, but there is a 1-in-2 chance of becoming a carrier. There is no known cure for Tay-Sachs Disease, and it is always fatal. It first appears in infancy with the baby losing motor control. Blindness and paralysis follow with death around ages 3 or 4. Tay-Sachs Disease can be diagnosed through amniocentesis prior to birth. A simple blood test prior to pregnancy will determine if one is a carrier.

Figure 5.2
Three forms of
clubfoot

**Equinovarus
(most severe)**

**Calcaneal Valgus
(most common)**

**Metatarsus Varus
(mildest)**

Phenylketonuria (PKU) is the only gene-based disorder that is completely treatable if detected early enough. PKU, a metabolic disorder, is the result of a recessive gene that inhibits production of phenylalanine hydroxylase which is necessary to convert the amino acid phenylalanine to tyrosine. Without this enzyme the child is unable to digest many foods including dairy products. Identification is done through a routine blood test at birth. Treatment consists of simply following a scientifically controlled diet that eliminates foods containing phenylalanine. It is interesting to note that the can of diet cola you may be consuming right now contains phenylalanine with a warning on the label. Left untreated PKU will result in severe mental retardation. However, if PKU is detected (about 1 week after birth), the devastating results can be entirely avoided with proper dietary precautions. In fact, many states in the United States mandate PKU testing of all newborns.

Spina bifida is a birth defect of the spinal column, caused by a weakened or absent formation of the vertebral arch. According to the March of Dimes Birth Defects Foundation (1984), about one in every 2,000 babies born each year has spina bifida ("open spine"). Spina bifida follows no particular law of inheritance, although it does appear to run in certain families. Families with one affected child have about a 1-in-40 chance of having a second with spina bifida. Families with two affected children have about a 1-in-20 chance of having a third child with the condition. Spina bifida may take three forms. The first may be so slight that only an x-ray of the spinal column will detect its presence. This form rarely bothers the child. In the second form, a lump or cyst which contains the spinal cord pokes through the open part of the spine. The lump may be surgically removed, permitting the baby to grow normally. In the third and most severe form of spina bifida the cyst holds deeper nerve roots of the spinal cord. Little or no skin protects the lump and spinal fluid may leak out. The site of this cyst is generally in the lower spine resulting in paralysis and loss of sensation to the legs, a permanent condition. Spina bifida can be detected during pregnancy through a combination of blood screening, ultrasound, and amniocentesis techniques.

Table 5.7 summarizes a variety of gene-based birth defects.

Environmental Factors

In recent years the effects of the general environment on prenatal development have attracted attention. The influence of radiation and chemical pollutants are areas of particular concern to parents of unborn children.

Table 5.7 Common Gene-based Birth Defects

Genetic Defect	Condition
Clubfoot	Equinovarus
	Calcaneal Valgus
	Metatarsus Varus
Sickle Cell Anemia	Anemia, pain, damage to vital organs, slow growth and motor development, possible death
Tay-Sachs Disease	Loss of motor control, blindness, paralysis, certain death
Phenylketonuria (PKU)	Severe mental retardation
Spina Bifida	Paralysis in legs, poor bladder and bowel control

Radiation

The environment's influence on development is evident in the effects of high doses of radiation. Radiation dosage is measured in units called *rads.* An exposure to the developing fetus of over 25 rads would be considered a high dosage. The fetus is most vulnerable during the first trimester of pregnancy. Excessive radiation has been implicated in *microcephaly* (small head and brain) and mental retardation. Therefore, exposure to x-rays early in pregnancy, especially repeated x-rays of the pelvic region, may put the developing fetus at risk. Radiation prior to pregnancy is also an area of concern. Freeman and Pescar (1982) reported that a few studies suggest a relationship between ovarian radiation and chromosomal defects, and between the buildup of rads over the years and genetic damage.

Concept 5.9 A variety of factors have been shown to affect later development of the fetus.

Chemical Pollutants

It is difficult to establish a direct causal link between *chemical pollutants,* the pregnant mother, and later developmental abnormalities in her offspring. A number of other variables may account for, or interact with, chemical pollutants to cause birth defects. Lead and mercury, however, have been conclusively linked to birth defects in humans (March of Dimes, 1984). There is speculative evidence that other pollutants such as acid rain, PCB, and chemicals such as agent orange contribute to an increased incidence of birth defects.

Medical Problems

The causes and effects of developmental difficulties in the offspring of mothers with various sexually transmitted diseases, infections, hormonal and chemical imbalances, Rh incompatibility, and severe stress are being researched. These conditions play a significant role in placing the unborn child at risk.

Concept 5.10 A number of maternal medical conditions may contribute to developmental difficulties in offspring.

Sexually Transmitted Diseases

In recent years there has been growing awareness and concern over a variety of sexually transmitted diseases. The ravages of genital herpes, chlamydia, gonorrhea, syphilis, and acquired immunodeficiency syndrome (AIDS) are a direct threat to the unborn child. Yarber (1987) noted that "sexually transmitted diseases (STD), of which AIDS is one, impair the health of more teenagers than do all other communicable diseases combined" (p. 8). Moreover, the National Research Council (1987) estimated that by age 19 about 63 percent of all American females and 78 percent of all American males have had at least one coital experience. Teens and young adults who are sexually active are at risk. The risks are great, and the consequences for the developing fetus of a mother with a sexually transmitted disease are even greater.

Genital herpes has become a serious health problem with an estimated 30 million sufferers in the United States (Yarber, 1993). A pregnant woman with an active case of genital herpes may infect her baby, resulting in permanent brain damage or death. The baby may be protected through a Caesarean delivery.

Chlamydia is a highly contagious sexually transmitted disease that may be passed on to a baby during a vaginal delivery. Although curable with certain antibiotics, it is difficult to diagnose. If left untreated chlamydia may result in sterility and premature and still births as well as infant pneumonia, eye infections, and blindness.

Gonorrhea is the number one reportable communicable disease in the United States with more than 2 million new cases documented each year (Yarber, 1993). Although curable with antibiotics, some strains of the bacteria have become resistant to treatment. Gonorrhea may result in ectopic pregnancies and eye damage to the newborn.

Maternal syphilis is easily cured with antibiotics if detected in the early stage. The newborn with congenital syphilis is likely to be stillborn or display severe illnesses. The long-term effects of maternal syphilis are still unclear, but preliminary data indicate a greater incidence of prematurity and later motor, sensory, and cognitive disabilities.

Acquired Immunodeficiency Syndrome (AIDS) is the newest and most deadly of the various sexually transmitted diseases. AIDS is a virus that attacks the body's immune system. It is transmitted through sexual contact, contaminated needles, and transfusions. Mothers with the AIDS virus are at risk of transmitting the virus during pregnancy or childbirth. The virus may also be transmitted by breastfeeding. Although only about 1 percent of all AIDS cases in the United States occurs in children, women testing positive for the AIDS antibody should not become pregnant.

Table 5.8. summarizes the possible effects of sexually transmitted diseases.

Table 5.8 Sexually Transmitted Diseases and Their Possible Effects

Sexually Transmitted Disease	Possible Effects on the Newborn Child
Acquired Immunodeficiency Syndrome (AIDS)	Fever, weight loss, lethargy, diarrhea, pneumonia, death
Chlamydia	Prematurity, still births, pneumonia, eye infections, blindness
Genital Herpes	Brain damage, death
Gonorrhea	Ectopic pregnancies, eye damage
Syphilis	Severe illnesses, nervous system damage, death

Maternal Infections

Perhaps the most significant diseases contracted by the mother that adversely affect her fetus are cytomegalovirus (CMV) and rubella contracted during the first trimester of pregnancy. Both of these diseases pass though the placenta to the fetus and can have serious debilitating effects.

CMV is a common infectious cause of birth defects including blindness, deafness, and mental retardation. Very little is known about this virus and its effects. It is still unclear whether the virus is introduced into the fetus by a primary infection to the mother during pregnancy or whether it may already be present genetically but in latent form. About 4 percent of pregnant women secrete the virus, but 95 percent of infected infants are asymptomatic. The remaining 5 percent will suffer a range of developmental difficulties ranging from mild to severe motor retardation in the form of speech and problems in gross and fine motor coordination [Wieczorek and Natapoff, 1981].

Rubella, sometimes called the "three-day measles," is caused by a mild, contagious virus. It is not the same as regular measles, which is called rubeola. Vaccination against rubella has been possible since 1969 and has greatly reduced the incidence of birth defects due to this virus. It should be noted, however, that those who received the vaccine during the late 1960s and early 1970s need to be retested for immunity, because not all vaccines were found to be lifelong. Vaccination should occur during childhood and not during pregnancy. A simple blood test called a "rubella titer" is available to determine whether a person has had rubella or is immune. Figure 5.3 depicts the decline in infectious rubella since 1969. The child born of a mother who has had rubella during the first trimester of pregnancy is likely to be deaf, blind, or mentally retarded due to interference with sensory and/or cognitive development during the embryonic or early fetal period.

Figure 5.3
Incidence of infec-
tious rubella

CENTERS FOR DISEASE CONTROL
RATE PER 100,000 POPULATION

Hormonal and Chemical Imbalances

An inadequate hormonal or chemical environment in the thyroid patient, for example, can result in congenital hypothyroidism and cre-
tinism in the infant due to a lack of thyroxine in the mother's blood
during the early months of pregnancy. Diabetes in the expectant mother
is a chronic chemical imbalance that may adversely affect a child's later
development. The inadequate production of insulin prevents the proper
metabolizing of sugar and other carbohydrates. Untreated diabetes can
result in mental retardation, circulatory and respiratory problems in the
infant, or even death. Many women are diabetic only during pregnancy.
As a result it is prudent for all expectant mothers to be regularly checked.

Rh Incompatibility

Rh incompatibility results from the incompatibility of blood types between mother and child. Although there is no direct link between the
bloodstream of the infant and that of the mother, there may be some
seepage of blood from the fetus to the mother during the later stages of
pregnancy. If an expectant Rh negative mother is carrying her first Rh
positive child, this seepage will cause the mother to produce antibodies
in her blood. The production of antibodies generally has no effect on the
first child. The time lag between the first and subsequent children, however, provides ample opportunity for the production of antibodies in the
mother. These antibodies may have a devastating effect on future pregnancies, by destroying the fetal red corpuscles of Rh positive babies.

Erythroblastosis fetalis is the name given to this condition, which is characterized by anemia and jaundice. Rh incompatibility occurs only in cases where the father is Rh positive and the mother is Rh negative. Routine blood tests and a *rhogam* injection immediately after birth of the first child will prevent the formation of antibodies. Rhogam is the gamma globulin component of blood obtained from an Rh negative person previously sensitized to the Rh factor. The rhogam neutralizes the Rh factor in the mother and prevents the buildup of antibodies. A rhogam injection must be given with each Rh positive pregnancy.

Maternal Emotional Stress

The effects of severe prolonged maternal emotional stress on the unborn child are another concern. Severe stress factors such as death of a loved one and marital problems have been associated with complications during pregnancy and fetal abnormalities. Although there is no direct link between the nervous system of the mother and the fetus, the mother's emotional state may influence development. Because the nervous system and the endocrine system communicate through the blood, the emotional trauma experienced by the mother is transferred from her cerebral cortex to the thalamus and hypothalamus. The autonomic nervous system acts on the endocrine system, which empties into the bloodstream. The mother's bloodstream then transports the endocrine secretions to the placenta through which some are passed into the fetal bloodstream and finally to its nervous system. This hypothesis is speculative, but it is clear that prolonged maternal stress may have detrimental effects. Children born of emotionally stressed mothers tend to be vulnerable to a variety of illnesses and physical problems throughout life (Bee, 1975). Rosenblith and Sims-Knight (1985) concluded that "considering both the relatively well-controlled animal research and the human studies with their verifying methodological problems, it seems likely that babies of women who feel stressed during pregnancy are adversely affected" (p. 140).

Teenage Pregnancy

In the United States alone more than a half million girls give birth each year. Babies born to teen mothers have a much higher risk of serious health problems than do children born of a fully mature mother. Teenage mothers as a group are more likely to have children born small-for-date or young-for-date. Low-birthweight babies are statistically more likely to suffer from a variety of developmental abnormalities including mental retardation, immature organ systems, thermoregulatory difficulties, learning difficulties, respiratory problems, and death. Furthermore, the maternal death rate from complications in pregnancy is much higher among girls under age 15 who give birth than among older mothers.

Additional risk factors often found in teenage pregnancies include psychological stress, low socioeconomic status, inadequate parenting behaviors, maternal drug and alcohol abuse, and poor or nonexistent medical care. The complex risks involved in teenage pregnancies need further investigation so that appropriate intervention strategies may be devised.

Toxoplasmosis

In addition to the infections, diseases, and special conditions already discussed as high-risk considerations, expectant parents need to be aware of *toxoplasmosis* so that they can protect their unborn children against the offending protozoan. Toxoplasmosis is amazingly prevalent. It has been estimated that 1 in every 1,000 infants and 1 in every 500 pregnant women are infected (Litch, 1978). Infected children, although often small-for-date at birth, may appear normal at birth and even into their 20s. But, the toxoplasma cysts may rupture at any time, releasing thousands of parasites that attack the eyes, heart, other internal organs, and central nervous system.

Toxoplasmosis is a more prevalent health problem than either rubella or PKU but its devasation to the unborn child has had little publicity. However, the parents of an unborn child can do some very specific things to protect their child from this infection. All beef, pork, and lamb should be cooked until well done because the protozoan cysts exist in the muscle of meat. Because the toxoplasma organisms are transmitted through cat feces, it is wise to avoid contact with cats during pregnancy.

The natural reservoir of the *Toxoplasma gondii sporozoan* is the mouse, and most cats come in contact with mice. The spores passed in the feces of infected cats can be inhaled or ingested. The symptoms of infection in humans are similar to the flu, but many times there are no symptoms at all. Persons who have been infected carry antibodies against toxoplasmosis. However, the fetus does not have the ability to make such antibodies and takes the effects of the infection full force. About 10 percent of the 3,000 infants infected with toxoplasmosis each year are severely brain damaged and suffer a variety of sensory and motor disabilities (Alford et al., 1975).

Prenatal Diagnosis

In recent years a variety of prenatal diagnostic procedures have become available and are frequently used to detect the presence of fetal developmental abnormalities. Among the most frequently used techniques are amniocentesis, ultrasound, and fetoscopy.

Concept 5.11   Prenatal diagnostic techniques are valuable tools for determining the status of the developing fetus.

Amniocentesis is a technique whereby a hollow needle is inserted into the pregnant woman's abdomen. It is an almost painless procedure which sounds much worse than it actually feels. A small amount of amniotic fluid is withdrawn though the needle and analyzed. Fetal cells are contained within the amniotic fluid and can be analyzed to detect any form of chromosomal abnormality, nearly 100 metabolic disorders, and some structural defects (March of Dimes, 1984).

Amniocentesis is generally performed between the 16th and 18th weeks of pregnancy. It can, however, be performed late in the pregnancy as a means of determining fetal maturity and the severity of Rh disease. Amniocentesis is an invasive procedure that has been known to cause miscarriages in a small but significant number of cases. Therefore, it should only be used for specific medical purposes and not for determining gender or for routine examination of the developing fetus.

Ultrasound is another prenatal diagnostic technique using high-frequency sound waves to determine the size and structure of the fetus. It also provides visual information about its position in the womb. Ultrasound is used in conjunction with amniocentesis as a means of guiding the physician when inserting the needle through the abdomen and into the uterus.

Fetoscopy is a third fetal diagnostic procedure. Fetoscopy is the most recent of the three prenatal diagnostic procedures and involves inserting a small camera directly into the womb. This enables the physician to view the fetus and take blood samples. Fetoscopy is frequently used after amniocentesis and ultrasound for diagnosis of still suspected blood diseases and fetal malformations.

Vigorous Activity during Pregnancy

Fundamental societal changes regarding vigorous exercise and the continual quest for fitness have prompted important questions concerning vigorous physical activity during pregnancy. Among them are: how will maternal exercise affect fetal development? will maternal exercise help or hinder delivery? and will maternal exercise influence infant development? Conclusive answers to each of these questions are not yet available, but a growing body of research has begun to shed some light on each.

A number of recent studies have examined the influence of vigorous activity on fetal development. Bonds and Delivoria-Papadopoulos (1985) reviewed a number of animal and human studies on the fetal effects of exercise and reported no negative findings. Lotgering et al. (1985) reported that in contrast to rather significant physiological changes in the exercising mother, and despite reduced uterine blood flow during maternal exercise, that physiological changes to the fetus are small. They state that "acute exercise normally does not represent a major stress for the fetus" (p. 30). Furthermore, Pijpers et al. (1984) found no significant changes in fetal heart rates, and no signs of fetal stress at the conclusion of moderate short-term maternal exercise. Collings et al. (1982) found small but significant increases in fetal heart rates measured during a maternal aerobic exercise program, but no differences in Apgar scores or fetal growth when compared to a non-exercising control group. Wolfe et al. (1989), on the other hand, reported temporary decreases in fetal heart rates (*bradycardia*) in a small but significant percent of fetuses of exercising mothers for 15 to 20 minutes after the mothers' exercise bouts. This raises the question of the possibility of fetal *asphyxia* (i.e., oxygen loss) in some developing fetuses.

Thus far the data tend to support exercise during pregnancy in terms of both fetal and maternal responses. Connelly Freyder (1989) concluded from her literature review that: "Although studies on exercise have been limited, the results have been favorable. Little, if any, negative effects on the mother and fetus have been documented" (p. 364). Further clarification is still needed on how much exercise, what types of exercise, and contraindications for maternal exercise during pregnancy. Guidelines for exercise during pregnancy are available from the American College of Obstetricians and Gynecologists (1985) and should be followed until these questions are resolved.

Concern over the effects of strenuous exercise on labor and delivery has little basis for support. Historically, there have been two distinct "opinions" about delivery in female athletes. One opinion held that extensive sport activity made the muscles of the pelvic floor rigid and led to difficulty during labor. The other opinion denied this supposition and emphasized the positive effect of increased abdominal strength particularly during the second stage of labor. The literature, however, does not support either claim. There appears to be no causal link between fitness levels and the length of labor.

With regard to the effects of maternal exercise on later infant development, women who continue endurance exercise at or near their preconception levels tend to gain less weight, deliver earlier, and have lighter-weight babies than their counterparts who stop exercising early in their pregnancy. Furthermore, Lotgering et al. (1984) in their review reported a number of studies that clearly linked maternal exercise to low-birthweight. They report that several studies have demonstrated decreases in birthweight of as much as 400 grams. They did note, however, that this may reflect the inadequate nutritional status of these women rather than the effect of physical activity itself. Further study needs to be done before any conclusive link can be established between exercise intensity, low-birthweight, and later developmental difficulties.

Concept 5.12   Mothers-to-be may continue to exercise throughout their pregnancies with the guidance of their physicians and careful self-monitoring.

Birth Process Factors

The average length of intrauterine life is 279 days from the day of conception to the day of birth. Two thirds of all expectant mothers give birth within 279 days, plus or minus a two-week period. The beginning of labor is marked by the passage of blood and amniotic fluid from the ruptured amniotic sac through the vagina and the onset of labor pains. There are three distinguishable stages of labor. In the first stage the neck of the uterus (the cervix) dilates to about four centimeters in diameter. Dilation is responsible for labor pains and may last for only one or two hours, or up to 18 to 24 hours. Labor is generally longer with the first child (*primiparas*) than for subsequent children (*multiparas*). When the cervix reaches two centimeters, full labor begins. It is at this point that the amniotic sac breaks and the fluid flows out of the mother. Complete dilation to about 10 centimeters marks the onset of the second stage of labor: the expulsion stage. During this stage the baby, through the continued increase in uterine pressure, is forced down the birth canal. This phase takes an average of 90 minutes for the first child and about half as long for subsequent children. The third stage of labor begins after the baby has emerged and continues until after the umbilical cord and placenta (afterbirth) have been delivered. During any stage of the birth process a number of obstetrical medications and obstetrical procedures may influence later development of the child.

Concept 5.13   Obstetrical medications and birthing procedures have an impact on the later development of the child.

Obstetrical Medication

A controversial issue among obstetricians and infant researchers involves the effects of obstetrical medication commonly used during the birth process. A paper published by Brackbill (1979), the sensational attention that it received in the popular press, and the subsequent rebuttal of her findings by many have done much to fuel this already heated debate. Basically, her argument is that drugs given during childbirth will impair the newborn and its subsequent development because of the structural and functional immaturity of the infant's nervous

Table 5.9 Function of Common Types of Predelivery and Delivery Drugs

Predelivery Drugs	Delivery Drugs
Oxytocics (premedication agents) Induce labor Augment labor Increase uterine tonus *Sedatives* (Demerol, meperidine) Reduce anxiety Reduce excitement Slow down labor	*General Analgesics* (inhalants, intravenous injections) Relieve fetal distress Speed up delivery Mother emotionally unsuited to remain awake Multiple births *Local Analgesics* (lumbar, spinal, caudal) Pain relief Relaxation

system at birth and because of the rapid absorption rate across the placenta. It is estimated, based on a variety of surveys, that 90 to 95 percent of all hospital births involve the use of some form of medication (Brackbill, 1979). Table 5.9 lists common types of predelivery, general, and local anesthetics used during delivery. These medications are used to initiate or augment labor (*oxytocics*), relieve pain (*analgesics*), and relieve anxiety (*sedatives*).

The results of several studies point to a relationship between drug use during labor and later development. There is compelling evidence that muscular strength and motor coordination are impaired as measured on infant development scales (Brackbill, 1970; Conway and Brackbill, 1970). Muller et al. (1971) and Goldstein et al. (1976) found a relationship between obstetrical drugs and lowered IQ scores. Brackbill (1979) contends that obstetrical drug use has had a significant effect on lowering the IQs of most Americans, by increasing the risk of anoxia and delaying the organization of the CNS. The extent of these influences is open to considerable debate and is dependent on a variety of factors, including type and combination of drugs, amount administered, and the time lag between administration and birth. It is safe, however, to say that drugs taken during the birth process put the newborn at risk. The extent and certainty of this risk is unclear, but it seems reasonable to assume that a drug-free birth or very judicious use of drugs during labor would do much to reduce the risk of later developmental difficulties.

Birth Entry

A variety of birth entry factors also have been shown to put the infant at risk. Among them are malpresentation, the use of forceps, and Caesarean section. About 4 in every 100 babies are born buttocks first or feet first (*breech birth*) and 1 out of 100 are in a crosswise position (transverse presentation). Parron and Eisenberg (1982) observed that

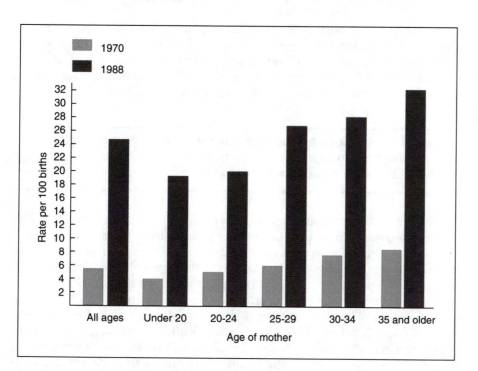

Figure 5.4
Changes in the rate of U.S. Caesarean deliveries by age per 100 births (U.S. Bureau of the Census, 1991)

breech or transverse fetal presentations are found in one-third to one-half of all infants delivered at less than 1,500 grams. These presentations can sometimes be altered by the attending physician or midwife. The danger in malpresentation, as with drug-assisted labor and umbilical cord difficulties, is anoxia. In fact, anoxia is generally considered to be the major cause of perinatal death and has been implicated as the cause of mental retardation, learning disabilities, and cerebral palsy.

Forceps are occasionally used to withdraw the baby from the birth canal. Today, the use of forceps is limited largely to emergency situations, but they were used routinely in obstetrics until the 1940s. Forceps are now used to speed delivery when the mother is displaying uncontrollable pushing, when the infant has a weak heartbeat, when the umbilical cord emerges before the head and endangers the baby's oxygen supply, or when there is a premature separation of the placenta. Forceps play a vital role in obstetrics as a lifesaving device, but their overuse and misuse, have had debilitating and lethal effects on both mothers and children.

A *Caesarean section* involves survival delivery of the baby. There has been a definite increase in the number of Caesarean operations over the past 30 years (Figure 5.4). In 1970 Caesarean deliveries comprised 5.5 percent of births. By 1988 that figure rose to 25 percent, (U.S. Bureau of the Census, 1991). The reasons for this seem to be associated with planning the exact delivery date, avoidance of pain (a general anesthetic is usually given), the advent of newer incision techniques leaving a smaller and less noticeable scar, and the desire to spare the fetus any distress. A Caesarean section is a major operation and in the past was considered only in cases of malpresentation, fetal distress, and failed use of forceps. Most obstetricians and medical societies recommend that it be used only when there are extenuating circumstances.

Concept 5.14 Both mother and father-to-be have an obligation to their unborn child to ensure its optimal development by monitoring those factors over which they can exercise control.

The birth process is an important beginning in the three-way bonding among mother, infant, and father. Because of this, parents frequently choose the method in which they wish to introduce their offspring into the world. The Lamaze and the Le Boyer methods of childbirth are two procedures from which prospective parents can choose. The Lamaze method centers on the mother and father. It uses conscious relaxation techniques that incorporate rhythmical breathing to block the sensations of pain. It relies on the mother's complete knowledge of what to expect during labor and delivery (Lamaze, 1976). The Le Boyer method focuses almost entirely on the infant. The aim is to simulate the conditions of the womb as closely as possible. Delivery occurs in a dimly lit room without loud noises. The baby is immediately immersed in a warm fluid solution and gradually, but gently, introduced into the world (Seifert & Hoffnung, 1987). Many hospitals have made dramatic changes in their delivery procedures. Birthing rooms, birthing chairs, and rooming-in are all widely popular procedures that reflect greater concern for the health and comfort of both mother and child.

Summary

This chapter discussed a wide variety of prenatal factors that impact on later development in general, and motor development in particular. There is growing realization among many prospective parents that they can do something to reduce the chances of putting their offspring at risk. Many now understand that poor choices in what expectant mothers ingest in the way of nutrients, alcohol, tobacco, drugs and medications can be devastating to unborn children. Many are now sensitive to the possible harmful effects of caffeine, saccharin, overexposure to radiation, noxious chemicals, and obstetrical medications. As a result there has been a resurgence of interest in "natural" childbirth techniques, rooming-in, and home births, and a return by many to a more responsible attitude about giving birth. More mothers are asserting their rights for drug-free pregnancies and are working knowledgeably with concerned obstetricians to produce the healthiest offspring possible.

The prenatal period is too important to be left to chance. An "intelligent" pregnancy and delivery, although not a guarantee, can do much to reduce the risk of problems for both mother and child.

Terms to Remember

High-risk pregnancy
Teratogen
Placental malnutrition
Maternal malnutrition
Undernourishment
Jaundice
Genital Herpes
Kernicterus
Street drugs
Fetal Alcohol Syndrome (FAS)
Fetal Alcohol Effects (FAE)
Mitosis
Chromosome damage
Down Syndrome
Genetic defect
Autosomal syndromes
Clubfoot
Equinovarus
Calcaneal Valgus
Metatarsus Varus
Asphyxia
Sickle Cell Anemia
Tay-Sachs Disease
Phenylketonuria (PKU)
Spina Bifida
Rads
Microcephaly
Caesarean Section

Chemical pollutants
Prenatal malnutrition
Fetal malnutrition
Malnourishment
Chlamydia
Gonorrhea
Maternal syphilis
Acquired Immunodeficiency
 Syndrome (AIDS)
Cytomegalovirus (CMV)
Rubella
Rh Incompatibility
Erythroblastosis Fetalis
Rhogam
Toxoplasmosis
Amniocentesis
Ultrasound
Fetoscopy
Bradycardia
Primiparas
Multiparas
Oxytocics
Analgesics
Sedatives
Breech Birth
Forceps

Critical Readings

Brackbill, Y. (1979). Obstetrical medication and infant behavior. In J. D. Osofsky (Ed.), *The Handbook of Infant Development,* New York: Wiley.

Chasnoff, I. J., Landress, H. J., & Barrett, M. E. (1990). The prevalence of illicit drug or alcohol use during pregnancy and discrepancies in mandatory reporting in Pinellas County, Florida. *The New England Journal of Medicine,* 26, 1202–1206.

Connelly Freyder, S. (1989). Exercising while pregnant. *The Journal of Orthopaedic and Sports Physical Therapy,* March, 358–365.

Dorris, M. (1989). The Broken Cord: *A Family's Ongoing Struggle with Fetal Alcohol Syndrome.* New York: HarperCollins.

Fink, J. R. (1989). Effects of crack and cocaine upon infants: A brief review of the literature. *Children's Legal Rights Journal,* 10, 2–10.

Freeman, R. K., & Pescar, S. C. (1982). *Safe Delivery: Protecting Your Baby During High Risk Pregnancy.* New York: McGraw-Hill.

Gittler, J., & McPherson, M. (1990). Prenatal substance abuse: An overview of the problem. *Children Today,* July–August, 3–7.

Henderson, S. E. (1985). Motor skills development. In D. Lane, and B. Stratford (Eds.), *Current Approaches to Down Syndrome,* London: Holt, Reinhart and Winston.

Parron, D., & Eisenberg, L. (1982). *Infants at Risk for Developmental Dysfunction,* Washington, D.C.: National Academy Press.

Streissguth, A. P. et al. (1991). Fetal alcohol syndrome in adolescents and adults. *Journal of the American Medical Association,* 265, 1961–1967.

Wolfe, L. A., Ohtake, P. J., Mottola, M. F., & McGrath, M. J. (1989). Physiological interactions between pregnancy and aerobic exercise. In K. B. Randolph (Ed.), *Exercise and Sport Science Reviews, Vol. 17,* Baltimore: Williams and Wilkens.

Chapter 6

Prenatal and Infant Growth

CHAPTER COMPETENCIES

Upon completion of this chapter you should be able to:

- *Discuss embryonic and fetal growth and biological maturation*
- *Describe and interpret the normal displacement and velocity graphs of infant growth*
- *Discuss proportional changes in segmental length from birth through childhood*
- *Speculate on prenatal time periods that are critical to normal growth*
- *Describe the process of prenatal growth from conception to birth*

Key Concept: The rate of growth from conception through infancy is unsurpassed throughout the rest of life.

This chapter focuses on the process of normal growth from conception through the period of infancy. It is important for the student of motor development to have a reference point from which to view the normal growth process. The approach taken here provides that reference point from the standpoint of the mythical "average" child. In other words, heights, weights, and other growth statistics are presented in terms of averages. There may be considerable normal variation from these figures as a result of the interaction between biological and environmental processes.

Prenatal Growth

Growth begins at the moment of conception and follows an orderly sequence throughout the prenatal period. Prechtl's (1986) studies of the motor development of the fetus demonstrated that prenatal movement and growth patterns are just as predictable during the fetal period as they are throughout infancy. The uniting of a mature sperm and ovum marks the beginning of this process. The ovum is one of the largest cells in the female body. It is about 0.004 of an inch in diameter and is just barely visible to the naked eye. The sperm, on the other hand is microscopic and one of the smallest cells in the male body. Fertilization occurs if one of the approximately 20 million sperm released from the male during intercourse meets and penetrates the ovum in the Fallopian tube. Once the sperm cell penetrates the outer membrane of the egg, fertilization occurs. Each parent contributes 23 chromosomes (barlike structures in cells that carry all of a person's genetic information). The 2 cell nuclei lie side by side for a few hours before they merge to form a *zygote* (the fertilized egg with 46 chromosomes). It is at this instant that one's genetic potential is determined. Realization of this potential will depend on many environmental as well as hereditary factors. The genetic inheritances of both mother and father are transferred to this single cell. The pattern for a variety of traits is now established, including eye and hair color, general body shape, and complexion. During the germinal period, the zygote splits into two cells through a process called *mitosis*. The 2 cells form 4 cells, and the 4 cells form 8. Three days after conception the zygote has grown into 32 cells, and after four days it consists of about 90 cells. Because all cells have the same genetic setup except for sex cells, the division of cells is not simultaneous, and stages in early embryonic life have been observed in which there is an odd number of cells (Sundberg & Wirsen, 1977). After the first three or four days of mitotic cell division, the zygote travels down the Fallopian tube to the uterus, where it attaches itself to the uterine wall. This implantation process marks the true onset of pregnancy, although the days of pregnancy are counted from the first day of the last menstrual bleeding. The ovum is normally fertilized within a day of ovulation, near the 14th day of the menstrual cycle. Therefore, during the first two weeks of what is considered pregnancy, the woman is not actually pregnant. Implantation generally occurs by the end of the first week after fertilization.

Concept 6.1   The union of ovum and sperm marks the point of conception and the determination of one's genetic inheritance.

Zygotic Period (Conception–1st week)

During the first week (period of the zygote) the fertilized egg remains practically unchanged in size. It lives off its own yoke and receives little outside nourishment. By the end of the first week the zygote is only a small round disk about 0.01 of an inch wide. The situation for the zygote is especially precarious during this time. Although the mother-to-be may not be aware that she is pregnant, her system will automatically attempt to slough off this foreign body, as it would any foreign matter. The expectant mother may continue to ingest a variety of chemical substances, drugs, alcohol, and tobacco that could prove damaging, if not lethal, to the zygote. Malina and Bouchard (1991) reported that, for a variety of reasons, approximately 50 percent of all fertilized eggs spontaneously abort during the first trimester. Although this statistic may appear alarmingly high, this process of spontaneous abortion helps to ensure that only the fittest of zygotes survive.

Concept 6.2   Pregnancy does not begin until the zygote is implanted on the uterine wall.

Embryonic Period (2nd week–2nd month)

The differentiation of embryonic cells into layers marks the end of the period of the zygote and the beginning of the period of the *embryo*. By the end of the first month there is a definite formation of three layers of cells. The *ectoderm*, from which the sense organs and nervous system develop, begins to form. The *mesoderm* accounts for the formation of the muscular, skeletal, and circulatory systems. The *endoderm* eventually accounts for the formation of the digestive and glandular systems (Table 6.1). Every part of the body develops from these three kinds of cells and is formed in rudimentary structure by the end of the embryonic period. Special cells form the *placenta*, through which nutritive substances will be carried and wastes removed. Another special layer of cells begins formation of the *amnion*, which will enclose the embryo except at the umbilical cord throughout the prenatal period.

The embryonic period is an especially important time in the formation of all of the body systems, and as such is a highly sensitive period for susceptibility to *congenital malformations*. Congenital malformation refers to a condition with which the infant is born, but does not refer to the specific defect. The risk of congenital malformations is greatest during the embryonic period. This period of rapid cell division is very vulnerable to changes in the sequence, rate, and timing of events. A wide variety of environmental factors (see Chapter 5 for a complete discussion) as well as the embryo's specific genetic composition determine its susceptibility to congenital malformations.

Table 6.1 Systems That Develop From Three Layers of Cells

Layer	Systems
Endoderm (inner layer)	Digestive system Respiratory system Glandular system
Mesoderm (middle layer)	Muscular system Skeletal system Circulatory system Reproductive system Central nervous system Sensory end-organs
Ectoderm (outer covering)	Peripheral nervous system Skin, hair, nails

Concept 6.3   The cell layers that will eventually form the various systems of the body are differentiated during the embryonic period.

By the end of the first month the embryo is about 1/4 of an inch long and weighs about 1 ounce. It is crescent shaped, with small bumps on its sides (limb buds). It has a tail and tiny ridges along the neck. These gill-like ridges mark the beginning of a primitive mouth opening, heart, face, and throat. By the end of the first month the embryo has a rudimentary circulatory system, and the heart begins to beat. Growth accelerates toward the end of the first month. The organism grows about 1/4 of an inch each week. By the end of the second month the embryo is about 1 1/2 inches long. The beginnings of the face, neck, fingers, and toes develop, and the embryo starts to take on a more human appearance. The limb buds lengthen, the muscles enlarge, and the sex organs begin to form. Brain development is rapid, and the head is very large in comparison to the rest of the body. The embryo is now firmly implanted in the uterine wall and receiving nourishment through the placenta and the umbilical cord. This marks the end of the embryonic period and the beginning of the fetal period of prenatal life (Figure 6.1).

Early Fetal Period (3rd–6th month)

The period of the *fetus* begins around the third month and continues until delivery. Although no new anatomical features appear during this period, this critical time for the fetus is easily influenced by a variety of factors over which it has no control. During the third month the fetus continues to grow rapidly. It is about 3 inches long by the end of the third month. Sexual differentiation continues, buds for the teeth emerge, the stomach and kidneys begin to function, and the vocal cords appear.

14 days

18 days

24 days

4 weeks

6 $\frac{1}{2}$ weeks

7 $\frac{1}{2}$ weeks

9 weeks

11 weeks

15 weeks

Figure 6.1
Embryos drawn to
actual size

By the beginning of the third month the first reflex actions are felt (DeVries, 1982). The fetus opens and closes its mouth, swallows, clenches its fist, and can even reflexively suck its thumb. The growth rate during the fourth month is the most rapid for the fetus. During this period it doubles in length to about 6 to 8 inches and weighs about 4 ounces. The hands are fully shaped, and the transparent cartilaginous skeleton begins to turn into bony tissue, starting in the middle of each skeletal bone and progressing toward the ends. The lower limbs, which lagged behind in their initial development, now catch up with the rest of the body. By the beginning of the fifth month the fetus has reached half of its birth length but only 10 percent of its birth weight. The fetus is now sloughing off skin and respiratory cells and replacing them with new ones. Sloughed off cells remain in the amniotic fluid, providing a basis for amniocentesis (refer to Chapter 5 for a brief discussion of this technique).

Concept 6.4   Movement first becomes apparent to the mother-to-be during the early fetal period.

At the beginning of the fifth month the fetus is about 8 to 10 inches long and weighs about 1/2 pound. Skin, hair, and nails appear. The internal organs continue to grow and assume their proper anatomical positions. The entire body of the fetus is temporarily covered with a very fine soft hair called *lanugo*. The lanugo on the head and eyebrows becomes more marked by the end of the fifth month and is replaced by pigmented hair. The lanugo is generally shed before birth, although some may still remain. The larger size and cramped quarters of the rapidly developing fetus generally result in considerable reflexive movement during the fifth month.

By the sixth month the fetus is about 13 inches long and weighs over a pound. During this month the eyelids, which have been fused shut since the third month, reopen and are completed. The *vernix caseosa* forms from skin cells. It is a fatty secretion that protects the thin and delicate skin of the fetus. There is little in the way of subcutaneous fat at this point, and the fetus appears red and wrinkled and resembles a very old and frail individual. An infant born prematurely during the sixth month has a very poor chance of survival even with the most sophisticated technology available. Although it can cry weakly and move about, it cannot perform the more basic functions of spontaneous breathing and temperature regulation. By the end of the sixth month, the fetus weighs approximately 2 pounds and is about 14 inches long. It is structurally complete but needs additional time for the various systems of the body to become functionally mature.

Later Fetal Period (7th–9th month)

From the seventh month to term the fetus triples its weight (Figure 6.2). A layer of adipose tissue begins to form under the skin and serves as both an insulator and food supplier. The lanugo hair is shed, along with much of the vernix fluid, and the nails often grow beyond the ends of the fingers and toes, necessitating an immediate manicure after birth to prevent scratching. During the seventh month the fetus is often quiet for long periods of time as if resting up for the "big event." The fetal brain becomes more active and assumes increasing control over the body systems. The majority of fetuses born at the end of the seventh month survive, although many require special handling during the early weeks after birth.

Concept 6.5 The last two months of fetal life are a time for filling out in preparation for birth.

During the eighth and ninth months the fetus becomes more active. The cramped quarters result in frequent changes in position, kicking, and thrusting of the legs and arms. During these last two months the skin's red coloration disappears as fatty deposits become more evenly distributed.

Figure 6.2
Summary of development during the fetal period

WEEK 12: Sex distinguishable. Eyelids sealed shut. Buds for deciduous teeth. Vocal cords. Digestive tract. Kidneys and liver secrete.

WEEK 16: Head about one third of total length. Nose plugged. Lips visible. Fine hair on body. Pads on hands and feet. Skin dark red, loose, wrinkled.

WEEK 20: Body axis straightens. Vernix caseosa covers skin as skin glands develop. Internal organs move toward mature positions.

WEEK 24–28: Eyes open. Taste buds present. If born, can breathe, cry, and live for a few hours without life support.

WEEK 28–40: Fat deposited. Rapid brain growth. Nails develop. Testes descend. Becomes viable.

The birth process is initiated by the placenta and contraction of the uterine musculature and not the fetus. Birth generally occurs after about 40 weeks of gestation. Normal variation in gestational age ranges from 38 to 42 weeks. At birth the normal term infant is about 19 to 21 inches long and weighs between 6 and 8 pounds. Table 6.2 includes a summary of development during the fetal period.

Infant Growth

The growth process during the first two years after birth is truly amazing. The infant progresses from a tiny, helpless, horizontal, relatively sedentary creature to a considerably larger, autonomous, vertical, active child. The physical growth of the infant has a very definite influence on

Table 6.2 Highlights of Prenatal Growth and Development

Age	Length	Weight	Major Events
Conception	1 cell	Less than 1 g	Genetic inheritance determined
1 week	0.01 in.	Less than 1 g	Germinal period, period of rapid cell differentiation
2 weeks	0.05 in.	1.5 g	Implantation in the uterus
1 month	0.25 in.	1 oz	Endoderm, mesoderm, and ectoderm formed; growth organized and differentiated
2 months	1.5 in.	2 oz	Rapid growth period, begins to take on human form; weak, reflex activity
3 months	3 in.	3 oz	Sexual differentiation; stomach and kidney function; eyelids fuse shut
4 months	6 to 8 in.	6 oz	Rapid growth period, first reflexive movements felt; bone formation begins
5 months	8 to 10 in.	8 oz	Half birth height; internal organ completion; hair over entire body
6 months	13 to 15 in.	1 to 2 lb	Eyes reopen; vernix caseosa forms; structurally complete but functionally immature
7 months	14 to 16 in.	2 to 4 lb	Rapid weight gain, adipose tissue deposited
8 months	16 to 18 in.	4 to 6 lb	Active period, fatty deposits distributed
9 months	19 to 21 in.	6 to 8 lb	Uterine contractions, labor and delivery

its motor development. The size of the head, for example, will influence the child's developing balance abilities. Hand size will influence the mode of contact with different-size objects, and strength development will influence the onset of locomotion.

Concept 6.6 Increases in body proportions are uneven and influenced by the principles of proximodistal and cephalocaudal development.

Neonatal Period (Birth–4 Weeks)

The neonatal period is generally considered to comprise the first two to four weeks of postnatal life. It is generally thought of as an "adjustive time-period to being born" (Krogman, 1980, p. 9). The typical full-term newborn is 19 to 21 inches long, but the head accounts for fully one fourth of that length. The proportionately large head size makes it difficult for the baby to gain and maintain equilibrium. The remaining body length is taken up with a 4-to-3 ratio of trunk to lower-limb length. The eyes are about half their adult size, and the body is about one 20th its eventual adult dimension (Figure 6.3).

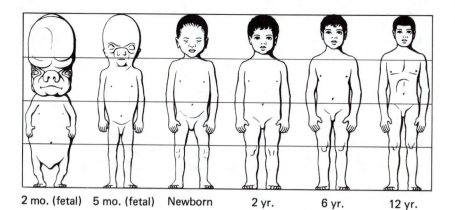

Figure 6.3
Changes in body form and proportion before and after birth

| 2 mo. (fetal) | 5 mo. (fetal) | Newborn | 2 yr. | 6 yr. | 12 yr. |

There is considerable normal variation in the weight of newborns, which may be attributed to a variety of environmental and hereditary factors. Birthweight is closely related to the socioeconomic and nutritional status of the mother. The birthweight of male infants is about 4 percent higher than that of females. Optimal growth requires proper nutrition, a positive state of health, and a nurturing environment. It is interesting to note, however, that low-birthweight babies and young-for-date babies tend to catch up to their age-mates if their deficiencies are not too severe. J. M. Tanner (1978), a physician, has devoted much time to the study of the growth characteristics of the infant. He noted that an individual's ultimate growth potential seemed to be determined early in life and could be amended under limited conditions if prematurity, illness, or malnutrition deflected the child from his or her normal growth curve. If an infant is moderately malnourished or ill, the growth rate will slow and then accelerate (or catch up) to the normal trajectory with an adequate diet or the termination of the illness. The rate will then slow down again. Under most conditions we see infants and children fitting into broadly determined ranges for height and weight, with little in the way of extremes at either end of the developmental continuum. Although the trajectory approximates the normal curve, low-birthweight children usually remain somewhat smaller than full-term children throughout life.

Figures 6.4 through 6.7 provide graphic representations of changes in body length and weight of both boys and girls from birth to age three. It is important to note that *body length* is the term used when it is measured from a recumbent position, the commonly accepted means of measurement from birth to age two or three. After that an erect standing measure is taken, and referred to as *height*. These growth charts, from the National Center for Health Statistics, indicate by age percentiles the growth patterns of infants and toddlers. Although height is genetically influenced, there is little relationship between birth length and attained adult height. However, by the second year the correlation raises to the mid to high 70s (Tanner, 1978).

Figure 6.4
USA female length by age percentiles: birth to 36 months (*Source:* National Center for Health Statistics, U.S. Government)

Early Infancy (4 Weeks–1 Year)

During the child's first year there are rapid gains in both weight and length. During the first six months, growth is mainly a process of "filling out," with only slight changes in body proportions. In fact, the "newborns" often pictured in advertisements are actually two or three months old, displaying a chubby look rather than the reddish, wrinkled look of the actual newborn. Birthweight is doubled by the fifth month, almost tripled by the end of the first year, and quadrupled by 30 months of age. Length increases to around 30 inches by the first birthday. By age 2 boys have attained about 50 percent of their adult height and girls about 53 percent (Bayley, 1954). After 6 months of age the thoracic region is larger than the head in normal children and increases with age. Infants suffering from malnutrition will have a weight deficit but generally have head sizes larger than the thoracic regions.

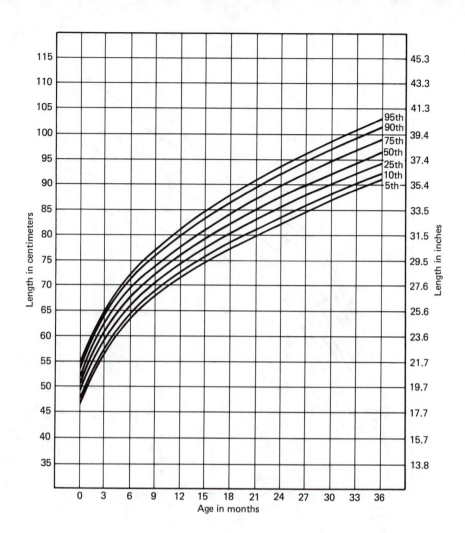

Figure 6.5
USA male length by
age percentiles:
birth to 36 months
(*Source:* National
Center for Health
Statistics, U.S.
Government)

Concept 6.7 Early infancy is characterized by rapid growth in length and substantial increases in subcutaneous tissue.

Later Infancy (1 Year–2 Years)

Physical growth during the second year continues at a rapid pace but at a slower rate than the first year. By age 2 the height of the average boy is about 35 inches. Girls are about 34 inches tall and weigh about 31 pounds, whereas boys average 32 pounds (National Center for Health Statistics, 1976). Height and weight have about a .60 correlation, showing a moderate degree of relationship between these two indices of physique. Because growth follows a directional trend (i.e., proximodistal and cephalocaudal), increase in size of the body parts is uneven. Upper arm growth precedes lower arm growth and hand growth. Therefore, from infancy to puberty the greatest amount of growth takes place in

Figure 6.6
USA female weight by age percentiles: birth to 36 months (*Source:* National Center for Health Statistics, U.S. Government)

the distal portions of the limbs. Head growth slows from infancy onward, trunk growth proceeds at a moderate rate, limb growth is faster, and growth of the hands and feet is most rapid.

Summary

Throughout the prenatal period a variety of environmental factors may influence and dramatically alter later development. The relationship between the unborn child and the mother is essentially one of parasite and host. The fetus uses the mother to supply all of its vital needs, including the intake of oxygen and nutrients and the expulsion of carbon

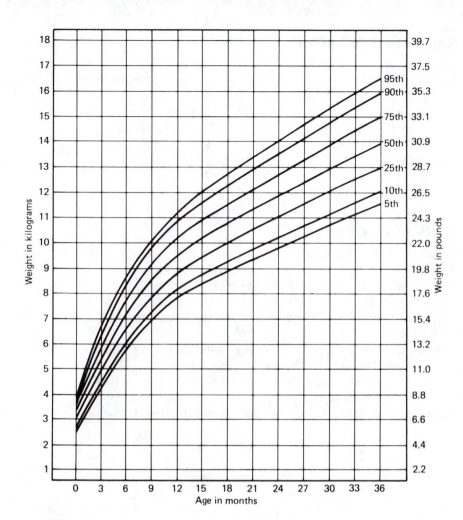

Figure 6.7
USA male weight by age percentiles: birth to 36 months (*Source:* National Center for Health Statistics, U.S. Government)

dioxide and other wastes. These nutrients are "screened" by the mother in her bloodstream. The condition and content of the circulatory systems of both mother and fetus are crucial to future growth and development.

The normal process of prenatal and infant growth is crucial to the motor development of the child. The length, weight, physique, and maturational level of the child plays an important role in his or her acquisition and performance of rudimentary movement patterns. The prenatal period and infancy set the stage for what is to come in the development of the young child's repertoire of fundamental movement and physical abilities.

Terms to Remember

Zygote

Mitosis

Embryo

Ectoderm

Mesoderm

Endoderm

Placenta

Amnion

Congenital malformation

Fetus

Lanugo

Vernix Caseosa

Body length

Height

Critical Readings

Allen, K. E., & Marotz, L. (1989). *Developmental Profiles: Birth to Six.* Albany, NY: Delmar.

Caplan, F. (1981). *The First Twelve Months of Life.* New York: Bantam.

Malina, R. M., & Bouchard, C. (1991). *Growth Maturation and Physical Activity* (Chapter 3). Champaign, IL: Human Kinetics.

Oppenheimer, S. B. (1980). *Introduction to Embryonic Development.* Boston: Allyn and Bacon.

Rosenblith, J. F., & Sims-Knight, J. E. (1985). *In the Beginning: Development in the First Two Years.* Monterey, CA: Brooks/Cole.

Sundberg, A. I., & Wirsen, C. (1977). *A Child is Born: The Drama of Life Before Birth.* New York: Delacorte.

Tanner, J. M. (1978). *Foetus into Man.* Cambridge, MA: Harvard University Press.

Chapter 7

Infant Reflexes and Rhythmical Stereotypies

CHAPTER COMPETENCIES

Upon completion of this chapter you should be able to:

- *Describe primitive and postural reflexes that appear before birth or during the first year, and explain the neural development that occurs with these changes*
- *Relate inhibition of specific reflexes and appearance of specific reactions to development of particular voluntary motor skills*
- *Distinguish between "primitive reflexes" and "postural reflexes"*
- *Speculate on the relationship of reflexes and rhythmical stereotypies to later voluntary movement behavior*
- *Identify and discuss several rhythmical stereotypies present in the human infant*
- *Speculate on the purpose and role of rhythmical stereotypies*
- *Devise your own infant reflex/stereotypy observational assessment instrument*

Reflex movements are evident in all fetuses, neonates, and infants to greater or lesser degrees, depending on their ages and neurological makeups. Reflex movements are involuntary reactions of the body to various forms of external stimulation. Most reflexes are subcortical in that they are controlled by the lower brain centers, which are also responsible for numerous involuntary life-sustaining processes such as breathing. Although not the topic of this chapter, equilibrium reflexes are mediated by the cerebral cortex. Voluntary motor control in the normal child is a function of the maturing cerebral cortex. Movements that are consciously controlled result from nerve impulses transmitted from the cerebral cortex along motor neurons.

Many early reflexes are related to infant survival (*primitive survival reflexes*), while others are precursors of voluntary movements that will appear between the ninth and fifteenth months after birth (*primitive postural reflexes*). Reflexive walking, swimming, crawling, and climbing movements were reported by Shirley (1931), McGraw (1939b), and Ames (1937). These reflexes are inhibited prior to the appearance of their voluntary counterparts, but their mere presence is an indication of how deeply locomotor activities are rooted within the nervous system.

Concept 7.1 Reflexes are the first forms of human movement and provide interesting insights into the process of development.

From about the fourth month of fetal life until the fourth month of infancy, most of a baby's movements are reflexive. Involuntary reactions result from changes in pressure, sight, sound, and tactile stimulation. These stimuli and the responses form the basis for the *information-gathering stage* of the reflexive movement phase. Reflexes, at this point in the child's life, serve as a primary information-gathering device for information storage in the developing cortex. As higher brain centers gain greater control of the sensorimotor apparatus the infant is able to process information more efficiently. This *information-processing stage* parallels Piaget's first three stages within his sensorimotor phase of development, namely, the use of reflexes, primary circular reactions, and secondary circular reactions.

Concept 7.2 Infant reflexive behaviors serve as a primary information-gathering source during the neonatal period.

Reflexive Behavior and Voluntary Movement

Two main functions of the primitive survival reflexes are to seek nourishment and protection. Several primitive reflexes during early infancy resemble later voluntary movements. These postural reflexes, as they are sometimes called, have been subjected to considerable debate over the past several years. It has been hypothesized and demonstrated that these reflex movements form the basis for later voluntary movement (Bower, 1976; McGraw, 1954; Thelen, 1980; Zelazo, 1976). As the cortex gradually matures, it assumes control over the postural reflexes of walking, climbing, swimming, and the like. In fact, Zelazo (1976) questioned the dualistic position of the anatomists in favor of a hierarchical view, stating, "Indeed, current behavioral and neurological research with infants challenges the validity and generality of the hypothesized independence between early reflexive and later instrumental behavior. An alternative hypothesis holds that the newborn's reflexes do not disappear but retain their identity within a hierarchy of controlled behavior" (p. 88).

Anatomists and neurologists, on the other hand, argue that there is a recognizable gap of up to several months between the inhibition of a postural reflex and the onset of voluntary movement (Kessen et al., 1970; Prechtl and Beintema, 1964; Pontius, 1973; Wyke, 1975). This time lag, they contend, clearly indicates that there is no direct link between postural reflexes and later voluntary movement. Therefore, Zelazo's view has been heavily criticized. Furthermore, anatomists and neurologists argue that the performance of reflexive movements and voluntary movements is controlled by entirely different brain centers. Bower (1976), however, contends that "such results pointed to the possibility that the reason abilities disappear is that they are not exercised" (p. 40).

Concept 7.3   There appears to be a link between early reflexive behaviors and later voluntary movement.

From these statements, and the research of the anatomists, one would think that there is little basis for assuming that the infant's first reflexive movements prepare him or her for later voluntary movement in a direct way. We know, however, that the results of early reflexive activity of the infant are internalized and that this information is stored for future use (Zelazo, 1976). Thelen (1983) further argued that studies do in fact demonstrate continuity between reflexive and voluntary walking. She contended, as did Bower (1976), that the period of inhibition disappears if the reflex is exercised. Thelen argued that the reflex disappears because leg mass increases. Preservation of the reflex strengthens the leg and lower body thus permitting the infant to continue the movement with little or no lag between the locomotor reflex and its voluntary counterpart. Explanations such as this account for at least an indirect link between the infant's postural reflexes and later voluntary movement. Anyone interested in the study of movement must have a clearer understanding of the very first forms of movement behavior.

The *neuromaturational theory* of motor development (Hebb, 1949; Eckert, 1987) holds that as the cortex develops it inhibits some of the functions of the subcortical layers and assumes ever-increasing neuromuscular control. The cortex joins in its ability to store information that is received by way of sensory neurons. This phenomena is evidenced in the phasing out of reflex behaviors and the assumption of voluntary movements by the infant. Concurrent formation of myelin prepares the body for the mature neuromuscular state. Movements become more localized as functional neural pathways serve isolated regions of the body with greater precision and accuracy.

More recent explanations of infant motor development (Thelen, 1986; Thelen et al., 1987) subscribe to a *dynamical systems theory,* which contends that neuromaturation serves as a rate-limiter to development and is only one of many rate-limiters influencing the emergence of controlled voluntary movement. The dynamics of the system itself shape movement, and a *rate-limiter* is something in the individual, task, and/ or environment that prevents or restricts coordinated movement from occurring with little central input. Such things as body proportions, insufficient myelination, body weight, or a host of environmental conditions inhibit or promote progress from the reflexive to the rudimentary movement phase of development.

Diagnosing Central Nervous System Disorders

It is common for a pediatrician to attempt to elicit primitive and postural reflexes in the neonate and young infant. If a reflex is absent, irregular, or uneven in strength, neurological dysfunction is suspected. The absence of normal reflexive movements or the prolonged continuation of various reflexes beyond their normal periods may also cause the physician to suspect neurological impairment.

Concept 7.4   Infant reflex behavior may be used as an effective diagnostic tool for assessing the integrity of the central nervous system.

The use of developmental reflexes as a tool for diagnosing central nervous system damage has been widespread. Over the years, scientists have compiled an approximate timetable for the appearance and inhibition of neonatal and infant behaviors. Prechtl and Beintema

(1964), for example, noted that the resting posture of the newborn is the flexed position. The flexors, in fact, are dominant over the extensors in the early part of infancy. Shortly, however, increased cortical control permits the normal neonate to raise its head from the prone position. Prechtl noted that: "An absence of the head-lifting response at the third day or later was highly correlated with other signs of neurological abnormalities. We may conclude therefore that normal babies are able to lift their chins when they are in the prone position" (p. 83).

Several other meaningful examples of this principle exist. The *doll-eye* movements of the neonate permit it to maintain constancy of the retinal image. When the head is tilted back, the eyes look down toward the chin, and when the head is tilted forward, the eyes look up toward the forehead. This response is almost always seen in premature infants and during the first day following birth in the normal neonate, after which it is replaced by voluntary eye movements. Perseveration of this reflex could indicate delayed cortical maturation.

One means of diagnosing possible central nervous system disorders, therefore, is through perseverating reflexes. It must be noted that complete absence of a reflex is usually less significant than a reflex that remains too long. Other evidence of possible damage may be reflected in a reflex that is too strong or too weak. A reflex that elicits a stronger response on one side of the body than on the other may also indicate central nervous system dysfunction. An asymmetrical tonic neck reflex, for example, which shows full arm extension on one side of the body and only weak extensor tone when the other side is stimulated, may also provide evidence of damage.

Inspection and evaluation of reflexive behaviors in the neonate should be done only by a trained examiner. The examinations provide physicians with a primary means of diagnosing central nervous system integrity in full-term, premature, and at-risk infants. Furthermore, they serve as a basis for intervention by physical and occupational therapists working with individuals displaying pathological reflexive behaviors beyond their expected periods of inhibition. Neurological dysfunction may be suspected when any one of the following conditions appear.

1. Perseveration of a reflex beyond the age at which it should have been inhibited by cortical control
2. Complete absence of a reflex
3. Unequal bilateral reflex responses
4. Responses that are too strong or too weak

Concept 7.5   Infant reflexes appear and are inhibited on a predictable schedule in terms of both rate and sequence.

Primitive Reflexes

Primitive reflexes are closely associated with the obtainment of nourishment and the protection of the infant. They first appear during fetal life and persist well into the first year. The following is a partial list of the numerous primitive reflexes exhibited by the fetus and the neonate. Their approximate times of appearance and inhibition are found in Table 7.1, which also includes information about postural reflexes.

Moro and Startle Reflexes

The Moro and startle reflexes may be elicited by placing the infant in a supine position and tapping on the abdomen, or by producing a feeling of insecurity of support (for instance, allowing the head to drop sharply backward a short distance). It may even be self-induced by a loud noise or the infant's own cough or sneeze. In the Moro reflex, there is a sudden extension and bowing of the arms and spreading of the fingers. The legs and toes perform the same actions, but less vigorously. The limbs then return to a normal flexed position against the body (Figure 7.1). The startle reflex is similar in all ways to the Moro reflex except that it involves flexion of the limbs without prior extension.

Figure 7.1
The Moro reflex:
(a) extension
phase, (b) flexion
phase

a

b

Table 7.1 Developmental Sequence and Approximate Rate for Appearance and Inhibition of Selected Primitive and Postural Reflexes

							Month						
Primitive Reflexes	0	1	2	3	4	5	6	7	8	9	10	11	12
Moro	X	X	X	X	X	X	X						
Startle								X	X	X	X		
Search	X	X	X	X	X	X	X	X	X	X	X	X	
Sucking	X	X	X	X									
Palmar-mental	X	X	X										
Palmar-mandibular	X	X	X	X									
Palmar grasping	X	X	X	X	X								
Babinski	X	X	X	X									
Plantar grasp	X	X	X	X	X	X	X	X	X	X	X	X	X
Tonic neck	X	X	X	X	X	X	X						
Postural Reflexes													
Labyrinthine righting			X	X	X	X	X	X	X	X	X	X	X
Optical righting							X	X	X	X	X	X	X
Pull-up				X	X	X	X	X	X	X	X	X	X
Parachute and propping					X	X	X	X	X	X	X	X	X
Neck righting	X	X	X	X	X	X	X	X	X	X	X		
Body righting							X	X	X	X	X	X	X
Crawling	X	X	X	X									
Stepping	X	X	X	X	X								
Swimming	X	X	X	X	X								

The Moro reflex is present at birth and during the first six months of life. The Moro reflex has been one of the most widely used tools in the neurological examination of the young infant. The reaction is most pronounced during the infant's first few weeks. The intensity of the response gradually decreases until it is finally characterized by a simple jerking motion of the body in response to the stimulus (startle reflex). Persistence of the reflex beyond the sixth month may be an indication of neurological dysfunction. An asymmetrical Moro reflex may indicate Erb's palsy or an injury to a limb.

Search and Sucking Reflexes

The search, or rooting, and sucking reflexes enable the newborn to obtain nourishment from its mother. Stimulation of the area around the mouth (search reflex) will result in the infant's turning its head toward the source of stimulation. The search reflex is strongest during the first three weeks and gradually gives way to a directed head turning response that becomes quite refined and appears to be a purposeful behavior to bring the mouth into contact with the stimulus. The search reflex is most easily obtained when the infant is hungry, sleeping, or in his or her normal feeding position. Stimulation of the lips, gums, tongue, or hard palate will cause a sucking motion (sucking reflex) in an attempt to ingest nourishment. The sucking action is usually rhythmically repetitive. If it isn't, gentle movement of the object within the mouth will produce sucking. The sucking reflex actually has two phases, the expressive phase and the suction phase (Sameroff, 1973). During the *expressive phase of sucking* the nipple is squeezed between the tongue and palate. During the *suction phase* negative pressure is produced in the mouth cavity. Leonard et al. (1980) studied the nutritive sucking of high-risk neonates in a neonatal intensive care unit of a large hospital. The purpose of their study was to determine if stimulation of the area around the mouth (*perioral stimulation*) would facilitate the searching, sucking, and swallowing reflexes. The results were positive, clearly indicating that producing such stimulation prior to feeding reduces the need for intravenous feeding of high-risk newborns.

Both of these reflexes are present in all normal newborns. The search reflex may persist until the end of the first year; the sucking movement generally disappears as a reflex by the end of the third month but persists as a voluntary response.

Hand-Mouth Reflexes

Two hand-mouth reflexes are found in the newborn. The *palmar-mental reflex*, elicited by scratching the base of the palm, causes contraction of the chin muscles, which lift the chin up. This reflex has been observed in newborns but disappears relatively early.

The *palmar-mandibular reflex*, or *Babkin reflex*, as it is sometimes called, is elicited by applying pressure to the palms of both hands. The responses usually include mouth opening, closing of eyes, and flexing

Figure 7.2
The palmar
grasping reflex

the head forward. This reflex begins decreasing during the first month after birth and usually is not visible after the third month.

Palmar Grasping Reflex

During the first two months, the infant usually has its hands closed tightly. Upon stimulation of the palm, the hand will close strongly around the object without use of the thumb. The grip tightens when force is exerted against the encircling fingers. The grip is often so strong that the infant is able to support his or her own weight when suspended (Figure 7.2). Also, the grip with the left hand is generally stronger than the right. Grasping also increases during sucking (von Bernuth and Prechtl, 1968).

The grasping reflex is normally present at birth and persists during the first four months. The intensity of the response tends to increase during the first month and slowly diminish after that. Weak grasping or persistence of the reflex after the first year may be a sign of delay in motor development or of hemiplegia, if it occurs on only one side.

Babinski and Plantar Grasp Reflexes

In the newborn the Babinski reflex is elicited by a stroke on the sole of the foot. The pressure causes an extension of the toes. As the neuro-muscular system matures, the Babinski reflex gives way to the plantar reflex, which is a contraction of the toes upon stimulation of the sole of the foot (Figure 7.3).

Figure 7.3
The plantar
grasping reflex

The Babinski reflex is normally present at birth but gives way around the 4th month to the plantar grasp reflex, which may persist until about the 12th month. The plantar grasp reflex may be most easily elicited by pressing the thumbs against the ball of the infant's foot. Persistence of the Babinski reflex beyond the sixth month may be an indication of a developmental lag.

Asymmetrical and Symmetrical Tonic Neck Reflexes

The asymmetrical tonic neck reflex is probably the most widely researched reflex in the therapeutic literature. To elicit it, the infant is placed by a trained examiner in a supine position, and the neck is turned so that the head is facing toward either side. The arms assume a position similar to the fencer's "on guard." That is, the arm extends on the side of the body toward which the head is turned, and the other arm assumes an acute flexed position. The lower limbs assume a position similar to the arms. The symmetrical tonic neck reflex may be elicited from a supported sitting position. Extension of the head and neck will produce extension of the arm and flexion of the legs. If the head and neck are flexed, the arms flex and the legs extend (Figure 7.4).

Both tonic neck reflexes may be observed in most premature infants, but they are not an obligatory response in newborns (that is, they do not occur each time the infant's head is turned). However, the 3- or 4-month-old infant assumes the asymmetrical position about 50 percent of the time and then this response gradually fades away. Persistence beyond the 6th month may be an indication of lack of control over lower brain centers by higher ones.

Figure 7.4
The asymmetrical
tonic neck reflex
(a) and the sym-
metrical tonic neck
reflex (b & c)

Swartz and Allen (1975) indicated that vestiges of the asymmetrical tonic neck reflex are apparent in some children and that this reflex can affect head position in the breast stroke of young swimmers. They further contend that reflexes do not totally disappear but are "integrated into the central nervous system largely through inhibition" (p. 311). If these reflexes are not properly inhibited, they may result in inadequate muscle tone, lack of independent movement of the head and extremities, midline problems, and difficulty in learning swimming strokes.

Postural Reflexes

Postural reflexes resemble later voluntary movements. Postural reflexes automatically provide for an individual's maintenance of an upright position in relation to his or her environment. They are found in all normal infants during the early postnatal months of life and may, in a few cases, persist through the first year. The following sections discuss postural reflexes that are of particular interest to the student of motor development. These reflexes are associated with later voluntary movement behavior and should be carefully studied by all concerned with the development of voluntary patterns of movement. (The approximate times of appearance and inhibition of these reflexes are also found in Table 7.1.)

Concept 7.6   Postural reflexes resemble, and may be linked to, later voluntary movements.

Labyrinthine and Optical Righting Reflexes

The labyrinthine and the optical righting reflexes may be elicited when the infant is held in an upright position and is tilted forward, backward, or to the side. The child will respond by attempting to maintain the upright position of the head by moving it in the direction opposite to the one in which its trunk is moved. For example, if the baby is held in a prone position and tilted downward, it will respond by raising the head upward (Figure 7.5). The optical righting reflex is the same as the labyrinthine reflex except that the eyes can be observed to follow the upward lead of the head. In the labyrinthine righting reflex, impulses arising in the otolith of the labyrinth cause the infant to maintain its head in proper alignment to the environment even when other sensory channels (i.e., vision or touch) are excluded.

The labyrinthine righting reflex makes its first appearance around the 2nd month and persists to about the 6th month, when vision generally becomes an important factor. The reflex continues into the first year as the optical righting reflex. The optical righting reflex, and its more primitive cousin, the labyrinthine righting reflex, help the infant achieve and maintain an upright head and body posture, and contribute to the infant's forward movement around the end of the first year.

Pull-Up Reflex

The pull-up reflex of the arms is an involuntary attempt on the part of the infant to maintain an upright position. When the infant is in an upright sitting position and held by one or both hands, it will flex its arms in an attempt to remain upright when tipped backward. It will do the same thing when tipped forward. The reflexive pull-up reaction of the arms usually appears around the 3rd or 4th month and often continues through the first year (Figure 7.6).

Parachute and Propping Reflexes

Parachute and propping reactions are protective movements of the limbs in the direction of the displacing force. These reflexive movements occur in response to a sudden displacing force or when balance can no longer be maintained. Protective reflexes depend on visual stimulation and thus do not occur in the dark. They may, in fact, be a form of a startle reflex.

The forward parachute reaction may be observed when the infant is held vertically in the air and then tilted toward the ground. The infant extends the arms downward in an apparent attempt to cushion the anticipated fall (Figure 7.7). The downward parachute reactions may be observed when the baby is held in an upright position and rapidly lowered toward the ground. The lower limbs extend, tense, and abduct. Propping reflexes may be elicited by pushing the infant off balance from a sitting position either forward or backward. The forward and down-

Figure 7.5
The labyrinthine righting reflexes from three positions: (a) upright, (b) tilted backward, and (c) prone

Figure 7.6
The pull-up reflex

Figure 7.7
The parachute reflex

ward parachute reactions begin to occur around the 4th month. The sideways propping reaction is first elicited around the 6th month. The backward reaction is first seen between the 10th and 12th months. Each of these reactions tends to persist beyond the first year and are necessary before the infant can learn to walk.

Figure 7.8
The neck righting
reflex (a) and the
body righting reflex
(b)

a   b

Neck and Body Righting Reflexes

The neck righting reflex can be observed when the infant is placed in
a supine position with the head turned to one side. The remainder of
the body moves reflexively in the same direction of the head. First the
hips and legs turn into alignment, followed by the trunk. In the body
righting reflex the reverse occurs. When tested from a side-lying position with the legs and trunk turned in one direction, the baby will turn
its head reflexively in the same direction and right the body in alignment with the head (Figure 7.8).

The neck righting reflex disappears around 6 months of age. The body
righting reflex emerges around the sixth month and persists to about
18 months of age. The body righting reflex forms the basis for voluntary
rolling that occurs from the end of the fifth month onward.

Crawling Reflex

The crawling reflex can be seen when the infant is placed in a prone
position and pressure is applied to the sole of one foot. It will reflexively
crawl, using both its upper and lower limbs. Pressure on the soles of

Figure 7.9
The crawling reflex

both feet will elicit a return of pressure by the infant. Pressure on the sole of one foot will produce returned pressure and an extensor thrust of the opposite leg (Figure 7.9).

The crawling reflex is generally present at birth and disappears around the 3rd or 4th month. There is a lag between reflexive crawling and voluntary crawling, which appears around the 7th month.

Primary Stepping Reflex

When the infant is held erect, with its body weight placed forward on a flat surface, it will respond by "walking" forward. This walking movement involves the legs only (Figure 7.10). The primary stepping reflex is normally present during the first six weeks and disappears by the fifth month. Zelazo (1976) and Bower (1976) studied how early and persistent practice of the primary stepping reflex affects the onset of voluntary walking behavior. The results of these investigations revealed that the age of independent walking was accelerated through conditioning of the stepping reflex in the experimental group; the control group did not show accelerated development. The implications of this important finding are enormous, but further research is necessary before we can confirm why perpetuating a reflex through persistent exercise accelerates the onset of voluntary behavior. An alternative hypothesis has been presented by Thelen (1983) that needs further testing. Essentially she proposes that conditioning of a reflex actually improves strength in the limbs exercised. Improved strength becomes the key to early voluntary walking rather than an improved memory trace which enables the baby to recall the movement pattern from memory.

Swimming Reflex

When placed in a prone position in or over water, the infant will exhibit rhythmical extensor and flexor swimming movements of the arms and legs. The movements are well organized and appear more advanced than any of the other locomotor reflexes. McGraw (1939) filmed reflexive swimming movements in the human infant as early as the 11th day

Figure 7.10
The primary step-
ping reflex

following birth. These involuntary movements generally disappear around the fourth month. McGraw discovered that a breath-holding reflex is elicited when the infant's face is placed in the water and that the swimming movements are more pronounced from this position. McGraw (1954) has since speculated on the theory that the infant's swimming reflex is a precursor to walking. "Basically the neuromuscular mechanisms which mediate the reflexive swimming movements may be essentially the same as those activated in the reflexive crawling and stepping movements of the infant" (p. 360). It is interesting to reflect on the relationship among the crawling, stepping, and swimming reflexes.

Rhythmical Stereotypies

Researchers have been interested in the many intriguing questions concerning infant reflexes for several decades. This research has important implications for the diagnosis of central nervous system disorders, and for the physical and occupational therapist working with individuals who display various pathological conditions. Furthermore, the study of the origin of reflexes and their relationship to later voluntary behaviors is forging new inroads into learning theory and how the human being organizes itself for the learning of new movement skills.

Concept 7.7 Infant rhythmical stereotypies provide evidence that human motor development is a self-organizing system that strives for increased motor control.

Only recently have investigators gone beyond cataloging and describing infant reflexive behaviors to explain what is going on. Esther Thelen is among the first to attempt to answer the many questions raised by the stereotypical behaviors of the infant. She studied *rhythmical stereotypies* in normal human infants to classify these movements and explain their occurrences. (Stereotypies are rhythmical behaviors performed over and over for their own sakes.) In children and adults stereotypies are regarded as evidence of abnormal behavior, but in infants they are quite normal.

Thelen (1979, 1981) observed and cataloged the rhythmical stereotypies of normal infants from four weeks to one year of age. Her observations revealed 47 stereotypical behaviors which have been subdivided into four groups: (1) movements of the legs and feet; (2) movements of the torso; (3) movements of the arms, hands, and fingers; and (4) movements of the head and face. According to Thelen (1979), "These behaviors showed developmental regularities as well as constancy of form and distribution. Groups of stereotypies involving particular parts of the body or postures had characteristic ages of onset, peak performance, and decline" (p. 699). Rhythmic movements of given body systems tended to increase just before the infant gained voluntary control of that system. Therefore, the maturational level of the infant appears to control rhythmical stereotypies. Recently, Thelen and her colleagues (Thelen, 1985; Thelen, Kelso, and Fogel, 1987) have argued that the presence of stereotypical behaviors in normal human infants is evidence of a self-organizing central motor program in control of infant motor development.

Legs and Feet

Thelen (1979) found that rhythmical kicking movements of the legs and feet were the earliest stereotypies observed. The majority of rhythmical kicking took place when infants were in either prone or supine positions. The supine position afforded infants the greatest amount of freedom with flexibility at both the hip and knee joints. When kicking from this back-lying position the babies' legs were bent slightly at the hips, knees, and ankles with moderate outward rotation at the hips.

From this position the infants could alternately kick the legs in what resembled a "bicycling" action. From the prone position alternate leg kicking was more restricted and occurred only from the knee joint. Thelen noted that stereotypies of the legs and feet began around the 4th week of age, earlier than for arms, and reached their peak occurrence between 24 and 32 months of age. Other forms of kicking discovered were foot rubbing from a related position, and single leg kicking from both prone and supine positions.

Torso

Thelen (1979) also observed several rhythmical stereotypies of the torso. The most common was from a prone position. The infant arched the back, lifted the arms and legs from the supporting surface, and rhythmically rocked back and forth in an airplane-like position. Another frequently observed stereotypy of the torso occurred from a hands-and-knee prone creeping position. From this position the infant moved the body forward by extending the upper position of the leg and keeping the lower leg stationary. The arms remained extended throughout but moved forward on the backward thrust of the legs.

Other common, but less frequently observed, rhythmical stereotypies of the torso included rhythmical actions from sitting, kneeling, and standing postures. From either a supported or unsupported sitting position, the infant rhythmically rocked the torso forward and back. Rhythmical stereotypies from a kneeling position included rocking back and forth, side to side, and up and down. Standing stereotypies were quite common and generally occurred from a support-standing position. The infant bent at the knees and performed a rhythmical up-and-down bouncing movement. Infants might also rhythmically rock forward and back and from side to side.

Arms, Hands, and Fingers

Rhythmical stereotypies of the arms, hands, and fingers were observed in all of the infants sampled by Thelen. Waving (actions without an object) and banging (actions with an object in the infant's grasp) were the most frequently observed. Both were actually the same motor pattern and involved rhythmical movement in a vertical action from the shoulder. Banging differed from waving only in that the infant made contact with the surface on the downward action. Rhythmical clapping of the hands in front of the body was another common stereotypy, as in arm sway. The arm sway stereotypy is elicited, however, only when the infant is grasping an object and involves shoulder-initiated action across the front of the body.

Head and Face

Rhythmical stereotypies of the head and face, according to Thelen (1979), are much less frequent. They involve actions such as rhythmical head shaking from side to side (''no'') and up and down (''yes''). Rhythmical sticking out of the tongue and drawing it back was routinely observed, along with non-nutritive sucking behaviors.

Of the 47 rhythmical stereotypies observed by Thelen, movements of the legs and feet were the most common, began the earliest, and peaked between 24 and 32 weeks of age. Arm and hand stereotypies are also very common but peaked somewhat later, between 34 and 42 weeks. Torso stereotypies, although common, are less frequent than movements of the legs and feet and the hands and arms. Furthermore, torso stereotypies from sitting, kneeling, or standing positions tend to peak later than the others.

Summary

Primitive reflexes, which are under the control of subcortical brain layers, are observed in the fetus from about the 18th week of gestation. Generally, reflexes serve the double function of helping the neonate to secure nourishment and protection. Many of the movements represent initial methods of gaining information about the infant's environment.

As neurological development proceeds in the normal fetus, and later in the normal neonate, reflexes appear and disappear on a fairly standard, though informal, schedule. The presence of a primitive or postural reflex is evidence of subcortical control over some neuromuscular functions. Although cortical control soon dominates, the function of the subcortex is never completely inhibited. Throughout life, it maintains control over such activities as coughing, sneezing, and yawning, as well as over the involuntary life processes. The cortex mediates more purposeful behavior, whereas subcortical behavior is limited and stereotyped.

Although it is not yet possible to determine whether there is a direct relationship between reflexive behavior and later voluntary movement, it is safe to assume that there is at least an indirect link. This link may be associated with the ability of the developing cortex to store information received from the sensory end-organs regarding the actual performance of the involuntary movement. Or it may be due to improved strength in the involuntarily (reflexively) exercised body part.

Terms to Remember

Primitive reflexes
Postural reflexes
Information encoding stage
Information decoding stage
Neuromaturational theory
Dynamical systems theory
Rate-limiter
Moro reflex
Startle reflex
Search reflex
Sucking reflex
Expressive sucking phase
Suction phase
Perioral stimulation
Palmar-mental reflex
Palmar-mandibular reflex

Palmar grasping reflex
Babinski reflex
Plantar grasp reflex
Asymmetrical tonic neck reflex
Symmetrical neck reflex
Labyrinthine righting reflex
Pull-up reflex
Parachute reflex
Propping reflex
Neck-righting reflex
Body-righting reflex
Crawling reflex
Primary stepping reflex
Swimming reflex
Rhythmical stereotypies

Critical Readings

Bobath, B., & Bobath, K. (1975). *Motor Development in the Different Types of Cerebral Palsy.* London: William Heinemann Medical Books Ltd.

Easton, T. A. (1972). On the normal use of reflexes. *American Scientist,* 60, 591–599.

Fiorentino, M. R. (1972). *Normal and Abnormal Development.* Springfield, IL: Charles C. Thomas.

Payne, G. (1985). *Infant Reflexes in Human Motor Development.* Lawren Productions Inc., Box 666, Mendocino, CA 95460. (videotape).

Thelen, E. (1981). Rhythmical stereotypies in normal human infants. *Animal Behavior,* 27, 699–715.

Thelen, E. (1981). Rhythmical behavior in infancy: An ethological perspective. *Developmental Psychology,* 17, 237–257.

Thelen, E., Kelso, J. A. S., & Fogel, A. (1987). Self-organizing systems and infant motor development. *Developmental Review,* 7, 39–65.

Wyke, B. (1975). The neurological basis of movement: A developmental review. In K. S. Holt (Ed.), *Movement and Child Development,* London: William Heinemann Medical Books.

Zelazo, P. (1976). From reflexive to instrumental behavior. In L. P. Lipsett (Ed.), *Developmental Psychobiology—The Significance of Infancy,* Hillsdale, N.J.: Lawrence Erlbaum.

Chapter **8**

Rudimentary Movement Abilities

CHAPTER COMPETENCIES

Upon completion of this chapter you should be able to:

- *Describe intertask "motor milestones" that lead to upright locomotion and visually guided reaching*
- *Distinguish between the reflex inhibition and the precontrol stages within the rudimentary movement phase of development*
- *Discuss historical and contemporary study of infant motor development*
- *List and describe the developmental sequence of acquisition of rudimentary stability, locomotor, and manipulative abilities*
- *Distinguish between "creeping" and "crawling" and describe the developmental process of each*
- *Discuss the interaction between maturation and experience on the acquisition of rudimentary movement abilities*
- *Devise your own rudimentary movement infant observational assessment instrument*

Key Concept: Mastery of the rudimentary movement abilities of infancy is a reflection of increased motor control and movement competence, brought about by factors within the task and the environment, as well as within the individual.

We are all products of specific genetic structures, and the sum total of the experiences we have had since conception. As such, a child is not a blank slate, ready to be molded and shaped to our whims or a precut pattern. Current research has made it abundantly clear that infants are able to process a great deal more information than we had ever suspected. Infants think and use movement as a purposeful, though initially imprecise, way of gaining information about their environments. Each child is an individual, and no two individuals will respond in exactly the same manner. The child's hereditary and experiential background, as well as the specific demands of the movement tasks, have a profound effect on the rate of attainment of the rudimentary movement abilities of infancy.

It is important to study motor development, beginning with the early movement experiences of infancy, to gain a better understanding of the development that takes place before children enter school and to learn more about the developmental concept of how humans learn to move.

Gaining control over musculature, learning to cope with the force of gravity, and moving in a controlled manner through space are major developmental tasks facing the infant. During the neonatal period, movement is ill defined and poorly controlled. Reflexes are gradually inhibited and the *reflex inhibition stage* begins. This period stretches throughout most of the infant's first year. The infant gradually moves toward controlled rudimentary movement that represents a monumental accomplishment in suppressing reflexes and integrating the sensory and motor systems into controlled purposeful movement.

As the primitive and postural reflexes of the previous phase begin to fade, higher brain centers take over many of the skeletal muscle functions of lower brain centers. The reflex inhibition stage essentially begins at birth. From the moment of birth the newborn is bombarded by sight, sound, smell, tactile, and kinesthetic stimulation. The task is to bring order to this sensory stimulation. Initial reflexive responses are inhibited throughout the first year until around the first birthday, when the infant displays remarkable progress in bringing a semblance of control to his or her movement.

The period from about 12 months to between 18 and 24 months represents a time for practice and mastery of the many rudimentary tasks initiated during the first year. The infant begins to bring his or her movements under control during this pre-control period. The *pre-control stage* spans roughly the period between the first and second birthdays. During this stage the infant begins to gain greater control and precision in movement. Differentiation and integration of sensory and motor processes become more highly developed, and the rate-limiters of early infancy become less pronounced.

As the infant makes crude but purposeful attempts at a variety of movement tasks, he or she should be encouraged. An environment that provides sufficient stimulation through abundant opportunities for practice and positive encouragement may prove beneficial in hastening development of the rudimentary stability, locomotor, and manipulative tasks that follow. The question, however, should be asked: What are the benefits of early motor skill acquisition? The answer is not at all clear, and it is difficult to build a reasonable case for doing so in normally developing infants.

Study of Infant Motor Development

The study of the rudimentary movement abilities of infancy received its impetus in the 1930s and 1940s, when a wealth of information was obtained from the observations of developmental psychologists. Many of these studies have become classics and have withstood the tests of time because of their careful controls and thoroughness. The works of H. M. Halverson, Mary Shirley, Nancy Bayley, and Arnold Gesell are particularly noteworthy.

The work of H. M. Halverson (1937) is probably the most comprehensive on the sequence of the emergence of voluntary grasping behavior during infancy. Through film analysis of infants from 16 to 52 weeks of age, he described three distinct stages of approach toward a cube, and the development of the use of fingers-thumb opposition in grasping behavior.

Mary Shirley's (1931) pioneering study of 25 infants from birth to age 2 enabled her to describe a sequential developmental progression of activities leading to upright posture and a walking gait. She noted that "each separate stage was a fundamental step in development and that every baby advanced from stage to stage in the same order" (p. 98). She also noted that although the sequence was fixed, individual differences were expressed in variations in the rates of development between infants.

Nancy Bayley (1935) conducted an extensive study similar to that of Shirley. As a result of her observations of infants, she was able to describe a series of emerging locomotor abilities progressing from reflexive crawling to walking down a flight of stairs using an alternate foot pattern. Based on this information Bayley developed a cumulative scale of infant motor development that has been widely used as a diagnostic tool to determine an infant's developmental status.

Arnold Gesell (1945) conducted extensive studies of infant motor development. He viewed posture (i.e., stability) as the basis of all forms of movement. Therefore, according to Gesell, any form of locomotion or infant manipulation is actually a closely related series of sequential postural adjustments.

The sequence of motor development is predetermined by innate biological factors that cut across all social, cultural, ethnic, and racial boundaries. This common base of motor development during the early years of life has caused many experts to speculate that some voluntary movements (particularly locomotor movements) are phylogenetic (Eckert, 1973), and that because these movements are maturationally based, they are not actually under voluntary developmental control (Hellebrandt et al., 1961). This view has often led to the erroneous assumption that infants and particularly young children acquire their movement abilities at about the same chronological age solely by the action of neural maturation and with little dependence on experience.

Concept 8.1   The sequence of infant motor development is predictable, but the rate is variable.

Although the sequence of skill acquisition is generally invariant during infancy and childhood, the rate of acquisition differs from child to child. This fact causes one to hypothesize that early motor development is not only a function of neurological maturation, but also a function of a self-organizing system involving the task, the environment, and the individual. As with the reflexive phase, neural maturation may only be one of a number of factors influencing the developmental rate of children's rudimentary movement abilities. In accordance with the hourglass model of motor development presented in Chapter 4, it is time to look beyond neural maturation as the sole means of explaining infant motor development. Researchers are now looking more closely at the transactional processes embodied in the task, the individual, and the environment through a self-organizing dynamical systems perspective (Thelen et al., 1987; Newell, 1992; Alexander et al., 1993).

From the moment of birth the infant is in a constant struggle to gain mastery over the environment in order to survive. During the earliest stages of development, the infant's primary interaction with the environment is through the medium of movement. The infant must begin to master three primary categories of movement for survival and effective and efficient interaction with the world. First, the infant must establish and maintain the relationship of the body to the force of gravity to achieve an upright sitting posture and an erect standing posture (*stability*). Second, the child must develop basic abilities in order to move through the environment (*locomotion*). Third, the infant must develop the rudimentary abilities of reach, grasp, and release to make meaningful contact with objects (*manipulation*).

Concept 8.2   Variations in the rate of infant motor development lends support to the proposition that development is a dynamical process within a self-organizing system.

The rudimentary movement abilities in the infant are the building blocks for more extensive development of the fundamental movement abilities in early childhood and the specialized movement skills of later childhood and beyond. These so-called rudimentary movement abilities are highly involved tasks for the infant. The importance of their development must not be overlooked or minimized. The question that arises is: Can factors in the environment enhance the development of those movement abilities? The answer is an unqualified yes. Rudimentary movement abilities are not genetically determined to the point where they are not susceptible to modification. Early enrichment does seem to influence later development, but further information is needed about the type, timing, degree, and duration.

Stability

The infant is in a constant struggle against the force of gravity in order to achieve and maintain an upright posture. Establishing control over the musculature in opposition to gravity is a process that follows a predictable sequence in all infants. The events leading to an erect standing posture begin with gaining control over the head and neck and proceed down to the trunk and the legs. Operation of the cephalocaudal principle of development is generally apparent in the infant's sequential progress from a lying position to a sitting posture and eventually to an erect standing posture. Table 8.1 provides a summary of the developmental sequence and the approximate age of onset of selected rudimentary stability abilities.

Concept 8.3   Stability is the most basic of the three categories of movement because all voluntary movement involves an element of stability.

Control of the Head and the Neck

At birth the infant has little control over the head and neck muscles. If the infant is held erect at the trunk, the head will drop forward. Around the end of the first month, the infant gains control over these muscles and is able to hold the head erect when supported at the base of the neck. By the end of the first month, the infant should be able to lift the chin off the crib when lying in a prone position. By the 5th month the infant should be able to lift the head off the crib when lying in a supine position.

Table 8.1 Developmental Sequence and Approximate Age of Onset of Rudimentary Stability Abilities

Stability Tasks	Selected Abilities	Approximate Age of Onset
Control of head and neck	Turns to one side	Birth
	Turns to both sides	1 week
	Held with support	First month
	Chin off contact surface	Second month
	Good prone control	Third month
	Good supine control	Fifth month
Control of trunk	Lifts head and chest	Second month
	Attempts supine-to-prone position	Third month
	Success in supine-to-prone roll	Sixth month
	Prone to supine roll	Eighth month
Sitting	Sits with support	Third month
	Sits with self-support	Sixth month
	Sits alone	Eighth month
	Stands with support	Sixth month
Standing	Supports with handholds	Tenth month
	Pulls to supported stand	Eleventh month
	Stands alone	Twelfth month

Control of the Trunk

After infants have gained mastery of the head and neck muscles, they begin to gain control of the muscles in the thoracic and lumbar regions of the trunk. The development of trunk control begins around the 2nd month. Control of the trunk muscles may be observed if you hold the infant off the ground by the waist and note the ability to make postural adjustments necessary to maintain an erect position.

By the end of the 2nd month, the infant should be capable of lifting the chest off the floor when placed in a prone position. After the infant is able to lift the chest, he or she begins to draw the knees up toward the chest and then kick them out suddenly as if swimming. This usually occurs by the 6th month. Another indication of increasing control over the trunk muscles is the ability to turn over from a supine to a prone position. This is generally accomplished around the 6th month and is easily done by flexing the hips and stretching the legs out at right angles to the trunk. Mastery of the roll from a prone to a supine position usually occurs somewhat later.

Sitting

Sitting alone is an accomplishment that requires complete control over the entire trunk. The infant of 4 months is generally able to sit with support in the lumbar region. The infant has control over the upper trunk but not the lower portion. During the next month or two the infant

Figure 8.1
Three stages in achieving independent sitting: third month (a), sixth month (b), and eighth month (c)

gradually gains control over the lower trunk. The first efforts at sitting alone are characterized by an exaggerated forward lean to gain added support for the lumbar region. Gradually, the ability to sit erect with a limited amount of support develops. By the 7th month the infant is generally able to sit alone completely unsupported. At this juncture he or she has now gained control over the upper half of the body (Figure 8.1). At the same time that the infant is learning to sit alone, he or she is developing control over the arms and hands—a further example of the cephalocaudal and proximodistal principles of development in operation.

Standing

Achievement of an erect standing posture represents a developmental milestone in the infant's quest for stability. It is an indication that control over the musculature has been gained to the extent that the force of gravity can no longer place such demanding restraints on movement. The infant is now on the verge of achieving upright locomotion (walking), a feat heralded by parents and pediatricians alike as the infant's most spectacular task of motor development.

The first voluntary attempts at standing occur around the 5th month. When held under the armpits and brought in contact with a supporting surface, the infant will voluntarily extend at the hip, straighten and tense the muscles of the legs, and maintain a standing position with considerable outside support. Around the 9th or 10th month the infant is able to stand beside furniture and support himself for a considerable period of time. Gradually, the infant begins to lean less heavily on the supporting object and can often be seen testing balance completely unsupported for a brief instant. Between the 11th and 12th months the infant learns to pull to a stand by first getting to the knees and then pushing with the legs while the upward extended arms pull down. Standing alone for extended periods of time generally takes place with walking alone and does not appear separately in most babies. The onset of an erect standing posture normally occurs somewhere between 11

Figure 8.2
Three stages in
gaining a standing
posture: sixth
month (a), tenth
month (b), and
twelfth month (c)

and 13 months (Figure 8.2). At this point the infant has gained considerable control over the musculature. He is able to accomplish the difficult task of rising from a lying position to a standing position completely unaided.

Locomotion

The infant's movement through space is dependent on emerging abilities to cope with the force of gravity. Locomotion does not develop independently of stability; it relies heavily on it. The infant will not be able to move about freely until the rudimentary developmental tasks of stability are mastered. The following are discussions of the most frequent forms of locomotion engaged in by the infant while learning how to cope with the force of gravity. These forms of locomotion are also summarized in Table 8.2.

Concept 8.4   Development of rudimentary locomotor abilities provides the infant with a means for exploring a rapidly expanding world.

Crawling

The crawling movements of the infant are the first attempts at purposeful locomotion. Crawling evolves as the infant gains control of the muscles of the head, neck, and trunk. In a prone position the infant may reach for an object in front of her, raising her head and chest off the floor. On coming back down, the outstretched arms pull her back toward the feet. The result of this combined effort is a slight sliding movement forward (Figure 8.3). The legs are usually not used in these early attempts at crawling. Crawling generally appears in the infant by the 6th month, but may appear as early as the 4th month.

Table 8.2 Developmental Sequence and Approximate Age of Onset of Rudimentary Locomotor Abilities

Locomotor Tasks	Selected Abilities	Approximate Age of Onset
Horizontal movements	Scooting	Third month
	Crawling	Sixth month
	Creeping	Ninth month
	Walking on all fours	Eleventh month
Upright gait	Walks with support	Sixth month
	Walks with handholds	Tenth month
	Walks with lead	Eleventh month
	Walks alone (hands high)	Twelfth month
	Walks alone (hands low)	Thirteenth month

Figure 8.3
Crawling

Creeping

Creeping evolves from crawling and often develops into a highly efficient form of locomotion for the infant. Creeping differs from crawling in that the legs and arms are used in opposition to one another. The infant's first attempts at creeping are characterized by very deliberate movements of one limb at a time. As the infant's proficiency increases, movements become synchronous and more rapid. Most efficient creepers utilize a *contralateral pattern* (right arm and left leg). See Figure 8.4 for a visual representation of contralateral creeping.

There has been considerable speculation about the importance of creeping in the infant's motor development and the "proper" method of creeping. The neurological organization rationale of Carl Delacato (1966) placed great importance on proper creeping and crawling techniques as a necessary stage in achieving cortical hemispherical dominance. Dominance of one side of the cortex is necessary, according to Delacato, for proper neurological organization. Faulty organization, it is hypothesized, will lead to motor, perceptual, and language problems

Figure 8.4
Creeping

in the child and adult. This hypothesis has been attacked by neurologists, pediatricians, and researchers in the area of child development. Few conclusions can be reached regarding alternative theories because little research has been conducted. Careful evaluation of the pros and cons of Delacato's rationale is necessary before making any definite conclusions.

Upright Gait

The achievement of upright locomotion depends on the infant's stability. The infant must first be able to control the body in a standing position before tackling the dynamic postural shifts required of upright locomotion. The infant's first attempts at independent walking generally occur somewhere between the 10th and 15th months and are characterized by a wide base of support, the feet turned outward, and the knees slightly flexed. These first walking movements are not synchronous and fluid. They are irregular, hesitant, and unaccompanied by reciprocal arm movements. In fact, they only vaguely resemble the mature walking pattern of early childhood. The advent of walking and other forms of upright locomotion is influenced primarily by maturation but may also be influenced by environmental factors. A child cannot move through space until he or she is developmentally ready. Special training before readiness is not likely to accelerate learning. If, however, the child's nervous system and musculature are developed to the point of readiness, we may expect to witness slight acceleration in the advent of upright locomotion when the infant receives the benefit of additional environmental supports (that is, encouragement and assistance of parents and furniture handholds). Physique, heredity, and environmental factors interact to determine the onset of independent walking in the child.

Shirley (1931) identified four stages that the infant passes through in learning how to walk unaided: "(a) an early period of stepping in which slight forward progress is made (3–6 months); (b) a period of standing with help (6–10 months); (c) a period of walking when led (9–12 months); (d) a period of walking alone (12–15 months)" (p. 18). As the infant passes through each of these stages and progresses toward a mature walking pattern, several changes occur. First, the speed of walking accelerates and length of the step increases. Second, the width of the step increases until independent walking is well established, and then decreases slightly. Third, the eversion of the foot gradually decreases until the feet are pointing straight ahead. Fourth, the upright walking gait gradually smooths out, the length of the step becomes regular, and the movements of the body become synchronous. Shortly after independent walking has been achieved, the toddler will experiment with walking sideways, backward (Eckert, 1973), and on tiptoes (Bayley, 1935).

Manipulation

As with stability and locomotion, the manipulative abilities of the infant evolve through a series of stages. In this section, only the most basic aspects of manipulation—reach, grasp, and release—will be considered. As with the sections on stability and locomotion, the manipulative abilities of the infant may be susceptible to early appearance even though the process is influenced greatly by maturation. If the child is maturationally ready, she will benefit from early opportunities to practice and perfect rudimentary manipulative abilities. Mussen et al. (1969) pointed out that:

> the child can be helped to master skills earlier than he ordinarily would through enrichment, but the timing of the enrichment is important. It is almost as bad to present enriching experiences before the child is ready to use them effectively as it is to deprive the child of these stimulations entirely (p. 178).

The following are the three general steps in which the infant engages during the acquisition of rudimentary manipulative abilities. Table 8.3 provides a summary of the developmental sequence and approximate age of onset of rudimentary manipulative abilities.

Concept 8.5   The emergence of rudimentary manipulative abilities provides the developing infant with the first meaningful contact with objects in the immediate environment.

Table 8.3 Developmental Sequence and Approximate Age of Onset of Rudimentary Manipulative Abilities

Manipulative Tasks	Selected Abilities	Approximate Age of Onset
Reaching	Globular ineffective reach	First to third month
	Definite corralling reach	Fourth month
	Controlled reach	Sixth month
Grasping	Reflexive grasp	Birth
	Voluntary grasp	Third month
	Two-hand palmar grasp	Third month
	One-hand palmar grasp	Fifth month
	Pincer grasp	Ninth month
	Controlled grasping	Fourteenth month
	Eats without assistance	Eighteenth month
Releasing	Basic release	Twelfth to fourteenth month
	Controlled release	Eighteenth month

Reaching

During the first 4 months, the infant does not make definite reaching movements toward objects, although she may attend closely to them visually and make globular encircling motions in the general direction of the object. Around the 4th month she begins to make the fine eye and hand adjustments necessary for contact with the object. Often the infant can be observed making alternating glances between the object and the hand. The movements are slow and awkward, involving primarily the shoulder and elbow. Later the wrist and the hand become more directly involved. By the end of the 5th month, the child's aim is nearly perfect, and she is now able to reach for and make tactual contact with objects in the environment. This accomplishment is necessary before she can actually take hold of the object and grasp it in the hand.

Grasping

The newborn will grasp an object when it is placed in the palm of the hand. This action, however, is entirely reflexive until about the 4th month. Voluntary grasping must wait until the sensorimotor mechanism has developed to the extent that efficient reaching and meaningful contact can take place. Halverson (1937) identified several stages in the development of prehension. In the first stage, a 4-month-old infant makes no real voluntary effort at tactual contact with object. In the second stage, the infant of 5 months is capable of reaching for and making contact with the object. He is able to grasp the object with the entire hand but not firmly. In the third stage, the child's movements are gradually refined so that by the seventh month the palm and fingers are coordinated. The child is still unable to effectively use the thumb and fingers. In the fourth stage, at about the 9th month, the child begins use of the forefinger in grasping. At 10 months reaching and grasping are coordinated into one continuous movement. In the fifth stage, efficient use of the thumb and forefinger comes into play at around 12 months. In the sixth stage, when the child is 14 months old, prehension abilities are very much like those of adults.

The developmental progression of reaching and grasping is complex. Landreth (1958) stated that six component coordinates appear to be involved in the development of prehension. Eckert (1987) neatly summed up these six developmental acts in the following statement:

> These acts involve transitions and include: (1) the transition from visually locating an object to attempting to reach for the object. Other transitions involve: (2) simple eye-hand coordination, to progressive independence of visual effort with its ultimate expression in activities such as piano playing and typing; (3) initial maximal involvement of body musculature to a minimum involvement and greater economy of effort; (4) proximal large muscle activity of the arms and shoulders to distal fine muscle activity of the fingers; (5) early crude raking movements in manipulating objects with the hands to the later pincer-like precision of control with the opposing thumb and forefinger; and (6) initial bilateral reaching and manipulation to ultimate use of the preferred hand. (pp. 122–123)

Releasing

The frantic shaking of a rattle is a familiar sight when observing a 6-month-old infant at play. This is a learning activity that is generally accompanied by a great deal of smiling, babbling, and obvious glee. Minutes later, however, the same infant may be observed shaking the rattle with obvious frustration and apparent rage. The reason for this abrupt shift in moods may be that at six months of age the infant has yet to master the art of releasing an object from grasp. The child has succeeded in reaching for and grasping the handle of the rattle but is not maturationally able to command the flexor muscles of the fingers to relax their grip on the object on command. Learning to fill a bottle with stones, building a block tower, hurling a ball, and turning the pages of a book are seemingly simple examples of a young child's attempts to learn to release, but when compared with earlier attempts at reaching and grasping, these are indeed remarkable advances. By the time the child is 14 months old, she has mastered the rudimentary elements of releasing objects from her grasp. The 18-month-old has well-coordinated control of all aspects of reach, grasp, and release (Halverson, 1937).

As the infant's mastery of the rudimentary abilities of manipulation (reach, grasp, and release) are developing, the reasons for handling objects are revised. Instead of manipulating objects simply to touch, feel, or mouth them, the child now becomes involved in the process of manipulating objects to learn more about the world in which he lives. The

Figure 8.5
Rudimentary
reaching (a),
grasping (b), and
releasing (c)

a   b   c

manipulation of objects becomes directed by appropriate perceptions in order to achieve meaningful goals (Figure 8.5).

The development of locomotor, stability, and manipulative movement abilities in infants is influenced by both maturation and learning. These two facets of development are interrelated, and it is through this interaction that the infant develops and refines rudimentary movement abilities. These movement abilities are necessary steppingstones to the development of fundamental movement patterns and specialized movement abilities.

Special Programs for Infants

In recent years experts and parents have debated the potential benefits of early intervention on the motor development of infants. Infant stimulation programs for at-risk babies have become increasingly popular due to the dramatic reduction in their mortality rates. Similarly, but for different reasons, infant aquatic programs have steadily gained in popularity as have land-based baby exercise programs. Care must be taken to separate fact from fiction and to carefully catalogue what we know about the effects of each of these programs on the motor development of the infant.

Infant Stimulation Programs

Developmental stimulation is a form of intervention for high-risk infants to provide enrichment through the various sensory modalities. This is done in an attempt to counteract conditions that may interfere with the infants' potential for full and productive lives (Denhoff, 1981). These programs are implemented to prevent postnatal factors associated with high-risk infants from seriously impairing later development.

Studies concerning postnatal factors affecting motor development center on how the postnatal environment, the neonatal/infant intensive care unit, influences subsequent development. Many researchers believe that the high-risk infant's surroundings may actually increase the risk of further developmental deficits. The bright lights, noises, blandness, and restricted handling found in neonatal/infant intensive care units may cause both sensory overload and sensory deprivation (Ulrich, 1984). Infant development is largely dependent upon learning from and interacting with the environment, and a hospital environment may restrict these processes from taking place.

Concept 8.6 Developmental stimulation programs for at-risk infants have the potential for enhancing later development.

Developmental stimulation, as a treatment for high-risk infants, is based on a number of assumptions concerning infant development and behavior. In the long run, the success of these programs will depend upon the validity of the theories underlying these assumptions and the ability of programs to provide appropriate services. The following is a list of some basic assumptions involved in high-risk infant stimulation taken from Denhoff (1981), Kopp (1982), Ulrich (1984), and Titzer (1992).

1. Infancy is a crucial period, and intervention will be effective only if it is started early in life.
2. Appropriate maternal and infant behavior is contingent upon interactions between mother and child.
3. Physical abilities can impinge upon, but do not necessarily interfere with development, if emotional and social growth can be maintained as nearly normal as possible.
4. Multiple caretakers in the early months may interfere with infant/parent attachment.
5. A disabled infant must be managed as a total person, with equal emphasis on physical, mental, and social-emotional elements.
6. The environment of the neonatal/infant intensive care unit is different from the intrauterine environment and deprives the preterm infant of the kinesthetic, tactile, and auditory stimulation it would normally have received in the third trimester.
7. The neonatal intensive care unit does not provide high-risk infants with the nurturing environment any newborn needs during early postnatal growth and development.
8. Infants can benefit from long-term stimulation programs.

The preceding assumptions place considerable emphasis on the infant-parent relationship and stress the need for parental involvement in early intervention. To enhance the overall well-being of a child, parents must be involved because so much of an infant's development is dependent upon family interaction. For this reason, virtually all programs of infant stimulation utilize parents as primary providers of treatment.

Ulrich (1984) reported the outcomes of a number of studies in which high-risk infants were provided stimulation in the form of rocking, stroking, talking and increased handling. Some of the improvements noted were increased weight gain, better motor and visual functioning, and improved performance on developmental tests of mental functioning. Ottenbacker (1983) reported similar results and further stated that most clinical studies indicate stimulation, in a variety of forms, can improve arousal level, visual exploratory behavior, motor development, and reflex integration in early human development. Some of the research reviewed reported no significant changes, but none reported negative effects.

From a pool of 1,010 very premature infants who were stimulated (i.e., born at less than 32 weeks of gestation) Ouden et al. (1991) conducted a national survey on 555 Dutch infants with no evidence of any disabilities. The study was conducted to determine whether age correction for preterm birth (adding the difference between normal and preterm birth to the infants' gestational age) should be applied during developmental diagnosis. The results of their investigation indicated that the development of the infants studied equaled the development of normal term children during their first year when the ages of the preterm children were corrected for gestational age. Furthermore, at 2 years of age, development was equal to or better than normal term children's development without correction. These researchers concluded that full correction for gestational age should be applied during the infant's first year to avoid unnecessary referral to developmental stimulation programs. The results of this study suggest that normal preterm infants may reach developmental milestones sooner than their full term counterparts because of early extrauterine stimulation. This supports the view that early development is not purely a process of cortical maturation, but is affected also by environmental stimuli. It would seem, therefore, that to the best of our current knowledge, the benefits derived from early stimulation for high-risk infants are real and not entirely related to maturational processes.

Infant Aquatic Programs

Infant swim programs have become increasingly popular over the past 30 years. Most communities with swimming facilities offer some form of aquatics for babies (Hicks-Hughes and Langendorfer, 1986). Parents enroll their children in infant swimming programs for varying reasons. Some want to "drownproof" their children. Others want babies to learn how to swim in the belief that this is a "critical period" for developing swimming skills. Still others enroll their babies for the sheer pleasure of interacting in a different medium and enhancing the bonding process. Although each of these reasons may have merit, aquatic programs for infants should be approached with caution.

Concept 8.7   Infant aquatic programs may be beneficial in terms of providing additional stimulation and promoting parent-child interaction, but they involve potential dangers that must be acknowledged.

Langendorfer (1987) points out that "regardless of age or skill, *no* person is completely water safe!" (p. 3). Parents who attempt to "drownproof" their children need to be alerted that this is literally not possible, and that constant vigilance is necessary when children are near the water. Langendorfer further indicated that there is no evidence to suggest that infant swimming enhances later development. The notion of a narrowly defined critical period for learning how to swim is not supported by available research.

Other problems associated with infant swim programs are hyponatremia (or infant water intoxication) and Giardia. *Hyponatremia* is a rare but serious condition activated by swallowing excessive amounts of water, which reduces the body's serum sodium level. Symptoms as reported by Burd (1986) include lethargy, disorientation, weakness, nausea, vomiting, seizures, coma, and death. *Giardia,* a problem much more common to infant swimming classes, is an intestinal parasite that may be transmitted between infants. It causes severe and prolonged diarrhea.

As a result of the misinformation about infant aquatics and potential problems, both the YMCA Division of Aquatics (1984) and the American Academy of Pediatrics (1985) published guidelines discouraging total submersion of infants and recommending that organized aquatic programs be limited to children over three years old. Infant aquatic programs that follow the guidelines outlined by the YMCA and the American Academy of Pediatrics can be pleasant and fun for both parent and child. The actual benefits and detriments of such programs, however, are not completely known and await further study.

Summary

Chapter **8**

During infancy the child's primary concerns are with self-gratification. Primitive reflexes serve the infant well in meeting basic survival needs, but as the child develops, other needs emerge. Among them is the characteristic need to "know." Development proceeds in a predictable sequence but at varying rates as control is gained first over head and trunk and then over the limbs. Sitting enables the infant to more effectively use the arms for exploration. Manipulative skills, including mouthing, allow use of the sensorimotor mechanisms to gain information. Movements become the symbols of the child's thought process because language is limited.

The motor achievements of the normal human infant are not only a function of neurological maturation, but also a function of a self-organizing system. Biology plays an important role in the predictable sequence of motor development. There is, however, considerable normal variation in the rate of development. Although neuromuscular maturation must occur for the infant to progress to the next developmental level, several environmental and task demand factors determine the rate. Environments that provide stimulation and opportunities for exploration encourage early acquisition of rudimentary movement patterns. Crawling, for example, is often the outgrowth of an ocular following pattern, while standing and an upright gait are reinforced by the presence of handholds in the child's environment.

Terms to Remember

Reflex inhibition stage
Pre-control stage
Locomotion
Manipulation
Stability
Crawling

Creeping
Contralateral pattern
Infant stimulation
Infant aquatic program
Hyponatremia
Giardia

Critical Readings

Alexander, R. et al. (1993). *Normal Development of Functional Motor Skills: The First Year of Life.* Tucson, AZ: Communication Skill Builders.

Bailey, D. B., & Wolery, M. (1989). *Assessing Infants and Preschoolers with Handicaps.* Columbus, OH: Charles E. Merrill.

Campos, J. J. et al. (1982). The emergence of self-produced locomotion. In D. D. Brecker (Ed.), *Intervention With At-Risk and Handicapped Infants.* Baltimore: University Park Press.

Newell, K. M. (Ed.) (1992). Theme issue on dynamical approaches to motor skill acquisition. *Journal of Motor Behavior,* 24, 1, 2–142.

Ouden, L. D. et al. (1991). Is it correct to correct? Developmental milestones in 555 'normal' preterm infants compared with term infants. *Journal of Pediatrics,* 118, 3, 399–404.

Thelen, E. (1986). Development of coordinated movement: Implications for early human development. In, M. G. Wade & H. T. A. Whiting (Eds.), *Motor Development in Children: Aspects of Coordination and Control.* Dordrecht, The Netherlands: Martinus Nyhoff.

Thelen E. et al. (1987). Self-organizing systems in infant motor development. *Developmental Review,* 7, 39–65.

Chapter **9**

Infant Perception

CHAPTER COMPETENCIES

Upon completion of this chapter you should be able to:

- *Discuss changes in perceptual functioning during infancy*
- *Describe various methods of studying infant perception*
- *Discuss developmental aspects of infant visual perception*
- *Describe developmental changes in visual acuity, accommodation, and peripheral vision*
- *Distinguish between the terms "binocularity," "fixation," and "tracking"*
- *Discuss the visual-cliff experiments and draw conclusions about infant depth perception*
- *Debate the question concerning infants' perception of color*
- *Trace the developmental aspects of form perception*
- *Describe various aspects of infant, auditory, olfactory and gustatory perception*

Key Concept: Perceptual development in infancy is intricately entwined with motor development, resulting in an interdependent system.

From the moment of birth, infants begin the process of learning how to interact with the environment. This interaction is a perceptual as well as a motor process. The term *perception* refers to "any process by which we gain immediate awareness of what is happening outside ourselves" (Bower, 1977, p. 1). The term *perceptual-motor* refers to the process of organizing incoming information with stored information which leads to an overt act or motor performance. All voluntary movement involves an element of perception. Students of motor development should be concerned with perceptual development, because of the important link between perceptual and motor processes.

To gain immediate information about the outside world, we must rely on our various senses. Newborns receive all sorts of stimulation (visual, auditory, olfactory, gustatory, tactual, and kinesthetic) through the various sense modalities. They make responses to these stimuli, but these responses have limited utility. Only when sensory stimuli can be integrated with stored information do these sensations take on meaning for the infant and truly warrant being called perceptions.

Newborns attach little meaning to sensory stimuli. For example, light rays impinging on the eyes register on the retinas and are transmitted to appropriate nerve centers in the sensory areas of the cortex. The newborn's reaction is simple (sensation)—if the light is dim the pupils dilate, and if the light is bright the pupils constrict and some of the stimulation is obscured (*consensual pupillary reflex*). Soon the neonate blinks as the stimulus approaches. These simple reflex actions persist throughout life, but in a very short time the infant begins to attach meaning to the visual stimuli received. Soon a certain face becomes "mother." An object is identified as having either three or four sides. The infant attends to certain stimuli and begins to apply basic meaning to them with the powers of visual perception.

Concept 9.1   Development of the perceptual system is more rapid than that of the motor system during infancy.

As with the development of movement abilities in the infant, the development of perceptual skills is a matter of both experience and maturation. Maturation plays an important role in the development of increased acuity of perception, but much improvement in acuity is due to experience. Learning opportunities afforded children and adults enhance the sophistication of their perceptual modalities. Similarly, only through experience will the infant be able to acquire many perception capabilities. The infant's perceptual development is basic to later functioning, and as we will see, is intricately intertwined with the motor system.

Methods of Studying Infant Perception

In the study of infant perceptual abilities a number of techniques are used to determine infants' responses to various stimuli. Because they cannot verbalize or fill out questionnaires, indirect techniques of naturalistic observation were, until recently, used as the primary means of determining what infants could see, hear, feel, and so forth. Each of these methods compares an infant's state prior to introduction of the stimulus with its state during or immediately following the stimulus. The difference between the two measures provides the researcher with an indication of the level and duration of the response to the stimulus. For example, if a uniformly moving pattern of some sort is passed across a neonate's visual field, repetitive following movements of the eyes occur (Atkinson & Braddick, 1982). The occurrence of these eye movements provides evidence that the moving pattern is perceived at some level by the newborn. Similarly, changes in the infant's general level of motor activity—turning the head, blinking the eyes, crying and so forth—have all been used by researchers as visual indicators of the infant's perceptual abilities.

Such techniques, however, have limitations. First, the observation may be unreliable in that two or more observers may not agree that the particular response actually occurred, or to what degree it occurred. Second, responses are difficult to quantify. Often the rapid and diffuse movements of the infant make it difficult to get an accurate record of the number of responses. The third, and most potent, limitation is that it is not possible to be certain that the infant's response was due to the stimulus presented or simply a change from no stimulus to a stimulus. The infant may be responding to aspects of the stimulus that are different than those identified by the investigator. Therefore, when observational assessment is used as a technique for studying infant perceptual abilities, care must be taken not to overgeneralize from the data, or to rely on one or two studies as conclusive evidence of a particular perceptual ability of the infant.

Concept 9.2   It is unwise to generalize from conclusions reached in some observational studies of infant perceptual development, even though the study techniques are sophisticated.

Observational assessment techniques have become much more sophisticated in recent years, reducing the limitations presented above. Film analysis of the infant's responses, heart and respiration rate monitors, and non-nutritive sucking devices are all used as effective tools in understanding infant perception. Film analysis permits researchers to carefully study the infant's responses over-and-over, and in slow motion. Precise measurements can be made of the length and frequency of the infant's attention between two stimuli. Heart and respiration rate monitors provide the investigator with the number of heartbeats or breaths taken when a new stimuli is presented. Numerical increases are used as quantifiable indicators of heightened interest in the new stimulus. Increases in *non-nutritive sucking* were first used as an assessment measure by Siqueland and DeLucia (1969). They devised an apparatus which connected a baby's pacifier to a counting device. As stimuli were presented, changes in the infant's sucking behavior were recorded. Increases in the number of sucks were used as an indicator of the infant's attention to, or preference for, a given visual display.

Two additional techniques of studying infant perception have come into vogue in recent years: habituation-dishabituation, and evoked potentials. In the *habituation-dishabituation* technique, a single stimulus is presented repeatedly to the infant until there is a measurable decline (habituation) in whatever attending behavior is being observed. At that point a new stimulus is presented, and any recovery (dishabituation) in responsiveness is recorded. If the infant fails to dishabituate and continues to show habituation with the new stimulus, then it is assumed that the baby is unable to perceive the new stimulus as different. The habituation-dishabituation paradigm has been used most extensively with studies of auditory and olfactory perception in infants.

Evoked potentials are electrical brain responses that may be related to a particular stimulus because of where they originate. Electrodes are attached to the infant's scalp. Changes in the electrical pattern of the brain indicates that the stimulus is getting through to the infant's central nervous system and eliciting some form of response.

Each of the techniques discussed above provide the researcher with evidence that the infant can detect or discriminate between stimuli. With these sophisticated observational assessment and electrophysiological measures we know that the neonate of only a few days is far more perceptive than previously suspected. However, these measures are only "indirect" indicators of the infant's perceptual abilities. Rigid adherence to a chronological age classification of these abilities is unwise.

Visual Perception

At birth, the infant's eyes have all of the parts necessary for sight and are almost completely formed. The fovea is incompletely developed and the ocular muscles are immature. These two factors result in poor fixation, focusing, and coordination of eye movements. The blinking and lacrimal apparatuses are poorly developed at birth, and the neonate is unable to shed tears for 1 to 7 weeks after birth. Also, it is debatable whether the newborn possesses color vision because of the amount of rhodopsin and iodopsin (visual purple) present in the rods and cones of the eye. Visual acuity, accommodation, peripheral vision, binocularity, fixation, tracking, color vision, and form perception develop rapidly during the early weeks and months following birth. Table 9.1 presents a list of the major developmental aspects of infant visual perception, along with the approximate age at which these abilities begin to emerge.

Table 9.1 Developmental Aspects of Selected Infant Visual Perceptual Abilities

Visual Quality	Selected Abilities	Approximate Age of Onset
Sensitivity to Light The visual apparatus is complete in the newborn and is first put to use by adjusting to varying intensities of the light source.	Consensual pupillary reflex (contraction and dilation of the pupils)	Birth 2 to 3 hours
	Strabismus	Birth to 14 days
	Turns head toward light source	Birth
	Closes eyes if light is bright	Birth
	Tightens eyelids when asleep	Birth
	More active in dim light than in bright light	Birth to 1 year
Visual Acuity The length of focus increases daily as the eye matures.	Organically complete visual apparatus	Birth
	Length of focus 4 to 10 in.	Birth to 1 week
	Length of focus about 36 in.	3 months
	Length of focus about 100 ft.	1 year
Accommodation Accommodation is dependent upon functional maturity of the lens.	Poor	Birth to 2 months
	Near adultlike	2 to 4 months

Table 9.1 continued

Peripheral Vision Peripheral vision improves rapidly in a horizontal direction.	15 degrees from center 30 degrees from center 40 degrees from center	Birth to 2 weeks 1 to 2 months 5 months
Fixation Fixation is monocular and essentially reflexive during the first weeks.	Fixates one eye on bright objects Fixates both eyes on bright objects Turns head from one stationary bright surface to another Follows an object in motion, keeping the head stationary Directs eyes toward an object	Birth 2 to 3 days 11 days 23 days 10 weeks
Tracking Tracking is first saccadic and gradually smooths out. Develops far sooner than the motor component.	Horizontal Vertical Diagonal Circular	Saccadic pursuit begins at birth Smooth pursuits begin by 2 months Sequence is fixed
Depth Perception Monocular vision at birth soon gives way to binocular vision and perception of depth.	Monocular vision Binocular vision Depth perception	Birth 2 months 2 to 6 months
Color Discrimination and Preference Inconsistent evidence. Color vision may be present at birth depending on the amount of rhodopsin and iodopsin present.	Color vision Color perception Prefers shape to color Color discrimination	Birth? 10 weeks 15 days 3 months
Form Perception Discrimination begins early and develops rapidly in complexity. The human face is the favorite object.	Prefers patterned objects to plain Imitates facial gestures Prefers human face Size and shape constancy Discriminates between two- and three-dimensional figures	Neonate Neonate Neonate 2 months 3 months 6 months

Contrast Sensitivity

The visual apparatus is anatomically complete at birth, although it may
be functionally immature. Vision is first used by the newborn in responding to various light intensities. At birth the newborn exhibits a
consensual pupillary reflex in which the pupils dilate or constrict in
response to the intensity of a localized light source. Hershenson (1964)
found that 2- to 4-day-old infants looked at medium-intensity lights
longer than at dim or high-intensity lights. Peeples and Teller (1975)
found that 2-month-old infants could discriminate between bars of light
against a black background almost as well as adults. The babies were
able to detect differences in brightness of as little as 5 percent, whereas
adults were able to make 1 percent discriminations. Additionally, it has
frequently been observed that newborns tighten their eyelids when
asleep in brightly lit rooms, and tend to be more active in dim light than
in bright. Perhaps this helps explain why infants are frequently more
active at night than during the daylight hours.

Visual Acuity, Accommodation, and Peripheral Vision

The eye grows and develops rapidly during the child's first two years.
In the infant, the cornea is thinner and more spherical than in the adult.
As a result the cornea is more refractive and the infant tends to be
slightly myopic at birth. Normal visual acuity is gradually achieved as
the cornea rounds out and the lens flattens. The term *visual acuity*
refers to the degree of detail that can be seen in an object. The newborn
has a focal distance of about 4 to 10 inches. The length of focus increases almost daily and is within the range of normal adult acuity by
the time the infant is 6 to 12 months old (Cohen et al., 1979; Aslin and
Dumais, 1980).

   Accommodation, the ability of the lens of each eye to vary its curvature to bring the retinal image into sharp focus, improves with age.
The study by Haynes et al. (1965) demonstrated that adult-like accommodation does not occur until around the fourth month. Banks (1980),
in a replication of the Haynes study, found partial accommodation at

one month and near adult-like focusing around the second month. These studies demonstrated that, until at least two months of age, infants are not able to bring objects into sharp focus.

Peripheral vision is the visual field that can be seen without a change in fixation of the eyes. Tronick's (1972) work suggests that the visual field of the 2-week-old is quite narrow (about 15 degrees from center), but expands to about 40 degrees from center by the 5th month. In line with Tronick (1972), Aslin and Salapatek (1975) found that 1- and 2-month-old infants had a visual field of about 30 degrees from center. Normal adult peripheral vision is about 90 degrees from center to either side.

Concept 9.5   Although myopic at birth, with a short focal distance and limited peripheral vision, the neonate responds to various light intensities.

Cohen et al. (1979) reported that "by 6 months of age both the infant's central and peripheral systems are quite mature" (p. 404). It appears, therefore, that visual acuity, accommodation, and peripheral vision improve dramatically as the eyes mature during early infancy. The interaction between these three developing systems is, at present, unknown.

Binocularity, Fixation, and Tracking

The topics of infant binocularity, fixation, and tracking have interested researchers for years. Prerequisite to efficient fixation and tracking behaviors is binocular vision. *Binocular vision* requires that the eyes work together in visually attending to a stationary object (*fixation*) or to a moving object (*tracking*).

Binocular vision, according to the theoretical framework originally presented by Worth in 1915 and discussed by Aslin and Dumais (1980), occurs at three levels: bifoveal fixation, fusion, and stereopsis. In order for *bifoveal fixation* to occur, the fovea of the two eyes must be aligned and directed at the same instant toward the object of visual regard. If bifoveal fixation is absent, then fusion and stereopsis can not occur.

Concept 9.6   Binocular vision occurs at three levels: bifoveal fixation, fusion, and stereopsis.

Fusion is the second level of binocular vision. Fusion is a process in which the images on the two retinas are combined into a single visual percept. When looking at an object each eye sends information to the retina and on to the brain from a different orientation. The two eyes are about 6 centimeters apart, so a direct line from each eye to the object is quite different. Krieg (1978) noted that the interocular distance between the two eyes increases by about 50 percent from birth to adulthood. Limited data suggests that infants have fusion by the fourth to sixth month of postnatal life (Aslin, 1977). Fusion is required for stereopsis to occur.

Stereopsis is the third level of binocularity, and enables one to detect depth. Stereopsis is based on the extent of retinal disparity or mismatch between the two eyes, and has been demonstrated in infants three months and older (Fox et al., 1980). Aslin and Dumais (1980) stated that "the presence of bifoveal fixation in infants does not guarantee that fusion and stereopsis are present" (p. 60). Therefore, although it is possible that these three levels of binocularity are hierarchical, it is also possible that they exist as three parallel functions interdependent upon one another. The primary developmental determinants of binocular vision, which makes fixation and tracking possible, are visual acuity, contrast sensitivity, accommodation, and the distance between the eyes (Aslin and Dumais, 1980).

Visual fixation is monocular at birth, probably because of the infant's poor visual acuity and contrast sensitivity. Also, visual-motor control of the two eyes is immature. These conditions improve rapidly during the first six months, suggesting improvement in the infant's ability to binocularly fixate (Atkinson & Braddick, 1982).

Concept 9.7   Saccadic eye movements govern visual tracking by the young infant.

Binocular tracking is the most basic aspect of visual-motor pursuit. Tracking involves directing the eyes from one line of sight to another. These eye movements are either of a high velocity (saccadic) or slow velocity (smooth pursuit). *Saccades* are quick movements of the eyes that involve a redirection of focus from one object of regard to another. Saccadic eye movements govern the object tracking of the very young infant. A series of saccadic movements are made as the infant tracks an object across the visual field. A variety of hypotheses are available for this yet unexplained phenomena (Aslin, 1984), but by the end of the second week of postnatal life the neonate is capable of making reliable saccadic tracking movements. Dayton and Jones (1964) were the first to demonstrate that the eye movements of the infant are totally saccadic until the end of the second month. However, Aslin (1981), using a very slow moving target, found evidence of smooth pursuits beginning by the sixth week of age. Although the exact timing of the onset of smooth pursuits is debatable, the sequence is clear. Smooth pursuits tracking behaviors first occur in a horizontal direction, followed by vertical, then diagonal, and finally circular (Field, 1976; Haith, 1966; Pratt, 1954).

Depth Perception

Perception of depth involves the ability to judge the distance of an object from oneself. Williams (1983) categorized depth perception into "static" and "dynamic" components. Static depth perception involves making depth or distance judgments with regard to stationary objects. Dynamic depth perception requires one to make distance judgments about moving objects.

Concept 9.8 Perception of depth by the infant is a function of experience as well as maturation.

Static depth perception has been extensively investigated in infants through the now classic *visual-cliff* experiments by Gibson and Walk (1960), and Walk (1966). In their research design, infants and animals capable of self-produced locomotion were encouraged to crawl across a thick sheet of glass that contained a variety of depth cues (Figure 9.1). The experiments concluded that mobile infants, even when coaxed, would not crawl across the "deep end" to their mothers. More recently, Svejda and Schmidt (1979) assessed the cardiac responses of pre-locomotor infants (mean age of 6.9 months) and locomotor infants (mean age of 7.1 months) as they were lowered to the shallow or to the deep side of the cliff. Pre-locomotor infants exhibited little or no difference in heart rate levels when lowered to either side. However, locomotor infants showed significant increases in heart rate responses to both sides, but a "more marked acceleration" on the deep side. The results of this experiment tends to confirm the Held and Hein (1963) and Walk (1978)

Figure 9.1
The visual cliff

Glass only

Glass over patterned surface

Deep side

Shallow side

Floor pattern seen through glass

hypotheses that the development of depth perception is in part a function of experience. It also indicates that sensorimotor feedback through early locomotor experience is sufficient to account for a developmental shift on the visual cliff between pre-locomotor and locomotor infants. Whether sensorimotor experiences are a necessary condition is still uncertain.

A number of investigations into *dynamic depth perception* have been conducted with infants in recent years. The reaching responses of young infants presented with moving stimuli have been carefully studied by von Hofsten (1979, 1982, 1986). The results of his investigations clearly demonstrated that infants as young as five days of age make what appear to be purposeful, but poorly controlled, reaching movements toward moving objects. Dynamic depth perception appears to be present in rather sophisticated form by the fourth month of post-natal life. von Hofsten (1986) stated that:

> Thus it seems without doubt that shortly before four months of age the infant starts to be able to use also the purely visual mode of control whereby the seen position of the hand is related to the seen position of the object (p. 174).

It must be remembered that at this point the motor system lags behind the perceptual system. Movements toward an object, though purposeful, are crude, demonstrating poor integration between the visual and motor systems. Adult-like reaching behaviors do not appear until around the sixth month when differentiation of muscle groups and integration with sensory systems begin to conjoin.

Color Perception

A large number of studies have been conducted over the years to determine if infants perceive color and are able to distinguish among different colors. Much of the experimentation prior to the 1960s yielded confusing and often conflicting results. Out of this research, however, came the realization that the infant responds to the brightness (i.e., *chromatic intensity*) of the colors presented prior to responding to hue. Hershenson (1964) was the first to demonstrate this in infants, prompting a new wave of studies that attempted to control for the brightness factor. As cited by Cohen et al. (1979), Oster (1975) found that by 10 weeks of age infants perceive colors over a large portion of the visible color spectrum. Schaller (1975) also found similar results with 11- to 12-week-old infants. These two experiments clearly demonstrated that infants as young as 10 weeks of age have the ability to perceive color. We do not know if infants younger than 10 weeks perceive color. The amount of *rhodopsin and iodopsin* present in the rods and cones may be insufficient for color vision. Similarly, we do not know categorically if the color perception of the infant is identical to that of adults, but limited evidence favors this notion.

Concept 9.9   Infants tend to respond more to the chromatic intensity of color than to the actual hue itself.

Bornstein et al. (1976) demonstrated that 4-month-old infants were capable of discriminating between blue, green, yellow, and red. Another experiment by Bornstein et al. (1976) with 3-month-olds yielded similar results. It appears, therefore, that infants as young as 3 months of age do have the ability to make adult-like color discriminations. The question concerning the "favorite" color of infants is open to further speculation and study. Spears (1964) noted that it is clear that babies as young as 15 days prefer colors to non-colors (i.e., unpatterned whites and grays), and that they prefer shape to color.

Form Perception

A number of investigators have examined *form perception* in infants. Form perception is the ability to distinguish between shapes and to discriminate among a variety of patterns. Haith (1980) found that newborns placed in a darkened room would look for subtle shadows and edges. Moreover, Kessen et al. (1972), in a similar experiment, reported that newborns responded only to vertical high-contrast edges. However, Haith found that they could also respond to horizontal lines. Fantz et al. (1975) reported that newborns were able to perceive form and preferred curved lines over straight lines. Salapatek (1975) reported that other researchers examining neonatal responses to squares, circles, and triangles found that the infants tend to fixate on a single line or edge at one month of age, but spent much more time scanning the figures at two months of age. Salapatek (1975) drew three important conclusions from the abundance of research on form perception in the newborn:

> First, before 2 months of age visual attention appears to be captured by a single or limited number of features of a figure or pattern. Second, before approximately 1 to 2 months of age there is little evidence that the arrangement or pattern of figural elements plays any role in visual selection or memory. Third, before 1 to 2 months, there is little evidence that the line of sight is attracted by anything more than the greatest number or size of visible contour elements per unit area, regardless of type or arrangement of elements. (p. 226)

Concept 9.10   Complexity governs the infant's visual attending behaviors, in that the infant prefers shape to color, and prefers complex shapes to simpler ones.

Infants over 3 months of age appear to exhibit a variety of sophisticated abilities with regard to form perception. Cohen et al. (1979) reported that several investigators have determined that infants can discriminate one pattern from another even when the pattern is placed in a variety of arrangements. Furthermore, "the evidence is reasonably convincing that at some point within the first 6 months of life infants can perceive multiple forms and can respond to, and prefer, a change in pattern arrangement" (Cohen et al., 1979, p. 412). Fantz (1963) found that 2-month-old infants prefer looking at the human face over all other simple stimuli. Cohen (1979) reported that by 6 months of age infants can distinguish among two-dimensional photographs of human faces. Clearly the ability of the infant to discriminate between shapes and patterns develops rapidly during this period, and has reached rather sophisticated levels by the end of the first 6 months of postnatal life.

Auditory, Olfactory, and Gustatory Perception

Available research data concerning the development of auditory, olfactory, and gustatory perception in the human infant are much less complete than for the visual modality. As with vision, the auditory abilities do not unfold exclusively without the influences of the environment. Environmental conditions influence the extent of development of audition. The ear is structurally complete at birth, and the infant is capable of hearing just as soon as the amniotic fluid drains (usually within a day or two after birth). The fetus responds to sound before birth (Bernard & Sontag, 1947). These responses, however, may be in response to tactile sensations created by the vibrations produced (Aslin et al., 1983). At present we do not know if the fetus is capable of hearing sound.

Concept 9.11   Although less widely studied, infant auditory, olfactory, and tactile-kinesthetic perceptions also influence the process of motor development.

Research indicates that the newborn is less sensitive to sound than adults. Aslin et al. (1983) reported that the difference is at least 10 decibels. Sensitivity to sound improves with age, and infants as young as 6 months are more sensitive to high-frequency sounds than neonates (Trehub et al., 1980). Infant auditory perception may be adult-like by 2 years of age (Schneider et al., 1980). The infant can localize sounds at birth and reacts primarily to loudness and duration (Trehub et al., 1991).

Crude pitch discriminations have been demonstrated by Leventhal and Lipsett (1964) as early as the first 4 days of postnatal life. Definite responses to tonal differences are seen around the 3rd month, and the infant reacts with obvious pleasure to a parent's voice by the 5th month (Leventhal and Lipsett, 1964).

The research on olfactory and gustatory perception is sparse. It is difficult to separate the developmental sequence of smell and taste simply because the nose and mouth are closely connected, and stimuli applied to one are likely to affect the other. The newborn does, however, appear to react to certain odors, although this may be due more to pain caused by the pungent odors than to smell. Lipsett et al. (1963) demonstrated that newborns less than 24 hours old made definite responses when exposed to a highly offensive odor. Engen and Lipsett (1965) showed that infants as young as 32 hours were able to discriminate between two different odors. McFarlane (1975) in studying infants less than a week old found that they could discriminate between the mother's breast pad and a clean pad, with a clear preference for mother's pad. Not one of the infants, however, could discriminate between his or her mother's breast pad and that of another. It may not be until the second week that recognition of mother's smell is developed. Newborns react to taste, preferring sweet tastes to sour ones and sour tastes to bitter ones. Table 9.2 presents a summary of the major developmental aspects of infant auditory, gustatory, and olfactory perception.

Summary

The study of infant perception has intrigued researchers for years. We now know that the newborn, neonate, and young infant is much more perceptually aware and capable than previously thought. Newer techniques for observing and recording infant responses to various stimuli have been responsible for a shift in our assumptions about the perceptual capabilities of the very young. Observational assessment techniques that utilize film analysis, heart and respiration monitors, nonnutritive sucking devices, and electrical brain impulse recorders are making new inroads into our understanding of the perceptual world of the infant.

The visual world of the infant has been the most extensively studied perceptual modality. The newborn's eyes are structurally complete, but functionally immature. Rapid progress is seen in the acquisition of a vast array of visual perceptual abilities. Although it is difficult to pinpoint when these abilities emerge, it is possible to chart the sequence of acquisition of many visual perceptual abilities. (Generalized application of observations to all infants should be avoided, however.) The motor developmentalist is especially interested in the visual modality because of its close, often essential, link to voluntary movement. Much

Table 9.2 Developmental Aspect of Selected Infant Auditory, Olfactory, and Gustatory Abilities

Perceptual Quality	Selected Abilities	Approximate Age of Onset
Auditory Perception The ear is structurally complete at birth, and the newborn can respond to sound.	Responds to loud, sharp sounds	Prenatal
	Ability to localize sounds	Birth
	Reacts primarily to loudness and duration	Birth
	Crude pitch discrimination	1 to 4 days
	Responds to tonal differences	3 to 6 months
	Reacts with pleasure to parent's voice	5 to 6 months
	Adult-like	24 months
Olfactory Perception The olfactory mechanism is structurally complete at birth, and the newborn responds crudely to various odors.	Responds to odors	Birth
	Reduced sensitivity upon repeated application of the stimuli (habituation)	Neonate
	Distinguishes between pleasant and unpleasant odors	2–3 days
	Shows preference for mother's odor	2 weeks
	Discrimination abilities improve with practice	Infancy
Gustatory Perception The newborn reacts to variation in sweet, sour, and bitter tastes. Little research data are available on this modality.	Shows preference in tastes (prefers sweet to sour, sour to bitter)	Neonate

movement behavior is governed by our perceptions. Although the visual perceptual world of the infant develops rapidly, the motor system tends to lag behind. It is not until later infancy that the motor system begins to catch up and a matching of perceptual and motor data occurs.

These other sensory modalities (auditory, gustatory, and olfactory), although important, are less clearly understood in the infant. Furthermore, their link to the motor system, although significant, is less crucial than vision. Therefore, the matching of perceptual and motor data in the infant and young child will probably continue to be a topic of keen interest to researchers and educators alike.

Terms to Remember

Perception
Sensation
Consensual pupillary reflex
Non-nutritive sucking
Dishabituation
Evoked potentials
Contrast sensitivity
Habituation
Visual acuity
Accommodation
Peripheral vision
Binocular vision
Fixation
Tracking
Bifoveal fixation

Fusion
Visual fixation
Binocular tracking
Saccades
Depth perception
Static depth perception
Visual cliff
Dynamic depth perception
Color perception
Chromatic intensity
Rhodopsin
Form perception
Auditory perception
Olfactory perception
Gustatory perception

Critical Readings

Aslin, R. N. (1984). Motor aspects of visual development in infancy. In P. Salapatek and L. B. Cohen (Eds.), *Handbook of Infant Perception.* New York: Academic Press.

Bower, T. G. R. (1977). *The Perceptual World of the Child.* Cambridge, MA: Harvard University Press.

Cohen, L. B. et al. (1979). Infant visual perception. In J. D. Osofky (Ed.), *Handbook of Infant Development* (pp. 393–438).

Cratty, B. J. (1986). *Perceptual and Motor Development in Infants and Children* (Chapter 11). Englewood Cliffs, NJ: Prentice-Hall.

Sekuler, R., & Blake, R. (1985). *Perception.* New York: Alfred A. Knopf.

Wade, M. G., & Whiting, H. T. A. (Eds.) (1986). *Motor Development in Children: Aspects of Coordination and Control* (Section 4: Perception and Action). Dordrecht, The Netherlands: Martinus Nijhoff Publishers.

Williams, H. G. (1983). *Perceptual and Motor Development* (Chapter 4). Englewood Cliffs, NJ: Prentice-Hall.

SECTION III

CHILDHOOD

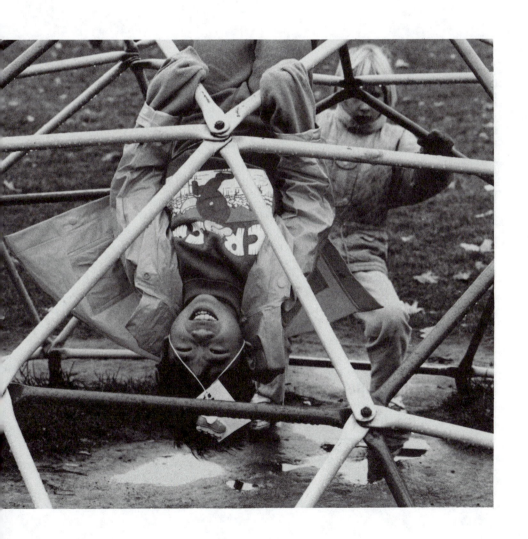

Chapter 10

Childhood Growth and Development

Key Concept: Development during the period of childhood is marked by steady, incremental changes in the cognitive, affective, and motor domains.

The period of childhood is marked by steady increases in height, weight, and muscle mass. Growth is not as rapid during this period as it is during infancy, and it slows gradually throughout childhood until the adolescent growth spurt. Childhood is divided here into the early childhood period of 2 to 6 years of age and the later childhood period from about 6 to 10 years of age. Figures 10.1 through 10.4 present height and weight growth charts for males and females from 2 to 18 years of age.

Figure 10.1
USA male stature by age percentiles: ages 2 to 18 years (*Source:* National Center for Health Statistics, U.S. Government)

Figure 10.2
USA female stature by age percentiles: ages 2 to 18 years (*Source:* National Center for Health Statistics, U.S. Government)

Growth in Early Childhood

During the early childhood years, growth in height and weight is not as rapid as it is during infancy. The growth rate decelerates slowly. By 4 years of age, the child has doubled his or her birth length, which represents only about one half the gain experienced during the first two years. The total amount of weight gained from 2 through 5 years of age is less than the amount gained during the first year of life. The growth process slows down after the first two years but maintains a constant rate until puberty. The annual height gain from the early childhood period to puberty is about 2 inches per year. Weight gains average 5 pounds per year. Early childhood, therefore, represents an ideal time for the child to develop and refine a wide variety of movement tasks ranging from the fundamental movements of early childhood to the sport skills of middle childhood.

Figure 10.3
USA male weight
by age percentiles:
ages 2 to 18 years
(*Source:* National
Center for Health
Statistics, U.S.
Government)

Concept 10.1 The rate of growth decelerates throughout early childhood resulting in average incremental gains in height and weight of about 2 inches and 5 pounds, respectively.

Gender differences may be seen in terms of height and weight, but they are minimal. The physiques of male and female preschoolers are remarkably similar when viewed from a posterior position, with boys being slightly taller and heavier. Boys have more muscle and bone mass than girls, and both show a gradual decrease in fatty tissue as they progress through the early childhood period. The proportion of muscle tissue remains fairly constant throughout early childhood at about 25 percent of total body weight (Eckert, 1987).

Figure 10.4

USA female weight by age percentiles: ages 2 to 18 years (*Source:* National Center for Health Statistics, U.S. Government)

Body proportions change markedly during early childhood because of the various growth rates of the body. The chest gradually becomes larger than the abdomen, and the stomach gradually protrudes less. By the time preschoolers reach first grade, their body proportions more closely resemble those of older children.

Bone growth during early childhood is dynamic, and the skeletal system is particularly vulnerable to malnutrition, fatigue, and illness. The bones ossify at a rapid rate during early childhood and have been shown to be retarded by as much as three years in growth in deprived children.

The brain is about 75 percent of its adult weight by age 3, and almost 90 percent by age 6. The midbrain is almost fully developed at birth, but it is not until age 4 that the cerebral cortex is completely developed.

The development of myelin around the neurons (*myelination*) permits the transmission of nerve impulses and is not complete at birth. At birth many nerves lack myelin, but greater amounts of myelin are laid down along nerve fibers as the child matures. Myelination is largely complete by the end of the early childhood period, allowing for the complete transference of nerve impulses throughout the nervous system. A child's movement patterns are increasingly complex following myelination of the cerebellum.

The sensory apparatus is still developing during the preschool years. The eyeball does not reach its full size until about 12 years of age. The *macula* of the retina is not completely developed until around the sixth year, and the young child is generally farsighted. Preschool children have more taste buds than adults. They are generously distributed throughout the insides of the throat and cheeks as well as on the tongue, causing greater sensitivity to taste. The eustachian tube, which connects the middle ear with the throat, is shorter and flatter in the child, causing greater sensitivity to ear infections and fluid retention.

Development in Early Childhood

Play is what young children do when they are not eating, sleeping, or complying with the wishes of adults. Play occupies most of their waking hours, and it may literally be viewed as the child's equivalent of work. Children's play is the primary mode by which they learn about their bodies and movement capabilities. It also serves as an important facilitator of cognitive and affective growth in the young child, as well as an important means of developing both fine and gross motor skills.

Young children are actively involved in enhancing their cognitive skills in a variety of ways. These early years are a period of important cognitive development and have been termed the "preoperational thought phase" by Piaget. During this time children develop cognitive functions that will eventually result in logical thinking and concept formulation. Young children are not capable of thinking from any point of view other than their own. They are extremely egocentric and view almost everything in terms of themselves. The perceptions of preschoolers dominate their thinking, and what is experienced at a given moment has great influence on them. During this preconceptual phase of cognitive development, seeing is, literally, believing. In the thinking and logic of preschool children, their conclusions need no justifications. Children at this age are unable to reconstruct their thoughts and show others how they arrived at their conclusions. Play serves as a vital means by which higher cognitive structures are gradually developed. It provides a multitude of settings and variables for promoting cognitive growth.

Affective development is also dramatic during the early childhood years. During this period children are involved in the two crucial social-emotional tasks of developing a sense of autonomy and a sense of initiative. Autonomy is expressed through a growing sense of independence, which may be seen in a child's delight in answering no to almost any direct question. For instance, even if a child wants to play outside he or she will often refuse an invitation to do so. This may be viewed as an expression of a new sense of independence and an ability to manipulate some factors in the environment rather than as an expression of sheer disobedience. A way in which to avoid this natural autonomous reaction is to rephrase the question "Do you want to go outside?" to form a positive statement such as "Let's go play outdoors." In this way, the child is not confronted with a direct yes-or-no choice. Care must be taken, however, to give children abundant situations in which expressions of their autonomy are reasonable and proper.

A young child's expanding sense of initiative is seen in curiosity, exploration, and very active behavior. Children engage in new experiences, such as climbing, jumping, running, and throwing objects, for their own sake and for the sheer joy of sensing and knowing what they are capable of doing. Failure to develop initiative and autonomy leads to feelings of shame, worthlessness, and guilt. The establishment of a stable self-concept is crucial to proper affective development in a young child because it has an effect on both cognitive and psychomotor functions.

Through the medium of play, young children develop a wide variety of fundamental locomotor, manipulative, and stability abilities. With a stable and positive self-concept, the gain in control over musculature is a smooth one. The timid, cautious, and measured movements of the 2-to-3-year-old gradually give way to the confident, eager, and often reckless abandon of the 4-and-5-year-old. Vivid imaginations make it possible for young children to jump from "great heights," climb "high mountains," leap over "raging rivers," and run "faster" than an assorted variety of "wild beasts."

Children of preschool age are rapidly expanding their horizons. They are asserting their personalities, developing their abilities, and testing their limits as well as the limits of their family and others around them. In short, they are pushing out into the world in many complex and wondrous ways. Caretakers must understand their developmental characteristics, their limitations, and their potentials. Only in this way can we effectively structure developmental experiences that truly reflect children's needs and interests and are within their levels of ability.

The following developmental characteristics represent a synthesis of findings from a wide variety of sources and are presented here to provide a more complete view of the total child during the early childhood years.

Physical and Motor Development Characteristics

1. Boys and girls range from about 33 to 47 inches in height and from 25 to 53 pounds in weight.
2. Perceptual-motor abilities are rapidly developing, but confusion often exists in body, directional, temporal, and spatial awareness.
3. Good bladder and bowel control are generally established by the end of this period, but accidents still occur.
4. Children during this period are rapidly developing fundamental movement abilities in a variety of motor skills. Bilateral movements such as skipping, however, often present more difficulty than unilateral movements.
5. Children are active and energetic and would often rather run than walk, but they still need frequent short rest periods.
6. Motor abilities are developed to the point that the children are beginning to learn how to dress themselves, although they may need help straightening and fastening articles of clothing.
7. The body functions and processes become well regulated. A state of physiological homeostasis (stability) becomes well established.
8. The body builds of both boys and girls are remarkably similar. A back view of boys and girls reveals no readily observable structural differences.
9. Fine motor control is not fully established, although gross motor control is developing rapidly.
10. The eyes are not generally ready for extended periods of close work due to farsightedness.

Cognitive Development Characteristics

1. There is constantly increasing ability to express thoughts and ideas verbally.
2. A fantastic imagination enables imitation of both actions and symbols with little concern for accuracy or the proper sequencing of events.
3. There is continuous investigation and discovery of new symbols that have a primarily personal reference.
4. The ''how'' and ''why'' of the child's actions are learned through almost constant play.
5. This is a preoperational thought phase of development, resulting in a period of transition from self-satisfying behavior to fundamental socialized behaviors.

Affective Development Characteristics

1. During this phase children are egocentric and assume that everyone thinks the way they do. As a result, they often seem to be quarrelsome and reluctant to share and get along with others.
2. They are often fearful of new situations, shy, self-conscious, and unwilling to leave the security of that which is familiar.
3. They are learning to distinguish right from wrong and are beginning to develop consciences.
4. Two- and 4-year-old children are often seen to be unusual and irregular in their behavior, while those who are 3 and 5 are often viewed as stable and conforming in their behavior.
5. Self-concept is rapidly developing. Wise guidance, success-oriented experiences, and positive reinforcement are especially important during these years.

Implications for the Developmental Movement Program

1. Plenty of opportunity for gross motor play must be offered in both undirected and directed settings.
2. Movement experiences should stress movement exploration and problem-solving activities to maximize the child's creativity and desire to explore.
3. The movement education program should include plenty of positive reinforcement to encourage the establishment of a healthy self-concept and to reduce the fear of failure.
4. Stress should be placed on developing a variety of fundamental locomotor, manipulative, and stability abilities, progressing from the simple to the complex as the child becomes "ready."
5. Interests and abilities of boys and girls are similar, with no need for separate activities during this period.
6. Plenty of activities designed specifically to enhance perceptual-motor functioning are necessary.
7. Advantage should be taken of the child's great imagination through the use of an assortment of activities, including drama and imagery.
8. Because of their often awkward and inefficient movements, be sure to gear movement experiences to their maturity levels.
9. Provide a wide variety of activities that require object handling and eye-hand coordination.
10. Begin to incorporate bilateral and crosslateral activities such as galloping and skipping after unilateral movements such as hopping have been fairly well established.

11. Encourage children to take an active part in the movement education program by "showing" and "telling" others what they can do to help overcome tendencies to be shy and self-conscious.
12. Activities should stress arm, shoulder, and upper body involvement.
13. Mechanically correct execution in a wide range of fundamental movements is the primary goal, without emphasis on standards of performance.
14. Do not stress coordination in conjunction with speed and agility.
15. Poor habits of posture are beginning. Reinforce good posture with positive statements.
16. Provide convenient access to toilet facilities and encourage the children to accept this responsibility on their own.
17. Provide for individual differences and allow for children to progress at their own rates.
18. Establish standards for acceptable behavior and abide by them. Provide wise guidance in the establishment of a sense of doing what is right and proper instead of what is wrong and unacceptable.
19. The developmental movement program should be prescriptive and based on each individual's readiness level.
20. A multisensory approach should be utilized; that is, one in which a wide variety of experiences are incorporated, using several sensory modalities.

Growth in Later Childhood

The period from the 6th through the 10th years of childhood is typified by slow but steady increases in height and weight and progress toward greater organization of the sensory and motor systems. Changes in body build are slight during these years. Childhood is more a time of lengthening and filling out prior to the prepubertal growth spurt that occurs around the 11th year for girls and the 13th year for boys. Although these years are characterized by gradual physical growth, the child makes rapid gains in learning and functions at increasingly mature levels in the performance of games and sports. This period of slow growth gives the child time to get used to his or her body and is an important factor in the typically dramatic improvement seen in coordination and motor control during the childhood years. The gradual change in size and the close relationship maintained between bone and tissue development may be important factors in increased levels of functioning.

Differences between the growth patterns of boys and girls are minimal during the middle years. Both have greater limb growth than trunk growth, but boys tend to have longer legs, arms, and standing heights during childhood. Likewise, girls tend to have greater hip widths and thigh sizes during this period. There is relatively little difference in physique or weight exhibited until the onset of the preadolescent period. Figures 10.5 and 10.6 depict this concept using 1973 data. Very little has changed since then according to current estimates (Malina & Bouchard, 1991). Therefore, in most cases, girls and boys should be able to participate together in activities.

During childhood there is very slow growth in brain size. The size of the skull remains nearly the same although there is a broadening and a lengthening of the head toward the end of childhood.

Concept 10.3   Growth in height and weight during later childhood is slow and steady, representing a time of lengthening and filling out prior to puberty.

Figure 10.5
Mean height of U.S. children by age and gender (*Source:* U.S. Department of Health, Education and Welfare, DHEW Publication No.— HSM-73–1605, January 1973)

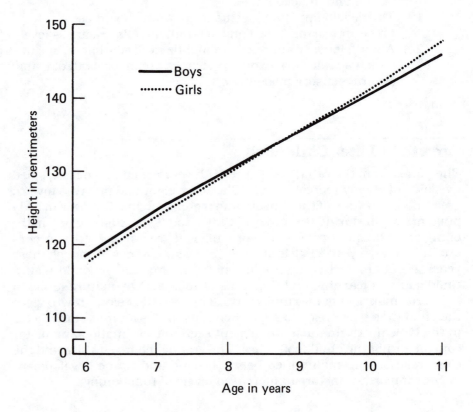

Perceptual abilities during childhood become increasingly refined. The sensorimotor apparatus is working in ever greater harmony so that by the end of this period the child can perform numerous sophisticated skills. Striking of a pitched ball, for example, improves with age and practice due to improved visual acuity, tracking abilities, reaction and movement time, and sensorimotor integration. A key to maximum development of more mature growth patterns in the child is utilization. Practice and experimentation with the maturing perceptual abilities will enhance the process of integration with the motor structures. Failure to have the opportunity for practice, instruction, and encouragement during this period will prevent many individuals from acquiring the perceptual and motor information needed to perform skillful movement activities.

Development in Later Childhood

Children in the elementary school years are generally happy, stable, eager, and able to assume responsibilities. They are able to cope with new situations and are anxious to learn more about themselves and their expanding world. Primary grade children take another big step when they enter first grade. Although first grade rarely represents a child's first separation from the home for a regularly scheduled, extended block of time, it is the first step out of the secure play environment of the home, nursery school, or day care center, into the world of older children and

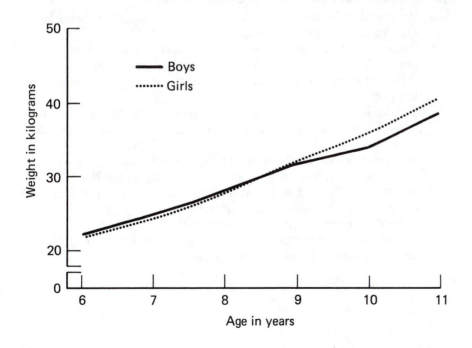

Figure 10.6
Mean weight of U.S. children by age and gender (*Source:* U.S. Department of Health, Education and Welfare, DHEW Publication No.—HSM-73–1605, January 1973)

adults. Entering a school represents the first time that many children are placed in group situations in which they are not the center of attention. It is a time when sharing, concern for others, and respect for the rights and responsibilities of others are established. Kindergarten is a readiness time in which to make the gradual transition from an egocentric, child-centered play world to the group-oriented world of adult concepts and logic. In the first grade, the first formal demands for cognitive understanding are made. The major milestone of the first- and second-grader is learning how to read at a reasonable level. The 6-year-old is generally developmentally ready for the important task of "breaking the code" and learning to read. The child is also developing the first real understanding of time, money, and numerous other cognitive concepts. By the second grade, children should be well able to meet and surmount the broader array of cognitive, affective, and psychomotor tasks placed before them.

The following is a listing of the general developmental characteristics of the child from age 6 to 10. It is presented here in order to provide a more complete view of the total child and represents a synthesis of current findings.

Concept 10.4 Boys and girls are similar in their growth patterns, with limb growth being greater than trunk growth throughout childhood.

Physical and Motor Development Characteristics

1. Boys and girls range from about 44 to 60 inches in height and 44 to 90 pounds in weight.
2. Growth is slow especially from age 8 to the end of this period. There is a slow but steady pace of increments, unlike the more rapid gains in height and weight during the preschool years.
3. The body begins to lengthen with an annual gain in height of only 2 to 3 inches and an annual gain in weight of only 3 to 6 pounds.
4. The cephalocaudal (head to toe) and proximodistal (center to periphery) principles of development, in which the large muscles of the body are considerably more developed than the small muscles, are quite apparent.
5. Girls are generally about a year ahead of boys in physiological development, and separate interests begin to emerge toward the end of this period.

6. Hand preference is firmly established with about 85 percent preferring the right hand and about 15 percent preferring the left.
7. Reaction time is slow, causing difficulty with eye-hand and eye-foot coordination at the beginning of this period. By the end they are generally well established.
8. Both boys and girls are full of energy but often possess low endurance levels and tire easily. Responsiveness to training, however, is great.
9. The visual perceptual mechanisms are fully established by the end of this period.
10. Children are often farsighted during this period and are not ready for extended periods of close work.
11. Most fundamental movement abilities have the potential to be well defined by the beginning of this period.
12. Basic skills necessary for successful play become well developed.
13. Activities involving the eyes and limbs develop slowly. Such activities as volleying or striking a pitched ball and throwing require considerable practice for mastery.
14. This period marks a transition from refining fundamental movement abilities to the establishment of transitional movement skills in lead-up games and athletic skills.

Cognitive Development Characteristics

1. Attention span is generally short at the beginning of this period but gradually extends. However, boys and girls of this age will often spend hours on activities that are of great interest to them.
2. They are eager to learn and to please adults but need assistance and guidance in making decisions.
3. Children have good imaginations and display extremely creative minds; however, self-consciousness seems to become a factor toward the end of this period.
4. They are often interested in television, computers, video games, and reading.
5. They are not capable of abstract thinking and deal best with concrete examples and situations during the beginning of this period. More abstract cognitive abilities are evident by the end of this period.
6. Children are intellectually curious and anxious to know "why."

Affective Development Characteristics

1. Interests of boys and girls are similar at the beginning of this period but soon begin to diverge.
2. The child is self-centered and plays poorly in large groups for extended periods of time during the primary years, although small group situations are handled well.
3. The child is often aggressive, boastful, self-critical, over-reactive, and accepts defeat and winning poorly.
4. There is an inconsistent level of maturity; the child is often less mature at home than in school.
5. The child is responsive to authority, "fair" punishment, discipline, and reinforcement.
6. Children are adventurous and eager to be involved with a friend or group of friends in "dangerous" or "secret" activities.
7. The child's self-concept becomes firmly established.

Implications for the Developmental Movement Program

1. There should be opportunities for children to refine fundamental movement abilities in the areas of locomotion, manipulation, and stability to a point where they are fluid and efficient.
2. Children need help in making the transition from the fundamental movement phase to the specialized movement phase.
3. Acceptance and affirmation tell children that they have stable and secure places in their schools and homes.
4. Abundant opportunities for encouragement and positive reinforcement from adults are necessary to promote continued development of positive self-concepts.
5. Opportunities and encouragement to explore and experiment through movement with their bodies and objects in the environment enhances perceptual-motor efficiency.
6. There should be exposure to experiences in which progressively greater amounts of responsibility are introduced to promote self-reliance.
7. Children learn to adjust to the rougher ways of the playground and neighborhood without becoming rough or crude themselves.
8. Opportunities for gradual introduction to group and team activities should be provided at the proper time.
9. Story plays, imaginary, and mimetic activities may be effectively incorporated into the program during the primary years because the children's imaginations are still vivid.

10. Activities that incorporate the use of music and rhythmics are enjoyable at this level and are valuable in enhancing fundamental movement abilities, creativity, and a basic understanding of the components of music and rhythm.

11. Children at this level learn best through active participation. Integration of academic concepts with movement activities provides an effective avenue for reinforcing academic concepts in science, mathematics, social studies, and the language arts.

12. Activities that involve climbing and hanging are beneficial to develop the upper torso and should be included in the program.

13. Discuss play situations involving such topics as taking turns, fair play, not cheating, and other universal values as a means of establishing a more complete sense of right or wrong.

14. Begin to stress accuracy, form, and skill in the performance of movement skills.

15. Encourage children to think before they engage in an activity. Help them recognize potential hazards as a means of reducing their often reckless behavior.

16. Encourage small-group activities followed by larger-group activities and team sport experience.

17. Posture is important. Activities need to stress proper body alignment.

18. Use of rhythmic activities to refine coordination is desirable.

19. Specialized movement skills are developed and refined toward the end of this period. Plenty of opportunity for practice, encouragement, and selective instruction is important.

20. Participation in youth sport activities that are developmentally appropriate and geared to the needs and interests of children should be encouraged.

Factors Affecting Child Growth and Development

Growth is not an independent process. Although heredity sets the limits of growth, environmental factors play an important role in the extent to which these limits are reached. The degree to which these factors affect motor development is not clear and needs further study. Nutrition, exercise, and physical activity are major factors affecting growth.

Nutrition

The potentially harmful effects of poor nutrition during the prenatal period were highlighted earlier. Among the factors influencing physical development during the prenatal period, nutrition is the most important. Numerous investigations have provided clear evidence that dietary deficiencies can have very harmful effects on growth during infancy and childhood. The extent of growth retardation obviously depends on the severity, duration, and time of onset of undernourishment. For example, if severe chronic malnutrition occurs during the child's first four years, there is little hope of catching up to one's age-mates in terms of mental development, because the critical brain growth period has passed.

Concept 10.5   Prolonged dietary deficiencies and excesses can have a serious impact on the growth patterns of children.

The physical growth process can be interrupted by malnutrition at any time between infancy and adolescence. Malnutrition may serve also as a mediating condition for certain diseases that affect physical growth. For example, lack of vitamin D in a diet can result in *rickets,* a softening and deformity of the bones that occurs as a result of lime salts in newly formed bones. Vitamin B-12 deficiencies may cause *pellagra* which is characterized by skin lesions, gastrointestinal, mitosal and neurologic symptoms. Chronic lack of vitamin C may lead to *scurvy,* a disease characterized by loss of energy, joint pains, anemia, and a tendency toward epiphyseal fractures. All are relatively rare in most modern developed countries, but the effects of *kwashiorkor,* a debilitating disease, are seen in many parts of the world where there is a general lack of food and good nutrition. In the child with kwashiorkor, growth retardation can be expected as well as a large, puffed-belly, sores on the body, and diarrhea.

Studies indicate that children suffering from *chronic malnutrition,* particularly during infancy and early childhood, never completely catch up to the growth norms for their age levels and suffer from what is known as *growth retardation.* This is apparent in developing nations where adult height and weight norms are considerably lower than those for industrialized nations. Nutritional status is linked to income level. Growth retardation can be found in all ethnic groups but its prevalence varies with sex, ethnic origin, and income level. Centers for Disease Control reported that almost 16 percent of infants from low-income families were anemic (Yip, 1989). Walter (1989) reported that anemic infants were significantly delayed in attaining the motor milestones typical of that age period. In fact, the American Academy of Pediatrics recommends that infant formula be iron fortified.

Popular opinion has it that children of low-income families generally have poor diets simply because food of low nutritional value is purchased. This simply is not true. The results of the Preschool Nutrition Survey (Owen et al., 1974) indicated that the "feeding style" of low-income families is important. The quantity of food available to all members is less in low-income families, and low-income parents tend to be more permissive about the eating habits of their children. The survey revealed that the quantity of food available increased with income level, and permissiveness about eating decreased.

Dietary excesses also affect the growth of children. In affluent countries, obesity is a major problem. Research has proposed an interesting hypothesis linking obesity and its intractability to dietary habits established during infancy and the preadolescent period. There is considerable concern among professionals over the high consumption of refined starches and sugars by children. The constant barrage of television commercials loudly extolling one junk food or another, the "fast food" addiction of millions, and the use of non-nutritive edibles as a reinforcer for good behavior all may have an effect on the nutritional status of children. The critical difference between adequate and inadequate nutrition has not been identified. The individual nature of the child, with his or her own unique biochemical composition, makes it difficult to pinpoint where adequate nutrition ends and malnutrition begins. It is, however, a serious question that needs further exploration. The welfare of a vast number of children is at stake.

Exercise and Injury

One of the basic principles of physical activity is the concept of use and disuse. According to this principle, a muscle that is used will *hypertrophy* (i.e., increase in size) and a muscle that is not used will *atrophy* (i.e., decrease in size). Anyone who has had a limb placed in a cast for several weeks knows about atrophy. In children, activity definitely promotes muscle development. Although the number of muscle fibers does not increase, the size of the fibers does increase. Muscles respond and adapt to greater amounts of stress. Maturation alone will not account for increases in muscle mass. An environment that promotes vigorous physical activity on the part of the child will do much to promote muscle development. Active children have less body fat in proportion to lean body mass. They do not have more muscle fibers; they simply have more muscle mass per fiber, and smaller fat cells.

Concept 10.6   Physical activity generally has a positive effect on growth, except in cases of excessive levels of exercise.

Although it is doubtful that an individual's basic physique can be altered, it is certain that improvements within limits can be made. A popular method of classification of adult physique was developed by Sheldon et al. (1940), and later extended to children by Peterson (1967). This much-used system classifies individuals on the basis of fat, muscle, and bone length. An *endomorphic* physique is one that is soft and rounded in physical features (pear shape). The *mesomorphic* physique is well muscled, with broad shoulders, narrow waist, and thick chest (V shape). The *ectomorphic* physique is characterized by a tall, thin, lean look (angular shape).

Within each classification a person is rated on a scale of 1 to 7, with 1 representing the least amount of a characteristic and 7 the most of a characteristic. Therefore, the three-number sequence of 1-7-1 would represent a person very low on endomorphy, very high on mesomorphy, and very low on ectomorphy. A 2-3-6 would typify a person low on endomorphy, with some mesomorphic characteristics, and high on ectomorphy (perhaps a high jumper, or middle distance runner). Sheldon et al. (1954) found that males could typically be classified at the middle of the scale (i.e., 3-4-4 or 4-4-3) and females rated higher in endomorphy and lower in mesomorphy (i.e., 5-3-3).

Although physical activity generally has positive effects on the growth of children, it may have some negative effects if carried to the extreme. Seefeldt and Gould (1980) indicated that several studies have reported reduced growth rates in the height and weight of young athletes involved in moderate to intensive training programs, but that the controls in these investigations were weak at best. Clarke (1974) and Tipton and Tcheng (1970), however, did report retarded growth in the height and weight of wrestlers. This was probably due to the unusually strenuous nature of training for this sport. Caine and Lindner (1984) raised the question of *growth plate injuries* to young long-distance runners. They reported that the literature is clear on the dangers of overusing a muscle. Overuse may result in epiphyseal injuries, and growth plate damage. Much more research needs to be conducted on the beneficial limits of strenuous physical activity during childhood. The critical point separating harmful and beneficial activity is not clear. The rapid rise of youth sports and the intensity of training leave many unanswered questions. We can, however, assume that strenuous activity carried out over an extended period of time may result in injury to muscle and bone tissue of the child. "Swimmer's shoulder," "tennis elbow," "runner's knees," and stress fractures are but a few of the ailments plaguing children who have exceeded their developmental limits. Exercise and activity programs for children must be supervised carefully. The potential benefits to the growth process are great, but individual limitations must be accommodated.

Concept 10.7   The critical line between beneficial and harmful amounts of physical exertion is not clear.

In summary, little evidence exists to support the notion that regular exercise has a direct effect on the length of bone growth (Malina and Bouchard, 1991). Bone growth is a hormonal process that is unaffected by activity levels. Exercise does, however, increase bone width and promote *bone mineralization,* which make for stronger, less brittle bones. Stress within the limits of the particular individual is beneficial to the bones. Chronic inactivity, on the other hand, has harmful effects on bone growth and may result in growth retardation.

Physical activity stimulates bone mineralization and muscle development and helps retard the depositing of fat. The vast majority of physical activity and athletic programs for children, not including marathon running, wrestling, and other heavy strength and endurance activities, have beneficial effects. Injury, whether acute or chronic, may have negative effects on growth, depending on the severity and location. Refer to Chapter 12, Physical Development of Children, for a further discussion of health-related fitness training.

Concept 10.8   Age of onset, duration, and severity determine how a variety of activity and nutrition factors influence later development.

Illness and Climate

A number of other factors influence the growth process, including illness and disease, climate, emotions, and handicapping conditions.

The standard childhood illnesses (chicken pox, colds, measles, and mumps) do not have a marked effect on the growth of the child. The extent to which illnesses and diseases may retard growth is dependent on duration, severity, and timing. Krogman (1980) reported that "there is some reason to use age three years as a cut-off point: before the age of three years the registry of health damage may be more marked and rebound may be slower" (p. 144). Often, the interaction of malnutrition and illnesses in the child makes it difficult to accurately determine the specific cause of growth retardation. However, the combination of conditions puts the child at risk and greatly enhances the probability of measurable growth deficits.

A great deal of literature has reported the differences in height, weight, and onset of adolescence among individuals of varying climates (Krogman, 1980). The interacting effects of nutrition and health as well as possible genetic differences (e.g., when comparing black Africans with white Americans) make it impossible to demonstrate a direct causal relationship between climate and physical growth. The available data suggest that American children born and raised in the tropics have more linear physiques, but grow and mature at a slower rate than American children raised in more temperate climates. It is however, difficult to relate climatic conditions to specific factors of growth and maturation. As noted by Malina and Bouchard:

> The effects of climate extend beyond temperature and include other components such as relative humidity, precipitation, and topography, as well as the effects on food production, availability of suitable conditions for infectious and parasitic disease vectors, and so on (p. 412).

Secular Trends

A positive *secular trend* reflects the tendency for children to be taller, heavier, and more mature at an earlier age than children one or more generations ago. The trend for secular increases is not universal. Increases in growth, maturation, and physical performance levels have been demonstrated in most developed countries. Developing nations throughout the world, however, have not demonstrated secular increases and in some cases have even shown decreases in stature. There may be many reasons for this, but it is largely a reflection of the limited improvements in lifestyle and nutritional habits from one generation to another.

Malina (1978) reported that secular changes in length and weight are slight at birth but become progressively more pronounced until puberty, when there is again a lessening of differences. The largest differences in height and weight are found from age 11 to 15 (the pubertal years) and are apparent across all socioeconomic classes and races in developed countries.

Concept 10.9 Although secular trends appear to have ceased in North America, this is not a universal phenomena.

Children today mature more rapidly than they did 100 years ago. The age at menarche, for example, decreased in European populations over the past century from an estimated range of 15.5 to 17.4 years to between 12.5 and 14 years (Eveleth and Tanner, 1976). Although secular trends in the maturation of boys are no doubt present, maturity data for them are lacking. It may be noted, however, that the average age at which voices begin to change for members of boys' choirs today is considerably lower (about 13 years) than that estimated for boys performing in choirs more than 100 years ago (about 18 years) (Daw, 1974).

Malina and Bouchard (1991) reported that the secular trend in size and maturation in the United States and many other developed nations has stopped. There have been few indications of secular trends in height, weight, and maturation in the past 20 years. This is probably due largely to the elimination of growth-inhibiting factors and a peaking of improved nutritional and health conditions.

Summary

Growth during childhood decelerates from the rapid pace characteristic of the first two years. The slow but steady increases in height and weight during childhood provide the child with an opportunity to coordinate perceptual and motor information. The child has time to lengthen, fill out, and gain control over his or her world. Numerous factors, however, can interrupt the normal developmental process. Nutritional deficiencies and excesses may influence growth patterns and have lasting effects on the child, depending on the severity and duration of the poor nutrition. Severe and prolonged illness also interrupts the growth process.

The effects of acute and chronic exercise at low and high intensity levels is of great interest to researchers and youth sport coaches. Physical exercise has a positive influence on the growth process. Little evidence exists to support the claim that physical activity can be harmful to children, except in cases of extreme training requirements. The problem, however, is knowing when "extremes" have been reached for each individual child. Climatic factors have also been shown to accelerate or decelerate growth in children. North American children today are taller and heavier than their counterparts of 100 years ago. Definite secular trends can be seen in many but not all cultures. Differences in lifestyle and dietary circumstances play an important role in the presence or absence of secular trends.

Terms to Remember

Myelination
Macula
Atrophy
Rickets
Pellagra
Scurvy
Kwashiorkor
Chronic malnutrition

Growth retardation
Hypertrophy
Endomorphic
Mesomorphic
Ectomorphic
Growth plate injuries
Bone mineralization
Secular trend

Critical Readings

Allen, K. E., & Marotz, L. (1989). *Developmental Profiles: Birth to Six* (Chapters 5–6). Albany, NY: Delmar.

Gabbard, C. (1992). *Lifelong Motor Development* (Chapters 2–4). Dubuque, IA: Wm. C. Brown.

Gallahue, D. L. (1993). *Developmental Physical Education for Today's Children.* Dubuque, IA: Brown & Benchmark.

Gallahue, D. L. (1993). Motor development and movement skill acquisition in early childhood education. In B. Spoder (Ed.), *Handbook of Research on the Education of Young Children* (pp. 24–41). New York: Macmillan.

Malina, R. M., & Bouchard, C. (1991). *Growth, Maturation and Physical Activity* (Chapters 4–10). Champaign, IL: Human Kinetics.

Seifert, K. L. (1993). Cognitive development in early childhood education. In B. Spoder (Ed.), *Handbook of Research on the Education of Young Children* (pp. 9–23). New York: Macmillan.

Time-Life, Successful Parenting Series. (1987). *Developing Your Child's Potential.* Alexandria, VA: Time-Life Books.

Time-Life, Successful Parenting Series. (1987). *Your Growing Child.* Alexandria, VA: Time-Life Books.

Walter, T. et al. (1989). Iron deficiency anemia: Adverse effects on infant motor development. *Pediatrics, 84,* 1, 7–17.

Yip, R. (1989). Iron nutritional status defined. In L. J. Filer (Ed.), Dietary Iron: *Birth to Two Years* (pp. 19–36). New York: Raven Press.

Chapter 11

Fundamental Movement Abilities

CHAPTER COMPETENCIES

Upon completion of this chapter you should be able to:

- *Compare and contrast intertask and intratask developmental sequences in selected fundamental movement skills*
- *Categorize performer's movement into developmental stages*
- *Demonstrate observational assessment skill in a variety of fundamental movement patterns*
- *Discuss the uses of a developmental sequence checklist for assessing motor development*
- *Distinguish between motor problems that students can assess and those they cannot*
- *Identify motor behavior characteristics of children who developmentally lag in motor skills*
- *Discuss the concept of a developmental sequence of fundamental movement skill acquisition*
- *Describe the meaning of the "initial," "elementary," and "mature" stages within the fundamental movement phase*
- *Distinguish between "among-child differences," "between-pattern differences," and "within-pattern differences" in movement skill acquisition*
- *Devise a fundamental movement observational assessment checklist as an individual or group evaluative tool*
- *Critically analyze the influences of opportunities for practice, encouragement, and instruction on the acquisition of fundamental movement abilities*

Key Concept: Although age-related, the acquisition of mature fundamental movement skills is not age-dependent because of numerous factors within the task itself, the individual, and the environment.

As children approach their second birthdays, marked changes can be observed in how they relate to their surroundings. By the end of the second year, they have mastered the rudimentary movement abilities that are developed during infancy. These movement abilities form the basis on which each child develops or refines the fundamental movement patterns of early childhood and the specialized movement skills of later childhood and adolescence. Children are no longer immobilized by their basic inability to move about freely or by the confines of their cribs or playpens. They are now able to explore the movement potentials of their bodies as they move through space (*locomotion*). They no longer have to maintain a relentless struggle against the force of gravity but are gaining increased control over their musculature in opposition to gravity (*stability*). They no longer have to be content with the crude and ineffective reaching, grasping, and releasing of objects characteristic of infancy but are rapidly developing the ability to make controlled and precise contact with objects in their environment (*manipulation*).

Young children are involved in the process of developing and refining fundamental movement abilities in a wide variety of stability, locomotor, and manipulative movements. This means that they should be involved in a series of coordinated and developmentally sound experiences designed to enhance knowledge of the body and its potential for movement. *Movement pattern* development is not specifically concerned with developing high degrees of skill in a limited number of movement situations, but rather with developing acceptable levels of proficiency and efficient body mechanics in a wide variety of movement situations. A *fundamental movement* involves the basic elements of that particular movement only. It does not include such things as the individual's style or personal peculiarities in performance. It does not emphasize the combining of a variety of fundamental movements into complex skills such as the lay-up shot in basketball or a floor exercise routine in gymnastics. Each movement pattern is first considered in relative isolation from all others, and then linked with others in a variety of combinations. The locomotor movements of running, jumping, and leaping, or the manipulative movements of throwing, catching, kicking, and trapping, are examples of fundamental movement abilities that are first mastered separately by the child. These movements are then gradually combined and enhanced in a variety of ways to become sport skills. The basic elements of a fundamental movement should be the same for all children.

The development of fundamental movement abilities is basic to the motor development of children. A wide assortment of movement experiences provide them with a wealth of information on which to base their perceptions of themselves and the world about them.

Developmental Sequence of Fundamental Movements

With the renewed interest in the study of motor development that began in the 1960s, several scales appeared that illustrated a relationship between age and motor performance. Johnson (1962) using a large sample of boys and girls from grades one through six, found that the mean scores on a variety of motor performance items showed a definite upward trend until the fifth grade. Cratty and Martin (1969) presented age-related sequences of acquisition for a variety of locomotor, manipulative, and perceptual abilities of 365 children ranging in age from 4 to 12 years. Williams's (1970) summary of the movement abilities of children between 3 and 6 years old revealed more advanced forms of movement with increases in age. Sinclair (1973) studied the motor development of 2- to 6-year-old children. The results of her longitudinal film analysis of 25 movement tasks at 6-month intervals lent further support to the basic assumption that movement is a developing process during the early childhood years.

Concept 11.1   Children have the developmental potential to be at the mature stage of most fundamental movement skills by about age six.

These normative studies of motor development are interesting and informative about the quantity or outcome of movement in that they tell "how far," "how fast," and "how many." They fail, however, to provide information about *qualitative change* that occurs as the child progresses toward more mature form. As a result, a number of investigators, all using film and computer techniques to analyze the intraskill aspects of a variety of fundamental movement patterns, began to collect data leading to a stage concept of motor development during early childhood (Wild, 1938; Halverson & Roberton, 1966, 1979; Seefeldt, 1972). Seefeldt and Haubenstricker (1976), and several others conducted important investigations into the *intraskill sequences* of a variety of fundamental movement tasks. Out of these investigations have come three popular methods of charting the stage classification of children in actual observational settings. The systems devised by Roberton (1978), Mc-Clenaghan and Gallahue (1978), and Seefeldt and Haubenstricker (1976) have been used successfully in observational assessment with young children. The Roberton method expands the stage theory to an analysis of the separate components of movement within a given pattern, and is commonly referred to as a *segmental analysis* approach. The Seefeldt method assigns an overall stage classification score (stage 1 through stage 5), and is referred to as a *total body configuration* approach.

Gallahue (1993) recently expanded and revised the McClenaghan-Gallahue (1978) method of identifying stages within the fundamental movement phase. In the book *Developmental Physical Education for Today's Children* he offers a practical, easy-to-use, and reliable system for classifying individuals at the initial, elementary, mature, or sport skill stages, along with a wide variety of developmentally appropriate movement experiences for each stage in 23 fundamental movement skills. This method encourages use of both the total body configuration and segmental analysis approaches to assessing fundamental movement pattern development. First, the examiner (teacher, coach, parent) observes the movement task using a total body assessment approach. This provides a general picture of the stage at which the individual, group, or class is performing a specific movement skill. If the movement is observed to be at the mature stage, further diagnostic observational assessment is not necessary. If, however, the fundamental movement skill is observed to be at the initial or elementary stage in a general sense, then further assessment is warranted. At this time a segmental assessment is conducted to identify specifically those body parts that are lagging behind. This method recognizes the differential rates of development within fundamental movement patterns as well as the need for an easy-to-apply tool for daily teaching situations.

Concept 11.2   Several effective techniques have been devised for observational assessment of fundamental movement patterns.

Not all movement patterns fit precisely into an arbitrary three-stage progression. The developmental aspects of some movements may be more completely described in four-, five-, or even eight-stage sequences, depending on the specific pattern and the level of sophistication of the observer. The three-stage approach is used in the following sections because it accurately and adequately fits the developmental sequence of most fundamental movement patterns and provides the basis for a reliable, easy-to-use, observational assessment instrument. Tables 11.1a–c provide a visual representation of the emergence sequence of selected fundamental stability, locomotor, and manipulative abilities.

Table 11.1a Sequence of Emergence of Selected Stability Abilities

Movement Pattern	Selected Abilities	Approximate Age of Onset
Dynamic Balance		
Dynamic balance involves maintaining one's equilibrium as the center of gravity shifts	Walks 1-inch straight line	3 years
	Walks 1-inch circular line	4 years
	Stands on low balance beam	2 years
	Walks on 4-inch wide beam for a short distance	3 years
	Walks on same beam, alternating feet	3–4 years
	Walks on 2- or 3-inch beam	4 years
	Performs basic forward roll	3–4 years
	Performs mature forward roll*	6–7 years
Static Balance		
Static balance involves maintaining one's equilibrium while the center of gravity remains stationary	Pulls to a standing position	10 months
	Stands without handholds	11 months
	Stands alone	12 months
	Balances on one foot 3–5 seconds	5 years
	Supports body in basic 3-point inverted positions	6 years
Axial Movements		
Axial movements are static postures that involve bending, stretching, twisting, turning, and the like	Axial movement abilities begin to develop early in infancy and are progressively refined to a point where they are included in the emerging manipulative patterns of throwing, catching, kicking, striking, trapping, and other activities	2 months–6 years
Walking		
Walking involves placing one foot in front of the other while maintaining contact with the supporting surface	Rudimentary upright unaided gait	13 months
	Walks sideways	16 months
	Walks backward	17 months
	Walks upstairs with help	20 months
	Walks upstairs alone—follow step	24 months
	Walks downstairs alone—follow step	25 months
Running		
Running involves a brief period of no contact with the supporting surface	Hurried walk (maintains contact)	18 months
	First true run (nonsupport phase)	2–3 years
	Efficient and refined run	4–5 years
	Speed of run increases, mature run*	5 years

*The child has the developmental "potential" to be at the mature stage. Actual attainment will depend on factors within the task, individual, and environment.

Table 11.1b Sequence of Emergence of Selected Locomotor Abilities

Movement Pattern	Selected Abilities	Approximate Age of Onset
Jumping Jumping takes three forms: (1) jumping for distance; (2) jumping for height; and (3) jumping from a height. It involves a one- or two-foot takeoff with a landing on both feet	Steps down from low objects	18 months
	Jumps down from object with one foot lead	2 years
	Jumps off floor with both feet	28 months
	Jumps for distance (about 3 feet)	5 years
	Jumps for height (about 1 foot)	5 years
	Mature jumping pattern*	6 years
Hopping Hopping involves a one-foot takeoff with a landing on the same foot	Hops up to 3 times on preferred foot	3 years
	Hops from 4 to 6 times on same foot	4 years
	Hops from 8 to 10 times on same foot	5 years
	Hops distance of 50 feet in about 11 seconds	5 years
	Hops skillfully with rhythmical alteration, mature pattern*	6 years
Galloping The gallop combines a walk and a leap with the same foot leading throughout	Basic but inefficient gallop	4 years
	Gallops skillfully, mature pattern*	6 years
Skipping Skipping combines a step and a hop in rhythmic alteration	One-footed skip	4 years
	Skillful skipping (about 20 percent)	5 years
	Skillful skipping for most*	6 years
Reach, Grasp, Release Reaching, grasping, and releasing involve making successful contact with an object, retaining it in one's grasp and releasing it at will	Primitive reaching behaviors	2–4 months
	Corralling of objects	2–4 months
	Palmar grasp	3–5 months
	Pincer grasp	8–10 months
	Controlled grasp	12–14 months
	Controlled releasing	14–18 months
Throwing Throwing involves imparting force to an object in the general direction of intent	Body faces target, feet remain stationary, ball thrown with forearm extension only	2–3 years
	Same as above but with body rotation added	3.6–5 years
	Steps forward with leg on same side as the throwing arm	4–5 years
	Boys exhibit more mature pattern than girls	5 years and over
	Mature throwing pattern*	6 years

*The child has the developmental "potential" to be at the mature stage. Actual attainment will depend on factors within the task, individual, and environment.

Table 11.1c Sequence of Emergence of Selected Manipulative Abilities

Movement Pattern	Selected Abilities	Approximate Age of Onset
Catching		
Catching involves receiving force from an object with the hands, moving from large to progressively smaller balls	Chases ball; does not respond to aerial ball	2 years
	Responds to aerial ball with delayed arm movements	2–3 years
	Needs to be told how to position arms	2–3 years
	Fear reaction (turns head away)	3–4 years
	Basket catch using the body	3 years
	Catches using the hands only with a small ball	5 years
	Mature catching pattern*	6 years
Kicking		
Kicking involves imparting force to an object with the foot	Pushes against ball; does not actually kick it	18 months
	Kicks with leg straight and little body movement (kicks *at* the ball)	2–3 years
	Flexes lower leg on backward lift	3–4 years
	Greater backward and forward swing with definite arm opposition.	4–5 years
	Mature pattern (kicks *through* the ball)*	5–6 years
Striking		
Striking involves sudden contact to objects in an overarm, sidearm, or underhand pattern	Faces object and swings in a vertical plane	2–3 years
	Swings in a horizontal plane and stands to the side of the object	4–5 years
	Rotates the trunk and hips and shifts body weight forward	5 years
	Mature horizontal pattern with stationary ball	6–7 years

*The child has the developmental "potential" to be at the mature stage. Actual attainment will depend on factors within the task, individual, and environment.

Movement Conditions

The fundamental movement phase of development has been extensively studied over the past several years. Most would agree that this phase follows a sequential progression that may be subdivided into stages. The cognitively and physically normal child progresses from one stage to another in a sequential manner that is influenced by both maturation and experience. Children cannot rely solely on maturation to attain the mature stage in their fundamental movement abilities. Environmental conditions that include opportunities for practice, encouragement, and instruction are crucial to the development of mature patterns of fundamental movement. Miller (1978) investigated the facilitation of fundamental movement skill learning in children 3 to 5 years of age. She found that programs of instruction can increase fundamental movement pattern development beyond the level attained solely through maturation. She also found that an instructional program in skill development was more effective than a free-play program and that parents working under the direction of a trained specialist can be as effective as physical education teachers alone in developing fundamental movement skills. Luedke (1980) found similar results, utilizing two different methods of instruction for the mature stage of throwing with fourth grade boys and girls. Both instructional groups were more proficient in terms of form and performance than a non-instructed control group. The interactions of the environment and the mover and the goal of the task and the mover have a dramatic impact on the observed developmental maturity of a fundamental movement task (Figure 11.1).

Concept 11.3   Progression to the mature stage of a fundamental movement pattern depends on a variety of experiential factors including opportunities for practice, encouragement, and instruction in an environment that is conducive to learning.

Natural conditions within the environment itself such as temperature, lighting, surface area, and gravity may influence the quantitative aspects of a movement task as well as the qualitative aspects. Similarly, artificial conditions such as the size, shape, color, and texture of objects may dramatically influence performance (Payne & Isaacs, 1991). Furthermore, conditions such as object velocity, trajectory, and weight may influence success in interceptions. The goal of the task itself is another important influencer of the observed developmental status of a fundamental movement task. If, for example, the focus is on accuracy in a throwing task such as with the game of darts, then it is reasonable to assume that the pattern of movement will be different than if the goal of the task was throwing for distance. Langendorfer (1988) observed two groups of subjects (children and adults) performing an overhand throwing pattern under two different goal conditions (force and accuracy). The results of his investigation indicated that "motor patterns are not absolutely robust to all environmental conditions, but some movers can accommodate their movements to shifting environmental constraints." The degree to which a mover is able to make adjustments to an altered goal will be influenced by several factors within the mover as well as the degree to which the task demands have changed. For example, an individual with limited ability to increase throwing velocity

ENVIRONMENTAL
CONDITIONS

GOAL OF THE
TASK

MOVER

OUTCOME
(development status of observed task)

Figure 11.1
The interactions
between the envi-
ronmental condi-
tions and the
mover, and the goal
of the task and the
mover will affect
the apparent devel-
opmental maturity
of a specific move-
ment task

(due to faulty body mechanics or lack of strength) will be able to make only minor adjustments when switching from an accuracy throwing task to a distance throwing task.

The link among the mover, the conditions of the environment, and the demands of the task itself is not completely understood. It is interesting to note that many of the developmental descriptions of the fundamental movement patterns that follow are laboratory-generated. They are hypothesized developmental sequences that are the products of research in artificial settings quite unlike the real world in which children move. Little is known, as of yet, about the changing ecology of the environment and its influence on the observed developmental status of movement in children. As we turn to methods of analyzing children's movement in more natural settings we may find these hypothesized stages of development to be somewhat different. This point is echoed by Roberton (1987) who indicated that researchers have frequently been so concerned with describing changes in the movement characteristics of their subjects that they have often failed to consider the powerful influences of other elements (i.e., conditions of the environment, and goal of the task) on the resulting observed developmental status of the fundamental movement pattern itself.

Developmental Differences

When observing and analyzing the fundamental movement abilities of children, it soon becomes apparent that there are various stages of development for each pattern of movement. It should also be obvious that differences in abilities exist among children, between patterns, and within patterns.

Concept 11.4 Although age-related, numerous differences are present among children, between patterns, and within patterns in the performance of fundamental movement tasks.

Among child differences should remind us of the principle of individuality in all learning. The sequence of progression through the initial, elementary, and mature stages is the same for most children. The rate, however, will vary, depending on both environmental and hereditary factors. Whether or not a child reaches the mature stage depends primarily on instruction, encouragement, and opportunities for practice. When these are absent, normal differences between children will be magnified.

Between pattern differences are seen in all children. A child may be at the initial stage in some movement tasks, the elementary in others, and the mature in still others. Children do not progress evenly in the development of their fundamental movement abilities. Play and instructional experiences will greatly influence the rate of development of locomotor, manipulative, and stability abilities.

Within pattern differences are an interesting and often curious phenomenon. Within a given pattern, a child may exhibit a combination of initial, elementary, and mature elements. For example, in the throw, the arm action may be at the elementary stage, while the leg action is at the mature stage and the trunk action at the initial stage. Developmental differences within patterns are common and usually the result of: (1) incomplete modeling of the movements of others, (2) initial success with the inappropriate action, (3) failure to require an all-out effort, (4) inappropriate or restricted learning opportunities, or (5) incomplete sensorimotor integration. Children exhibiting within pattern differences should be assessed utilizing the segmental analysis approach. This will permit the observer to accurately determine the stage of development of each body segment. With this knowledge, appropriate intervention strategies can be mapped out.

Creative, diagnostic teaching can do much to aid the child in the balanced development of his or her fundamental movement abilities. Observational assessment of the child's movement abilities will enable the teacher to plan experiences and instructional strategies that will help the child establish mature patterns of movement. Once movement control has been established, these mature patterns may be further refined in terms of force production and accuracy in the specialized movement phase. Failure to achieve proficiency in a wide variety of fundamental movement abilities will inhibit the development of efficient and effective movement skills that may be applied to game, sport, and dance activities that are characteristic of a child's culture.

Fundamental Stability Movements

Stability is the most fundamental aspect of learning to move. It is through this dimension that children gain and maintain a point of origin for the explorations that they make in space. Stability involves the ability to maintain one's relationship to the force of gravity. This is true even though the nature of the application of the force may be altered as the requirements of the situation change, causing the general relationship of the body parts to the center of gravity to be altered. Movement experiences designed to enhance children's stability abilities enable them to develop flexibility in postural adjustments as they move in a variety of different and often unusual ways relative to their centers of gravity, lines of gravity, and bases of support.

Concept 11.5 Stability is the most fundamental aspect of learning to move, because all movement involves an element of stability.

The ability to sense a shift in the relationship of the body parts that alters one's balance is required for efficient stability. The ability to compensate rapidly and accurately for these changes with appropriate movements is also essential. These compensatory movements should ensure maintenance of balance, but they should not be overdone. They should be made with only those parts of the body required for balance rather than with the entire body. Children's stability abilities should be flexible so that they may make all kinds of movements under all sorts of conditions and still maintain their fundamental relationship to the force of gravity.

It should be noted here that the term stability as used in this text goes beyond the catch-all terms of ''non-locomotor'' or ''non-manipulative'' movements. The movement category of stability encompasses these terms but further implies maintenance of body control in movements that place a premium on balance. All movement involves an element of stability when viewed from the balance perspective. Therefore, strictly speaking, all locomotor and manipulative activities are, in part, stability movements. Certain fundamental movements may, however, be separated from all others that require the controlled maintenance of equilibrium. Table 11.2 summarizes the usual sequence of emergence of several fundamental stability abilities.

Axial movements and various static and dynamic balance postures are considered here as the major components of stability. Axial, or non-locomotor, movements are orientation movements of the trunk or limbs while in a static position. Twisting, turning, bending, stretching, and swinging are all axial movements.

Postures are other body positions that place a premium on the maintenance of equilibrium while in a position of static or dynamic balance.

Table 11.2 Developmental Sequence for Axial Movements

I. Axial Movements
   A. Initial stage
      1. Exaggerated base of support
      2. Momentary loss of balance
      3. Visual monitoring of body and model when possible
      4. Combined movements appear jerky and segmented
      5. Lack of fluid transition from one level or plane to another
      6. Only one to two actions possible at a time
   B. Elementary stage
      1. Good balance
      2. Appropriate base of support
      3. Requires visual model
      4. Does not have to monitor own body
      5. Good coordination of similar movements
      6. Poor transition in dissimilar movements
      7. Can combine two to three actions into one fluid movement
   C. Mature stage
      1. Smooth, rhythmical flow
      2. Sequences several movements with ease
      3. Vision unimportant
      4. Appears totally in control
      5. Can combine four or more movements into one fluid movement
II. Developmental Difficulties
   A. Visually monitoring body
   B. Visually mimicking a model
   C. Poor rhythmical coordination
   D. Segmented combination of movements
   E. Loss of balance
   F. Lack of smooth transition in flow of movement
   G. Inability to perform at various tempos
   H. Inability to perform at different levels

Standing, sitting, inverted supports, rolling, stopping, dodging, and landing, as well as beam walking, stick balancing, and one-foot balances, are dynamic or static balance postures.

Axial Movements

Axial movements are movements of the trunk or limbs that orient the body while it remains in a stationary position. Bending, stretching, twisting, turning, swinging, swaying, reaching, lifting, pushing, and pulling are axial movements. They are often combined with other movements to create more elaborate movement skills. Skilled performances in diving, gymnastics, figure skating, and modern dance typically incorporate a variety of axial movements along with various locomotor movements. Axial movements are included with a variety of manipulative skills in soccer, baseball, football, and track and field.

Figure 11.2
Stages of axial movement development

INITIAL

ELEMENTARY

MATURE

Little is known about the developmental sequence of axial movements (Figure 11.2). To date, few film analyses or observational studies have been conducted with children. Ozmun and Robertson (1992), however, completed a preliminary cross-sectional investigation of the total body pushing action with 15 three- to seven-year-olds. The results of

Fundamental Movement Abilities   **235**

their study identified a stage sequence of progression to the mature stage of pushing. The initial stage was identified as having the feet together and pushing from either an upright position or from a forward body lean. The elementary stage was identified as having the feet staggered with the front foot off the surface and the body leaning forward. The mature stage of the total body pushing action was identified as having the feet staggered with both feet on the surface with the legs bent and the body leaning forward.

The following discussion represents a proposed developmental sequence for axial movements in general. It is based on observation of numerous children and is subject to further verification and refinement.

Body Rolling

Body rolling postures, although actually locomotor in nature, require inordinate amounts of balance control. Considerable disturbance of the fluid in the semicircular canals results from rolling actions; therefore, they are regarded as fundamental stability movements. Body rolling movements may involve rolling forward, sideways, or backward. In each, the body is momentarily inverted and must maintain positional control as it travels through space. The sport skills of the forward and backward somersault are elaborations of the fundamental forward and backward rolling patterns. Walkovers and handsprings are sophisticated combinations of rolling patterns combined with transitional inverted supports.

Developmental studies of body rolling are limited (Williams, 1980; Wickstrom, 1983; Roberton & Halverson, 1984). The following proposed sequence is based on these studies (Table 11.3, Figure 11.3).

Dodging

Dodging is a fundamental stability pattern of movement that combines the locomotor movements of sliding with rapid changes in direction. Dodging involves rapid shifts in direction from side to side and requires good reaction time and speed of movement. Extensive developmental studies of dodging have not been conducted with children. However, observational assessment of children and the work of Roberton and Halverson (1984) does provide the basis for the following sequence (Table 11.4, Figure 11.4).

One-foot Balance

The one-foot balance is probably the most common measure of static balance ability. Several investigators have studied the one-foot balance in subjects with their eyes open or closed and the arms at the sides, folded, or on the hips (Cratty, 1986; De Oreo, 1971, 1980; Eckert and Rarick, 1975). Performance trends for balancing on one foot are reported in a later chapter. The following appears to be the developmental sequence gleaned from these performance investigations, but it is subject to verification and refinement (Table 11.5, Figure 11.5).

Table 11.3 Developmental Sequence for Body Rolling

I. Body Rolling
  A. Initial stage
    1. Head contacts surface
    2. Body curled in loose "C" position
    3. Inability to coordinate use of arms
    4. Cannot get over backward or sideways
    5. Uncurls to "L" position after rolling forward
  B. Elementary stage
    1. After rolling forward, actions appear segmented
    2. Head leads action instead of inhibiting it
    3. Top of head still touches surface
    4. Body curled in tight "C" position at onset of roll
    5. Uncurls at completion of roll to "L" position
    6. Hands and arms aid rolling action somewhat but supply little push-off
    7. Can perform only one roll at a time
  C. Mature stage
    1. Head leads action
    2. Back of head touches surface very lightly
    3. Body remains in tight "C" throughout
    4. Arms aid in force production
    5. Momentum returns child to starting position
    6. Can perform consecutive rolls in control
II. Developmental Difficulties
  A. Head forcefully touching surface
  B. Failure to curl body tightly
  C. Inability to push off with arms
  D. Pushing off with one arm
  E. Failure to remain in tucked position
  F. Inability to perform consecutive rolls
  G. Feeling dizzy
  H. Failure to roll in a straight line
  I. Lack of sufficient momentum to complete one revolution

Beam Walking

The beam walk is the most frequently measured fundamental dynamic balance ability. A variety of investigations have been conducted using walking boards that vary in length, width, and height from the supporting surface (De Oreo, 1971, 1980; Goetzinger, 1961; Seashore, 1949). Considerable information concerning the performance abilities of children from year to year is available, but little is known about the developmental sequence of the beam-walking process itself. The following developmental sequence is based on observational assessment of numerous children and is subject to refinement and verification (Table 11.6, Figure 11.6).

Figure 11.3
Stages of body
rolling development

INITIAL

ELEMENTARY

MATURE

Inverted Supports

Inverted supports involve postures in which the body assumes an upside-down position for a number of seconds before the movement is discontinued. Stabilization of the center of gravity and maintenance of the line of gravity within the base of support apply to the inverted posture as well as to the erect standing posture. An inverted supporting posture, however, utilizes either the head, hands, forearms, or upper arms (or a combination) as the base of support. The shoulders are above the point of support. The tip-up, tripod, headstand, and handstand are examples of skills that incorporate the fundamental pattern of the inverted support. To date, no developmental studies have been conducted with inverted supports. The following represents a developmental sequence based on observation of numerous children, and is subject to verification and refinement (Table 11.7, Figure 11.7).

Table 11.4 Developmental Sequence for Dodging

I. Dodging
  A. Initial stage
      1. Segmented movements
      2. Body appears stiff
      3. Minimal knee bend
      4. Weight is on one foot
      5. Feet generally cross
      6. No deception
  B. Elementary stage
      1. Movements coordinated but with little deception
      2. Performs better to one side than to the other
      3. Too much vertical lift
      4. Feet occasionally cross
      5. Little spring in movement
      6. Sometimes outsmarts self and becomes confused
  C. Mature stage
      1. Knees bent, slight trunk lean forward (ready position)
      2. Fluid directional changes
      3. Performs equally well in all directions
      4. Head and shoulder fake
      5. Good lateral movement
II. Developmental Difficulties
  A. Inability to shift body weight in a fluid manner in direction of dodge
  B. Slow change of direction
  C. Crossing feet
  D. Hesitation
  E. Too much vertical lift
  F. Total body lead
  G. Inability to perform several dodging actions in rapid succession
  H. Monitoring body
  I. Rigid posture

Fundamental Locomotor Movements

Locomotion is a fundamental aspect of learning to move effectively and efficiently within one's environment. It involves projection of the body into external space by altering its location relative to fixed points on the surface. Activities such as walking, running, jumping, hopping, sliding, and skipping are considered fundamental locomotor movements. Performance of these movements must be sufficiently flexible so that they can be altered as the requirements of the environment demand without detracting from the purpose of the act. The child must be able to: (1) use any one of a number of types of movements to reach the goal, (2) shift from one type of movement to another when the situation demands, and

Figure 11.4
Stages of the
dodging pattern

INITIAL

ELEMENTARY

MATURE

Table 11.5 Developmental Sequence for the One-foot Balance

I. One-foot Balance
  A. Initial Stage
    1. Raises nonsupporting leg several inches so that thigh is nearly parallel with contact surface
    2. Either in or out of balance (no in-between)
    3. Overcompensates ("windmill" arms)
    4. Inconsistent leg preference
    5. Balances with outside support
    6. Only momentary balance without support
    7. Eyes directed at feet
  B. Elementary stage
    1. May lift nonsupporting leg to a tied-in position on support leg
    2. Cannot balance with eyes closed
    3. Uses arms for balance but may tie one arm to side of body
    4. Performs better on dominant leg
  C. Mature stage
    1. Can balance with eyes closed
    2. Uses arms and trunk as needed to maintain balance
    3. Lifts nonsupporting leg
    4. Focuses on external object while balancing
    5. Changes to nondominant leg without loss of balance
II. Developmental Difficulties
  A. Tying one arm to side
  B. No compensating movements
  C. Inappropriate compensation of arms
  D. Inability to use either leg
  E. Inability to vary body position with control
  F. Inability to balance while holding objects
  G. Visually monitoring support leg
  H. Overdependence on outside support

(3) alter each movement as the conditions of the environment change. Throughout this process of alteration and modification, attention must not be diverted from the goal. For example, the locomotor pattern of walking may be used singularly, or it may be used in conjunction with manipulative or stability movements. The walking pattern can be elaborated upon by including object handling, such as bouncing a ball, and walking on a balance beam. Development and refinement of the following locomotor patterns in children is essential since it is through these movements that they explore the world.

Figure 11.5
Stages of the one-
foot balance

INITIAL

ELEMENTARY

MATURE

Table 11.6 Developmental Sequence for the Beam Walk

I. Beam Walk
  A. Initial stage
    1. Balances with support
    2. Walks forward while holding on to a spotter for support
    3. Uses follow-step with dominant foot lead
    4. Eyes focus on feet
    5. Body rigid
    6. No compensating movements
  B. Elementary stage
    1. Can walk a 2-inch beam but not a 1-inch beam
    2. Uses a follow-step with dominant foot leading
    3. Eyes focus on beam
    4. May press one arm to trunk while trying to balance with the other
    5. Loses balance easily
    6. Limited compensating movements
    7. Can move forward, backward, and sideways but requires considerable concentration and effort
  C. Mature stage
    1. Can walk a 1-inch beam
    2. Uses alternate stepping action
    3. Eyes focus beyond beam
    4. Both arms used at will to aid balance
    5. Can move forward, backward, and sideways with assurance and ease
    6. Movements are fluid, relaxed, and in control
    7. May lose balance occasionally
II. Developmental Difficulties
  A. Overdependence on spotter
  B. Visually monitors stepping leg
  C. Tying one arm in
  D. Rigid, hesitant movement
  E. Failure to actually negotiate the problem of balance
  F. Inability to perform without holding on to a spotter
  G. Poor rhythmical coordination of both sides of body
  H. Overcompensating for loss of balance

Concept 11.6 Fundamental locomotor movements involve projecting the body into space in a horizontal, vertical, or diagonal plane.

Figure 11.6
Stages of the beam walk

INITIAL

ELEMENTARY

MATURE

Table 11.7 Developmental Sequence for Inverted Supports

I. Inverted Supports
  A. Initial stage
     1. Able to maintain triangular, low-level, three-point balance positions
     2. Able to assume inverted three-point postures for up to three seconds
     3. Poor kinesthetic feel for unseen body parts
     4. Minimal coordinated control of movements
  B. Elementary stage
     1. Can maintain controlled triangular three-point and low two-point contacts with surface
     2. Able to hold balance for three seconds or longer with frequent brief addition of another balance point
     3. Gradual improvement in monitoring of unseen body parts
  C. Mature stage
     1. Good surface contact position
     2. Good control of head and neck
     3. Good kinesthetic feel for body part location
     4. Appears to be in good control of body
     5. Maintains inverted low- and high-level two- and three-point balance positions for three or more seconds
     6. Comes out of static posture under control
II. Developmental Difficulties
  A. Inability to accurately sense location and position of body parts not visually monitored
  B. Inability to keep line of gravity within base of support
  C. Inadequate or exaggerated base of support
  D. Overbalancing by shifting the body's weight too far forward
  E. Inability to hold inverted balance position for three seconds or longer

Walking

Walking has often been defined as the process of continually losing and regaining balance while moving forward in an upright position. The walking pattern has been extensively studied in infants, children, and adults. The onset of walking behavior in the infant depends primarily on maturation but is also influenced by the environmental factors such as the availability of handholds. Burnett and Johnson (1971) indicated that the average age for achieving independent walking is 12 1/2 months, with a range of from 9 to 17 months. Once independent walking has been achieved, the child progresses rapidly to the elementary and mature stages. Several authors have described the walking pattern and indicated that mature walking is achieved sometime between the fourth and the seventh year (Eckert, 1987; Grieve and Gaer, 1966; Guttridge, 1939; Saunders et al., 1953; Wickstrom, 1983; Williams, 1983). Many

Figure 11.7
Stages of inverted support development

INITIAL

ELEMENTARY

MATURE

Table 11.8 Developmental Sequence for Walking

I. Walking
  A. Initial stage
     1. Difficulty maintaining upright posture
     2. Unpredictable loss of balance
     3. Rigid, halting leg action
     4. Short steps
     5. Flat-footed contact
     6. Toes turn outward
     7. Wide base of support
     8. Flexed knee at contact followed by quick leg extension
  B. Elementary stage
     1. Gradual smoothing out of pattern
     2. Step length increased
     3. Heel-toe contact
     4. Arms down to sides with limited swing
     5. Base of support within the lateral dimensions of trunk
     6. Out-toeing reduced or eliminated
     7. Increased pelvic tilt
     8. Apparent vertical lift
  C. Mature stage
     1. Reflexive arm swing
     2. Narrow base of support
     3. Relaxed, elongated gait
     4. Minimal vertical lift
     5. Definite heel-toe contact
II. Developmental Difficulties
  A. Inhibited or exaggerated arm swing
  B. Arms crossing midline of body
  C. Improper foot placement
  D. Exaggerated forward trunk lean
  E. Arms flopping at sides or held out for balance
  F. Twisting of trunk
  G. Poor rhythmical action
  H. Landing flat-footed
  I. Flipping foot or lower leg in or out

subtle changes continue to occur in the walking pattern, but they are not observable through unaided visual assessment. Sophisticated film analysis and electromyography techniques must be used in order to detect progress in walking skill beyond this point (Wickstrom, 1983). Gad-Elmawla's 1980 dissertation is used as the basis for description of the following developmental sequence in the walking pattern (Table 11.8, Figure 11.8).

Figure 11.8
Stages of the
walking pattern

INITIAL

ELEMENTARY

MATURE

Running

Running is an exaggerated form of walking. It differs principally from
the walk in that there is a brief flight phase during each step, in which
the body is out of contact with the supporting surface. The flight phase
is first seen around the second birthday. Prior to that the run appears

Table 11.9 Developmental Sequence for Running

I. Running
  A. Initial stage
    1. Short, limited leg swing
    2. Stiff, uneven stride
    3. No observable flight phase
    4. Incomplete extension of support leg
    5. Stiff, short swing with varying degrees of elbow flexion
    6. Arms tend to swing outward horizontally
    7. Swinging leg rotates outward from hip
    8. Swinging foot toes outward
    9. Wide base of support
  B. Elementary stage
    1. Increase in length of stride, arm swing, and speed
    2. Limited but observable flight phase
    3. More complete extension of support leg at takeoff
    4. Arm swing increases
    5. Horizontal arm swing reduced on backswing
    6. Swinging foot crosses midline at height of recovery to rear
  C. Mature stage
    1. Stride length at maximum; stride speed fast
    2. Definite flight phase
    3. Complete extension of support leg
    4. Recovery thigh parallel to ground
    5. Arms swing vertically in opposition to legs
    6. Arms bent at approximate right angles
    7. Minimal rotary action of recovery leg and foot
II. Developmental Difficulties
  A. Inhibited or exaggerated arm swing
  B. Arms crossing the midline of the body
  C. Improper foot placement
  D. Exaggerated forward trunk lean
  E. Arms flopping at the sides or held out for balance
  F. Twisting of the trunk
  G. Poor rhythmical action
  H. Landing flat-footed
  I. Flipping the foot or lower leg in or out

as a fast walk with one foot always in contact with the supporting surface. The initial stage of the running pattern does not depend on mature walking (Broer & Zernicke, 1979). Many young children begin to run before they master the mature walking pattern. The mature running pattern is fundamental to successful participation in a variety of sport-related activities. The running pattern has been extensively studied by a number of investigators (Seefeldt et al., 1972; Wickstrom, 1983; Roberton & Halverson, 1984; Roberton, 1985). The four-stage developmental sequence hypothesized by Roberton has been collapsed into three stages and is used here (Table 11.9, Figure 11.9).

Figure 11.9
Stages of running
pattern

INITIAL

ELEMENTARY

MATURE

Table 11.10 Developmental Sequence for Jumping from a Height

I. Jumping from a Height
  A. Initial stage
    1. One foot leads on takeoff
    2. No flight phase
    3. Lead foot contacts lower surface prior to trailing foot leaving upper surface
    4. Exaggerated use of arms for balance
  B. Elementary stage
    1. Two-foot takeoff with one-foot lead
    2. Flight phase, but lacks control
    3. Arms used ineffectively for balance
    4. One-foot landing followed by immediate landing of trailing foot
    5. Inhibited or exaggerated flexion at knees and hip upon landing
  C. Mature stage
    1. Two-foot takeoff
    2. Controlled flight phase
    3. Both arms used efficiently out to sides to control balance as needed
    4. Feet contact lower surface simultaneously with toes touching first
    5. Feet land shoulder-width apart
    6. Flexion at knees and hip congruent with height of jump
II. Developmental Difficulties
  A. Inability to take off with both feet
  B. Twisting body to one side on takeoff
  C. Exaggerated or inhibited body lean
  D. Failure to coordinate use of both arms in the air
  E. Tying one arm to side while using the other
  F. Failure to land simultaneously on both feet
  G. Landing flat-footed
  H. Failure to flex knees sufficiently to absorb impact of landing
  I. Landing out of control

Jumping from a Height

The movements involved in jumping from a low height are somewhat similar to those found in the jump for distance and the jump for height particularly at the initial stage. The jump from a low height has been studied by a few investigators (Bayley, 1935; McCaskill & Wellman, 1938) who have concentrated on the takeoff, flight phase, and landing aspects of the pattern. The description of stages that follows is based on this research and on observation of numerous children. It is, therefore, subject to refinement and verification (Table 11.10, Figure 11.10).

Figure 11.10
Stages of the jump from a height

INITIAL

ELEMENTARY

MATURE

Vertical Jumping

Jumping for height, or the vertical jump, has been studied by several investigators in recent years (Martin & Stull, 1969; Myers et al., 1977; Poe, 1976; Wickstrom, 1983; Williams, 1983). The jump for height involves projecting the body vertically into the air from a one- or two-foot takeoff with a landing on both feet. The developmental sequence proposed by Myers et al. (1977), based on film analysis, is presented here (Table 11.11, Figure 11.11).

Table 11.11 Developmental Sequence for Vertical Jumping

I. Vertical Jumping
  A. Initial stage
    1. Inconsistent preparatory crouch
    2. Difficulty in taking off with both feet
    3. Poor body extension on takeoff
    4. Little or no head lift
    5. Arms not coordinated with the trunk and leg action
    6. Little height achieved
  B. Elementary stage
    1. Knee flexion exceeds 90-degree angle on preparatory crouch
    2. Exaggerated forward lean during crouch
    3. Two-foot take off
    4. Entire body does not fully extend during flight phase
    5. Arms attempt to aid in flight (but often unequally) and balance
    6. Noticeable horizontal displacement on landing
  C. Mature stage
    1. Preparatory crouch with knee flexion from 60 to 90 degrees
    2. Forceful extension at hips, knees, and ankles
    3. Simultaneous coordinated upward arm lift
    4. Upward head tilt with eyes focused on target
    5. Full body extension
    6. Elevation of reaching arm by shoulder girdle tilt combined with downward thrust of non-reaching arm at peak of flight
    7. Controlled landing very close to point of takeoff
II. Developmental Difficulties
  A. Failure to get airborn
  B. Failure to take off with both feet simultaneously
  C. Failure to crouch at about a 90-degree angle
  D. Failure to extend body, legs, and arms forcefully
  E. Poor coordination of leg and arm actions
  F. Swinging of arms backward or to the side for balance
  G. Failure to lead with eyes and head
  H. One-foot landing
  I. Inhibited or exaggerated flexion of hips and knees on landing
  J. Marked horizontal displacement on landing

Horizontal Jumping

The jump for distance is an explosive movement requiring coordinated performance of all parts of the body. This is a complex movement pattern in which it is difficult to inhibit the tendency to step forward on one foot. Instead the takeoff and landing must be with both feet. The horizontal jumping pattern has been extensively studied (Wickstrom, 1983; Seefeldt et al., 1972; Roberton & Halverson, 1984; Clark & Phillips, 1985). The developmental sequence proposed by McClenaghan (1976), based on film analysis, is used here (Table 11.12, Figure 11.12).

Figure 11.11
Stages of the vertical jumping pattern

INITIAL

ELEMENTARY

MATURE

Table 11.12 Developmental Sequence for Horizontal Jumping

I. Horizontal Jumping
  A. Initial stage
      1. Limited swing; arms do not initiate jumping action
      2. During flight, arms move sideward-downward or rearward-upward to maintain balance
      3. Trunk moves in vertical direction; little emphasis on length of jump
      4. Preparatory crouch inconsistent in terms of leg flexion
      5. Difficulty in using both feet
      6. Limited extension of the ankles, knees, and hips at takeoff
      7. Body weight falls backward at landing
  B. Elementary stage
      1. Arms initiate jumping action
      2. Arms remain toward front of body during preparatory crouch
      3. Arms move out to side to maintain balance during flight
      4. Preparatory crouch deeper and more consistent
      5. Knee and hip extension more complete at takeoff
      6. Hips flexed during flight; thighs held in flexed position
  C. Mature stage
      1. Arms move high and to rear during preparatory crouch
      2. During takeoff, arms swing forward with force and reach high
      3. Arms held high throughout jumping action
      4. Trunk propelled at approximately 45-degree angle
      5. Major emphasis on horizontal distance
      6. Preparatory crouch deep, consistent
      7. Complete extension of ankles, knees, and hips at takeoff
      8. Thighs held parallel to ground during flight; lower leg hangs vertically
      9. Body weight forward at landing
II. Developmental Difficulties
  A. Improper use of arms (that is, failure to use arms opposite the propelling leg in a down-up-down swing as leg flexes, extends, and flexes again)
  B. Twisting or jerking of body
  C. Inability to perform either a one-foot or a two-foot takeoff
  D. Poor preliminary crouch
  E. Restricted movements of arms or legs
  F. Poor angle of takeoff
  G. Failure to extend fully on takeoff
  H. Failure to extend legs forward on landing
  I. Falling backward on landing

Hopping

Hopping is similar to the jump for distance and the vertical jump but both the takeoff and the landing are on the same foot. The hop has been studied by Seefeldt & Haubenstricker (1976), Roberton and Halverson (1984), and Halverson and Williams (1985). The four-stage developmental sequence proposed by Halverson and Williams is summarized here and condensed into three stages (Table 11.13, Figure 11.13).

INITIAL

ELEMENTARY

MATURE

Figure 11.12
Stages of the horizontal jumping pattern

Table 11.13 Developmental Sequence for Hopping

I. Hopping
  A. Initial stage
      1. Non-supporting leg flexed 90 degrees or less
      2. Non-supporting thigh roughly parallel to contact surface
      3. Body upright
      4. Arms flexed at elbows and held slightly to side
      5. Little height or distance generated in single hop
      6. Balance lost easily
      7. Limited to one or two hops
  B. Elementary stage
      1. Non-supporting leg flexed
      2. Non-supporting thigh at 45-degree angle to contact surface
      3. Slight forward lean, with trunk flexed at hip
      4. Non-supporting thigh flexed and extended at hip to produce greater force
      5. Force absorbed on landing by flexing at hip and by supporting knee
      6. Arms move up and down vigorously and bilaterally
      7. Balance poorly controlled
      8. Generally limited in number of consecutive hops that can be performed
  C. Mature stage
      1. Non-supporting leg flexed at 90 degrees or less
      2. Non-supporting thigh lifts with vertical thrust of supporting foot
      3. Greater body lean
      4. Rhythmical action of non-supporting leg (pendulum swing aiding in force production)
      5. Arms move together in rhythmical lifting as the supporting foot leaves the contact surface
      6. Arms not needed for balance but used for greater force production
II. Developmental Difficulties
  A. Hopping flat-footed
  B. Exaggerated movements of arms
  C. Exaggerated movement of non-supporting leg
  D. Exaggerated forward lean
  E. Inability to maintain balance for five or more consecutive hops
  F. Lack of rhythmical fluidity of movement
  G. Inability to hop effectively on both left foot and right foot
  H. Inability to alternate hopping feet in a smooth, continuous manner
  I. Tying one arm to side of body

Galloping and Sliding

Galloping and sliding involve the combination of two fundamental movements, the step and the hop, with the same foot always leading in the direction of movement. The movement is called a gallop when the person is moving forward or backward, and a slide when he or she is progressing sideward. Sapp (1980) and Williams (1983) described a developmental sequence for galloping that may also be applied to sliding (Table 11.14, Figure 11.14).

Figure 11.13
Stages of the hop-
ping pattern

INITIAL

ELEMENTARY

MATURE

Table 11.14 Developmental Sequence for Galloping and Sliding

I. Galloping and Sliding
  A. Initial stage
    1. Arrhythmical at fast pace
    2. Trailing leg often fails to remain behind and often contacts surface in front of lead leg
    3. Forty-five-degree flexion of trailing leg during flight phase
    4. Contact in a heel-toe combination
    5. Arms of little use in balance or force production
  B. Elementary stage
    1. Moderate tempo
    2. Appears choppy and stiff
    3. Trailing leg may lead during flight but lands adjacent to or behind lead leg
    4. Exaggerated vertical lift
    5. Feet contact in a heel-toe, or toe-toe, combination
    6. Arms slightly out to side to aid balance
  C. Mature stage
    1. Moderate tempo
    2. Smooth, rhythmical action
    3. Trailing leg lands adjacent to or behind lead leg
    4. Both legs flexed at 45-degree angles during flight
    5. Low flight pattern
    6. Heel-toe contact combination
    7. Arms not needed for balance; may be used for other purposes
II. Developmental Difficulties
  A. Choppy movements
  B. Keeping legs too straight
  C. Exaggerated forward trunk lean
  D. Overstepping with trailing leg
  E. Too much elevation on hop
  F. Inability to perform both forward and backward
  G. Inability to lead with non-dominant foot
  H. Inability to perform to both left and right
  I. Undue concentration on task

Leaping

The leap is similar to the run in that there is a transference of weight from one foot to the other, but the loss of contact with the surface is sustained, with greater elevation and distance covered than in the run. Leaping involves using greater amounts of force to produce more height and to cover a greater distance than in a run. Biomechanical studies have been conducted on the hurdle event in track, but there is a dearth of information about the developmental aspects of the leaping pattern. The description of stages that follows is based on observational assessment of numerous children and is subject to refinement and verification (Table 11.15, Figure 11.15).

Figure 11.14
Stages of the
sliding pattern

INITIAL

ELEMENTARY

MATURE

Table 11.15 Developmental Sequence for Leaping

I. Leaping
   A. Initial stage
      1. Child appears confused in attempts
      2. Inability to push off and gain distance and elevation
      3. Each attempt looks like another running step
      4. Inconsistent use of takeoff leg
      5. Arms ineffective
   B. Elementary stage
      1. Appears to be thinking through the action
      2. Attempt looks like an elongated run
      3. Little elevation above supporting surface
      4. Little forward trunk lean
      5. Stiff appearance in trunk
      6. Incomplete extension of legs during flight
      7. Arms used for balance, not as an aid in force production
   C. Mature stage
      1. Relaxed rhythmical action
      2. Forceful extension of takeoff leg
      3. Good summation of horizontal and vertical forces
      4. Definite forward trunk lean
      5. Definite arm opposition
      6. Full extension of legs during flight
II. Developmental Difficulties
   A. Failure to use arms in opposition to legs
   B. Inability to perform one-foot takeoff and land on opposite foot
   C. Restricted movements of arms or legs
   D. Lack of spring and elevation in push-off
   E. Landing flat-footed
   F. Exaggerated or inhibited body lean
   G. Failure to stretch and reach with legs

Skipping

The skipping action puts two fundamental movement patterns, the step and the hop, together into a combined pattern of movement. Seefeldt and Haubenstricker (1976) as well as Halverson and Roberton (1979) have studied the skipping pattern and reported a three-stage developmental sequence which serves as the basis of the following description. The skip is a continuous flow of the step and hop involving rhythmical alteration of the leading foot (Table 11.16, Figure 11.16).

Figure 11.15
Stages of the
leaping pattern

INITIAL

ELEMENTARY

MATURE

Table 11.16 Developmental Sequence for Skipping

I. Skipping
   A. Initial stage
      1. One-footed skip
      2. Deliberate step-hop action
      3. Double hop or step sometimes occurs
      4. Exaggerated stepping action
      5. Arms of little use
      6. Action appears segmented
   B. Elementary stage
      1. Step and hop coordinated effectively
      2. Rhythmical use of arms to aid momentum
      3. Exaggerated vertical lift on hop
      4. Flat-footed landing
   C. Mature stage
      1. Rhythmical weight transfer throughout
      2. Rhythmical use of arms (reduced during time of weight transfer)
      3. Low vertical lift on hop
      4. Toe-first landing
II. Developmental Difficulties
   A. Segmented stepping and hopping action
   B. Poor rhythmical alteration
   C. Inability to use both sides of body
   D. Exaggerated movements
   E. Landing flat-footed
   F. Exaggerated, inhibited, or unilateral arm movements
   G. Inability to move in a straight line
   H. Inability to skip backward and to side

Fundamental Manipulative Movements

Gross motor manipulation involves an individual's relationship to objects and is characterized by giving force to objects and receiving force from them. Propulsive movements involve activities in which an object is moved away from the body. Fundamental movements such as throwing, kicking, striking, and rolling a ball are examples. Absorptive movements involve activities in which the body or a body part is positioned in the path of a moving object for the purpose of stopping or deflecting that object. Fundamental movements such as catching and trapping are examples. The essence of manipulative movements is that

Figure 11.16
Stages of the skip-
ping pattern

INITIAL

ELEMENTARY

MATURE

they combine two or more movements and are generally used in conjunction with other forms of movement. For example, propulsive movements are generally a composite of stepping, turning, swinging, and stretching. Absorptive movements generally consist of bending and stepping.

Concept 11.7 Fundamental movements categorized as manipulative involve giving force to objects and/or receiving force from them.

Through the manipulation of objects children are able to explore the relationship of moving objects in space. These movements involve making estimates of the path, distance, rate of travel, accuracy, and mass of the moving object. At the point of contact a check on previous estimates is possible. Through such types of experimentation children learn the nature and effect of the movement of objects. Because manipulative patterns commonly combine both locomotor and stabilizing movements, efficient use of them should not be expected at the same time that locomotor and stability abilities are developing. Only after these patterns have been fairly well established do we begin to see the emergence of efficient manipulative movements. The following is a description of several manipulative patterns of movement.

Ball Rolling

Rolling an object is another fundamental movement pattern that has not been methodically studied. Ability in ball rolling has most often been assessed by accuracy in knocking down bowling pins rather than from the standpoint of form. Numerous sport and recreational activities utilize the fundamental patterns found in rolling. Bowling, curling, shuffleboard, and the underhand pitch in softball employ variations of the pattern found in mature rolling. The developmental sequence that follows is based on observational assessment of numerous children and is subject to verification and further refinement (Table 11.17, Figure 11.17).

Overhand Throwing

The overhand throw has been studied extensively over the past several years (Wild, 1938; Deach, 1951; Seefeldt et al., 1972; McClenaghan & Gallahue, 1978; Haubenstricker et al., 1983; Roberton, 1978, 1984), with attention focused on form, accuracy, and distance. The components of the throw vary depending on which of these three factors the thrower is concentrating on and the starting position that is assumed. When viewing the overhand throw from the standpoint of the process or form, the developmental sequence depicted in Table 11.18 and Figure 11.18 is apparent.

Table 11.17 Developmental Sequence for Ball Rolling

I. Ball Rolling
   A. Initial stage
      1. Straddle stance
      2. Ball is held with hands on the sides, with palms facing each other
      3. Acute bend at waist, with backward pendulum motion of arms
      4. Eyes monitor ball
      5. Forward arm swing and trunk lift with release of ball
   B. Elementary stage
      1. Stride stance
      2. Ball held with one hand on bottom and the other on top
      3. Backward arm swing without weight transfer to the rear
      4. Limited knee bend
      5. Forward swing with limited follow-through
      6. Ball released between knee and waist level
      7. Eyes alternately monitor target and ball
   C. Mature stage
      1. Stride stance
      2. Ball held in hand corresponding to trailing leg
      3. Slight hip rotation and trunk lean forward
      4. Pronounced knee bend
      5. Forward swing with weight transference from rear to forward foot
      6. Release at knee level or below
      7. Eyes are on target throughout
II. Developmental Difficulties
   A. Failure to transfer body weight to rear foot during initial part of action
   B. Failure to place controlling hand directly under ball
   C. Releasing the ball above waist level
   D. Failure to release ball from a virtual pendular motion, causing it to veer to one side
   E. Lack of follow-through, resulting in a weak roll
   F. Swinging the arms too far backward or out from the body
   G. Failure to keep eyes on target
   H. Failure to step forward with foot opposite hand that holds ball
   I. Inability to bring ball to side of the body

Catching

The fundamental movement pattern of catching involves use of the hands to stop tossed objects. The elements of the underhand and overhand catch are essentially the same. The major difference is in the position of the hands upon impact with the object. The underhand catch is performed when the object to be caught is below the waist. The palms of the hands and the wrists are turned upward. When the object is above the waist, the palms face away from the individual in the direction of the flight of the object.

INITIAL

ELEMENTARY

MATURE

Figure 11.17
Stages of the ball
rolling pattern

Table 11.18 Developmental Sequence for Overhand Throwing

I. Throwing
  A. Initial stage
    1. Action is mainly from elbow
    2. Elbow of throwing arm remains in front of body; action resembles a push
    3. Fingers spread at release
    4. Follow-through is forward and downward
    5. Trunk remains perpendicular to target
    6. Little rotary action during throw
    7. Body weight shifts slightly rearward to maintain balance
    8. Feet remain stationary
    9. There is often purposeless shifting of feet during preparation for throw
  B. Elementary stage
    1. In preparation, arm is swung upward, sideward, and backward to a position of elbow flexion
    2. Ball is held behind head
    3. Arm is swung forward, high over shoulder
    4. Trunk rotates toward throwing side during preparatory action
    5. Shoulders rotate toward throwing side
    6. Trunk flexes forward with forward motion of arm
    7. Definite forward shift of body weight
    8. Steps forward with leg on same side as throwing arm
  C. Mature stage
    1. Arm is swung backward in preparation
    2. Opposite elbow is raised for balance as a preparatory action in the throwing arm
    3. Throwing elbow moves forward horizontally as it extends
    4. Forearm rotates and thumb points downward
    5. Trunk markedly rotates to throwing side during preparatory action
    6. Throwing shoulder drops slightly
    7. Definite rotation through hips, legs, spine, and shoulders during throw
    8. Weight during preparatory movement is on rear foot
    9. As weight is shifted, there is a step with opposite foot
II. Developmental Difficulties
  A. Forward movement of foot on same side as throwing arm
  B. Inhibited backswing
  C. Failure to rotate hips as throwing arm is brought forward
  D. Failure to step out on leg opposite the throwing arm
  E. Poor rhythmical coordination of arm movement with body movement
  F. Inability to release ball at desired trajectory
  G. Loss of balance while throwing
  H. Upward rotation of arm

Several researchers have investigated the development of catching abilities in children (Guttridge, 1939; Whiting, 1969; Pederson, 1973; McClenaghan & Gallahue, 1978; Haubenstricker et al., 1983; Roberton & Halverson, 1984). The following developmental sequence of catching is based on these and McClenaghan's (1976) study (Table 11.19, Figure 11.19).

INITIAL

Figure 11.18
Stages of the over-
hand throwing pat-
tern

ELEMENTARY

MATURE

Table 11.19 Developmental Sequence for Catching

I. Catching
   A. Initial stage
      1. There is often an avoidance reaction of turning the face away or protecting the face with arms (avoidance reaction is learned and therefore may not be present)
      2. Arms are extended and held in front of body
      3. Body movement is limited until contact
      4. Catch resembles a scooping action
      5. Use of body to trap ball
      6. Palms are held upward
      7. Fingers are extended and held tense
      8. Hands are not utilized in catching action
   B. Elementary stage
      1. Avoidance reaction is limited to eyes closing at contact with ball
      2. Elbows are held at sides with an approximately 90-degree bend
      3. Since initial attempt at contact with child's hands is often unsuccessful, arms trap the ball
      4. Hands are held in opposition to each other; thumbs are held upward
      5. At contact, the hands attempt to squeeze ball in a poorly-timed and uneven motion
   C. Mature stage
      1. No avoidance reaction
      2. Eyes follow ball into hands
      3. Arms are held relaxed at sides, and forearms are held in front of body
      4. Arms give on contact to absorb force of the ball
      5. Arms adjust to flight of ball
      6. Thumbs are held in opposition to each other
      7. Hands grasp ball in a well-timed, simultaneous motion
      8. Fingers grasp more effectively
II. Developmental Difficulties
   A. Failure to maintain control of object
   B. Failure to "give" with the catch
   C. Keeping fingers rigid and straight in the direction of object
   D. Failure to adjust hand position to the height and trajectory of object
   E. Inability to vary the catching pattern for objects of different weight and force
   F. Taking eyes off object
   G. Closing the eyes
   H. Inability to focus on, or track the ball
   I. Improper stance, causing loss of balance when catching a fast-moving object
   J. Closing hands either too early or too late
   K. Failure to keep body in line with the ball

Kicking

Kicking is a form of striking in which the foot is used to impart force to an object. Precise variations of the kicking action may be accomplished by making adjustments with the kicking leg and by bringing the arms and trunk into play. The primary factors that influence the type of kick used are: (1) the desired trajectory of the ball and (2) the height of the

INITIAL

Figure 11.19
Stages of the
catching pattern

ELEMENTARY

MATURE

ball when it is contacted. The fundamental kicking pattern for a stationary ground ball is the only common striking movement that does not use the arms and hands directly. The developmental aspects of kicking a stationary ball have been studied extensively by Deach (1951) and Seefeldt and Haubenstricker (1981). The developmental sequence that follows (Table 11.20, Figure 11.20) is based on these studies and the work of McClenaghan (1976).

Fundamental Movement Abilities   **271**

Table 11.20 Developmental Sequence for Kicking

I. Kicking
  A. Initial stage
    1. Movements are restricted during kicking action
    2. Trunk remains erect
    3. Arms are used to maintain balance
    4. Movement of kicking leg is limited in backswing
    5. Forward swing is short: there is little follow-through
    6. Child kicks "at" ball rather than kicking it squarely and following through
    7. A pushing rather than a striking action is predominant
  B. Elementary stage
    1. Preparatory backswing is centered at the knee
    2. Kicking leg tends to remain bent throughout the kick
    3. Follow-through is limited to forward movement of the knee
    4. One or more deliberate steps are taken toward the ball
  C. Mature stage
    1. Arms swing in opposition to each other during kicking action
    2. Trunk bends at waist during follow-through
    3. Movement of kicking leg is initiated at the hip
    4. Support leg bends slightly on contact
    5. Length of leg swing increases
    6. Follow-through is high; support foot rises to toes or leaves surface entirely
    7. Approach to the ball is from either a run or leap
II. Developmental Difficulties
  A. Restricted or absent backswing
  B. Failure to step forward with nonkicking leg
  C. Tendency to lose balance
  D. Inability to kick with either foot
  E. Inability to alter speed of kicked ball
  F. Jabbing at ball without follow-through
  G. Poor opposition of arms and legs
  H. Failure to use a summation of forces by the body to contribute to force of the kick
  I. Failure to contact ball squarely, or missing it completely (eyes not focused on ball)
  J. Failure to get adequate distance (lack of follow-through and force production)

Trapping

Trapping an object is actually a form of catching in which the feet or the body is used to absorb the force of the ball instead of the hands and arms. Trapping is a skill that must be highly refined in order for an individual to successfully play soccer. With young children, however, trapping should be viewed very generally, that is, as the ability to stop a ball without use of the hands or arms. A developmental sequence for trapping in children follows. It is based on observational assessment of numerous children and is subject to verification and further refinement (Table 11.21, Figure 11.21).

INITIAL

Figure 11.20
Stages of the
kicking pattern

ELEMENTARY

MATURE

Table 11.21 Developmental Sequence for Trapping

I. Trapping
   A. Initial stage
      1. Trunk remains rigid
      2. No "give" with ball as it makes contact
      3. Inability to absorb force of the ball
      4. Difficulty getting in line with object
   B. Elementary stage
      1. Poor visual tracking
      2. "Gives" with the ball, but movements are poorly timed and sequenced
      3. Can trap a rolled ball with relative ease but cannot trap a tossed ball
      4. Appears uncertain of what body part to use
      5. Movements lack fluidity
   C. Mature stage
      1. Tracks ball throughout
      2. "Gives" with body upon contact
      3. Can trap both rolled and tossed balls
      4. Can trap balls approaching at a moderate velocity
      5. Moves with ease to intercept ball
II. Developmental Difficulties
   A. Failure to position body directly in path of ball
   B. Failure to keep eyes fixed on ball
   C. Failure to "give" as ball contacts body part
   D. Failure to angle an aerial ball downward toward feet
   E. Causing body to meet ball instead of letting ball meet body
   F. Inability to maintain body balance when trapping in unusual or awkward positions

Striking

The first striking movements (other than kicking) appear in young children whenever they hit objects with implements. Swinging at a ball on the ground, on a batting tee, or in flight is a familiar act to most children. Only a limited amount of scientific investigation has been conducted on the developmental aspects of striking in children (Deach, 1951; Halverson and Roberton, 1966, 1984; Seefeldt & Haubenstricker, 1976). The developmental sequence proposed by Seefeldt and Haubenstricker (1976) is summarized below (Table 11.22, Figure 11.22).

INITIAL

Figure 11.21
Stages of the trap-
ping pattern

ELEMENTARY

MATURE

275

Table 11.22 Developmental Sequence for Striking

I. Striking
  A. Initial stage
    1. Motion is from back to front
    2. Feet are stationary
    3. Trunk faces direction of tossed ball
    4. Elbow(s) fully flexed
    5. No trunk rotation
    6. Force comes from extension of flexed joints in a downward plane
  B. Elementary stage
    1. Trunk turned to side in anticipation of tossed ball
    2. Weight shifts to forward foot prior to ball contact
    3. Combined trunk and hip rotation
    4. Elbow(s) flexed at less acute angle
    5. Force comes from extension of flexed joints. Trunk rotation and forward movement are in an oblique plane
  C. Mature stage
    1. Trunk turns to side in anticipation of tossed ball
    2. Weight shifts to back foot
    3. Hips rotate
    4. Transfer of weight is in a contralateral pattern
    5. Weight shift to forward foot occurs while object is still moving backward
    6. Striking occurs in a long, full arc in a horizontal pattern
    7. Weight shifts to forward foot at contact
II. Developmental Difficulties
  A. Failure to focus on and track the ball
  B. Improper grip
  C. Failure to turn side of the body in direction of intended flight
  D. Inability to sequence movements in rapid succession in a coordinated manner
  E. Poor backswing
  F. "Chopping" swing

Dribbling

Dribbling a ball with one hand is a fundamental movement pattern that has only recently received attention in the literature on children (Wickstrom, 1983; Williams, 1983; Payne & Isaacs, 1991). Dribbling is a complicated task requiring precise judgment of an object's distance, force, and trajectory. Dribbling is preceded by ball bouncing and catching. Good figure-ground and depth perception are also required for efficient dribbling. The following proposed developmental sequence is based on Wickstrom's work (1983) and on observational assessment of numerous children. It is subject to further refinement (Table 11.23, Figure 11.23).

INITIAL

ELEMENTARY

MATURE

Figure 11.22
Stages of the striking pattern

Table 11.23 Developmental Sequence for Dribbling

I. Dribbling
  A. Initial stage
    1. Ball held with both hands
    2. Hands placed on sides of ball, with palms facing each other
    3. Downward thrusting action with both arms
    4. Ball contacts surface close to body, may contact foot
    5. Great variation in height of bounce
    6. Repeated bounce and catch pattern
  B. Elementary stage
    1. Ball held with both hands, one on top and the other near the bottom
    2. Slight forward lean, with ball brought to chest level to begin the action
    3. Downward thrust with top hand and arm
    4. Force of downward thrust inconsistent
    5. Hand slaps at ball for subsequent bounces
    6. Wrist flexes and extends and palm of hand contacts ball on each bounce
    7. Visually monitors ball
    8. Limited control of ball while dribbling
  C. Mature stage
    1. Feet placed in narrow stride position, with foot opposite dribbling hand forward
    2. Slight forward trunk lean
    3. Ball held waist high
    4. Ball pushed toward ground, with follow-through of arm, wrist, and fingers
    5. Controlled force of downward thrust
    6. Repeated contact and pushing action initiated from fingertips
    7. Visual monitoring unnecessary
    8. Controlled directional dribbling
II. Developmental Difficulties
  A. Slapping at ball instead of pushing it downward
  B. Inconsistent force applied to downward thrust
  C. Failure to focus on and track ball efficiently
  D. Inability to dribble with both hands
  E. Inability to dribble without visually monitoring ball
  F. Insufficient follow-through
  G. Inability to move about under control while dribbling

Volleying

Volleying is a form of striking in which an overhand pattern is used. It resembles the two-handed set shot that was once popular in basketball and is similar to the overhead set shot used in power volleyball. Use of balloons and beach balls for volleying practice prior to using volleyballs is recommended as a means of promoting success and proper body mechanics. The developmental sequence that follows is based on observation of children and is subject to verification and refinement (Table 11.24, Figure 11.24).

INITIAL

ELEMENTARY

MATURE

Figure 11.23
Stages of the drib-
bling pattern

279

Table 11.24 Developmental Sequence for Volleying

I. Volleying
  A. Initial stage
    1. Inability to accurately judge path of ball or balloon
    2. Inability to get under the ball
    3. Inability to contact ball with both hands simultaneously
    4. Slaps at the ball from behind
  B. Elementary stage
    1. Failure to visually track ball
    2. Gets under the ball
    3. Slaps at ball
    4. Action mainly from hands and arms
    5. Little lift or follow-through with legs
    6. Unable to control direction or intended flight of ball
    7. Wrists relax and ball often travels backward
  C. Mature stage
    1. Gets under the ball
    2. Good contact with fingertips
    3. Wrists remain stiff and arms follow through
    4. Good summation of forces and utilization of arms and legs
    5. Able to control direction and intended flight of ball
II. Developmental Difficulties
  A. Failure to keep eyes on ball
  B. Inability to accurately judge flight of ball and to properly time movements of body
  C. Failure to keep fingers and wrists stiff
  D. Failure to extend all of the joints upon contacting ball (lack of follow-through)
  E. Inability to contact ball with both hands simultaneously
  F. Slapping at ball
  G. Poor positioning of body under ball

Summary

The fundamental movement pattern phase of development follows a sequential progression. The cognitively and physically normal child, under optimal circumstances, will progress through the initial, elementary, and mature stages in a sequential manner. Developmental sequences for several fundamental movements have been identified through biomechanical assessment of children at different age levels. Developmental sequences have also been proposed, based on film, videotape, and observational assessments of numerous children. The fundamental movement phase of development is greatly influenced by the environment. Conditions within the environment and the goal of the task create a variety of between child, between pattern, and within pattern differences. Developmental sequences have been proposed and are

INITIAL

Figure 11.24
Stages of the volleying pattern

ELEMENTARY

MATURE

undergoing validation. A thorough knowledge of these developmental sequences enables one to be more effective in diagnosing movement problems and programming meaningful movement experiences.

Terms to Remember

Movement pattern	Within pattern differences
Fundamental movement	Locomotion
Qualitative change	Manipulation
Intraskill sequences	Stability
Segmental analysis	Axial movement
Total body configuration	Posture
Between child differences	Gestures
Between pattern differences	

Critical Readings

Haubenstricker, J., & Seefeldt, V. (1986). Acquisition of motor skills during childhood. In Seefeldt, V. (Ed.), *Physical Activity and Well-Being*. Reston, VA: AAHPERD.

Haubenstricker, J., Seefeldt, V., & Branta, C. (1983). *Preliminary validation of a developmental sequence for the standing long jump.* Paper presented at the Annual Convention of the AAHPERD, Minneapolis.

Ozmun, J. C., & Robertson, L. D. (1992). *Motor skill characteristics of force production in young children.* Paper presented at the Annual Convention of ACSM, Dallas. (Contact author for a copy.)

Payne, V. G., & Isaacs, L. D. (1991). *Human Motor Development: A Lifespan Approach* (Chapter 13). Mountain View, CA: Mayfield.

Roberton, M. A., & Halverson, L. E. (1984). *Developing Children: Their Changing Movement*. Philadelphia: Lea and Febiger.

Wickstrom, R. L. (1983). *Fundamental Motor Patterns*. Philadelphia: Lea and Febiger.

Chapter **12**

Physical Development of Children

CHAPTER COMPETENCIES

Upon completion of this chapter you should be able to:

- *Demonstrate knowledge of data available on performance scores and motor pattern changes during childhood*
- *Describe gender differences and similarities in motor development*
- *Discuss changes in movement dimensions such as balance, timing, or force production/control*
- *Demonstrate knowledge of major changes in body composition and physiological functioning in males and females*
- *Discuss the effect of exercise on body systems and body composition such as bone and muscle development and cardiorespiratory capacity*
- *Draw conclusions concerning the merits and/or liabilities of strength and endurance training for prepubescent males and females*
- *Distinguish between health-related and performance-related fitness during childhood*
- *Interpret velocity curves on various parameters of children's fitness*
- *Identify gender differences and similarities in motor performance*

Key Concept: The physical fitness of children has been assessed through a variety of laboratory and field-based measures and may be improved through the application of appropriate training techniques.

The health-related fitness and motor fitness of children should be of great concern to all and not just the physical educator, coach, and physician. For the past several decades the fitness levels of boys and girls in North America have received considerable attention in the professional and lay literature. This attention was originally highlighted by the results of minimum muscular efficiency tests (Kraus-Weber) administered to several thousand American and European children during the 1950s. This historic study indicated that the performances of American children were significantly poorer than those of their European counterparts. In fact, more than 55 percent of the Americans failed the test, as compared to less than 10 percent of the European youths. Although the comparison has been criticized for several reasons, it pointed out the important fact that American children are often in poor physical condition.

As a result of the Kraus and Hirschland study (1954), then President Dwight D. Eisenhower established the President's Council on Youth Fitness (now the President's Council on Physical Fitness and Sports—PCPFS) to upgrade the physical fitness of our nation's children. Since that time the PCPFS and others concerned with youth fitness have made many important contributions toward that goal. The American Alliance for Health, Physical Education, Recreation, and Dance (AAHPERD) became a leader in surveying the fitness of American youth through the development and promotion of a national youth fitness test. This test, with revisions, became the basis for decade-by-decade comparisons in 1965, 1975, and 1985. The AAHPERD Youth Fitness Test (1980), and the AAHPERD Health-Related Physical Fitness Tests (1980) were probably the most widely used standardized physical fitness tests throughout the United States during the 1980s. Now, a new generation of field-based fitness measures compete to be the nation's premier youth fitness test battery. *The President's Challenge* (PCPFS), *Physical Best Fitness Test* (AAHPERD), *AAU Physical Fitness Test* (AAU), and *Fitnessgram* (Institute for Aerobics Research, Inc.) are among several test batteries available for use by field professionals.

Concept 12.1 A variety of available field measures claim to measure various aspects of children's physical fitness.

Noted professionals as well as fitness organizations report that a great many children are unfit (Baranowski et al., 1992; Kuntzleman & Reiff, 1992; Updyke, 1992; NASPE 1992). Moreover, the National Children and

Youth Fitness Study (Ross & Gilbert, 1985) revealed that more than one-third of the children and youth tested (ages 10 to 18) were not sufficiently active in their daily lives for aerobic benefit. A second survey (National Children and Youth Fitness Study II, 1987) of children 6 to 9 years old showed that they were heavier and fatter than their counterparts of 20 years ago.

Two primary factors seem to have contributed greatly to this state of affairs. First, the need to enhance fitness in the United States has centered on adults. Until recently, relatively little research has been focused on the fitness needs of children. As a result, our knowledge of the fitness of children and their capacity for work has been limited.

Concept 12.2   Conventional wisdom suggests that today's children are unfit, but little conclusive evidence exists to either support or deny this assertion.

A second assumption has been that children are naturally active and get plenty of vigorous physical exercise as a normal part of their daily routines. However, apartment living, city dwelling, and the ubiquitous television set have created sedentary lifestyles for many children. Blair, however, (1992) takes exception to this position:

> Anyone who has taught or raised children should know that they are
> physically active. Nevertheless, we have been bombarded by
> propaganda over the past 35 years in both the professional and lay
> literature that deplores the status of youth fitness in the United States
> (p. 120).

There are three primary reasons why it makes little sense to argue whether children are fit or unfit. First, we have not completely or adequately defined ''physical fitness.'' As simple as this may seem, there has been considerable debate as to what constitutes ''physical fitness.'' In fact, a recent article by Gutin, Manos, and Strong (1992) pointed out that defining the terms ''health'' and ''fitness'' was a necessary first step toward establishing children's fitness standards. Here we are in the last years of the twentieth century and we still have not agreed on the meaning of the term physical fitness even though definitions have been proposed for nearly 100 years.

Second, there is an absence of proven, valid, and reliable gold standards for assessing physical fitness in the laboratory. *Gold standard* is a term used to refer to an ultimate and universally accepted measure of a particular quality. To date, laboratory gold standards have not been established for most measures of physical fitness. This makes it difficult to conclusively establish the validity of common field measures of fitness. Baranowski et al. (1992) in their two recommendations for future research in physical activity and physical fitness recommended that: (1) gold standard laboratory measures and corresponding valid field measures be developed and (2) valid measures of health-related fitness that are applicable to laboratory, field, and clinical settings be identified.

Third, specific criteria for determining who is "physically fit" or "physically unfit" have yet to be established. Classifying one as being fit or unfit is based more on supposition and hunches, rather than on scientifically determined standards. Specific numerical levels have been established as guidelines for determining mental retardation, high cholesterol, obesity, and a number of other educational and health issues. It follows then that criteria can and should be established for minimal physical fitness levels necessary for good health. Until this is accomplished, we are doing little more than tilting at windmills in the youth fitness debate. In fact, Seefeldt and his colleagues (1989) questioned the basic assumptions underlying physical fitness testing of children, and claim that it has resulted in a 30-year history of misguided efforts.

With these limitations in mind we will now turn to a discussion about what we do know about the health-related and performance-related aspects of children's physical fitness. The information that follows is based on information gleaned from laboratory, field, and clinical settings.

Health-Related Fitness

Extensive studies in the area of physical fitness have been conducted over the past several years, and we are gradually piecing together what is known about the physical fitness of children (Falls & Pate, 1993). A review of the literature on fitness, however, reveals a marked lack of information on children under 6 years of age. The reasons for this are many. Most tests of physical fitness require the individual to go "all out" and perform at his or her maximum. Anyone familiar with young children will recognize the difficulty of this situation. The problems lie in: (1) being able to sufficiently motivate the youngster for maximal performance, (2) accurately determining whether a maximum effort has been achieved, and (3) overcoming the fears of anxious parents. Experts working with young children have an almost untouched area for the study of physical fitness. Carefully controlled, patient research will yield much valuable information. In fact, new inroads are being made in conducting treadmill tests on preschool children, an area historically fraught with methodological difficulties (Delozier et al., 1988).

Cardiovascular endurance, muscular strength, muscular endurance, joint flexibility, and body composition are the components of health-related fitness. Each of these components is discussed briefly in the following paragraphs in terms of what is known at the present time.

Aerobic Endurance

Aerobic endurance is an aspect of muscular endurance, specific to the heart, lungs, and vascular system. It refers to the ability to perform numerous repetitions of a stressful activity requiring considerable use of the circulatory and respiratory system. *Maximal oxygen consumption* (VO_2 max) refers to the largest quantity of oxygen an individual can consume during physical work while breathing air at sea level. It is a measure of one's maximum ability to transmit oxygen to the tissues of the body. An increase in one's aerobic capacity is an excellent indicator of a higher energy output. Astrand (1952) indicated that up to a 20 percent improvement in VO_2 max is possible. One's genetic inheritance plays a crucial role in the capacity to consume oxygen. Maximal oxygen consumption tends to improve as a function of age until about 18 to 20. Improvement thereafter is primarily a function of training. Females possess about 75 percent of the capacity of males to consume oxygen. The differences between males and females prior to puberty are largely unexplored. Oxygen consumption in children has been investigated by relatively few researchers, and the results have often been conflicting because of the questionable reliability and reproducibility of VO_2 max measures with children. However, recent attempts have been made to develop and establish clinical guidelines for measuring aerobic factors with pediatric populations (Rowland, 1993).

Maximal aerobic power as measured by maximal oxygen consumption is a universally accepted means of measuring status and change in cardiovascular fitness. It is not, however, universally accepted or understood how to express maximal aerobic ability in relation to body size. The literature concerning the aerobic capacity of children, particularly under the age of 6, is limited. Young children make difficult subjects, and the testing environment is restricted by the extent of their interest in putting forth a maximal effort. Bailey et al. (1978) indicated that knowing how maximal aerobic power relates to body mass and body size is very important when dealing with children. "In fitness training studies on children there is a problem in determining if changes and maximal aerobic power are a result of training, growth or both, since increasing size may result in changes similar to the training effect" (p. 140–141). Bailey and his colleagues studied 200 Canadian boys for 10 years beginning when the boys were 7 years old. The subjects received no special instruction or opportunities other than performing yearly treadmill tests of their aerobic capacities. The results of this study revealed yearly increases in their oxygen utilization. However, when the data were expressed in terms of the amount of oxygen utilized in proportion to body weight (i.e., liters per minute per kilogram of body weight) no consistent pattern with increasing age emerged. This finding indicates that the aerobic capacity of an individual is related in part to body weight and in part to age.

Andersen et al. (1978) conducted a 9-year longitudinal study of aerobic capacity with Norwegian boys and girls ranging in age from 8 to 12 years. The results of this investigation indicated that gains in aerobic power were greater than could be expected from growth in body size alone. Fitness expressed on the basis of body weight and on lean body mass increased as the children became older. The authors attributed this linear trend toward improved aerobic capacity over time, and without special training, to informal environmental stimulation and not simply to changes in body size.

Over the years several laboratory studies have been conducted with children to determine their VO_2 max values. Pate and Blair (1978) in their review of two decades of studies concluded that values ranging from 45 to 55 milliliters of oxygen per kilogram of body weight had been consistently reported in the United States. Krahenbuhl et al. (1985) in a more recent review of 29 longitudinal studies found similar mean values. They also noted that VO_2 max relative to weight remained stable for boys from year to year, but declined for girls as they advanced in years. It is interesting to note that a minimum VO_2 max threshold value of 42 has been recommended for adults (Cooper 1968), and according to Simons-Morton et al. (1987) in their review of children and fitness, "it appears that most children are well above this level" (p. 297).

Heart rate responses to exercise are sometimes used as crude measures of cardiovascular endurance in young children because of the difficulty in gathering accurate VO_2 max data. Normal resting heart rates in children range from approximately 60 to 80 beats per minute. Maximum exercise heart rates in children have been reported to range from about 150 to 230 beats per minute. Mrzena and Macuek (1978) tested children 3 to 5 years old on the treadmill. Each subject was required to walk or run for 5 minutes at a level grade with the treadmill set at three different speeds (3, 4, and 5 km/h). The highest heart rates were recorded at 142 beats per minute. Another group performed the treadmill task at 4 km/h while the grade was increased from 5° to 10° to 15°. This group produced heart rates averaging 162 beats per minute. Investigators noted that when the treadmill speed was increased to 6 km/h and the inclination to 20°, "the children were not able to increase the step frequency and lost their balance" (p. 31). The average maximum aerobic capacity of preschool children is certainly greater than the scores obtained in this experiment, but maturity of movement as well as the psychological and emotional state of the young child determine the degree of cooperation and effort during testing.

In an investigation by Parizkova (1977), heart rates of 160 beats per minute were recorded in a bench-stepping task with 3-year-old children. The children had considerable difficulty maintaining the cadence of 30 steps per minute on the low bench without the investigator's assistance. The children in this investigation also had difficulty maintaining the task even though normal play heart rates of young children often exceed 200 beats per minute. Cumming and Hnatiuk (1980) reported that normal maximal heart rates for children range from 180 to 234 beats per minute. This investigation again reminds us of the extreme difficulty in achieving a maximal effort for a sustained period of time with young children.

A study by Montoye (1970) used a 3-minute step test to evaluate an entire community. The results of Montoye's investigation indicate that resting, exercise, and recovery heart rates decrease with age between ages 10 and 20 and to a lesser degree between ages 20 and 35. Children are capable of working at much higher heart rates than previously expected.

Although it is now clear that children are capable of achieving maximal heart rates at or above those of adults, it is doubtful that such levels are reached during the daily routines of the vast majority of children. Gilliam and his colleagues (1981) confirmed this hypothesis in an experiment in which they monitored the heart rate patterns of 6- and 7-year-olds during a two-month summer period. The results of this investigation in which 22 boys and 18 girls wore small heart monitoring devices for 12 hours during their normal daily routine revealed:

> The voluntary activity patterns of the children studied may not be adequate, in terms of duration and intensity, to promote cardiovascular health. . . . our data and others' show children . . . very seldom experience physical activity of high enough intensity to promote cardiovascular health. Furthermore, our data show that boys are more active than girls (p. 67).

The National Children and Youth Fitness Study II (1987) collected data on more than 4,500 children in grades one through four on 5 health-related fitness items. This study represents the most rigorously controlled national sampling of the fitness of children under 10 years of age to date. Data were collected by a small, highly trained field staff. The data are thought to be highly reliable and representative of a broad cross section of the children of the United States (Errecart et al., 1987). Based on the results of these field tests, estimates of the various health-related components of fitness comparisons can be made by age and by gender. Figure 12.1 provides a graph of the mean scores for boys and girls ages 6 and 7 on the half-mile walk/run, and the mean scores for boys and girls ages 8 and 9 on the mile walk/run. Analysis of this graph reveals that boys are superior to girls in terms of mean times for both the half-mile and the mile walk/run at all ages. Furthermore, boys appear to maintain their margin of aerobic superiority at all ages.

An area of study that has received increased attention in recent years deals with the *aerobic trainability* of prepubescent children in terms of their potential for making significant gains in VO_2 max scores. Because it has been widely documented that adults respond to training protocols, it is commonly believed that children can produce similar physiologically measurable training effects. To date, however, studies

Figure 12.1
Half-mile walk/run (left) and one mile walk/run (right): mean scores for males and females 6–7 and 8–9, in minutes and seconds (drawn from data, *Source:* Ross, J. G., et al. [1987]. "The National Children and Youth Fitness Study II: New Health-Related Fitness Norms." *Journal of Physical Education, Recreation and Dance, 58,* 66–70)

examining this phenomena have yielded inconsistent findings. Vaccaro and Mahon (1987) raised the question of whether adult criteria can be applied to children. In fact, they noted that "studies in children are contradictory with regard to the effects of exercise training on the cardiorespiratory system" (p. 353). This view has been supported by a number of investigators (Borms, 1986; Bar-Or, 1989; Katch, 1983). Borms (1986) indicated that although children often demonstrate improvements in their running performance in terms of time or distance covered, this frequently occurs without corresponding improvements in VO_2 max. To compound matters, Borms further suggested that early maturers may be more susceptible to positive training effects than average or late maturers. In addition, Bar-Or contends that children's aerobic trainability is less than one would expect prior to puberty. Katch (1983) hypothesizes that a "triggering" effect is absent before puberty due to insufficient circulating androgens. Recently, a meta-analysis of the quantitative effects of aerobic training on the VO$_2$ max scores of children was completed by Payne and Morrow (1993). Their investigation, which included 30 studies that met inclusionary criteria, revealed that:

> In the most rigorously controlled studies (pre/post test), subjects improved less than 2 ml.kg-1.min-1. When contrasting studies with 'sufficient' and 'insufficient' training protocols, significance was not achieved. These findings indicate that many current practices concerning children's fitness should be viewed with skepticism (p. 3).

Concept 12.3   The potential for measurable aerobic trainability in prepubescent children has yet to be conclusively documented.

In summary, there is considerable research available on the topic of children's trainability, but the issue remains controversial (Pate & Ward, 1990; Payne & Morrow, 1993; Rowland, 1985). The practice of increasing the amount of a child's vigorous physical activity as a means of enhancing aerobic endurance is endorsed by many leading professionals and national professional associations. To date, the data do not conclusively support this hypothesis. Training protocols that produce significant training effects in children should be studied, and the specific attributes of those being trained must be identified.

Muscular Strength

Muscular strength is the ability of the body to exert force. In its purest sense, it is the ability to exert one maximum effort. Children engaged in daily active play are enhancing their leg strength by running and bicycling. Their arm strength is developed through such activities as lifting, carrying objects, handling tools, and swinging on the monkey bars. Strength may be classified as isotonic, isometric, or isokinetic. *Isometric strength* involves exerting force on an immovable object. The muscle contracts, but there is little change in its length. *Isotonic strength* refers to the ability of a muscle to go through its full range of motion. The muscles involved contract, but they also shorten and lengthen during the activity. A barbell curl and a bench press are examples of isotonic strength activities. *Isokinetic strength* involves contracting a muscle and maintaining that contraction through its full range of motion. Isokinetic strength is measured by use of special machines that accommodate resistance at a set velocity as the muscle works.

In laboratory situations *strength* is commonly measured by using a dynamometer or tensiometer. These devices are highly reliable when utilized by trained personnel. *Dynamometers* are calibrated devices designed to measure grip strength, leg strength, and back strength. *Tensiometers* are more versatile than dynamometers in that they permit measurement of many different muscle groups. The classic longitudinal studies conducted by Clarke (1971) utilized 18 different cable tensiometer tests and revealed yearly strength increments in boys between 7 and 17 years. After age 12 or 13, girls tend to differ markedly from boys in their strength levels. According to Corbin (1980), girls without training tend to level off at this age, but boys continue to gain in strength. It seems probable that the strength levels of preschool and primary grade boys and girls are similar, with the edge being given to boys based on their tendency to be slightly taller and heavier than girls. Unfortunately, virtually nothing is known about the muscular strength of the young child.

Concept 12.4   Although incremental, strength gains during childhood are not linear; therefore, estimating strength scores in later years based on scores achieved during childhood offers little in the way of predictive validity.

Relatively few longitudinal investigations have been conducted on the development of strength in children at all ages. However, the information that is available indicates consistency in the development of strength in children over time. In fact, strength has been shown to increase more rapidly than muscle size during childhood (Armussen, 1973; Bar-Or, 1989; Sale, 1989). This is probably due to the improved skill and coordination with which a maximal contraction may be performed. This indicates the interrelationship between strength, coordination, and motor performance in children.

Although strength is a relatively stable quality throughout childhood, predicting strength levels at later years from measures taken in childhood has met with little success. The "strong" child at age 8, for example, will not necessarily make the greatest gains in strength from childhood through adolescence. Neither will the "weak" child necessarily make the least gains in strength from childhood through adolescence. Rapid change in body size, which is positively correlated with strength, and individual variability of growth patterns make prediction a precarious venture.

Muscular Endurance

Muscular endurance is the ability of a muscle or a group of muscles to perform work repeatedly against moderate resistance. Muscular endurance is similar to muscular strength in the activities performed but it differs in emphasis. Strength-building activities require overloading the muscles to a greater extent than endurance activities. Endurance-building activities require less of an overload on the muscle but more repetitions. Therefore, endurance may be thought of as the ability to continue in strength performance. Children performing sit-ups, push-ups, and pull-ups are actually engaged in endurance activities even though strength is required for any movement to begin. These three activities are among the most often used measures of muscular endurance, and according to Montoye (1970), they are among the best tests available. There are, however, problems with pull-up measures because of body weight (Pate et al., 1987). The entire body weight must be lifted, and many children are unable to accomplish such a task. Therefore, a modified pull-up test is now frequently used.

Concept 12.5   Endurance levels of children approach and often exceed those of adults when adjusted for body weight.

The daily uninhibited play routines of young children are excellent examples of endurance that most adults would be unable to duplicate. *Relative endurance* refers to the child's endurance level adjusted to body weight. It stands to reason that an adult's gross levels of endurance and fitness are generally greater than those of the child, but when body weight is factored into the total fitness score, the differences are less pronounced.

The results of the bent knee sit-up test and the flexed arm hang test administered in both the AAHPERD Youth Fitness Test (1980) and the CAHPER Manitoba Physical Fitness Performance Test (1980) revealed age changes in muscular endurance. On both of these measures, boys and girls showed a tendency toward considerable improvement during childhood. The National Children and Youth Fitness Study II (1987) measured the strength/endurance of boys and girls age 6 to 9. Abdominal strength/endurance was assessed by a 60-second bent-knee sit up test (Figure 12.2). Upper body strength/endurance was tested through performance of a modified pull-up test (Figure 12.3). The results of the sit-up test (Figure 12.4) indicated that the mean scores for boys were slightly superior to girls at all ages. Both groups made steady improvements in terms of their abdominal strength/endurance from year to year.

With regard to upper body strength/endurance boys were again slightly ahead of girls in the average number of completed modified pull-ups. Boys continued to improve with age while girls tended to level off in their average performance (Figure 12.5).

Flexibility

Joint flexibility is the ability of the various joints of the body to move through their full range of motion. There are two types of flexibility: static and dynamic. *Static flexibility* is the range of motion achieved by a slow and steady stretch to the limits of the joints involved. *Dynamic flexibility* is the range of motion that is achieved when rapidly moving a body part to its limits (Williams, 1993).

Figure 12.2
The modified sit-up
test

Figure 12.3
The modified pull-
up test

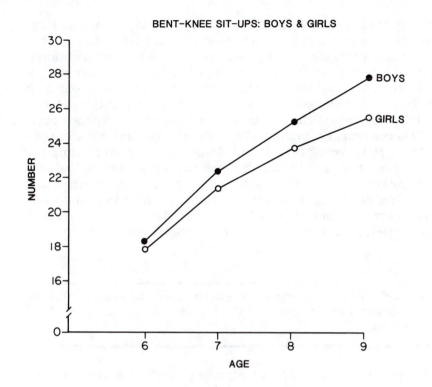

Figure 12.4
Modified sit-ups: mean scores for males and females 6–9 years, number in 60 seconds (drawn from data, *Source:* Ross, J. G., et al. [1987]. "The National Children and Youth Fitness Study II: New Health-Related Fitness Norms." *Journal of Physical Education, Recreation and Dance,* 58, 66–70)

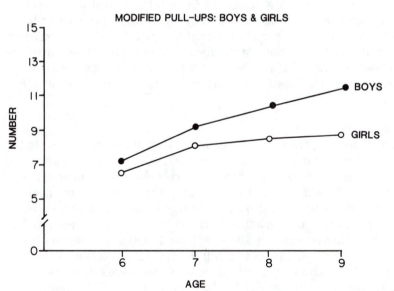

Figure 12.5
Modified pull-ups: mean scores for males and females 6–9, number completed (drawn from data, *Source:* Ross, J. G., et al. [1987]. "The National Children and Youth Fitness Study II: New Health-Related Fitness Norms." *Journal of Physical Education, Recreation and Dance,* 58, 66–70)

Flexibility is joint specific and can be improved with practice. Hupperich and Sigerseth (1950) indicated, however, that dynamic flexibility in the shoulder, knee, and thigh joints decreases with age in children as evidenced by their investigation of girls 6, 9, and 12 years of age. Their investigation revealed also that static flexibility increased with age. Clarke (1975) reviewed the research on flexibility and concluded that flexibility begins to decline in boys around age 10 and in girls around age 12. This confirms Leighton's (1956) study of the flexibility of boys ages 10 to 18. His investigation revealed that the common assumption that boys have a high level of flexibility during childhood and adolescence is questionable. Boys showed no consistent pattern of increasing or maintaining flexibility with age, but did show a definite tendency toward decreased flexibility with age. DiNucci (1976) reported that girls performed better than boys on five different measures of flexibility at all ages.

Concept 12.6   Activity levels offer a better guide to joint flexibility than chronological age, because of the highly specific nature of this fitness component.

The National Children and Youth Fitness Study II (1987) tested thousands of children 6 to 9 years of age for flexibility. A sit-and-reach test (Figure 12.6) was used as a measure of joint flexibility in the lower back and hip area. Mean scores clearly favored the girls. They tended to be slightly more flexible than boys at all ages. Girls showed little improvement with age, but neither did they regress. The boys, however, were on the average slightly less flexible at age 9 than they were at age 6 (Figure 12.7).

Body Composition

Body composition is defined as the proportion of lean body mass to fat body mass. Relative fatness can be determined through a variety of means. *Hydrostatic weighing* (underwater) techniques, although the most accurate, are seldom used in studying the body composition of children. Instead, *skinfold calipers* are the preferred method, even though the accuracy of measurement is sometimes questionable (Lohman, 1986). Measurement sites include the triceps, subscapular region, and the medial portion of the calf (Figure 12.8). National surveys of body fatness have shown that children of all ages are fatter than they were 20 years ago (Gortmaker et al., 1987; Pate et al., 1985; Ross et al., 1987). This trend toward increased fatness of American youth probably reflects changes in physical activity patterns and nutritional habits.

Figure 12.6
The sit-and-reach
test

Figure 12.6 The sit-and-reach test

Concept 12.7 Over the past 20 years, a number of factors have contributed to a secular trend toward higher body fat percentages among children living in the United States.

With regard to activity patterns, Parizkova (1972, 1973, 1977) demonstrated repeatedly that young athletes are less fat than their more sedentary age-mates. Conversely, it has been repeatedly documented that obese children are significantly less active than their lean peers (Bandini, 1987; Romanella et al., 1991; Rowland, 1991).

The reasons for adoption of a sedentary lifestyle among children are many, but the implications are clear. Lower activity levels result in increased body fat percentages, while higher activity levels tend to promote lower body fat levels. The activity habits of a lifetime are formed during childhood. Parents, teachers, and other significant individuals in a child's environment can make a difference in activity levels both by example and by positive encouragement. Ward and Bar-Or (1986)

Figure 12.7
Sit-and-reach:
mean scores for
males and females
6–9 years, in
inches (drawn from
data, *Source:* Ross,
J. G., et al. [1987].
"The National Chil-
dren and Youth Fit-
ness Study II: New
Health-Related Fit-
ness Norms."
*Journal of Physical
Education, Recrea-
tion and Dance,* 58,
66–70)

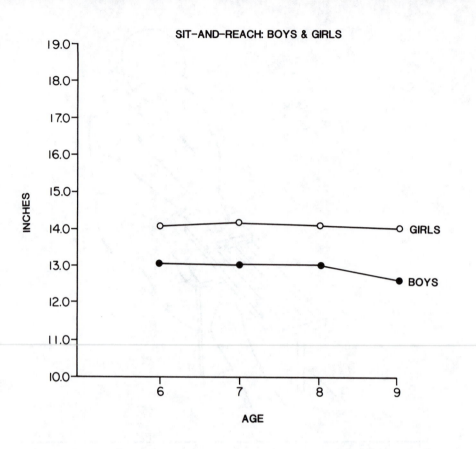

Figure 12.8
Triceps and sub-
scapular skinfold
caliper measure-
ment sites

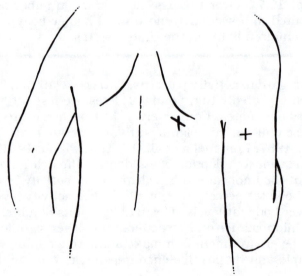

after reviewing 13 school-based obesity intervention programs reported that the success of these programs was dependent upon the following elements.

1. Multidisciplinary, integrating behavior modification, nutrition education, and physical activity
2. Structured physical activity opportunities 4 to 5 times per week, with encouragement and incentives for after-school activities
3. Team approach, with the participation of the school nurse, guidance counselor, lunchroom supervisor, and physical education teacher
4. Parental involvement, in order to achieve continuity and to coordinate home support for the development of new behaviors (Bar-Or, 1987, p. 306)

Ward et al. (1987) found that a multi-component intervention program with obese children could serve as a valuable means of reducing health risks associated with obesity. Parents, classroom teachers, health workers, and physical education teachers all play important roles in reversing the trend toward increased body fatness in children. Working as a team, they stand the best chance of successfully intervening (Ross et al., 1987).

The National Children and Youth Fitness Study II (1987) represents the latest large-scale, nationally representative sampling of 6- to 9-year-olds in terms of body composition. Skinfold measurements were made at three body landmarks (triceps, subscapular, and medial calf skinfolds) by use of a Lange skinfold caliper. In comparison to the National Health Examination Survey and data from the National Center for Health Statistics, both the boys and the girls of the 1980s have higher percentages of body fat than their counterparts of the 1960s (Ross et al., 1987). Furthermore, there is a definite tendency for increased body fatness in both males and females as they advance in years from 6 to 9, with females leading males at all ages (Figure 12.9).

Children's Fitness Training

During the last few years our knowledge base has expanded dramatically in the area of children's fitness training. Although we still have many unanswered questions, research is beginning to show that children are capable of much more in terms of aerobic conditioning, strength and endurance enhancement, and flexibility improvement than previously thought (Roberts, 1993). Although we do not have adequate information at this time to clearly delineate the physical activity patterns of children, we do know that the active child can make significant health-related fitness gains.

Figure 12.9
Sum of triceps, subscapular and medial calf skinfolds: mean scores for males and females 6–9, in millimeters (drawn from data, *Source:* Ross, J. G., et al. [1987]. "The National Children and Youth Fitness Study II: New Health-Related Fitness Norms." *Journal of Physical Education, Recreation and Dance,* 58, 66–70)

BODY COMPOSITION: BOYS & GIRLS

Aerobic Training

The demonstrable effects of children's *aerobic training* programs are sometimes questionable (Payne & Morrow, 1993). Some studies have reported increases in VO_2 max with training in children (Brown et al., 1972; Massicotte and MacNab, 1974; Vrijens, 1978). However, several studies have failed to show a training effect with children (Cumming & Friesen, 1967; Cumming et al., 1969; Daniels & Oldridge, 1971; Ekbolm, 1969). This discrepancy is probably due to the fact that children are not predisposed to all-out physical exertion. The use of scientific gadgets, the pain, and the time involved in data collection all make the results of any training study with children subject to further verification. Training effects have seldom been reported in elementary physical education programs that focused on aerobic endurance. This, according to Simons-Morton et al. (1987), may be due to a number of factors including (1) naturally high levels of activity, (2) insufficient intensity in the training program, or (3) failure of all children to participate fully in the program. However, Pate and Blair (1978), Chausow et al. (1984), Krahenbuhl et al. (1985), and Savage et al. (1986) have all reported positive responses to training in laboratory settings where the frequency, intensity, and duration could be controlled and progress could be more carefully monitored. Therefore, it appears that prepubescent children can make positive adaptations to increased aerobic demands, and that failure to do so is related to factors other than the child's inherent inability to adapt.

Concept 12.8 A child's aerobic capacity has the potential to increase with training under specific laboratory conditions.

A second important consideration in aerobic training programs for children deals with aerobic activity carryover into adolescence and adulthood. Shepard (1984), Pate and Blair (1978), and others have hypothesized that active children become active adults. Unfortunately, little data exist to support this claim. It seems, however, that vigorous activity during childhood alone is not the key to later activity patterns. Developing the movement skills necessary to participate in lifetime fitness activities for fun, success, and enjoyment is essential if we expect to see real activity carryover from childhood to adulthood. The notion of "no pain—no gain" simply will not work with most children. We must strive to make children's aerobic training highly enjoyable, and promote skill development so that aerobic conditioning becomes a natural outcome of a healthy lifestyle.

A third issue of importance to aerobic conditioning with children centers on the question of just how much is enough to promote the functional health of the child. Although we now know that the child is capable of far more than we previously thought, we do not know the optimal intensity, frequency, and duration of activity necessary to produce health benefits. Although we can produce a training effect as measured by the ability of the cardiovascular system to adapt to increased stress, we do not know how much is required to produce lasting health benefits. Recent studies with adults (Kallel & Sorlie, 1979; Paffenbarger et al., 1986) provide convincing evidence for moderate activity levels of a regular nature over time as an essential promoter of positive health. Perhaps it is not the level of one's physical fitness *per se* that affects cardiovascular health, but the fact that one takes part in moderate levels of physical activity as a part of the daily activity pattern. At this juncture, we simply do not know if these results are applicable to children. Gilliam and Macconnie (1984) stated that "programs and research efforts should be designed to study the long-range effects of physical activity and dietary intervention programs on CHD (coronary heart disease) risk in children" (p. 183). We do know, however, that overuse injuries, burnout, and high attrition rates are associated with high-intensity children's programs that fail to stress skill and learning enjoyment (Andrish, 1984; Gould, 1987). Much needs to be done to determine optimal levels of activity and appropriate conditions for maximum carryover of benefits into adulthood.

Cardiovascular endurance in children can be improved in much the same way as it is in adults. However, the extent to which they can improve is still open to speculation. A recent meta-analysis of 28 studies that aerobically trained children concluded that: "Results indicated that reported changes in VO_2 max in children are small to moderate and are a function of the experimental design used." (Payne & Morrow, p. 305). Children need motivation, familiarity with pacing, and opportunities to engage in intensive physical work over time. The primary concern of the parent and teacher should not be how to improve maximum oxygen utilization (VO_2 max) but how to develop movement abilities and motivate the child so that he or she improves as a function of a daily self-programmed regimen of vigorous physical activity. The teacher of preschool and primary grade children needs to focus on developing and refining fundamental movement abilities. The intermediate and upper grade teacher needs to apply these movement abilities to a variety of game, sport, and dance activities that enhance cardiovascular endurance and other fitness components.

Strength Training

It has been widely assumed that prepubescent children will not benefit significantly from a monitored strength training program. Please refer to Table 12.1 for a description of common terms used in resistance training (NSCA, 1985). Early negative findings led many people to believe that strength training programs were ineffective because of low levels of circulating androgens (male sex hormones) in prepubescent boys and in females of all ages (Vrijens, 1978; Legwold, 1982, 1983). In fact, a 1983 position paper by the American Academy of Pediatrics concluded that prepubescent strength training, although acceptable if properly supervised, was largely ineffective. However, Bar-Or (1983) asked, if women, who have low levels of testosterone, are capable of making significant strength gains, then why can't prepubescent children make similar gains? A number of recent studies clearly point out that children are capable of making significant strength gains in properly conducted and supervised programs of sufficient duration and intensity (Cahill, 1986; Duda, 1986; Sewell & Micheli, 1984). These investigations and others prompted the American Academy of Pediatrics (1990) to update their position statement to recognize the efficacy of prepubescent strength training (AAP, 1990). With proper supervision strength training can benefit prepubescent children in terms of strength enhancement (Micheli, 1988; Blimkie, 1989), injury reduction (Hejna, 1982) and improved performance (Malina, 1986; Sale, 1989). It should be noted, however, that "strength training" is different from "weight lifting." *Strength training* involves the use of progressive resistance techniques using the body, weights, or machines to improve one's ability to exert or resist a force. *Weight lifting* is a sport in which one attempts to lift the maximum number of pounds possible. Weight lifting is not recommended for prepubescent children (Micheli, 1988; National Strength and Conditioning Association, 1985).

Table 12.1 Terms Commonly Used in Strength Training

RESISTANCE TRAINING: Any method used to overcome or bear force.

STRENGTH TRAINING: The use of resistance to increase the ability to overcome or bear force. Various devices, including machines, weights, or one's body may be used as a means of increasing strength.

WEIGHT TRAINING: The use of free weights (barbells, dumbbells), stationary weights, or machines to increase strength.

WEIGHT LIFTING: A competitive sport sometimes referred to as "power lifting" in which the participant attempts to lift the maximum weight possible in prescribed events (Olympic snatch, clean and jerk, squat, bench press, and dead lift).

Concept 12.9 Prepubescent children can, under certain conditions, make significant gains in muscular strength in properly designed and carefully supervised resistance training programs.

Hormonal control of protein synthesis in muscle tissue involves the complex interaction of many *anabolic hormones* (muscle-enhancing) and *catabolic hormones* (muscle-destroying). One of the most important anabolic hormones is *growth hormone* (GH), which is found in prepubescent children. According to Bernuth et al. (1985) "exercise has been found to be the most potent stimulus for GH release in children" (p. 100). It seems, therefore, that children have at least some of the hormones necessary for muscle hypertrophy. Most studies, however, examining prepubescent weight training have found no evidence of muscle hypertrophy following a training program (Ozmun et al., in press; Ramsay et al., 1990; Blimkie et al., 1989; Weltman et al., 1986). Only one investigation has claimed to have observed muscle hypertrophy in a prepubescent population (Mersch & Stoboy, 1989). These results, however, require verification as the subjects involved only two sets of identical twins.

Testosterone has been the primary sex hormone associated with the tremendous gains in muscular strength seen in adolescent males. Like growth hormone, it is an anabolic hormone, but it is not clear whether it enhances muscular development by direct action on muscle tissue or by an indirect inhibition of the catabolic action of other hormones (Kuoppasaline & Adlercreutz, 1985). It is, however, the combination of testosterone and growth hormone that enhances protein synthesis and inhibits protein destruction in muscle tissue, contributing to an increase in muscle size and strength (Tanner, 1978). Therefore, although females of all ages and prepubescent males have low levels of circulating androgens, they possess other anabolic hormones such as growth hormone that can facilitate protein synthesis and result in significant strength increases under sufficiently enhanced levels of training.

Prepubescent children can increase their strength through resistance training due to enhanced stimulation of the central nervous system beyond that which would occur with normal growth and maturation. The term *neuromuscular adaptation* is used for changes that result from training. When the body is subjected over time to significant amounts of anatomical or physiological stress, the natural reaction is to adapt to the new conditions. It has been demonstrated that a short term weight training program results in neuromuscular adaptations with prepubescent participants (Ozmun et al., in press; Ramsay et al., 1990; Blimkie et al., 1989). There are, however, special considerations for the preadolescent involved in a strength training program.

The possibility that weight training harms the still-growing *epiphyseal growth plates* in young bones is a concern. Indeed, these cartilaginous structures, by their soft and spongy nature, are susceptible to injury, especially from excessive weight bearing, shearing forces, and chronic stress (Micheli, 1984; Micheli & Melhonian, 1987). The potential vulnerability of the growth plates through excessive stress must not be minimized. In fact, a high correlation exists between damage to these areas and children involved in weight lifting (Gumbs et al., 1982). As a result, the National Strength and Conditioning Association (1985) and the American Academy of Pediatrics (1990) recommend that prepubescent athletes avoid the sport due to the immaturity of their bones.

Another prime cause of epiphyseal damage in children engaged in weight training and chronic stress activities is improper training techniques. In addition, some weight training equipment may be unsuitable with or without proper technique. Most machine-type resistance equipment is made to adult body proportions, with little or no consideration given to youth proportions.

Epiphyseal growth plate injuries due to overuse have also been reported in children participating in certain sports. Distance running, gymnastics, and distance swimming have the potential for causing overuse injuries in the prepubescent athlete. In fact, overuse injuries are beginning to be reported in sports such as soccer as playing seasons continue to increase in length.

In summary, it appears that prepubescent strength training can, if properly supervised, produce significant strength gains in boys and girls. One must be careful, however, to use this information with care. Damage to the epiphyseal growth end plates of the long bones may occur if the young body is pushed too far. At this juncture it is not possible to determine the extent to which any one individual may be pushed in training before damage is done. As a result, carefully supervised weight training programs that emphasize proper technique and actively discourage maximal lifts are recommended. Programs should also utilize equipment adapted to child's size and stress low resistance training. In no case should prepubescent athletes be encouraged or permitted to engage in weight lifting (i.e., "max-out").

Flexibility Training

Besides strength and endurance training, another key health-related fitness component considered essential to injury prevention is joint flexibility. Improving the range of motion about the various joints of the body plays an important role in enhancing movement performance. Historically, it was believed that any type of weight training would decrease an individual's flexibility by not allowing the muscle to work through the full range of motion. The isokinetic weight training equipment of today is designed to solve this problem. With the principle of variable resistance, an intricate system of cams and pulleys compensates for the inherent weak areas in a joint's range of motion. Flexibility can be maintained or even augmented with proper technique and certain types of weight training equipment (Duda, 1986).

Concept 12.10   Children frequently exhibit decreased levels of joint flexibility during the prepubescent growth spurt because bone growth precedes muscle and tendon growth.

Micheli and Micheli (1985) reported less flexibility in males and females during the prepubescent growth spurt. The reason for this is that bone growth precedes muscle and tendon growth. As a result, musculotendinous units tighten. It is essential for the prepubescent athlete to engage in a good stretching program along with any form of strength or endurance training to help counter the tendency for reduced flexibility. Overuse injuries such as "swimmer's shoulder" are related to a lack of flexibility. Do not assume that endurance activities such as running and swimming promote flexibility. The young performer must be encouraged to engage in a proper stretching program prior to and after any endurance workout to minimize the possibility of injury to the area around the joints.

Health-Related Fitness and Movement Abilities

The interaction between the components of health-related fitness and physical activity is obvious. Performance of any movement task whether it be at the rudimentary, fundamental, or sport skill level requires varying degrees of cardiovascular fitness, muscular strength, muscular endurance, and joint flexibility. All movement involves exerting force to overcome inertia. To exert that force, one must possess some degree of muscular strength. If a movement task is to be performed repeatedly, as in dribbling a ball, muscular endurance is also required. If the action is to be repeated over an extended period of time at a rapid pace, as in dribbling a ball up and down a basketball court, both cardiovascular endurance and flexibility are required. Reciprocity in building the components of physical fitness is evident in that performance of movement activities maintains and develops higher levels of physical fitness. The components of physical fitness are inseparable from movement activity. Rarely, if ever, is a movement activity performed that does not involve some aspect of strength, muscular endurance, or flexibility.

Concept 12.11   One's health-related fitness, motor fitness, and movement abilities are interrelated; each influences the other in the ''real'' world and operates in isolation only in the research laboratory.

It is not possible under normal conditions to isolate the basic components of skill performance. However, tests have been devised that, by their very nature, require more of one component of fitness than of another. Through this indirect means of measuring health-related fitness we are able to determine estimates of one's functional health (Table 12.2).

Motor Fitness

Considerable research has been conducted on the motor skill performance of the adolescent, adult, and skilled performer. The literature is replete with information dealing with their performance levels, biomechanics, and neurophysiological capabilities, but relatively little has been done with preschool and elementary school age children. The situation is much the same as with health-related fitness. Only recently have investigators begun to more closely analyze the motor fitness of children. Studies on the specific factors that make up the child's *motor fitness* indicate that a well-defined structure is present during early childhood but that these factors may differ somewhat from those of older age groups (Peterson et al., 1974; Seefeldt, 1980). There is a statistically determined structure of motor abilities in children generally consisting of four or five items depending on the age level investigated (Bergel, 1978; Peterson et al., 1974; Rarick & Dobbins, 1975). *Movement control factors* of balance (both static and dynamic balance) and coordination (both gross motor and eye-hand coordination), coupled with the *force production* factors of speed, agility, and power, tend to emerge as the components that most influence motor performance. The movement control factors (balance and coordination) are of particular importance during

Table 12.2 Common Measures of Children's Health-Related Fitness and a Synthesis of Findings

Health-Related Fitness Components	Common Tests	Specific Aspect Measured	Synthesis of Findings
Cardiovascular endurance	Step test	Physical work capacity	VO_2 max estimates are tenuous with young children. Children can achieve maximum VO_2 values similar to adults when corrected for body weight. Maximal heart rates decrease with age. Trend for improved VO_2 max values in both boys and girls with age. Girls level off after age 12 or so. Boys continue to improve.
	Distance run	Aerobic endurance	
	Treadmill stress test	Max VO_2	
	Bicycle ergometer	Max VO_2	
Muscular strength	Hand dynamometer	Isometric grip strength	Annual increase for boys from age 7 on. Girls tend to level off after age 12. Boys slow prior to puberty, then gain rapidly throughout adolescence. Boys superior to girls at all ages.
	Back and leg dynamometer	Isometric back and leg strength	
	Cable tensiometer	Isometric joint strength	
Muscular endurance	Push-ups	Isotonic upper body endurance	Similar abilities throughout childhood slightly in favor of boys on most items. Lull in performance prior to age 12. Large increases in boys from 12 to 16, then a leveling off. Girls show no significant increases without special training after age 12.
	Sit-ups	Isotonic abdominal endurance	
	Flexed arm hang	Isometric upper body endurance	
	Pull-ups	Isotonic upper body endurance	
Flexibility	Bend and reach	Hip joint flexibility	Flexibility is joint specific. Girls tend to be more flexible than boys at all ages. Flexibility decreases with reduced activity levels.
	Sit and reach	Hip joint flexibility	
Body composition	Hydrostatic weighing	Percent body fat	Children at all ages have higher percentages of fat than their age-mates of 20 years ago. Active children are leaner than obese children at all ages. Obese children are less active than non-obese children.
	Skinfold calipers	Estimate of percent body fat	
	Body mass index	Estimate of percent body fat	
	Electrical impedance	Estimate of percent body fat	

early childhood when the child is gaining control of his or her fundamental movement abilities. The force production factors (speed, agility, and power) become more important after the child has gained control of his or her fundamental movements and passes into the specialized movement phase of later childhood.

Concept 12.12   The components of motor fitness may be grouped into movement control factors and force production factors.

As with the components of health-related fitness, one's motor fitness is intricately interrelated with movement skill acquisition. One depends in large part on the other. Without adequate motor fitness, a child's level of skill acquisition will be limited, and without adequate skill acquisition, the level of motor fitness attainment will be impeded. The components of motor fitness are discussed here and synthesized in Table 12.3.

Coordination

Coordination is the ability to integrate separate motor systems with varying sensory modalities into efficient patterns of movement. The more complicated the movement tasks, the greater the level of coordination necessary for efficient performance. Coordination is linked to the motor fitness components of balance, speed, and agility, but not closely aligned with strength and endurance (Barrow & McGee, 1978). Coordinated behavior requires the child to perform specific movements in a series quickly and accurately. Movement must be synchronous, rhythmical, and properly sequenced in order to be coordinated.

Concept 12.13   Coordinated movement requires integration of sensory and motor systems into a congruent and harmonious action pattern.

Eye-hand and eye-foot coordination are characterized by integrating visual information with limb action. Movements must be visually controlled and precise in order to project, make contact with, or receive an external object. Bouncing, catching, throwing, kicking, and trapping all require considerable amounts of visual input integrated with motor output to achieve efficient coordinated movement.

Gross body coordination in children involves moving the body rapidly while performing various fundamental movement skills. Peterson et al. (1974) indicated that measures such as the shuffle run, 30-yard dash, various hopping and skipping tests, and the standing long jump require high levels of gross body coordination. Gross body coordination

Table 12.3 Common Measures of Children's Performance-Related Fitness and a Synthesis of Findings

Motor Fitness Component	Common Tests	Specific Aspect Measured	Synthesis of Findings
Coordination	Cable jump	Gross body coordination	Year by year improvement with age in gross body coordination. Boys superior from age 6 on in eye-hand and eye-foot coordination.
	Hopping for accuracy	Gross body coordination	
	Skipping	Gross body coordination	
	Ball dribble	Eye-hand coordination	
	Foot dribble	Eye-foot coordination	
Balance	Beam walk	Dynamic balance	Year by year improvement with age. Girls often outperform boys, especially in dynamic balance activities until about age 8. Abilities similar thereafter.
	Stick balance	Static balance	
	One-foot stand	Static balance	
Speed	20-yard dash	Running speed	Year by year improvement with age. Boys and girls similar until age 6 or 7, at which time boys make more rapid improvements. Boys superior to girls at all ages.
	30-yard dash	Running speed	
Agility	Shuttle run	Running agility	Year by year improvement with age. Girls begin to level off after age 13. Boys continue to make improvements.
	Side straddle	Lateral agility	
Power	Vertical jump	Leg strength and speed	Year by year improvement with age. Boys outperform girls at all age levels.
	Standing long jump	Leg strength and speed	
	Distance throw	Upper arm strength and speed	
	Velocity throw	Upper arm strength and speed	

and eye-hand and eye-foot coordination appear to improve with age in a roughly linear fashion. Also, boys tend to exhibit better coordination than girls throughout childhood (Frederick, 1977; Van Slooten, 1973).

Balance

Balance is the ability to maintain the equilibrium of one's body when it is placed in various positions. Balance is basic to all movement and is influenced by visual, tactile-kinesthetic, and vestibular stimulation.

Vision plays an important role in balance with young children. Cratty and Martin (1969) found that boys and girls age 6 and under could not balance on one foot with their eyes closed. By age 7, however, they were able to maintain balance with their eyes closed, and balancing ability continued to improve with age. Use of the eyes enables the child to focus on a reference point in order to maintain balance. The eyes also enable the young child to visually monitor the body during a static or dynamic balance task.

Concept 12.14   Balance is critical to all movement behavior and is influenced by a variety of sensory mechanisms.

Tactile and kinesthetic abilities play an important role in balance. The famous rod-and-frame experiments conducted by Wapner and Werner (1957) emphasize the importance of the tactile and kinesthetic senses. Verticality of a luminous rod in a frame was predicted by subjects seated in a darkened room and tilted to one side. The hypothesis was that children do not have control of their kinesthetic abilities to the point that they can compensate for changes in body tilt and that they rely on visual information for accurate prediction of verticality. The experiment by Comalli et al. (1959) confirmed this hypothesis and revealed that in subjects from 6 to 16 years of age the rod appeared to be vertical when it was actually tilted in the same direction as the individual. Older subjects (age 16 to age 50) were able to more accurately locate the apparent vertical plane but often overcompensated and predicted verticality of the rod in the opposite direction. It is evident that tactile and kinesthetic abilities tend to improve with age and contribute to balance more in adults than in children (Parker, 1980).

Balance is profoundly influenced by the vestibular apparatus. The fluid contained in the *semicircular canals* and the *otolith* plays a key role in helping an individual maintain equilibrium. The receptors in the semicircular canal respond to changes in angular acceleration (dynamic and rotational balance), while the otolith receptors respond to linear accelerations (static balance). The movements of *macula* (hairs) in either the otolith or the semicircular canals trigger nerve impulses by changing the electrical potential of adjoining nerve cells (Parker, 1980). Movement of the body and gravity are sensed by these vestibular receptors to keep the individual aware of both static and dynamic postural changes and changes in acceleration. The vestibular apparatus coordinates with the visual, tactile, and kinesthetic systems in governing balance. It appears that vestibular development in terms of balance occurs very early in life and that the vestibular apparatus is structurally complete at birth. However, the body musculature and the other sensory modalities involved in maintaining balance must mature and be integrated with vestibular clues to be of any use to the child in maintaining either static or dynamic balance.

Balance is often defined as static or dynamic. *Static balance* refers to the ability of the body to maintain equilibrium in a stationary position. Balancing on one foot, standing on a balance board, and performing a stick balance are common means of assessing static balance abilities. Research on the static balance abilities of children shows a linear trend toward improved performance from ages 2 through 12 (DeOreo, 1971; Keogh, 1965; Van Slooten, 1973). Prior to age 2 children generally are not able to perform a one-foot static balance task, probably because of their skill-developing abilities to maintain a controlled upright posture. DeOreo (1980) indicated that clear-cut boy-girl differences are not as apparent in static balance performance tasks as they are with other motor performance tasks. In fact, girls tend to be more proficient than boys until about age 7 or 8, whereupon the boys catch up. Both sexes level off in performance around age 8, prior to a surge in abilities from age 9 to age 12.

Dynamic balance refers to the ability to maintain equilibrium when moving from point to point. Balance beam walking tests are used most often as measures of dynamic balance in children. The available literature on dynamic balance indicates a trend similar to that for static balance. Girls are often more proficient than boys until age 8 or 9, whereupon they perform at similar levels (DeOreo, 1971; Frederick, 1977). Both slow in their progress around age 9, before making rapid gains to age 12 (Goetzinger, 1961; Heath, 1949).

Speed

Speed is the ability to cover a short distance in as brief a time period as possible. Speed is influenced by *reaction time* (the amount of elapsed time from the signal "go" to the first movements of the body) as well as *movement time* (the time elapsed from the initial movement to completion of the activity). Reaction time depends on the speed with which the initial stimulus is processed through the efferent and afferent neural pathways and is integrated with the initial response pattern. Reaction time improves in children as they get older.

Cratty (1986) reported that the information available on simple reaction time indicates that it is about twice as long in 5-year-olds as it is in adults for an identical task and that there is rapid improvement from age 3 to age 5. These developmental differences are probably due to neurological maturation, variations in the information-processing capabilities of children and adults, as well as to environmental and task considerations.

Speed of movement in children is most generally measured through various tests of running speed. Frederick (1977), who tested the running speeds of five groups of children 3 to 5 years of age on the 20-yard dash, found linear improvement with age but no gender differences. In a study of the running speed of elementary school children, Keogh (1965) found that boys and girls are similar in running speed at ages 6 and 7, but boys were superior from ages 8 to 12. Both boys and girls improve with age at a rate of about 1 foot per second per year from ages 6 to 11

(Cratty, 1979). Keogh also found similar improvements and boy-girl differences in the 50-foot hop for speed, although girls tended to perform better than boys on hopping and jumping tasks requiring greater precision and accuracy of movement.

Fifty-yard sprint run scores are recorded as part of the AAU Physical Fitness Program (1993). These data are viewed as highly representative of the running speed of children and adolescents because of the very large sample size, geographical distribution, and randomization techniques utilized. Both boys and girls are reported to make annual incremental improvements with males slightly outperforming females at all ages (Figure 12.10). Similarity in performance on the sprint run does not appear to carry over into the adolescent years (see Chapter 17, Figure 17.11). Males continue to make dramatic improvements throughout the teen years, while females tend to regress slightly after age 14. Both factors are associated with pubescent male strength increases, limb length increases and body fat decreases, and female body fat increases.

Figure 12.10
50-yard sprint run, mean scores for males and females 6–12 years, in seconds (drawn from data courtesy of: AAU Physical Fitness Program [1993], Indiana University, Bloomington, IN)

Speed of movement generally improves until about age 13 in both boys and girls. After this, however, girls tend to level off and even regress, while boys tend to continue improving throughout the adolescent years. The movement speed of both boys and girls may be encouraged during childhood and beyond through vigorous physical activity that incorporates short bursts of speed.

Concept 12.15   Reaction time and movement time influence movement speed, agility, and power, which tend to advance linearly during childhood, but require special training afterward for continued improvement.

Agility

Agility is the ability to change the direction of the body rapidly and accurately. With agility, one can make quick and accurate shifts in body position during movement. An assortment of agility runs have been used as indirect measures of agility. Unfortunately, the wide variety of ways in which these scores have been obtained makes it impossible to compare studies. Scores from the 30-foot shuttle run are typically used as a measure of agility. Figure 12.11 depicts mean shuttle run scores for both boys and girls 6 to 17 years of age. Annual incremental improvements are seen throughout childhood with an edge given to boys at all ages.

Power

Power is the ability to perform a maximum effort in as short a period as possible. Power is sometimes referred to as "explosive strength" and represents the product of force divided by time. This combination of strength and speed is exhibited in children's activities that require jumping, striking, throwing for distance, and other maximum efforts. The speed of contraction of the muscles involved, as well as the strength and coordinated use of these muscles, determine the degree of power of the individual.

Because power involves a combination of motor abilities, it is difficult, if not impossible, to obtain a pure measure of this component. The often-used throwing and jumping measures give only an indirect indication of power because of the skill required for both of these tasks. Frederick (1977), however, found significant yearly increments in vertical jump, standing long jump, and distance throwing tasks for children ages 3 through 5. The boys outperformed the girls on all measures at all age levels. The same results were found by Keogh (1965) for boys and girls from 6 to 12 years of age and by Van Slooten (1973) for children 6 to 9 years of age on the throw for distance, but with gender differences magnified beyond age 7. Luedke's (1980) excellent review of the literature on throwing supports these results.

Figure 12.11
30-foot shuttle run, mean scores for males and females 6–17 years, in seconds (drawn from data courtesy of: AAU Physical Fitness Program [1993], Indiana University, Bloomington, IN)

Figure 12.12 represents mean standing long jump scores for boys and girls 6 to 17 years of age. This figure is based on a national sampling of thousands of children taking the AAU Physical Fitness Test (Updyke, 1993). These data are considered to be highly representative of standing long jump abilities because of the sample size and randomization techniques used. Boys outperform girls at all ages. The gap that begins to widen after age 10 increases in magnitude throughout adolescence.

Similar linear improvements and differences between boys and girls have been demonstrated in the standing long jump from age 3 through 5 (Frederick, 1977), from age 6 through 12 (Keogh, 1965), and from age 10 through 17 (Ross & Gilbert, 1985). Differences in throwing velocity based on age and gender have also been shown in samples of children from age 6 to 14 years old (Glassow & Kruse, 1960; Luedke, 1980). However, differences from age to age and between sexes are closely related to yearly strength and speed of movement increments as well as to the varying sociocultural influences on boys and girls.

Figure 12.12
Standing long jump, mean scores for males and females 6–17 years, in feet and inches (drawn from data courtesy of: AAU Physical Fitness Program [1993], Indiana University, Bloomington, IN)

Summary

Although specific questions remain unanswered, there is general agreement regarding the advisability of vigorous physical activity in children. The growth patterns of almost all the internal organs are in proportion to the remainder of the body. Hence the lungs, heart, and so forth, are able to cope with the demands placed on them. Proportional to their mass, young children can transport and utilize oxygen volumes comparable to adults. There seems to be no appreciable difference in the fatigue patterns between children and high school youth and adults. The general consensus among researchers is that a sound heart cannot be injured by vigorous physical activity. Of course, precautionary measures need to be taken for a child with a suspected or known cardiac and/or pulmonary dysfunction.

Muscular strength, muscular endurance, and flexibility are also components of health-related fitness. They affect one's state of health in much the same way as does aerobic endurance. Good levels of fitness tend to reduce vulnerability to numerous physical ailments. The components of health-related fitness improve with age but not in a linear fashion. There is a strong tendency to make small gains during early and later childhood, followed by a lull during the preadolescent period.

During adolescence boys often make rapid gains in all measures of fitness, while girls tend to level off and sometimes decline in their performance scores after age 15.

The motor fitness components of coordination and balance are closely aligned with the development of movement control during early childhood. Once good control has been established, the child is able to focus on improvement in the force components of motor fitness. Speed, agility, and power improve dramatically during later childhood, as balance and coordination improve during early childhood. There is a linear trend for improvement in all measures of motor fitness. The motor fitness levels of both boys and girls improve with age and effort, with boys outperforming girls at all levels except during the prepubescent period.

Terms to Remember

Health-related fitness
Dynamic flexibility
Aerobic endurance
Aerobic trainability
Maximal oxygen consumption
Heart rate response
Muscular strength
Weight lifting
Joint flexibility
Static flexibility
Dynamic flexibility
Body composition
Hydrostatic weighing
Skinfold calipers
Aerobic training
Strength training
Anabolic hormones
Catabolic hormones
Growth hormone
Testosterone
Neuromuscular adaptation
Epiphyseal growth plates

Isotonic strength
Isometric strength
Isokinetic strength
Dynamic strength
Electrical impedance
Motor fitness
Coordination
Balance
Semicircular canals
Otolith
Macula
Movement control factors
Force production factors
Static balance
Dynamic balance
Dynamometer
Tensiometer
Reaction time
Movement time
Muscular endurance
Agility
Power

Critical Readings

American Academy of Pediatrics (1990). Strength training, weight and power lifting, and body building by children and adolescents. *Pediatrics,* 85, 801–803.

Bandini, L. G. (1987). *Energy expenditure in obese and nonobese adolescents.* (Ph.D. thesis). Cambridge, MA: Massachusetts Institute of Technology.

Baranowski, T. et al. (1992). Assessment, prevalence, and cardiovascular benefits of physical activity and fitness in youth. *Medicine and Science in Sports and Exercise,* 24, 6, S237–S247.

Bar-Or, O. (1983). *Pediatric Sports Medicine for the Practitioner* (Chapter 1). New York: Springer-Verlag.

Bar-Or, O. (1989). Trainability of the prepubescent child. *Physician and Sportsmedicine,* 17, 5, 65–83.

Blair, S. N. (1992). Are American children and youth fit? The need for better data. *Research Quarterly for Exercise and Sport,* 63, 2, 120–123.

Borms, J. (1986). The child and exercise: An overview. *Journal of Sports Science,* 4, 1, 3–20.

Corbin, C. B. & Pangrazi, R. P. (1992). Are American children and youth fit? *Research Quarterly for Exercise and Sport,* 63, 2, 96–106.

Delozier, M. G., Gutin, B., & Basch, C. E. (1988). Conducting treadmill tests on preschool children—Strategies and techniques. *Journal of Physical Education, Recreation and Dance,* October, 83–87.

Falls, H. B., & Pate, R. R. (1993). Status of physical fitness in U.S. children. In M. L. Leppo (Ed.), *Healthy from the Start: New Perspectives on Childhood Fitness.* Washington, DC: Eric Clearinghouse on Teacher Education.

Gutin, B., Manos, T., & Strong, W. (1992). Defining health and fitness: First steps toward establishing fitness standards. *Research Quarterly for Exercise and Sport,* 63, 2, 128–132.

Katch, V. L. (1983). Physical conditioning of children. *Journal of Adolescent Health Care,* 3, 241–246.

Kuntzleman, C. T. & Reiff, G. G. (1992). The decline in American children's fitness levels. *Research Quarterly for Exercise and Sport,* 63, 2, 107–111.

NSCA Journal. (1985). National strength and conditioning association position paper on prepubescent strength training, 7, 4, 27–31.

Payne, G. V. & Morrow, J. R. (1993). Exercise and VO_2 max in children: A meta-analysis. *Research Quarterly for Exercise and Sport,* 64, 305–313.

Research Quarterly for Exercise and Sport. (1987). Review and commentary: Children and fitness, 58, 295–333.

Roberts, S. O. (1993). Trainability of prepubescent children: Current theories and training considerations. In M. L. Leppo (Ed.), *Healthy from the Start: New Perspectives on Childhood Fitness.* Washington, DC: Eric Clearinghouse on Teacher Education.

Romanella, N. E. et al. (1990). Physical activity and attitudes in lean and obese children and their mothers. *International Journal of Obesity,* 15, 407–414.

Ross, J. G. & Pate, R. R. (1987). The national children and youth fitness study II. *Journal of Physical Education Recreation and Dance,* 58, 49–96.

Rowland, T. W. (1991). Effects of obesity on aerobic fitness in adolescent females. *American Journal of Diseases of Children,* 145, 764–768.

Seefeldt, V. & Voegel, P. (1989). Physical fitness testing of children: A thirty-year history of misguided efforts? *Pediatric Exercise Science,* 1, 4, 295–302.

Updyke, W. (1992). In search of relevant and credible physical fitness standards for children. *Research Quarterly for Exercise and Sport,* 63, 2, 112–119.

Vaccaro, P. & Mahon, A. (1987). Cardiorespiratory responses to endurance training in children. *Sports Medicine,* 4, 352–363.

Chapter 13

Childhood Perception and Perceptual-Motor Development

CHAPTER COMPETENCIES

Upon completion of this chapter you should be able to:

- *Discuss changes in perceptual functioning during childhood*
- *Analyze the relationship and interaction between perceptual and motor development*
- *Identify motor behavioral characteristics of children who developmentally lag in motor skills*
- *Analyze the effect of cognitive processing differences within and across age groups on motor skill development and performance*
- *Evaluate cognitive processing demands on motor skill performance*
- *Discuss the developmental aspects of visual acuity, figure-ground perception, depth perception, and visual motor coordination, and their interaction with motor performance*
- *Demonstrate an understanding of perceptual training and its impact on the skill learning process*
- *Define the term "perceptual-motor" and diagram the perceptual-motor process*
- *Describe the perceptual-motor components and give examples of each*
- *Distinguish between various forms of perceptual-motor training and provide a rationale for each*
- *Draw conclusions from perceptual-motor research findings regarding what we know about its relationship to cognitive development and academic achievement*

Study of the perceptual process and perceptual-motor development attempts to answer the age-old question of how we come to know our world. The nature of the perceptual process and its impact on movement and cognition have been topics of considerable interest to researchers and educators for years. From the moment of birth, children begin to learn how to interact with their environment. This interaction is a perceptual as well as a motor process. This chapter focuses on developmental aspects of visual perception and perceptual-motor behavior during childhood. The importance of developing both perceptual and perceptual-motor abilities is discussed along with factors that influence their emergence.

Perceptual Development in Childhood

By the time children reach 2 years of age, the ocular apparatus is mature. The eyeball is near its adult size and weight. All anatomical and physiological aspects of the eye are complete, but the perceptual abilities of young children are still incomplete. Although children are able to fixate on objects, track them, and make accurate judgments of size and shape, numerous refinements still need to be made. A young child is unable to intercept a tossed ball with any degree of control. Difficulty with letter and number reversals is common, and a child's perception of moving objects is poorly developed, as are figure-ground perceptual abilities, perception of distance, and anticipatory timing.

The extent to which movement plays a role in visual perceptual development is debatable. Held and his colleagues (1963, 1965), Smith and Smith (1966), and Riesen and Aarons (1959) all speculated on the importance of movement in the development and refinement of visual perceptual abilities. They conducted investigations based on the hypothesis that self-produced movement is both necessary and sufficient for *visual-motor adjustment* to occur within a visually altered environment. They contended that without movement, visual perceptual adjustments will not occur and that the muscles and the motor aspect of the nervous system are intimately involved with perception and are dependent on one another. The concept of a relationship between movement activity and perceptual development has also been indirectly supported by the decline in performance on perceptual and motor deprivation experiments (Hebb, 1949; Riesen & Aarons, 1959), and experiments testing visual perceptual adjustments to optically rearranged environments (Held & Blossom, 1961; Held & Mikaelian, 1964; Hoepner, 1967; Gallahue, 1982). The gist of this research has lead to what Payne and Isaacs (1991) termed the "movement hypothesis" which according to Schaffer (1985) is the "notion that individuals must attend to objects that move in order to develop a normal repertoire of visual-spatial skill" (p. 233).

Concept 13.2   Movement has been shown to be a sufficient condition for the development of selected visual perceptual abilities, but it has not been demonstrated to be a necessary condition.

The fact remains, however, that the results of each of these experiments are speculative at best when applied to the development of perceptual abilities in children. At this juncture we still do not know the extent to which movement plays a role in perceptual development. It is, however, probably safe to say that movement is a "sufficient" condition for encouraging the development of perceptual abilities. Whether it is in fact a "necessary" condition is doubtful (Gallahue, 1982).

Although it is doubtful that self-produced movement is a necessary condition for development of a child's visual perceptual abilities, there is little doubt that the developmental level of his or her visual perceptual abilities will affect the performance levels of movement skills. It is important that we become familiar with the child's developing perceptual abilities and understand the impact of perception on movement skill learning and refinement. Visual acuity, figure-ground perception, depth perception, and visual-motor coordination are important visual qualities that are developmentally based and influence movement performance. Table 13.1 provides a summary of these qualities and a hypothesized developmental sequence.

Visual Acuity

Visual acuity is the ability to distinguish detail in objects. The finer the details that can be distinguished the better one's visual acuity, and vice versa. Visual acuity may be measured in both static and dynamic settings. *Static visual acuity* is the degree of distinguishable detail that one is able to detect when both the individual and the object of visual regard are stationary. Static visual acuity is most commonly measured by use of a Snellen eye chart. A Snellen assessment is expressed in fractions. An individual with a 20/20 rating is able to distinguish objects at a distance of 20 feet in the same manner as others with normal vision

Table 13.1 Selected Developmental Aspects of Children's Visual Perception

Visual Quality	Selected Abilities	Approximate Age
VISUAL ACUITY	Rapid Improvement	5–7
The ability to distinguish detail	Plateau	7–8
in static and dynamic settings	Rapid Improvement	9–10
	Mature (Static)	10–11
	Plateau (Dynamic)	10–11
	Mature (Dynamic)	11–12
FIGURE-GROUND PERCEPTION	Slow Improvement	3–4
The ability to separate an	Rapid Improvement	4–6
object from its surroundings	Slight Spurt	7–8
	Mature	8–12
DEPTH PERCEPTION	Frequent Judgment Errors	3–4
The ability to judge distance	Few Judgment Errors	5–6
relative to oneself	Rapid Improvement	7–11
	Mature	By age 12
VISUAL-MOTOR COORDINATION	Rapid Improvement	3–7
The ability to integrate use of	Slow Slight Improvement	7–9
eyes and hands in terms of	Mature	10–12
object tracking and		
interruption		

at the same distance of 20 feet. An individual with a 20/200 rating is able to distinguish at 20 feet what others with normal vision could distinguish at 200 feet.

Dynamic visual acuity is the ability to distinguish detail in moving objects. It is less frequently assessed than static visual acuity for various reasons but it is of interest to anyone required to make precise judgments based on visually guided tracking. The baseball player preparing to strike or catch a ball needs to have good dynamic visual acuity, as does the volleyball player or skeet shooter. Dynamic visual acuity is measured by flashing checkerboard targets with varying levels of grid precision on a screen. These targets travel horizontally at varying speeds, and the individual indicates when the "small checks" can be seen in the moving object.

Williams (1983) reported that static visual acuity is mature by age 10 and, in general, is less well developed in 5- and 6-year-olds. Rapid improvement occurs between 5 and 7 years of age, with little change seen from ages 7 to 9, followed by rapid improvement between ages 9 and 10. By age 12 static visual acuity is generally adult-like (Whiting, 1974).

Dynamic visual acuity appears to mature somewhat later than its static visual acuity. Morris (1977) found improvement in individuals up to 20 years of age. Williams (1983) reported that dynamic visual acuity becomes increasingly refined during three separate time periods: 5 to 7 years, 9 to 10 years, and 11 to 12 years of age. Furthermore, boys display better visual acuity (both dynamic and static) than girls at all ages. This information may help us better understand why it is essential to adjust the skill requirements in a sport such as baseball if we expect children to sustain their interest over time. The fact that girls often lag behind their male counterparts can probably be attributed to socialization factors (fewer opportunities for practice and less active encouragement). This may also explain why girls tend to do less well on object interception tasks, and tend to drop out of these sports earlier. Adult leaders must modify the rules to enhance the potential for success and sustained participation for both boys and girls at various developmental levels.

Concept 13.3   Vision is the primary sensory modality and plays an important role in the process of motor development.

Figure-Ground Perception

Figure-ground perception is the ability to separate an object of visual regard from its surroundings. Gallahue (1968) demonstrated that various combinations of blending and/or distracting backgrounds influenced the abilities of 6-year-olds to distinguish objects of visual regard from their surroundings. Combinations that caused a maximum amount of blending and distraction were most disruptive of the children's abilities to distinguish a figure from its background in the performance of a simple stepping test. Conditions in which only color blending or visual distractors were present were less disruptive. With regard to the developmental nature of visual figure-ground perception, Williams (1983), interpreting data from Frostig et al. (1966), reported stable figure-ground perception between 8 and 10 years of age. Prior to that, however, slow improvement occurs between 3 and 4 years, with large improvement seen from 4 through 6 years. Smaller changes were reported from ages 6 to 7 followed by a slight spurt between 7 and 8 years. Williams (1983) further suggested that figure-ground perception becomes increasingly refined from 8 to 13 years and may even continue to improve to 17 or 18 years of age. One may conclude that mature figure-ground perception involves elements of attention as well as visual-motor maturation.

The significance of visual figure-ground perception is obvious. Along with good dynamic visual acuity, figure-ground perception enables the performer not only clearly to distinguish an object, but to separate it from its background. Such a highly refined skill is essential to the batter or outfielder in baseball, the wide-receiver or quarterback in football, or the performer on the uneven bars in gymnastics. The ability to clearly extract the object of regard (*figure*) from its background (*ground*) is essential for success. It is important to recognize that this perceptual quality is still developing in children. Modifications of the task requirements or manipulating the background against which certain movement tasks are performed may do much to enhance motor performance.

Depth Perception

Depth perception is one of the most intriguing aspects of visual perception. Depth perception allows us to see three-dimensionally, an astonishing feat when you consider that separately our retinas function two-dimensionally but when combined provide a visual image complete with minute depth cues. These cues to depth are both monocular and binocular.

Monocular depth cues are those that can be picked up by one eye. Such things as size, texture gradient, shading, convergence, overlap, proportionality, and linear perspective are common monocular cues to depth. Each of these are used by the artist to give the "illusion" of depth on canvas. They also give us important three-dimensional visual cues to depth.

Binocular depth cues require both eyes to work in concert. *Retinal disparity,* an important component of depth perception, refers to the fact that an object of visual regard is viewed from a slightly different angle by each eye. Therefore, the image projected on each retina is slightly different, and the information passed on to the visual area of the cortex results in binocular disparity. Hence, the images that we receive have depth.

Little is known about the developmental aspects of depth perception. Williams (1983) however, reported that binocularity and depth perception improve from 2 through 5 years of age. She also indicated that by age 7 children can accurately judge depth with monocular cues. Based on this and the extensive literature on infant depth perception it is probably safe to conclude that depth perception begins developing in a very basic way during the first months of infancy, but that it continues to improve throughout early childhood. It is doubtful whether depth perception in general can be improved through special training. It is however, possible that depth perception in specific situations can be improved (Sage, 1984).

Teachers, parents, and coaches need to consider the visual perceptions of depth when teaching new ball skills. Ball size, color, and texture as well as distance, trajectory, and speed play important roles in providing depth cues for successful object interceptions (Isaacs, 1980; Payne, 1985; Payne and Isaacs, 1991). One need only observe the child who turns his or her head to avoid an approaching ball to see why depth cues are important to successful catching. Turning the head to one side eliminates binocular vision and forces the child to depend on monocular cues. All too often these monocular cues are insufficient to make the accurate and refined adjustments required for mature catching. As a result the child reverts to a less mature scooping catching pattern, or the ball hits the child's face or chest before it is stopped or dropped. Successful object interception requires making use of all the depth cues available, especially during the early stages of skill development.

Visual-Motor Coordination

Visual-motor coordination refers to the ability to track and make interception judgments about a moving object. The development of visual abilities begins early in infancy and continues to improve with age. Morris (1980) indicated that by ages 5 or 6 children can accurately track moving objects in a horizontal plane, and that by ages 8 or 9 they can track balls moving in an arc. Payne and Isaacs (1987) noted that "as dynamic visual acuity improves, so does the ability to track fast-moving objects because whenever an object is moving at an angular velocity at which smooth eye movements are no longer possible, the pursuit task becomes a function of dynamic visual acuity" (p. 191). Williams (1983) reported that accurate perception of movement continues to develop to about 10 to 12 years of age.

Object interception is the second aspect of visual-motor coordination. Object interception, or *coincidence-anticipation timing* as it is frequently referred to in motor learning literature, involves the ability to match estimates of an object's location with a specific motor response. For example, the batter in baseball must estimate where the ball will be at a certain point in time and simultaneously activate the motor system to bring the bat into contact with the ball at just the right moment. Object interception abilities improve greatly with age and practice (Dorfman, 1977). At this point it is difficult to propose a developmental model for object interception ability because of the vast number of confounding variables. However, observation of numerous children attempting to hit pitched balls leads us to conclude that younger children and less experienced individuals make numerous judgment errors, but older children and more experienced persons make fewer errors. Experience clearly appears to be an essential element in making accurate estimates of object interception. The question of whether experience alone or maturation of the visual-motor apparatus in conjunction with experience is responsible for improved judgments awaits further study.

Perceptual Training

The fact that an individual's visual perceptual sophistication is intricately related to success in the performance of numerous movement skills makes it essential for the teacher or coach to be aware of the developmental nature of children's visual abilities. The perceptual requirements of fundamental manipulative skills that involve imparting force to an object or receiving force from an object are especially great. When working with young children we must make appropriate adjustments in the equipment to accommodate the developmental levels of their perceptual abilities. Simply changing the weight or size of balls by using foam, fleece, plastic, or soft rubber is likely to have a dramatic influence on the degree of success experienced. Making modifications in the color and size of the objects will also have an impact.

Concept 13.4 Practice in perceptual-motor activities may enhance perceptual-motor abilities, but there is insufficient evidence to claim that improved perceptual-motor abilities will enhance academic achievement.

Modifying the rules of play to permit greater clarity and consistency of perception, time to react, or ease of tracking is also recommended. For example, in baseball, using a pitching machine set at a predetermined speed and trajectory will help children develop their tracking skills. Hitting a ball off a tee will enable younger children to experience greater success and to focus on developing a level swing without compounding the complexity of the task with object-tracking.

A third consideration in perceptual training is to recognize that the mechanics of the movement itself are influenced by the perception levels required for successful performance. If the visual requirements are great the mechanics are more likely to be complicated. The mechanics of a tennis serve are more difficult than those for swimming or skipping.

Finally, individuals who work with children must recognize that a child's perceptual development *and* motor development are crucial to successful movement performance. We must adjust our level of expectations to the perceptual as well as the physical maturity of each individual.

Perceptual-Motor Development in Children

The visual perceptual abilities of young children are not the same as those of adults. The child's visual world is in the developmental stages and is therefore restricted. The development of perceptual abilities significantly inhibits or enhances a child's movement performance. From the previous section we have seen that the converse of this may be true, that is, movement performance may significantly inhibit or enhance the development of children's perceptual abilities. The child restricted in perceptual development often encounters difficulties in performing perceptual-motor tasks.

The realization that the process of perception is not entirely innate prompts one to hypothesize that the quality and quantity of movement experiences afforded young children are related to some extent to the development of their perceptual abilities. The initial responses of young children are motor responses, and all future perceptual and conceptual data are based, in part, on these initial responses. Young children must establish a broad base of motor experiences in order for higher learning to develop properly. Meaning is imposed on perceptual stimulation through movement. The matching of perceptual and motor data is thought by many to be necessary for the child to establish a stable spatial world (Barsch, 1965; Kephart, 1971). The more motor and perceptual learning experiences that children have, the greater the opportunity to make this "perceptual-motor match" and to develop a plasticity of response to various movement situations.

Unfortunately, the complexity of our modern society often deters the development of many perceptual-motor abilities. The environment in which today's children are raised is so complicated and dangerous that they are constantly being warned not to touch or to avoid situations that offer great amounts of motor and perceptual information. The environment of today's children is also too passive and sedentary. Many children grow up in large cities, apartment buildings, cramped day care centers, and school environments that do not encourage or promote learning through movement. Too few children in contemporary society climb trees, walk fences, jump streams, or ride horses. They miss many of the experiences that children ought to have to develop their movement abilities. Children who spend time watching television or playing computer games develop sedentary, passive habits. The absence of varied movement experiences and the adaptations that come with practice and repetition can stifle motor development.

Concept 13.5   Children frequently lag in their perceptual-motor learning because of environmental restrictions.

Artificial means must be devised to give children additional experiences and practice in the perceptual-motor activities that modern society cannot provide naturally. Substitute experiences may have positive effects on the development of visual perceptual abilities in children. The physical education teacher should be an essential person in the educational curriculum. A sound, developmentally based physical education program will encourage children's perceptual-motor skills and promote many of the basic readiness skills required for success in school.

What Is "Perceptual-Motor"?

The hyphen in the term *perceptual-motor* is there for two specific reasons. First, it signifies the dependency of voluntary movement activity upon some forms of perceptual information. All voluntary movement involves an element of perceptual awareness resulting from some sort of sensory stimulation. Second, the hyphen indicates that the development of one's perceptual abilities is dependent, in part, on motor activity. Perceptual-motor abilities are learned. As such, they use movement as an important medium in which learning occurs.

The quality of movement performance depends on the accuracy of an individual's perceptions and his ability to interpret these perceptions into a series of coordinated movement acts. The terms "eye-hand coordination" and "eye-foot coordination" have been used for years to express the dependency of efficient movement on the accuracy of sensory information. The individual on the free throw line has numerous forms of sensory input that must be sorted out and expressed in the final perceptual-motor act of shooting the basketball. If the perceptions are accurate, and if they are blended into a coordinated sequence, the basket is made. If not, the player misses the shot. All voluntary movements involve the use of one or more sensory modalities to greater or lesser degrees. Until recently we did not fully appreciate the important contributions movement experiences make toward the development of perceptual-motor abilities.

The term perception means "to know" or "to interpret information." Perception is the process of organizing incoming information with stored information, which leads to a modified response pattern. Perceptual-motor development may be described as a process of attaining increased skill and functional ability by using sensory input, sensory integration, motor interpretation, movement activation, and feedback. These elements are described below.

1. *Sensory Input:* receiving various forms of stimulation by way of specialized sensory receptors (visual, auditory, tactile, and kinesthetic receptors) and transmitting this stimulation to the brain in the form of a pattern of neural energy.
2. *Sensory Integration:* organizing incoming sensory stimuli and integrating it with past or stored information (memory).
3. *Motor Interpretation:* making internal motor decisions (recalibration) based on the combination of sensory (present) and long-term memory (past) information.
4. *Movement Activation:* executing the actual movement (observable act) itself.
5. *Feedback:* evaluating the movement act by way of the various sensory modalities (visual, auditory, tactile, and/or kinesthetic) which in turn feed information back into the sensory input aspect of the process, thus beginning the cycle over again.

The Perceptual-Motor Components

Although movement experiences in regular physical education programs are by general definition perceptual-motor activities, programs that focus on reinforcing perceptual-motor quality are significantly different in emphasis from those that focus on gross motor quality. In remedial and readiness programs emphasis is on improving specific perceptual-motor components, so movement activities are grouped according to the perceptual-motor qualities they enhance, namely, body awareness, spatial awareness, directional awareness, and temporal awareness. Activities designed to enhance these abilities are used in regular physical education programs, but the primary objective is movement skill acquisition rather than on perceptual-motor acquisition.

The development and refinement of children's *spatial worlds* and *temporal worlds* are two of the primary contributions of perceptual-motor training programs. The jargon used in programs across North America varies greatly. There seems to be general agreement, however, that the following perceptual-motor qualities are among the most important to be developed and reinforced in children.

Concept 13.6 Developmentally based physical education programs have the potential to enhance perceptual-motor functioning.

Body Awareness. The term *body awareness* is often used in conjunction with the terms body image and body schema. Each term refers to the developing capacity of a child to accurately discriminate among her body parts. The ability to differentiate among body parts and to gain a greater understanding of the nature of the body occurs in three areas. The first is knowledge of the body parts—being able to accurately locate the parts of the body on oneself and on others. Second is knowledge of what the body parts can do. This refers to the child's developing recognition of how the body performs a specific act. Third is knowledge of how to make the body parts move efficiently. This refers to the ability to reorganize the body parts for a particular motor act and to perform a movement task.

Body image has to do with the internalized picture that a child has of his or her body, and the extent to which that image matches reality. Self-perceptions of height, weight, shape, and individual features affect how we compare ourselves to others. Establishing a realistic body image is important in childhood and thereafter. Anorexia and bulimia have been clearly linked to unrealistic body images and are now concerns for children. In addition, there appears to be a close link between body image and self-esteem (Marsh & Peart, 1988; Marsh et al., 1991).

Spatial Awareness. *Spatial awareness* is a basic component of perceptual-motor development that may be divided into two subcategories: (1) knowledge of how much space the body occupies and (2) the ability to project the body effectively into external space. Knowledge of how much space the body occupies and the body's relationship to external objects may be developed through a variety of movement activities. With practice and experience, the child progresses from his egocentric world of locating everything in external space relative to himself (*subjective localization*) to establishing an objective frame of reference (*objective localization*). The child also learns to deal with the concepts of self-space and general space. Self-space refers to the area immediately surrounding an individual bounded by how far one can extend his or her body from a fixed point on the ground. General space refers to that which is beyond a person's self-space. For example, preschoolers tend to determine the locations of objects relative to where they are standing (subjective localization in one's self-space). Older children are able, however, to locate objects relative to their proximity to other nearby objects without regard to the location of their bodies (i.e., objective localization in general space).

The concepts of subjective localization and self-space are closely akin to Piaget's preoperational thought phase of development. The concepts of objective localization and general space are identified with higher cognitive structures in his concrete operations phase. Refer to Chapter 2 for a discussion of Jean Piaget's phases and stages of cognitive development, and the role that movement plays in each of his developmental phases.

The spatial awareness of adults is generally adequate, despite occasional difficulties in locating the relative positions of various objects. For example, when reading a road map while traveling through unfamiliar territory, many people become confused as to whether they are traveling north, south, east, or west. It can be difficult to turn either way while looking at a map, without almost literally placing oneself on the map. The absence of familiar landmarks and the impersonality of the road map make it difficult to objectively localize oneself in space relative to this particular task. Young children encounter much the same difficulty but on a broader scale. They must first learn to orient themselves subjectively in space and then proceed ever so carefully to venture out into unfamiliar surroundings in which subjective clues are useless. Providing children with opportunities to develop spatial awareness is an important attribute of a good, developmentally based physical education program that recognizes the importance of perceptual-motor development.

Directional Awareness.   An area of great concern to many classroom teachers is that of *directional awareness*. Through directional awareness children are able to give dimension to objects in external space. The concepts of left—right, up—down, top—bottom, in—out, and front—back are enhanced through movement activities that place emphasis on direction. Directional awareness is commonly divided into two subcategories: laterality and directionality.

Laterality refers to an internal awareness or feel for the various dimensions of the body with regard to their location and direction. A child who has adequately developed the concept of laterality does not need to rely on external cues for determining direction. She does not need, for example, to have a ribbon tied to her wrist as a reminder about which is left and which is right. She does not need to rely on cues such as the location of a watch or a ring to provide information about direction. The concept seems so basic to most adults that it is difficult to conceive how anyone could fail to develop laterality. However, we need only look into the rear-view mirror of a car to have directions reversed and sometimes confused. Backing up a trailer hitched to a car or parallel parking are experiences that most of us avoid because it is difficult to decide whether to turn the wheel to the left or right. The pilot, astronaut, and deep-sea diver must possess a high degree of laterality or ''feel'' for determining up from down and left from right.

Directionality is the external projection of laterality. It gives dimension to objects in space. True directionality depends on adequately established laterality. Directionality is important to parents and teachers because it is a basic component of learning how to read. Children who do not have fully established directionality will often encounter difficulties in discriminating among various letters of the alphabet. For example, the letters b, d, p, and q are all similar. The only difference lies in the direction of the ''ball'' and the ''stick'' that make up the letters. The child without fully established directionality encounters considerable difficulty in discriminating among several letters of the alphabet. Entire words may even be reversed. The word ''cat'' may be read as ''tac,'' or ''bad'' may be read as ''dab'' because of the child's inability to project direction into external space. Some children encounter difficulty in the top—bottom dimension, which is more basic than the left—right dimension. They may write and see words upside down and are totally confused when it comes to reading.

It should be pointed out that establishing directional awareness is a developmental process that relies on both maturation and experience. It is perfectly normal for the 4- and 5-year-old to experience confusion in direction. We should, however, be concerned for the 6- and 7-year-old child who consistently experiences these problems because this is the time when most schools traditionally begin instruction in reading. Adequately developed directional awareness is one important readiness skill necessary for success in reading, and movement is one way in which this important perceptual-motor concept may be developed.

Temporal Awareness. The preceding discussion of the various aspects of perceptual-motor development dealt with the child's spatial world. Body awareness, spatial awareness, and directional awareness are closely interrelated and combine to help the child make sense of his spatial dimensions. *Temporal awareness,* on the other hand, concerns the acquisition of an adequate time structure in children. It is evoked and refined at the same time the child's spatial world is developing.

Temporal awareness is intricately related to the coordinated interaction of various muscular systems and sensory modalities. The terms eye-hand coordination and eye-foot coordination have been used for years to reflect the interrelationship of these processes. We refer to an individual with a well-developed time dimension as coordinated. One who has not fully established this dimension is often regarded as clumsy or awkward.

Everything that we do possesses an element of time. There is a beginning point and an end point, and no matter how minute, there is a measurable span of time between the two. It is important that children learn how to function efficiently in this time dimension as well as in the space dimension. Without one, the other cannot develop to its fullest potential.

Rhythm is the basic and most important aspect of developing a stable temporal world. The term has many meanings but is described here as the synchronous recurrence of events related in such a manner that they form recognizable patterns. Rhythmic movement involves the synchronous sequencing of events in time. Rhythm is crucial in the performance of any act in a coordinated manner. Cooper (1982) tape-recorded the sounds of outstanding performers completing the movement patterns of selected sport skills. The sounds were transcribed into musical notations, illustrating that recordable rhythmical elements were present. The recorded rhythms of these outstanding athletes were beaten out on a drum in several teaching situations with beginners, who learned the movements of the champions more rapidly than they did when standard teaching techniques were used. Cooper and Andrews (1975) concluded that "it appears that beginning performers can profit by listening to and emulating certain elements of the rhythmic pattern of the good performers. Teachers should take full advantage of this phenomenon" (p. 66). Surely this statement applies to children as well as athletes. We must recognize the rhythmic elements in all efficient movements.

H. Smith (1970) indicated that children begin to make temporal discriminations through the auditory modality before the visual and that there is transfer from the auditory to the visual but not the reverse. Activities that require children to perform movement tasks to auditory rhythmic patterns should begin when they are young and remain a part of their daily lives. The activity possibilities are endless. Moving to various forms of musical accompaniment ranging from drumbeats to instrumental selections contribute to temporal awareness.

Perceptual-Motor Training

During the 1960s and 1970s several *perceptual-motor training* programs were established throughout North America. These programs were given considerable exposure in the popular press. Based on these articles and the claims of some, many people formed the impression that perceptual-motor programs were panaceas for the development of cognitive and motor abilities. Considerable confusion and speculation developed over the values and purposes of perceptual-motor training programs. Programs adhering to one technique or another emerged almost overnight. All too often, people were inadequately trained, ill informed and, frankly, not clear on just what they were trying to accomplish. The smoke has now cleared, and concerned educators have taken a closer, more objective look at perceptual-motor training programs and their role in the total educational spectrum. Instead of claiming they are panaceas or adhering to one training technique or another, many are viewing perceptual-motor programs as important facilitators of *readiness development.* Perceptual-motor activities are being recognized as important contributors to the general readiness of children for learning. The contribution of perceptual-motor activities to specific perceptual readiness skills is being closely reexamined.

Concept 13.7   Perceptual-motor training programs can be effective when viewed as readiness programs that assist young children in learning to learn.

Readiness programs may be classified as concept developing and concept reinforcing. *Concept development programs* are generally designed for children who have been limited or restricted in their experiential backgrounds (e.g., socioeconomic class, prolonged illness, ethnic background, or excessive television). Head Start programs and Frostig's (1969) developmental program are examples of concept-developing programs, in which a variety of multisensory experiences including perceptual-motor activities are used to develop fundamental readiness skills.

Concept reinforcement programs are those in which movement is used in conjunction with traditional classroom techniques to develop basic cognitive understandings. In this type of program, movement is used as an aid or vehicle for reinforcing cognitive concepts presented in the nursery school or primary grade classroom.

Concept 13.8   There is insufficient evidence to support the efficacy of perceptual-motor training programs designed to remediate childhood learning disabilities.

Remedial training programs are the third and most controversial type of perceptual-motor training program. They have been established as a means of alleviating perceptual inadequacies and increasing academic achievement. Programs have been developed by Delacato (1959), Getman (1952), Kephart (1971), and others to aid cognitive development through perceptual-motor remediation techniques. The avowed purpose of these programs is to enhance academic achievement. There is, however, little solid support for this claim although abundant testimony and opinions are available. In fact, a meta-analysis of more than 180 research studies designed to measure the efficacy of perceptual-motor training on academic achievement and cognition clearly reveals that such programs make little or no "direct" contribution to these areas (Kavale & Mattson, 1983). Additionally, the Council for Learning Disabilities (1987) published a position statement dealing with the measurement and training of perceptual and perceptual-motor functions. This statement said, in part, that:

> There is little or no empirical support for claims that the training of perceptual and perceptual-motor functions improves either academic performance or the perceptual-motor functions of learning disabled individuals. Therefore, such training must be characterized at best as experimental and nonvalidated" (p. 350).

Figure 13.1 presents an overview of the various types of perceptual-motor training programs.

Readiness and Remediation

Research indicates that as children pass through the normal developmental stages, their perceptual abilities become more acute and refined. This is due partly to the increasing complexity of the neuromuscular apparatus and sensory receptors and partly to children's increasing ability to explore and move through the environment. Piaget's (1954) work has traced the gradual development of perception from crude, meaningless sensations to impressions of a stable spatial world. His stages of development rely heavily on motor information as a primary information-gathering device. As the perceptual world unfolds, children seek stability and reduce variability as far as possible. They learn to differentiate among things that can be ignored, things that are easily predictable, or things that are wholly unforeseen and must be observed and examined to be understood, according to Piaget and others. Movement plays an important role in this process of developing perceptual readiness for cognitive tasks. Table 13.2 compares Piaget's (1952) stages of development with those proposed by Kephart (1971) and by these authors.

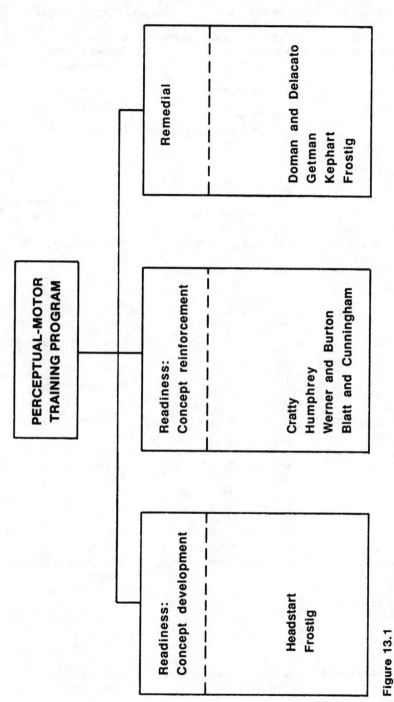

Figure 13.1
Three types of perceptual-motor training programs

Table 13.2 Comparison of Piaget's, Kephart's, and Gallahue's Phases and Stages of Development

Approximate Chronological Age	Piaget's Cognitive Phases and Stages	Kephart's Developmental Sequences	Gallahue's Phases and Stages of Motor Development
0 to 6 months	**Sensorimotor Phase** Use of reflexes Primary circular reactions Coordination of prehension and vision, secondary circular reactions	**Reflexive Stage** **Motor Stage** Rudimentary motor pattern development	**Reflexive Phase** Encoding stage Decoding stage
6 to 12 months	Secondary schemata Discovery of new means, tertiary circular reactions	Balance Receipt and propulsion Globular form	**Rudimentary Phase** Reflex inhibition stage
1 to 2 years	Beginnings of insight and cause/effect relationships Egocentric organization Perceptive movement	**Motor-Perceptual Stage** Laterality Hand-eye coordination Gross motor pattern development Syncretic form Form recognition	Precontrol stage
2 to 4 years	**Preoperational Thought Phase** Perceptually oriented, period from self-satisfying behavior to rudimentary social behavior Awareness of a conceptual hierarchy, beginnings of cognition		**Fundamental Movement Phase** Initial stage Elementary stage
4 to 6 years	Beginning abstractions	**Perceptual-Motor Stage** Directionality Eye-hand coordination **Perceptual Stage** Form perception Constructive form Form reproduction	Mature stage
7 to 10 years	**Concrete Operations Phase** Additive composition, reversibility, associativity, identity, deductive reasoning Relationships Classification	Perceptual Cognitive Stage	**Specialized Movement Phase** Transition stage
11 years and over	**Formal Operations Phase** Intellectual maturity Symbolic operations Abstract thinking Propositional thinking	Cognitive Perceptual Stage Cognitive Stage	Application stage Lifelong utilization stage

The majority of our perceptions, and visual perceptions in particular, result from the elaboration and modification of these basic reactions by experience and learning. When we speak of children being perceptually ready to learn, we are, in fact, referring to a point in time in which they have sufficiently developed their basic perceptual and conceptual learning capacities.

Achieving perceptual readiness for learning is a developmental process in which perceptual-motor activities play an important part. Specific perceptual readiness skills, such as visual perceptual readiness for reading, may be affected by the quality and quantity of a child's perceptual-motor experiences, but this has not been conclusively demonstrated in controlled research studies.

The process of being able to read (and accomplish other important tasks) involves a number of abilities including visual perceptual ability. The reading process may be considered in terms of three basic areas: language, skill, and perception. Considerable research has been conducted in the first two areas, but scholars are just beginning to explore the third. The perceptual phase of reading involves the identification and recognition of words on a printed page. Form and shape perception may be enhanced through movement as well as directional awareness of up, down, left, and right. All are important factors associated with word identification and recognition.

The greatest amount of perceptual-motor development takes place between ages 3 and 7. These are the crucial years preceding and during the time that most children begin to learn to read. A child is perceptually ready to read when she has acquired a sufficient backlog of information to encode and decode sensory impressions at a given point in time. Ideally, the child's previous learning experiences were numerous and of high quality. A sufficient number of children enter first grade lagging in their perceptual abilities to warrant programs in readiness training that utilize perceptual-motor development activities as one of many avenues for intervention. The physical education portion of the school day can play an important role in helping many of these children catch up with their peers.

Perceptual-Motor Research Findings

Research efforts continue to document the virtues of perceptual-motor training programs on readiness and remedial aspects of perceptual and cognitive development. Each new research effort stimulates new questions and problems. The results that are available are not conclusive, but there is ample evidence to suggest that perceptual-motor training programs are making positive contributions to the motor and perceptual development of children. In reviewing the literature, one may discover several generalizations that lend support to and have specific implications for the educator and parent concerned with the prevention and remediation of perceptual-motor learning disabilities. Some of the findings that arise out of this research are summarized below.

1. Not all learning disabilities are perceptual-motor in nature. Some may be due to problems in perceptual functioning. Others may be due to problems in concept formulation.
2. Perceptual-motor deficits may or may not lead to learning disabilities in a given child. Despite this fact, diagnosis and remediation of perceptual problems are worthwhile if only for the expanded competencies, both physical and emotional (self-concept), that may result from such intervention.
3. Diagnostic tools for assessment are at this time rather primitive. Distinct elements in the perceptual-motor spectrum have yet to be identified. Diagnostic tests cannot yet validly isolate separate factors.
4. Low-level functional deficits (perceptual-motor tasks) seem to be associated with high-level functional deficits (perceptual-cognitive tasks). This is to say that children who perform poorly on tasks of high complexity (reading and arithmetic) also tend to perform poorly on tasks of low complexity (laterality, directionality, midline). This link, however, has not been proven to be causal, and therefore must be assumed to be casual.
5. Intramodal abilities develop before intermodal abilities. This means that children learn to use each of the senses separately before they interrelate them and use more than one mode at a time.
6. The most efficient learning mode seems to be visual although learning is enhanced when information is presented to or processed by two or more modes at the same time. That is, children are likely to learn more if information is presented kinesthetically, visually, and auditorially at the same time than if it is presented through only one mode at a time.
7. Not all children are at the same perceptual level on entering the first grade. Perceptual development is a process of both maturation and experience, and children therefore develop at their individual rates.
8. Adequate perception (auditory, visual, tactile-kinesthetic) is prerequisite to success in school. Inaccurate perceptions may lead to difficulties in academic concept formation. Perceptual readiness is an important aspect of total readiness for learning.
9. Perceptual abilities may be improved through specialized training.

10. Pre-assessment of perceptual-motor skills may be useful at the preschool or kindergarten level as a means of providing subjective clues to readiness lags in children.
11. Developmentally based physical activity programs provide many of the movement experiences that enhance a child's perceptual-motor abilities.

In conclusion, when we say that a child is "ready" to learn, we are, in fact, referring to a point in time when the child, through both maturation and learning, has developed sufficient perceptual and motor abilities to benefit measurably from higher-order perceptual and cognitive tasks. Movement experiences are a means by which these capabilities can be developed and refined. Myers and Hammill (1982) in their recommendations for needed perceptual-motor research insisted that three basic issues be addressed.

1. The characteristics of children for whom training has been demonstrated to be beneficial must be identified.
2. The optimal amount and type of training necessary to produce real perceptual and/or motor growth must be determined.
3. The fact that perceptual-motor processes can actually be improved as a result of training must be demonstrated (p. 416).

Children learn by doing. Teachers encourage children's perceptual-motor skills by providing varied programs of success-oriented movement experiences appropriate for the developmental level of each child.

Assessing Perceptual-Motor Development

During the past several years numerous measures of perceptual-motor development have been constructed. Generally, these tests were developed as measures for children who had been classified as "slow learners," "neurologically impaired," or as having "attention deficit disorder" (ADD). They have been used with varying degrees of success. The classroom teacher and physical education teacher are often the first to pick up "subjective" cues of possible perceptual-motor difficulties in preschool and primary grade children. The validity of these subjective observations must not be discounted or minimized. On the contrary, the careful daily observation of a child's behavior can be very valuable and reliable in detecting potential lags in development. A child who shows signs of possible developmental problems should be referred to the school psychologist for testing. The results of the testing should be shared with parents and the teachers with whom the child comes in contact. The adults can form an effective team to eliminate or diminish the difficulty.

The checklist of cues in Table 13.3 may aid the teacher in assessing children with potential perceptual-motor problems. The checklist is designed to serve only as a subjective indicator of possible perceptual-motor difficulties. There is very little interrelationship among these variables, and there is no predictable pattern for determining difficulties. A teacher who observes a child's weaknesses in several of these items should seek further information through more objective evaluation procedures.

Concept 13.9 Both formal and informal devices for assessing perceptual-motor functioning are available to provide important cues to developmental difficulties in children.

Summary

Perceptual-motor training programs possess many of the same elements as reputable developmentally based physical education programs. Many of the movement skills taught in a perceptual-motor curriculum, either readiness or remedial, parallel those taught in regular developmental physical education classes. The goals of each program are obviously different. A primary goal of the developmental physical activity program is to enhance movement control through practice and instruction in a variety of movement skills, while the goal of the perceptual-motor program is to enhance perceptual-motor qualities through practice and instruction in a variety of movement activities.

Perceptual-motor training programs that purport to enhance academic achievement or to promote specific readiness for schoolwork do so amid considerable controversy and a lack of research support. Public testimony and opinion have served for years as the basis of support for perceptual-motor training programs. This is not adequate. However, the value of perceptual-motor experiences to a general state of readiness should not be dismissed. Enhancement of body, spatial, directional, and temporal awareness as a means of guiding the child toward improved movement control and efficiency in fundamental movement is worthwhile in itself. Practice in perceptual-motor activities may, under certain conditions, enhance perceptual-motor abilities. Whether these abilities have a direct effect on academic performance is highly questionable. One can be assured, however, that they do play an important role in developing and refining the child's movement abilities.

Table 13.3 Checklist of Possible Perceptual-Motor Dysfunctions

1. Has trouble holding or maintaining balance. _____
2. Appears clumsy. _____
3. Cannot carry body well in motion. _____
4. Appears to be generally awkward in activities requiring coordination. _____
5. Does not readily distinguish left from right. _____
6. In locomotor skills, performs movements with more efficiency on one side than the other. _____
7. Reverses letters and numbers with regularity. _____
8. Is unable to hop or skip rhythmically. _____
9. Has difficulty making changes in movement. _____
10. Has difficulty performing combinations of simple movements. _____
11. Has difficulty in gauging space with respect to the body, and collides with objects and other children. _____
12. Tends to be accident-prone. _____
13. Has poor hand-eye coordination. _____
14. Has difficulty handling the simple tools of physical activity (beanbags, balls, and other objects that involve a visual-motor relationship). _____
15. Has persistent poor general appearance. _____
    (a) Shirt tail always out. _____
    (b) Shoes constantly untied. _____
    (c) Fly constantly unzipped. _____
    (d) Socks bagged around ankles. _____
    (e) Hair uncombed. _____
16. Is inattentive. _____
17. Does not follow directions; is able to follow verbal but not written directions, or vice versa. _____
18. Has speech difficulties. _____
    (a) Talks too loudly. _____
    (b) Talks too softly. _____
    (c) Slurs words. _____
    (d) Leaves off ends of words. _____
    (e) Uses immature sentence structure. _____
19. Poor body posture. _____
20. Has hearing difficulties. _____
    (a) Frequently turns head to one side. _____
    (b) Holds or prefers one ear over the other. _____
21. Has difficulty negotiating stairs. _____
22. Daydreams excessively. _____
23. Is excessively messy in work. _____
    (a) Goes out of the lines. _____
    (b) Inconsistency of letter size, etc. _____
    (c) General sloppiness. _____
24. Is unable to copy objects (words, numbers, letters, etc.). _____

A comparison of Gallahue's phases of motor development to Kephart's developmental sequence and Piaget's cognitive phases of development was presented in Table 13.2. Careful review of these models reveals the interrelated nature of the perceptual, motor, and cognitive processes. The magnitude of this relationship and the conditions necessary for improved functioning in each area await further well-controlled scientific research.

Terms to Remember

Visual-motor adjustment
Perception
Visual perception
Static visual acuity
Dynamic visual acuity
Figure-ground perception
Figure
Ground
Depth perception
Monocular depth cues
Binocular depth cues
Retinal disparity
Visual-motor coordination
Visual tracking
Object interception
Coincidence-anticipation
Perceptual-motor
Sensory input
Sensory integration

Motor interpretation
Movement activation
Feedback
Temporal world
Spatial world
Body awareness
Spatial awareness
Subjective localization
Objective localization
Directional awareness
Laterality
Directionality
Temporal awareness
Rhythm
Perceptual-motor training
Readiness development
Concept development programs
Concept reinforcement programs
Remedial training programs

Critical Readings

Bower, T. G. R. (1977). *The Perceptual World of the Child*. Cambridge, MA: Harvard University Press.

Council on Learning Disabilities (1987). The CLD position statements: Measurement and training of perceptual and perceptual-motor functions. *Journal of Learning Disabilities*, 20, 6, 347–350.

Kavale, K., & Mattson, P. D. (1983). One jumped off the balance beam: Meta-analysis of perceptual-motor training. *Journal of Learning Disabilities*, 16, 165–173.

Sage, G. H. (1984). *Motor Learning and Control: A Neuropsychological Approach* (Chapter 9). Dubuque, IA: Wm. C. Brown.

Williams, H. G. (1983). *Perceptual and Motor Development* (Chapter 4). Englewood Cliffs, NJ: Prentice-Hall.

Zeki, S. (1992). The visual image in mind and brain. *Scientific American*, 267, 69–76.

Chapter 14

Childhood Self-Concept Development

CHAPTER COMPETENCIES

Upon completion of this chapter you should be able to:

- *List and describe sociocultural correlates that may affect motor development*
- *Distinguish similarities, differences, and relationships among various terms used in the study of self-concept*
- *Describe the developmental aspects of self-concept*
- *Demonstrate how movement competence is related to self-esteem*
- *Analyze similarities and differences of movement competence on social status in males and females*
- *List the consequences of a negative self-concept*
- *Propose means of enhancing self-esteem through movement*
- *Describe problems associated with assessing self-concept*

Key Concept: Self-concept is a multidimensional construct linked to perceived physical competence throughout childhood and beyond.

Do you remember when you were a child with nothing to do but play for hours and hours each day? Do you remember the excitement of that first climb to the top of the monkey bars, your first successful ride on a two-wheeler, or your first swim all the way across a pool? We can all remember how good it felt to succeed and can probably even remember how it felt to fail. The successes and failures of childhood may seem remote and meaningless to us now, but they were important events that influenced what and who we are today. Many of these events centered around early play experiences. The feelings children have about themselves are greatly determined by their play experiences, both successful and unsuccessful.

Children are active, energetic, and emerging beings. Many of their lives are spent in play and active exploration of an ever-expanding world. The so-called play world of children occupies large portions of their days and is of central importance. It is a primary means by which children learn more about themselves, their bodies, and their potential for movement. Many basic affective concepts have their roots in the carefree, exhilarating world of play.

Self-concept is an important aspect of a child's affective behavior that is influenced through the world of games, play, and vigorous movement. A stable, positive self-concept is so crucial to a child's ability to function effectively, that its development cannot be left to chance. The important contributions that movement and vigorous physical activity can make to forming a positive self-concept should not be overlooked. As adults we should be genuinely interested in the development of good self-concepts in our children. In this chapter we will examine self-concept development and the potential of physical activity for enhancing self-esteem.

What Is Self-Concept?

The topic of "self" has been a central focus of the psycho-social literature for more than a hundred years. The now classic work of William James (1890/1963) undergirds much of the current work on the developing self. A variety of terms have been used with "self" as a hyphenated prefix (Figure 14.1). As a result considerable confusion has existed over meanings, similarities, and differences. We will attempt to clarify these often subtle differences before examining the role of movement in the establishment of a positive view of self. There is considerable overlap and cross-use among these terms as they are commonly used in the literature today.

Self-concept, as used here, is the umbrella term under which several other variations of self are categorized. Self-concept is generally viewed as one's awareness of personal characteristics, attributes, and limitations, and the ways in which these qualities are both like and unlike those of others. Self-concept is how one views herself or himself without passing personal judgment or comparison with others. On the other hand, *self-esteem* is the value that one attaches to his or her

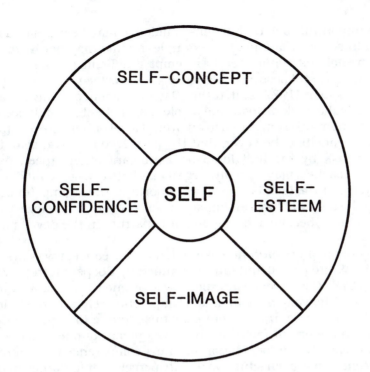

Figure 14.1
Terms commonly
used to describe
one's perception of
self

unique characteristics, attributes, and limitations. Weiss (1987) indicated that "self-esteem represents the evaluation and effective component of one's self-concept: that is, it refers to the qualitative judgments and feelings attached to the descriptions one assigns to self" (p. 88). Whereas self-concept is merely one's perceptions of self, self-esteem is the value one places on those perceptions.

James (1890) was the first modern scholar to attempt to decipher the elusive meaning of self-esteem. His now famous formula concluded that one's feelings of self-worth (self-esteem) are equal to the ratio of one's accomplishments to one's potential for achievement. The closer the success to potential ratio is to 1.0, the nearer one is to his or her ideal self. Perhaps Coopersmith (1967) defined self-esteem best when he stated that "self-esteem is a personal judgment of worthiness that is expressed in the attitudes the individual holds toward himself" (p. 5). Although the terms are linked, self-esteem is not the same as self-confidence.

Self-confidence denotes one's belief in his or her ability to carry out a mental, physical or emotional task. It is one's anticipated ability to master particular challenges and to overcome obstacles or difficulties. Self-confident persons believe that they can cause things to happen in accordance with their desires. Self-confidence as used here means the same as Bandura's (1982) term *self-efficacy,* which he defines as "the conviction that one can successfully execute the behavior required to produce the [desired] outcome" (p. 39).

It is important to note that self-confidence may be unrelated to self-esteem in some situations. For example, a child may not have a sufficient level of self-confidence to attempt a difficult gymnastics movement, but may still possess a high level of self-esteem. In support of this notion Diskstein (1977) stated that "self-confidence involves carrying off a particular task or fostering a role. Level of self-confidence at any one moment may be unrelated to an overall level of self-esteem" (p. 136). One must conclude, however, that the perceived importance of the activity or task by the individual or significant others (peer, parents, teachers, coaches) may actually forge a link between self-confidence and self-esteem. If the task is viewed as important, then competence in executing the task will have an impact on self-esteem. Therefore, the term "competence" becomes an important construct in the development of self-esteem.

The notion of *competence* as related to self-concept was first introduced by White (1959) and later expanded by Coopersmith (1977) and Harter (1978). Competence may be viewed as one's actual ability to meet particular achievement demands. Competence refers to one's level of mastery which may range from poor to adequate to superior. Competence is an important factor in the development of one's self-concept. More specifically, the perception of one's competence (i.e., *perceived competence*) in a given situation and its perceived importance may have a significant impact on one's actual competence, self-confidence, self-esteem, and self-concept (Figure 14.2). Estimates of perceived physical competence (i.e., ability) have been shown to contribute to children's achievement motivation (Weiss & Horn, 1990). In other words, low estimates of physical ability are likely to lead to attrition in youth sport participation, whereas high levels of perceived ability are likely to motivate children to continue sports participation.

Self-Concept: Global or Multidimensional?

A question that has intrigued theorists and researchers for decades involves the general nature or specificity of one's self-concept; that is, is self-concept a global trait, or can it be differentiated into various components? A strong case can be made for both views and research can be cited to support both positions. It seems entirely possible that one possesses both a differentiated concept of self and a global self-concept. In support of this, Rosenberg (1979) insisted that the two are not identical, stating, "Both exist within the individual's phenomenal field as separate and distinguishable entities and each can and should be studied in its own right" (p. 20). Rosenberg (1982) in a later paper makes the telling point that: "Although widely overlooked in self-esteem studies, it is fairly obvious that a person's global self-esteem is not based solely on his assessment of his constituent qualities. His self-esteem is based

Figure 14.2
A hierarchical view
of self-concept de-
velopment

```
┌─────────────────────────────┐
│        SELF-CONCEPT         │
│  The value-free description │
│      attached to oneself    │
└─────────────────────────────┘
```

```
┌─────────────────────────────┐
│         SELF-ESTEEM         │
│  The value (worth) attached │
│     to one's self-description│
└─────────────────────────────┘
```

```
┌─────────────────────────────┐
│       SELF-CONFIDENCE       │
│   The belief in one's ability to │
│       carry out a task      │
└─────────────────────────────┘
```

```
┌─────────────────────────────┐
│         COMPETENCE          │
│    Actual success in meeting │
│  specific achievement demands│
└─────────────────────────────┘
```

```
┌─────────────────────────────┐
│     PERCEIVED COMPETENCE    │
│  One's feelings of potential for │
│   success in meeting specific │
│     achievement demands     │
└─────────────────────────────┘
```

on his self-assessments of qualities that count'' (p. 536). In other words, global self-concept is the product of one's perception of his or her competence in areas that have personal meaning. It is unaffected by one's self-assessment of competence in areas that have little or no personal significance. It follows, therefore, that if being good at games, play activities, and sports is important to a child, then success in these areas will have an impact on his global self-concept. If, however, these attributes are not perceived as being personally meaningful, then they will have little impact.

Concept 14.1 Global self-concept is the product of one's perceptions of competence in areas that have personal meaning.

In modern North American society, being good in games, play activities, and sports is of high positive value to both boys and girls. Competence in these areas is important in terms of social acceptance and status within the peer group. Moreover, adults frequently give children the impression that their competence in physical endeavors is closely linked to their acceptance and value within the family or team unit. In a society that places high positive value on success in games and sport, it is reasonable to assume that one of the important components of global self-concept is *movement competence* and that movement competence plays a crucial role in positive self-esteem development.

Harter (1978, 1982a) and Harter and Connell (1984), studying the developmental aspects of self-concept, attempted to isolate three self-evaluative dimensions of competence. The Self-Perception Profile for Children (Harter, 1985) and the Pictorial Scale of Perceived Competence and Social Acceptance for Young Children (Harter & Pike, 1984) subdivide perceived competence into cognitive and physical (movement) domains, along with measures of social acceptance and general self-worth. Harter (1982) found that children in grades 3 through 9 make clear distinctions among categories. However, Harter and Pike (1984) did not find the same to be true with younger children (ages 4 to 7). These children tended to lump cognitive and physical competence together into a category of ''general competence,'' and to view social acceptance (by the peer group and mother) as important. Also, they did not possess concepts of general self-worth. It appears, therefore, that the notion of movement competence has significant implications for children from about the third grade onward. Prior to that time children tend to view themselves as either competent or incompetent with little distinction between the physical and cognitive domains. Recently, however, Marsh et al. (1991) investigated the multidimensional structure of self-concept in children 5 to 8 years of age. The results of this study which used the

Self-Description Questionnaire (Marsh, 1990), revealed that when appropriately measured, self-concepts are better differentiated by young children than previously assumed. Therefore, we can conclude that when properly measured, self-concept is multidimensional in young children as well as older children, adolescents and adults.

Concept 14.2 Movement competence plays an important role in self-concept development, because children generally value being good in games, sports, and play activities.

A person is unique because of his or her self-concept and view of the world. The sum of life experiences and the person's feelings about these experiences contribute to this mental model. We find out about ourselves in many ways. By choosing, trying things out, experimenting, and exploring, we discover who we are, what we can do, and what we cannot do. Not only do we discover who we are, but through our experiences we contribute to the making or formation of our unique identities.

Developmental Aspects of Self-Concept

A person's self-concept is learned, and it begins to develop at least at birth. In fact, some authorities argue that the emotional state of the expectant mother, ranging from relaxed and happy to tense and unhappy, may have a dramatic affect on the unborn child. Emphasizing this point, Yamamoto (1972) stated that:

> Some studies have suggested that stress experiences by a pregnant mother can alter the movements of the fetus from normal to hyperactive—the mother should know that a physically healthy child has a greater chance for adequate psychological development, since the concept of a child's physical self plays an important part in the entirety of the self-concept (pp. 181–182).

The early months of infancy mark the first tangible beginnings of self-concept development. The tenderness, warmth, and love from the parent to the child convey the first feelings of value and affection. The infant's sense of well-being is affected by the parent's emotional state and attention to his or her physical needs. The fulfillment of psychological needs is just as important, for the infant needs to establish a sense of trust, security, recognition, and love. Trust is a basic issue to be resolved in the early parent-infant relationship. Mothers and fathers create a sense of trust in their children by combining sensitive care with a firm sense of personal reliability.

Concept 14.3 Self-concept is learned during childhood and is resistant to change once it is fully established.

Self-concept is established in the infant and young child through the affirmation of others. Children increase their competence under the care of loving, capable, and nurturing adults. Werner (1989a; 1989b) in her 30-year longitudinal study of 698 "high-risk" individuals from infancy onward, clearly identified the importance of the presence of at least one consistent, nurturing, unconditionally accepting adult in a child's life in order for successful adaptation to occur. Erik Erikson (1963, 1980) was among the first to recognize the importance of establishing a sense of trust during a child's early years. His stage of "trust versus mistrust" (discussed in greater detail in Chapter 2) is rooted in the child's developing sense of being loved and valued in a world that has constancy and permanence.

Concept 14.4 Parents, teachers, and coaches are significant others in the lives of children, and as such play important roles in the development of their self-concepts.

The toddler experiences the satisfaction of mastering the art of walking successfully or solving a problem with a new toy. The development of a sense of autonomy is an important facilitator of a positive self-concept, influenced greatly by central adults in the life of the child. The dependency of children on significant others is temporary, and it is the temporary nature dependence that leads them to the exploratory behaviors and mastery attempts of early childhood and beyond. Adults have unique opportunities to reinforce the ways in which children learn about themselves by providing opportunities for self-discovery and by consistently accepting the individuality of each child. During this period caretakers should respect a child's need for freedom and independence within carefully defined limits.

Much of what the young child learns is imitative, and this learning is not restricted to overt action. Feelings and attitudes can also be learned through imitation. As a result, the moods and emotions of a central adult affect many of the attitudes and feelings that the child develops.

As a child's social world and the influence of others expands, he develops a greater sense of independence. Upon entering school he begins to shift his frame of reference from the home and family to the school and the teacher. The number of significant others that affect his developing self increase as teachers and peers begin to exert greater influence. The teacher becomes a primary model for the child, and there is a great desire to please. Martinek and Zaichkowsky (1977) found that the teacher's expectations of a child's performance level had a definite impact on self-concept from the second through the sixth grades. A study by Zaichkowsky et al. (1975) revealed that the teacher's levels of expectancy for children in physical activities were positively correlated with self-concept scores. Furthermore, Schempp et al. (1983) found that an atmosphere in which children were encouraged to make decisions promoted the development of positive self-concepts, attitudes, creativity, and motor skills. Those who were expected to do well and involved in decision making had higher self-concept scores than those who were expected to do poorly or not involved in decision making. The implications of these findings are enormous when applied to the teacher/learner or coach/athlete dyads.

Older children feel good about accomplishing new and difficult tasks, establishing independence, and performing meaningful work to earn money. The thoughtful parent recognizes the importance of the peer group at this level and gradually helps the child develop a sense of mature independence.

A person's sense of worth and effectiveness develops chiefly through successful experiences in coping, according to Maynard (1973). Coping skills are essential for confidence. One must be willing to accept oneself as well as others who are different. Children and adults who can cope are adaptable rather than rigid in their behavior. They are diligent, can concentrate on a task, and can work through difficulties. Self-confidence is developed through the joy of finding what one does well— of doing anything really well. Movement skill and fitness acquisition are important avenues by which self-confidence may be enhanced. They are especially important for most children, because many of their daily life experiences are centered around the need for efficient and effective movement.

The work of Damon and Hart (1986) argues strongly. For the developmental nature of self-concept, as revealed in a 3-year longitudinal study of self-understanding in children 4 through 18. Their results also lend support to the basic assumption that an individuals sense of self tends to be stable over time.

Movement Competence and Self-Esteem

Limited research has been conducted in the area of movement and self-esteem. It has long been considered a "sloppy" area in which to do study, for a variety of reasons. First, it is difficult to isolate the possible variables that influence the self. Second, the criterion measures of self-esteem that are used are often suspect in terms of their validity. Third, the manner in which numerous tests were constructed was often "weird," according to McCandless (1976). Research in the area of movement and self-esteem is now, however, beginning to reflect a concern for these difficulties and to deal effectively with them. Several investigations into the effects of movement on the self-concept of children are just emerging.

The perception of competence is one of the most important variables underlying motivation (White, 1959; Harter, 1978; Duda, 1986; Crawford, 1989). Harter's expansion on White's theory of competence motivation (Harter, 1980) argues that the quality of one's experiences is the critical determinant for the developing of competence. Competence is a facilitator of confidence, and confidence fosters a positive view of self. Demonstrating competence leads to pride and joy, but failing to demonstrate competence leads to shame and self-doubt. A child's perceived competence affects her continued interest in an activity and in further mastery attempts. When applied to physical activity, Harter's theory of competence motivation means that if an individual perceives himself as physically competent he will continue to participate in physical activities. If, however, he perceives himself to be physically incompetent, he will limit participation and suspend mastery attempts.

Concept 14.5 Perceived competence and actual competence promote self-confidence, which has the potential for enhancing dimensional aspects of one's self-esteem and self-concept.

The development of perceived competence is a primary goal of youth sport participation (Gould, 1984; Horn, 1984; Fox, 1988; Knoppers, 1992). Several studies have demonstrated the importance of perceived competence for continued participation in sport (Crawford, 1989; Feltz & Petlichkoff, 1983; Gould, 1984; Marsh, 1985; Roberts et al., 1981). Physical activity can enhance or limit self-concept development in children, because it is a central focus in their lives. Both boys and girls place great value on competence in physical activities, and this is an essential factor in global self-esteem (Harter, 1983; Weiss, 1987).

Zaharopoulos and Hodge (1991) examined differences between adolescent athletes and non-athletes and gender. The results of their cross-sectional study indicated that athletes differed significantly from non-athletes in physical ability self-concept, but not in global self-concept. Additionally, females did not differ from males in physical ability self-concept. These findings support the concept of multidimensionality in self-concept, but refute the notion that sport participation enhances self-concept in general. These results confirmed the results of an earlier investigation by Marsh and Peart (1988).

The relationship between a child's social status and his movement competence has been a subject of interest to researchers for many years. Numerous studies point out that there is a link between high positive peer group acceptance and ability in games and sports, especially for boys. Athletic skill is paramount for many boys, predicated upon motor coordination, strength, size, and physical maturity (Tudenham, 1951). Recently however, several investigations have pointed out that girls have less positive perceptions of their physical competence than boys (van Wersch et al., 1990; Fox, et al., 1985; Granleese et al., 1988; Marsh, 1985).

Skill level is often controlled by factors outside the child's influence. Such things as physical stature, health-related conditions, experience, and the quality of instruction make it impossible for many children to meet the values of their peer groups. As a result, they feel inferior and rejected and develop poor self-images. Personal insecurity and social maladjustment often have their roots in this area.

Schoolyards, gymnasiums, and play environments provide excellent opportunities for positive self-concept development. A child's perceived competence as well as her actual competence in the physical, cognitive and affective domains are important facilitators of positive self-concept development (Harter, 1978). With regard to the physical domain, Roberts et al. (1981) tested fourth and fifth graders, and Harter (1982) tested sixth graders who were either non-participants or participants in organized youth sport programs. The results of their independent investigations indicated that participants perceive themselves as more competent in games and sports than non-participants. Ulrich (1987) however, found somewhat different results in her study of younger children in grades K through 4. She compared children's perceptions of physical competence, their actual motor competencies, and their participation in youth sport programs. Her results revealed that the perceived physical competencies of young children were not significantly related to their participation in organized sports. However, their actual motor competencies were significantly related to sport participation. It seems that while older children are clearly influenced by their perceptions of physical competence and participation, younger children may not be. Reasons for this difference are as yet unexplained.

Consequences of a Poor Self-Concept

A poor self-concept is reflected in the feelings of "I can't," "I'm always wrong," or, "I'm worthless." Children who feel bad about themselves and the world they know are not likely to feel better about parts of the world they do not know. As a result, they are often indifferent or fearful about exploring new territory. It does not look inviting and appears hostile and full of possibilities for humiliation and defeat. This threatening new world does not lure the child out but thrusts in on her, invading those few places in which she feels secure. A child with a negative self-concept regards unfamiliar experiences with fear.

Concept 14.6   A negative self-concept can have devastating effects on all aspects of a child's life.

A child who feels worthless due to repeated failures often falls back on the strategy of deliberate failure, which serves as a self-protective device. Children who view themselves as failures will not even be tempted to try new tasks.

Children with poor self-concepts are also negatively affected by what they think others think of them. Children, as well as adults, tend to live up to the expectations of others, or at least to what these expectations are perceived to be. Teachers are of tremendous importance in shaping children's basic attitudes toward themselves in relation to school. During the elementary years significant correlations exist between children's perceptions of their teachers' feelings toward them and their own self-images. Teachers who emphasize positive self-concepts tend to be associated with students who hold positive views of themselves. Using such terms as stupid, dumb, always wrong, bad boy or girl, troublemaker, and lousy is harmful to children. These spoken words, as well as our unspoken indications of disapproval, dismay, disgust, anger, and surprise, influence what children think others think of them. Given enough negative information, a child soon adapts to a negative role. A cycle of failure and perceived expectation of failure is established.

Children with poor self-images are rarely cheered when they succeed. Their perceptions of themselves as non-achievers, combined with their convictions that others perceive them in the same manner, are difficult to change when success is infrequent. Even when normal patterns of failure are broken occasionally with success, children with poor self-images regard the successes as temporary and believe that things will certainly go wrong soon.

The influence of a poor self-concept on the learning process can be tremendous. High anxiety, underachievement, behavior problems, learning difficulties, and delinquency are among the problems. Brookover et al. (1967) concluded from their extensive research on self-concept and achievement that the assumption that human ability is the most important factor in achievement is questionable, and that a student's attitudes limit or extend the level of achievement in school. Students' perceptions of themselves as "learners" or "non-learners" affect academic achievement levels. Low achievement is often due to a child's definition of himself as a non-learner. He resists learning because it is inconsistent for him, in his view, to learn. A child who feels that he cannot achieve may negate or reduce his actual ability, which may be average, above average, or even higher. Conversely, a child with a success-oriented outlook plunges into a project or takes on a new challenge with every expectation of achievement.

The role of physical activity in self-concept development must not be minimized, but questions remain. Does increased movement competence lead to improved self-esteem? Does one's level of self-esteem influence achievement? Physical educators and coaches, for the most part, have adopted the behavioristic point of view that improved levels of movement competence lead to enhanced self-esteem. This behavioristic model has not been sufficiently tested. Physical education teachers and coaches who emphasize competitiveness and reward the more skillful athletes may actually do little to enhance perceptions of physical competence among those who are less skillful (van Wersch et al., 1990). On the other hand, many educators have adopted a cognitive view of learning that promotes student self-discovery and perceived competence through developmentally appropriate activities (Bigge & Shermis, 1992). Teachers and coaches who adopt a developmental model of education and adapt their instruction to the individual needs of children may in fact be enhancing perceived competence and promoting further mastery attempts in all students (Gallahue, 1993). In fact, self-concept enhancement has been an established goal for most teachers and coaches who subscribe to a developmental skill and fitness model of instruction. One's level of self-esteem can be a factor in influencing achievement, and achievement can be an important factor in influencing self-esteem (Weiss, 1987).

Concept 14.7 Perceived physical competence can be enhanced through success-oriented, developmentally based movement programs.

Movement Techniques for Enhancing Self-Esteem

Children who have difficulty performing many fundamental skills that are basic to proficient performance in games and sports encounter repeated failures in their everyday play experiences. As a result, they often have trouble seeing themselves as worthy beings. Taylor (1980) stated that "one of the best and easiest pathways to a strong self-concept is through play. Play offers opportunities to assist the child in all areas of development. Its importance can be found in how he [the child] perceives himself, his body, his abilities and his relationships with others" (p. 133). Educators and parents need to determine how to utilize the movement activities of children to encourage the formation of stable, positive self-concepts.

For several years the senior author of this book conducted a developmental physical education program designed to make positive contributions to the self-concepts of children from ages 4 to 12 years. The "Challengers" program catered to children who were experiencing difficulty in everyday play. A large percentage of the children were referred to the four-day-a-week program because of problems in school adjustment, peer relations, self-confidence, and emotional immaturity. The others did not possess any apparent difficulties in these areas. Informal research with the children consistently demonstrated self-concept increases as measured by standardized indicators of self-esteem in a significant majority of the children. Throughout the operation of the Challengers program, common sense principles regarding self-concept enhancement through movement were employed. The following paragraphs are a delineation of these principles.

Concept 14.8   Success-oriented movement experiences play an important role in self-concept enhancement.

Success

The most important thing that we can do is to help children develop proper perspectives on success and failure in their daily lives. Because of the egocentric nature of children, it is very difficult for them to accept both success and failure. Success is that feeling of "I can," "I did it," or "Look at me" that we love to see in children. It is the sense of accomplishment that accompanies mastering a new skill, executing a good move, or making a basket. Failure is that feeling of "I can't," "I don't know how," or "I am always wrong." It is the feeling of frustration and hopelessness that often follows failure to master a skill or execution of a poor move.

We need to help children develop a balance between success and failure. We need to bolster self-worth so that when they fail to achieve something, they will not be completely defeated. A backlog of successful experiences will help develop that "I can" attitude. Success is very important, particularly at the initial stages of learning. We need only look at ourselves and our tendencies to continue activities at which we are successful. This basic principle of learning theory is applicable to both children and adults. We need to take the importance of success into consideration when working with young children, by using teaching methods that emphasize success.

The use of problem solving or guided discovery in teaching new movement skills enables all children to experiment and explore their movement potentials. Children become involved in the process of learning instead of being solely concerned with the product. This child-centered, success-oriented approach allows for a variety of solutions or "correct" answers. The teacher and the children are more concerned about individual solutions to a problem than finding the one best way.

The astute teacher of young children recognizes that there is no best way of performing at this level of development. The wise teacher instead focuses on helping children learn more about their bodies and how they move and fostering more mature patterns of movement. For example, the teacher may structure a challenge such as, "How can you balance on three body parts?" or "Who can balance on three body parts?" The number of possible solutions is great and so is the range of difficulty. All children gain increased knowledge of how to move and balance their bodies. The teacher, through questioning or movement challenges, also avoids imposing predetermined models of what performances should be and how they should look.

Individualizing instruction is another way of emphasizing success for each child. Individualized instruction takes into account the uniqueness of each learner and provides every child with opportunities to achieve at his or her particular level of ability. Although it is often difficult because of large classes and limited staff, time, and facilities, teachers should try to individualize whenever possible. The typical nursery school program does a tremendous job of individualizing instruction by employing an open classroom approach with a variety of interest centers. Too often, however, children entering elementary school are faced with the rigid structure of traditional classroom and gymnasium programs that assume that all children are at the same level in their interests, abilities, and motivation for learning. Not all children are "typical" first-graders. Within any given class, children exhibit a wide range of cognitive, affective, and motor abilities. Greater attention to individual needs, interests, and abilities will do much to strengthen the success potential of each child.

Traditional methods of teaching movement are valuable, especially at higher skill levels, but teachers often dominate and require all students to perform at certain levels or emulate particular models. Some children may have considerable difficulty achieving desired standards of performance. Teacher-dominated methods rarely provide success-oriented experiences for everyone. Although these methods should be included in the movement activity program, they should not be stressed too early in the learning process. Teachers of young children should allow for individual differences in readiness rates and abilities to learn new movement skills.

Movement programs that make use of problem-solving approaches and individualized instruction whenever possible make positive contributions to self-concept development. But what actually is involved in using these success-oriented approaches?

Developmentally appropriate movement experiences that are challenging and properly sequenced are very beneficial for children. As educators and parents, we help children form good self-images by encouraging them to establish reasonable expectations of themselves and by clearly outlining our own intentions (Figure 14.3).

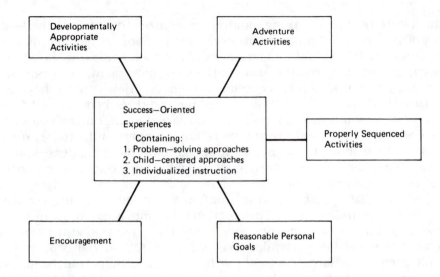

Figure 14.3
Five important factors to consider when utilizing success-oriented experiences to enhance self-concept development

Developmentally Appropriate Activities

Children are not miniature adults ready to be programmed for the whims and wishes of adults. They are growing and developing beings with needs, interests, and capabilities that are quite different from those of adults. Too often, we fall into the trap of trying to create miniature athletes out of 6- and 7-year-olds without first developing the children's fundamental movement abilities. Too often, we force children to specialize in the development of their movement abilities at early ages. They become involved in competitive athletics before they are ready to handle the physical and emotional demands. Competition is not evil or something to be removed from the lives of children, but it must be kept within the proper perspective. Parents and coaches should not be preoccupied with winning games. Instead, they should focus on the balanced, wholesome, and healthful development of children under wise guidance. The needs, interests, and capabilities of each child must be carefully considered.

Concept 14.9   Movement activities that are both developmentally appropriate and properly sequenced can contribute to self-concept enhancement.

Sequencing of Tasks

A third factor involved in using a success-oriented approach to enhancing self-concepts is understanding the sequencing and difficulty of a movement task. The proper sequencing of movement activities is crucial in determining a child's sense of success or failure. For example, a child should learn to do a handstand by first mastering, in order, a tripod, a frogstand, and a headstand. Too often, parents and teachers neglect to develop fundamental movement abilities before proceeding to higher level skills. Instead of looking at the development of movement skills from the point of view of the child, we look at movement from the perspective of a mature athlete. It is much better to begin at a lower level where a child's chances for experiencing success are greater, and then proceed to develop skill upon skill in a logical sequential progression. Success at the initial stages of learning will not only encourage continued performance, but will promote continued mastery attempts, and generate success at later stages. Children who attempt difficult tasks without the proper basic skills may not succeed and may give up entirely. It is important that we analyze movement activities in which children engage and determine logical sequences for accomplishing them.

Competition should not be introduced too early in the learning process. Because competition determines winners and losers, it may be prematurely discouraging or overly encouraging. It is also a distraction from sound skill development. Postpone competitive situations until each child can make a sound appraisal of his or her ability and equate success with effort and skill rather than with winning or losing.

Reasonable Expectations

A fourth area in which we can influence a child's developing self is in helping him establish reasonable expectations of his abilities. Young children see the world in extremes: black or white, good or bad, right or wrong. It is important to help children develop attitudes about success based on personal goals rather than absolute scores. Children need to establish reasonable expectations for themselves. We help by offering goals that are challenging but commensurate with their skill levels and interests. For example, lowering the basket or reducing the size of the basketball will provide children with more opportunities for success than insisting on the use of a regulation ball and putting the standard at the regulation 10-foot height. When success is achieved, new goals need to be established to keep the activity challenging.

Adventure Activities

We can also have an impact on the self-concepts of children in the area of adventure challenge activities. Children need to experience the thrill of climbing, hanging, balancing, riding, and crawling through objects. They need the feeling of mastery that comes from succeeding at activities that require courage and imagination.

The teacher, by using voice inflection and stimulating the young child's imagination, can create an atmosphere of challenge and adventure. Imaginary obstacles may be put in the path of an activity. The balance beam can be transformed into a "narrow log" across a "shark-infested pond." Through adventure activities, both real and imagined, children learn more about their own bodies and overcome challenges.

Encouragement

We influence a child's developing self-concept through communication of our expectations and support. We must describe how we feel about the child's accomplishments and potential. Praise and positive encouragement must be used judiciously because children will regard them as meaningless if overdone. We can communicate our feelings to children by praise for a job well done, with a pat on the back, or a smile. We need to convey messages that "you are loved" and "you are worthwhile." Remember that it is often not so much what we say to children that influences their feelings about themselves as how we treat them. Children tend to value themselves to the degree that they are valued. The way we feel about children actually builds in (or builds out) self-confidence and a sense of self-worth. Children build their pictures of themselves from the words, attitudes, body language, and judgments of those around them.

Concept 14.10   Encouragement, not unbridled praise, is an important facilitator of self-esteem enhancement as well as increased competence.

By providing children with a nurturing climate of acceptance and experiences of success, negative attitudes can be changed to high self-esteem. When we make a specific statement regarding inappropriate behavior, we should restrict our comments to the behavior instead of making generalized criticisms of the child as a person. For example, it is much better to say "I am worried about your difficulties with sharing" rather than "nobody likes a stingy person." Similarly, it is dangerous to label children as "stupid," "bad," or "a motor moron." They often believe the labels that are attached to them and inadvertently act out their expected roles. We should not link undesirable behavior with a personal lack of worth. We should not make children feel that they are personally worthless because their academic achievements or sports performances do not meet our expectations.

There is no place for devastating remarks in teacher–child communication. The teacher's role is not to injure but to prevent injury and to heal. Encouragement in the development of one's movement skills and level of physical fitness plays an important role in helping children develop stable, positive self-concepts.

Assessing Self-Concept in Children

Problems in accurately assessing self-concept have plagued psychologists for years. The validity of a vast majority of measures of self is questionable, and the reliability of the information is often subject to criticism (Wylie, 1979). In spite of these obvious limitations, a number of self-report measures have become available in recent years. The basic assumption underlying any self-report measure is that the respondent is the only individual qualified to reveal his or her feelings and that these responses provide an accurate and truthful indication of how that person feels.

Concept 14.11 A child's self-concept is difficult to measure or assess with scientific accuracy.

The problems that surround self-concept assessment in children are many. Zaichkowsky et al. (1980) have indicated that "attitudes toward the self do not become generalized until about 8 years of age. Up until that time they are more a function of the immediate situation" (p. 157). This, combined with the additional problems of reading level, comprehension, and the testing environment, makes it questionable whether the assessment of self-concept prior to age 8 or 9 can be of practical, let alone research, value. Nevertheless, a variety of self-concept measures suitable for use with children have been devised. A list of selected self-concept measures may be found at the end of this chapter. The Self-Perception Profile for Children devised by Harter (1985) and The Pictorial Scale of Perceived Competence and Social Acceptance for Young Children by Harter and Pike (1984) hold particular promise.

Summary

Self-concept is an important aspect of the affective development of children. The concepts that children have of themselves are based on their self-perceptions and their perceptions of what others think of them. Their self-concepts are in the developmental stages and are profoundly influenced by their daily life experiences. Adults must encourage the development of positive and stable self-concepts in children, because once they are firmly established, they are difficult to change. Combs and Snygg (1959) alluded to the stability of self-concept beyond its developmental stages:

> Once established in a given personality, the perceived self has a high degree of stability. The phenomenal self with the self-concept as its core represents our fundamental frame of reference, our anchor to reality; and even an unsatisfactory self-organization is likely to prove highly stable and resistant to change. This stability has been repeatedly demonstrated in modern research (p. 130).

Because of the importance of vigorous play in the lives of children and the high value placed on physical ability by children and adults, movement serves as an important facilitator of a positive self-concept. Sound principles of growth and development must be adopted and followed to provide children with success-oriented experiences that minimize the failure potential.

We must employ developmentally appropriate movement experiences that are within the ability level of the individual. We must be sure that new movement tasks are learned in the proper sequence, based on sound teaching progressions. We must also help children establish reasonable goals for performance within the limits of their abilities. We must be sure also to provide encouragement and to incorporate adventure activities into their lives. Although movement is only one avenue by which a positive self-concept may be fostered, we must recognize that it is important for most children.

Terms to Remember

Self-concept
Self-esteem
Self-confidence
Self-efficacy
Competence
Perceived competence
Movement competence
Movement confidence

Critical Readings

Duda, J. (1986). Towards a developmental theory of children's motivation in sport. *Journal of Sport and Exercise Psychology, 9,* 130–145.

Feltz, D. L., & Petlichkoff, (1983). Perceived competence among interscholastic sport participants and dropouts. *Canadian Journal of Applied Sport Science, 8,* 231–235.

Fox, K. (1988). The child's perspective in PE. Part I. The psychological dimensions in PE. *British Journal of Physical Education,* 19, 34–38.

Fox, K., Corbin, C. B., & Couldry, W. H. (1985). Female physical estimation and attraction to physical activity. *Journal of Sport Psychology,* 7, 125–136.

Granleese, J., Trew, K., & Turner, I. (1988). Sex differences in perceived competence. *British Journal of Sport Psychology,* 27, 181–184.

Harter, S. (1983). Developmental perspectives on the self system. In P.H. Mussen (Ed.), *Handbook of Child Psychology,* New York: Wiley, p. 274–385.

Knoppers, A. (1992). Personal and social skills. In V. Seefeldt & E. W. Brown (Eds.), *Program for Athletic Coaches Education,* Dubuque, IA: Brown & Benchmark.

Marsh, H. W. (1985). Age and sex effects in multiple dimensions of preadolescent self-concept: A replication and extension. *Australian Journal of Psychology,* 37, 197–204.

Marsh, H. W. et al. (1991). Self-concepts of young children 5 to 8 years of age: Measurement and multidimensional structure. *Journal of Educational Psychology,* 83, 3, 377–392.

Roberts, G. C., Kleiber, D. A., & Duda, J. L. (1981). An analysis of motivation in children's sport: The role of perceived competence in motivation. *Journal of Sport Psychology,* 3, 206–216.

Weiss, M. R. (1987). Self-esteem and achievement in children's sport and physical activity. In D. Gould & M. R. Weiss (Eds.), *Advances in Pediatric Sport Science: Volume II, Behavior Issues,* Champaign, IL: Human Kinetics.

Werner, E. E. (1989). Children of the garden island. *Scientific American,* April, 106–111.

Werner, E. E. (1989). High-risk children in young adulthood: A longitudinal study from birth to 32 years. *American Journal of Orthopsychiatry,* 59, 1, 72–81.

White, R. (1959). Motivation reconsidered. The concept of competence. *Psychological Review,* 66, 297–323.

van Wersch, A., Trew, K., & Turner, I. (1990). Pupils' perceived physical competence and its implications for the new PE curriculum. *Research Supplement of the Physical Education Association of Great Britain and Northern Ireland,* 7, 1–5.

Selected Measures of Self-Concept in Children

Braken, B. A. (1992). Multidimensional Self Concept Scale. Pro-Ed, Austin: TX.

Brown, L., & Alexander, J. (1991). Self-Esteem Index. Pro-Ed, Austin: TX.

Connell, J. P. (1985). A new multidimensional measure of children's perceptions of control. *Child Development,* 56, 1018–1041.

Harter, S. (1982). The perceived competence scale for children. *Child Development,* 53, 87–97.

Harter, S. (1985). *Manual for the Self-Perception Profile for Children* (Revision of the Perceived Competence Scale for Children). Denver: University of Denver.

Harter, S., & Pate, R. (1984). The pictorial scale of perceived competence for young children. *Child Development,* 55, 1969–1982.

Martinek, T., & Zaichkowsky, L. D. (1977). *Manual for the Martinek-Zaichkowsky Self-Concept Scale for Children.* Jacksonville, IL: Psychologists and Educators, Inc.

Piers, E. V. (1969). *Manual for the Piers-Harris Children's Self-Concept Scale,* Nashville, TN: Counselor Recordings and Tests.

ADOLESCENCE

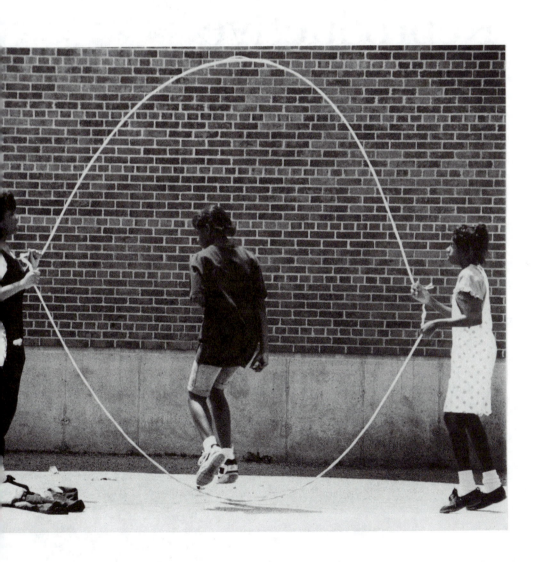

Chapter **15**

Adolescent Growth, Puberty, and Reproductive Maturity

CHAPTER COMPETENCIES

Upon completion of this chapter you should be able to:

- *Describe and interpret the normal curve and displacement and velocity graphs of human growth*
- *Describe variations in biological maturity within and across genders*
- *Discuss characteristics of the adolescent growth spurt*
- *Analyze factors associated with the onset of puberty*
- *Describe hormonal factors that affect puberty*
- *Chart the sequence of events leading to reproductive maturation*
- *Discuss the concept of adolescent reproductive sterility*
- *List and describe how the stages of pubic hair growth are used as a maturity assessment technique*

The period of time that makes up what we know as "adolescence" is affected by both biology and by culture. It is affected by biology in that the end of childhood and the onset of adolescence are marked by the beginnings of sexual maturation. It is affected by culture in that the end of adolescence and the beginning of adulthood are marked by financial and emotional independence from one's family. As a result, the adolescent years have been reshuffled over time. In North American society today the period of adolescence is significantly longer than it was 100 or even 50 years ago. The earlier onset of *puberty* (the start of sexual maturation) coupled with a longer period of dependence on family has caused us to view adolescence in a much broader perspective.

Secular trends in biological maturation over the past 100 years have dramatically lowered the average age of puberty. However, economic and socio-cultural trends over that same period have dramatically extended the average age of adolescence beyond the "teen" years. Whereas adolescence used to span the years from 13 to 18, it now begins as early as age 10 and does not end until about age 20 or beyond.

Concept 15.1   The period of adolescence has lengthened due to the combined effects of biology and culture.

During adolescence tremendous changes are occurring. The adolescent growth spurt, the onset of puberty, and sexual maturation are the primary biological markers of adolescence. Each of these will be discussed in the sections that follow.

Adolescent Growth

The onset of adolescence is marked by a period of accelerated increases in both height and weight. The age of onset, duration, and intensity of this growth spurt is genetically based and will vary considerably from individual to individual. One's *genotype* (growth potential) establishes the boundaries for individual growth. However, an individual's *phenotype* (environmental conditions) will have a marked influence on the achievement of this growth potential.

Concept 15.2 The onset, duration, and intensity of the growth spurt are controlled by one's genotype, while growth potential is influenced by one's phenotype.

An adolescent's genotype will play the determining role in linear body measures, skeletal maturation, sexual maturation, and body type. Final adult standing height, trunk, arm, and leg length are ultimately determined by genetic factors. Similarly, bone ossification, the onset of puberty, and the manner in which fat is distributed around the body are all products of genotype. Each of these may be modified to a certain extent but an individual cannot go beyond his or her inherited potential. On the other hand, the environment will influence how close one comes to his or her genetic potential. Such things as body weight, skinfolds, and circumferences are all subject to significant modification.

Concept 15.3 Secular trends in biological maturation have lowered the average age of puberty in North America.

Height

Because of the interaction of genotype with the environment there is considerable variability in the growth process among individuals during the adolescent period. There is, however, a definite period of accelerated growth at the end of childhood known by a variety of terms including "adolescent growth spurt," "period of preadolescent acceleration," and "circumpubertal period." This period of "growing like a weed" begins prior to sexual maturation; therefore, for our purposes, we will refer to it as the "adolescent growth spurt."

Concept 15.4 The adolescent growth spurt marks the first visual indicator of the onset of puberty.

The *adolescent growth spurt* is a time period that lasts about 4 1/2 years. Males, on the average, begin their growth spurts around age 11, reach their *peak height velocity* by age 13, and taper off by age 15. Peak height velocity refers to the maximum annual rate of growth in height during the adolescent growth spurt. Females are about two years advanced, beginning their spurts around age 9, peaking in velocity at age 11, and tapering off by age 13 (Malina & Bouchard, 1991). It is not uncommon to show a one-year incremental gain in height during the period of peak velocity of 6 to 8 inches or more. Further growth continues at the end of the adolescent growth spurt but at a much slower rate. Males appear to reach their mature adult heights at around age 18. Females are reported to attain their maximum heights at around age 16 (Malina & Bouchard, 1991). These ages, however, are only approximate indicators of when maximum heights are attained. There is considerable variation among individuals in the attainment of maximum statures, and most growth studies cease when the subjects leave high school, preventing follow-up beyond the school years. Growth in stature frequently continues at a modest rate for both males and females several years beyond high school.

Concept 15.5   The adolescent growth spurt lasts about four years, beginning in females about two years earlier than in males.

It should be noted that the adolescent growth spurt is highly variable from individual to individual. Some will have completed the process before others have begun. The results are clearly evident in the typical youth sport setting where "midgets" and "giants" are frequently grouped together with little or no accommodation for maturation variations. Remember, development is age-influenced but it is not age-dependent. Overreliance on chronological age as a guide for youth sport team selection is unwise and inconsistent with what we know about motor development and quality education. We must, therefore, use standards other than age for team selection.

Figure 15.1 provides a longitudinal view of the growth patterns of two individuals (the Gallahue children, David Lee and Jennifer). From childhood through adolescence annual height, weight, and girth measurements were taken. Although a longitudinal view of just two individuals does not provide a complete picture of the growth process, Figure 15.1 does provide us with a typical height velocity curve of two individuals. Notice how at age 9, Jennifer, an average maturer, was actually taller than her brother was at that age, but how by age 10 David Lee was a full 4 inches taller than his sister at that age. Notice also that between age 9 and 11, David Lee (an early maturer) grew a full 12 inches in height, whereas his sister grew only by about 3 inches during the same period. Jennifer's adolescent growth spurt was at its greatest velocity between 11 and 12 years of age when she grew 3 inches before slowing down at menarche and plateauing by age 16. Similarly David Lee's velocity curve slowed down although he continued to make small annual incremental height gains to age 19.

Events within the adolescent growth spurt are interdependent. For males the period of most rapid growth coincides with the appearance of secondary sex characteristics such as axillary and pubic hair. For females the peak velocity in growth tends to occur prior to menarche. Females with an early growth spurt tend to reach menarche earlier than those with a later growth spurt (Tanner, 1989).

Figure 15.1
Longitudinal velocity curves for height for a single male and a single female from childhood through adolescence (* = date of menarche for Jennifer, onset of axillary hair development for David Lee)

LONGITUDINAL VELOCITY CURVES FOR HEIGHT MALE AND FEMALE

DAVID LEE

JENNIFER

INCHES

AGE

Concept 15.6 Adult height can be predicted from adolescent growth data with reasonable accuracy.

The attainment of maximal adult height is of interest to most adolescents. Males are frequently concerned about being too short and females often fret about being too tall. A number of prediction formulas are available, and mature adult height is correlated with height prior to the preadolescent growth spurt. Therefore, if a child was in the 50th percentile prior to puberty he or she is likely to continue to be at the same percentile after puberty. Krogman (1980) recommends the following formulas for predicting approximate adult height.

Males: 2 × height at age 2 = adult height
Females: 2 × height at 1 1/2 years = adult height

Attainment of adult height is dominated by one's genotype, and under normal circumstances, only minimally influenced by the environment. (On the other hand, one's attained adult weight is strongly influenced by environmental factors.) Early maturers tend to be shorter as adults than predicted from their childhood statures, and late maturers tend to be taller (Krogman, 1980). Table 15.1 provides a percentile equivalent chart for height in inches for males and females 12 to 17 years of age. This chart may be used to predict adult height and to determine an individual's percentile equivalent in comparison with other youth from the United States. For example, a male at the 25th percentile at age 12 (57.8 inches) will probably remain within that percentile and can expect to attain a height of about 67 inches by age 17. This would make him about 2 inches shorter than the average 17-year-old North American male (69.1 inches) and about 3 inches taller than the average North American female (64.1 inches). Conger and Peterson (1984) indicated that once an early maturer and a late-maturing age-mate passed the period of accelerated adolescent growth that "their comparative standings in height are most likely to return to those of preadolescence" (p. 94). The genetic influence on stature is strong and unless significant long-term changes are made in diet and lifestyle during the growing years there will be little variability from the predicted growth channel (Tanner, 1975). Figure 15.2 depicts mean height scores for males and females using data from the 1993 AAU Physical Fitness Test. These mean scores have remained essentially identical for the entire 13-year history in which these data have been collected, thereby indicating no secular changes from 1980 through 1993.

Table 15.1. Height in Inches of Youths Aged 12–17 Years by Gender and Age at Last Birthday[1]

		Percentile						
Gender and Age	Mean	5th	10th	25th	50th	75th	90th	95th
Males								
12 years	60.0	54.6	55.7	57.8	60.0	61.9	64.0	65.2
13 years	62.9	57.2	58.3	60.4	62.8	65.4	68.0	68.7
14 years	65.6	59.9	60.9	63.2	66.1	68.1	69.8	70.7
15 years	67.5	62.4	63.7	65.7	67.8	69.3	71.0	72.1
16 years	68.6	64.1	65.2	67.0	68.7	70.4	72.1	73.1
17 years	69.1	64.1	65.7	67.2	69.2	70.9	72.6	73.7
Females								
12 years	61.1	55.8	57.4	59.5	61.2	63.0	64.6	65.9
13 years	62.5	57.8	58.9	60.7	62.6	64.4	66.0	66.9
14 years	63.5	59.6	60.5	61.9	63.5	65.2	66.7	67.4
15 years	63.9	59.6	60.3	62.0	63.9	65.8	67.2	68.1
16 years	64.0	59.7	60.7	62.4	64.2	65.6	67.2	68.1
17 years	64.1	60.0	60.9	62.3	64.3	65.9	67.4	68.1

[1]Source: U.S. Public Health Service. Vital and Health Statistics, Series 11, No. 124, Height and Weight of Youths, 12–17. United States: January 1973.

A new and somewhat frightening potential for both growth retardation and enhancement has surfaced in the last few years. Steroid use by adolescents during the growing years has been found to have permanent effects on stature (Taylor, 1987). Steroid use by prepubertal children may cause the epiphyses of the long bones to fuse prematurely (American College of Sports Medicine Position Statement on the Use and Abuse of Anabolic-Androgenic Steroids in Sports, 1987). Certain steroid products, however, have been safely prescribed by physicians for years to stimulate growth in males with uncomplicated short statures. Taylor (1987) reported that:

> Clear evidence that heavy steroid use can reduce the ultimate height of adolescents is lacking. It is safe to say only that self-prescribed use of supra therapeutic doses of steroids by adolescents can have powerful effects on maturation processes and that these effects may lead to either increased or decreased adult stature (p. 147).

Concept 15.7 Steroid use for therapeutic and growth-enhancing purposes can affect the growth potential of the adolescent in as yet unexplained ways.

CROSS-SECTIONAL VELOCITY CURVES FOR HEIGHT
CHILDHOOD-ADOLESCENCE

Figure 15.2
Height mean
scores for males
and females 6–17,
1993 (data cour-
tesy of AAU Phys-
ical Fitness
Program [1994], In-
diana University,
Bloomington, IN)

MALES

FEMALES

HEIGHT IN INCHES

AGE

Growth retardation is frequently seen in asthmatic children due to heavy usage of corticosteroid drugs to expand the bronchial passages. Further research is necessary to determine the long-term effects of steroid use on adolescent stature. The dosage, duration, and types of steroids used must be investigated before conclusions can be drawn.

Weight

Weight changes during adolescence are great. For both males and females, increases in weight tend to follow the same general curves as for increases in height. Peak weight velocity, the period during the adolescent growth spurt when weight gain is the greatest, is generally greater in boys than in girls. Also, it appears that peak weight velocity occurs closer to peak height velocity in boys than in girls (Malina & Bouchard, 1991). Weight gain in adolescent males is primarily due to increases in height and muscle mass. Fat mass tends to remain relatively stable at this time. In females, however, adolescent weight gain is due largely to increases in fat mass and height, and to a lesser degree to increases in muscle mass. Skeletal maturation, increases in both muscle and fat tissue, and organ growth all contribute to the weight gains of adolescence for both males and females.

Concept 15.8   Weight gains during adolescence roughly approximate the curves for height, but weight is much more affected by environmental factors.

Overreliance on adolescent weight curves is unwise because weight reflects a combination of developmental events and as a result is limited in its information value. For example, failure to gain weight or actual loss of weight may be a reflection of an adolescent's increased attention to diet and exercise and not a cause for alarm. Failure to make incremental gains in height, however, would be a cause for concern. Weight gain throughout adolescence will be affected by diet, exercise, gastric motility, and general lifestyle factors as well as by hereditary factors. We know that youth in the United States have greater percentages of body fat than their counterparts of 20 years ago (NCYFS, 1985, 1987). This average higher body fat percentage has been attributed to the sedentary lifestyle and unhealthy eating patterns of many members of our society.

By the age of 10, males have attained approximately 55 percent of their final adult weights, and females have attained 59 percent (Heald & Hung, 1970). Prior to age 10 the average weights of both males and females are almost identical with males being only slightly heavier. However, during the adolescent growth spurts females are frequently heavier than their male age-mates. Females tend to weigh more than males until about age 14 whereupon their weight gains begin to level off. Males, however, continue to make significant gains in weight until about age 22. Figures 15.3a & b depict a definite secular trend in weight from childhood through adolescence for both males and females.

Figure 15.3A
Secular trend in weight mean scores for males 6–17, 1980 and 1993 (data courtesy of: AAU Physical Fitness Program [1994] Indiana University, Bloomington, IN)

You should disregard height/weight tables published prior to 1960. Secular trends in both height and weight have been repeatedly documented and reported in the literature (Krogman, 1980; NCYFS, 1985, 1987). The reasons for this include changes in the health and nutritional status of youth, socio-economic factors, genetic factors, and changes in activity patterns. Whatever the case, weight is of considerable importance to the adolescent. The constant bombardment from the media and our obsession with the "perfect body" has raised the weight consciousness of the typical adolescent to the point of obsession. Care must be taken to help the adolescent understand the changing nature of his or her body and not to overstep the fine line between a healthy regard for weight control and an obsessive preoccupation with weight gain.

Figure 15.3B
Secular trend in
weight mean
scores for females
6–17, 1980 and
1993, (data cour-
tesy of: AAU Phys-
ical Fitness
Program [1994] In-
diana University,
Bloomington, IN)

Heart and Lungs

The remarkable changes in height and weight are easily observed during
adolescence, but what about other less apparent but equally important
changes? Growth of the heart and lungs is dramatic and is a primary
factor in the increased functional capacity of the adolescent.

The heart increases by about one-half in size and almost doubles in
weight during adolescence (Malina & Bouchard, 1991). Females have
slightly smaller hearts than males during childhood, begin accelerated
growth of the heart earlier, and attain significantly smaller total growth
by the end of adolescence. Although heart rate is related to overall body
size we see a gradual lowering of heart rate throughout the entire growth
process. By age 10 male resting heart rates are on the average 3 to 5
beats per minute slower than those for females. By late adolescence
males have an average resting heart rate of 57 to 60 beats per minute,

compared to females at 62 to 63 beats per minute (Malina & Bouchard, 1991). Systolic blood pressure rises steadily throughout childhood, and accelerates rapidly during puberty before settling down to its adult value by the later period of adolescence (Katchadourian, 1977).

Growth of the lungs parallels heart growth during adolescence. Both the size of the lungs and their respiratory capacity increase rapidly during puberty after a period of gradual growth during childhood. Respiration rates decrease throughout childhood and puberty for both males and females. However, *vital capacity* (the amount of air that can be inhaled with a single breath) increases much more rapidly in boys from about age 12 onward even though males and females are almost identical in this measure prior to puberty (Katchadourian, 1977). Dramatic gender differences may be attributed to the larger heart size and traditionally more aerobically active lifestyles of males.

Physical differences between males and females are just that—differences, and nothing else. For one to ascribe "superiority" or "inferiority" to one gender over the other on the basis of biological differences is absurd. On the other hand, those who deny the relevance of basic physical gender differences apart from reproductive functions are naive. Fundamental genetic differences between males and females are irrevocably established at conception and heightened during the adolescent period. Significant differences in height, weight, body proportions, and functional capacity of the heart and lungs can be expressed only in terms of population averages, and there is considerable overlap between the sexes. The only way in which males and females are truly unique is in reproductive functions. To understand this uniqueness we must understand the process of puberty and sexual maturation.

Puberty

The onset of puberty is generally termed *pubescence*. Pubescence is the earliest period of adolescence, generally about 2 years in advance of sexual maturity. During pubescence secondary sex characteristics begin to appear, sex organs mature, changes in the endocrine system begin to occur, and the adolescent growth spurt begins.

Concept 15.9   Menarche is the primary event of female puberty, but it does not mark reproductive maturity, which may be delayed by as much as two years.

The highlight of puberty in females is marked by a clearly distinguishable event, menarche. *Menarche,* or the first menstrual flow, generally occurs between 12.5 and 13.5 years of age in the average North

American female (Wieczorek & Natapoff, 1981). The development of mature ova follows menarche by as much as 2 years; therefore, puberty is not complete in females until sexual maturity has been attained.

The highlight of puberty in males is less distinct than it is for females. In a clinical sense, it is marked by the first *ejaculation* (the sudden discharge or ejection of semen) but as with menarche this milestone does not truly mark reproductive maturity. Only when live sperm are produced is reproductive maturity attained. Live sperm generally appear in boys between 13 and 16 years of age (Wieczorek and Natapoff, 1981).

Onset of Puberty

During the period of infancy and childhood both boys and girls develop at highly similar rates. There are few differences in height, weight, heart and lung size, and body composition is essentially the same. By age 10 children have attained about 80 percent of their adult height and a little over half of their adult weight. But as children begin their second decade, there are dramatic changes not only in measures of growth but in sexual maturation as well. The onset of puberty marks the transition from childhood to sexual adulthood. Exactly when this process begins and what starts the process is not clearly understood. We do know, however, that the timing of the process is highly variable and may begin as early as age 8 in females and age 9 in males, or as late as ages 13 and 15, respectively (Katchadourian, 1977). The general sequence of events that mark puberty is much more predictable than specific dates on which they will occur.

Sequentially, for the male adolescent, growth spurt is preceded by testicular growth and coincides with enlargement of the penis. This is generally followed by the first appearance of pubic hair. *Axillary hair* (hair under the arms) formation soon follows, along with a deepening of the voice. Mature sperm formation and sexual maturation occur shortly after, followed by the appearance of facial hair and increased body hair.

The sequence of puberty for females is also predictable. There is a close correlation between the female growth spurt and breast development (Katchadourian, 1977). Budding of the nipples occurs prior to budding of the breasts. Breast bud development coincides with the beginning of pubic hair formation, followed by growth of the genitalia. Axillary hair formation and menarche soon occur followed by the development of mature ova and the capacity for becoming pregnant. A tendency toward acne and slight deepening of the voice are the final events of female sexual maturation. Table 15.2 provides a visual representation of the sequence of events marking puberty and an approximate timetable. Many of the events of puberty overlap and should not be expected to occur in specific time frames.

Table 15.2. Sequence of Events Marking Puberty

Males	Females	Approximate Age of Onset
First Testicular Growth	Beginning of Growth Spurt	9–10
	Budding of Nipples	10–11
Beginning of Growth Spurt	Budding of Breasts	11–12
Start of Pubic Hair Growth	Start of Pubic Hair Growth	
	Growth of Genitalia	
	Peak of Growth Spurt	12–13
	Axillary Hair Formation	
	Menarche	
Penile and Testicular Peak of Growth Spurt		13–14
Axillary Hair Formation	Mature Ova Production	14–15
Deepened Voice	(End of Puberty)	
Mature Sperm Production	Acne	15–16
(End of Puberty)	Deeper Voice	
	Mature Pubic Hair & Breast Development	
Facial Hair	Cessation of Skeletal Growth	16–17
Body Hair		
Mature Pubic Hair Development		
Cessation of Skeletal Growth		18–19

Hormonal Influences

The onset of puberty may be influenced by a variety of factors, but genetics plays a dominant role. For example, Chinese females tend to achieve menarche earlier than females of European origin (Conger & Peterson, 1984), and the events of puberty are much more closely related between identical twins than among non-identical twins and non-related age-mates (Tanner, 1989). Factors within the environment may also have a dramatic impact on puberty. Although incompletely understood, stress, nutritional status, general health, and metabolism all appear to affect the onset and duration of puberty in some as yet unexplained manner.

Concept 15.10   The onset of puberty is regulated by heredity and may be influenced by nutrition, illness, climate, and emotional stress.

The endocrine system plays a critical role in the growth and maturation process. Malina (1986) reports that, "endocrine secretions are themselves strongly influenced by genetic mechanisms. . . . The nervous system, in turn, is intimately involved in regulating endocrine secretions" (p. 24). There appears to be a complex interaction among the endocrine system, the nervous system, and the gonads leading to puberty. The hormones from the endocrine system are responsible for "translating the instructions of the genes into the reality of the adult form" (Tanner, 1962, p. 112).

The pituitary gland, located below the brain, appears to be of critical importance. When the *hypothalamus* (a central regulating nerve center in the brain) matures, it secretes hormones that in turn stimulate the anterior pituitary gland to begin releasing *gonadotropin (GnRH) hormones*. The hormones released by the anterior pituitary gland have a stimulating effect on other endocrine glands, resulting in the release of other growth and sex hormones. The release of sex-related hormones initiates maturation of the gonads. *Estrogens* (female hormones) account for initiation of the events of female puberty. Malina (1986) quotes Wierman and Crowley (1986) as stating that:

> at this time, however, no definite statement can be made as to the precise trigger (or triggers) of sexual maturation. Although the final common pathway of this effect is clearly mediated by modulation of hypothalamic secretion of GnRH, little else is clear (p. 235).

Reproductive Maturity

The onset of the preadolescent growth spurt and puberty marks the transition from childhood to reproductive maturity. The physical changes and appearance of secondary sex characteristics are frequently a cause for heightened interest in one's body and a dramatically increased level of self-consciousness. If young adolescents appear preoccupied with matters of sex it is because a whole host of dramatic and rapid changes are occurring right before their eyes. The young adolescent frequently feels like a spectator in his or her own growth process. Each day seems to bring about changes that are whispered about, giggled over, and closely scrutinized. The wise adult will be sensitive to these physical changes and the impact that they have on the social and emotional development of the individual. The journey from childhood to reproductive maturity follows a predictable pattern for both males and females. The student of motor development will want to be knowledgeable about these events and will learn to recognize physical changes that offer cues to physical maturity. Many of these have been discussed in the previous sections on growth and puberty. This section will, therefore, focus on a brief overview of sexual maturation in females and males, and a reliable technique for maturational assessment.

TABLE 15.3. Stages in Female Breast and Pubic Hair Development

Breast Development	Pubic Hair Development
Stage	
1. Prepubertal—Flat appearance like that of a child	Prepubertal—Absence of pubic hair
2. Small raised breast bud	Sparse amount of downy hair mainly at sides of the labia
3. Enlargement and raising of the breast and areola	Increased amount of hair with pigmentation, coarsening, and curling
4. Areola and nipple form a contour separate from the breast	Adult hair, but limited in area
5. Adult breast—areola is in the same contour as the breast	Adult hair with horizontal upper border

Adapted from photos: Tanner, J. M. (1962). Growth At Adolescence, *Oxford, England: Blackwell Scientific.*

Females

Breast growth marks the first visible sign of the female journey to sexual maturity. *Breast development* begins around age 11 and is completed around age 15, although it may begin as early as age 8 and not end until age 18 (Katchadourian, 1977). Breast development has been described by Tanner (1962) and is outlined in Table 15.3, along with female pubic hair development. These stages can be useful as reliable developmental landmarks of sexual maturity.

Pubic hair is usually the second sign of progress toward sexual maturity. On the average, hair growth begins between 11 and 12 years of age, and the triangular adult pattern of growth is established by about age 14. The stages of pubic hair development developed by Tanner (1962) provide useful indices of sexual development.

Changes in the *female genitalia* are usually the third step in progress toward reproductive maturity. The external sex organs (i.e., the vulva, mons, labia, and clitoris) all increase in size and become sensitive to stimulation. Changes in a female's exterior genitalia are not as useful for clinically assessing maturity as indices of pubic hair growth and breast development.

The internal sex organs of the female also undergo considerable change. The uterus and ovaries increase in weight. The uterus makes dramatic weight gains, becomes larger, and "develops an intricate and powerful musculature" (Katchadourian, 1977, p. 59). The vagina increases in size, and the ovaries, although structurally complete at birth, continue to moderately gain weight throughout adolescence.

The average age of menarche for females in the United States is earlier than any other population studied, and is reported to be about 12.8 years of age (Malina & Bouchard, 1991). It may, however, range from as early as 9 years of age to as late as 18 (Katchadourian, 1977). Menarche occurs after the peak of the growth spurt and about 2 years after the start of breast development, but it does not mark the beginning of reproductive maturity. Generally, up to 1 1/2 years may pass from the first menstrual cycle until the young female is physiologically capable of conception (Conger & Peterson, 1984). This lag is known as the period of *relative sterility of puberty*. It is, however, unwise to assume that this is a "safe" period from conception. Individual differences between menarche and reproductive maturity are great, and no safe period can be guaranteed.

Males

Puberty begins in males with growth of the *testes*. Increased testicular growth begins around 11 1/2 years of age and may range from ages 10 to 14 (Tanner, 1962). Growth continues until somewhere between ages 14 and 18 (Katchadourian, 1977). As the male reproductive gland, the testes produce *sperm* and male sex hormones. The ability of the male to ejaculate seminal fluid is largely a function of the prostate gland which becomes much larger during puberty. Ejaculation is a psychological as well as a physiological event and occurs most frequently in the young male through nocturnal seminal emissions and masturbation beginning at about age 12 to 16 (Katchadourian, 1977). Clearly this increase in sexual behavior is associated with rising levels of testosterone. Mature sperm are not contained in the ejaculate until approximately ages 15 to 17.

Concept 15.11   The ability to ejaculate seminal fluid is a primary event of male puberty, but reproductive maturity requires mature sperm production.

Pubic hair growth begins as early as age 10 or as late as age 15. As with female pubic hair growth, Tanner (1962) developed a five-stage pubic hair scale for males (Table 15.4). Mature, stage 5, pubic hair distribution continues into the mid-20s in males, and the area is less clearly defined than in females.

The external *male genitalia*, the penis and scrotum, change little in appearance throughout childhood. Penis growth begins about a year after the first onset of testicular and pubic hair growth. The scrotum first becomes larger followed by lengthening and then thickening of the penis (Tanner, 1962). See Table 15.4 for the stages of male genital development first described by Tanner (1962). It is important to note that the size and shape of a male's penis is unrelated to physique, race, and virility (Masters & Johnson, 1970).

Table 15.4. Stages in Male Genital and Pubic Hair Development

Genital Development	Pubic Hair Development
Stage	
1. Prepubertal—Size of testes and penis like that in early childhood	Prepubertal—Absence of pubic hair
2. Testes enlarge and scrotal skin darkens and becomes coarse	Sparse amount of downy hair mainly at the base of the penis
3. Continuation of Stage 2, along with increase in penis length	Increased amount of hair with pigmentation, coarsening, and curling
4. General enlargement in penis size and scrotal skin pigmentation	Adult hair, but limited in area
5. Adult genitalia	Adult hair with spread to the thighs and horizontal upper border

Adapted from photos: Tanner, J. M. (1962). Growth At Adolescence, *Oxford, England: Blackwell Scientific.*

Secondary sex characteristics such as axillary hair, facial hair, and deepening of the voice are all associated with progress toward reproductive maturity. Axillary and facial hair usually begin to appear about two years after the growth of pubic hair. Facial hair, an important "badge" of manhood, first appears on the upper lip. It then starts to grow on the upper cheek in an area parallel with the lower ear, and then under the lower lip. In the final stage, facial hair growth spreads to the lower face and chin creating a full beard (Katchadourian, 1977). Axillary hair appears in concert with facial hair, and body hair continues to spread until well after puberty.

Maturity Assessment

A *maturity assessment* is a means of determining how far one has progressed toward physical maturation. A variety of techniques, including circumpubertal, skeletal, and dental assessments, measure the progress of a particular body part or system toward maturity. Unfortunately, these maturity assessments are seldom used in routine preparticipation physical examinations of young athletes. The omission is unfortunate because young athletes could be more fairly equated for competition. Chronological age is the most frequently used measure of maturity. Throughout this text we have continually referred to the individuality and extreme variability of the growth process, particularly during later childhood and early adolescence. Although existing maturity assessments are expensive, time consuming, and inconvenient, developmental standards based on factors other than chronological age should be used to assess and place young athletes. Some process of equating youth for participation and competition should be devised in order to reduce the incidence of athletic injuries.

Concept 15.12   Maturity assessment scales offer reliable and valid devices for equating athletes, limiting training, and reducing injuries.

Caine and Broekhoff (1987) presented a convincing argument for including a standardized maturity assessment in the preparticipation physical examination that every youth should undergo prior to sports participation. They argued that maturity assessments can be used to match adolescents for contact sports, and to determine when youth are experiencing growth spurts, which make them more susceptible to injury. Caine and Broekhoff (1987) argued that the stages of circumpubertal maturation proposed by Tanner (1962) can be easily and effectively used. To accommodate social-cultural mores and avoid embarrassment, parents can be asked to assess the circumpubertal maturity of their children or young athletes can rank their maturity levels with reference to the pubic hair scales. Duke et al. (1980) and Kreipe and Geivanter (1983) both reported moderate to high correlations between self-assessed stages and physician-assessed stages of pubic hair development.

The benefits of maturity assessment are obvious. First, it can aid in injury reduction serving as a basis for matching athletes for contact sports. Second, it can serve as a means of limiting or disqualifying individuals for participation in contact sports. Third, it can be used to identify rapid growth periods and to justify reductions in training regimens in long-term, high-intensity sports such as cross country, swimming, gymnastics, and ballet.

Summary

The period of adolescence has gradually expanded due to biological and cultural factors to the point where it now encompasses the child's second decade. Dramatic growth increments, the onset of puberty, and reproductive maturation are highlights of the adolescent period.

Adolescent growth in height and weight follows a predictable pattern although there is considerable variability in the onset and duration of the preadolescent growth spurt. Wide variations in stature are typical among preadolescents and have many ramifications for athletic participation and social acceptance.

The onset of puberty is generally considered to coincide with the start of the growth spurt. Puberty is influenced by a variety of genetic factors operating in concert with environmental circumstances.

Puberty and reproductive maturity are not the same thing. Reproductive maturity occurs somewhat after the onset of puberty. Menarche in females and ejaculation in males do not indicate the arrival of reproductive maturity. The development of mature ova and the production of sperm are the hallmarks of reproductive maturity.

Maturity assessments can be used as an effective aid for equating young athletes for competition and reducing the risk of injury. Circumpubertal assessment measures although not without difficulties are reliable and valid means of determining maturity levels.

Terms to Remember

Puberty
Genotype
Phenotype
Preadolescent growth spurt
Vital capacity
Pubescence
Menarche
Ejaculation
Axillary hair
Hypothalamus
Gonadotropin (GnRH)

Estrogens
Breast development
Pubic hair
Female genitalia
Relative sterility of puberty
Testes
Sperm
Male genitalia
Secondary sex characteristics
Maturity assessment
Androgens

Critical Readings

Katchadourian, H. (1977). *The Biology of Adolescence*. San Francisco: W. H. Freeman.

Krogman, W. M. (1980). *Child Growth*. Ann Arbor: The University of Michigan Press.

Malina, R. M. (1986). Physical growth and maturation. In V. Seefeldt (Ed.), *Physical Activity and Well-Being*. Reston, VA: AAHPERD.

Malina, R. M., & Bouchard, C. (1991). *Growth Maturation and Physical Activity* (Chapters 16 & 17). Champaign, IL: Human Kinetics.

Prior, J. C. (1990). Reproduction: Exercise-related adaptations and the health of women and men. In C. Bouchard et al. (Eds.). *Exercise Fitness and Health: A Consensus of Current Knowledge* (Chapter 57). Champaign, IL: Human Kinetics.

Chapter **16**

Specialized Movement Abilities

CHAPTER COMPETENCIES

Upon completion of this chapter you should be able to:

- *Demonstrate observation skills of specialized movement abilities*
- *Discuss relationships between motor-skill regression and environmental complexity*
- *Discuss the effects of athletic competition on growth and development of children and adolescents*
- *Demonstrate the relationship between specialized movement abilities and fundamental movement abilities*
- *Describe the developmental sequence of specialized movement skills*
- *Demonstrate an understanding of the concept of fostering improvement through movement control, emotional control, and learning enjoyment*

Key Concept: The development of specialized movement skills is highly dependent upon opportunities for practice, encouragement, and quality instruction.

Specialized movement skills are mature fundamental movement patterns that have been refined and combined to form sport skills and other specific and complex movement skills. Specialized movement skills are task specific, but fundamental movements are not.

Most children have the potential by about age 6 to perform at the mature stage of most fundamental movement patterns and to begin the transition to the specialized movement phase. Neurological makeup, anatomical and physiological characteristics, and visual perceptual abilities are sufficiently developed to function at the mature stage in most fundamental movement skills. There are a few obvious exceptions to this generalization, namely striking a moving object and volleying, because of the sophisticated perceptual-motor requirements of these tasks. However, many adolescents lag in their movement capabilities because of limited opportunities for regular practice, poor or absent instruction, and little or no encouragment. We are all familiar with teens and adults who throw balls at the elementary stage or jump for distance using movement patterns characteristic of a 2- or 3-year-old child. Older children, adolescents, and adults should be able to perform fundamental movements at the mature stage. Failure to develop mature forms of fundamental movements has direct consequences on an individual's ability to perform task-specific skills at the specialized movement phase. Successful progression through the transition, application, and lifelong utilization stages in a particular movement task depends on mature levels of performance at the fundamental movement phase (Figure 16.1). A person could hardly expect to be successful at softball if his fundamental striking, throwing, catching, or running abilities were not at

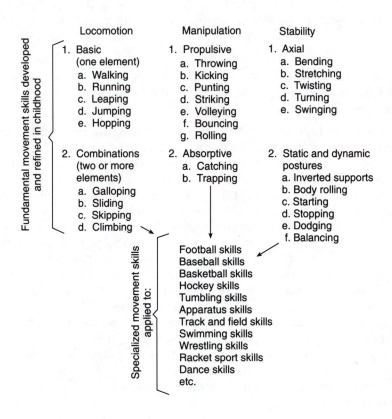

Figure 16.1
Mature fundamental movement skills must be developed before the introduction of sport skills

mature levels. There is a definite *proficiency barrier* (Seefeldt, 1980) between the fundamental movement phase and the specialized movement phase of development. The transition from one phase to another depends on the application of mature patterns of movement to a wide variety of movement skills. If the patterns are less than mature, ability will be impaired.

Concept 16.1   Mature fundamental movement development is prerequisite to successfully incorporating corresponding specialized movement skills into one's movement repertoire.

This chapter focuses on the specialized movement skill phase of development. Two important points should be kept in mind. First, even though a person may be cognitively and affectively ready to advance to this phase, progression depends on successful completion of specific aspects of the previous phase. Second, progress from one phase to another is not an all-or-none proposition. One is not required to be at the mature stage in all fundamental movements before advancing to subsequent stages. While a 12-year-old who specialized early in gymnastics may be performing at highly sophisticated levels in several locomotor and stability movements, she may not be able to throw, catch, or kick a ball with the proficiency expected for her age and developmental level.

Developmental Sequence of Specialized Movements

After the child has achieved the mature stage in a particular fundamental movement pattern, little change occurs in the "form" of that movement ability during the specialized movement phase. Refinement of the pattern and stylistic variations in form occur as greater skill (precision, accuracy, and control) is achieved, but the basic pattern remains unchanged (Wickstrom, 1983). However, dramatic improvements in performance based on increased physical abilities may be seen from year to year. As the adolescent improves in strength, endurance, reaction time, speed of movement, coordination, and so forth, we can expect to see improved performance scores. Chapters 12 and 17 provide detailed discussions and comparisons of the physical abilities and the performance scores of children and adolescents, respectively.

Within the specialized phase, there are three separate but often overlapping stages. The onset of stages during this phase of development depends on neuromuscular, cognitive, and affective factors within the individual. Specific factors within the task and the individual as well as conditions within the environment stimulate movement from one stage to another.

A person's fundamental movement patterns are little changed after they reach the mature stage, and physical capabilities influence only the extent to which specialized movement skills are acted out in sport, recreational, or daily living situations. Therefore, *specialized movement skills* are mature fundamental movements that have been adapted to the specific requirements of a sport, recreational, or daily living activity. The extent to which these abilities are developed depends on a combination of conditions within the task, the individual, and the environment.

A key to successful teaching at the specialized movement skill phase, whether the students are skilled adolescents or unskilled adults, is recognizing conditions that may limit or enhance development. Once these conditions have been identified for each individual, teaching becomes more a matter of reducing the limiting conditions and maximizing the enhancing conditions than simply stressing mechanically "correct" execution of the skill. The three stages within the specialized movement phase are outlined below.

Concept 16.2   Progress through the stages within the specialized movement skill phase depends on the foundation of movement patterns previously established during the fundamental movement phase.

Transition Stage

This stage is characterized by the individual's first attempts to refine and combine mature movement patterns. With children, there is heightened interest in sport and standards of performance. Children generally enjoy pitting their developing movement skills against those of others. During this stage children are attracted to several different types of sports and do not feel limited by physiological, anatomical, or environmental factors. Leaders begin to emphasize accuracy and skill in the performance of games, lead-up activities, and a wide variety of sport-related movements. During this stage the individual works at "getting the idea" of how to perform the sport skill. Skill and proficiency are limited.

Application Stage

During this stage the individual becomes more aware of personal physical assets and limitations and, accordingly, focuses on certain types of sports. Emphasis is on improving proficiency. During this stage practice is the key to developing higher degrees of skill. The movement patterns characteristic of the beginner during the transition stage smooth out. More complex skills are refined and are used in official sports and designated recreational activities for both leisure and competition.

Lifelong Utilization Stage

During this stage the individual reduces the scope of his athletic pursuits by choosing a few activities to engage in regularly in competitive, recreational, or daily living settings. Further specialization and skill refinement occur in this "fine-tuning" stage. Lifetime activities are chosen on the basis of personal interests, abilities, ambitions, availability, and past experiences. Opportunities to participate are limited in this stage because of increased responsibilities and time commitments.

Many individuals do not go through the development and refinement of specialized movement skills in the sequence presented above. Children are often encouraged to refine their skills in a particular sport at an early age. Early participation in sports is not detrimental, but premature specialization may have a high cost. The development of a broad range of mature fundamental movement patterns could be sacrificed, thereby limiting the potential for participation in a wide variety of activities.

Youth Sport

Under ideal conditions, the transitional movement skill stage begins around ages 7 or 8. With their growing interest in performance capabilities and sport, increasing cognitive sophistication, and improved group interaction children are more attracted to organized competition. The growth in youth sport participation over the past 20 years has been phenomenal. An estimated 20 to 35 million children in the United States participate in youth sports (Seefeldt et al., 1992). Virtually every community in the sample group provided some form of competitive activity for youth. In fact, it would be hard to find any sizable community in North America today that does not provide competitive sport experiences for its youth outside the school setting as well as school-sponsored programs. Youth sport is big, it is popular, and it is here to stay.

Concept 16.3   Sport participation is important to millions of children and adolescents, who need competent leadership and developmentally appropriate experiences.

Youth sport can have detrimental as well as beneficial effects, all of which have been fully discussed over the years. See the *Program for Athletic Coaches' Education: PACE* (Brown & Benchmark, 1993), and *American Coaching Effectiveness Program: ACEP* (Human Kinetics, 1993) for up-to-date and highly practical sources of information. Sport allows individuals at the transition and application stages to improve their skills and get plenty of vigorous physical activity in competitive situations. Competitive sport, however, should not be regarded as the only skill outlet for children. Non-competitive and leisure-time activities such as hiking, canoeing, fishing, jogging and the like, as well as various forms of cooperative recreation and dance, are also beneficial for youth. Tables 16.1 through 16.9 provide an overview of several sport skills and the various fundamental locomotor, manipulative, and stability movements that are involved in the performance of these skills.

Table 16.1 Basketball Skills

Fundamental Movements	Specialized Movement Skills	
Manipulation		
Passing	Chest pass	Shovel pass
	Overhead pass	Push pass
	Baseball pass	
Shooting	Lay-up shot	Jump shot
	Two-hand set shot	
Bouncing	Stationary dribbling	Bounce pass
	Moving dribbling	
Catching	Pass above the waist	Rebounding
	Pass below the waist	Pass to the side
		Jump ball reception
Volleying	Tipping	
	Center jump	
Locomotion		
Running	In different directions while dribbling	
	In different directions without ball	
Sliding	Guarding while dribbling	
Leaping	Lay-up shot	
	Pass interception	
Jumping	Center jump	Rebounding
	Tip-in	Catching a high ball
Stability		
Axial movements	Pivoting	
	Bending	
Dynamic balance	Compensation for rapid changes in direction, speed, and level of movement	
Dodging	Feinting with the ball	

Table 16.2 Contemporary Dance Skills

Fundamental Movements	Specialized Movement Skills
Locomotion	
Walking	Contemporary dance is a movement form which utilizes a
Running	movement vocabulary specific to the particular creative
Leaping	effort being expressed. The choreographer utilizes
Jumping	movement as a vehicle of expression. Therefore,
Hopping	fundamental locomotor and stability movements serve
Galloping	as the means for conveying concepts and ideas.
Sliding	
Skipping	
Stability	
Axial movements	Bending, stretching, twisting, turning, reaching, lifting, falling, curling, pushing, pulling
Static and dynamic balance	Numerous balance skills requiring synchronizing rhythm and proper sequencing of movement

Table 16.3 Football Skills

Fundamental Movements	Specialized Movement Skills	
Manipulation		
Throwing	Forward pass	Lateral
	Centering	
Kicking	Place kick	Field-goal kicking
	Punting	
Catching	Pass above the waist	Over the shoulder
	Pass below the waist	Across the midline
	Pass at waist level	Hand-off
Carrying	Fullback carry	
	One-arm carry	
Locomotion		
Running	Ball carrying	
	Pursuit of ball carrier	
Sliding	Tackling	Blocking
Leaping and jumping	Pass defense	Pass reception
Stability		
Axial movements	Blocking	
	Tackling	
Static and dynamic balance	Blocking	Rolling
	Stances	Pushing
	Dodging a tackle	

Table 16.4 Softball/Baseball Skills

Fundamental Movements	Specialized Movement Skills	
Manipulation		
Throwing	Overhand throw for accuracy	
	Overhand throw for distance	
	Underhand toss	
	Overhand pitch	
	Underhand pitch	
Catching	Above-waist ball	Grounder
	Below-waist ball	Across midline
	Fly ball	Line drive
Striking	Batting	
	Bunting	
Locomotion		
Running	Base running	
	Fielding	
Sliding	Fielding	
	Base sliding	
Leaping	Base running	Fielding
Jumping	Fielding	
Stability		
Axial movements	Batting	
	Fielding	
	Pitching	
Dynamic balance	Compensation for rapid changes in direction, speed, and level of movement	

Changing a Well-Learned Technique

When a student or athlete displays well-learned but improper technique in performing a skill, you are faced with the dilemma of determining whether to attempt to change the habit or to leave it alone. The individual may be experiencing success with the technique, but you know that proper execution would be more efficient and successful. A well-learned technique is difficult and time-consuming to change because any new learning requires taking an unconscious advanced skill and returning it to the conscious level (beginning and intermediate stages). Under stress and in conditions where rapid decisions are required, the athlete is likely to revert to the incorrect technique. Only after considerable practice will the incorrect response be replaced by the correct

Table 16.5 Soccer Skills

Fundamental Movements	Specialized Movement Skills	
Manipulation		
Kicking	Instep kick	Inside of foot kick
	Toe kick	Outside of foot kick
	Heel kick	Dribbling
	Corner kick	Passing
	Goal kick	Goalie punt
Striking	Heading	
	Juggling	
Catching	Goalie skills	
Throwing	Throw-in	
	Goalie throw	
Trapping	Sole trap	
	Double-knee trap	
	Stomach trap	
	Single-knee trap	
	Chest trap	
Locomotion		
Running	With ball	
	Without ball	
Jumping and leaping	Heading	
Sliding	Marking	
Stability		
Axial movements	Goalie skills	
	Field play skills	
Dynamic balance	Tackling	
	Dodging opponent	
	Feinting with ball	

action at the advanced fine-tuning stage. In deciding whether to change an individual's technique, the teacher or coach needs to consider the following issues.

1. Determine if there is sufficient time to make the change (in terms of weeks and months, not hours and days).
2. Determine if the individual wants to make the change.
3. Be certain that the individual understands why the change is being made.
4. Be certain that the individual realizes that performance will regress prior to improvement.
5. Provide a supportive, encouraging environment.
6. Structure practice sessions that will gradually bring the learner from the initial to the intermediate and finally back to the fine-tuning stage.

Table 16.6 Track and Field Skills

Fundamental Movements	Specialized Movement Skills	
Manipulation		
Throwing	Shot put	Hammer
	Discus	
	Javelin	
Locomotion		
Running	Dashes	Pole-vault approach
	Middle distances	High-jump approach
	Long distances	Long-jump approach
Leaping takeoff	Low hurdles	Running long-jump
	High hurdles	Pole-vault takeoff
Jumping	High jump	
	Long jump	
Vertical jump	High jump	
Stability		
Axial movements	Pivoting and twisting (shot put, discus, javelin, and hammer)	
Dynamic balance	Compensation for rapid changes in speed, direction, and level of movement	

Table 16.7 Racquet Sport Skills

Fundamental Movements	Specialized Movement Skills	
Manipulation		
Striking	Forehand shot	Lob shot
	Backhand shot	Smash
	Overhead shot	Corner shot
	Sweep	Drop shot
Locomotion		
Running	Net rush	
	Ball retrieval	
Sliding	Lateral movement to ball	
Stability		
Axial movements	An aspect of all strokes (twisting, stretching, pivoting)	
Dynamic balance	Compensation for rapid changes in direction, level, and speed of movement	

Table 16.8 Volleyball Skills

Fundamental Movements	Specialized Movement Skills	
Manipulation		
Striking	Overhand serve	Spike
	Underhand serve	Dink
Volleying	Set-up	
	Dig	
Locomotion		
Sliding	Lateral movement	
Running	Forward	
	Backward	
Vertical jump	Diagonal	
	Spike	
Stability		
Axial movements	Found in general play (stretching, twisting, turning, falling, reaching)	
Dynamic balance	Rapid changes in speed, level, and direction of movement	

Concept 16.4 It is essential for the instructor to know the learner in order to make a difference in motor development and movement skill learning.

Knowing the Learner

It is vitally important for you as the teacher or coach to know your learners and to recognize that each comes to you with a different set of physical, mental, emotional, and social capabilities. You must accommodate an awesome number of individual differences when planning skill learning and practice sessions. Some of these individual differences are easy to detect, others are not. However, it is to your advantage to be aware of as many factors as possible. Important points to remember are listed below.

1. People learn at different rates.
2. Each person's potential for performance excellence is unique.
3. Fundamental movement and perceptual-motor abilities must be mastered before the sport skill is attempted.
4. Responses to instructional approaches vary among learners.
5. Responses to winning and losing vary among individuals.

Table 16.9 Gymnastic Skills

Fundamental Movements	Specialized Movement Skills	
Locomotion		
Running	Approach	
Vertical jumping	Back flip	
	Front flip	
Skipping	Skip step	
Leaping	Various stunts	
Stability		
Axial movements	One or more found in numerous stunts and apparatus skills (bending, stretching, twisting, turning, falling, reaching, pivoting)	
Static balance	Integral part of all stationary tricks and landing on dismounts	
Inverted supports		Tip-up headstand
		Tripod handstand
Body rolling	Forward roll	Back walkover
	Backward roll	Front walkover
Dynamic balance	Compensation for changes in direction, level, and speed of movement	

6. Responses to praise and criticism, reward and punishment vary among individuals.
7. Former sport-related experiences vary among individuals.
8. Variations in home life experiences influence people differently.
9. Strengths in some areas can compensate for deficiencies in other areas.
10. Attention spans and concentration abilities vary among individuals and groups.
11. The developmental levels of individuals vary, resulting in dissimilar potential for learning and performance.
12. There is no uniformity in the physical potential of individuals (particularly during the preteen and early teenage years).
13. Individuals display greater or lesser degrees of gross and fine motor skills depending on past experiences and inherited factors.
14. The ability to analyze, conceptualize, and solve problems varies from person to person.

Types of Sport Skills

Sport skills may be classified in a variety of ways. One classification scheme uses the terms externally paced and internally paced to describe the nature and intent of the activity itself.

Externally Paced Skills

Externally paced skills involve making responses to changes in environmental cues, as in trap and skeet shooting. These environmental changes are generally fast and unpredictable. Rapidity and flexibility in decision making are required of the athlete. Sports such as tennis, basketball, and football are examples of other externally paced activities. The coach needs to organize practice sessions that promote rapid decision making and adaptive behaviors in a variety of game-like situations.

Concept 16.5   A movement skill should be viewed in the context in which it will be performed in the "real" world to have ecological validity.

Internally Paced Skills

Internally paced skills require fixed responses to a given set of conditions. The athlete moves at his or her own pace through the activity and has time to recognize and respond to the conditions of the environment. Internally paced activities generally place a great deal of emphasis on accuracy, consistency, and repetition of performance. Target shooting, as well as bowling, golf, archery, and gymnastics are generally regarded as internally paced activities. Coaches need to provide ample opportunities for repetition under environmental conditions that duplicate, as nearly as possible, the actual competitive environment.

In both internally paced and externally paced sport skills the teacher/coach needs to:

1. Identify the type of activity (i.e., externally or internally paced)
2. Establish a practice environment that is consistent with the nature of the activity
3. Introduce externally paced activities under internally paced conditions first (i.e., control the environment and conditions of skill practice first)
4. Introduce situations that require responses to sudden and unpredictable cues in externally paced activities as skill develops
5. Strive for greater consistency, duplication, and elimination of environmental influences for internally paced activities as skill develops

6. Encourage each individual to "think through" the activity in the early stages of learning
7. Encourage each individual to screen out unnecessary cues as skill develops

Levels in Movement Skill Learning

All movement skill learning, whether internally paced or externally paced, involves a hierarchial sequence. The sequential progression in the development and refinement of movement skills may be classified into three general levels. Each of these levels represents a period during which both the learner and the instructor have specific, identifiable tasks and responsibilities (Magill, 1993; Sage, 1984; Lawther, 1977; Gentile, 1972; Fitts & Posner, 1967; Fitts, 1962).

Concept 16.6   Movement skill learning is age-independent, and it follows a predictable sequence progressing from the beginning or "novice" level, to the intermediate or "practice" level, and finally to the advanced or "fine-tuning" level.

Beginning Level

The *beginning*, or "novice level," as it is sometimes called, is the first stage in learning a new movement skill. During this stage the movements of the individual are generally slow, uncoordinated, and jerky. He pays conscious attention to every detail of the activity. During this stage he begins to construct a mental plan of the activity and actively tries to understand the skill. Because he pays such close attention to the details of the task itself, performance is poor. The early onset of fatigue, due more to the mental requirements of the task than to the task itself, is often apparent. During this stage the learner tends to pay attention to all available information and is unable to "screen" out the relevant from the irrelevant.

The teacher or coach at this early level of movement skill learning needs to be aware of the conscious cognitive requirements of this stage. The intent, at this level, is to provide the learner with the gross general framework of the skill activity. The instructor needs to:

1. Introduce the major aspects of the skill only (be brief)
2. Provide for visual demonstrations of the skill
3. Permit the learner to try out the skill
4. Provide plenty of opportunity for exploration of the skill itself and self-discovery of general principles of the skill
5. Recognize that this is primarily a cognitive stage and that the learner only needs to get the general idea at this stage

6. Compare the new skill, when possible, to a similar skill with which the athlete may be familiar
7. Provide immediate, precise, and positive feedback concerning the skill
8. Focus on process, and avoid situations that emphasize performance

Intermediate Level

The *intermediate* or "practice level" as it is often called, begins after the performer comprehends the general idea of the skill and is able to perform it, albeit somewhat roughly. The learner at this stage has a better understanding of the skill. As the mental image of the skill becomes fixed, conscious attention to the skill details diminishes. More attention is devoted to the goal or product of the skill than to the process itself. The poorly coordinated, jerky movements so evident in the preceding stage gradually disappear. The individual gains a "feel" for the skill as kinesthetic sensitivity increases. As a result, there is less reliance on verbal and visual cues and greater reliance on muscle sense.

The teacher or coach during the practice stage focuses on greater skill development. Practice conditions promote skill refinement and maximize feedback. To accomplish this the instructor needs to:

1. Provide numerous opportunities for practice
2. Provide opportunities for skill refinement in a supportive, non-threatening environment
3. Devise practice situations that progressively focus on greater skill refinement
4. Schedule short, fast-paced practice sessions with frequent breaks before implementing longer sessions with few breaks
5. Analyze skills and provide constructive criticism
6. Structure quality practice sessions that focus on quality performance (i.e., "perfect practice makes perfect")
7. Accommodate frequent differences in the rates of skill development
8. Allow for individual differences in the rate of skill development
9. Focus attention on the whole skill whenever possible
10. Set up practices that simulate the intensity and demands of competitive conditions

Advanced Level

The *advanced*, or "fine-tuning" level, as it is sometimes called, is the third and final stage of learning a new movement skill. The performer who is at this stage has a complete understanding of the skill. The mental image is highly developed, and the athlete pays little attention to the cognitive aspects of the task. In fact, individuals at this level often have difficulty describing how they peform an activity. They often resort to a "let me show you," or a "do it like this" statement followed by actual performance of the skill. The performer at this stage is refining and fine-tuning the skill. In sports where movement is the key element, it is smooth, fluid, and highly coordinated. In sports like archery, in which the absence of movement is most highly valued, there is a general appearance of ease, mastery, and total control. The performer is able to screen irrelevant information and is not bothered by distractions. There is excellent timing and anticipation of movements and the action appears automatic, although in reality it is a finely tuned skill requiring only a minimum of conscious cortical control.

Instructors of individuals at the advanced stage of movement skill learning must focus on additional refining, maintaining the skill, and providing selected feedback. In order to do this the teacher or coach needs to:

1. Structure practice opportunities that promote intensity and enthusiasm
2. Be available to provide encouragement, motivation, and positive support
3. Offer suggestions and tips on strategy
4. Structure practices that duplicate competitive situations
5. Help the athlete anticipate her actions in game-like situations
6. Know the athlete as an individual and be able to adjust methods to meet her needs
7. Provide feedback that focuses on specific aspects of the skill
8. Avoid asking the athlete to think about execution of the skill, which might result in "analysis paralysis"

Each stage in the movement skill learning process requires concerned, knowledgeable, and sensitive teaching. The instructor must understand the characteristics of each learner at all three stages and structure sessions that are most effective for enhancing performance. The acquisition of skill is a process that takes time. The teacher and coach make maximum effective use of the time available. Organized, effective practice sessions geared to the skill levels of the learners are crucial.

Fostering Improvement

By age 8 most children have the potential to be at the transitional skill stage. Emphasis on skill improvement at this time results from the increase in the child's performance potential. The learner and the teacher (i.e., the parent, instructor, therapist or coach) are becoming more concerned with the degree of skill, accuracy, and form used in performing a movement task. The teacher's foremost purpose is to help the learner improve in accordance with her developmental needs and potential. The operational goal of improvement helps teachers to see all students (whether they are children, adolescents, or adults) at their actual developmental levels. By assessing current levels of motor behavior and providing meaningful and enjoyable learning experiences, developmental teachers will foster improvements.

The operational goal of improvement encompasses three other concepts that guide teachers. The first of these concepts is *movement control* in which teachers reflect their knowledge of the three categories of movement (stability, locomotion, and manipulation) and the phases of motor development. Teachers also incorporate variation and presentations that move from the general to the specific in their plans. By condensing information into the concept of movement control, teachers have a basis for analyzing their own effectiveness in improving the skills of their students.

The second concept under the goal of improvement is *emotional control.* Teachers are concerned with how learners understand themselves and others. Teachers rely heavily on appropriate communication skills in themselves and in their students. These communication skills include self-discipline as well as experiences through which learners can develop responsibility and self-control. The concept of emotional control gives teachers a guide for evaluating past experiences and designing new experiences.

The third and final concept is *learning enjoyment.* This concept also gives teachers a guide for evaluating their programs with improvement in mind. The objective here is for teachers to stimulate an eagerness to learn within each individual. Success-oriented experiences and opportunities to receive praise and recognition positively reinforce the learner's view of learning. By making the learning of new movement skills enjoyable, teachers foster intrinsic motivation within the individual.

The overall goal of improvement, with its three emphases of (1) movement control, (2) emotional control, and (3) learning enjoyment, provides teachers with a compact philosophical construct that can serve as an operational guide to teaching action. This construct can and should be modified. Its purpose is not to limit parents, teachers, and coaches but to empower them by providing operational guidelines to assure that teaching is meaningful, relevant, and fun. Every teacher must rely on some sort of philosophical construct. Without one, a teacher might impose inappropriate performance expectations on his students. The purpose of the suggested philosophical construct is to provide teachers with a basis for keeping instructions realistic, practical, and meaningful.

The refinement of specialized movement abilities occurs in three stages. In the transitional stage, it is crucial that a smooth shift be made from mature fundamental movement patterns to corresponding sport skills. This transition will be hampered if the individual has not developed mature patterns necessary for performance of the sport skills. Teachers must be alert to the proficiency with which the individual executes a sport skill and not give in to the temptation of ignoring incorrect form as long as the outcome is satisfactory. All too often the teachers and coaches focus on the product rather than on the process. There is no legitimate reason for failing to use the mature, mechanically correct, pattern in the performance of a sport skill. Use of a mature pattern of movement will, in the long run, enhance movement performance. However, once proficiency has been achieved, has become relatively automatic, and has been applied to numerous sport situations, it is entirely appropriate to encourage unique individual variations.

At the application stage, attention is focused on greater degrees of precision, accuracy, and control. Performance scores generally improve at a rapid rate, and the individual is keenly aware of the specific advantages and limitations of his or her body. The individual at this level is also influenced by a variety of social, cultural, and psychological factors in selecting specific sport, dance, and recreational activities for regular involvement.

The lifelong utilization stage is a continuation and further refinement of the previous stage. It is the pinnacle of the phases and stages of motor development. This stage encompasses lifetime sport and recreational activities. Failure to develop and refine the fundamental and specialized skill abilities of the previous stages will restrict any person's ability to reach this stage.

The goal of the instructor concerned with the motor development and movement education of youth is to foster improvement in such a way that there is an orderly and developmentally sound progression through the fundamental movement and specialized skill phases. Improvement in movement control, emotional control, and learning enjoyment serves as a practical philosophical construct around which to plan and implement meaningful learning experiences.

Terms to Remember

Specialized movement skill
Proficiency barrier
Transition stage
Application stage
Lifelong utilization stage
Externally paced skills
Internally paced skills

Beginning/novice level
Intermediate/practice level
Advanced/fine-tuning level
Movement control
Emotional control
Learning enjoyment

Critical Readings

Christina, R. W., & Corcos, D. M. (1988). *Coaches Guide to Teaching Sport Skills*. Champaign, IL: Human Kinetics.

Haubenstricker, J. L., & Seefeldt, V. D. (1986). Acquisition of motor skills during childhood. In V. Seefeldt (Ed.), *Physical Activity and Well-being*. Reston, VA: AAHPERD.

Martens, R. (1990). *Successful Coaching*. Champaign, IL: Human Kinetics.

Sawyer, T. (Ed.) (1992). Coaching education in North America. *Journal of Physical Education, Recreation and Dance, 63,* 33–64. (Series of articles on 5 coaching education programs).

Seefeldt, V., & Brown, E. W. (Eds.) (1992). *Program for Athletic Coaches' Education*. Dubuque, IA: Brown & Benchmark.

Seefeldt, V. et al. (1992). *Overview of Youth Sports Programs in the United States*. New York: Carnegie Council on Adolescent Development.

Physical Development of Adolescents

Key Concept: Although there are differences between genders as well as within genders on measures of health-related and performance-related fitness, adolescent males and females have the potential to make significant improvements through participation in regular vigorous physical activity.

Health-related fitness and performance-related fitness change rapidly during adolescence. Both males and females are capable of making significant increments in all measures of fitness. This chapter will examine these changes. The first section is devoted to the components of health-related fitness. Results of the 1985 National Children and Youth Fitness Study (NCYFS) are the primary source of data because of the validity of the sample and the reliability of the data. All the figures presented in this section are based on the mean sample scores for each health-related fitness item tested. There is considerable variability in performance scores on all items at all age levels.

The information presented in the discussion and figures on performance-related fitness is based on a synthesis of post-1960 studies reported by Haubenstricker and Seefeldt (1986). These data were selected because they are considered the best representative sampling available of changes in motor skill performance.

The reader is encouraged to study the figures and tables throughout this chapter carefully. It will be of far more value to you to gain a conceptual grasp of the meaning implied in the slopes of the curves, than to memorize specific data points.

Health-Related Fitness

The health-related fitness of youth has been a topic of considerable interest in recent years. It has been suggested that today's North American youth are unfit in comparison to their age-mates of years ago and their peers from other nations (see Chapter 12). To date we do not have sufficient hard data collected and reported in a scientifically acceptable manner to make a strong case for this claim. At the present time no reliable data permit us to make accurate comparisons across generations or across cultures. The problem exists primarily in sampling and data collection techniques. Prior to the publication of the National Children and Youth Fitness Study (1985, 1987) large-scale, population-based field studies used *convenience samples.* Although thousands of children and youth were tested on a variety of fitness items, little attention was given to sampling procedures. As a result the data tend to be suspect and are not suitable for generalizations across ages and the population as a whole. For example, it is altogether possible that participants in some locations were more highly motivated by the testing than others.

As a result, performance scores could be biased in favor of more highly motivated participants. Furthermore, in convenience samples little attention is given to geographical representation, rural versus urban settings, and private versus public school populations, all of which may have dramatic effects.

Concept 17.1   Field assessments of physical fitness are frequently unsuitable for the formulation of generalizations because of questionable underlying assumptions, sampling procedures, and data collection techniques.

Another inherent difficulty with nationally normed field test fitness data published prior to the NCYFS (1985, 1987) is inherent in the test administration itself. Data were collected by different examiners at each site, usually by trained physical education professionals. Also, all students in the convenience sample method were receiving physical education, a factor that may have skewed the data upward. It is difficult, if not impossible, to assure consistency among testers. Therefore, *interrater reliability* (objectivity) and *intrarater reliability* (consistency) tend to be poor.

A third problem in comparing generational scores rests in the test items themselves. Comparison can be made only among items that are performed and administered in exactly the same manner. Changing the protocol, even slightly, for an assessment item may result in drastically inflated or deflated scores.

With these concerns in mind we have chosen to use the NCYFS (1985) data as a basis for our discussion about the health-related fitness of adolescents. Additional data sets are on the horizon, but to date the NCYFS data are the most valid and reliable. The NCYFS is based on a *stratified random sample* of 5,140 males and 5,135 females from 25 randomly selected counties in the United States. Over 88 percent (4,539) of the randomly selected males completed the test battery, and exactly 83 percent (4,261) females completed the testing (Errecart et al., 1985). The high participation rate and the definitive manner in which the sample was obtained contributed greatly to the validity and generalizability of the results. Reliability of the NCYFS was insured by a highly trained field staff of 10 individuals who "directly" supervised administration of all of the assessment measures given by trained teachers (Ross et al., 1985). The NCYFS (1985) results represent the best field data available in terms of validity of the sample and reliability of the data. Each of the sections that follow discuss the various health-related components of fitness in respect to these data. Comparisons, where appropriate, are made with norms from the 1980 AAHPERD Health-Related Physical Fitness Test (HRPFT). You will note that, in general, HRPFT scores are better than NCYFS scores. This may be due to the sampling

Table 17.1 Common Measures of Adolescent Health-Related Fitness and a Synthesis of Findings

Health-Related Fitness Component	Common Measures	Synthesis of Findings
Aerobic endurance	1-Mile Walk/Run	Males and females both improve at a near parallel rate
		Males are faster than females at all ages
		Males continue to improve until late adolescence
		Females regress and plateau from mid-adolescence onward
		Males show rapid yearly increments until late adolescence
Muscular strength/ endurance	Modified Sit-ups	Females improve at a less rapid rate than males
		Females tend to plateau in performance during mid-adolescence
		Males outperform females at all ages
	Pull-ups	Females average less than one pull-up throughout adolescence
		Males demonstrate slow gains prior to puberty followed by rapid gains throughout adolescence
		Males significantly outperform females at all ages

and test administration issues discussed earlier. When comparing the two tests (HRPFT and NCYFS), carefully observe the slope of the two curves. In most cases, the slopes are remarkably similar, thereby strengthening the validity of the data for both tests in terms of changes over time. Care should be taken to note where age differences in the slopes of the two lines exist. These differences may reflect variations in activity patterns between the two studies due to sociocultural shifts in activity levels over time. Table 17.1 provides a synthesis of findings from the NCYFS (1985).

Table 17.1 continued

Health-Related Fitness Component	Common Measures	Synthesis of Findings
Joint flexibility	Sit-and-reach	Females outperform males at all ages Females make yearly incremental improvements until late adolescence Males regress during early adolescence followed by rapid improvement
Body Composition	Skinfold Calipers	Females have a higher percent body fat than males at all ages Female body fat percentages increase rapidly during early and mid-adolescence followed by a plateau in late adolescence Males increase in percent body fat during late childhood and the pre-adolescent period Males decrease in percent body fat during early adolescence and maintain low fat levels throughout adolescence

Aerobic Endurance

Cardiovascular or aerobic endurance is related to the functioning of the heart, lungs, and vascular system. One's aerobic capacity may be evaluated in the laboratory through a variety of stress tests that require the subject to exert an all-out effort to go into oxygen debt. These "max" tests as they are known are most generally performed on a treadmill or bicycle ergometer. The VO_2 max score is obtained as the result of exhaustive exercise. Although measuring VO_2 max is the preferred method of determining aerobic capacity, large longitudinal population studies using treadmill and ergometer tests are nonexistent. Instead, research has focused on *population samples* across ages using field test estimates of aerobic endurance. As a result the 1-mile walk/run has emerged as the most popular field test item with adolescents. Updyke and Willett (1989) and Updyke (1992) in a 10-year retrospective study of various fitness components found that aerobic fitness declined annually among a large cross-sectional convenience sample of children and youth.

Concept 17.2 Field-based population studies of health-related fitness yield more valid and reliable data than convenience samples, thus giving a truer picture of the fitness of youth.

Based on the 1985 National Children and Youth Fitness Study (NCYFS) as depicted in Figure 17.1, males on the average continue to improve in aerobic endurance until age 16, whereupon they regress slightly through age 18. These results are similar to mean mile walk/run times on the 1980 AAHPERD Health Related Physical Fitness Test (HRPFT). However, the males tested in the HRPFT regressed slightly between ages 10 and 11, followed by steady improvement through age 14. This in turn was followed by a general plateauing of scores through age 17. It is difficult to explain the discrepancy in the slope of the two curves (Figure 17.2) at age 11, but this may be a function of the sampling techniques employed. (The HRPFT used a convenience sampling technique, whereas the NCYFS utilized a stratified random sampling technique.) Nevertheless, the similar slope of the two curves demonstrates that

Figure 17.1
One mile walk / run: mean scores for males and females 10–18 years, in minutes and seconds (drawn from data, *Source:* Ross, J. G., et al. [1985]. "The National Children and Youth Fitness Study: New Standards for Fitness Measurement." *Journal of Physical Education, Recreation and Dance,* 56, 1, 62–66)

MILE WALK/RUN: MALES & FEMALES

males improve in their mile walk/run times with age. The fact that the boys in the NCYFS continued to improve until age 16 may be reflective of differences in aerobic activity patterns among boys between those sampled in the HRPFT and those in the NCYFS. Note, however, that for both tests, males, with age, tend to plateau after age 16 in their performance on the mile walk/run test. This should be viewed with concern in that it reflects a tendency toward more sedentary activity patterns of the older adolescent. It is interesting to note that the dropoff in scores coincides with the age at which most males are eligible to drive and work.

With regard to the performance of females on the mile walk/run test of aerobic endurance, the results are of similar concern. Although we might expect the male to outperform his female counterpart due to a variety of anatomical and physiological variables, we would hope to see a descending slope (i.e., lower times) over a longer period of time. Based on the results of the NCYFS, the female is closest to her male counterpart on the mile walk/run at age 10, and the gap between males and females remains roughly parallel until age 14. It widens, however, at a dramatic rate from then on (Figure 17.1). Although females performing on both the NCYFS and the HRPFT tended to improve with age until around 13 or 14 years, there was a decided tendency to regress and plateau in performance. The 18-year-old female is at almost the same level as her 12-year-old counterpart.

Data from the HRPFT tend to support that published in the NCYFS. However, females in the HRPFT peaked at an earlier age and regressed at a more rapid rate than those tested in the NCYFS (Figure 17.3). Perhaps there is room for cautious optimism in that comparison of the two

MILE WALK/RUN: MALES

Figure 17.2
Comparison of one mile walk / run scores between NCYFS and HRPFT: mean scores for males 10–17 years, in minutes and seconds

Figure 17.3
Comparison of one mile walk/run scores between NCYFS and HRPFT: mean scores for females 10–17 years, in minutes and seconds

MILE WALK/RUN: FEMALES

slopes may indicate a tendency of females later in the 1980s to be more active aerobically than their peers early in the decade. The rapid rise and sustained popularity of aerobic dance and other rhythmic exercise classes may be at least partially responsible for the less severe rate of regression.

Muscular Strength and Endurance

Modified sit-ups and chin-ups are frequently used as field measures of *abdominal isotonic strength/endurance.* They are isotonic in that the muscles go through a full range of motion while in a contracted state. They are related to strength because a significant force is overcome, and they are related to endurance because a maximum number of repetitions is recorded. From 6 to 9 years of age both boys and girls are similar in their performance scores on the bent-knee sit-up test. However, from age 10 onward males improve at a much more rapid rate than their female counterparts (NCYFS, 1985). Figure 17.4 depicts males improving at a near linear rate from ages 11 to 16 with a tendency to level off and slightly regress from ages 16 to 18. This is clearly in conflict with the general notion (i.e., not supported by data) that males peak in terms of strength shortly after puberty.

Figure 17.5's presentation of scores for chin-ups, a measure of upper trunk strength and endurance, provides additional support for the contention that strength increases at a near linear rate for boys from about

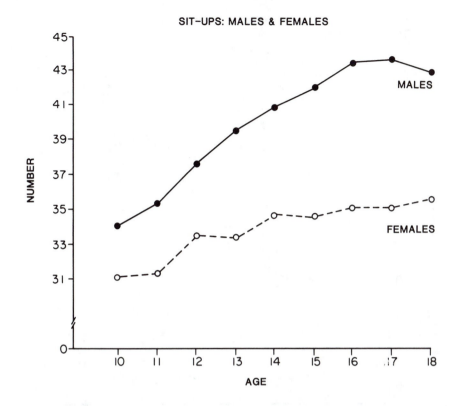

SIT–UPS: MALES & FEMALES

MALES

FEMALES

NUMBER

AGE

Figure 17.4
Bent-knee sit-ups:
mean scores for
males and females
10–18 years,
number in 60 sec-
onds (drawn from
data, *Source:* Ross,
J. G., et al. [1985].
"The National Chil-
dren and Youth Fit-
ness Study: New
Standards for Fit-
ness Measure-
ment." *Journal of
Physical Education,
Recreation and
Dance,* 56, 1,
62–66)

age 12 (the approximate age of onset of male puberty) through approximately age 18. Comparing mean scores from published norms on bent-
knee sit-ups in the HRPFT reveals similar conclusions, although the
boys tested on the HRPFT outperformed their age-mates on the NCYFS
(Figure 17.6).

Concept 17.3 Females are comparable to males in abdominal
strength and endurance prior to puberty, but males make significantly more rapid gains throughout adolescence.

In terms of female *upper body strength/endurance* the data are
somewhat different. Females appear to be quite weak in this area
throughout childhood and adolescence. There appears to be no peaking
followed by a plateau and gradual decline as previously thought. Rather,
there is a consistently flat curve indicating low levels of upper body
strength/endurance at all ages. Females, however, seem to fare somewhat better on measures of abdominal endurance as measured by the
NCYFS. Mean score values for the bent-knee sit-up test improve slightly
with age. In terms of abdominal strength/endurance, older adolescents

Figure 17.5
Chin-ups: mean
scores for males
and females 10–18
years, number com-
pleted (drawn from
data, *Source:* Ross,
J. G., et al. [1985].
"The National Chil-
dren and Youth Fit-
ness Study: New
Standards for Fit-
ness Measure-
ment." *Journal of
Physical Education,
Recreation and
Dance,* 56, 1,
62–66)

CHIN-UPS: MALES AND FEMALES

tend to score slightly higher than their younger counterparts. Mean score values for bent-knee sit-ups on the HRPFT revealed similar results, although females tended to perform at a higher level at all ages on the HRPFT (Figure 17.7).

In terms of strength and endurance the sudden upsurge in performance by boys during adolescence may be explained by their increased muscularity brought about by high levels of testosterone. Furthermore, the tendency on the part of males at all ages to "go all out" on measures of fitness may account for the vast discrepancy between males and females. Females did not improve at such a rapid rate perhaps because of greater amounts of fatty tissue in proportion to lean muscle mass. The tendency on the part of females to level off during mid and later adolescence could also be a matter of motivation and lack of all-out enthusiasm rather than of purely physiological factors. These are important points to consider. One must be careful to avoid the implication that no matter how hard females try to improve their performances on measures of strength and endurance they will fail. In fact, the data using motivated females suggests the opposite.

Figure 17.6
Comparison of
bent-knee sit-up
scores between
NCYFS and HRPFT:
mean scores for
males 10–17 years,
number in 60 sec-
onds

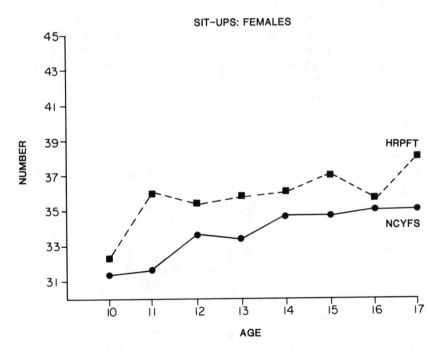

Figure 17.7
Comparison of
bent-knee sit-up
scores between
NCYFS and HRPFT:
mean scores for fe-
males 10–17 years,
number in 60 sec-
onds

Concept 17.4 Males tend to make rapid gains in muscular strength and endurance throughout adolescence, while females tend to peak at the onset of puberty and regress slightly by the end of adolescence.

The flexed arm hang, an *isometric strength endurance* measure, was administred to both males and females in the Manitoba Physical Fitness Performance Test (CAPHER, 1980). It too revealed age differences between the genders. Males tended to improve slightly from age 5 onward, with a preadolescent lull followed by rapid improvement through age 18. Females, on the other hand, improved somewhat until age 11 or 12, whereupon they achieved a plateau until age 15, and showed a slight decline thereafter. Hunsicker and Reiff (1977) reported similar findings with American girls on the flexed arm hang. The performance of boys and girls was quite similar from age 5 to age 8, but began to diverge radically after that in favor of the boys.

The often dramatic differences exhibited between males and females and the span of years in which improved performances can be expected on measures of muscular strength and endurance should be examined carefully. Although males on the average can be expected to outperform females in measures of strength and endurance due to anatomical, physiological, and biomechanical advantages, there is not an adequate biological explanation of differences in the span of years over which relative improvements may be seen. A reasonable explanation may be based on social, cultural, and child-rearing differences between males and females. Although North American culture has become more tolerant of females being involved in vigorous physical activity, it is apparent that discrepancies remain in the opportunities, encouragement, and instruction available to them.

Flexibility

The sit-and-reach test has become the standard field measurement of *joint flexibility*. Data from the NCYFS (1985) clearly indicate that on the average females make near linear improvements in sit-and-reach scores from ages 10 to 16, followed by a slight decline. Females at all ages outperform their male counterparts on this measure (Figure 17.8). Reasons for this discrepancy have not been adequately explained, but may center around anatomical differences as well as sociocultural variances in activity patterns favoring joint flexibility in females.

It is interesting to note the slight dropoff in sit-and-reach scores for males around age 12. This may be associated with the prepubescent growth spurt during which time the long bones are growing faster than the muscles and tendons. As a result performance of the sit-and-reach regresses until the muscles and tendons catch up. Note also, that both males and females begin to plateau and regress slightly in their flexibility scores around age 17. Decreases in joint flexibility during this period are clearly associated with a general decrease in the activity levels

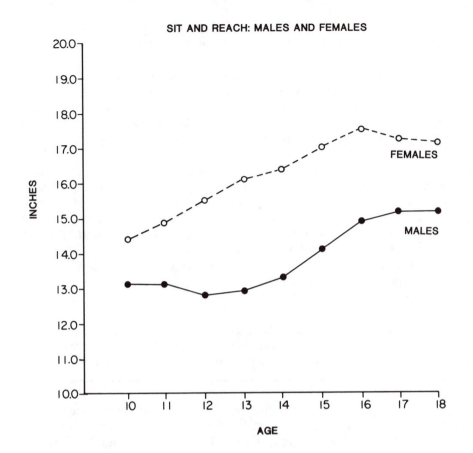

SIT AND REACH: MALES AND FEMALES

Figure 17.8
Sit-and-reach: mean scores for males and females 10–18 years, in inches (drawn from data, *Source:* Ross, J. G., et al. [1985]. "The National Children and Youth Fitness Study: New Standards for Fitness Measurement." *Journal of Physical Education, Recreation and Dance,* 56, 1, 62–66)

of the older adolescent and with aging. In fact, a high level of joint flexibility may be maintained well into adulthood and beyond if appropriate activities are maintained. In other words the phrase "use it or lose it" applies. Based on the NCYFS, loss of flexibility begins around age 17.

Concept 17.5   As a population, females display greater joint flexibility throughout adolescence than their male counterparts, but both tend to regress over time due to reduced activity patterns rather than age.

Body Composition

Body composition (percent body fat) is now considered by many to be a health-related aspect of fitness. Previously, total body weight was used by insurance companies as an indicator of functional health. However, total body weight is a poor predictor of body composition because it does not reflect the distribution and composition of one's body weight. Total body weight is the sum of muscle, skeletal, organ, and fat masses. To accurately assess one's body composition, the percent of body fatness needs to be separated from the other components of one's total body weight.

Hydrostatic weighing is currently the most accurate method of determining percent body fat. It involves submerging an individual under water and calculating his underwater weight from which an accurate estimate of percent body fat can be calculated. Accurate hydrostatic weighing is not a practical measure for field-based assessments of body composition.

Electrical impedance techniques hold great promise for the future. They are less inconvenient than hydrostatic weighing, but involve sophisticated equipment not frequently available in most field settings. Therefore, despite their limitations, *skinfold calipers* have become the preferred method of estimating percent body fat in the field. The reliability of the caliper technique has been frequently challenged, but when administered by trained personnel it may yield fairly accurate results. Body composition data from the NCYFS (1985) is based on the use of skinfold calipers.

Concept 17.6   As a population, females steadily gain in percent body fat measurements from preadolescence through adolescence.

Figure 17.9 illustrates tremendous developmental differences in body composition between males and females. Females show a sharp increase in body fatness from ages 10 to 11, followed by a less sharp but steady increase to age 15, which is in turn followed by a tapering off through age 18. The sharp rise between 10 and 11 years of age may be explained by the female prepubescent growth spurt which begins around this time. The steady increase until about age 15 is the result of the pubertal process of becoming a woman.

Males have dramatically different measurements of percent body fat during adolescence. The preadolescent shows a definite increase in body fatness from 10 to 12 years of age. The typically chunky sixth grader enters his growth spurt and shows a dramatic decrease in adiposity and increase in muscle mass. Increases in male sex hormones account for this increase in muscularity and decrease in body fat. Males continue to display significantly lower levels of body fatness throughout the high school years.

Concept 17.7   Male body fat percentages increase during the preadolescent period, decline sharply at puberty, and level off throughout adolescence.

BODY COMPOSITION: MALES AND FEMALES

Figure 17.9
Sum of triceps and subscapular skinfolds: mean scores for males and females, in millimeters (drawn from data, *Source:* Ross, J. G., et al. [1985]. "The National Children and Youth Fitness Study: New Standards for Fitness Measurement." *Journal of Physical Education, Recreation and Dance*, 56, 1, 62–66)

It is interesting to note that on the average today's adolescents are fatter than their counterparts of previous generations, according to body fat measurements with skinfold calipers (Kuntzleman and Reiff, 1992). This suggests that there is indeed a trend toward increased fatness among different generations of American youth. Data published by the National Center for Health Statistics (NCHS) in the 1960s were the result of a national probability sample. When compared with the results of the NCYFS:

> It can be assured that the skinfold data from the NCYFS and NCHS projects are equally representative of the population of American youth, but at two different points in time. If we discount possible differences in measurement techniques, the differences in skinfold thickness may be explained by the passage of time: American children have become fatter since the 1960s (Pate et al., 1985, p. 72).

Although we may not be able to critically compare the previously discussed measures of health-related fitness generationally, we can make such a comparison in terms of percent body fat. The message is clear: *American children have become fatter since the 1960s.* Regular vigorous physical activity can alter body composition. Exercise coupled with caloric regulation will result in an increase in lean body mass and a decrease in percent body fat in children, adolescents, and adults. The extent to which body composition can be altered is dependent on the degree and length of training. Alterations in body composition are not necessarily permanent. As activity levels decrease, body fat percentages increase. Parizkova (1982) demonstrated a significant relationship between physical activity levels and lean body mass percentages. Also, several researchers (Bandini et al., 1990; Bar-Or, 1983; Romanella et al., 1991; Moore et al., 1991) noted that intensity of activity is significantly lower in obese children, adolescents, and adults. Clearly, increased levels of physical activity coupled with moderation in caloric intake are keys to reducing the trend toward increased fatness.

Concept 17.8 Differences between males and females on measures of health-related and performance-related fitness are just that, differences, explainable by a variety of anatomical, physiological, and sociocultural factors.

Performance-Related Fitness

The *motor fitness* components of speed, power, agility, balance, and coordination are generally considered to be the performance- or skill-related components of fitness. These differ considerably from the health-related components of fitness in that they are genetically dependent, resistant to major environmental (experiential) modifications, and relatively stable. Also, these traits are closely related to skillful performance in a variety of sports.

Quantitative changes in a variety of gross motor skills have been studied by several investigators over the past several decades. As a result we have a wealth of information on the performance capabilities of males and females from childhood to adulthood. In fact, it is even possible to compare performance scores between generations and arrive at some tentative conclusions concerning secular trends in motor performance on selected skills. Haubenstricker and Seefeldt (1986) presented data summaries for four motor performance items that have been assessed by a variety of investigators prior to 1960 and since 1960. Three of these—running for speed, jumping for distance, and throwing for distance—are summarized in the following sections, and presented in Table 17.2.

Table 17.2 Common Measures of Adolescent Motor Fitness and a Synthesis of Findings

Motor Fitness Component	Common Measures	Synthesis of Findings
Speed	30- to 60-yard dash	Boys and girls are similar throughout childhood
		Boys outperform girls at all ages
		Males make more rapid improvement after puberty than females
		Males make significant annual gains throughout childhood and adolescence
		Females tend to plateau in mid-adolescence
Muscular power Lower trunk	Jump for distance	Boys and girls are similar throughout childhood
	Jump for height	Boys slightly outperform girls during childhood, but the gap widens significantly at male puberty
Muscular power Upper trunk	Throw for distance	Males make significant annual increments throughout adolescence
		Females begin to plateau during early adolescence and regress by mid-adolescence
Balance		Males and females make significant qualitative, as well as quantitative improvements with age
Static balance	Stabilometer Stick balance 1-foot balance	
Dynamic balance	Beam walk	Males make rapid improvement at all ages but especially after puberty
		Females and males improve with age throughout childhood and adolescence
		Females tend to outperform males during childhood on both static and dynamic measures
		Males and females are similar on both static and dynamic measures throughout adolescence with no clear advantage for either

Running Speed

Running speed may be assessed across studies that use different distances by converting dash times (usually 30- to 60-yard dashes) to units of yards covered per second. In order to further standardize measurements Haubenstricker and Seefeldt (1986) reported that only those studies that utilized a stationary start were included. The results of these comparisons led them to conclude that:

> There is systematic improvement in the running speed of children during the middle and late childhood years. This improvement in running speed continues during the teenage years for males. The running speed of post-1960 females increases until age 15, after which time it appears to plateau (pp. 67–69).

Figure 17.10 graphically depicts changes in running speed with age from childhood through adolescence based on studies conducted after 1960. Running speed is similar in boys and girls, only slightly favoring the boys, throughout childhood. However, beginning at about age 12 males begin to make more rapid improvements while their female age-mates begin to plateau. Reasons for the early plateauing on the part of

Figure 17.10
Age changes in running speed: mean scores for males and females 5–17 years, from post-1960 studies (drawn from data from Haubenstricker, J., and Seefeldt, V. [1986]. "Acquisition of Motor Skills During Childhood." In Seefeldt, V. [Ed.] *Physical Activity and Well-Being.* Reston, VA: AAHPERD)

adolescent females may be explained, in part, in terms of early maturation and lower levels of personal motivation as compared to their late-maturing and often more highly motivated male age-mates. Figure 17.11 illustrates comparable results in actual age changes in running the 100-yard dash.

Concept 17.9 The gap between males and females widens considerably in favor of males from puberty onward on measures of speed and power.

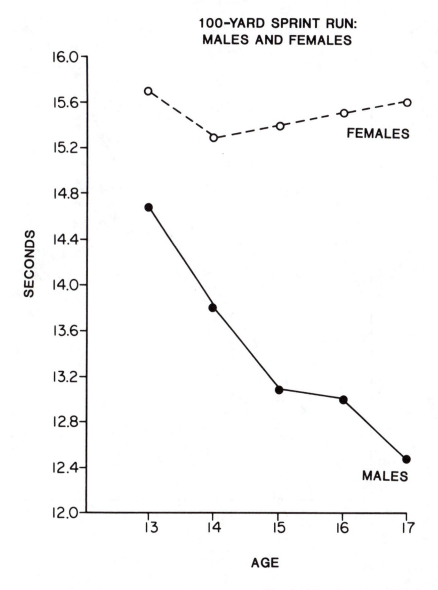

100-YARD SPRINT RUN: MALES AND FEMALES

Figure 17.11
100-yard sprint run mean scores for males and females 13–17 years, in seconds (drawn from data, *Source:* Ross, J. G., et al. [1985]. "The National Children and Youth Fitness Study: New Standards for Fitness Measurement." *Journal of Physical Education, Recreation and Dance,* 56, 1, 62–66)

Jumping for Distance

Jumping for distance, a purported measure of muscular power has been assessed in a large number of studies. Haubenstricker and Seefeldt (1986) in summarizing the post-1960 performance scores of children and adolescents 5 to 17 years of age found that males only slightly outperform females, and that there is steady improvement for both from ages 5 to 14 (Figure 17.12). After that females begin to level off and may even decline. Males, however, continue to improve at a linear rate to

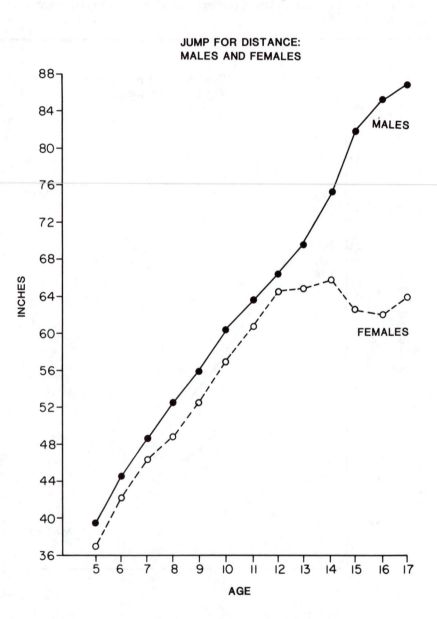

Figure 17.12
Age changes in standing long jump: mean scores for males and females 5–17 years, from post-1960 studies (drawn from data, *Source:* Haubenstricker, J., and Seefeldt, V. [1986]. "Acquisition of Motor Skills During Childhood." In Seefeldt, V. [Ed.] *Physical Activity and Well-Being.* Reston, VA: AAHPERD)

about age 17 (Figure 17.13). The discrepancy between males and females on the standing long jump that begins to appear after age 12 and the widening gap may be explained in a variety of ways. First, jumping for distance incorporates an element of strength. Males from puberty onward demonstrate dramatic strength gains, whereas their female counterparts, because of low levels of circulating androgens, tend to level off in their strength. Therefore, a widening of the gap at this time is to be expected. The tendency of females to regress may also be explained by lack of motivation or increasingly sedentary lifestyles. Changes in body proportions and lower centers of gravity may also contribute to these changes.

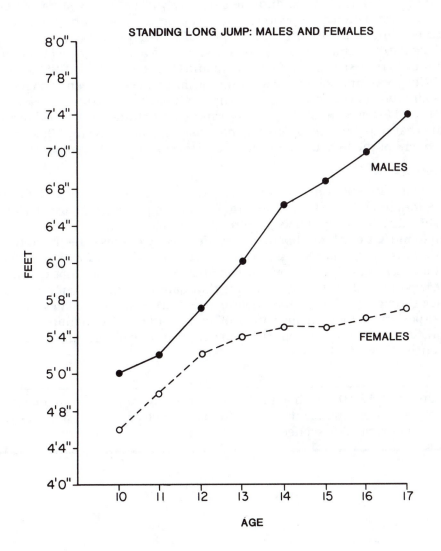

Figure 17.13
Standing long jump mean scores, for males and females 10–17 years, in feet (drawn from data, *Source:* Ross, J. G., et al. [1985]. "The National Children and Youth Fitness Study: New Standards for Fitness Measurement." *Journal of Physical Education, Recreation and Dance,* 56, 1, 62–66)

Throwing for Distance

Throwing for distance is a fequently used measure of muscular power in the upper extremities. As with running for speed and jumping for distance, skill enters into the equation. Those who run, jump, or throw at the mature stage are likely to score well on performance measures that incorporate these skills. The contribution of a mature pattern is no more evident than in throwing for distance. Immature throwers are at a distinct disadvantage. Therefore, significantly lower mean performance scores for females throughout childhood and adolescence may be due to lower skill levels and weakness in the upper arm and shoulder girdle area. Figure 17.14 clearly shows significant differences between males and females at all ages, and the gap only widens with age. Males experience a significant upsurge in performance scores around age 13 corresponding roughly with the onset of puberty. Females, however, demonstrate a much more gradual increase to age 15 followed by a tendency to regress slightly. Reuschlein and Haubenstricker (1985) offered the best explanation for these dramatic differences between genders. In their study of the throwing patterns of 4th, 7th, and 10th graders, 51, 61, and 70 percent of the males, respectively, threw with ''good form'' at what may be considered the mature stage, but only 15, 19, and 23 percent of the females, respectively, threw at the mature stage.

Balance

Williams (1983) in her review of age and gender differences in balance performance found that in general balance improves from ages 3 to 18. Difficulty, however, exists in directly comparing the abundant information that exists on balance. A wide variety of measures have been used over the years to assess both *static balance and dynamic balance,* and, as a result, comparisons between studies are not possible. It is possible, however, to conclude that balance tends to improve with age through childhood and adolescence. Furthermore, females tend to outperform males on measures of both static and dynamic balance during childhood, but appear to have no clear advantage during adolescence (Williams, 1983).

Concept 17.10   Although females tend to outperform males on measures of balance during childhood, no clear pattern appears to exist during adolescence.

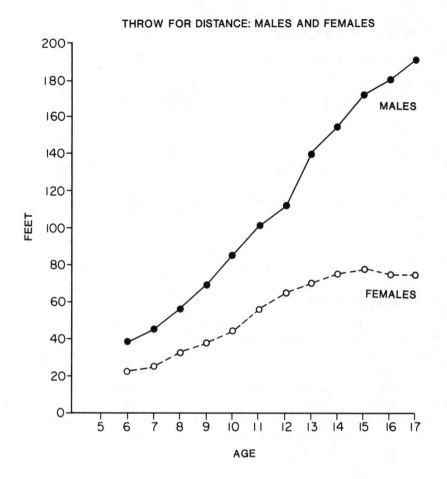

THROW FOR DISTANCE: MALES AND FEMALES

Figure 17.14
Age changes in throwing for distance: mean scores for males and females 6–17 years, from post-1960 studies (drawn from data, *Source:* Haubenstricker, J., and Seefeldt, V. [1986]. "Acquisition of Motor Skills During Childhood." In Seefeldt, V. [Ed.] *Physical Activity and Well-Being.* Reston, VA: AAHPERD)

MALES

FEMALES

FEET

AGE

Summary

The health-related and performance-related fitness of the adolescent changes dramatically from the beginning of the adolescent period to later adolescence. In general, boys and girls are similar throughout childhood on most measures of fitness. The onset of the preadolescent growth spurt marks the beginning of a rapid acceleration in fitness scores for males. This may be associated with a variety of physical as well as social and cultural factors. Females do not display the same rapid improvements as do their male counterparts. There is a decided tendency for adolescent females to improve at a slower rate to about age 15 where they frequently begin to plateau and sometimes regress.

Health-related fitness measures are susceptible to considerable improvement in both males and females. As activity patterns change, we hope for the better, we can anticipate changes in the slope of the performance curves for both males and females. Highly motivated individuals score significantly better on all measures of fitness than the mean score performances reported for population samples.

Terms to Remember

Convenience sample
Interrater reliability
Intrarater reliability
Stratified random sample
Aerobic endurance
Population sample
Field test
Abdominal isotonic strength/
    endurance
Upper body strength/endurance
Isotonic strength/endurance
Joint flexibility

Body composition
Hydrostatic weighing
Electrical impedance
Skinfold calipers
Secular trend
Motor fitness
Running speed
Jumping for distance
Throwing for distance
Static balance
Dynamic balance

Critical Readings

Corbin, C. B., & Pangraz, R. P. (1992). Are American children and youth fit? *Research Quarterly for Exercise and Sport,* 63, 96–106.

Gutin, B. et al. (1992). Defining health and fitness. *Research Quarterly for Exercise and Sport,* 63, 128–131.

Haubenstricker, J., & Seefeldt, V. (1986). Acquisition of motor skills during childhood. In V. Seefeldt (Ed.), *Physical Activity and Well-Being.* Reston, VA: AAHPERD.

Meredith, C. N., & Dwyer, J. T. (1991). Nutrition and exercise: Effects on adolescent health. *Annual Review of Public Health 1991,* 12, 309–333.

Chapter **18**

Adolescent Socialization

CHAPTER COMPETENCIES

Upon completion of this chapter you should be able to:

- *List and describe sociocultural correlates that may affect motor development*
- *Evaluate relationships between sociocultural correlates and motor development*
- *Define the term "adolescence" in terms of biological and sociocultural factors*
- *Demonstrate knowledge about the process of cultural socialization*
- *Discuss the structure of socialization and its implications for the motor behavior of adolescents*
- *List and describe the primary factors that influence cultural socialization*
- *Discuss the role of sport and physical activity on cultural socialization*
- *Describe the impact of physical activity and sport on affiliation, self-esteem, attitude formation, and moral growth*

Key Concept: The process of motor development occurs in social settings through play, games, physical activity, and sport, and is therefore influenced by the cultural setting of the individual.

The term "adolescence" is difficult to define. Not only is it a period of rapid physical change, but it is also a period of social and psychological transition from childhood to adulthood. Different rates of social and psychological maturation are as clearly evident as the variability in physical maturation discussed in previous chapters.

The period of adolescence has lengthened in North America not only for biological reasons, but also because of fundamental societal changes. Compulsory education and longer collegiate and graduate school commitments have increased the duration of financial dependence on parents for many young Americans. The shift from an agrarian to an industrialized state, and the emergence of a technological society, have also extended the period of adolescence. Adolescence is indeed a period of preparation for life, and as life has become more complex, the preparatory period has lengthened.

Adolescent behavior is essentially exploratory. This exploratory behavior should not be viewed as unimportant for it helps adolescents to find their places in society. Exploratory behavior carries high risks. As a result, adolescence is often seen as a turbulent time full of heartaches and problems.

It is naive to assume that the period of adolescence will be as smooth and placid as childhood. This is a time of questioning, challenging, exploring, and critically examining the actions of peers and adults. These pursuits are essential if the adolescent is to make a successful transition from childhood to adulthood. Adolescents should not be expected to display unquestioning obedience to authority. Wise adult leadership, positive role models, and nurturing guidance are essential to the healthy and productive psychosocial process of development through these tumultuous years.

Concept 18.1   Adolescence is characterized by exploration and experimentation, processes which may have lifelong consequences.

To combat the rising and often life-threatening problems of adolescence one must critically examine the causes prior to offering viable solutions. Teen alcohol and drug abuse, pregnancy, delinquency, and suicide are major problems among the teen cultures of many contemporary societies. The choices that are made in these areas have powerful implications and lifelong consequences. Problems in these areas frequently signal failures of the family, peers, schools, and society at large to help adolescents make intelligent and responsible choices in the transition to adulthood.

In this chapter we will examine critical aspects in the process of adolescent socialization. Each of these areas may be significantly influenced by the process of motor development.

Concept 18.2 Socialization involves modifying one's behavior to meet the expectations of a group.

The Structure of Socialization

Cultural socialization is a term that refers to the modification of one's behavior to conform to the expectations of a group. Sage (1986) defined it as "the process by which persons learn the skills, attitudes, values, and behaviors that enable them to participate as members of the society in which they live" (p. 344). Socialization is a lifelong process by which an infant becomes an adult in a cultural setting.

The structure of socialization is dependent upon three factors: status, roles, and norms. *Status* refers to one's position in society. Status is variable in that one may actually have several positions. Adolescents have different levels of status conferred upon them as sons, daughters, students, and athletes. They learn to play the roles associated with the status levels that have been established. Therefore, a *role* is an individual behavior that one employs to fulfill a status. It is the "job description" (status) interacting with the "interpretation of the job" (role). The manner in which a person acts out her role as a daughter, student, or athlete is reflected by the status of that role and certain norms of behavior. *Norms* are standards of behavior expected of all members of a given society. Societal norms are the means by which cultural transmission occurs. Sons and daughters should "act" like "sons and daughters," students should "act" like "students," and athletes should "act" like "athletes." These standards of behavior may change from society to society, but they remain relatively constant within a given society.

Concept 18.3 Cultural socialization is dependent upon the interaction of status, roles, and norms.

Socialization is an active process and should not be viewed as the mere internalization of status, roles, and norms. Although this is important, socialization is more than the passive stamping of society on the individual. We are dynamic, ever-developing beings, and as such we bring a wealth of individual differences to the process of socialization. Cultural socialization should be viewed as an interactive process between society and the individual.

Influencing Factors

Many factors influence the process of socialization, including people, institutions, and activities. Each of these are briefly discussed in the following paragraphs.

People

Family members, peers, friends, and significant adults play critical roles in the social development of the adolescent. The family structure has changed considerably in the last generation and will probably continue to evolve in response to societal pressures. Today, only about one family in four conforms to the traditional family stereotype of the two-parent, one-marriage, multiple-child family with mother as the primary caregiver and homemaker and father as the sole wage earner (Conger and Peterson, 1984). Instead a variety of family patterns may be found: two-income families, single-parent families, childless couples, blended families, and combined non-married households. As a result the role of the "family" in social development has changed. Nevertheless fully 98 percent of all children are still raised in "families" and 79 percent of these children live with two parents (U.S. Department of Commerce, Bureau of the Census, 1987).

The family remains the dominant agent of socialization throughout childhood and well into adolescence. It is responsible, among other things, for fostering a sense of autonomy, love, and trust in the adolescent. It also has tremendous influence in introducing children to physical activity and sport. The socioeconomic status of the family, for example, affects the activity choices of children and youth. Greenspan (1983) found that young swimmers, skiers, and gymnasts tended to come from upper-middle class families, but that young wrestlers, baseball players, and boxers tended to come from lower income homes. Similarly, Greendorfer (1977) and Greendorfer and Lewko (1978) found that family members play a critical role in sport selection and involvement. Parental attitudes, encouragement, and personal participation were found to be important factors in activity selection.

Concept 18.4   The process of socialization is influenced by family members, teachers, coaches, and special friends.

As adolescence approaches and childhood wanes, the dominance of the family is frequently diminished by a rise in the influence of the peer group. Building strong ties to a peer group is a first giant step toward autonomy for the adolescent. With respect to socialization into physical activity and sport, the peer group is dominant during childhood, adolescence, and early adulthood (Greendorfer, 1977). Adolescents participate in sports for group affiliations as well as for skill mastery and opportunities to compete. Parents and coaches need to recognize that activity selection and participation is often less a matter of a desire to compete than it is a matter of wanting to fit in and belong.

Special friends and significant adults outside the family frequently play important roles in the process of adolescent socialization. The influence of these individuals sometimes even overshadows that of the family and the peer group. The respected friend or the revered coach affect the social maturation of the adolescent. Peer counseling and modeling behaviors of respected mentors offer promise as effective techniques for inspiring behavioral changes in adolescents (Carnegie Report, 1987).

Institutions

Adolescents come into contact with a variety of societal institutions that affect how they are socialized into the culture. The school is probably the primary agent if for no other reason than that it occupies the greatest portion of the day for the longest period of time. The school physical education program is responsible for developing fundamental movement and sport skills in the activities of the culture. It is charged with informing children about fitness and helping them develop the skills necessary for healthy lives. While the physical education program has great potential to be a significant socializing agent, it frequently dampens enthusiasm for vigorous physical activity and skill development (Vogel, 1986; Seefeldt, 1987). Programs that are not relevant to students' needs or interests, or are poorly taught and fail to promote learning enjoyment, are doomed to failure.

Concept 18.5   Sport and physical activity have the potential to be powerful socializing agents.

Youth organizations such as the YMCA, YWCA, Boys and Girls Clubs, and a host of youth sport leagues play key roles in adolescent socialization. Youth sport programs are a significant cultural modifier in modern

North American society. An estimated 16 million children between the ages of 6 and 16 participate in non-school-sponsored sports programs (Martens, 1986).

Youth organizations such as the Boy Scouts and the Girl Scouts along with the church are also important institutions of socialization for many children and youth. These agencies promote ethical and moral character. They help youngsters develop values and civic responsibility.

Activities

The activities engaged in by children and adolescents are important in cultural socialization. Children's play, games, and sports activities are key elements in the socialization process. In fact, social development is an often stated objective of physical education (Greendorfer, 1987). Although the research base for this claim is sparse, empirical evidence tends to support the notion that cultural attitudes and values can be transmitted (in some undefined and almost mystical way) through physical activity. The influence of physical activity on psychosocial development will be examined further in the section that follows.

Physical Activity and Socialization

The role of physical activity in the form of play, games, and sport cannot be understated. Growth and motor development do not take place in a vacuum, but rather in a social setting that includes physical activity. The need for group affiliation is a frequently cited reason for participation in peer play and sport (Greendorfer, 1987). Another reason is the enhancement of self-esteem through increased movement competence and confidence (Weiss, 1987). Physical activity as a socializing agent is a powerful influence on attitude formation (Sage, 1986) and moral development (Weiss & Bredemeier, 1986).

Concept 18.6 Games, play, and sport offer opportunities for affiliation and group identity formation.

Affiliation

One of the most compelling forces of later childhood and adolescence is the need to belong. An adolescent's need to be identified as a member of a team or club often sparks interest in physical activity (Seefeldt et al., 1992). The popularity of peer play and youth sport is in large part attributable to the need for affiliation. In fact, when adolescents were asked why they were involved in peer play activity Coakley (1983) reported that one of the most frequently cited reasons was "reaffirmation of friendships" (p. 438). Winning is not often the initial reason for engaging in peer play, but when play is converted to organized sport, winning does become an overriding goal of activity involvement (Sage, 1986).

The need for affiliation, fun, and success must be fulfilled in any sport program. In fact, based on a survey of 8,000 youths who responded to a sport participation and attrition questionnaire tabulated for age, gender, and race, "to have fun" was reported to be the primary reason for sport participation for all groups (Seefeldt et al., 1992). Athletes must have opportunities to compete and excel, but fun and fellowship must not be ignored in a relentless quest to be "number one." Overemphasis on competition is frequently cited as a reason for dropping out of sport activities, along with burnout induced by overtraining and inadequate instruction. It has been estimated that the annual dropout rate for all youth sports is about 35 percent (Gould, 1987).

Sport offers many benefits to its participants, but a healthy balance between competition and cooperation must be maintained. Recognition of the primary need for affiliation should alert teachers, coaches, and parents to the value of play, games, and sport as socializing agents.

Self-Esteem

Self-esteem development begins at birth and is generally stabilized by adolescence (Wylie, 1979; Campbell, 1984). The nature of self-esteem development and the influences of physical activity on the developing self were discussed in Chapter 14 (Childhood Self-Concept Development). Historically, self-concept has been viewed as a global trait, but more recently it has been viewed as a trait that may be factored into several components representing the psychomotor, cognitive, and affective domains (Harter, 1982). Terms such as "movement competence," movement confidence," and "perceived physical competence" refer to dimensional aspects of self-concept related to one's physical sense of self.

Concept 18.7   Self-esteem and achievement are linked, but it is difficult to document that there is a causal relationship.

Physical activity as part of an adolescent's total constellation of behavior provides one important avenue by which self-concept may be reinforced. Weiss (1987) cautioned, however, that:

> A continuing controversy among educators pertains to the causal relationship between self-esteem and achievement. Specifically, does achievement or gains in competence lead to enhanced self-esteem, or does self-esteem influence achievement? That is, does a high level of self-esteem increase the likelihood for successful accomplishment? (pp. 103–104).

In terms of adolescent socialization, the question posed by Weiss, although interesting and in need of clarification, is moot. Regardless of whether self-esteem influences achievement, or achievement influences self-esteem, physical activity plays an important but largely undetermined role in this process. Certainly, we have adequate field data to support the reciprocal concepts. In either case, a stable, positive view of self is an essential aspect of the adolescent socialization process, and physical activity plays a part.

Attitude Formation

A major function of socialization is the transference of the attitudes and values of a culture to its citizens. Basically, an *attitude* is a feeling of like or dislike about something. It is a learned behavior that has placed a value on something or someone. Kenyon (1968) defined an attitude as "a latent and nonobservable complex but relatively stable behavioral disposition reflecting both direction and intensity of feeling toward a particular object, whether it be concrete or abstract" (p. 567). An attitude is an emotion, based on a cognitive knowledge or belief, that results in a behavior that may be either positive or negative (Figure 18.1).

Concept 18.8   Attitude formation is a major function of cultural socialization.

As learned behaviors, attitudes are acquired in a social context, and as such they may be taught, modified, and shaped. Acquisition of an attitude involves three things: compliance, identification, and internalization (Kellman, 1968). *Compliance* is associated with doing something in the hope of getting a favorable response from someone else. For example, a young athlete, although not inclined to stretch out before a training run does so because the coach is watching. *Identification* requires one to adopt the attitude or behavior of another. The runner stretches out in preparation for her training run even when the coach is not around because she knows the coach wants her to do so. *Internalization* deals with taking on a behavior as part of one's value system. Our runner now stretches out prior to her training run because of her own desire to do so.

Physical activity in the form of peer play, games, and sport can mold positive attitudes. Attitudes, when grouped together into the often elusive constructs of "character," "sportsmanship," and "fair play," contribute to the moral development and integrity of the individual.

Moral Growth

Moral behavior within a sport context is called *sportsmanship*. It is commonly believed that participation in sport develops character and instills the moral ideals of a culture in the young athletes. Sport has

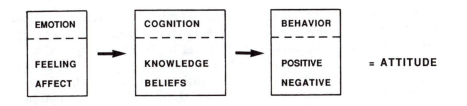

EMOTION		COGNITION		BEHAVIOR	
FEELING		KNOWLEDGE		POSITIVE	= ATTITUDE
AFFECT		BELIEFS		NEGATIVE	

Figure 18.1
Components of attitude formation

great potential for developing moral behavior because of the variety of emotions and unpredictable situations that arise (Coakley, 1990). Sport provides an ideal setting in which to teach the qualities of honesty, loyalty, self-control, and fairness.

Participants distinguish between the "conventional" aspects of sportsmanship and the "moral" aspects. Weiss and Bredemeier (1986) note that "social-conventional behaviors are those which conform to prescribed social norms and are intended to maintain social organization" (p. 373).

Concept 18.9   Moral growth may be fostered through games, play, and sport.

Therefore, shaking hands and congratulating opponents after a contest are not examples of moral behaviors but of accepted standards of conventional behavior. "Moral behaviors are those which are concerned with the physical or psychological welfare of others and the protection of rights and responsibilities" (Weiss & Bredemeier, 1986, p. 375). Refraining from lying, cheating, and intimidating opposing players are moral decisions governed by respect for the rights of others.

Moral development enhances the strength of the conscience. Kohlberg (1981, 1984), a cognitive developmentalist building on the work of Piaget (1932), proposed a three-level hierarchial model of moral development that can be subdivided into six stages. The first level is known as *Preconventional Morality*. The preconventional level is characteristic of the preschool and primary grade child. At this level the child is egocentric, avoids punishment, and responds to power. In stage 1 of this level, the child operates on a "whatever feels good is okay" philosophy. In stage 2, the concept of "it is okay as long as you don't get caught" predominates. At the *Conventional Morality Level* there is a real desire to win approval and to please others. Being liked and conforming to group norms are important individual goals at stage 3 of this level. At stage 4, the law and order stage, the individual recognizes that behavior is governed by the rules of society and that laws define what is right. Operation at the conventional level is typical of the childhood and adolescent period. In fact, some experts suggest that most people do not get beyond stage 4. At the *Postconventional Morality Level* the individual is inner-directed rather than other-directed. At stage 5, the social contract stage, the individual recognizes that what is "right" is what is agreed on by the whole of society, and that some laws are unjust and can be changed. Personal behavior at this level is not regulated by law but by personal decisions about right and wrong. At stage 6, the universal ethical principle stage, the individual exhibits the highest level of morality, according to Kohlberg. At this stage the individual determines right and wrong within a logical, consistent, and universal framework. The dignity and worth of all of humankind is recognized (Figure 18.2).

Concept 18.10   Moral dissonance provides a "climate" for moral reasoning which may lead to moral behavior.

Moral development is not automatic but requires social settings in which moral dilemmas can be provoked, worked out, and restructured. Play activities, games, and sport offer ideal settings in which all levels of moral behavior can be observed and developed and real moral growth can occur. Unless the thought process is stimulated dissonance (i.e., incongruity, or lack of agreement between "what is" and "what should

Figure 18.2
Kohlberg's stages of moral development

be'' thought about) will not occur. If dissonance does not occur, it is unlikely that moral growth will take place. Figure 18.3 provides a schematic representation of the steps leading to moral behavior.

Summary

Socialization is a lifelong process that is particularly important during the period of adolescence. Cultural socialization is influenced by status, roles, and societal norms of behavior. Adolescents are confronted with changing status and an increasing number of roles to play. Adolescents are shaped by society, and society is shaped by them.

A variety of societal factors affect the process of adolescent socialization. Other people, institutions, and activities serve as primary socializing agents. Physical activity is an important arena of adolescent socialization. The games, play, and sport of one's culture offer opportunities for affiliation, self-esteem enhancement, attitude formation, and moral growth.

The process of development is continual and multi-faceted. Motor development both influences and is influenced by the process of cultural socialization.

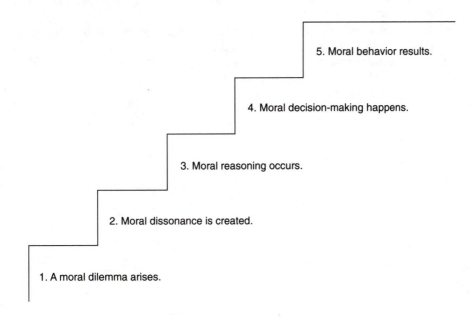

5. Moral behavior results.

4. Moral decision-making happens.

3. Moral reasoning occurs.

2. Moral dissonance is created.

1. A moral dilemma arises.

Figure 18.3
The steps leading to moral behavior (*Source:* Gallahue, D. L. (1993). *Developmental Physical Education for Today's Children.* Dubuque, IA: Brown & Benchmark)

Terms to Remember

Cultural socialization
Status
Roles
Norms
Attitude
Compliance
Identification

Internalization
Sportsmanship
Morality
Preconventional morality
Conventional morality
Postconventional morality

Critical Readings

Bredemeier, B. J., & Shields, D. L. (1987). Moral growth through physical activity: A structural/developmental approach. In D. Gould and M. R. Weiss (Eds.), *Advances in Pediatric Sport Sciences (Vol. 2: Behavioral Issues)*. Champaign, IL: Human Kinetics.

Coakley, J. J. (1987). Children and the sport socialization process. In D. Gould and M. R. Weiss. *Advances in Pediatric Sport Sciences. (Vol. 2: Behavioral Issues)*. Champaign, IL: Human Kinetics.

Coakley, J. J. (1990). *Sport in Society: Issues and Controversies*. Boston, MA: Times Mirror/Mosby.

Sage, G. H. (1986). Social development. In V. Seefeldt (Ed.), *Physical Activity and Well-Being*. Reston, VA: AAHPERD.

Seefeldt, V., et al. (1992). *Overview of Youth Sports Programs in the United States*. New York: Carnegie Council on Adolescent Development.

Weiss, M. R., & Bredemeier, B. J. (1986). Moral development. In V.Seefeldt (Ed.), *Physical Activity and Well-Being*. Reston, VA: AAHPERD.

SECTION **V**

ADULTHOOD

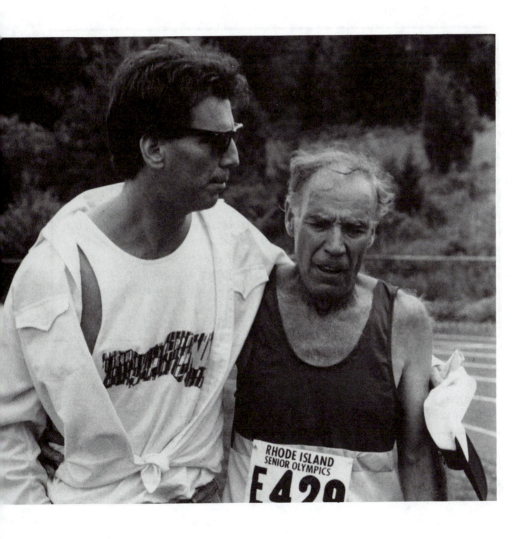

Chapter **19**

Physiological Changes in Adults

CHAPTER COMPETENCIES

Upon completion of this chapter you should be able to:

- *Discuss the limitations of generalizing about declines during the adult years*
- *Describe how the interaction among characteristics of the individual, the nature of the task, and the environmental conditions affects the motor performance of adults*
- *Discuss how the concepts of task specificity, interindividual variability, and intraindividual variability influence the success levels of adult motor performance*
- *Describe the theories of aging related to cellular changes, the human immune system, and homeostasis*
- *Identify age-related changes in the musculoskeletal system*
- *Identify age-related changes in the central nervous sytem*
- *Identify age-related changes in the circulatory and respiratory systems*
- *Identify age-related changes in the sensory systems*

Key Concept: Throughout adulthood, changes in the body's physiological systems may influence motor performance and may represent a mechanism of the aging process.

As we enter adulthood, we experience a number of physical and physiological changes that affect our behavior. Likewise, as we continue through the life span process, changes in our affective and cognitive abilities alter how we respond to our environment. As discussed in earlier chapters, these domains are not mutually exclusive, but are intricately interrelated. These relationships are evident when an older individual compensates for an age-related slowing of reaction time by using different cognitive strategies to accomplish a task. We also see the association between the different domains when older individuals experience declines in self-competency and self-esteem as age-related changes in muscular strength begin to limit their abilities to perform functional daily living skills.

Concept 19.1 As we advance through adulthood, aspects from the motor, cognitive, and affective domains interact to affect motor behavior.

When we generalize about behavior and performance across the life span we usually make the observation that individuals experience continual improvement from infancy through adolescence, a leveling off during young adulthood, a slow decline during middle adulthood, and a much greater decline during older adulthood. There is, however, a major problem when we describe a complex event like human development in such simplistic terms. This oversimplified perception of the aging process can place unrealistic expectations on young children and unnecessary limitations on older adults. In adulthood some functions follow the generalistic pattern, but other characteristics show no signs of deterioration, and some show the capacity for continual improvement. Spirduso and MacRae (1990) point out that variability in the motor performance of adults increases with each decade of life. "The descriptions of 'average' behavior for specific age groups grow less and less accurate for an individual's performance as the age of the group increases" (p. 183).

The motor behavior exhibited by an individual is dependent upon the interaction of a number of variables categorized by: (1) the nature of the task, (2) the environmental conditions, and (3) the cognitive, affective, and psychomotor characteristics of the individual. The nature of a task involves such elements as degree of difficulty, duration, and the need for speed or accuracy. An older adult whose vision has weakened may not be able to perform a specific task successfully if it involves speed. If, however, there are no time requirements, the individual may complete the task with a high degree of success.

Concept 19.2 While many age-related changes reflect general trends, individual characteristics play a major role in determining whether a person follows those trends.

Examples of the environmental conditions that may influence motor behavior include room temperature, lighting, floor surface texture, and degree of familiarity of surroundings. An older individual with an age-related slowing of the circulatory system will likely feel quite uncomfortable in a cool room. Discomfort and stiffness could limit his ability to complete required tasks.

The third category related to motor behavior pertains to the state of the individual. In reference to the cognitive domain, the ability to understand skill instructions is vital to the successful completion of a motor task. An inability to follow verbal instructions may be the result of an age-related loss in hearing, which could prevent or restrict pertinent information from reaching otherwise healthy processing centers of the brain. On the other hand, an older person who appears to have trouble understanding verbal instructions may suffer from Alzheimer's disease (a disease that greatly affects cerebral functioning). Affective domain characteristics that may influence motor behavior include motivation, peer relationships, and self-confidence. An older adult who has recently lost a spouse or a close friend may lack the motivation to be physically active or to try hard in the performance of a motor task he regards as unimportant. Finally, in the motor domain, physiological changes play a crucial role in the performance of a motor task. Older adults usually experience declines in muscular strength, vision, and other systems. These age-related changes will be discussed in greater detail later in this chapter.

Concept 19.3   Individual characteristics, demands of the task, and environmental circumstances are major factors in determining the level of success experienced by the adult in performance of a motor task.

In reviewing various aspects of motor performance in the adulthood years, key principles begin to emerge. The first of these is that the maturity or success of the performance of a motor task is *task specific*. The generalization that the motor performance of an individual will deteriorate with age may be true for some tasks but certainly not for all. The degree of performance success depends upon the specific demands of the task. Does the task require speed of movement, accuracy, or both? Does the task require a specific amount of joint flexibility or cardiovascular endurance? Does the task require a great deal of memorization? As we mentioned earlier in this chapter, certain physiological systems will experience age-related functional decline through adulthood, while other physiological systems may remain relatively unchanged. If the demands of a particular task require an individual to use a physiological system that is in decline, his performance may be less than ideal. If, however, the motor task demands require the use of physiological systems that are healthy, no physiological limitations should prevent him from performing the task successfully. Other limiting factors (i.e., environmental constraints) may impair task performance, but these also follow the concept of task specificity. A high degree of room illumination may be necessary for the completion of one task, while it may have little or no bearing on whether another task is completed successfully.

Concept 19.4   The aging of various physiological systems varies among adults and within individual adults.

A second principle that emerges from this review is that there is a tremendous amount of *inter-individual variability* in how people age. Both genetics and lifestyle play vital roles in determining the life spans of individuals. A person who has a lineage of nonagenarians (persons 90 years of age or older, but less than 100) probably has in her genetic blueprint the makings of a long life. Her lifestyle choices will affect whether her longevity will reach its genetic potential. Level of physical activity, smoking, stress, drug abuse, and diet are important lifestyle variables that impact the number of years we live. Similarly, in the area of motor performance in adults, a certain physiological system may deteriorate more slowly in one individual than in another because of genetic differences. If a motor task requires a high degree of muscular strength, for example, the person who genetically loses muscular strength at a slower rate may have an easier time completing the task than a person whose ancestors tended to experience strength loss more rapidly. An individual's lifestyle choices may affect various physiological systems and, in turn, may influence the performance of a motor task dependent on the healthy functioning of those physiological systems. A number of additional variables affect the outcomes of motor tasks. We cannot isolate a single variable and predict the likelihood of success. We can, however, realize that genetic blueprints and lifestyles vary widely and consequently affect the motor performances of specific tasks in different ways, depending upon requirements of the tasks.

This leads into the next principle of *intra-individual variability.* Individual physiological systems do not necessarily experience age-related declines at the same rate. Certain physiological characteristics will begin to decline in early adulthood, while others wait until later. Still other characteristics will not experience declines at all. Generalizing about the overall developmental rate of an individual without taking into consideration variations among her personal characteristics may limit her movement potential.

Combining the three principles of task specificity, inter-individual variability, and intra-individual variability with the knowledge that motor performance can vary in accordance with the task, the environment, and the individual provides us with the foundation to evaluate the motor performance of adults from an individual basis rather than a generalistic approach. A percentage of the adult-aged population will face limitations and stereotyping when their performances are evaluated with a generalistic approach. As with children and adolescents, the motor performance of adults should be assessed using individual characteristics following their individual developmental rates.

Why Do We Age?

A number of theories seek to provide the answer to the age-old question of "Why do we age?" Many early theorists suggested that the human body simply wears out through the wear and tear of daily living. They compared the human body to a machine that breaks down and wears out parts with continual use (and sometimes abuse). The performance of the machine deteriorates, and it eventually ceases to operate. This analogy suggests that deterioration is a continual process. While this may be the case with some human characteristics, it is not representative of the total aging process. Numerous investigations have demonstrated that the use of the human body (i.e., through exercise and physical activity) can slow, stop, or in some cases reverse aspects of age-related deterioration.

Concept 19.5 Changes at the cellular level, at the immune system level, and/or in the interaction of the physiological systems may represent the underlying causes of aging.

More recently, a number of theories have been presented to address the question of why we age. The level at which these theories approach the aging question range from the cellular to the whole organism.

At the cellular level we are interested in what happens to the integrity of the cells of the human body during aging. Every part of the body is structured of cells. Each cell has a specific function and possesses the genetic material to accomplish that function. Cells divide and increase in number for growth, maturation, and/or maintenance of a particular organ or tissue. What has been demonstrated is that the number of times a cell can divide is limited. Hayflick (1965) observed that connective tissue cells divided approximately 50 times. It is possible that the cells are programmed genetically to shut down after a certain number of replications. Another possibility is that the genetic material that dictates cell function may change or mutate as time passes. As these mutated cells increase, either through ongoing cell mutation and/or replication during cell division, they may cause deterioration in the tissue or organ. Depending upon the function of the affected organ or tissue, deficits may appear in motor performance, overall health, or both. The likelihood of such deficits increases when these cellular changes occur in more than one organ or tissue.

A second approach to understanding why we age involves the function of the human immune system, which consists of the lymph nodes, spleen, thymus, and lymphoid tissue in the tonsils and intestine. The purpose of the immune system is to protect us from various organisms that enter the body. With age, the human immune system gradually decreases in effectiveness. This increases the vulnerability of older adults to illnesses and extends their recovery times. In addition, the immune system of an older individual may, in fact, begin to target healthy organ and tissue cells for destruction, as if they were "bad" cells. These immune system malfunctions may represent the process by which we age.

A third possible explanation as to why we age involves the concept of *homeostasis*. Homeostasis refers to the maintenance of stability in the physiological systems and their interrelationships. Homeostasis is the state in which various systems of the body (i.e., sensory, digestive, and cardiovascular) work in harmony to keep the body in normal, healthy condition. The human body is an incredibly complex network of systems that carry out their functions both independently and in combination. Guyton (1991) states that the cells of the organs and tissues within the interrelated systems benefit from a homeostatic state and contribute to its maintenance. This harmonious state is maintained until a particular system or group of systems malfunctions or cannot contribute to the maintenance of homeostasis. The degree to which negative consequences are manifested depends upon the ability of the other systems to adapt and the degree to which the dysfunctional system is unable to contribute to the homeostatic network. A moderate level of dysfunction in a particular system may impair health and the ability to carry out functional daily living skills. A high level of disruption leads to death.

There appears to be a reciprocal relationship between aging and the maintenance of a homeostatic state. With age, the balance among the systems involved in homeostasis is less stable and more vulnerable to disruption. Individual systems appear to experience age-related decreases in their ability to contribute to the homeostatic equilibrium. Subsequently, age-related characteristics begin to emerge. Greater susceptibility to illnesses, longer recovery times from illnesses, and greater limitations in motor performance become more prevalent.

Physiological Changes in the Adult Musculoskeletal System

The human skeleton is multifaceted in its function. It protects internal organs, gives form to the body, acts as levers from which muscles attach, provides a reserve site for calcium, and develops blood cells in the bone marrow. Skeletal muscles excited by the central nervous system move most of the bones of the body. In addition, the muscles, tendons, and ligaments provide stability to the articulating joints throughout the body.

Skeleton

Various changes within the skeletal structure appear as a person ages. Many individuals experience a shortening in stature. This "shrinkage" may be attributed to one or more causes. As we age the discs that separate the vertebrae of the spinal column undergo various changes. In a healthy state, intervertebral discs possess jelly-like nuclei. The vertebral discs of older adults often lose a portion of the water content important for shock absorption, and the disks become more fibrous. This, along with changes in bone mineral density in the vertebrae, results in compression of the discs. Disk compression reduces the length of the vertebral column and causes the subsequent loss of overall height. Other contributors to age-related height loss include spinal misalignment and poor posture. Curving of the spine may result from a reduction of the shock-absorption capacity of the vertebral disks. Postural problems may reflect weakening in the muscles that support the spine and thorax (rib cage). While these conditions appear in many older adults, they are not inevitable. While a certain amount of vertebral water content loss may occur, the muscles supporting the spine and thorax can maintain strength through physical activity and proper exercises. In addition, the loss of bone mineral content may be prevented or slowed through proper treatment.

Concept 19.6   Osteoporosis represents a potentially debilitating disease that requires the attention of individuals at all stages of adulthood.

The disease *osteoporosis* may contribute to height reduction in older adults, but its other consequences can be much more devastating. Osteoporosis is characterized by a reduction of *bone mineral density* severe enough to increase vulnerability to fractures of the bone (Figure 19.1). In healthy bone, the ongoing process of bone mineral production and absorption maintains a balance in calcium metabolism regulated by the endocrine system. With age, that balance between absorption and production becomes less stable, and more bone mineral content is absorbed than is produced. While this imbalance normally leads to a

Figure 19.1
Bone loss due to osteoporosis

Neck
of Femur

Magnified internal view of bone formation
of healthy adult femur.

Magnified internal view of bone formation
of osteoporotic adult femur.

slight age-related loss in bone density, osteoporosis accelerates the process. As the bone mineral content is reduced, the bones become increasingly porous and fragile. Fractures can occur within a bone, causing that bone to compress. These compression fractures are often seen in the spinal column of older adults with osteoporosis. Normal weight-bearing stress on the spinal column causes tiny fractures in the individual vertebrae. As more and more fractures occur, the vertebrae become more compressed and the position of the thorax is altered. This positional change can adversely affect the functions of the lungs and other internal organs directly below the thorax region. In addition, postural deviations and spinal deformities are common with osteoporosis (Figure 19.2).

Figure 19.2
Skeletal changes
with osteoporosis
(*Source:* F. Kaplan,
*Clinical Symposia
CIBA* 35, No. 5,
1983. Reprinted by
permission)

Progressive Spinal Deformity in Osteoporosis

Age
55 years

Age
65 years

Age
75 years

Compression fractures of thoracic vertebrae lead to loss of height and progressive thoracic
kyphosis (dowager's hump). Lower ribs eventually rest on iliac crests, and downward pressure
on viscera causes abdominal distention

While individuals with osteoporosis are more vulnerable to fractures
within a bone, fractures *of* the bone also represent a major concern. As
the bone mineral content declines and bones become more porous, the
individual with osteoporosis is at great risk of bone breakage as a result
of minimal trauma. We often hear reports of older adults falling and
breaking their hips. Even the force experienced from a fairly mild fall
may be sufficient to break a brittle femur ravaged by osteoporosis. Of
additional concern is that osteoporotic bones heal at a much slower rate
than healthy bones.

Osteoporosis can occur in both men and women, but it is present in
a much higher rate in postmenopausal women. Hormonal changes experienced by women following menopause may disrupt bone mineral
formation. Other factors that play a role in maintaining bone density
are calcium intake and weight-bearing physical activity. Calcium plays
an important role in regulating bone metabolism, and weight-bearing
stress aids in building and maintaining bone density. Hormonal changes,
the reduction of calcium intake, and restrictions in weight-bearing exercises place an individual at risk for significant bone mineral loss.

It has been demonstrated that astronauts in space suffered substantial bone mineral loss after only a few weeks in a weightless environment. Upon arriving back to earth's gravitational pull and performing various exercises, they recovered most but not all of their pre-flight bone density. This phenomenon confounds the situation for the older adult who is recovering from a hip fracture. The weight-bearing restrictions placed on the broken hip for healing purposes can further increase bone mineral loss.

Drinkwater has called osteoporosis the "silent thief of the golden years" (1992). Outward signs of the disease are usually not evident until the vertebrae experience compression fractures. Posture deviations become apparent, or the individual begins to experience back pain from spinal misalignment. However, since the late 1970s diagnostic technology has been able to safely and accurately identify an individual's bone density. Because osteoporosis is preventable, using such technology to monitor bone density is essential and should begin in early adulthood. Comparing an individual's bone density with a bone density standard for healthy young adults will tell a physician if that person is subject to an accelerated bone loss rate. Treatment can minimize future bone loss. While osteoporosis is preventable, it is not reversible as of yet. However, diagnosis and treatment can restrict further bone loss, even in those individuals whose bone mineral stores are depleted.

Treatment for osteoporosis involves hormonal replacement for postmenopausal women, increasing calcium intake, and, of particular interest to the movement specialist, increasing weight-bearing exercises. Drinkwater points out a principle of specificity that applies to weight-bearing activities. Weight-bearing stress must be directed to a specific bone area for that bone to be affected. This is valuable information for movement professionals planning physical activities for individuals with osteoporosis.

Muscles and Joints

Muscular strength is essential for the performance of motor skills, whether they are related to high-level athletic performance or daily functional living. With age the structure and function of skeletal muscles change. Structurally, muscle mass decreases as the number and size of muscle fibers decline through the late middle and older adulthood years. Functionally, a decrease in muscular strength seems to parallel this loss in muscle tissue. The general adulthood pattern for muscle strength is represented by a peak in strength at about 25 to 30 years, a plateau until approximately 50 years, and a gradual decline until about 70 years, followed by a much sharper strength decline in the succeeding years (Figure 19.3). Cross-sectional data indicate an approximate 20 percent loss in strength by the 6th decade and a more drastic 40 percent strength loss in the 7th and 8th decades. Longitudinal data appear to support the loss of strength in the older adult years, but indicate that significant strength declines are not manifested until the early older adulthood years rather than the late middle adulthood years.

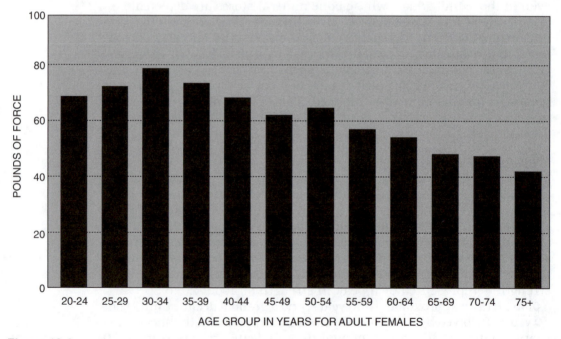

Figure 19.3
Muscular strength across adulthood (adult male and female mean right grip strength measures) Data graphed from Mathiowetz et al. (1985)

While the previous paragraph outlined a generalistic viewpoint regarding the age-related muscle performance, several variables should be considered concerning the performance of an individual. While a loss of muscle mass or *muscle atrophy* appears to occur with age, muscle atrophy also occurs as a result of inactivity. Inactivity-induced atrophy can occur at any age, and is not just a function of growing old. There is substantial evidence that adults who maintain physically active lifestyles experience much smaller declines in muscular strength than their non-active peers. In subjects 90 years or older, it has been demonstrated that a strength training program improves muscular strength and increases muscle mass (Fiatarone et al., 1990). Clearly, an individual's lifestyle represents a key variable in determining whether her muscular strength capacity will follow or deviate from the general curve.

Another important consideration about strength involves the requirements of a particular task. While the term "muscular strength" is often used to describe the muscle functions of a particular movement task, most skills require some combination of muscular strength and muscular endurance. It has been demonstrated that muscular endurance is less affected by aging than is muscular strength. In fact, Dummer et al. (1985) found no significant differences between the muscular endurance of young adult swimmers and older adult swimmers. Their findings indicate that it may be possible to offset age-related declines in muscular endurance by engaging in physically active lifestyles. It likewise makes us aware that an older adult may be more likely to complete muscular endurance-related motor tasks than muscular strength-related tasks.

While a general trend in age-related changes in muscle function is apparent, tremendous inter-individual variability exists. The loss of muscle mass often seen with increasing years is also affected by the adult's levels of physical activity and muscle usage. In addition, the muscle function demands of various tasks influence task performance outcome.

Joints and connective tissues appear to undergo age-related changes. Joints become less flexible. In general terms, joint flexibility peaks for young adults in their 20s and gradually declines. Much of the reduction of flexibility can be attributed to water loss in the connective tissue resulting in greater stiffness of ligaments and tendons. There is also an age-related loss in the water content of the cartilage tissue. A loss of flexibility, and in some cases a loss of joint stability, can be of significant consequence to the older adult in carrying out everyday functional living tasks. Physically active lifestyles and stretching exercises appear to retard age-related loss in joint flexibility.

At the extreme end, age-related joint diseases such as osteoarthritis not only place limitations on certain movements but can totally restrict them as well. Osteoarthritis is the most prevalent form of arthritis in people who are 50 years of age or older, and at least half of the population over 60 years of age show some symptoms of the disease. Treatment involves therapy to maintain joint activity and flexibility, relief of pain and other symptoms, and in extreme cases, total joint replacement surgery.

Central Nervous System

The components of the central nervous system (CNS) are the brain and spinal cord, with the neuron representing the basic unit by which signals are transmitted. There are approximately 100 billion neurons in the human brain requiring an incredibly complex network of neuronal connections. The three primary elements of the neuron are the cell body, axon, and dendrite (Figure 19.4).

Dendrites carry signals to the cell body, while axons carry signals away. Signal transmissions throughout the CNS are both electrical and chemical in nature. Electrical signals travel along dendritic branches to the cell body and then along the axon. The transmission of the signal from one neuron to another involves altering the electrical signal to a chemical signal and then back to an electrical signal. This occurs at the junction between two neurons. The chemical substances released during this event are called *neurotransmitters.*

Figure 19.4
Structure of the neuron

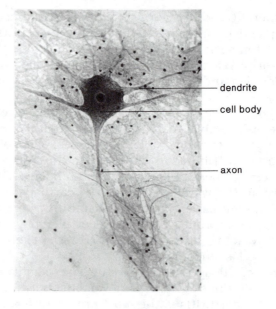

dendrite

cell body

axon

Concept 19.7 Age-related structural changes in the central nervous system may result in decrements of various functions.

A number of age-related changes occur in the CNS. Structurally, the brain experiences a continual loss of neurons that are not replaced. We are born with all of our nerve cells, and when they die they are not replaced. We lose thousands of brain cells each day without generating replacements. Consequently, the brain of the older adult is smaller and weighs less than the brain of a younger adult. In addition, the size of the ventricles or brain cavities increase, particularly during older adulthood. While this age-related neuronal loss is sufficient to decrease brain size and weight, some sections of the brain are less susceptible to neuron decreases than others. The cerebral cortex experiences a 10 to 20 percent loss of mass between the ages of 20 to 90, while other sections of the brain may undergo as much as a 50 percent loss in mass. Therefore, any functional changes that may occur as a result of neuronal loss should be considered specific to certain regions.

While it should follow that the loss of millions of neurons through adulthood would affect behavior, this assumption ignores the adaptable nature of the brain or what is called *brain plasticity*. Neurons are continually dying, but there is evidence that living neurons develop compensatory dendritic branches to help maintain connections that may otherwise deteriorate. Although the pathway connections may be maintained, the strength of the signal may be reduced or distorted when fewer neurons are involved in the signal transmission. In addition, signals that deviate slightly from their designated courses may not be corrected. The ultimate changes in behavior due to neuron loss remain unclear. While compensation mechanisms may maintain signal pathways, the quality of those signals may be compromised.

Other manifestations that appear to be age-related are abnormal formations including *neurofibrillary tangles, senile plaques*, and an accumulation of *lipofuscin*. These formations are often referred to as *age markers* because they appear in the older brain and increase in number as the brain continues to age. Neurofibrillary tangles occur when long, thin fibers that transport chemical substances to all parts of the neuron become twisted and entangled. It is thought that these neurofibrillary tangles may contribute to a slowing of CNS responsiveness (Rybash et al., 1991) and may play a role in the eventual death of the neuron in which they are housed. Senile plaques are spherical formations composed of substances remaining from degenerated neurons. The plaques are located outside of the neuron and may interfere with normal neuronal transmission by disrupting the synaptic juncture. Experts suggest that senile plaques may play a role in memory loss. Neurofibrillary tangles and senile plaques are also present in large quantities in the brains of individuals with Alzheimer's disease. Lipofuscin is a brownish or yellowish pigment that appears in neurons as the brain ages. The effects of lipofuscin on neuronal function have not been confirmed, but there is a greater concentration of the pigment around less active neurons. Therefore, the presence of lipofuscin may retard or inhibit cell activity.

As mentioned earlier, neurotransmitters are instrumental in the sending and receiving of neuronal signals. They are chemical substances that regulate the passage of signals across the synaptic junction. As the brain ages, this biochemical activity is often affected. The amount of neurotransmitter available as the signal reaches the synapse may be reduced, and the signal may decrease in strength. Extreme deficiencies of the neurotransmitter Dopamine is characteristic of Parkinson's disease.

Finally, the aging brain is susceptible to *hypoxia,* a condition in which the brain receives an inadequate amount of oxygen. Nerve cells of the brain are particularly vulnerable to oxygen deficits which affects their function and longevity. With age, the circulation of oxygen-carrying blood gradually declines due to structural changes in the circulatory system and decreases in physical activity. The movement specialist must remember that increasing the level of physical activity in the older adult can enhance the blood flow to the brain, and in turn, increase the amount of oxygen reaching the nerve cells.

Circulatory and Respiratory Systems

The circulatory system involves the heart, blood vessels, and blood delivering nutrients to and removing wastes from the organs and tissues of the body (Figure 19.5). The nose, mouth, pharynx, larynx, trachea, bronchi, and lungs comprising the respiratory system serve the body's organs and tissues by providing oxygen and eliminating carbon dioxide (Figure 19.6). Both systems must function properly to keep the body healthy, and they play important roles in the performance of many tasks. Sufficient oxygen and nutrient delivery and waste transport are necessary for muscle fibers, neurons, and all cells of the body to carry out their appointed functions.

Concept 19.8   Declines in an adult's circulatory and respiratory functions may be the result of age, disease, lifestyle, or combinations of the three.

While a number of changes take place in the main organs and tissues of the circulatory and respiratory systems as adults age, it is extremely difficult to determine the underlying cause or causes of these

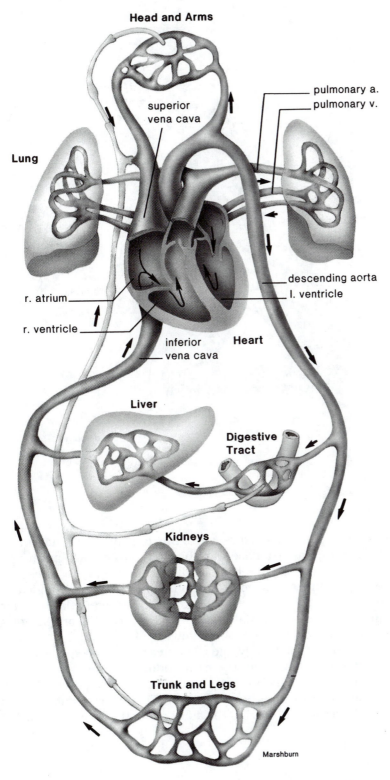

Figure 19.5
Characteristics of the circulatory system (*Source:* From Sylvia S. Mader, *Understanding Human Anatomy and Physiology*. Copyright © 1991 Wm. C. Brown Communications, Inc., Dubuque, IA. All rights reserved. Reprinted by permission.)

Head and Arms

superior vena cava

pulmonary a.
pulmonary v.

Lung

descending aorta
l. ventricle

r. atrium

r. ventricle

inferior vena cava

Heart

Liver

Digestive Tract

Kidneys

Trunk and Legs

Marshburn

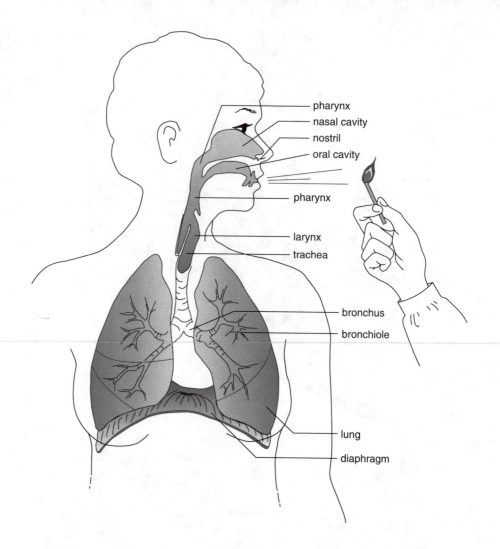

Figure 19.6
Characteristics of
the respiratory
system

pharynx
nasal cavity
nostril
oral cavity
pharynx
larynx
trachea
bronchus
bronchiole
lung
diaphragm

changes. Lifestyle choices, disease, aging, or some combination thereof contribute to changes that occur in these two systems. Separating these variables and delineating their individual effects on the systemic changes represents an arduous and sometimes impossible endeavor, but certain factors are more easily identified as age-related, lifestyle-associated, or disease-initiated. When possible the origins of these changes will be addressed in the following discussion.

As the adult human body ages, the heart and blood vessels tend to undergo changes that affect their functions. Arteries serve as the primary pathways by which oxygenated blood is pumped to the various organs and tissues throughout the body. The arterial walls contract to keep the blood moving. During the adult years the arterial walls become less elastic and more rigid, representing a condition known as *arterio-sclerosis.* An increase in calcification and a buildup of collagen connective tissue in the arteries cause arteriosclerosis, which occurs as a result of aging rather than disease. A second condition, *atheroscle-rosis,* is also seen in adults as they become older, but it represents a cardiovascular disease rather than the normal aging process. Atherosclerosis occurs when fatty deposits begin to collect within arteries. If the deposits do not completely close off the arterial openings, they create sites on the arterial walls on which blood clots can form. Both arteriosclerosis and atherosclerosis affect the performance of the circulatory system. With both conditions there is an increase in blood pressure and a decrease in the amount of oxygen and nutrients reaching the cells of the body. This may impair the performance efficiency of the organs and tissues.

Other circulatory changes seen in adults as they age include changes in the valves of the heart and vessels. Valves within the circulatory system become thicker and less elastic. As a result, they work less efficiently.

A number of age-related changes are observed in the organs involved in respiration. The function of the lungs tends to increase through adolescence, plateau in the third decade, and gradually decline thereafter. While this decline follows an age-related pattern, the reduction during the fourth and fifth decades tends to be linked to factors such as an increase in body weight rather than to actual changes in the tissues. Other age-related variables that influence lung function include reduced levels of muscular strength in the muscle groups that aid in respiration. Postural problems often experienced by older adults may anatomically restrict the expansion capabilites of the lungs. Curvatures of the spine can compress the thorax and push the lungs against other internal organs, impairing the work of the lungs and the other crowded organs.

Maximal oxygen uptake (VO_2 max) represents the best physiological measure of total body endurance. It serves to evaluate the greatest amount of oxygen that reaches the tissues during a maximum exercise effort by an individual. The general age-related trend in maximal oxygen uptake levels begins with a continual increase during childhood and adolescence. A plateauing during the 20s is followed by a gradual decline of approximately 1 percent for each subsequent year. Much of this continuous loss during middle adulthood can be attributed to other age-associated conditions such as a decline in the amount of blood pumped by the heart to the tissues and a loss of muscle mass. However, it has been demonstrated that the annual 1 percent loss in VO_2 max can be reduced by as much as one half if a person maintains a physically active lifestyle and constant body composition (Heath, Hagberg, Ehsani, & Holloszy, 1981).

Sensory Systems

We gain information about the environment through various sensory systems. Different sensory receptors send to the central nervous system information about taste, smell, vision, touch, pain, and sound, to name a few sensations. Some sensory systems play crucial roles in motor performance, in particular visual, auditory, and proprioception.

Concept 19.9   Age-related changes in the eyes and ears can result in insufficient or distorted visual, auditory, and proprioceptive transmissions to the brain.

Visual System

For many if not most movement skills, vision represents the dominant sensory system. Vision occurs when the eye receives light rays that have been reflected by objects in the visual field. As the light rays reach the eye, they are refracted as they pass through the cornea, aqueous humor, pupil, lens, and vitreous humor before the image reaches the retina (Figure 19.7). Refraction involves a process of bending the light rays. The degree to which the rays are bent depends upon the transparency of the eye structures and the angles of light rays as they enter the eye. The cornea is the fibrous, transparent covering of the eyeball. The aqueous humor is a watery solution located in a chamber just behind the cornea and in front of the pupil and lens. Muscles attached to the iris contract or relax to determine pupil size. The size of the pupil regulates the amount of light that passes through the crystalline lens and into the vitreous body. The vitreous body holds a jelly-like fluid called the vitreous humor. After the light rays have been refracted through the various transparent medium, they form an image on the retina, the inner membrane of the eyeball. The retina transfers the image by way of the optic nerve to the cortex of the brain.

With age, the eye tends to undergo a number of structural and functional changes that affect the quality of vision. Visual quality is generally maintained during the early adulthood years, but anatomical changes that begin to occur during middle adulthood have a gradual but detrimental affect on visual abilities. However, such declines during these middle adulthood years rarely limit the ability to carry out everyday tasks. During the older adulthood years the visual decrements experienced in middle adulthood become more pronounced and have a greater impact on functional and adaptive abilities.

As the eye ages, the cornea begins to flatten somewhat, increases in thickness, and develops surface waviness and irregularities. These changes in the curvature of the outer eye alter the pathway of the light rays entering the eye and diminish the accuracy of the refractory process. The amount of light that eventually reaches the lens is reduced by

Vitreous humor

Cornea

Pupil

Lens

Aqueous humor

Optic nerve

Retina

Kasnot

Figure 19.7
Structure of the eye (*Source:* From John W. Hole, *Human Anatomy and Physiology*,
6th edition. Copyright © 1993 Wm. C. Brown Communications, Inc., Dubuque, IA.
All rights reserved. Reprinted by permission.)

the age-related changes in the constricting and dilating properties of the
eye muscles regulating pupil size. The eyes of older adults do not respond to changes in light intensity as rapidly as those of young adults.
When light is dim, the pupils of older adults do not open as widely as
they did in previous years. This condition is known as *senile miosis*.
The amount of light received by the lens of an older person with senile
miosis can range from one tenth to one third that of younger adults. The
lens undergoes a variety of changes, particularly in the older adult years.
The clear, transparent lens characteristic of young adulthood gradually
yellows in older adulthood. This decline in lens transparency results in
a filtering effect and a reduction in the amount of light that ultimately
reaches the retina. The lenses of the older adult also thicken and decrease in flexibility, which affects how light waves are projected on the
retina.

Another problem that occurs with age is cataract formation. *Cataracts* result in a clouding of the lens and can result in complete lens opaqueness. There is some cataract formation in an estimated 95 percent of adults over the age of 70. Cataracts are treatable through a corrective or surgically implanted lens. Left untreated cataracts will result in a reduction or elimination of light rays refracted to the retina.

With age the clear gelatinous vitreous humor shows signs of becoming more liquid in consistency and may develop patches of cloudiness. In addition, the retina loses rods and cones. Rod receptor cells of the retina are particularly important for adapting visually to the dark. Thus, older adults often experience a gradual decline in light and dark adaptation. Cone receptor cells are essential for color vision, so the ability to discriminate colors is often diminished in the older adult. An accumulation of lipofuscin has also been noted in the retinas of older adults.

Structural changes of the eye that begin during middle adulthood and increase in later years often affect the visual function of the eyes. About the age of 40, the ability of an individual to focus at close distances tends to decline. This condition is called *presbyopia*. As an individual ages this condition worsens. This onset of presbyopia during middle adulthood is generally attributed to age-related changes in the lens, which also cause increased glare sensitivity. In addition, the ability to track moving objects also becomes a problem, generally attributed to weaker eye muscle and focusing abilities.

Auditory System

While the auditory system does not serve as a primary sensory system for the completion of most motor tasks, auditory information can be extremely valuable in providing feedback in a number of movement situations. Hearing takes place when vibrating sound waves enter the ears and, through a complex process, are transformed into neuronal signals sent to the brain for processing. Audible sound waves travel from their source to the outer ears of a person. The outer ear consists of the pinna (the visible ear structure on both sides of the head) and the external auditory canal. The sound vibrations travel down the external auditory canal until they come in contact with the tympanic membrane (ear drum). The tympanic membrane begins vibrating in accordance with the vibration characteristics of the sound waves. These vibrations are transferred to three connected middle ear bones and subsequently transmitted to the fluid environment of the inner ear. The vibrations that reach the inner ear stimulate the sound sensitive organ of Corti which conveys the sensations down the cochlear nerve to the brain (Figure 19.8).

As adults grow older their ears undergo a number of structural changes that may impair the quality of their hearing. Various membranes and organs throughout the ear tend to become less flexible. This loss of flexibility can dampen the sound vibrations as they move from

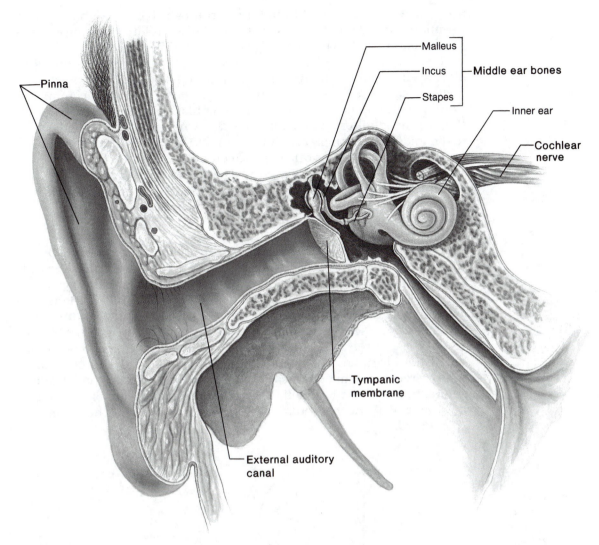

Figure 19.8
Structure of the ear (*Source:* From John W. Hole, *Human Anatomy and Physiology*, 6th edition. Copyright © 1993 Wm. C. Brown Communications, Inc., Dubuque, IA. All rights reserved. Reprinted by permission.)

the external to the inner ear. Hearing loss associated with aging is referred to as *presbycusis*. In addition to membrane changes that may decrease the quality of hearing, presbycusis can result from a loss of cells in the auditory nerve or other organs instrumental in transmitting or interpreting sound waves. A decline in the amount of blood flow to various parts of the ear can contribute to hearing loss as well. In addition to presbycusis, older adults may experience *tinnitus*, a persistent ringing or buzzing noise in the ears. While these age-related changes are somewhat permanent in nature, certain strategies can be explored to improve an older person's hearing. When age-related hearing loss becomes noticeable, a visit to a physician should be scheduled.

The prevalence and consistency of *cerumen* (earwax) changes in older adults. Due to the drying and thinning of tissue in the external auditory canal, a greater amount of cerumen is likely to accumulate. Cerumen also becomes thicker. An accumulation of cerumen can block the external auditory canal, affecting the transmission of sound waves to the middle and inner ears. Such a condition can be treated by a physician, and hearing loss due to cerumen buildup can be restored.

Hearing assistance devices can be beneficial in many cases. It is important, however, to recognize that hearing aids amplify all sounds and may serve to confuse rather than help some individuals.

Proprioception

Proprioception refers to a sense of body awareness and position. One of the primary methods of receiving proprioceptive information is through the vestibular system. The primary function of the vestibular system is to provide information concerning head movement and position. Various components of the vestibular system are located in each inner ear and include the semicircular canals, the utricle, and the saccule (Figure 19.9). These three structures are filled with a fluid called endolymph. When the head moves the endolymph moves as well and stimulates sensory receptor hair cells located within the vestibular structures. The stimulation of these hair cells initiates the transmission of neural signals by way of the vestibular nerve to various parts of the brain and spinal cord.

Figure 19.9
Components of the vestibular system (*Source:* From Sylvia S. Mader, *Understanding Human Anatomy and Physiology.* Copyright © 1991 Wm. C. Brown Communications, Inc., Dubuque, IA. All rights reserved. Reprinted by permission.)

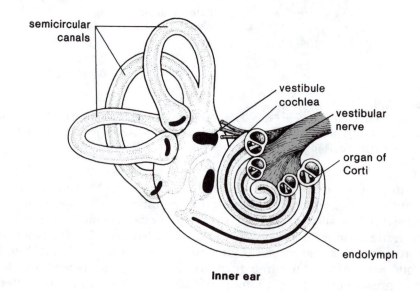

semicircular canals

vestibule
cochlea

vestibular nerve

organ of Corti

endolymph

Inner ear

In older adults losses have been noted in the number of sensory cells located within the saccule, utricle, and semicircular canals. In addition, the nerves that transmit messages from the vestibular structures to the brain experience some age-associated degeneration. How these changes influence the motor behavior of an older individual remains subject to speculation. Older adults often experience vertigo and dizziness. While these conditions may be attributed to age-related changes in the vestibular system, they may likewise occur as a result of certain medications, various diseases, or changes in posture.

Summary

As adults age, they experience a number of changes, many of them detrimental to motor performance. While many of these declines in performance occur as a result of the aging process, others are related to task demands and environmental conditions. The underlying reasons why we age may include changes in cells and/or in whole physiological systems. It is important to recognize that while aging patterns seem to follow a general trend, individual rates of aging may vary widely. Some of these age-related changes can be observed in the musculoskeletal system, the central nervous system, the circulatory and respiratory systems, and the sensory systems. While many of these observed changes may be a direct result of the aging process, other causes may include disease and lifestyle habits.

Terms to Remember

Task specificity
Inter-individual variability
Intra-individual variability
Homeostasis
Osteoporosis
Bone mineral density
Muscle atrophy
Brain plasticity
Neurofibrillary tangles
Senile plaques
Lipofuscin

Age markers
Neurotransmitters
Hypoxia
Arteriosclerosis
Atherosclerosis
Senile miosis
Cataracts
Presbyopia
Presbycusis
Tinnitus
Cerumen

Critical Readings

Dacey, J., & Travers, J. (1991). *Human Development across the Lifespan*. Dubuque, IA: Wm. C. Brown.

Gabbard, C. (1992). *Lifelong Motor Development* (Chapter 11). Dubuque, IA: Wm. C. Brown.

Hazzard, W. R., Andres, R., Bierman, E. L., & Blass, J. P. (Eds.). (1990). *Principles of Geriatric Medicine and Gerontology*. New York: McGraw-Hill.

Rybash, J. M., Roodin, P. A., & Santrock, J. W. (1991). *Adult Development and Aging* (2nd ed.). Dubuque, IA: Wm. C. Brown.

Saxon, S. V., & Etten, M. J. (1987). *Physical Change and Aging* (2nd ed.). New York: Tiresias Press.

Spirduso, W. W. (1986). Physical activity and the prevention of premature aging. In V. Seefeldt (Ed.), *Physical Activity and Well-Being* (pp. 142–160). Reston, VA: AAHPERD.

Chapter 20

Motor Performance in Adults

CHAPTER COMPETENCIES

Upon completion of this chapter you should be able to:

- *Discuss the relationship among aging physiological systems, psychological factors, environmental conditions, and task requirements of motor performance through adulthood*
- *Describe age-associated changes in reaction time and discuss intervention strategies that may reduce the differences in reaction time observed between older and younger adults*
- *Discuss balance and postural changes observed in older adults and describe methods that may increase their stability*
- *Recognize the susceptibility and potential dangers of falls in older adulthood*
- *Discuss age-related variations in gait patterns and their underlying causes*
- *Discuss intervention methods to assist older adults in the performance of daily living activities*
- *Recognize that high-level motor performance can occur at any age*

When we see an adult throwing a frisbee, typing a letter, rebounding a basketball, walking with the aid of a walker, or going for a run in the park, we are observing motor performance. The movement tasks of adults range from everyday activities to specialized skills. Some tasks require a high level of accuracy, others require a high degree of speed, while still others may dictate a combination of speed and accuracy.

Concept 20.1 Observed declines in motor performance through adulthood may be the result of physiological degeneration, psychological factors, environmental conditions, task requirements, disease, lifestyle, or combinations of these elements.

As we advance in age, we observe a number of changes in the performance of various movement tasks. Most of these changes involve a decline in successful task accomplishment. These detrimental changes in motor performance may be the result of age-related degeneration of physiological systems, age-associated psychological factors, the changing environment, task demands, or some combination of these four variables. It is important, however, to reemphasize the point made by Spirduso and MacRae (1990) that variability in the motor performance of adults can be very high. The interaction of several variables, some age-related, will dictate whether an individual will experience a decline in a specific movement task.

As discussed in the previous chapter, the aging process results in a number of physiological changes. Some of those changes may have little or no impact on the actual behavior of an aging adult. Certain task demands may not place major burdens on physiological systems that have deteriorated, or demands placed on a declining system may be accommodated by one or more of the healthy physiological systems. Other physiological changes, however, may result in an observable decline in the performance of various motor skills. A particular impaired system may play such a primary role in the performance of a certain motor task that other systems cannot provide sufficient compensation. The interaction of two or more declining physiological systems may have a detrimental effect on the performance of specific movements as well.

The environment in which the movement task is performed may play a role in the level of performance success. The amount of light that illuminates a room, the firmness of the floor surface, and the surrounding air temperature represent examples of environmental conditions that could affect performance. Certain environmental circumstances may be detrimental to the execution of a particular movement whether the performer is a child, young adult, or old adult. Other environmental conditions may inhibit performance only when they interact with a declining physiological system or systems. For example, an older adult standing in a dimly lit room may not be able to catch a tossed ball. While his inability to catch the ball may represent an age-associated decline in the skill of catching, it may also be the result of a low level of illumination interacting with age-associated changes in the structure and function of his eyes. Increasing the level of lighting in the room should enable him to catch a tossed ball with little or no difficulty.

The requirements that define how the task is to be performed may interact with certain age-related characteristics to reduce the level of performance efficiency or success. An older adult may have trouble performing a task that requires both speed and accuracy, but no difficulty if the same task requires only accuracy. Changes in the musculoskeletal and central nervous systems may affect the speed at which a task is attempted, but not necessarily its accurate completion.

While the reasons behind age-related changes in motor performance are many and varied, some behavioral changes are consistently observed. These include decreased reaction times, diminished maintenance of balance and postural control, and alterations in walking patterns.

Concept 20.2   Reaction time is an important component in many motor performance tasks.

Reaction Time

The study of *reaction time* (RT) has long been a vital aspect in the understanding of motor behavior in humans. RT represents the time delay between the presentation of a stimulus and the initial activation of the appropriate muscle groups to carry out that task. The measurement of RT provides insight into the internal processes taking place during voluntary movement.

Concept 20.3   Reaction time can be separated into different components, each of which may be affected by various age-related changes.

Reaction time can be described by various means. Non-fractionated RT is measured by recording the time between the presentation of a stimulus and the first initiation of the movement. *Fractioned RT* represents an attempt to break the complete RT process into various components. Generally, fractioned RT investigations dissect the total RT process into the two components of premotor RT and motor RT. Premotor RT represents the time between the onset of the signal and the first indication of electrical activity (as measured by electromyography) in the muscles used to carry out the task. Motor RT follows premotor RT and refers to the time between the first indication of electrical activity and the initiation of the movement (Figure 20.1).

Although much more difficult to accomplish, premotor RT may be further sectioned into reception time, motor integration time, and motor overflow time. As a signal travels (via light waves, sound waves, etc.) from its origin through the environment and is picked up by one or more

Figure 20.1
Components of fractionated reaction time

of the body's sensory systems, it reaches part of the brain that will either attach meaning to the signal or discard it as meaningless. The time it takes to execute this phase represents reception time. Once meaning has been attached to the signal, it is followed by activity in the motor cortex of the brain which helps determine the movement that is needed to respond to the signal. This part of the process represents the motor integration time. The time difference between this motor cortex activity and the first indication of electrical activity in the muscles used to carry out the task is referred to as the motor overflow time. While the process involved in RT is amazingly complex, it is equally amazing that, when the signal and movement task are fairly simple, the time involved in the RT process is generally less than 1 second.

In addition to investigating the various components of RT, researchers have attempted to alter the environmental conditions under which RT is observed. RT may be examined under such circumstances as multiple choice responses (i.e., responding one way to a green light and a different way to a red light), different sensory systems receiving the signal to begin a task (i.e., vision-light, hearing-bell, etc.), or the intensity of the signal to begin a task (i.e., vision-bright or dim, hearing-loud or soft).

Concept 20.4 Certain intervention strategies can reduce age differences in reaction time.

It has been consistently demonstrated that RT diminishes with age. Early cross-sectional studies indicated that RT reaches its peak somewhere in the early to mid-20s, begins a slow drop through the middle adulthood years, and declines sharply during older adulthood (Pierson and Montoye, 1958; Hodgkins, 1963). However, even these early investigations indicated that the variability in RT is large when people grow older. More recently it has been demonstrated that RT studies placing greater control on certain variables will elicit much smaller age differences than previous studies. Factors such as providing a familiar signal to start the task, allowing sufficient opportunities to practice the specific task involved in the investigation, and enhancing the quality of the starting signal represent ways to greatly reduce age-related differences (Spirduso and MacRae, 1990), particularly in RT studies that deal with a single signal and a single response. Reduction of age-related differences in RT when more complex signals and responses are involved is generally less significant.

While factors such as practice and the quality and familiarity of the signal help minimize age differences in RT, it remains that younger adults consistently have faster RT than older adults. The breadth of the age-related difference depends on factors associated with each individual's physiological and psychological characteristics, the environment in which the task is performed, and the nature of the task itself.

Physiologically, several possibilities might contribute to slower responses as a person ages. Spirduso (1986) suggested that "to some extent psychomotor tasks requiring speed may be considered a behavioral window through which the central nervous system's integrity may be viewed" (p. 153). As discussed in the previous chapter, the central nervous system undergoes a number of age-related changes ranging from a loss of brain cells to decreases in blood flow and, subsequently, the amount of oxygen that reaches the brain. These central nervous system changes can be harmful in all aspects, but particularly in the central components of the RT process. The functioning quality of the brain, influenced by the amount of blood and nutrients it receives, has the potential to affect the RT components of reception time, motor integration time, and motor overflow time.

Reception time can be impaired by age-associated changes in the systems that receive sensory information requiring a quick response. Decreases or distortions in the light waves or sound waves received by an aging visual system or auditory system, respectively, could be responsible for an increase in the amount of time it takes to transmit pertinent information to the processing centers of the brain. Additionally, the motor time component of RT may be slowed by a decline in the time required to activate the muscles of an aging muscular system.

Psychologically, a number of factors, either individually or in interaction with other variables, have the potential to slow an older adult's ability to respond quickly. Dacey and Travers (1991) suggest that variables such as motivation, depression, and anxiety may be important factors in RT difference between older and younger adults. The older adult, because of greater number of lifetime experiences, may not emphasize tasks requiring quick responses. An older adult may be more motivated to perform a task accurately rather than rapidly, while a younger adult may emphasize speed and sacrifice accuracy. This involves a phenomenon referred to as the *speed-accuracy trade-off*. The speed-accuracy trade-off is a principle that describes the trend toward a decline in the accuracy of a movement when its speed is increased (Schmidt, 1988). An older adult experiencing a state of depression may be less motivated to perform to her potential on a given task. Older adulthood is a time when factors such as health problems or the death of a spouse or friends create the potential for a psychologically depressed state. Older adults may also experience a sense of anxiety when asked to perform a task with which they may not be familiar.

Altering the environment can, in many cases, aid the older adult in performing a movement task requiring a quick response. As discussed in the previous chapter, many older adults experience a loss in rod cells of the retina causing problems with visually adapting to the dark. An older individual attempting to perform a movement task in a dimly lit room will probably perform the task slowly and with reduced accuracy. However, when the lighting is increased, the amount of light transmitted by the eyes to the processing centers of the brain is heightened and the RT process is enhanced. When movement instructions or signals are auditory in nature, increasing the amplitude or altering the frequency of auditory information increases the possibility that more information will reach the brain and enhance the RT process.

Modifying specific task requirements or conditions enhances the performance speed of older adults. As mentioned earlier in this chapter, providing opportunities to practice a movement task improves the RT of older adults. Practice, likewise, helps reduce any anxiety that an individual may have when attempting a task that is unfamiliar. Reducing the number of possible movements from which to select following a signal is also a proven means of boosting the RT of older adults.

In addition to environmental conditions and task requirements, many investigators have found that a person's level of physical activity can play a key role in determining RT status (Burley, 1944; Spirduso, 1975; Kroll & Clarkson, 1977; Spirduso & Clifford, 1978; Baylor & Spirduso, 1988). In an interesting study comparing the RT of young physically active men (YA), young non-physically active men (YNA), old physically active men (OA), and old non-physically active men (ONA) Spirduso (1975) found that the RT of the OA men were quite similar to RT of the YNA men. Of even greater importance, however, was the finding of a marked difference between the OA and ONA men. Kroll and Clarkson (1977) offer some explanation for the faster performances of the OA subjects. They suggest that good central nervous system circulation, which is necessary for optimal brain cell longevity and processing efficiency, is maintained through exercise. Spirduso (1975) adds that inactivity for both young and old adults may contribute to the wear and tear of the central nervous system due to the accumulated effects of increased blood pressure and higher lipofuscin concentrations. She concludes that "the best protection against senile involution of brain cells in cerebral activity is exercise, which unlike mental activity, stimulates metabolism, respiration, blood circulation, digestion, and glands of external secretion" (p. 439). Physical activity may, likewise, enhance the functioning of some neurotransmitter systems of older adults (Spirduso, 1986). While representing a positive influence on the central RT functions of the brain, exercise appears to promote better functioning of the more peripheral components of RT as well. Physical activity fosters healthy blood circulation to the extremities. Increased circulation provides for adequate extremity temperatures which are important for the rapid transmission of nerve signals to the muscles.

Balance and Postural Control

As mentioned earlier in this chapter, the RT process usually involves a time factor of less than 1 second depending upon the complexity of the circumstances. Some motor performance tasks do not require fast RTs for their successful completion, while other tasks do. The ability to maintain one's *balance* and *postural control* efficiently appears to require an adequately functioning RT process. However, RT is only one of many factors that interact for the purposes of maintaining balance and the control of posture. Woollacott and Shumway-Cook (1990) suggest that multiple neural and biomechanical factors work together to achieve the goal of balance. They list the following components that may play an influential role in the control of an individual's balance: (1) postural muscle response synergies; (2) visual, vestibular, and somatosensory systems; (3) adaptive systems; (4) muscle strength; (5) joint range of motion; and (6) body morphology.

Concept 20.5　Several factors serve as interacting components in the maintenance of balance and posture.

Postural muscle response synergies refer to the timing and sequencing of the activation of muscle groups needed to maintain balance or postural control. Several muscle groups in both the lower body and upper body may be called upon to maintain a controlled upright posture or to regulate balance smoothly in a variety of movement situations. The visual system provides valuable information regarding body position in relationship to the environment, while the vestibular and somatosensory systems contribute sensory input regarding body and head position in relation to gravity and joint position awareness. Adaptive systems allow for the modification of sensory input and motor output when changes take place in the task requirements or in the characteristics of the environment. The strength of the muscles at the ankle, knee, and hip must be adequate to be able to either maintain a specific postural position or to control the restoration of balance when equilibrium is disturbed. The range of motion of the body's various joints determines how restrictive or free a movement can be when that movement requires a high degree of balance. Finally, body morphology elements such as height, center of mass, foot length, and body weight distribution affect the biomechanical function of maintaining stability.

Concept 20.6　Older adults display different motor patterns than younger adults when attempting to regain stability after their balance has been disturbed.

With age, the process of maintaining postural control and balance becomes less efficient, particularly in the older adult. For many older adults the decrements in controlling posture may represent irreversible changes (Crilly et al., 1989). It has been demonstrated that when the stability of older adults is disturbed, the restoration process is often different and less effective than the process exhibited by younger adults (Woollacott et al., 1986). One difference is the timing of the muscle activation. When a person is standing upright and something causes him to lose his balance and begin to sway backwards, the balance recovery procedure generally involves the activation of the ankle dorsiflexors followed by the activation of the knee extensors. The muscle activation response in younger adults tends to be quicker than the muscle response of older adults. Some older adults have even demonstrated a reversal of the muscle activation pattern when attempting to restore balance. They may occasionally activate the knee extensor muscle group first followed by the ankle dorsiflexors. In addition, in an attempt to restore balance, some older adults may incorporate additional muscle groups (i.e., muscles of the hip) not utilized by younger adults, or activate the agonist muscle group (i.e., knee extensors) and the antagonist muscle group (i.e., knee flexors) at the same time (Manchester et al., 1989), an occurrence that has been observed in very young children (Forssberg & Nashner, 1982). This cocontraction of the agonist and antagonist muscle groups by older adults may represent a strategy of compensation for the inability to fine-tune the postural control to the same degree as young adults (Woollacott et al., 1988).

The proper functioning of the vestibular and visual systems and their interactions appear to be critical in the postural control differences of older and younger adults. It has been demonstrated that as long as these two systems are intact and able to receive and transmit accurate sensory information, the ability of older adults to recover from disturbed balance is similar to that of younger adults. However, when the amount of visual and vestibular input available to both younger and older adults is substantially reduced, the ability of older adults to restore stability following a loss in balance is much weaker than that of younger adults (Woollacott et al., 1986; Teasdale et al., 1991).

Concept 20.7   Intervention strategies can be incorporated to increase the stability of older adults.

While many adults experience age-related declines in postural and balance control that may become irreversible (particularly in the older adulthood years), various intervention possibilities may be useful in reducing the magnitude of the decline, promoting compensation strategies, or both. While age-associated physiological changes in the vestibular and visual systems may be difficult or impossible to counter, alterations in the environment may provide for stronger sensory stimuli. For example, when an older adult is standing or moving on a soft surface the amount or quality of sensory information sent from the joint, muscle, and vestibular receptors to the processing centers may be decreased. A firmer surface, however, may allow for sharper and more distinct sensory input, particularly for the joint and muscle receptors of the ankles. From a visual standpoint, an increase in room illumination could enhance the number of light waves that reach and are transmitted by the retina.

An increase in muscular strength may moderate the degree of instability of older people. Increases in muscular strength following training programs have been observed at all levels of adulthood. As mentioned in the previous chapter, even adults who were in their 90s experienced muscular strength gains following a strength training program. Adequate levels of muscular strength in the lower and upper legs are particularly important for both the maintenance of balance and the avoidance of falls resulting from balance disruptions (Whipple et al., 1987). The consequences of a fall can be substantially more devastating for the older adult than for someone younger (Tinetti, 1990), as will be discussed later in this chapter.

As previously mentioned, a second musculoskeletal-associated factor that may play an influential role in maintaining balance is the range of motion of the body's joints. While the joint flexibility of older adults tends to be more restricted than that of younger adults (Shephard et al., 1990), participation in physical activity and exercise has been shown to improve the range of motion of older adults and close the flexibility gap usually observed between young and old adulthood (Rikli & Edwards, 1991; Dummer et al., 1985).

Falls

Falls represent a major concern for many elderly individuals. Falling is much more common and serious when an adult is older than during early adulthood. Each year approximately 30 percent of adults over the age of 65 experience a fall. Many will endure multiple falls during a 1-year period. With age, the likelihood of falling increases. While the majority of falls experienced by older adults are minor and do not result in injury, more serious falls may result in soft tissue injuries, fractures, the development of psychological fears, or death.

Concept 20.8   Hip fractures resulting from falls are a major concern for older adults.

Soft tissue injuries can range from various degrees of contusions (bruising) to muscle sprains and strains that could reduce an older individual's mobility and restrict her level of independence. Of even greater concern to older adults is the threat of falls that result in fractures. Fractures may occur at the humerus or wrist when the arm is outstretched in an attempt to cushion or stop a fall. These fractures, however, generally do not decrease mobility. *Hip fractures*, on the other hand, are much more devastating. Fractures of the hip, which are experienced by over 200,000 Americans a year (Tinetti, 1990), result in an extensive time period of immobility, greater dependency on others for daily living functions, and heightened possibility of institutional care. Debilitating circumstances such as these may account for a 12 to 20 percent death rate in individuals during the year following hip fractures (Jackson & Lyles, 1990). Many fractures in older adults can be attributed to osteoporosis. The loss of bone mass from *osteoporosis* not only makes bones weaker and more prone to fractures, but also lengthens the time required for recovery. Another problem associated with hip fractures includes a susceptibility to instability and deformity of the fracture site (Jackson & Lyles, 1990).

While a number of physical injuries can occur as a result of falls, older adults may also develop a sense of fear and/or depression after falling. Approximately half of individuals who have fallen admit to a certain level of fear (Tinetti, 1990). The fear level of these older individuals may lead to overprotectiveness and unnecessary restrictions of mobility and independence. An older adult may begin to avoid even his everyday functional tasks such as bathing and dressing. Depression may accompany the sense of fear and compound the psychological effects of a fall.

A number of factors link falls with the death of older adults. As mentioned earlier in this chapter, the majority of falls are not serious. However, falls do kill a small percentage of persons. More common are deaths that occur from fall-related injuries or from circumstances created by a fall. For example, an older adult who fractures her hip in a fall may experience a decline in overall health due to a long-term reduction in mobility and a decreased ability to care for herself. This may eventually lead to death. Finally, multiple falls in an older individual may indicate underlying factors that elevate the risk of death (Dunn et al., 1992). Age-related and disease-related declines in a number of physiological systems may make a person more susceptible to falls. In these instances falling reveals rather than causes more serious health problems. These health problems may be moving an older adult closer to death.

Concept 20.9 A number of circumstances predispose the older adult to falls.

A number of interacting factors appear to predispose older individuals to falling. Many of these factors are physiological in origin while others relate to the environments in which falls take place. Task demands can, likewise, play a role in creating a precarious situation. Physiological factors may include age- or disease-associated changes in various sensory systems, the central nervous system, or the musculoskeletal system. Environmental conditions often involve potentially hazardous circumstances interacting with declining or drug-impaired physiological systems. The demands of certain tasks may require an individual to move beyond a comfort zone of stability making him vulnerable to other forces. A list of risk factors for falling and some potential intervention strategies can be found in Table 20.1.

Table 20.1 Risk Factors for Falling and Possible Intervention Strategies

Possible Risk Factors of the Older Adult	Possible Intervention Strategies
• Decrease in muscular strength	strength training exercises assistance devices (canes, walkers, handrails)
• Decrease in joint flexibility	active lifestyles stretching exercises
• Decrease in visual abilities	increased room lighting reduced glare eye glasses surgical treatments
• Decrease in auditory abilities	removal of cerumen hearing assistance devices
• Decrease in proprioception	firm walking surfaces proper footwear enhanced visual environment avoid uneven surfaces assistance devices (canes, walkers, handrails)
• Slowing of reaction time	active lifestyles focused attention on task allowance for practice of task increased motivation
• Medication	awareness of drug side effects awareness of drug interaction side effects

As discussed in the previous chapter, declines in the visual, auditory, and vestibular system are common in adults as they age. These declines add to the jeopardy that older adults face in relation to falling. Falls can occur when an individual trips over a hazardous object because she is unable to see it in a dimly lit room. The inability to distinguish the sounds that are made by the feet on different types of floor surfaces may reduce or eliminate certain feedback that is beneficial in maintaining stability. Improper functioning of the vestibular system may result in dizziness and place the person at risk for falling.

A slowing or disruption of the central nervous system can increase an older person's vulnerability to falling. Rapid RT may help a person catch his balance to avoid a fall when stability is lost. Under similar circumstances, a somewhat slower RT may restrict the restoration of balance causing the person to outstretch his arm and break the fall. While this action may cushion the impact of a fall, it places the person at risk for a fracture of the wrist or humerus. An older adult with an even slower RT may be unable to extend her arms quickly enough to break the fall and may land directly on an unprotected hip (Jackson & Lyles, 1990). Additional central nervous system conditions such as Parkinson's disease and strokes increase the older adult's susceptibility to falls.

Adequate muscular strength (particularly in the lower extremities) is important for maintaining balance and restoring lost stability. Age-related loss in muscle mass and a subsequent loss in strength can be detrimental to maintaining balance and preventing falls (Whipple et al., 1987). Arthritis of lower extremity joints can also decrease fall prevention strategies.

As the health of older adults declines, medication is often prescribed for a variety of conditions. A number of medications predispose the older adult to falling. Certain sedatives and antidepressants can increase the risk of falling, while taking more than one drug at the same time without knowledge of the drug interaction consequences also represents a potential problem.

An older person's home or work environment can present a number of hazards that increase the likelihood of falling. Falls can occur when a person climbs or descends stairs, bathes, moves in and out of a wheelchair, or trips over electrical cords, low furniture, or small pets. Other falls may occur as a result of shoes that fit poorly. Additional environmental hazards include low levels of room illumination, surfaces that produce glare when light strikes them, and soft, uneven, or unstable floor surfaces. It is possible that the optical patterns on floors and stairs may contribute to falling due to a decline in the older adult's visual perception process (Tinetti, 1990).

The demands of certain tasks can place older adults in situations in which they are at greater risk for falling, particularly when the tasks require intense concentration. Attention to balance may be diverted. Reaching for an object high on a shelf while using a stepladder, bending over and attempting to lift a heavy object, or carrying a full laundry basket down a flight of stairs are potentially hazardous tasks for older adults. Older individuals who participate in more physically active lifestyles appear to have an increased incidence of falls (Tinetti, 1990). Reasons probably include greater exposure to hazardous circumstances and increased intensity in active participation.

Gait

Walking appears to be a very simple, almost automatic task performed without much effort. It is, in fact, a very complex skill requiring the interaction of the central nervous system, the body's muscles and joints, several sensory systems, gravitational forces, and environmental circumstances. Age-related and/or disease-related changes in one or more physiological systems can interact with physical and/or environmental conditions to cause decrements in the *gait* process. Neurologically, gait utilizes an intricate combination of voluntary and reflexive action. The muscles and joints of the ankle, knee, pelvis, and to some degree the trunk and shoulder, are vital ingredients in an efficient walking pattern. The gait process makes use of information obtained through the visual, auditory, and vestibular systems, as well as others. The forces related to the earth's gravitational pull are involved with the continual altering of the body's center of gravity and the constant reestablishing of the base of support during the walking cycle. Environmental conditions such as walking surface or objects placed in the path of a walker can alter the gait pattern.

The walking cycle or gait pattern has two phases: the *swing phase* and the *support phase*. Generally speaking, when one leg is in the swing phase, the other leg is in the support phase. The swing phase begins when the toe pushes off the ground surface and ends when the heel strikes the ground surface. During the swing phase, the leg moves through the air in a pendulum-like motion. The support phase begins when the heel first strikes the ground surface and ends when the toe pushes off the ground surface. During the entire support phase the foot maintains contact with the ground surface. In addition to the support and swing phases, there is a brief time in the walking cycle when both feet contact the ground surface at the same time. This is referred to as a period of double support and is the major characteristic that differentiates running from walking. Other elements of walking include stride length, stride frequency, stride width, toe-floor clearance during the swing phase, arm swing, and hip and knee rotation.

Concept 20.10   Differences in the gait patterns of older adults and younger adults often originate in different walking speeds.

As individuals move into older adulthood, a variety of gait characteristics undergo changes. It has been reported that older adults may differ from younger adults in several walking components. Older adults characterized as healthy, have displayed decreases in *stride length*, increases in the *double support period*, reductions in *toe-floor clearance*, alterations of the strategies used when the foot clears obstacles on the floor, and decreases in *gait velocity* (Chen et al., 1991; Wall et al., 1991; Elble et al., 1991; Ferrandez et al., 1990). However, some investigators reported that many of the declines or reductions observed in the walking patterns of older adults can be attributed to slower paces, rather than to particular physiological problems (Ferrandez et al., 1990; Elble et al., 1991). While a slower walking speed appears to be characteristic of an older person's gait and may cause a number of other decreases in gait efficiency, intervention strategies such as weight training can improve the gait speed of older adults (Fiatarone et al., 1990).

While it is speculative to state that age alone causes declines in the gait cycle, a number of diseases that often afflict older adults contribute to gait problems. Disorders of the central nervous system such as Parkinson's disease, multiple sclerosis, tumors, or strokes can affect balance control and, in turn, the quality of the gait pattern (Koller & Glatt, 1990). Orthopedic conditions such as arthritis and bunions, which are often experienced by older adults, may also alter an individual's gait pattern.

Activities of Daily Living

Concept 20.11   Older adults may have difficulty carrying out daily living activities without some environmental modifications.

A multitude of movement-oriented tasks that individuals carry out throughout their lives are required for basic everyday needs. *Daily living activities* such as getting out of bed, getting dressed, bathing, and preparing meals are just a few of the many tasks that require the attention of adults. While most young- and middle-aged adults take for granted the ease with which these tasks are performed, many older adults find them difficult. Older adults demonstrate less efficient movement patterns when attempting to rise from the floor to a standing position

(VanSant, 1990). When attempting to stand from a horizontal position, an older adult may break down the process into discrete segments (i.e., sit up, get onto all fours, move to a kneeling or a squatting position, then pull up to a standing position). Younger adults tend to move from a horizontal position to a standing position in one fluid motion. This *segmental approach* demonstrated by an older adult may be evident when he rises to a standing position from a bed or a chair.

While some age-related movement patterns in certain daily living activities have been noted, it has also been observed that greater efficiency in those movement patterns can be achieved when the task conditions are modified. VanSant (1990) points out that altering environmental conditions, such as varying the height of objects (chair, bed, etc.), can increase the variability in an older person's motor performance. In addition, Hart et al. (1990) found that by providing assistance modifications to various household items, older adults were able to put on their shoes, get on and off the toilet, pour from a teapot, and turn on the tap with less difficulty and greater speed.

Elite Performance

Concept 20.12 A physically active lifestyle throughout adulthood can benefit an individual in a variety of motor performance-related aspects.

The quantity of motor performance activity observed at all levels of adulthood is extremely variable. The health status of various physiological systems, past and present lifestyles, genetic characteristics, environmental conditions, and task demands interact to generate a range of movement outcomes (performed extremely well, performed adequately, or performed poorly). Upon examining cross-sectional and longitudinal track and field accomplishments of masters-level athletes Stones and Kozma (1982) suggested that non-age related factors such as amount and quality of training, frequency and quality of competitive experience, motivation, and injury proneness may affect the performance trends through adulthood. It has also been suggested that the level of age-associated performance declines may be activity-specific (Salthouse, 1976; Stones & Kozma, 1980, 1981, 1986). Salthouse (1976) stated that "when one refers to slowing with age it is necessary to be quite specific about the activity to which one is referring because different activities decline at different rates" (p. 349).

Many of the age-related changes discussed in this chapter and the previous chapter can cause motor performance declines. However, evidence continues to mount that many adults who remain physically active and adapt and compensate for changing environmental and task demands inhibit the typical age-related declines much more effectively than their sedentary peers.

Concept 20.13 Certain individuals may be able to perform motor tasks at elite levels regardless of their age.

There are, also, those older adults who continue to perform certain motor tasks at extraordinarily high levels. While the records of *master athletes* are consistently poorer than the records of their younger counterparts, their performances are nonetheless noteworthy, and, in many cases, better than the performances of younger non-elite athletes. A few master athletes remain competitive in their sports. Two notable examples in the sport of track and field/road racing are Priscilla Welch of Great Britain and Carlos Lopes of Portugal. In her 40s, Priscilla Welch has run times of 16 minutes, 20 seconds for a 5-kilometer race, 32 minutes, 25 seconds for a 10-kilometer race, and 2 hours, 31 minutes, 14 seconds for the marathon (Tacstats/USA, 1992). Welch's times place her in world class standing in any age group. In his late 30s Carlos Lopes was the winner of the gold medal in the marathon at the 1984 Olympic Games. In addition to his Olympic feat, Lopes has held master age group (35, 36, and 37 years) world records for the 5-kilometer race and the 10-kilometer race (Mundle et al., 1992). Other notable master track and field age records are listed in Table 20.2.

Summary

A number of factors affect how adults perform motor tasks. These factors include the health status of various physiological systems, psychological characteristics, the changing environment, task demands, or some combination thereof. With age we see declines in motor performance. These declines may be attributed to aging, disease, lifestyles, or a combination of these elements. Reaction times tend to slow. Intervention strategies that reduce reaction time decrements include allowing practice of a task, increasing the intensity of the stimulus, using a task that is already familiar to the individual, and participating in a physically active lifestyle. The maintenance of balance and posture decreases in efficiency with age, and particularly in older adulthood.

Table 20.2 Selected Masters Track and Field Age Records

Event	Men Age (years)	Record*	Year
100-meters	35	10.28 (sec.)	1987
	40	10.6	1989
	50	11.2	1987
	60	12.0	1977
	70	13.0	1987
	80	15.3	1991
	90	19.9	1975
One mile	35	3:54.13 (min.)	1991
	40	4:05.39	1989
	50	4:32.2	1975
	60	5:04.9	1991
	70	5:32.4 (indoor)	1987
	80	6:43.3	1983
	90	13:43.6	1986
10,000-meters	35	27:24.4 (min.)	1982
	40	28:30.88	1991
	50	31:01.9	1991
	60	34:14.88	1991
	70	38:26	1989
	80	45:44.4	1987
	90	71:40.78	1989
Long jump	35	8.50 (meters)	1991
	40	7.54	1988
	50	6.66	1990
	60	6.07	1982
	70	4.98	1991
	80	3.79	1990
	90	2.44	1990
High jump	35	2.16 (meters)	1974
	40	2.06	1985
	50	1.85	1983
	60	1.62	1990
	70	1.48	1984
	80	1.20	1982
	90	1.04	1990

Declines in muscle strength and control, the sensory systems, joint flexibility, and physical characteristics interact to alter the balance and posture process. Poorer balance as well as other conditions increase an older person's susceptibility to falling. For the older adult, falling can result in serious consequences, such as hip fractures. The walking pattern of older adults often differs from that of younger adults. However, many of the observed differences result from slower walking speeds.

Table 20.2 (continued)

Event	Women Age (years)	Record*	Year
100-meters	35	11.6 (sec.)	1979
	40	12.2	1969
	50	13.1	1984
	60	13.9	1989
	70	16.2	1981
	80	20.93	1989
One mile	35	4:17.33 (min.)	1985
	40	4:54.69	1983
	50	5:29.83	1987
	60	6:46.30	1987
	70	7:26.0	1989
10,000-meters	35	31:35.52 (min.)	1988
	40	33:50.02	1986
	50	38:18.4	1986
	60	42:18	1990
	70	50:28.33	1989
	80	107:2	1987
Long jump	35	6.50 (meters)	1974
	40	6.13	1985
	50	5.04	1979
	60	4.36	1986
	70	3.45	1991
	80	2.00	1989
High jump	35	1.88 (meters)	1988
	40	1.65	1988
	50	1.47	1970
	60	1.27	1991
	70	1.13	1987
	80	0.88	1989

*wind assisted marks not included
Adapted from: Mundle, P., Dietderich, S., & Harvey, R. (1992). Masters age records for 1991. *North Hollywood, CA: National Masters News.*

When the walking speed is increased, many differences disappear. Daily living activities are often more challenging for older adults than for their younger counterparts. However, altering environmental conditions can increase the speed and decrease the difficulty level of many daily living activities. Although we note many age-associated declines in motor performance, a number of individuals remain physically active and, in some cases, perform motor tasks at exceptionally high levels.

Terms to Remember

Reaction time

Fractionated reaction time

Speed-accuracy tradeoff

Balance

Postural control

Falls

Hip fractures

Osteoporosis

Gait

Swing phase

Support phase

Stride length

Double support period

Toe-floor clearance

Gait velocity

Daily living activities

Segmental approach

Master athletes

Critical Readings

Gabbard, C. (1992). *Lifelong Motor Development* (Chapter 11). Dubuque, IA: Wm. C. Brown.

Payne, G. V., & Isaacs, L. D. (1991). *Human Motor Development: A Lifespan Approach* (Chapter 15). Mountain View, CA: Mayfield.

Rybash, J. M., Roodin, P. A., & Santrock, J. W. (1991). *Adult Development and Aging* (2nd ed.) (Chapter 4). Dubuque, IA: Wm. C. Brown.

Spirduso, W. W., & MacRae, P. G. (1990). Motor performance and aging. In J. E. Birren & K. W. Schaie (Eds.), *Handbook of the Psychology of Aging* (3rd ed.) (pp. 188–200). San Diego: Academic Press.

Woollacott, M. H., & Shumway-Cook, A. (1990). Changes in posture control across the life span: A systems approach. *Physical Therapy, 70,* 799–807.

Chapter **21**

Psychosocial Development in Adults

CHAPTER COMPETENCIES

Upon completion of this chapter you should be able to:

- *Discuss the relationship between the motor and psychosocial domains*
- *Describe Erikson's theory of psychosocial development with regard to the adult*
- *Describe Levinson's seasons of life theory with regard to the adult*
- *Discuss the effects of exercise on select psychological factors of middle-aged and old-aged adults*
- *Discuss the importance of a physically active lifestyle as it is related to activity theory and disengagement theory*
- *Describe how remaining physically active can enhance the retirement process*
- *Define ageism and recognize its various forms*
- *Describe the importance of health and physical activity as important predictors of longevity and successful aging*

Key Concept: An adult's level of physical activity affects his psychological and sociological states; in turn, psychological and sociological factors such as self-concept and peer relationships influence his commitment to a physically active lifestyle.

Various aspects of the motor domain influence the psychological state and the social characteristics of adults. Exercise, a physically active lifestyle, and the ability to carry out daily living skills are movement-oriented factors that can have a positive effect on how adults feel about themselves and how others view them. Progressive declines in motor performance, a decrease in muscular strength, and an inability to accomplish household tasks represent motor domain conditions that can negatively influence the psychological perspectives and social interactions of adults. In numerous situations the motor domain interacts with the psychosocial domain. When an individual elevates her self-esteem and body image following several months of weight training or when adults gather for early morning exercise walks at a city mall, we see the positive influences of motor performance on psychosocial behavior. When individuals with impaired motor functions must be admitted to nursing care facilities and are depressed or insecure, we see the negative influences. Experiences encountered throughout adulthood have the potential to affect a number of psychosocial features. Certain psychological factors that may change during the adult years include self-concept, body image, self-esteem, perception of locus of control, moods of depression, and fears. The development, maintenance, and loss of relationships; the concept of retirement; and ageism are socialization experiences often faced by adults as they grow older.

Concept 21.1 In a number of situations aspects of the motor domain interact with aspects of the psychosocial domain.

Theories of Adult Psychosocial Development

As presented in Chapter 2, Erik Erikson developed a stage approach to the psychosocial development of human beings, sometimes referred to as "The Eight Ages of Man." Each stage represents a *crisis state* that must be resolved before advancement to the next stage. Movement from stage to stage comes about through individual needs and societal demands. Erikson's theory proposes that inadequate resolution of a stage crisis will hinder future development at higher stages. While the successful resolution of each stage crisis is the mechanism for developmental change, Dacey and Travers (1991) point out that Erikson's stages are based on the ideal, and individuals rarely if ever complete each stage perfectly. It is, however, an important component of the theory that the closer an individual gets to a *crisis solution* at each stage, the greater her progress.

Concept 21.2 Erik Erikson's theory of psychosocial development has important implications for the adult at any age.

The first five stages of Erikson's theory address early infancy through adolescence. The last three stages are focused on the phases of early, middle, and late adulthood. In this section we will attempt to further define Erikson's final stages as outlined in Chapter 2. Table 21.1 recaps the three adulthood stages. In early adulthood Erikson identifies the crisis as one of *intimacy* vs. *isolation*, and it takes place between 18 to 25 years. This period of early adulthood life represents a time when adult friendships are established and an intimate relationship with a member of the opposite sex develops. Erikson suggests that if an individual is unable to form friendships and/or establish that one intimate relationship, then feelings of isolation form.

Generativity vs. *stagnation* represents the crisis facing adults during the latter stages of early adulthood through the middle adulthood years. Generativity refers to the usefulness individuals provide to themselves and to society. Achieving generativity provides an individual with a sense of personal fulfillment. Teachers, ministers, and medical professionals are involved in occupations that have inherent generativity attributes. It is how individuals perceive their levels of usefulness, however, that determines whether generativity is achieved. Erikson suggests that stagnation occurs when adults perceive they are unable to contribute to the betterment of society, even in a small way. Feelings of boredom develop often followed by a self-indulgent time period known as a midlife crisis.

Table 21.1 Erik Erikson's Adulthood Stages of Psychosocial Development

Stage	Adulthood Years	Psychosocial Process
First Adulthood Stage	Young Adulthood (18–25 years)	Acquiring a sense of intimacy vs. isolation
Second Adulthood Stage	Adulthood (25–65 years)	Acquiring a sense of generativity vs. self-absorption
Third Adulthood Stage	Older Adulthood (65 and older)	Acquiring a sense of integrity vs. despair

The final stage of Erikson's eight stages involves the crisis of *integrity* vs. *despair*. When an older adult takes a retrospective look at his life he is likely to experience a sense of integrity or despair. If he has lived a contributing, productive, and meaningful life, he can rest in the perception that he has achieved personal integrity. If he has regrets over poor choices and realizes that opportunities to make amends are minimal, he may feel a sense of despair.

Concept 21.3 Daniel Levinson's life structure theory provides insight into developmental eras and periods of transitions throughout adulthood.

Through a series of interviews with middle-aged men representing a variety of occupations and socioeconomic levels, Daniel Levinson acquired material for the creation of a theory of adult development and a subsequent book entitled *The Seasons of a Man's Life* (1978). Further research by Levinson (1986) led him to expand his theory to include women. Levinson uses as the foundation of his theory the concept of *life structure*. Life structure can be defined as the underlying design or pattern of an individual's life at any given time. The two most important aspects of the life structure are choices made about marriage and family and choices made about career. These choices help define the development of individuals at any particular time in the life structure. Levinson's theory incorporates four *eras* or seasons of an individual's life. Overlapping time frames between the eras are referred to as *transition* periods. The four developmental eras are childhood and adolescence (birth to 22 years), early adulthood (17 to 45 years), middle adulthood (40 to 65 years), and older adulthood (60 years and older). The overlap between the first and the second era is identified as the early adult transition. Overlaps between the second and third era, and the third and final era are called the midlife transition and the late adult transition, respectively. Figure 21.1 provides a visual display of Levinson's eras and transitions in sequence.

The latter part of the first era represents the onset of adulthood and the origins of independence and responsibility. During the early adult transition period, the relationships between family members and friends change in response to a person's desire for greater individualism and the need to find a niche in the adult world. Upon arrival in the early adulthood era, the individual begins to establish and raise her family, choose an occupation related to her strengths, and pursue ambitions that have been cultivated over the years. While this season of life represents a time of excitement and enthusiasm, it can also depict a time of high stress. Combining the experiences of establishing a new marriage, raising young children, and embarking on a new career can have a cumulative effect on a young adult's stress level. Toward the end of

Figure 21.1
Levinson's eras and transitions throughout adulthood (Reprinted by permission of the publishers from *Themes of Work and Love in Adulthood* by Neil J. Smelser and Erik H. Erikson, Cambridge, MA.: Harvard University Press, Copyright © 1980 by the President and Fellows of Harvard College.)

early adulthood, Levinson suggests that the individual attempts to advance in her chosen occupation—an important task during this period.

Upon reaching midlife transition adults begin to face some difficult questions about the past, present, and future. Concerns about slow progress toward the achievement of original goals may arise and doubts about future opportunities may develop. Physical signs of aging begin to appear. Changes in vision develop, and physical fitness levels decline and start to limit the amount of activity in which individuals are involved. During midlife transition Levinson notes that adults will either redefine their goals based on their current situations or begin to experience stagnation.

The realization that progress can be made in spite of age-related declines makes for a smoother step into the middle adulthood era. During middle adulthood, Levinson states that people recognize the importance of working with younger co-workers and serving as *mentors*. Because a person's professional goals have been achieved or modified, he has a greater sense of security and wants to help others reach their goals. This curtailment of personal ambitions allows for an increase in family involvement.

Levinson's transition into late adulthood can represent a time of trepidation. While many physical characteristics have declined gradually to this point, sharper drops become apparent during the late adulthood years. Acceptance of the aging process allows older adults to experience this era in a state of contentment. Similar to Erikson's last stage, Levinson's final season involves the advancement toward a sense of integrity.

Psychological Factors

There are many ways that the experiences in the motor domain interact with the psychological characteristics of adults. An often used method to explore this motor-psychology relationship is the examination of psychological factors following exercise or association with physical activity. Factors such as a sense of well-being, awareness of body image, perception of locus of control, and states of depression have been improved following participation in an exercise program. Individuals of a middle and/or old adulthood-age group are often targeted as subjects for such interaction investigations.

Concept 21.4   Exercise can have beneficial effects on a number of psychological variables associated with aging.

A *sense of well-being* serves as somewhat of a general term representing some type of positive change in a person's attitude (Hird & Williams, 1989). Following 14 weeks of an aerobic program Perri and Templer (1985) noted significant improvements in the self-concepts of older adults. In addition, men and women between the ages of 55 and

85 years have demonstrated heightened perceptions of self-concept at the conclusion of an 8-month dance/movement program (Berryman-Miller, 1988). However, other investigations examining the relationship between exercise and a sense of well-being have shown no changes following any exercise intervention (Table 21.2). Hird and Williams (1989) point out that some instruments used to measure various aspects of well-being may be too insensitive to subtle changes while others may lead the subjects to give answers that may not represent their true feelings.

Body image is another psychological factor that has been shown to improve following involvement in an exercise program or higher levels of physical activity. Body image refers to the subjective pictures individuals have of themselves created through their own observations and the reactions of others (Thomas, 1989). Loomis and Thomas (1991) examined body attitudes of older women who lived at home and women who resided in nursing facilities. They found that the women living in nursing facilities reported greater dissatisfaction with their body images than did the individuals living at home. The investigators concluded that greater opportunities for participation in physical activity and exercise should be made available to the nursing facility residents. Other body image investigations are summarized in Table 21.2.

Locus of control can be defined as a person's perception of her impact on events (Thomas, 1989). An individual with an internal locus of control perceives that she can influence events, while a person with an external locus of control believes that events are unaffected by her involvement and happen by chance. The investigation by Perri and Templer (1984) described earlier in this chapter resulted in an enhanced perceived internal locus of control by the adults who participated in the 14-week aerobic program. Other locus of control studies with middle-aged and old-aged adults have not been as conclusive (see Table 21.2). Further research is needed in this area before more definitive conclusions can be drawn.

Depression in adult populations may stem from numerous causes: a decrease in self-esteem due to the loss of employment, hormonal changes following menopause, or a reduction in the ability to carry out daily living skills due to failing health. Valliant and Asu (1985) examined men and women between the ages of 50 and 80 years who participated in different levels of exercise programming. Subjects included structured exercisers, self-imposed exercisers, social exercisers, and non-exercisers. The investigators found that the structured group exhibited a reduction in depression following the 12-week program. However, as with some of the psychological factors previously discussed in this chapter, other investigations failed to demonstrate positive exercise-related effects on depression (see Table 21.2). Further study in this area is required to clarify the impact of exercise on depression.

Table 21.2 Overview of Research Examining the Relationship between Physical Activity and Psychological Factors

Research Study	Subjects: Sex and Age	Fitness Program	Psychological Effect Studied	Instrument	Outcome
Barry et al. (1966)	Males & Females 55–78 yrs. M = 69.5	Ergometer 3×/wk., 3 mos.	Personality	Myers-Briggs Type Indicator	No change
			Memory	Short Term Retention	No change
			Mental functioning	Ravens Progressive Matrices: Simple Addition	No change
Blumenthal et al. (1982)	Males & Females 65–85 yrs. M = 69.3 Old-old = ≥ 70 Young-old = ≤ 70	Ergometer 3×/wk., 16 wks.	Type-A behavior	Jenkin's Activity Survey	No change
			Active, vigorous, impulsive, dominant, sociable, reflectable	Thurstone Temperament Schedule	No change
				General Health Survey	↑Mood, satisfaction, self-concept, achievement
				POMS	↓Anger
Coleman et al. (1985)	Females 55–81 yrs.	Swimming, walking, aerobics, flexibility 3×/wk.	Locus of control	Rotter's Locus of Control Scale	No difference from control
Elsayed et al. (1980)	Males 24–68 yrs. Young: M = 35 Old: M = 53	Progressive running, self-selected recreation, 3×/wk., 16 wks.	Fluid intelligence	Culture Fair Intelligence Test Scale 3, Form A	↑ in 3 of 5 measures
			Crystallized intelligence	Cattell 16-PF Factor B	No change

Study	Sample	Activity	Variable	Measure	Result
Hogan & Santomier (1984)	Males & Females M = 67.0 years	Swimming 5×/wk., 12 wks.	Self-efficacy	Swim Skills Efficacy Scale	↑Self-efficacy
Perri & Templer (1985)	Males & Females 60–79 yrs. M = 65.6	Walking, jogging 3×/wk., 14 wks.	Depression	Zung's SDS	No change
			Anxiety	Zuckerman's MAACL (anxiety)	No change
			Self-concept	Fitt's Tennessee Self-Concept Scale	↑Self-concept
			Locus of control	Rotter's Locus of Control Scale	↑Internal locus of control
			Memory	Key Auditory Verbal Training Test	No change
Powell (1974)	Male & Female Mental Patients 59–89 yrs. M = 69.3	Brisk walking/calisthenics 5×/wk., 12 wks.	Mental functioning	Raven's Progressive Matrices	↑Mental functioning
			Memory	Memory for Designs Test	No change
				Wechsler Memory Scale	↑Memory
			Behavior	Nurses observation Geriatric Assessment Scale	No change
					No change
Riddick & Freitag (1984)	Females 50–70 yrs.	Exercise & dance routines 2×/wk., 8 wks.	Body image	My Body Index	↑Body image
Rottella & Bunker (1978)	Males	Tennis	Locus of control	Rotter's Locus of Control Scale	No difference from control

Table 21.2 continued

Research Study	Subjects: Sex and Age	Fitness Program	Psychological Effect Studied	Instrument	Outcome
Sidney & Shephard (1976)	Males & Females Males $M = 66.2$ yrs. Females $M = 65.7$ yrs.	Walking/jogging 0–4 wk., 14 wks.	Trait anxiety	Taylor's Manifest Anxiety Scale	↓Anxiety
			Body image	Kenyon's Body Image Scale	↑Body image (high-frequency low-intensity group)
				McPherson's Real Me Test	↑Body image (all groups except low-frequency/low-intensity)
			Self-concept, mood, goal achievement	Life Satisfaction Index	No change (only low-frequency/low-intensity)
Stamford et al. (1974)	Male & Female Mental patients $M = 71.5$ yrs. Continuous hospitalization $M = 21$ yrs.	Walking 5×/wk., 12 wks.	Intelligence	Wechsler Adult Intelligence Scale Digit Span Test General Information Test	No change No change ↑Intelligence
			Sensitivity, self-concept, judgment, impulse, regulation	Draw-A-Person Test	No change
Valliant & Asu (1985)	Males & Females 50+ yrs.	Calisthenics, flexibility 2×/wk., 12 wks.	Depression	MMPI Depression Scale	↓Depression
			Locus of control	Rotter's Scale	No change
			Self-esteem	Coopersmith Self-Esteem Inventory	No change
			Fear	Motivational Analysis	No change
			Assertiveness	Motivational Analysis	No change

From Andrew C. Ostrow, Aging and Motor Behavior, Copyright © 1989 Benchmark Press Inc. Reprinted by permission of Wm. C. Brown Communications, Inc., Dubuque, Iowa. All Rights Reserved.

Socialization Factors

For many years social scientists have focused on two approaches, the *activity theory* and the *disengagement theory*, to help describe the optimal process of aging in regard to relationships with other people (Dacey & Travers, 1991). Activity theory suggests that as adults grow older they require interaction with other people and continued physical activity to be happy and satisfied. Disengagement theory is the inverse of activity theory. Disengagement theory suggests that as people age they begin to lose relationships, gradually abandon past interests, and eventually withdraw from society. Disengagement theory argues that the curtailment in social interaction is necessary for older adults to accept society's disengagement of them. Acceptance of this society-individual separation allows older individuals to maintain a sense of integrity in their late adulthood years.

Concept 21.5 Activity theory and disengagement theory provide opposing approaches to successful aging.

Maintaining a physically active lifestyle often requires interaction with individuals of different age groups in a variety of social environments. While these conditions run contrary to disengagement theory, they are consistent with activity theory. Remaining physically active in a social setting represents the activity theory's two primary conditions of sustaining or improving one's health status while preserving or developing relationships. As has been noted in the last few chapters, participation in physical activity encourages older adults to remain attached to society rather than to detach from it.

Concept 21.6 Retirement represents a process rather than a single event.

The theories of activity and disengagement represent a general view of the aging process from a socialization standpoint. An event that represents more of a specific sociological milestone in an older adult's life is *retirement*. Retirement is an interesting phenomenon that some people savor, some tolerate, and some resent. It has been postulated that adults advance through seven phases of retirement (Williamson et al., 1980) (Figure 21.2).

The first step is referred to as the remote phase. The remote phase describes a period of time when workers put little thought into retirement planning. It often represents a state of denial in that they have no

Figure 21.2
Seven phases of retirement

End of retirement

Retirement

VII — Termination phase

VI — Stability phase

V — Reorientation phase

IV — Disenchantment phase

III — Honeymoon phase

The Retirement Event

Preretirement

II — Near phase

I — Remote phase

expectations of not working. As they move to the near phase of retirement, workers begin pre-retirement planning. Pre-retirement matters may include financial planning, health maintenance, and leisure activities. Once the designated day of retirement occurs it is followed by what is termed the honeymoon phase. At this time, retirees receive much gratification from their newly acquired free time. New retirees may be inclined to overcompensate for opportunities they could not pursue earlier in their lives. The euphoric high experienced during the honeymoon phase is followed by a letdown period called the disenchantment phase. When the day-to-day pattern of retirement living commences, the retiree may experience loss of purpose, reductions in feelings of self-worth, and longings for job-related activities and friends. These feelings may be due to unrealistic expectations about retirement. Making adjustments to counter the disenchantment perspective advances the retiree to the reorientation phase, characterized by a time when options are explored and decisions made regarding realistic expectations of retirement. This is followed by the stability phase in which the retiree makes situational adjustments based upon the expectations determined during the previous phase. A final step is recognized as the termination phase, which represents the development of a time of dependency. The retiree may find it necessary to rely on others due to declines in health, physical abilities, or finances. In the latter case, it may be necessary to return to work, which concludes the retirement period. Time frames or ages are not included in these various phases because of the uniqueness of each individual's physical, emotional, and financial circumstances.

Some experts question the necessity for a phase-type approach suggesting that retirement reflects a lengthy series of adjustments, similar to other life transitions (Rybash, Roodin, & Santrock, 1991). In either case, aspects of the motor domain can serve beneficial or detrimental roles at various times of the retirement process. Maintaining a physically active lifestyle may reduce the apprehension about the life changes manifested by retirement. The participation in lifelong sports or leisure pursuits such as golf, tennis, cycling, or hiking can make potentially difficult retirement-based transitions somewhat smoother by providing challenge and enjoyment to the retiree within a framework that can be regulated by realistic expectations. In addition, as described in several examples in previous chapters, remaining physically active as long as possible may help delay the onset of health impairment and dependency on others for the performance of daily living skills.

Concept 21.7   Ageism can be detrimental to an older adult's developmental process.

Another social phenomenon that adults often face as they advance in years is *ageism,* which involves stereotyping (negatively or positively) or discriminating against older adults on the basis of prejudice (Rybash et al., 1991). A perception that all old people have physical and cognitive deficits and should be treated like children is an example of ageism. It may also involve a dislike for older persons because they are perceived to be of minimal value to society or to represent a drain on societal resources. Without exploring the underlying bases of such perceptions, suffice it to say that they represent serious misconceptions. Table 21.3 provides several common misperceptions about older populations, many of them related to health status and physical capabilities. Ageism represents, at best, a level of ignorance about the individual value of each person of advanced age, and, at worst, a destructive tool that can damage the opportunities and even lives of older adults.

Successful Aging

It has been proposed that the concept of *successful aging* requires the components of survival (longevity), health (lack of disability), and life satisfaction (happiness) (Palmore, 1979). In an attempt to determine items that may serve as predictors of successful aging, two longitudinal aging studies were initiated at Duke University. The first began in 1955 and observed 276 men and women (aged 60 to 90 years) every 2 to 4 years until 1976. The second investigation began in 1968 with 502 men

Table 21.3 Common Misperceptions about Older Adults

Examples of Misperceptions Based on Negative Stereotypes

1. Most older persons are poor.
2. Most older persons are unable to keep up with inflation.
3. Most older people are ill-housed.
4. Most older people are frail and in poor health.
5. The aged are impotent as a political force and require advocacy.
6. Most older people are inadequate employees; they are less productive, efficient, motivated, innovative, and creative than younger workers. Most older workers are accident-prone.
7. Older people are mentally slower and more forgetful; they are less able to learn new things.
8. Older persons tend to be intellectually rigid and dogmatic. Most old people are set in their ways and unable to change.
9. A majority of older people are socially isolated and lonely. Most are disengaging or disengaged from society.
10. Most older persons are confined to long-term care institutions.

Examples of Misperceptions Based on Positive Stereotypes

1. The aged are relatively well off; they are not poor, but in good economic shape. Their benefits are generously provided by working members of society.
2. The aged are a potential political force that votes and participates in unity and in great numbers.
3. Older people make friends very easily. They are kind and smiling.
4. Most older persons are mature, experienced, wise, and interesting.
5. Most older persons are very good listeners and are especially patient with children.
6. A majority of older persons are very kind and generous to their children and grandchildren.

From S. Lubomudrov, "Congressional Perceptions of the Elderly: The Use of Stereotypes in the Legislative Process," in Journal of Gerontology, 27:77–81, 1987. Copyright © The Gerontological Society of America.

and women (aged 45 to 70 years) and was also completed in 1976 (Shock, 1985). Palmore (1979, 1982) examined the data from the first Duke longitudinal study of aging and identified several significant factors that could be classified as predictors of longevity and of successful aging.

Significant predictors of successful aging for both men and women included the motor domain characteristics of physical functioning and number of physical activities. In regard to the more specific factor of longevity, several components from the motor domain represented significant predicting factors. For both men and women the physical functioning rating (representing the level of physical function ability in everyday tasks) was a significant predictor. A second significant predictor for men and women was each subject's self-rating of his or her health. For women, a significant longevity predictor was the number of activities involved in which required physical mobility.

Concept 21.8   Lifestyle characteristics can represent important determinants of longevity and successful aging.

One implication that arises from the results of these investigations is that a physically active lifestyle is a key element in the pursuit of successful aging. The value of remaining physically active throughout adulthood should not be underestimated and should be reinforced at all ages of the life span.

Summary

Both Erik Erikson and Daniel Levinson devised theoretical frameworks for the conceptualization of adult psychosocial development. Many aspects of the psychosocial domain interact often and in a number of ways with various characteristics of the motor domain. This is observed in many circumstances in which exercise is involved. Factors such as a sense of well-being, body image, locus of control, and depression may be influenced by an adult's involvement in physical activity. Maintaining a physically active lifestyle may also prove beneficial in the attainment of a sense of integrity during the latter stages of psychosocial development. Older adults, however, will face major decisions about retirement and may encounter ageism that could limit potential opportunities. Older adults who maintain good health and remain physically active can enhance their retirement circumstances while dispelling myths about older adult stereotypes. Health status and levels of physical activity are also recognized as predictors of longevity and successful aging.

Terms to Remember

Crisis state
Crisis solution
Intimacy
Isolation
Generativity
Stagnation
Integrity
Despair
Life structure
Eras
Transitions

Mentors
Sense of well-being
Body image
Locus of control
Depression
Activity theory
Disengagement theory
Retirement
Ageism
Successful aging

Critical Readings

Dacey, J. & Travers, J. (1991). *Human Development Across the Lifespan* (Chapters 18, 20, & 22). Dubuque, IA: Wm. C. Brown.

Hird, J. S. & Williams, J. M. (1989). The psychological effects of chronic exercise in the elderly. In A. C. Ostrow (Ed.), *Aging and Motor Behavior* (pp. 173–200). Indianapolis, IN: Benchmark Press.

Palmore, E. (1979). Predictors of successful aging. *The Gerontologist,* 19, 427–431.

Palmore, E. (1982). Predictors of the longevity difference: A 25-year follow-up. *The Gerontologist,* 22, 513–518.

Rybash, J. M., Roodin, P. A., & Santrock, J. W. (1991). *Adult Development and Aging* (2nd ed.) (Chapters 9–11). Dubuque, IA: Wm. C. Brown.

SECTION **VI**

PROGRAMMING

Chapter **22**

Developmental Physical Activity: A Curricular Model

CHAPTER COMPETENCIES

Upon completion of this chapter you should be able to:

- *Individualize physical activity instruction to accommodate the developmental levels of each learner*
- *Plan physical activity programs for all age groups*
- *Demonstrate awareness of within-age individual differences in planning physical activity programs for any portions of the life span*
- *Diagram the sequential basis for a developmentally-based physical education program*
- *Discuss what is meant by the term "developmental physical education" and how it is related to scientific study of motor development*

Key Concept: The utility of knowledge concerning the process of motor development from infancy through adulthood can be found in movement skill learning programs that are developmentally based.

Throughout the discussions in the preceding chapters, we have continually focused on the developmental stages that infants, children, adolescents, and adults pass through in their motor development. The thesis of this entire text has centered on the process of motor development and factors that impinge on its normal sequential progression. If the phases and stages of motor development presented in Chapter 4 and elaborated on throughout this text have any real meaning, we should be able to construct a curricular model congruent with these phases. This curricular model should embody the first and foremost key concept of this text, namely that: "motor development is progressive change in motor behavior throughout the life cycle, brought about by interaction among the requirements of the task, the biology of the individual, and the conditions of the environment" (p. 3). Additionally, it should serve as a "blueprint for action;" it should comprise the basic structure around which instructional lessons are planned and carried out by the teacher, therapist, or coach in the activity room, gymnasium, or swimming pool, or on the playing field. What has been discussed in the preceding chapters is of little value if we cannot apply it to the lives of real people. The value of theory and research that fails to foster models for implementation is limited at best. Curricular models that are not based on sound research and theory are equally worthless. It is, therefore, the purpose of this chapter to propose a developmentally based, dynamic curricular model for implementing developmentally appropriate movement experiences for children, adolescents, and adults.

Curricular Models in Physical Activity

A variety of curricular models are used in implementing movement skill learning programs for infants, children, adolescents, and adults. Obviously, the developmental model will be discussed and advocated here. The developmental approach to physical education aims to instruct individuals in the use of their bodies so that they can execute a wide variety of fundamental movements efficiently and effectively throughout life, and apply these basic abilities to a wide range of specialized movement skills for daily living, recreational, or competitive sport needs.

At the heart of the developmental model is emphasis on learning that utilizes individually appropriate movement tasks in an environment that promotes increased movement competence at all levels. Games, sports, and dances from the traditional content areas of physical education serve as vehicles or tools for improving skill. Please refer to Figure 22.1 for a visual representation of the dynamical nature of the developmental model advocated here.

The developmental approach also teaches individuals to move with awareness of how and why they move. Movement education programs that use the movement concepts originally proposed by Laban and Lawrence (1947) possess many of the characteristics embodied in the developmental model. These movement concepts are important but, like the content areas of physical education, should serve as vehicles by which appropriate movement skills are selected, developed and refined.

L The instructor (i.e. Parent/Teacher/Coach/Therapist) determines what type of *Learning* is desired (i.e. What are the age-appropriate goals or competencies?)

I The instructor assesses, recognizes and respects the *Individuality* of the learner (i.e. What is developmentally appropriate as determined by some form of assessment?)

T The instructor adjusts the goal of the learning *Task* to suit the needs of the individual (i.e. Task Analysis based on the above needs of the learner)

E The instructor manipulates the conditions of the *Environment* by making specific curricular decisions. (i.e. To facilitate increased motor control, movement skill learning and movement competence)

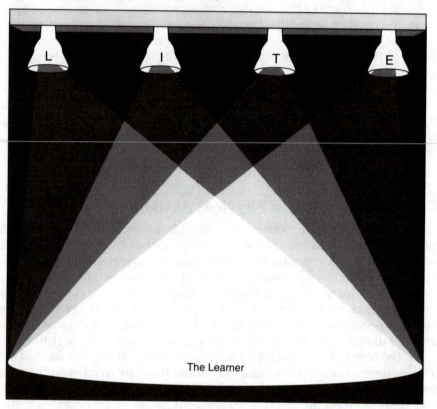

The Learner

The developmental model presented here recognizes the validity of many curriculum rationales. It does, however, place the individual rather than the content areas or movement concepts, at the center of the curricular process. The text *Developmental Physical Education for Today's Children* (Gallahue, 1993) represents an attempt to unite both the traditional and movement analysis approaches to teaching children's physical education.

To facilitate presentation of the developmental model, we will first review the three categories into which movement may be classified, and the appropriate movement skill themes that may be extracted from each category. Then we will briefly discuss the three major content areas of physical activity and the elements of movement education. We will then look at the stages in the process of movement skill learning and the implications for emphasizing indirect or direct methods of teaching. The elements of cognitive concept learning will also be discussed. Finally, a model will be presented for individuals at the fundamental movement phase, and for those at the specialized movement phase of their movement skill development. No scope and sequence charts, lesson plans, or suggestions for developmentally appropriate activities are provided here. The reader is instead referred to a variety of resources for that information including: Carlisle and Cole (1994), and Gallahue (1993).

Categories of Movement and Movement Skill Themes

The three *categories of movement* as they relate to motor development have been discussed extensively. Briefly, a "category of movement" is a classificatory scheme based on common underlying principles of movement. Locomotion, manipulation, and stability are used here to represent these underlying principles. Although others have used the term non-locomotor rather than stability as a category of movement, we have chosen to give recognition to the term stability as a movement category. Doing so is not arbitrary or without support from others. Smith and Smith (1962), Riggs (1980), and Keough and Sugden (1985) have all chosen to classify movement behavior into the categories of locomotion, manipulation, and stability. These three categories serve as the organizing centers of the developmental curriculum and as the basis for the formation of movement skill themes (Figure 22.2).

A *developmental skill theme* is a particular fundamental movement or sport skill around which a specific lesson or series of lessons is organized. In the developmental curriculum a category of movement serves as the organizing center of each unit of the curriculum, while skill themes serve as the organizing centers of the daily lesson plan. Each category of movement is briefly reviewed here, and a few examples of possible skill themes are given.

Concept 22.1   The developmental physical education curriculum utilizes a movement skill theme approach for the learning of fundamental and specialized movement skills.

Figure 22.2
Selected funda-
mental movement
skill themes

Fundamental Stability Movements Stressed	Fundamental Locomotor Movements Stressed	Fundamental Manipulative Movements Stressed
Bending	Walking	Throwing
Stretching	Running	Catching
Twisting	Jumping	Kicking
Turning	Hopping	Trapping
Swinging	Skipping	Striking
Inverted supports	Sliding	Volleying
Body rolling	Leaping	Bouncing
Landing	Climbing	Ball rolling
Stopping		Punting
Dodging		
Balancing		

Stability

Stability refers to the ability to maintain one's balance in relationship to the force of gravity even though the nature of the application of the force may be altered or parts of the body may be placed in unusual positions. The classification of stability extends beyond the concept of balance and includes various axial movements and postures in which a premium is placed on controlling one's equilibrium. Stability is the most basic form of human movement. It is fundamental to all efficient movement and permeates the categories of locomotion and manipulation. Bending, stretching, pivoting, dodging, and walking on a balance beam are examples of skill themes that may be incorporated into the daily lesson plan at the fundamental or sport skill phase of development.

Locomotion

Locomotion refers to changes in the location of the body relative to fixed points on the ground. To walk, run, hop, jump, slide, or leap is to be involved in locomotion. The movement classification of locomotion develops in conjunction with stability, not apart from it. Fundamental aspects of stability must be mastered before efficient forms of locomotion may occur. The vertical jump, rebounding, and high jumping are examples of skill themes that may be incorporated into the daily lesson plan at the fundamental or sport skill phase of development.

Manipulation

Gross-motor manipulation is concerned with giving force to objects and absorbing force from objects by the use of the hands or feet. The tasks of throwing, catching, kicking, trapping, and striking are included under the category of manipulation. Manipulation also refers to the fine motor controls required for tasks such as buttoning, cutting, printing, and writing. The scope of this book, however, has been limited to gross motor aspects of manipulation. Large muscle manipulative abilities tend to develop somewhat later than stability and locomotor abilities. This is due, in part, to the fact that most manipulative movements incorporate elements of both stability and locomotion. Throwing a ball, passing a football, and pitching a baseball are examples of skill themes within the manipulative category of movement.

Content Areas of Physical Activity

Fundamental movements and sport skills within the three categories of movement outlined above may be developed and refined through the three major *content areas* of physical activity: "games and sports," "rhythms and dance," and "self-testing activities." Learning how to participate in particular games, dances, or self-testing activities is a means of developing stability, locomotor, and manipulative abilities appropriate to the developmental level of the individual. Teachers must not lose sight of this goal. Every activity used in the program should be selected on the basis of what it can contribute to developing and refining certain movement abilities and to the fitness components. The primary objective of the learner may be having fun, but the basic objectives of instructors should involve teaching the children how to move and learn through movement. Incorporating fun as a motivation tool is an important objective of any good educational program. However, when fun becomes the primary objective of the program for the teacher, then the program ceases to be educational and becomes little more than a recreation period.

Concept 22.2 The traditional content areas of physical activity, when viewed from the developmental perspective, are a means to an end, namely learning to move and learning through movement, rather than as ends in themselves.

Games and Sports

Games and sports are used to enhance movement abilities appropriate to each child's developmental level. They are often classified into subcategories that proceed from the simple to the complex as follows.

1. Low organized games and relays
2. Lead-up games
3. Official sports

Rhythm and Dance

Rhythm and dance are important content areas of the movement program. All coordinated movement is rhythmical and involves the temporal sequencing of events and the synchronizing of actions. Rhythmic dance activities are generally categorized into the following sub-categories:

1. Rhythmic fundamentals
2. Creative dance
3. Folk and square dance
4. Social dance

Self-Testing

Self-testing is the third major content area of the program representing a wide variety of activities in which children work on their own and can improve their performances through their own efforts. Self-testing activities may be classified in a variety of ways. The following is a common classification scheme for typical self-testing activities.

1. Fundamental movement activities
2. Sport skill activities
3. Physical fitness activities
4. Stunts
5. Tumbling
6. Small (hand) apparatus
7. Large apparatus

Achieving effectiveness and efficiency in each of the three categories of movement at either the fundamental or specialized movement skill phase is the primary reason for incorporating games, dance, and self-testing activities in the program. The degree to which this is achieved depends on the particular developmental level of the learners and the teacher's expertise in structuring developmentally appropriate movement experiences. Games, dances, and self-testing activities serve only as the vehicles by which these experiences are applied.

Movement Concepts of Movement Education

Fundamental movements and sport skills within the three categories of movement may be elucidated in terms of *movement concepts.* The development of particular movement concepts—*effort, space,* and *relationships*—is the central focus of many movement education programs and is omitted from most traditional physical education programs. In the developmental curriculum, the concepts of movement are included and represent an emphasis of the program along with the three content areas discussed in the preceding section. The primary focus of the developmental curriculum is on fundamental and specialized movement skill development through implementation of movement skill themes. These skill themes are applied to the understanding and application of movement concepts and the content areas of physical activity.

Concept 22.3 The movement concepts of movement education provide the learner with a conceptual framework for learning.

A brief explanation of the three movement concept areas in relationship to movement skill development follows and is summarized in Table 22.1.

Table 22.1 The Movement Concepts of Movement Education

Effort (How the body moves with varying amounts of—)	Space (Where the body moves at different—)	Relationships (Moving with—)

—Force
  strong
  light
  moderate
 	
—Time
  fast
  slow
  medium
  sustained
  sudden
 	
—Flow
  free
  bound
	—Levels
	  high/medium/low
	
	—Directions
	  forward/backward
	  diagonally/sideward
	  up/down
	  various pathways
	  (curved, straight,
	    zig-zag, etc.)
	
	—Ranges
	  body shapes (wide,
	    narrow, curved,
	    straight, etc.)
	  body spaces (self-space
	    and general space)
	  body extensions (near/
	    far, large/small, with
	    and without
	    implements)
		—Objects (or people)
		  over/under
		  in/out
		  between/among
		  in front/behind
		  lead/follow
		  above/below
		  through/around
		
		—People
		  mirroring
		  shadowing
		  in unison
		  together/apart
		  alternating
		  simultaneously
		  partner/group

Effort

The concept of *effort* deals with "how" the body moves. Individuals need to learn about the concept of effort. Effort may be subdivided into three categories, with the possibility for a wide variety of movement experiences combined with locomotor, manipulative, and stability movements.

1. *Force* refers to the degree of muscular tension required to move the body or its parts from place to place or to maintain its equilibrium. Force may be heavy, light, or moderate.
2. *Time* refers to the speed at which movement takes place. A movement may be fast or slow, gradual or sudden, erratic or sustained.
3. *Flow* refers to the continuity or coordination of movements. A movement may be smooth or jerky, free or bound.

Space

The concept of *space* deals with "where" the body moves. Movers need to understand where and how their bodies can move in space. The following movement concepts of space can be directly related to all locomotor, manipulative, and stability movements.

1. *Level* refers to the height at which a movement is performed. A movement may be performed at a high, medium, or low level.
2. *Direction* refers to the path of movement. Movement may occur in a forward, backward, diagonal, up, down, left, or right direction, or it may be in a straight, curved, or zigzag pattern.
3. *Range* refers to the relative location of one's body (self-space/general space) and how various extensions of the body (wide/narrow, far/near, long/short, large/small) are used in movement.

Relationships

The concept of relationships deals with both "how and where" the body moves in harmony with objects and other people. The concept of relationships is important to understand and experience through the medium of movement.

1. *Objects* refers to stationing oneself in different positions to objects. Object relationships may be over/under, near/far, on/off, behind/in front, alongside, front/back, underneath/on top, in/out, between/among, and so on.
2. *People* refers to moving in various forms with people. People relationships include solo, partner, group, and mass movement.

Levels of Movement Skill Learning

The content areas and the movement concepts just discussed may be implemented in a variety of ways. The instructor must, however, be aware that individuals tend to pass through typical learning levels as they develop and refine new movement skills. These levels are based on two developmental concepts: the acquisition of movement abilities progresses from the simple to complex and individuals proceed gradually from general to specific in the development and refinement of their abilities. With these two concepts and the models of Fitts and Posner (1967), Gentile (1972), and Lawther (1977), it is possible to view learning a skill as a phenomenon that occurs in the sequence depicted in Figure 22.3. When involved in developing new stability, locomotor, or manipulative skills that are to be used in games, rhythm, or self-testing activities, we all generally go through the following sequence of learning experiences.

1. We first develop a conscious cognitive awareness of the general elements of the task, and *explore* the movements involved in the task in relative isolation to one another. The learner does not have control of movement but gets used to the task and forms a gross general framework of the pattern or skill.
2. We *discover* ways and means of executing each of these movements better through indirect means such as the observation of others, pictures, films, or books. During this aspect of achieving a gross general framework, the learner begins to gain control and to coordinate the task. It becomes relatively automatic.
3. We *combine* the isolated movements with others and experiment with them in various ways. This is a practice stage in which separate tasks are integrated, explored, and utilized in varying ways.
4. We *apply* best ways of combining each of these movements through a variety of lead-up games, informal competitions, and presentations. This aspect of practice is more specific and detailed than the previous stage, with more attention given to utilizing several entire skill-related tasks.
5. We produce a *refined performance* of the selected movements and execute the particular activity through formal or informal means of competition or through leisure-time pursuits. This is often called the automatic or skill diversification stage, and is a time for refining and smoothing performance.
6. We *individualize* or personalize the movement skill in accordance with our particular needs, interests, strengths, and limitations.

Figure 22.3
Levels and stages of learning a new movement skill (*Source:* Gallahue, D. L. [1993]. *Developmental Physical Education for Today's Children.* Dubuque, IA: Brown & Benchmark)

Concept 22.4 The levels of learning a new movement skill are age-independent, and as such may be used as a guide for effective teaching with children, adolescents, and adults.

This sequential progression of learning a new movement skill is similar for adolescents and adults as well as for children. The adolescent and adult are frequently at the specialized skill phase and may spend less time with exploration, discovery, and the combination of new skills, and more time in the application and refined performance aspects of the sequence. Preschool and primary grade children at the fundamental movement pattern phase of development spend a great deal of time exploring, discovering, and combining new movements and less time with the application of best ways of moving and the refined performance of activities.

Facilitating Exploration

Exploration represents the first level of the movement skill learning hierarchy. In order to take advantage of this level, the teacher focuses on indirect teaching approaches that encourage exploration. The *movement exploration technique* of teaching movement helps enhance knowledge of the body and its potential for movement in space. Individuals are encouraged to explore and experiment with the movement potentials of their bodies. Accuracy and skill in performance are not stressed. The leader refrains from establishing a model of performance for the particular movement being explored. Instead, the leader presents participants with a series of movement questions or challenges and gives them time to solve these problems as they see fit. Any "reasonable" solution to the problem is regarded as correct. At this time, there is no "best" method of performance that the leader attempts to elicit. The leader is more concerned with creative involvement in the learning process.

Movement exploration experiences are concerned less with the product of the movement act and more with acceptable execution of fundamental movements. However, the process of learning during the act is of great importance. The leader is not particularly concerned with whether the ball goes in to the hoop, how high Chet can jump, or how far Ruth can throw. The leader is interested in guiding participants to achieve some degree of success within the levels of their own particular abilities. The leader also places importance and value on their ability to think and act independently.

This is not to imply that success or goal-directed behavior is not important. On the contrary, movement exploration techniques are particularly appropriate for young children and novice learners because they structure the environment for success simply by considering all reasonable solutions to the movement problems as correct. Success and goal-directed behavior are individual standards that do not require emulation of a model or competition with others but permit achievement within the limits of one's own abilities. The individual is continually encouraged to experiment with endless variations that influence the performance of all locomotor, manipulative, and stability movements in both the content areas (games, rhythms, and self-testing activities) and the movement concept areas (effort, space, and relationships).

Concept 22.5   Developmentally based teaching recognizes the learner's current level of movement skill learning and makes adjustments to facilitate the learning process.

Developmental Physical Activity   **515**

Facilitating Discovery

Discovery represents the second classification of the movement skill learning hierarchy. Movement experiences that incorporate discovery may be included in the lesson by the leader in an indirect manner similar to the use of movement exploration techniques. The *guided discovery* method of teaching is often used when the learner is in the process of finding solutions. The use of this technique requires the leader to avoid establishing a model for "correct" performance at the outset of the experience. Instead, the leader poses problems in the form of questions or challenges. These questions zero in on movement pattern development rather than on skill development. The movement exploration method utilizes *problem-solving* techniques as a tactic in developing movement abilities. Gilliom (1970) defined problem solving as "original thinking, an individual's technique of productive thinking, his techniques of inquiry, which is characterized by (1) a focus on an incomplete situation, (2) the freedom to inquire, and (3) the desire to put together something new to him, on his own, to make the incomplete situation into a complete one" (p. 21).

It is the method employed by the individual in solving problems posed by the leader that causes exploration and guided discovery to be considered separately here. Whereas movement exploration considers all solutions correct in the absence of a performance model, the guided discovery technique incorporates an observation phase into the total experience. The observation phase takes the form of observing the solutions of fellow learners, the leader, or individuals on film in relation to the problem presented. Only after the learners have had an opportunity to solve the problem within the limits of their own understanding and ability is the observation phase utilized.

Instead of making problems entirely open-ended, as in movement exploration, the leader gradually narrows the questions to prompt the learners to discover for themselves how to perform the particular movement under consideration. The absence of one best solution at this stage allows for the performance of several "best" ways. After applying solutions to the problem, the learners evaluate their solutions in light of those of others. They are then given an opportunity to reassess their solutions in light of the performance of others (Figure 22.4).

Facilitating Combination

Combination represents a transitional category in the hierarchical sequence of learning. Movement experiences that use a combination of movement patterns or skills are incorporated into the lesson by the leader through the use of both indirect and direct styles of teaching.

Indirect combination is a logical extension of the movement exploration and guided discovery approaches. These experiences differ only in that activities involving stability, locomotion, and manipulation are combined through the problem-solving approaches used at the exploration and discovery stages of learning.

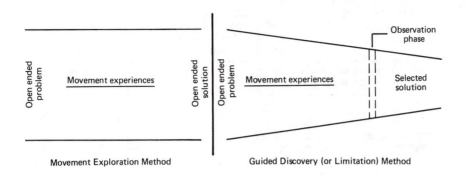

Figure 22.4
Differences be-
tween movement
exploration and the
guided discovery
teaching tech-
niques, both of
which utilize indi-
rect methods

Concept 22.6 Both indirect and direct styles of teaching can be effective, but an instructor should adopt a style based on knowledge about the learner as an individual.

Direct combination experiences follow a more traditional approach to developing and refining combinations of stability, locomotor, and manipulative movements. Traditional teaching approaches involve establishing models for correct performance through explanation, and demonstrating skills to be learned before they are practiced. The learners then duplicate the movement characteristics of the model as nearly as possible within the limits of their abilities in a short practice session or drill. The teacher then stops the group, and the model is presented again along with general comments concerning problems that the group as a whole may be encountering. The group is then involved in an activity that incorporates these skills. The leader circulates among the learners and aids individuals who may be having difficulty executing the skills proficiently. Direct combination experiences require a model for performance to be established before the movement experience begins, while indirect combination experiences do not. The task and the command styles of teaching as proposed by Mooston and Ainsworth (1991) are two of the most commonly used teacher-directed methods (Figure 22.5).

Facilitating Application

Application represents the fourth level of the learning hierarchy. To take advantage of this level of experience, the leader should help the students to make conscious decisions concerning the best methods of performing the numerous combinations of stability, locomotor, or manipulative skills. Rather than refining combinations of fundamental movements, learners begin to select and apply preferred ways of moving in a wide variety of sport, game, and dance activities. Application experiences follow the same direct progression as direct combination experiences: explanation, demonstration, and practice, followed by general and specific correction and drill. Application experiences, however, employ activities that are more advanced than those used in the combination stage. These experiences generally take the form of advanced

Figure 22.5
At the combination
stage of movement
skill learning, the
instructor often uti-
lizes both indirect
and direct methods
of teaching

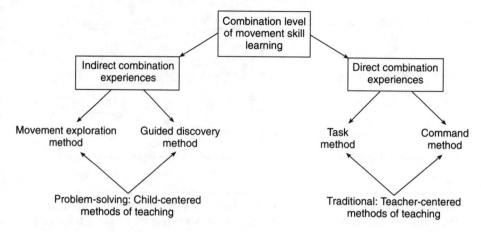

lead-up activities to dual, team, and individual sports, not low organized games and sport skill practice. Lead-up activities combine two or more selected skills into an approximation of the official sport. Advanced lead-up activities used during this period incorporate numerous elements of the official sport, modified in terms of the time, equipment, and facilities required. The desired combination of specialized movement skills to be performed in the official sport is adopted during this period.

Facilitating Refined Performance

Refined performance is the fifth level in the movement skill learning hierarchy. Individuals at this stage are ready to pit their skills and abilities against those of others. Refined performance as used here refers to the actual implementation of activities from the application stage in youth sports, interscholastic sports, intramurals, and informal recreational activities. As the performance becomes more refined, the leader places greater emphasis on accuracy and form in performing in a single, best way.

Concept 22.7   The highest form of movement skill learning occurs when learners personalize their movement repertoires to reflect individual needs, interests, strengths, and limitations.

Facilitating Individualization

The process of individualization is unique to each performer. The individual at this level is able to make fine adjustments in her performance to personalize and maximize performance. Adjustments are made based on body size, weight, limb length, fitness level, motor abilities, and other factors that may influence her level of performance. The distinctive features of one's golf game, lay-up shot, or swimming style represent the individualized level of movement skill learning. Occasional breakthroughs in skill performance come about at this level. The individual critically examines her strengths and weaknesses and thoroughly conceptualizes the skill, which enables her to create entirely new ways of moving. The Fosberry method of high jumping pioneered by olympic gold medalist Bill Fosberry, a once traditional high jumper in the 1960s, and the basketball wizardry of Michael Jordan in the 1990s are two examples. Both athletes were able to individualize skills in their respective sports, and in doing so vastly improved their performances.

In short, the person at the individualized stage uses both inductive and deductive thought processes in concert with her movement abilities to maximize individual performance potentials. To be able to adapt movements to the demands of the environment and to put a personal stamp on movement skills represents the zenith of the movement skill learning hierarchy. It is the essence of becoming a *skillful mover*.

Cognitive Concept Learning

Movement skill learning, at the fundamental or specialized movement skill levels, is an active process intricately interrelated with cognition. Movement skill learning cannot occur without the benefit of higher thought processes. All voluntary movement requires an element of cognition. The more complex the movement task, the more complicated the cognitive processing involved. As movement skills are learned, *cognitive maps*, or mental images, are formed. These images are retained in memory, ready to be recalled and recreated instantly. As skill continues to improve, performance appears to involve little or no conscious thought. Although movement skill performance is not automatic in the true sense of the word, the skill becomes so thoroughly ingrained that it appears to be. For example, when we walk from place to place we give scant attention to how, when, and exactly where we place one foot in front of the other. We do not consciously think about how our arms swing in opposition to our leg action or how we stride forward in an alternating heel-toe fashion. All of these processes have been so thoroughly learned that they appear to be automatic because they do not require conscious attention. Try, however, to walk on ice, in sand, or with a heavy backpack. The different set of conditions under which the task is performed will cause you, for a short while, to consciously attend to the modified requirements of the task until a new cognitive map has been formed and put into memory. It is critically important for leaders to help individuals learn both the skill concepts and the movement concepts associated with how their bodies can and should move. By doing so, we materially aid them in forming cognitive maps of fundamental and specialized movement skills.

Concept 22.8   Learning is a process that occurs from the inside out through trial and error, exploration and discovery.

Jean Piaget (1952, 1969) was among the first to demonstrate a link between motor processes and cognitive learning. Piaget's work highlighted the important role that movement plays in the cognitive development of infants and young children. His phases of development clearly illustrate the connection between movement and early cognition. Furthermore, the achievement of competence within the preoperational phase and the concrete operations phase that follow are considerably aided through the process of movement.

An important outgrowth of Piaget's work has been a cognitive theory of learning that emphasizes the **process** aspects of learning and not simply the product. Cognitive theory views learning as a process that involves experimentation, exploration, and individual decision making; a process that necessitates the reconstruction of incorrect events into a new, correct, whole. Piaget's view of learning underscores importance of indirect, exploratory, guided-discovery, and problem-solving approaches to learning, particularly for those at the beginning or novice levels of learning a new movement skill.

Movement activities have frequently been used by classroom teachers, as well as physical education teachers, to reinforce academic concepts associated with mathematics, language arts, science, and social studies. The evidence is clear; the use of movement as a means of reinforcing academic concepts works—in terms of both information learned and information retained over an extended period of time. Cognitive concept learning is a viable outcome of the developmentally based physical education program. It takes into account each individual's levels of cognitive development and motor development. It recognizes that the motor and cognitive domains are intertwined and enjoy a reciprocal relationship.

Concept 22.9   Movement skill learning is an active process, influenced by factors within the task, the individual, and the environment.

Cognitive concept learning, therefore, is defined as the process by which information is organized, put into memory, and made available for recall and application to a variety of settings. In a movement sense, cognitive concept learning utilizes movement activities to aid in the retention, recall, application, and use of one or more of the cognitive concept components that follow.

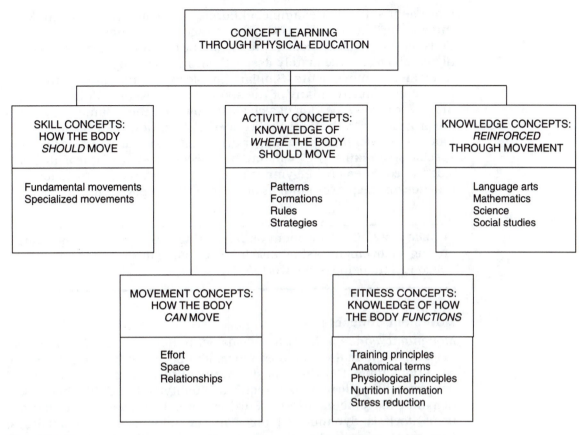

Figure 22.6
The components of cognitive concept learning (*Source:* Gallahue, D. L. [1993]. *Developmental Physical Education for Today's Children.* Dubuque, IA: Brown & Benchmark)

There are several aspects of cognitive concept learning from a movement sense (Figure 22.6). Each is briefly discussed in the following paragraphs with a view toward how it may be put to use in the developmental physical education curriculum.

Skill Concepts

Skill concept learning deals specifically with how the body **should** move. Teachers and coaches must recognize that problems associated with insufficient instructional time, large classes, immaturity in some children, and task complexity make it quite difficult to attain the goal of developing skillful movers within the confines of the instructional class. Therefore, it is essential for children and adults to learn how their bodies should move in the performance of fundamental and specialized movement skills. For example, children are frequently unable to kick, throw, or dribble a ball at the mature stage. Unfortunately, the instructional portion of the school day fails, for one or more of the reasons mentioned above, to adequately assist them in becoming skillful in these fundamental movements. Similarly, adolescents and adults often find it difficult to master many of the sport skills presented during the regular instructional portion of a class. If, however, these same individuals are provided with the vital skill concepts about how their bodies should move when kicking, throwing, or dribbling a ball, or when performing specific sport skills, they will have the necessary tools for learning outside the confines of the gymnasium. They will have the tools for skill practice on the playground, at home, or on the sport team.

Concept 22.10   Movement skill learning involves more than mastering a movement task; it also involves using movement as a means of conceptualizing one's world.

Movement Concepts

Movement concept learning deals with how the body **can** move. Seldom, in the real world, does movement occur under the exact same conditions time after time. Most movement tasks in games, sport, and dance are dynamic in nature, requiring fluidity and flexibility in the participant's movement patterns. Furthermore, the ecology of the environment itself is dynamic. Changes in the playing surface, facilities, equipment, and number of participants make it virtually impossible to address all the possibilities. The dynamic nature of movement, the changing ecology of the environment, and the situational requirements of the task make it absolutely essential for learners to understand how their bodies can move.

We should introduce the learning of a new movement skill first under static conditions in which the environment and the task itself are stable and unchanging. Such an atmosphere is essential at the beginning/ novice level of new movement skill learning. We must be mindful, however, that this movement skill will seldom be performed in isolation or under the same static conditions in which it is originally learned. This fact highlights the importance of movement concept learning as an essential aid to learning the many and varied ways in which the body is capable of moving in the performance of a single fundamental movement skill or a group of skills chained together as specialized sport skills.

The environment in which we move is dynamic and constantly changing. It demands plasticity or adaptability of movement. To equip young learners with the ability to move in a variety of ways in all sorts of circumstances, we need to be certain that they have ample opportunities to experiment with and explore the movement concepts of *effort*, *space*, and *relationships*. By experiencing how the body can move (effort), where the body can move (space), and with whom and with what the body can move (relationships), children become versatile dynamic movers—movers capable of responding with skill and precision, but also with plasticity, to the endless variety of movement circumstances in which they move every day.

Activity Concepts

Activity concept learning deals with **where** the body should move. Activity concepts center on the learning of patterns, formations, rules, and strategies for effective participation in game, sport, and dance activities. Developmental physical education recognizes the importance of activity concept learning as a means of providing learners of all ages with a knowledge base for effective participation in recreational and competitive settings outside of the physical education class. Therefore, when we help children learn the activity concepts involved in six-a-side soccer, kickball, or the Electric Slide, we are providing them with essential tools of understanding where they should position themselves, how to respond to elements of the activity, and the rules and strategies for successful participation. Activity concepts must be geared to each learner's levels of motor, cognitive, and affective development. The concepts must be both age-group appropriate and individually appropriate.

Although activity concepts can and should be taught in a systematic manner, they are not the main focus of the lesson. The primary focus of the developmental lesson is on movement skill learning and fitness enhancement, not on playing games or engaging in competition. Activity concepts provide the learner with the tools for effective participation in games, dances, and sports that take place primarily outside of the instructional program.

Concept 22.11   Cognitive concept learning through active movement provides the learner with the tools for learning how to learn.

Fitness Concepts

Fitness concept learning deals with **what** one needs to do in order to gain and maintain a healthy lifestyle. Because of the physiological requirements for achieving training effects, fitness enhancement is not a realistic goal in physical education programs that do not provide sufficient frequency, intensity, and time. Individuals must, however, learn essential fitness concepts for healthful living and develop appreciation for how to incorporate these concepts into their daily lives.

Learners of all ages need to understand and have opportunities to apply the principles of fitness training. It is important for them to know not only the components of health-related and performance-related fitness, but also how each may be enhanced. It is essential that children begin to learn and apply basic anatomical terms such as "abdominals," "biceps," and "triceps," as well as physiological terms such as "target heart rate," "threshold of training," and "ballistic stretching." All learners should know about the link between proper nutrition, fitness, and good health. Because of the stressful nature of many of our lives, it is becoming increasingly important to teach basic principles of relaxation and stress reduction.

Fitness concepts can be effectively integrated into the developmental physical education program. They must, however, be integrated in a manner that is both developmentally sound and pedagogically valid. In other words, it is important to recognize the cognitive comprehension level of your students, and to tailor fitness concepts to that level of understanding. Also, it is essential that a curricular sequence of progression be adopted that builds concept upon concept, and avoids the trap of teaching the same thing year after year with little or no consideration given to curricular progression.

Academic Concepts

Academic concept learning involves using movement activities as a means of reinforcing concepts in language arts, mathematics, science, and social studies. Movement activities have repeatedly been shown to be an effective means for helping individuals grasp, through the use of additional sensory modalities (primarily the tactile and kinesthetic modes), concepts that were heretofore taught only in the two-dimensional, auditory-visual environment of the classroom.

In order for academic concept learning to be effective in the gymnasium, two things must be done. First, you must take time to talk with classroom teachers and, when possible, to visit the classrooms. This will provide you with valuable information on what is being taught, when it is being presented, and how the children respond. You will need to discuss in specific terms what you can do to supplement and reinforce the classroom curriculum. Such a procedure has an added bonus in garnering support for your program. Classroom teachers who know that you are interested in what they are trying to accomplish have a tendency to be more receptive to what you are trying to achieve. You will gain allies in the support and promotion of your program when you show interest in the classroom teachers' programs.

Second, you must teach for transfer. In other words, you must help the student make the link between what is being taught in the classroom and how it can be applied in the gymnasium. It is not enough to assume that students will make this link themselves. When teaching for transfer it is important to utilize the gymnasium as a medium of demonstrating the relevancy of academic concepts. For example, the importance of learning fractions can easily be demonstrated when you teach students how to compute batting averages or win-loss percentages. The ethnic heritage of cultures from around the world can be described through games and folk dances characteristic of various cultures. Stories can be told through small group mini-plays that emphasize movement components. Academic concept learning can be effectively reinforced in the gymnasium. It should be a byproduct of good teaching that accommodates and responds to the needs of the whole person.

A Developmental Curricular Model

Unfortunately, programs stressing specialized movement skill development for young children abound throughout North America. Specialized skill development places primary emphasis on refined performance and little emphasis on the other aspects of the learning sequence outlined above. There is nothing inherently wrong with skill specialization, but we must ask ourselves whether skill specialization in the preschool and elementary school is really in the best interests of most children. If so, it should only supplement a developmental curriculum in the form of after-school activities. Specialized skill development should never overshadow or replace the primary purpose of the regular physical education program at the preschool and elementary school levels which is to develop and refine fundamental movement skills and introduce a wide variety of sport skills. We must involve all individuals in a series of coordinated movement experiences that go beyond the learning of isolated skills and the in-school playing of specific sports. The developmental model of physical education is based on the proposition that the development of movement abilities occurs in distinct but often overlapping "phases" (reflexes, rudimentary movement abilities, fundamental movement patterns, and specialized movement abilities) in each of the "categories of movement" (stability, locomotion, and manipulation). This is achieved through participation in skill themes that are applied to "content areas" of physical education (self-testing, games and sports, and rhythmics), "components of physical fitness" (health-related and performance related), and "cognitive concepts" of movement (skill concepts, movement concepts, activity concepts, fitness concepts, academic concepts). Concepts are applied at the appropriate levels of "movement skill learning" (exploration, discovery, combination, application, refined performance, individualization) recognized through the implementation of various "indirect" (movement exploration and guided discovery) and "direct" (command and task) teaching approaches (Figure 22.7).

Concept 22.12   The developmental curricular model places the learner at the heart of the teaching-learning process.

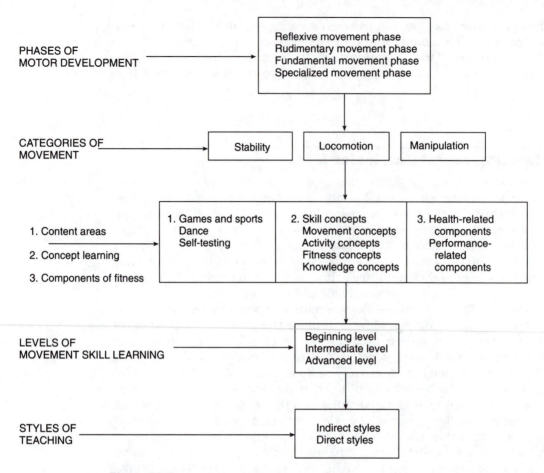

Figure 22.7
Outline of the conceptual framework for the developmental physical education program (*Source:* Gallahue, D. L. [1993]. *Developmental Physical Education for Today's Children.* Dubuque, IA: Brown & Benchmark)

Fundamental Phase

Developmental teaching recognizes that preschool and primary grade children are generally involved in developing and refining their fundamental movement abilities in the three categories of movement. These categories are the organizing centers of the curriculum and skill themes at this level. Each pattern of movement found under these three categories can be treated in relative isolation from the others (see Figure 22.1). These fundamental movements are the basis for sport skill movements. They are developed and refined at the exploration, discovery, and combination stages of learning through indirect styles of teaching that make use of games, rhythms, and self-testing activities and the application of effort, space, and relationship concepts (Figure 22.8).

GRADE LEVEL ⟶ Pre-kindergarten and primary grades

USUAL PHASE OF
MOTOR DEVELOPMENT ⟶ Fundamental movement phase ····· Initial stage
Elementary stage
Mature stage

CATEGORIES OF
MOVEMENT ⟶

Stability	Locomotor	Manipulative

FUNDAMENTAL MOVEMENT
SKILL THEMES ⟶

Axial movements	Walking	Throwing
Static balancing	Running	Catching
Dynamic balancing	Jumping	Kicking
Landing	Skipping	Trapping
Stopping	Climbing	Striking
Dodging		

APPLIED TO:
1. Content areas ⟶
2. Concept learning
3. Physical fitness

1. Self-testing
Dance
Games

2. Movement concepts
Skill concepts
Knowledge concepts

3. Health-related fitness
Performance-related fitness

TYPICAL LEVEL OF
MOVEMENT SKILL LEARNING ⟶ Beginning/novice level

PRIMARY
TEACHING STYLES ⟶
(but not limited to these)

Indirect styles

Exploratory approach
Guided discovery approach
Limitation approach

Figure 22.8
Implementing the developmental model in the pre-kindergarten and primary grades
level (*Source:* Gallahue, D. L. [1993]. *Developmental Physical Education for Today's Children.* Dubuque, IA: Brown & Benchmark)

Specialized Phase

When the developmental model is applied to older children, adolescents and adults, the focus of the curriculum generally changes from the fundamental movement phase to the specialized movement skill phase of development. Individuals are constantly combining various stability, locomotor, and manipulative patterns of movement in a wide variety of sport skills. Because of this, it becomes impossible to implement movement skill themes that focus on only one category of movement. Instead, at this level, skill themes are viewed in the context of the sport area to which they are being applied. The game of softball, for example, becomes a "sport skill theme" and involves combinations and elaborations of fundamental manipulative abilities (throwing, catching, striking), locomotor abilities (base running and sliding), and stability abilities (twisting, turning, and stretching). The teacher at this level focuses on developing skills related to a particular sport theme. This approach is applied to the various content areas and activity concepts (rules, strategies, understandings, and appreciation) of physical education. The teacher recognizes that the learner's goals at this level are to combine skills and apply the "best" ways of performing; therefore, the teacher uses direct teaching methods (Figure 22.9).

Chapter 22

Summary

For too many years parents, teachers, coaches, and therapists, as well as the general population, have had only a vague notion of the importance of balanced motor development and movement education for infants, children, adolescents, and adults. The developmental model presented here is based on the phases of motor development. Movement experiences and teaching methodologies that recognize the dynamic developmental level of the individual are used. Games, dance, and self-testing activities as well as concepts of effort, space, and relationships are regarded as the means of achieving increased skill rather than as ends in themselves. Learning to move is too important to be left to chance or to the whims of untrained persons. Leaders with knowledge of (1) the phases of motor development, (2) how individuals learn, and (3) how to implement developmentally appropriate programs are vital in developing the movement and physical competence in learners of all ages.

	Stability	Locomotor	Manipulative

GRADE LEVEL ⟶ Intermediate and upper elementary grades

USUAL PHASE OF MOTOR DEVELOPMENT ⟶ Specialized movement phase ┄┄┄┄ Transitional stage / Application stage

CATEGORIES OF MOVEMENT ⟶

1. Sport skill units
2. Sport skill themes ⟶

1. Basketball skills
   Dance skills
   Volleyball skills
   Soccer skills
   Gymnastics skills
   etc.

2. Combination and elaborations of stability, locomotor, and manipulative skills

APPLIED TO:
1. Content areas
2. Concept learning
3. Physical fitness ⟶

1. Self-testing
   Dance
   Games and sports

2. Skill concepts
   Activity concepts
   Fitness concepts

3. Health-related fitness
   Performance-related fitness

TYPICAL LEVEL OF MOVEMENT SKILL LEARNING ⟶ Intermediate/practice level

PRIMARY TEACHING STYLES (but not limited to these) ⟶ Direct styles

Limitation approach
Task approach
Command approach

Figure 22.9
Implementing the developmental model in the intermediate and upper elementary grades (*Source:* Gallahue, D. L. [1993]. *Developmental Physical Education for Today's Children.* Dubuque, IA: Brown & Benchmark)

Terms to Remember

Developmental approach
Movement analysis approach
Categories of movement
Developmental skill
Stability
Locomotion
Manipulation
Content areas
Games and sports
Rhythms
Self-testing
Movement concepts
Effort
Space
Relationships
Force
Time
Flow
Level

Direction
Range
Levels of movement skill learning
Exploration
Discovery
Application
Refined performance
Individualization
Movement exploration technique
Guided-discovery technique
Problem-solving
Indirect combination
Direct combination
Skillful mover
Skill concepts
Activity concepts
Academic concepts
Fitness concepts

Critical Readings

Balan, C. M. & Davis, W. E. (1993). Ecological task analysis—An approach to teaching physical education. *Journal of Physical Education, Recreation and Dance,* 64, 9, 54–61.

Carlisle, C. & Cole, S. (1994). *Skillful Movers.* Dubuque, IA: Brown & Benchmark.

Gallahue, D. L. (1993). *Developmental Physical Education for Today's Children.* Dubuque, IA: Brown & Benchmark.

Magill, R. A. (1993). *Motor Learning: Concepts and Applications* (Chapters 7–9). Dubuque, IA: Brown & Benchmark.

Mooston, M. & Ainsworth, S. (1991). *Teaching Physical Education.* Columbus, OH: Charles E. Merrill.

Chapter **23**

Assessing Motor Behavior

CHAPTER COMPETENCIES

Upon completion of this chapter you should be able to:

- *Describe the various characteristics of a well-developed assessment instrument*
- *Discuss various ways to categorize and select assessment instruments*
- *Identify motor assessment instruments that target the age populations of infants, toddlers, and preschoolers*
- *Identify motor assessment instruments that target the age populations of preschoolers, elementary children, middle school youth, and high school adolescents*
- *Identify motor assessment instruments that target the age population of adults*
- *Discuss the concept of naturalistic approaches to assessment*

Key Concept: Motor assessment of developmental levels is essential if developmentally appropriate physical activity programming is to be a reality for infants, children, adolescents, and adults.

   Assessment serves a very important purpose in the area of motor development. Evaluating various aspects of an individual's motor behavior enables the movement specialist to monitor developmental changes, identify developmental delays, and gain insight into instructional strategies. There is no dearth of assessment instruments that purport to measure motor abilities. Hundreds of formal tests exist, both published and unpublished, designed with the measurement of various motor behavior characteristics in mind. There are also assessment methods that represent a less formal, more naturalistic approach to the evaluation of an individual's motor characteristics. The challenge for the evaluator is to identify the most appropriate assessment procedures and instruments for the individual or group to be assessed.

Characteristics of Assessment Instruments

A well-designed assessment instrument should have high *reliability, validity,* and *objectivity.* A test that is reliable will provide consistent scores from one test administration to the next. A valid test is one that measures what it claims to measure. Test validity is determined by experts (content validity), comparison to other tests measuring similar characteristics (criterion validity), or multivariate statistical methods (construct validity). An objective test will yield similar results when it is administered by different testers on the same individual.

Concept 23.1   High values of reliability, validity, and objectivity are important characteristics of assessment instruments.

Assessment instruments can be categorized in various ways. *Norm-referenced tests* are based on a statistical sampling of hundreds or even thousands of individuals. They permit one to compare an individual against a statistical sample that is intended to be representative of the population at large. Caution, however, should be used when interpreting results from norm-referenced tests. Test norms are generally population-specific; that is, one can not generalize beyond the population on which the norms were generated. *Criterion-referenced tests,* on the other hand, incorporate a pre-established standard to which the individual's scores are compared. The standard represents a performance goal. The individual either achieves the standard or does not. No comparison to other persons is made.

Concept 23.2   Assessment instruments can be categorized as norm-referenced, criterion-referenced, product-oriented, and/or process-oriented.

Assessment tools can also be classified as either *product instruments* or *process instruments.* Product instruments are quantitative in nature and focus on the outcome or end result of a particular performance. Examples of product-oriented scores include how far a ball is thrown, how fast a child runs, and how much weight an adult lifts. Mechanics and technique are not considered with product instruments. Process instruments, on the other hand, focus on the form, style, or mechanics used to perform the desired skill. Little attention is directed to the result of the skill performance. Of these two types of assessments the product instruments are by far the most prevalent.

Concept 23.3   Several critical factors must be considered before an assessment instrument is selected.

When selecting an assessment instrument it is important to remember that one category of test is not inherently better than another. A norm-referenced test may address the needs of a particular population more adequately than a criterion-referenced test. Under a different set of conditions the converse may be true. The same can be said of the process-product comparison. A process instrument may be the better choice for assessing the motor skill patterns of a preschool-aged child who is not disabled, but a product-oriented approach may be more appropriate with an adult who has experienced a stroke. Selecting the most appropriate assessment instrument requires consideration of the reasons why the evaluation is being performed, the instrument's characteristics, the relevance of the procedure to the individual's circumstances, and the capabilities of the evaluator.

Formal Assessment Instruments

As previously mentioned in this chapter there are numerous assessment instruments available that attempt to measure motor behavior. As space does not allow a review of all available tests, this section will focus on a select few that represent assessment approaches with various age groups.

Concept 23.4   A variety of assessment instruments have been developed for the motor performance measurement of infants, toddlers, and preschoolers.

Infancy—Early Childhood

Medical and allied health professionals routinely conduct motor assessments of infants, toddlers, and preschoolers. With the passage of Public Law 99-457 (1986) by the federal government, which amended the 1975 Education of the Handicapped Act by expanding services to children from birth to 2 years of age with developmental disabilities, education professionals began to play a greater role in the assessment of the very young. The following assessment instruments are designed to measure motor behavior aspects of infants, toddlers, and preschoolers. *Screening tests* are often used with the very young child. These tests are designed to provide a relatively quick and simple means of differentiating normal infants or children from those who may not be developing normally.

Apgar Assessment. Virginia Apgar (1953) developed the Apgar screening test as a quick and reliable method of assessing the newborn immediately after birth. An Apgar rating is made 1 minute after birth with subsequent ratings given 5 or more minutes after delivery. Infants are assigned a value of 0, 1, or 2 for each of the following items: (1) heart rate, (2) respiratory effort, (3) irritability, (4) muscle tone, and (5) color. The maximum total score is 10. Infants with low Apgar ratings generally require immediate attention if they are to survive. Table 23.1 provides a summary of the five items and how they are scored. Apgar scores appear to be quite reliable. The test was standardized by Apgar and James (1962) on 27,715 infants. The standardization showed that infants with the lowest Apgar scores had the highest mortality rates and that the device was useful in predicting infant mortality.

Table 23.1 Scoring the Apgar Screening Test

Item tested	Scoring		
	2	1	0
Heart rate	100–140 bpm	Under 100	No heartbeat
Respiratory effort	Regular breathing and lusty crying	Irregular or shallow breathing	No breathing
Reflex irritability (measured by a slap to the soles of the feet)	Lusty crying when soles of feet are slapped	No crying but grimace or movement when soles of feet are slapped	No reaction when soles of feet are slapped
Muscle tone	Spontaneously flexed arms and legs resist attempts at extension	Spontaneously flexed arms and legs offer little resistance from attempts at extension	Completely flaccid
Color[1]	Entirely pink	Some pink	Other than pink

[1]This is the most controversial item in the test. Few infants receive a 2 at one minute, and the item is, of course, invalid with dark-skinned babies.

Denver Developmental Screening Test. The Denver Developmental Screening Test (DDST) constructed by Frankenburg and Dodds (1967) has long been a helpful device used to screen infants and young children. The *Denver II* (Frankenburg, Dodds & Archer, 1990; 1992) replaces the DDST as the latest version of this popular assessment drive. The norms have been updated, language items increased, and a subjective test behavior rating scale added. The DDST is one of the most widely used standardized tests for evaluating the motor development of young children. Both gross and fine motor skills are assessed along with language and personal-social skills. The 125 items on the test are scaled according to their normal developmental order of appearance in children. Seldom are more than 25 of the 125 items administered in order to provide a profile of the child's developmental level. Table 23.2 provides a brief overview of the test and some of the items assessed.

Table 23.2 Sample Items from the Denver II

Area Tested	Sample Items Measured
Gross motor (32 items measured)	Rudimentary stability abilities: control of head, neck, trunk, rolling over, sitting, standing with support, pulling to stand, cruising, standing alone, walking Fundamental manipulative abilities: kicking, throwing, tricycle riding, catching Fundamental locomotor abilities: jumping in place, long-jumping, hopping Fundamental stability abilities: balancing on one foot, heel-toe walk
Fine motor (30 items measured)	Rudimentary manipulative abilities: reaching, grasping, and releasing, cube stacking, scribbling, copying, draw-a-person
Language (39 items measured)	Vocalizing, laughing, squealing, sound imitation of speech sounds, rudimentary combining words, following directions, recognizing colors, defining words
Personal-social (24 items measured)	Smiling, feeding, drinking from cup, imitating housework, helping in house, removing garment, putting on clothing, washing and drying hands, playing interactive games, separating from mother easily, dressing without supervision

The DDST has been standardized on a sample of 1,036 children ranging in age from 2 weeks to 6 years. It has received criticism as being unrepresentative (Buros, 1971). Herkowitz (1978) has stated that:

> Although easy to administer, and capable of being used by relatively untrained testers—the DDST is not so reliable or valid as its authors had hoped. Its use for children under 30 months old should be discouraged because of questionable reliability at that age (p. 168).

The DDST should only be used as a gross screening measure that may provide some clues to potential developmental delays of a child and should not, at this time, be considered as a valid or reliable instrument for research or placement purposes.

Bayley Scales of Infant Development. The Bayley Scales of Infant Development (BSID) (Bayley, 1969) is a revision of Bayley's (1935) earlier work, which attempted, through behavioral assessment, to measure the intellectual development of the child. Very little relationship was found between the infant's score on mental scales and later intelligence or later performance on mental scales. As a result, the current BSID purports to assess only the child's developmental status from 1 month of age to 2+ years.

The BSID is divided into three separate scales: mental, motor, and infant behavior record. Table 23.3 presents a brief overview of these three scales and the general items measured. The mental scale contains 163 items. The motor scale consists of 81 items measuring progressive change in gross motor abilities such as sitting, standing, walking, and stair climbing, and fine motor abilities. Materials for the motor scale can be expensive and require special equipment.

The BSID scales are probably the best standardized behavioral assessment techniques available for infants. They have had the most extensive use as a research instrument of any of the infant assessment scales and have proven to be helpful in determining the developmental status of individual infants at a given age. When administered and interpreted by a trained examiner, they can be a valuable research tool.

The Peabody Developmental Motor Scales. The Peabody Developmental Motor Scales (PDMS) is designed to assess fine motor and gross motor development of children from birth to 83 months of age. Fine motor characteristics evaluated include manual dexterity, eye-hand coordination, and grasping. Gross motor items include reflexes, locomotor skills, non-locomotor skills, and balance. The PDMS is both a norm-referenced and a criterion-referenced instrument.

 Concept 23.5   Several assessment instruments have been developed for the motor performance measurement of preschoolers, elementary-aged children, middle school-aged youth, and adolescents.

Table 23.3 General Description of the Items Measured on the Bayley Scales of Infant Development

Scale	Items Assessed
Mental scale	Sensory-perceptual acuities Object discrimination Object constancy Memory Learning Problem solving Vocalization Verbal communication Generalizations and classifications
Motor scale	Control of the body Gross motor coordination Fine motor coordination
Infant behavior record	Administered after the mental and motor scales. Assesses the child's social development, interests, emotions, energy, and tendencies to approach or withdraw from situations.

Early Childhood—Adolescence

Motor assessment can be particularly important during the preschool and school years. Development can be monitored year after year through proper evaluation scheduling. A well-planned assessment schedule can yield valuable information for individualized instructional strategies as students advance through their preschool, elementary, middle school, and high school years. The following assessment instruments were designed with the preschool and school-aged child in mind.

The Purdue Perceptual-Motor Survey. The Purdue Perceptual-Motor Survey (PPMS) developed by Roach and Kephart (1966) is not a true test. It serves more as a behavioral assessment survey that provides the examiner with an opportunity to observe a broad spectrum of behaviors. In fact, Roach and Kephart note that "at its present level of development the survey should be regarded merely as an instrument which allows the examiner to observe a series of perceptual-motor behaviors and to isolate areas which may need further study" (pp. 10–11). The survey is based on Kephart's theory that all learning is based on the sensorimotor experiences of childhood.

The PPMS is designed for children from 6 to 10 years of age, but is often used with both younger and older children in an effort to gain some clues concerning possible perceptual-motor problems. Table 23.4 outlines the various components of the survey and how they are measured.

Table 23.4 Test Items from the Purdue Perceptual-Motor Survey

Items Assessed	Method
Balance and posture walking	Walking forward, backward, sideways on board; performing a series of eight tasks evaluating ability to jump, hop, and skip while maintaining balance
Body image and differentiation	Identification of body parts, imitation of movement, obstacle course activities, Kraus-Weber Test, angels-in-the-snow
Perceptual-motor match performing	Making circle, double circle, lateral line, and vertical line on chalkboard; eight rhythmic writing tasks
Ocular control	Ocular pursuits of both eyes, right eye, left eye, and convergence
Form perception square	Seven geometric forms are drawn on sheet of paper: circle, cross, triangle, horizontal diamond, vertical diamond, and divided rectangle

The PPMS has been used successfully for several years to discriminate between children who are experiencing problems in their motor development and those who are not. Surveys, however, do not provide for detailed evaluation of specific characteristics. Interpretation and generalization of results can, therefore, be limited. Despite these shortcomings, the PPMS may be of use by the evaluator as an observational assessment instrument that may offer some important clues to the perceptual and motor functioning of the child.

Bruininks-Oseretsky Test of Motor Proficiency. The Bruininks-Oseretsky Test of Motor Proficiency (BOTMP) was developed by Bruininks (1978) as an "individually administered test that assesses the motor functioning of children from 4+ to 14+ years of age" (p. 11). The BOTMP is composed of 8 subtests designed to measure important aspects of motor behavior. Table 23.5 provides an overview of the BOTMP. The gross motor skill and fine motor skill sections of the test may be administered separately and will yield separate composite scores. In order to arrive at a composite score for the entire battery of tests, a combination gross and fine motor skills test must be taken along with the separate gross motor items and separate fine motor items. A short form of the BOTMP is also available. It has, however, been suggested that the BOTMP short form be used only as a screening device and not for diagnostic or placement purposes (Verderber & Payne, 1987).

Table 23.5 Test Items from the Bruininks-Oseretsky Test of Motor Proficiency

Area Tested	Subtest	Items
Gross motor skills	1. Running—Designed to measure running speed	Shuttle run
	2. Balance (8 items)—Designed to measure static and dynamic balance abilities	Static balance (3 items) Dynamic balance (5 items)
	3. Bilateral coordination (8 items)—Designed to measure simultaneous coordination of upper and lower limbs	Foot and finger tapping (3 items) Jumping in place (4 items) Drawing lines and crosses simultaneously (1 item)
	4. Strength (3 items)—Designed to measure upper arm and shoulder girdle strength, abdominal strength, and leg strength	Standing broad jump Sit-ups Knee push-ups (boys under 8 and all girls) Full push-ups (boys 8 and older)
Gross and fine motor skills	5. Upper limb coordination (9 items)—Designed to measure gross and fine eye-hand coordination	Ball bounce and catch (2 items) Catching tossed ball (2 items) Throwing a ball (1 item) Touching swinging ball (1 item) Precise upper limb movements (3 items)
Fine motor skills	6. Response speed (1 item)—Designed to measure response to a moving object	Yardstick drop (1 item)
	7. Visual-motor control (8 items)—Designed to measure coordination of eye-hand movements	Cutting (1 item) Drawing and copying (7 items)
	8. Upper limb speed and dexterity (8 items)—Designed to measure hand and finger dexterity, hand speed, and arm speed	Penny placing (2 items) Card sorting (1 item) Bead stringing (1 item) Peg displacing (1 item) Lines and dots (3 items)

The BOTMP has good potential for assessing the motor proficiency of children. It can be of value as a research tool, and an aid for identifying children with special needs. There is also a corresponding developmental curriculum package called Body Skills that can be purchased separately from the test. Feasibility, however, with the BOTMP can be a problem as it can be very time consuming to administer the test, and children are generally tested individually.

Fundamental Movement Pattern Assessment Instrument. The Fundamental Movement Pattern Assessment Instrument (FMPAI) designed by McClenaghan (1976), later published by McClenaghan and Gallahue (1978), and expanded by Gallahue (1993) is a carefully developed observational assessment instrument. It is used to classify individuals at the "initial," "elementary," or "mature" stage of development first using a total body configuration approach, followed by an individual segmental analysis approach. The original version assessed five primary fundamental movements (throwing, catching, kicking, running, and jumping). The expanded version is designed to assess more than 20 fundamental movement patterns. The developmental sequence for each of these movements is based on a review of the biomechanical literature on each fundamental movement.

The FMPAI is an easy-to-administer, easy-to-use, subjective motor development test designed to measure the present status of children and to assess change over time. It attempts to view the quality of the child's movement, and is based on documented developmental sequences for acquiring selected fundamental movement abilities. The FMPAI does not, however, yield a quantitative score, nor can it be used for comparing one child to another. This instrument is intended instead to assess developmental changes over time, using observational assessment as a valid and reliable method of data collection and comparison among individuals.

Developmental Sequence of Fundamental Motor Skills Inventory. The Developmental Sequence of Fundamental Motor Skills Inventory (DSFMSI) assessment instrument was developed by Seefeldt and Haubenstricker (1976) and Haubenstricker et al. (1981). The DSFMSI categorizes each of 10 fundamental motor patterns into 4 or 5 stages. The fundamental movements of walking, skipping, hopping, running, striking, kicking, catching, throwing, jumping, and punting have been studied. These developmental sequences are based on combinations of longitudinal and cross-sectional data obtained from film analysis. Children are observed and matched to both visual and verbal descriptions of each stage. Individuals are classified along a continuum from stage 1 (immature) to stage 5 (mature) (Payne and Isaacs, 1991).

Test of Gross Motor Development. The Test of Gross Motor Development (TGMD) was developed by Ulrich (1985) as a means of assessing selected movement skills in children 3 to 10 years of age. Selected locomotor and manipulative skills comprise the 12-item test. Locomotor skills include running, galloping, hopping, leaping, horizontal jumping, skipping, and sliding. Manipulative skills include 2-hand striking, stationary ball bouncing, catching, kicking, and overhand throwing.

Administration of the TGMD takes approximately 15 minutes per child. A manual with a clear set of test instructions is available. The TGMD is easy to administer, and can be used with a minimum amount of special training. It provides both norm-referenced and criterion-referenced interpretations, and places emphasis on the sequence and qualitative aspects of gross motor skill acquisition rather than on the product and quantitative aspects of performance. A set of instructional videos titled *Assessment of Fundamental Motor Skills* (Ignico, 1994) is also available that corresponds with the use of the TGMD. These videotapes enable viewers to develop their observational assessment skills, and are highly recommended as a means of improving interrater and intrarater reliability.

Test of Motor Impairment-Henderson Revision. The Test of Motor Impairment-Henderson Revision (TOMI-H) is designed to provide insight into a child's level of motor deficiency. Four age bands (5–6 years, 7–8 years, 9–10 years, and 11 years and upward) are used to identify which items are to be measured. Each age band consists of 8 items representing both fine and gross motor tasks. The TOMI-H was found to be highly consistent with the BOTMP with regard to motor impairment decisions (Riggen et al., 1990).

Ohio State University Scale of Intra Gross Motor Assessment. The Ohio State University Scale of Intra Gross Motor Assessment (O.S.U. SIGMA) was developed to measure basic locomotor and manipulative skills of children ages 2 1/2 to 14 years. Additional test items include stair and ladder climbing. Accompanying the O.S.U. SIGMA is an instructional program called the Performance Base Curriculum. The Performance Base Curriculum provides activities that correspond to the developmental levels identified in the O.S.U. SIGMA.

Basic Motor Ability Tests-Revised. The Basic Motor Ability Tests-Revised (BMAT-R) developed by Arnheim and Sinclair (1979) consists of a battery of 11 tests designed to measure a variety of motor functions. These include eye-hand coordination, static and dynamic balance, fine and gross motor control, agility, and joint flexibility. Norms are reported for males and females aged 4 to 12 years. The authors of the BMAT-R reported that a group of up to 5 children can be assessed by a single test administrator in approximately 30 minutes.

Adults

The motor performance of adults is quite variable, and that variability increases with advancing age. Assessing motor characteristics of the adult is a key ingredient in establishing intervention strategies for the maintenance of functional abilities or the perpetuation of an active lifestyle.

Concept 23.6 Several assessment instruments have been developed for the motor performance measurement of adults.

Functional Fitness Assessment for Adults Over 60 Years. The Functional Fitness Assessment for Adults Over 60 Years (FFAA) is a field test that measures a combination of health-related physical fitness components and motor performance characteristics. Areas of investigation include flexibility, endurance, strength, balance, gait, reaction time, and posture. Test items are designed to relate to the daily functions of the older adult. In addition, the FFAA can be administered by individuals not necessarily trained in clinical settings.

Scales of Activities of Daily Living. Numerous instruments exist that purport to assess functional ability in activities of daily living (ADL). These activities include basic self-care skills such as eating, dressing, toileting, grooming, and functional mobility. Law and Letts (1989) conducted a critical review of scales of ADL and compared the purpose, clinical utility, reliability, and validity of 13 instruments. For greater detail on specific scales of ADL the reader is advised to refer to the Law and Letts study.

Naturalistic Approaches to Assessment

The majority of the previously discussed assessment instruments require formal, structured settings in which to evaluate individuals. Distance that is to be covered during a run, and size of ball to be tossed, are examples of how structured tests establish restrictions to the way motor performance is measured. Some assessment instruments are so specific that they dictate what is to be stated when directions are given.

Concept 23.7 Naturalistic approaches to assessment increase the opportunity to evaluate an individual's motor performance from a much broader perspective that encompasses the relationship between the task goal, the environment, and the performer.

By eliminating all but one or two environmental conditions from a particular task, the scope of the individual's ability cannot be truly measured. In addition, an individual's motor performance observed within the structured setting of a test condition may not be indicative of the person's performance in a more natural, realistic situation. Two approaches that attempt to accommodate both the individual being tested and the environmental conditions that may influence motor performance are ecological task analysis and interdisciplinary play-based assessment.

Ecological Task Analysis

Ecological task analysis (ETA) examines performance in light of the relationships among the task goal, the environment, and the performer. Davis and Burton (1991) describe 4 steps in establishing an ETA. The first step is selecting and presenting the task goal. This involves determining the function(s) of the task or what will be accomplished by the task. The second step is to allow the child or adult who is being tested the opportunity to choose the skill, the movement pattern, and when the task requires, the implement to complete the task. The third step involves giving the individual guidance by emphasizing the goal of the task and stressing attention to the environmental conditions corresponding to the task. Guidance may also be provided by manipulating certain task dimensions so as to make the task more difficult without altering the task goal. The fourth step involves providing direct instruction regarding the individual's skill selection and movement form. This incorporates more traditional forms of instruction such as giving a demonstration of the proper skill mechanics.

Ulrich (1988) developed an assessment model that addresses many of the ETA's considerations. His model uses striking an object as the example task. He provides numerous conditions under which an object may be struck. Aspects that may be manipulated include the striking implement, the movement of the ball, the size of the ball, and the conditions under which the individual is observed (formal test, informal play, or structured play). An example of the task conditions and sample score sheet can be seen in Tables 23.6a and 23.6b.

Ecological task analysis represents a very promising approach to the assessment of motor behavior characteristics. It increases the opportunity to evaluate an individual's motor performance from a very broad perspective.

Interdisciplinary Play-Based Assessment

A second assessment approach that attempts to evaluate individuals in a more naturalistic setting is interdisciplinary play-based assessment (IPBA). Used primarily with young children IPBA utilizes a team of professionals with varying areas of expertise. Team members may represent the areas of psychology, physical therapy, occupational therapy, special education, and adapted physical education. Collectively, the team observes the child interacting with a parent, parents, or family members. Following the interaction session the assessment team discusses their observations and uses an interdisciplinary approach in determining diagnosis and educational planning and placement.

The IPBA approach takes seriously the philosophy that the developmental domains of behavior are interrelated. For a more in-depth discussion on IPBA the reader is urged to read *Transdisciplinary Play-Based Assessment: A Functional Approach to Working with Young Children* by T. W. Linder (1990).

Table 23.6 Ulrich's Developmental Task Analysis Model for Striking

Task Conditions	Proposed Sequence
A. Striking Implement	1 — $A_1 B_1 C_1$
1. Hand	2 — $A_1 B_1 C^2$
2. Lightweight racquetball racquet	3 — $A_1 B_1 C_3$
3. Narrow plastic bat	4 — $A_1 B_2 C_1$
	5 — $A_1 B_2 C_2$
B. Ball Movement	6 — $A_1 B_2 C_3$
1. Stationary on batting tee	7 — $A_1 B_2 C_1$
2. Slow underhand toss from 15 feet	8 — $A_1 B_3 C_2$
3. Overhand toss from 15 feet	9 — $A_1 B_3 C_3$
	10 — $A_2 B_1 C_1$
C. Ball Size	11 — $A_2 B_1 C_2$
1. 12-inch lightweight ball	12 — $A_2 B_1 C_3$
2. 8-inch lightweight ball	13 — $A_2 B_2 C_1$
3. 4-inch lightweight ball	14 — $A_2 B_2 C_2$
	15 — $A_2 B_2 C_3$
	16 — $A_2 B_3 C_1$
	17 — $A_2 B_3 C_2$
	18 — $A_2 B_3 C_3$
	19 — $A_3 B_1 C_1$
	20 — $A_3 B_1 C_2$
	21 — $A_3 B_1 C_3$
	22 — $A_3 B_2 C_1$
	23 — $A_3 B_2 C_2$
	24 — $A_3 B_2 C_3$
	25 — $A_3 B_3 C_1$
	26 — $A_3 B_3 C_2$
	27 — $A_3 B_3 C_3$

(Source: *Ulrich, D. A. [1988].* JOPERD, *59, 43–47.*)

Summary

The process of motor assessment is important in monitoring developmental changes, identifying developmental delays, and providing insight into instructional strategies. A number of assessment instruments exist that purport to measure various aspects of motor behavior. The characteristics of a well-developed test should include strong reliability, validity, and objectivity. Assessment instruments may be classified as norm-referenced, criterion-referenced, process-oriented, and/or product-oriented.

Assessment tools exist for individuals from birth to adulthood. Evaluation instruments for infants to preschoolers include the Apgar Assessment, Denver Developmental Screening Test, Bayley Scales of Infant

Table 23.6b Test of Basic Striking Competence (Scoring Example)

Observational Contexts and Behavioral Criteria

Name _____

Age _____

Classroom _____

Scoring Key

0—Absent

1—Emerging

2—Mastered

Task Conditions	| 1 Formal Test | Eyes focus on ball (a)	Hip and shoulder rotation (b)	Contralateral weight transfer (c)	Contacts ball (d)	1 Context Score	| 2 Informal Play | Eyes focus on ball (a)	Hip and shoulder rotation (b)	Contralateral weight transfer (c)	Contacts ball (d)	2 Context Score	| 3 Structured Play | Eyes focus on ball (a)	Hip and shoulder rotation (b)	Contralateral weight transfer (c)	Contacts ball (d)	3 Context Score	Total Condition Score
1. A_1 B_1 C_1	2	1	2	2	7	2	1	1	1	5	2	0	1	1	4	16
2. A_1 B_1 C_2	2	1	2	1	6	2	1	1	1	5	2	0	1	1	4	15
3. A_1 B_1 C_3	2	1	1	1	5	2	1	1	1	5	1	0	1	1	3	13
4. A_1 B_1 C_1	1	1	1	1	4	1	1	1	1	4	1	0	1	1	3	11
5. A_1 B_2 C_2	1	1	1	0	3	1	1	0	0	2	1	1	0	0	2	7
6. A_1 B_2 C_3	1	1	1	0	3	1	1	0	0	2	1	0	0	0	1	5
7. A_1 B_3 C_1	1	0	1	0	2	1	0	1	0	2	1	0	0	0	1	5
8. A_1 B_3 C_2	1	0	0	0	1	1	0	0	0	1	1	0	0	0	1	3
9. A_1 B_3 C_3	1	0	0	0	1	1	0	0	0	1	0	0	0	0	0	2
10. A_2 B_1 C_1	2	0	0	1	3	1	0	0	1	2	1	0	0	1	2	7
11. A_2 B_1 C_2	1	0	0	1	2	1	0	0	0	1	1	0	0	0	1	4
12. A_2 B_1 C_3	1	0	0	0	1	1	0	0	0	1	1	0	0	0	1	3
13. A_2 B_2 C_1	0	0	0	0	0	0	0	0	0	0	0	0	0	0	0	0
14. A_2 B_2 C_2	0	0	0	0	0	0	0	0	0	0	0	0	0	0	0	0
15. A_2 B_2 C_3																
16. A_2 B_2 C_3																
17. A_2 B_2 C_3																
18. A_2 B_2 C_3																
19. A_2 B_2 C_3																
20. A_2 B_2 C_3																
21. A_2 B_2 C_3																
22. A_2 B_2 C_3																
23. A_2 B_2 C_3																
24. A_2 B_2 C_3																
25. A_2 B_2 C_3																
26. A_2 B_2 C_3																
27. A_2 B_2 C_3																
Total Context Score					38/216 18%					31/216 14%					23/216 11%	

Total Striking Competence Score   92/648 14%

Development, and Peabody Developmental Motor Scales. For school-aged children assessments include the Purdue Perceptual-Motor Survey, Bruininks-Oseretsky Test of Motor Proficiency, Fundamental Movement Pattern Assessment Instrument, Developmental Sequence of Fundamental Motor Skills Inventory, Test of Gross Motor Development, Test of Motor Impairment-Henderson Revision, O.S.U. Scale of Intra Gross Motor Assessment, and Basic Motor Ability Tests-Revised. Adult assessment instruments include the Functional Fitness Assessment for Adults Over 60 Years and a number of activities of daily living scales.

A more naturalistic approach to assessment attempts to examine an individual's motor performance in light of the relationships among the task goal, the environment, and the performer. Examples of this approach include Ecological Task Analysis and Interdisciplinary Play-Based Assessment.

Terms to Remember

Reliability
Validity
Objectivity
Norm-referenced tests
Criterion-referenced tests
Product instruments
Process instruments
Apgar Assessment
  Screening tests
Denver Developmental Screening
  Test
Bayley Scales of Infant
  Development
Peabody Developmental Motor
  Scales
Purdue Perceptual-Motor Survey
Bruininks-Oseretsky Test of Motor
  Proficiency

Fundamental Movement Pattern
  Assessment Instrument
Developmental Sequence of
  Fundamental Motor Skills
  Inventory
Test of Gross Motor Development
Test of Motor Impairment-
  Henderson Revision
O.S.U. Scale of Intra Gross Motor
  Assessment
Basic Motor Ability Tests-Revised
Functional Fitness Assessment for
  Adults Over 60 Years
Scales of Activities of Daily Living
Ecological Task Analysis
Interdisciplinary Play-Based
  Assessment

Critical Readings

Davis, W. E. (1984). Motor ability assessment of populations with handicapping conditions: Challenging basic assumptions. *Adapted Physical Activity Quarterly*, 1, 125–140.

Davis, W. E., & Burton, A. W. (1991). Ecological task analysis: Translating movement behavior theory into practice. *Adapted Physical Activity Quarterly*, 8, 154–177.

Frankenburg, W. K. et al. (1990). *Denver II Technical Manual*. Denver, CO: Denver Developmental Materials, Inc.

Frankenburg, W. K. et al. (1992). The Denver II: A major revision and restandardization of the Denver Development Screening Test. *Pediatrics*, 89, 1, 91–97.

Gallahue, D. L. (1983). Assessing motor development in young children. *Studies in Educational Evaluation*, 8, 247–252.

Haubenstricker, J. (1978). A critical review of selected perceptual-motor tests and scales currently used in the assessment of motor behavior. In D. M. Landers & R. W. Christina (Eds.), *Psychology in Motor Behavior and Sport* (pp. 536–543). Champaign, IL: Human Kinetics.

Herkowitz, J. (1978). Assessing the motor development of children: Presentation and critique of tests. In M. V. Ridenour (Ed.), *Motor Development—Issues and Applications* (pp. 175–187). Princeton, NJ: Princeton.

Linder, T. W. (1990). *Transdisciplinary Play-based Assessment: A Functional Approach to Working with Young Children*. Baltimore: P. H. Brookes.

Paget, K. D., & Bracken, B. A. (1983). *The Psychoeducational Assessment of Preschool Children* (Chapters 11 & 12). New York: Greene & Stratton.

Self, P. A., & Horwitz, F. D. (1979). The behavioral assessment of the neonate: An overview (pp. 126–164). In J. D. Osofsky (Ed.), *The Handbook of Infant Development*. New York: Wiley.

APPENDIX A

Equivalent Measures

English-Metric

1 inch = 2.54 centimeter
1 foot = 0.3048 meter
1 yard = 0.9144 meter
1 mile = 1.6093 kilometers

1 ounce = 28.349 grams
1 pound = 0.53 kilograms
1 short ton = 0.907 metric ton

1 fluid ounce = 29.573 milliliters
1 pint = 0.473 liter
1 quart = 0.946 liter
1 gallon = 3.785 liters

Metric-English

1 centimeter = 0.3937 inch
1 meter = 3.281 feet
1 meter = 1.0936 yards
1 kilometer = 0.6214 mile

1 gram = 0.35 ounce
1 kilogram = 2.2046 pounds
1 metric ton = 1.1 short ton

1 milliliter = .06 cubic inch
1 liter = 61.02 cubic inch
1 liter = 0.908 dry quart
1 liter = 1.057 liquid quart

APPENDIX B

Inches-Centimeters: Conversion Table

IN	CM	IN	CM	IN	CM
1/32	.08	24	61.0	52	132.1
1/16	.16	25	63.5	53	134.6
1/8	.32	26	66.0	54	137.2
1/4	.64	27	68.6	55	139.7
1/2	1.27	28	71.1	56	142.2
1	2.5	29	73.7	57	144.8
2	5.1	30	76.2	58	147.3
3	7.6	31	78.7	59	149.9
4	10.2	32	81.3	60	152.4
5	12.7	33	83.8	61	154.9
6	15.2	34	86.4	62	157.5
7	17.8	35	88.9	63	160.0
8	20.3	36	91.4	64	162.6
9	22.9	37	93.8	65	165.1
10	25.4	38	96.5	66	167.6
11	28.0	39	99.1	67	170.2
12	30.5	40	101.6	68	172.7
13	33.0	41	104.1	69	175.3
14	25.5	42	106.7	70	177.8
15	38.1	43	109.2	71	180.3
16	40.6	44	111.8	72	182.9
17	43.2	45	114.3	73	185.4
18	45.1	46	116.8	74	188.0
19	48.2	47	119.4	75	190.5
20	50.8	48	121.9		
21	53.3	49	124.5		
22	55.9	50	127.0		
23	58.4	51	129.5		

APPENDIX C

Pounds-Kilograms: Conversion Table

LB	Kg	LB	Kg	LB	Kg	LB	Kg
1	0.54	26	11.77	51	23.10	76	34.42
2	0.90	27	12.23	52	23.55	77	34.87
3	1.35	28	12.68	53	24.00	78	35.32
4	1.81	29	13.13	54	24.46	79	35.77
5	2.26	30	13.59	55	24.91	80	36.24
6	2.71	31	14.04	56	25.36	81	36.69
7	3.17	32	14.49	57	25.82	82	37.14
8	3.62	33	14.94	58	26.27	83	37.59
9	4.07	34	15.40	59	26.72	84	38.05
10	4.50	35	15.85	60	27.18	85	38.50
11	4.98	36	16.30	61	27.63	86	38.95
12	5.43	37	16.76	62	28.08	87	39.41
13	5.88	38	17.21	63	28.53	88	39.86
14	6.34	39	17.66	64	28.99	89	40.31
15	6.79	40	18.12	65	29.44	90	40.77
16	7.24	41	18.57	66	29.89	91	41.22
17	7.70	42	19.02	67	30.35	92	41.67
18	8.15	43	19.47	68	30.80	93	42.12
19	8.60	44	19.93	69	31.25	94	42.58
20	9.06	45	20.38	70	31.71	95	43.03
21	9.51	46	20.83	71	32.16	96	43.48
22	9.96	47	21.29	72	32.61	97	43.94
23	10.41	48	21.74	73	33.06	98	44.39
24	10.87	49	22.19	74	33.52	99	44.84
25	11.32	50	22.65	75	33.97	100	45.30

Bibliography

Chapter 1

Bayley, N. (1935). The development of motor abilities during the first three years. *Monographs of the Society for the Research in Child Development, 1,* 1–26.

Bloom, B. S. et al. (1956). *Taxonomy of Educational Objectives: Handbook I: Cognitive Domain.* New York: David McKay.

Branta, C., Haubenstricker, J., & Seefeldt, V. (1984). Age changes in motor skill during childhood and adolescence. In R. L. Terjung (Ed.), *Exercise and Sport Science Reviews,* Vol. 12. Lexington, MA: Collamore Press.

Clark, J. E., Phillips, S. J., & Petersen, R. (1989). Developmental stability in jumping. *Developmental Psychology, 25,* 929–935.

Clark, J. E., & Whitall, J. (1989). What is motor development? The lessons of history. *Quest, 41,* 183–202.

Clark, J. E., Whitall, J., & Phillips, S. J. (1988). Human interlimb coordination: The first 6 months of independent walking. *Developmental Psychology, 21,* 445–456.

Clarke, H. H. (1971). *Physical Motor Tests in the Medford Boys Growth Study.* Englewood Cliffs, NJ: Prentice-Hall.

Coakley, J. (1987). Children and the sport socialization process. In D. Gould, & M. Weiss (Eds.), *Advances in Pediatric Sport Science: Vol. 2: Behavioral Issues.* Champaign, IL: Human Kinetics.

Ellis, M. J. (1973). *Why People Play.* Englewood Cliffs, NJ: Prentice-Hall.

Gesell, A. (1928). *Infancy and Human Growth.* New York: Macmillan.

Gesell, A. (1929). Learning and growth in identical twins. *Genetic Psychology Monographs, 6,* 1–124.

Gesell, A., & Thompson, H. (1934). *Infant Behavior: Its Genesis and Growth.* New York: McGraw-Hill.

Greulich, W. W., & Pyle, S. I. (1959). *Radiographic Atlas of Skeletal Development of the Hand and Wrist.* Stanford, CA: Stanford University Press.

Halverson, H. M. (1931). An experimental study of prehension in infants by means of systematic cinema records. *Genetic Psychology Monographs, 10,* 107–286.

Halverson, H. M. (1937). Studies of the grasping responses in early infancy. *Journal of Genetic Psychology, 51,* 437–449.

Halverson, L. E. (1966). Development of motor patterns in young children. *Quest, 6,* 44–53.

Halverson, L. E., & Roberton, M. A. (1966). *A study of motor pattern development in young children.* Paper presented at the March 1966 national convention of the AAHPER, Chicago, IL.

Halverson, L. E., Roberton, M. A., & Harper, C. J. (1973). Current research in motor development. *Journal of Research and Development in Education, 6,* 56–70.

Halverson, L. E., & Williams, H. (1985). Developmental sequences for hopping over distance: A prelongitudinal study. *Research Quarterly for Exercise and Sport, 56,* 37–44.

Keogh, J., & Sugden, D. (1985). *Movement Skill Development.* New York: Macmillan.

Kephart, N. C. (1960). *The Slow Learner in the Classroom.* Columbus, OH: Charles E. Merrill.

Krathwohl, D. R., Bloom, B., & Masia, B. (1964). *Taxonomy of Educational Objectives. Handbook II: Affective Domain.* New York: David McKay.

Kugler, P. N., Kelso, J. A. S., & Turvey, M. T. (1980). On the concept of coordinative structures as dissipative structures: I. Theoretical lines of convergence. In G. E. Stelmach, & J. Requin (Eds.), *Tutorials in Motor Behavior,* New York: North Holland.

Lockhart, A. (1964). What's in a name? *Quest, 2,* 9–13.

Logsdon, B. et al. (1984). *Physical Education for Children: A Focus on the Teaching Process.* Philadelphia Lea & Febiger.

Magill, R. A. (1993). *Motor Learning—Concepts and Applications.* Dubuque, IA: Wm. C. Brown.

McGraw, M. B. (1935). *Growth: A Study of Johnny and Jimmy.* New York: D. Appleton-Century.

McGraw, M. B. (1940). Neural maturation as exemplified in achievement of bladder control. *The Journal of Pediatrics, 16,* 580–590.

Piaget, J. (1952). *The Origins of Intelligence in Children.* New York: International Universities Press.

Piaget, J. (1964). Development and learning. *Journal of Research in Science Teaching, 2,* 176–186.

Rarick, G. L. (1981). The Emergence of the Study of Human Motor Development. In G. A. Brooks (Ed.), *Perspectives on the Academic Discipline of Physical Education.* Champaign, IL: Human Kinetics.

Schaie, K. W., & Baltes, P. B. (1975). On sequential strategies in developmental research: Description or explanation. *Human Development, 18,* 384–390.

Seefeldt, V. (1972). *Discussion of walking and running.* Unpublished paper, Michigan State University.

Seefeldt, V., & Haubenstricker, J. (1982). Patterns, phases, or stages: An analytical model for the study of developmental movement. In J. A. S. Kelso, & J. E. Clark (Eds.), *The Development of Movement Control and Coordination.* New York: Wiley.

Shirley, M. M. (1931). *The First Two Years: A Study of Twenty-Five Babies: Vol. 1: Postural and Locomotor Development.* Minneapolis: University of Minnesota Press.

Smoll, F. L. (1982). Developmental kinesiology: Toward a subdiscipline focusing on motor development. In J. A. S. Kelso, & J. E. Clark (Eds.), *The Development of Movement Control and Coordination* (pp. 319–354). New York: Wiley.

Tanner, J. M. (1962). *Growth at Adolescence.* Oxford, England: Blackwell Scientific Publications.

Tanner, J. M., & Whitehouse, R. (1975). *Assessment of Skeletal Maturity and Prediction of Adult Height.* New York: Academic Press.

Thelen, E. (1986). Development of coordinated movement: Implications for early human development. In M. G. Wade, & H. T. A. Whiting (Eds.), *Motor Development in Children: Aspects of Coordination and Control.* Boston: Martinus Nijhoff.

Thelen, E. (1986). Treadmill-elicited stepping in seven-month-old infants. *Child Development, 57,* 1498–1506.

Thelen, E., & Cooke, D. W. (1987a). Relationship between newborn stepping and later walking: A new interpretation. *Developmental Medicine and Child Neurology, 29,* 380–393.

Thelen, E., Kelso, J. A. S., & Fogel, A. (1987b). Self-organizing systems and infant motor development. *Developmental Review, 7,* 39–65.

Thelen, E., & Ulrich, B. D. (1991). Hidden skills: A dynamic systems analysis of treadmill stepping during the first year. *Monographs of the Society for Research in Child Development, 56,* (1, Serial No. 223).

Thomas, J. R., & Thomas, K. T. (1989). What is motor development: Where does it belong? *Quest, 41,* 203–212.

Wetzel, N. C. (1948). *The Wetzel Grid for Evaluating Physical Fitness.* Cleveland: NEA Services.

Wickstrom, R. L. (1983). *Fundamental Motor Patterns*. Philadelphia: Lea & Febiger.

Wild, M. (1938). The behavior pattern of throwing and some observations concerning its course of development in children. *Research Quarterly*, 9, 20–24.

Williams, H. G. (1983). *Perceptual and Motor Development*. Englewood Cliffs, NJ: Prentice-Hall.

Chapter 2

Alexander, R. et al. (1993). *Normal Development of Functional Motor Skills*. Tucson, AZ: Communication Skill Builders.

Bernstein, N. (1967). *The Co-Ordination and Regulation of Movements*. Oxford, England: Pergamon Press.

Delacato, C. (1966). *Neurological Organization and Reading*. Springfield, IL: Charles C. Thomas.

Erikson, E. (1963). *Childhood and Society*. New York: W. W. Norton.

Erikson, E. (1980). *Identity and the Life Cycle*. New York: W. W. Norton.

Freud, A. (1945). *The Ego and Mechanisms of Defense*. New York: International Universities Press.

Freud, S. (1927). *The Ego and the Id*. New York: W. W. Norton.

Gallahue, D. L. (1993). *Developmental Physical Education for Today's Children*. Dubuque, IA: Brown & Benchmark.

Gesell, A. (1928). *Infancy and Human Growth*. New York: Macmillan.

Gesell, A. (1945). *The Embryology of Behavior*. New York: Harper.

Havighurst, R. (1953). *Human Development and Education*. New York: Longmans Green.

Havighurst, R. (1972). *Developmental Tasks and Education*. New York: David McKay.

Havighurst, R., & Levine, R. (1979). *Society and Education*. Reading, MA: Allyn & Bacon.

Kamm, K. et al. (1990). A dynamical systems approach to motor development. *Physical Therapy*, 70, 763–774.

Kugler, P. N., Kelso, J. A. S., & Turvey, M. T. (1982). On the control and coordination of naturally developing systems. In J. A. S. Kelso & J. E. Clark (Eds.), *The Development of Motor Control and Coordination* (pp. 5–78). New York: Wiley.

Lefrancois, G. (1993). *The Lifespan*. Belmont, CA: Wadsworth.

Lerner, P. M. (1986). *Concepts and Theories of Human Development*. Reading, MA: Addison-Wesley.

Maier, H. W. (1978). *Three Theories of Child Development*. New York: Harper & Row.

McClenaghan, B., & Gallahue, D. L. (1978). *Fundamental Movement: A Developmental and Remedial Approach*. Philadelphia: Saunders.

Peterson, R., & Felton-Collins, V. (1986). *The Piaget Handbook for Teachers and Parents*. New York: Teachers College Press.

Piaget, J. (1952). *The Origins of Intelligence in Children*. New York: International Universities Press.

Piaget, J. (1954). *The Construction of Reality and the Child*. New York: Basic Books.

Piaget, J. (1969). *The Psychology of the Child*. New York: Basic Books.

Piaget, J. (1974). Development and learning. In R. E. Riple, & V. N. Rockcastle (Eds.), *Piaget Rediscovered*. Ithaca, NY: Cornell University Press.

Roberton, M. A. (1977). Stability of stage categorization across trials: Implications for the stage theory of overarm throw development. *Journal of Human Movement Studies*, 3, 49–59.

Seefeldt, V. (1979). Development of motor patterns: Implications for elementary school physical education. In C. Nadeau et al. (Eds.), *Psychology of Motor Behavior and Sport–1979*. Champaign, IL: Human Kinetics.

Wadsworth, B. J. (1979). *Piaget's Theory of Cognitive Development*. New York: Longman.

Wild, M. (1938). The behavioral pattern of throwing and some observations concerning its course of development in children. *Research Quarterly*, 3, 20.

Chapter 3

Baker, S. A., & Mednick, B. R. (1984). *Influences on Human Development: A Longitudinal Perspective*. Boston: Kluwer-Nijhoff.

Bayley, N. (1935). The development of motor abilities during the first three years. *Monograph of the Society for Research on Child Development*, 1, 1–26.

Bolby, J. (1958). The nature of the child's tie to his mother. *International Journal of Psychoanalysis*, 39, 350–373.

Bower, T. G. R. (1974). *Development in Infancy*. San Francisco: W. H. Freeman.

Bower, T. G. R. et al. (1970). Demonstration of intention in the reaching behavior of neonate humans. *Nature*, 228–234.

Branta, C. et al. (1987). Gender differences in play patterns and sport participation of North American youth. In D. Gould, & M. Weiss (Eds.), *Advances in Pediatric Sport Sciences: Volume 2: Behavioral Issues*. Champaign, IL: Human Kinetics.

Bredenkamp, S. (Ed.) (1987). *Developmentally Appropriate Practice in Early Childhood Programs Serving Children From Birth Through Age 8*. Washington, DC: National Association for the Education of Young Children.

Bril, B. (1985). Motor development and cultural attitudes. In H. T. A. Whiting, & M. G. Wade (Eds.), *Themes in Motor Development*. Dordrecht: The Netherlands: Martinus Nyhoff Publishers.

Bruch, H. (1940). Energy expenditure in obese children. *American Journal of Disease in Children*, 60, 5.

Bruch, H. (1979). *The Golden Cage—The Enigma of Anorexia Nervosa*. New York: Vintage Books.

Bruner, J. S. (1965). *The Process of Education*. Cambridge, MA: Harvard University Press.

Carmichael, L. (1925). Heredity and environment: Are they antithetical? *Journal of Abnormal and Social Psychology*, 20, 245–260.

Chess, S., & Thomas, A. (1973). Temperament in the normal neonate. In J. C. Westman (Ed.), *Individual Differences in the Child*. New York: Wiley.

Crawford, J. W. (1982). Mother-infant interaction in premature and full-time infants. *Child Development*, 53, 957–962.

Davies, P., & Stewart, A. L. (1975). Low birth-weight infants: Neurological sequelae and later intelligence. *British Medical Bulletin*, 31, 85–91.

DeMyer, W. (1974). Congenital anomalies of the central nervous system. In D. B. Tower (Ed.), *The Nervous System*. New York: Raven.

Dennis, W. (1935). The effect of restricted practice upon the reaching, sitting and standing of two infants. *Journal of Genetic Psychology*, 47, 17–32.

Dennis, W. (1940). Does culture appreciably affect patterns of infant behavior? *Journal of Social Psychology*, 12, 307–317.

Dennis, W. (1960). Causes of retardation among institutional children: Iran. *Journal of Genetic Psychology*, 96, 47–59.

Dennis, W., & Najarian, P. (1957). Infant development under environmental handicap. *Psychology Monographs*, 71, 7.

Diamond, M. P. et al. (1991). Effect of acute physiological elevations of insulin on circulating androgen levels in nonobese women. *Journal of Endocrinol Metabolism*, 72, 883–887.

Dietz, W. H. (1983). Do we fatten our children at the television set? Obesity and television viewing in children and adolescents. *Pediatrics*, 75, 807–812.

Dietz, W. H. (1986). Prevention of childhood obesity. *Pediatric Clinics of North America*, 33, 823–833.

Documenta, G. (1970). Scientific tables. In K. Dierm, & C. Lentner (Eds.), *Scientific Tables*. Barie, Switzerland: Ciba-Geigy.

Drillien, C. M. (1964). *Growth and Development of the Prematurely Born Infant*. Edinburgh, Scotland: Livingstone.

Drillien, C. M. (1970). The small-for-dates infant: Etiology and prognosis. *Pediatric Clinics of North America*, 17, 9–23.

Drillien, C. M. et al. (1980). Low birth weight children at early school age. *Developmental Medicine and Child Neurology*, 22, 26–47.

Eisenberg, R. B. et al. (1966). Habituation to an acoustic pattern as an idea of differences among neonates. *Journal of Auditory Research*, 6, 239–248.

Enos, W. F. et al. (1955). Pathogenesis of coronary disease of American soldiers killed in Korea. *Journal of the American Medical Association*, 158, 912–914.

Fomon, S. J. et al. (1982). Body composition of reference children from birth to age 10 years. *American Journal of Clinical Nutrition*, 35, 1169–1175.

Freud, A. (1965). *Normality and Pathology in Childhood: Assessment of Development*. New York: International Universities Press.

Gallahue, D. L. (1993). *Developmental Physical Education for Today's Children*. Dubuque, IA: Brown & Benchmark.

Gallahue, D. L., Milchrist, P., Morris, H. H., Ozmun, J., & Medalha, J. (1994). *Cross-cultural considerations in the motor performance of young children*. Paper presented at the National Convention of AAHPERD, Denver.

Gerber, M. & Dean, R. F. A. (1957). Gesell tests of African children. *Pediatrics*, 20, 1055–1065.

Gesell, A. (1945). *The Embryology of Behavior*. New York: Harper.

Gesell, A. (1954). The ontogenesis of infant behavior. In L. Carmichael (Ed.), *Manual of Child Psychology*. New York: Wiley.

Gesell, A., & Thompson, H. (1929). Learning and growth in identical twins. *Genetic Psychology Monographs*, 6, 1–124.

Hasselmeyer, E. G. (1964). The premature neonates' response to handling. *American Nurses Association*, 11, 15–24.

Havinghurst, R. (1972). *Developmental Tasks and Education*. New York: David McKay.

Henry, F. M. (1960). Influence of motor and sensory sets: Reaction, latency, and speed of discrete movement. *Research Quarterly*, 31, 459–468.

Henry, F. M., & Rogers, D. (1960). Increased response latency for complicated movements and a memory drum theory of neuromotor reaction. *Research Quarterly*, 31, 448–468.

Hess, E. H. (1959). Imprinting. *Science*, 130, 133–141.

Hilgard, J. R. (1932). Learning and maturation in preschool children. *Journal of Genetic Psychology*, 41, 36–56.

Hinton, G. E. (1992). How neural networks learn from experience. *Scientific American*, 267, 3, 144–151.

Johnson, M. L. et al. (1956). Relative importance of inactivity and overeating in the energy balance of obese high school girls. *American Journal of Clinical Nutrition*, 4, 37.

Kaufman, D. A. (1975). Fundamentals of fat. *The Physical Educator*, 32, 77–79.

Kennell, J. H. et al. (1974). Maternal behavior one year after early and extended post partum contact. *Developmental Medicine and Child Neurology*, 16, 172–179.

Kennell, J. H. et al. (1979). Parent-infant bonding. In J. D. Osofsky (Ed.), *The Handbook of Infant Development*. New York: Wiley.

Klopper, P. et al. (1964). Maternal imprinting in goats. *Proceedings of the National Academy of Science*, 52, 911.

Kopp, C. B. (1982). The role of theoretical frameworks in the study of at-risk and handicapped young children. In D. D. Bricker (Ed.), *Intervention With At-Risk and Handicapped Infants*. Baltimore: University Park Press.

Kopp, C. B., & Kaler, S. R. (1989). Risk in infancy: Origins and implications. *American Psychologist*, 44, 224–230.

Kopp, C. B., & Parmelee, A. H. (1979). Prenatal and perinatal influence on infant behavior. In J. D. Osofsky (Ed.), *The Handbook of Infant Development*. New York: Wiley.

Korner, A. F. et al. (1975). Effects of waterbed flotation on premature infants: A pilot study. *Pediatrics*, 56, 361–367.

Korner, A. F. et al. (1982). Effects of waterbeds on the sleep and motility of the theophylline treated preterm infants. *Pediatrics*, 70, 864–869.

Lamb, M. E. et al. (1985). *Infant-Mother Attachment*. Hillsdale, NJ: Lawrence Erlbaum Associates.

Leifer, A. et al. (1963). Effects of mother-infant separation on maternal attachment behavior. *Child Development*, 43, 1203–1218.

Linder, C. W. et al. (1982). Exercise, serumlipids, and cardiovascular disease—risk factors in children. *Pediatric Clinics of North America*, 29, 1341–1355.

Lipton, E. L. et al. (1961). Autonomic function in the neonate. *Psychosomatic Medicine*, 23, 472–484.

Lorenz, K. (1966). *On Agression*. New York: Harcourt Brace Jovanovich.

Lubcheno, L. O. et al. (1963). Sequalee of premature birth. *American Journal of Disease of Children*, 106, 101–115.

Malina, R. M., & Bouchard, C. (1991). *Growth Maturation and Physical Activity*. Champaign, IL: Human Kinetics.

Mayer, J. (1968). *Overweight: Causes, Cost and Control*. Englewood Cliffs, NJ: Prentice-Hall.

McGraw, M. B. (1935). *Growth: A Study of Johnny and Jimmy*. New York: Appleton-Century.

McGraw, M. B. (1939). Later development of children specially trained during infancy. *Child Development*, 10, 1.

McNamera, J. J. et al. (1971). Coronary artery disease in combat casualties in Vietnam. *Journal of the American Medical Association*, 216, 1186–1187.

Millman, M. (1980). *Such a Pretty Face: Being Fat in America*. New York: Norton.

Minuchin, D. et al. (1978). *Psychosomatic Families—Anorexia Nervosa in Context*. Cambridge, MA: Harvard University Press.

Mossberg, H. O. (1989). 40 year follow-up of overweight children. *Lancet*, ii, 491–493.

Osofsky, J. D., & Conners, K. (1979). Mother infant interaction: An integrative view of a complex system. In J. D. Osofsky (Ed.), *The Handbook of Infant Development*. New York: Wiley.

Ounsted, M., & Ounsted, C. (1973). On fetal growth rate. In *Clinics in Developmental Medicine*. London: William Heinemann Medical Books.

Pace, P. W. et al. (1991). Ethics of obesity treatment: Implications for dietitians. *Journal of the American Dietetic Association*, 91, 1258–1260.

Payne, V. G., & Isaacs, L. D. (1991). *Human Motor Development: A Lifespan Approach*. Mountain View, CA: Mayfield.

Robson, K. (1967). The role of eye-to-eye contact in maternal-infant attachment. *Journal of Child Psychology and Psychiatry and Allied Disciplines*, 8, 13–25.

Rosenbaum, J. et al. (1989). Obesity in childhood. *Pediatric Review*, 11, 43–55.

Rothenberg, A. (1976). Understanding the anorectic student. *Today's Education*, 65, 48–49.

Rubin, R. A. et al. (1973). Psychological and educational sequel of prematurity. *Pediatrics*, 53, 352–363.

Schumer, F. (1983). *Abnormal Psychology*. Lexington, MA: D. G. Heath.

Sciafani, A. D. Dietary obesity. In A. J. Stunkard (Ed.), *Obesity*, Philadelphia: W. B. Saunders.

Seefeldt, V. (1975). *Critical learning periods and programs of intervention*. Paper presented at the National Convention of the AAHPERD, Atlantic City, NJ.

Selkoe, D. J. (1992). Aging brain, aging mind. *Scientific American*, 267, 134–142.

Shirley, M. (1931). *The First Two Years: A Study of Twenty-Five Babies*. Minneapolis: University of Minnesota Press.

Solkoff, N. et al. (1969). Effects of handling on the subsequent development of premature infants. *Developmental Psychology*, 1, 765–768.

Spitz, R. (1945). Hospitalism: An inquiry into the genesis of psychiatric conditions in early childhood. *Psychoanalytic Analysis of the Child*, 1, 53–74.

Stein, E. A. et al. (1981). Coronary risk factors in the young. *Annual Reviews of Medicine*, 52, 601–613.

Stunkard, A. J. et al. (1986). A twin study of human obesity. *Journal of the American Medical Association*, 256, 51–54.

Stunkard, A. J. et al. (1990). The body-mass index of twins who have been reared apart. *New England Journal of Medicine*, 322, 1483–1487.

553

Susser, M. et al. (1972). Birthweight, fetal age and perinatal mortality. *American Journal of Epidemiology*, 96, 197–204.

Thorndike, E. L. (1913). *The Psychology of Learning*. New York: Teachers College.

Ulrich, B. D. (1984). The effects of stimulation programs on the development of high risk infants: A review of research. *Adapted Physical Activity Quarterly*, 1, 68–80.

Warkany, J. et al. (1961). Intrauterine growth retardation. *American Journal of Diseases of Children*, 102, 462–476.

Wellman, B. (1937). Motor achievements of preschool. *Childhood Education*, 13, 311–316.

Westman, J. C. (Ed.) (1973). *Individual Differences in Children*. New York: Wiley.

Williams, H. G. (1983). *Perceptual and Motor Development*. Englewood Cliffs, NJ: Prentice-Hall.

Zonta, L. A. et al. (1987). Genetic analysis of human obesity in an Italian sample. *Human Heredity*, 37, 129–139.

Chapter 4

Bigge, M. L., & Shermis, S. S. (1992). *Learning Theories for Teachers*. New York: Harper Collins Publishers.

Gallahue, D. L. (1994). Motor development. In J. Winnick (Ed.), *Adapted Physical Education and Sports*. Champaign, IL: Human Kinetics.

Haubenstricker, J., & Seefeldt, V. (1986). Acquisition of motor skills during childhood. In V. Seefeldt (Ed.), *Physical Activity and Well-Being*. Reston, VA: AAHPERD.

Kamm, K., Thelen, E., & Jensen, J. (1990). A dynamical systems approach to motor development. *Physical Therapy*, 70, 12, 763–775.

Lerner, R. M. (1986). *Concepts and Theories in Human Development*. New York: Random House.

Roberton, M. A., & Halverson, L. E. (1984). *Developing Children— Their Changing Movement*. Philadelphia: Lea & Febiger, 1–16.

Seefeldt, V., & Haubenstricker, J. (1982). Patterns, phases, or stages: An analytic model for the study of developmental movement. In J. A. S. Kelso, & J. E. Clark (Eds.), *The Development of Movement Control and Coordination*. New York: Wiley.

Chapter 5

Alford, C. A. et al. (1975). Toxoplasmosis: Silent congenital infection. In S. Krogman, & A. A. Gershon (Eds.), *Infections in the Fetus and the Newborn Infant*. New York: Alan R. Liss.

American College of Obstetricians and Gynecologists (1985). *Exercise During Pregnancy and the Postnatal Period*. Washington, DC: AC06.

Bee, (1975). *The Developing Child*. New York: Harper & Row.

Bonds, D. R., & Delivoria-Papadopoulos, M. (1985). Exercise during pregnancy—potential fetal and placental metabolic effects. *Annals of Clinical and Laboratory Science*, 15, 29–99.

Brackbill, Y. (1970). Continuous stimulation and arousal level in infants: Additive effects. Proceedings, 78th Annual Convention, American Psychological Association, 5, 271–272.

Brackbill, Y. (1979). Obstetrical medication and infant behavior. In J. D. Osofsky (Ed.), *The Handbook of Infant Development*. New York: Wiley.

Chasnoff, I. J., Landress, H. J., & Barrett, M. E. (1990). The prevalence of illicit drug or alcohol use during pregnancy and discrepancies in mandatory reporting in Pinellas County, Florida. *The New England Journal of Medicine*, 26, 1202–1206.

Collings, et al. (1982). Maternal and fetal responses to a maternal aerobic exercise program. *American Journal of Obstetrics and Gynecology*, 145, 6, 702–707.

Connelly Freyder, S. (1989). Exercising while pregnant. *The Journal of Orthopaedic and Sports Physical Therapy*, March, 358–365.

Conway, E., & Brackbill, Y. (1970). Delivery medication and infant outcomes. Monographs of the Society for Research in Child Development, 35, 24–34.

Dorris, M. (1989). *The Broken Cord: A Family's Ongoing Struggle with Fetal Alcohol Syndrome*. New York: Harper Collins.

Eichorn, (1979). Physical development: Current foci of research. In J. Osofsky, (Ed.), *The Handbook of Infant Development*. New York: Wiley.

Fink, J. R. (1989). Effects of crack and cocaine upon infants: A brief review of the literature. *Children's Legal Rights Journal*, 10, 4, 2–10.

Ford, E. T. H. (1973). *Human Chromosomes*. New York: Academic Press.

Freeman, R. K., & Pescar, S. C. (1982). *Safe Delivery: Protecting Your Baby During High Risk Pregnancy*. New York: McGraw-Hill.

Gallahue, D. L. (1983). Assessing Motor Development in Young Children. In B. Spodek (Ed.), *Studies in Educational Evaluation*. New York: Macmillan.

Gallahue, D. L. (1994). Motor development. In J. Winnick (Ed.), *Adapted Physical Education and Sport*. Champaign, IL: Human Kinetics.

Gittler, J., & McPherson, M. (1990). Prenatal substance abuse: An overview of the problem. *Children Today*, July–August, 3–7.

Goldstein, K. M. et al. (1976). The effects of prenatal and perinatal complications on development at one year of age. *Child Development*, 47, 613–621.

Hagberg, B. M. (1975). Pre-, peri-, and postnatal prevention of major neuropediatric handicaps. *Neuropediatrics*, 6, 331–338.

Henderson, S. E. (1985). Motor skills development. In D. Lane, and B. Stratford (Eds.), *Current Approaches to Down Syndrome*. London: Holt, Reinhart and Winston.

Hoyt, L. (1981). Effects of marijuana on fetal development. *Journal of Drug Education*, 12, 113–123.

Lamaze, F. (1976). *Painless Childbirth*. London: Burke.

Litch, S. (1978). *Towards Prevention of Mental Retardation in the Next Generation*. Fort Wayne, IN: Fort Wayne Printing.

Lotgering, F. K. et al. (1984). The interactions of exercise and pregnancy. A review. *American Journal of Obstetrics and Gynecology*, 149, 5, 560–568.

Lotgering, F. et al. (1985). Maternal and fetal responses to exercise during pregnancy. *Physiological Reviews*, 65, 1:1–36.

Malina, R. M., & Bouchard, C. (1991). *Growth, Maturation and Physical Activity*. Champaign, IL: Human Kinetics.

March of Dimes Birth Defects Foundation (1988). *Birth Defects*. White Plains, NY.

March of Dimes Birth Defects Foundation (1986). *Sexually Transmitted Disease*. White Plains, NY.

March of Dimes Birth Defects Foundation (1985). *Drugs, Alcohol, Tobacco Abuse During Pregnancy*. White Plains, NY.

March of Dimes (1984). *Public Health Education Information Sheet*. White Plains, NY.

McGowan, B. (1979). Translating children's needs into rights. *Junior League Review*, September 12–18.

Muller, P. F. et al. (1971). Prenatal factors and their relationship to mental retardation and other parameters of development. *American Journal of Obstetrics and Gynecology*, 109, 1205–1210.

Naeye, R. L. et al. (1969). Urban poverty: Effects of prenatal nutrition. *Science*, 166, 1026.

Nora, J. J., & Fraser, F. C. (1974). *Medical Genetics: Principles and Practices*. Philadelphia: Lea & Febiger.

Parron, D., & Eisenberg, L. (1982). *Infants at Risk for Developmental Dysfunction*. Washington, DC: National Academy Press.

Pijpers, J. E. et al. (1984). Effect of short-term maternal exercise on maternal and fetal cardiovascular dynamics. *British Journal of Obstetrics and Gynecology*, 91, 1081–1086.

Rosenblith, J. F., & Sims-Knight, J. E. (1985). *In the Beginning: Development in the First Two Years*. Monterey, CA: Brooks/ Cole.

Rosett, H. L., & Sander, L. W. (1979). Effects of maternal drinking on neonatal morphology and state. In J. Osofsky, (Ed.), *The Handbook of Infant Development*. New York: Wiley.

Samuel, M. D., & Samuels, N. (1979). *The Well Baby Book*. New York: Summit Books.

Seifert, K. L., & Hoffnung, R. J. (1987). *Child and Adolescent Development*. Boston: Houghton Mifflin.

Streissguth, A. P. et al. (1991). Fetal alcohol syndrome in adolescents and adults. *Journal of the American Medical Association, 265,* 15, 1961–1967.

U.S. Bureau of the Census (1990).

Wieczorek, R. R., & Natapoff, N. N., *A Conceptual Approach to the Nursing of Children*. Philadelphia: J. B. Lippincott.

Williams, S. R. (1988). Nutrition for high-risk populations. In S. R. Williams, & B. S. Worthington-Roberts (Eds.), *Nutrition Throughout the Life Cycle*. St. Louis: Times Mirror/Mosby College Publishing.

Witti, F. P. (1978). Alcohol and Birth Defects. *FDA Consumer, 22,* 20–23.

Wolfe, L. A., et al. (1989). Physiological interactions between pregnancy and aerobic exercise. In K. B. Randolph (Ed.), *Exercise and Sport Science Reviews, Volume 17*. Baltimore, MD: Williams and Wilkens.

Worthington-Roberts, B. S. (1988). Maternal nutrition and the course and outcome of pregnancy. In S. R. Williams, & B. S. Worthington-Roberts (Eds.), *Nutrition Throughout the Life Cycle*. St. Louis: Times Mirror/Mosby College Publishing.

Yarber, W. (1987). AIDS: What Young Adults Should Know. Indianapolis, IN: Indiana State Board of Health.

Yarber, W. L. (1993). *STDs and HIV*. Reston, VA: AAHPERD.

Chapter 6

Allen, K. E., & Marotz, L. (1989). *Developmental Profiles: Birth to Six*. Albany, NY: Delmar.

Bayley, N. (1954). Some increasing parent-child similarities during the growth of children. *Journal of Educational Psychology, 45,* 1–21.

Caplan, F. (1981). *The First Twelve Months of Life*. New York: Bantam.

DeVires, J. I. P. et al. (1982). The emergence of fetal behavior in qualitative aspects. *Early Human Development, 7,* 301–322.

Krogman, W. M. (1980). *Child Growth*. Ann Arbor: University of Michigan Press.

Malina, R. M., & Bouchard, C. (1991). *Growth Maturation and Physical Activity*. Champaign, IL: Human Kinetics.

National Center for Health Statistics. (1976). Washington, DC: U.S. Department of Health, Education and Welfare (ARA), 25, 76–1120, June 22.

Oppenheimer, S. B. (1980). *Introduction to Embryonic Development*. Boston: Allyn & Bacon.

Prechtl, H. F. R. (1986). Prenatal motor development. In M. G. Wade, & H. T. A. Whiting (Eds.), *Motor Development in Children: Aspects of Coordination and Control*. Dordrecht, The Netherlands: Martinus Nijhoff Publishers.

Rosenblith, J. F., & Sims-Knight, J. E. (1985). *In the Beginning: Development in the First Two Years*. Monterey, CA: Brooks/Cole.

Sundberg, A. I., & Wirsen, C. (1977). *A Child is Born: The Drama of Life Before Birth*. New York: Delacorte.

Tanner, J. M. (1978). *Foetus into Man*. Cambridge, MA: Harvard University Press.

Chapter 7

Ames, I. I. (1937). The sequential patterning of prone progression in the human infant. *Genetic Psychology Monographs, 19,* 409–460.

Bobath, B., & Bobath, K. (1975). *Motor Development in the Different Types of Cerebral Palsy*. London: William Heinemann Medical Books Ltd.

Bower, T. G. R. (1976). *Development in Infancy*. San Francisco: W. H. Freeman.

Easton, T. A. (1972). On the normal use of reflexes. *American Scientist, 60,* 591–599.

Eckert, H. (1987). *Motor Development*. Indianapolis: Benchmark Press.

Fiorentino, M. R. (1972). *Normal and Abnormal Development*. Springfield, IL: Charles C. Thomas.

Hebb, D. O. (1949). *The Organization of Behavior*. New York: Wiley.

Kessen, W. et al. (1970). Human infancy: A bibliography and guide. In P. H. Mussen (Ed.), *Manual of Child Psychology*. New York: Wiley.

Leonard, E. et al. (1980). Nutritive sucking in high risk neonates after perioral stimulation. *Physical Therapy, 60,* 299–302.

McGraw, M. B. (1939). Later development of children specially trained during infancy. *Child Development, 10,* 1.

McGraw, M. B. (1939). Swimming behavior of the human infant. *Journal of Pediatrics, 15,* 485–490.

McGraw, M. B. (1954). Maturation of behavior. In L. Carmichael (Ed.), *Manual of Child Psychology*. New York: Wiley.

Payne, G. (1985). *Infant Reflexes in Human Motor Development*. Lawren Productions, Inc.: Box 666, Mendocino, CA 95460. (videotape)

Pontius, A. A. (1973). Neuro-Ethics of walking in the newborn. *Perceptual and Motor Skills, 37,* 235–245.

Prechtl, H. F. R., & Beintema, D. J. (1964). *The Neurological Examination of the Full Term Newborn Infant*. London: William Heinemann Medical Books.

Sameroff, A. (1973). Reflexive and operant aspects of sucking behavior in early infancy. In J. F. Bosma (Ed.), *Oral Sensation and Perception Development in the Fetus and Infant*. Springfield, MO: Charles C. Thomas.

Shirley, M. (1931). *The First Two Years. A Study of Twenty-Five Babies. 1. Postural and Locomotor Development*. Minneapolis: University of Minnesota Press.

Swartz, D., & Allen, M. (1975). Residual reflex patterns as a basis for diagnosing stroke faults. In J. P. Clarys, & L. Levillie (Eds.), *Swimming II*. Baltimore: University Park Press.

Thelen, E. (1979). Rhythmical stereotypies in normal human infants. *Animal Behavior, 27,* 699–715.

Thelen, E. (1980). Determinants of amount of stereotyped behavior in normal human infants. *Ethology and Sociobiology, 1,* 141–150.

Thelen, E. (1981). Kicking, rocking, and waving: Contextual analysis of rhythmical stereotypies in normal human infants. *Animal Behavior, 29.*

Thelen, E. (1981). Rhythmical behavior in infancy: An ethological perspective. *Developmental Psychology, 17,* 237–257.

Thelen, E. (1981). Rhythmical stereotypies in normal human infants. *Animal Behavior, 27,* 699–715.

Thelen, E. (1985). Developmental origins of motor coordination: Leg movements in human infants. *Developmental Psychobiology, 18,* 1–22.

Thelen, E. (1986). Development of coordinated movement. Implications for early motor development. In M. G. Wade, and H. T. A. Whiting (Eds.), *Motor Development in Children: Aspects of Coordination and Control*. Dordrecht, The Netherlands: Martinus Nyhoff.

Thelen, E. et al. (1985). Rhythmical behavior in infancy: An ethological perspective. *Developmental Psychology, 17,* 237–257.

Thelen, E., Kelso, J. A. S., & Fogel, A. (1987). Self-organizing systems and infant motor development. *Developmental Review, 7,* 39–65.

Von Bernuth, H. G. L., & Pretchtl, H. R. R. (1968). Reflexes and their relationship to behavioral state in the newborn. *Acta Pediatric Scandanavia, 57,* 177–185.

Wyke, B. (1975). The neurological basis of movement: A developmental review. In K. S. Holt (Ed.), *Movement and Child Development*. London: William Heinemann Medical Books.

Zelazo, P. (1976). From reflexive to instrumental behavior. In L. P. Lipsett (Ed.), *Developmental Psychobiology—The Significance of Infancy*. Hillsdale, NJ: Lawrence Erlbaum.

Chapter 8

Alexander, R. et al. (1993). *Normal Development of Functional Motor Skills: The First Year of Life*. Tucson, AZ: Communication Skill Builders.

American Academy of Pediatrics Committee on Sports Medicine. (1985). Weight training and weight lifting: Information for the pediatrician. *News and Comments*, 33, 7–8.

Bailey, D. B., & Wolery, M. (1989). *Assessing Infants and Preschoolers with Handicaps*. Columbus, OH: Charles E. Merrill.

Bayley, N. (1935). The development of motor abilities during the first three years. *Monograph of the Society for Research on Child Development*, 1, 1–26.

Burd, B. (1986). Infant swimming classes: Immersed in controversy. *The Physician and Sports Medicine*, 14, 3, 239–244.

Campos, J. J. et al. (1982). The emergence of self-produced locomotion. In D. D. Bricker (Ed.), *Intervention With At-Risk and Handicapped Infants*. Baltimore: University Park Press.

Delacato, C. (1966). *Neurological Organization and Reading*. Springfield, IL: Charles C. Thomas.

Denhoff, E. (1981). Current status of infant stimulation enrichment programs for children with developmental disabilities, *Pediatrics*, 67, 32–36.

Eckert, H. (1973). Age change in motor skills. In G. L. Rarick (Ed.), *Physical Activity: Human Growth and Development*. New York: Academic Press.

Eckert, H. (1987). *Motor Development*. Indianapolis: Benchmark Press.

Gesell, A. (1945). *The Embryology of Behavior*. New York: Macmillan.

Halverson, H. M. (1937). Studies of the grasping responses in early infancy. *Journal of Genetic Psychology*, 51, 437–449.

Hellebrandt, F. et al. (1961). Physiological analysis of basic motor skills. *American Journal of Physical Medicine*, 40, 14–25.

Hicks-Hughes, D., & Langendorfer, S. (1986). Aquatics for the young child. A survey of selected programs. *National Aquatics Journal*, 2, 2, 12–17.

Kopp, C. B. (1982). The role of theoretical frameworks in the study of at-risk and handicapped. In D. D. Bricker (Ed.), *Intervention with At-Risk and Handicapped Infants*. Baltimore: University Park Press.

Landreth, C. (1958). *The Psychology of Early Childhood*. New York: Alfred A. Knopf.

Langendorfer, S. (1987). Separating fact from fiction in preschool aquatics. *National Aquatics Journal*, 3, 1, 2–4.

Newell, K. M. (Ed.) (1992). Theme issue on dynamical approaches to motor skill acquisition. *Journal of Motor Behavior*, 24, 1, 2–142.

Ottenbacker, K. (1983). Developmental implications of clinically applied vestibular stimulation. *Physical Therapy*, 63, 338–341.

Ouden, L. D., et al. (1991). Is it correct to correct? Developmental milestones in 555 'normal' preterm infants compared with term infants. *Journal of Pediatrics*, 118, 3, 399–404.

Shirley, M. (1931). *The First Two Years: A Study of Twenty-Five Babies*, 1. Postural and Locomotor Development. Minneapolis: University of Minnesota Press.

Thelen, E. (1986). Development of coordinated movement: Implications for early human development. In M. G. Wade, & H. T. A. Whiting (Eds.), *Motor Development in Children: Aspects of Coordination and Control*. Dordrecht, The Netherlands: Martinus Nyhoff.

Thelen, E. et al. (1987). Self-organizing systems in infant motor development. *Developmental Review*, 7, 39–65.

Titzer, R. (1992). *A review of the effects of infant stimulation programs*. Unpublished paper, Indiana University.

Ulrich, B. D. (1984). The effects of stimulation programs on the development of high risk infants: A review of research. *Adapted Physical Activity Quarterly*, 1, 68–80.

YMCA Division of Aquatics (1984). *YMCA Guidelines for Infant Swimming*. Chicago: YMCA of the U.S.A.

Chapter 9

Aslin, R. N. (1977). Development of binocular fixation in human infants. In D. F. Fisher et al. (Eds.), *Eye Movements: Cognition and Visual Perception*. Hillsdale, NJ: Erlbaum.

Aslin, R. N. (1981). Development of smooth pursuit in human infants. In D. F. Fisher et al. (Eds.), *Eye Movements: Cognition and Visual Perception*. Hillsdale, NJ: Erlbaum.

Aslin, R. N. (1984). Motor aspects of visual development in infancy. In P. Salapatek & L. B. Cohen (Eds.), *Handbook of Infant Perception*. New York: Academic Press.

Aslin, R. N. et al. (1983). Auditory development and speech perception in infancy. In P. H. Mussan (Ed.), *Handbook of Child Psychology*. New York: Wiley.

Aslin, R. N., & Dumais, S. T. (1980). Binocular vision in infants: A review and a theoretical position. *Advances in Child Development and Behavior*, 15, 53–94.

Aslin, R. N., & Salapatek, P. (1975). Saccadic localization of peripheral targets by the very young human infant. *Perception and Psychophysics*, 17, 292–302.

Atkinson, J., & Braddick, O. (1982). Sensory and perception capacities of the neonate. In P. Stratton (Ed.), *Psychobiology of the Human Newborn*, New York: Wiley.

Banks, M. (1980). The development of visual accommodation during early infancy. *Child Development*.

Bernard, J., & Sontag, L. W. (1947). Fetal reactivity to tonal stimulation: A preliminary report. *Journal of Genetic Psychology*, 70, 205–210.

Bornstein, M. H. et al. (1976). The categories of hue in infancy. *Science*, 191, 201–202.

Bower, T. G. R. (1977). *The Perceptual World of the Child*. Cambridge, MA: Harvard University Press.

Cohen, L. B. et al. (1979). Infant visual perception. In J. D. Osofsky (Ed.), *The Handbook of Infant Development*. New York: Wiley.

Cratty, B. J. (1986). *Perceptual and Motor Development in Infants and Children*. Englewood Cliffs, NJ: Prentice-Hall.

Dayton, G. O., & Jones, M. H. (1964). Analysis of characteristics of fixation reflexes in infants by use of direct current electroculography. *Neurology*, 14, 1152–1157.

Engen, T., & Lipsett, L. P. (1965). Decrement and recovery of responses of olfactory stimuli in the human neonate. *Journal of Comparative and Physiological Psychology*, 59, 312–316.

Fantz, R. L. (1963). Pattern vision in newborn infants. *Science*, 140, 296–297.

Fantz, R. L. et al. (1975). Early visual selectivity. In L. B. Cohen, & P. Salapatek (Eds.), *Infant Perception From Sensation to Cognition*. New York: Academic Press.

Field, J. (1976). The adjustment of reaching behavior to object distance in early infancy. *Child Development*, 47, 304–308.

Fox, R. et al. (1980). Stereopsis in Human Infants. *Science*, 207, 323–324.

Gibson, E. J., & Walk, R. B. (1960). The visual cliff. *Scientific American*, 4, 67–71.

Haith, M. M. (1966). The response of the human newborn to visual movement. *Journal of Experimental Child Psychology*, 3, 235–243.

Haith, M. M. (1980). *Rules That Babies Look By*. Hillsdale, NJ: Erlbaum.

Haynes, H. et al. (1965). Visual accommodation in human infants. *Science*, 148, 525–530.

Held, R., & Hein, A. (1963). Movement-produced stimulation in the development of visually guided behavior. *Journal of Comparative Physiological Psychology*, 56, 872–876.

Hershenson, M. (1964). Visual discrimination in the human newborn. *Journal of Comparative Physiological Psychology*, 158, 270–276.

Kessen, W. et al. (1972). The visual response of the human newborn to linear contour. *Journal of Experimental Child Psychology*, 13, 9–20.

Krieg, K. (1978). *Tonic convergence and facial growth in early infancy.* Unpublished Senior honors Thesis, Indiana University.

Leventhal, A., & Lipsett, L. P. (1964). Adaption, pitch discrimination and sound vocalization in the neonate. *Child Development, 37,* 331–346.

Lipsett, L. P. et al. (1963). Developmental changes in the olfactory threshold of the neonate. *Child Development, 34,* 371–376.

McFarlane, A. (1975). Olfaction in the development of social preference in the human neonate. In *Parent-Infant Interaction.* Amsterdam: CIBA Foundation Symposium 33.

Oster, H. S. (1975). *Color Perception in Ten-Week Old Infants.* Paper presented at the Annual meeting of the Society for Research in Child Development, Denver.

Peeples, D. R., & Teller, D. Y. (1975). Color vision and brightness discrimination in two-month-old human infants. *Science, 189,* 1102–1103.

Pratt, K. C. (1954). The neonate. In L. Carmichael (Ed.), *Manual of Child Psychology.* New York: Wiley.

Salapatek, P. (1975). Pattern vision in early infancy. In L. B. Cohen, & P. Salapatek (Eds.), *Infant Perception.* New York: Academic Press.

Schaller, M. J. (1975). *Chromatic vision in human infants: Coordinated fixation to hues of varying intensity.* Paper presented at the meeting of the Society for Research in Child Development, Denver.

Schneider, B. A. et al. (1980). High-frequency sensitivity in infants. *Science, 207,* 1003–1004.

Sekuler, R., & Blake, R. (1985). *Perception.* New York: Alfred A. Knopf.

Siqueland, E. R., & DeLucia, C. A. (1969). Visual reinforcement of non-nutritive sucking in human infants. *Science, 165,* 1144–1146.

Spears, W. C. (1964). Assessment of visual preference and discrimination in the 4-month old infant. *Journal of Comparative Physiological Psychology, 57,* 381–386.

Svejda, M., & Schmidt, D. (1979). *The role of self-produced locomotion on the onset of fear of heights on the visual cliff.* Paper presented at the Society for Research in Child Development, San Francisco.

Trehub, S. E. et al. (1980). Infants' perception of melodies: The role of melodic contour. *Child Development, 55,* 821–830.

Trehub, S. E. et al. (1991). Observational measures of auditory sensitivity in early infancy. *Developmental Psychology, 27,* 40–49.

Tronick, (1972). Stimulus control and the growth of the infants' effective visual field, *Perception and Psychophysics, 11,* 373–375.

von Hofsten, C. (1979). Development of visually guided reaching: The approach phase. *Journal of Human Movement Studies, 5,* 160–178.

von Hofsten, C. (1982). Eye-hand coordination in newborns. *Developmental Psychology, 18,* 450–461.

von Hofsten, C. (1986). The emergence of manual skills. In M. G. Wade, & H. T. A. Whiting (Eds.), *Motor Development in Children: Aspects of Coordination and Control.* Dorbrecht, The Netherlands: Martinus, Nijhoff.

Wade, M. G., & Whiting, H. T. A. (1986). *Motor Development in Children: Aspects of Coordination and Control.* Dordrecht, The Netherlands: Martinus Nijhoff Publishers.

Walk, R. D. (1966). *The Development of Depth Perception in Animal and Human Infants.* Monograph of the Society for Research in Child Development, 31, 5.

Walk, R. D. (1978). Depth perception and experience. In R. D. Walk, & A. Pick (Eds.),*Perception and Experiences.* New York: Plenum Press.

Williams, H. G. (1983). *Perceptual and Motor Development.* Englewood Cliffs, NJ: Prentice-Hall.

Chapter 10

Allen, K. E., & Marotz, L. (1989). *Developmental Profiles. Birth to Six.* Albany, NY: Delmar.

Caine, D. J., & Lindner, K. (1984). Growth plate injury: A threat to young distance runners? *Physician and Sports Medicine,* 12, 4, 118–124.

Clarke, D. (1974). Predicting certified weight of young wrestlers. *Medicine and Science in Sports,* 6, 52–57.

Daw, S. F. (1974). Age of boy's puberty in Leipzig, 1727–49, as indicated by voice breaking in J. S. Bach's choir members. *Human Biology,* 46, 381–384.

Eckert, H. (1987). *Motor Development.* Indianapolis: Benchmark Press.

Eveleth, P. B., & Tanner, J. M. (1976). *Worldwide Variation in Human Growth.* Cambridge, MA: Cambridge University Press.

Gabbard, C. (1992). *Lifelong Motor Development.* Dubuque, IA: Wm. C. Brown.

Gallahue, D. L. (1993). *Developmental Physical Education for Today's Children.* Dubuque, IA: Brown & Benchmark.

Gallahue, D. L. (1993). Motor development and movement skill acquisition in early childhood education. In B. Spodek (Ed.), *Handbook of Research on the Education of Young Children.* New York: Macmillan.

Krogman, W. M. (1980). *Child Growth.* Ann Arbor: University of Michigan Press.

Malina, R. M. (1978). Secular changes in growth and performance. In R. S. Hutton (Ed.), *Exercise and Sport Science Reviews,* 6, 206–235.

Malina, R. M., & Bouchard, C. (1991). *Growth, Maturation and Physical Activity.* Champaign, IL: Human Kinetics.

Owen, G. M. et al. (1974). A Study of the Nutritional Status of Preschool Children in the United States. USDHEW, 53 Part II, Supplement.

Peterson, K. L. (1967). *Atlas for Somatotyping Children.* The Netherlands: Royal Vagorcum Ltd.

Seefeldt, V., & Gould, D. (1980). Physical Fitness Guidelines for Preschool Children. In Proceedings of the National Conference on Physical Fitness and Sports for All, Washington, DC: President's Council on Physical Fitness and Sports, 5–19.

Seifert, K. L. (1993). Cognitive development and early childhood education. In B. Spodek (Ed.), *Handbook of Research on the Education of Young Children.* New York: Macmillan.

Sheldon, W. H. et al. (1940). *The Varieties of Human Physique.* New York: Harper.

Sheldon, W. H. et al. (1954). *Atlas of Man.* New York: Harper.

Time-Life, Successful Parenting Series. (1987). *Developing Your Child's Potential.* Alexandria, VA: Time-Life Books.

Time-Life, Successful Parenting Series. (1987). *Your Growing Child.* Alexandria, VA: Time-Life Books.

Tipton, C., & Tcheng, T. K. (1970). Iowa wrestling study. *Journal of the American Medical Association,* 214, 1269–1274.

Walter, T. et al. (1989). Iron deficiency anemia: Adverse effects on infant motor development. *Pediatrics,* 84, 1, 7–17.

Yip, R. (1989). Iron nutritional status defined. In L. J. Filer (Ed.), *Dietary Iron: Birth to Two Years.* New York: Raven Press.

Chapter 11

Bayley, N. (1935). The development of motor abilities during the first three years. *Monograph of the Society for Research òn Child Development,* 1, 1–26.

Broer, M. R., & Zernicke, R. F. (1979). *Efficiency of Human Movement.* Philadelphia: W. B. Saunders.

Burnett, C. N., & Johnson, E. W. (1971). Development of Gait in Childhood, Part II. *Developmental Medicine and Child Neurology,* 13, 207–212.

Clark, J. E., & Phillips, S. J. (1985). A developmental sequence of the standing long jump. In J. E. Clark, and J. H. Humphrey (Eds.), *Motor Development: Current Selected Research*. Princeton, NJ: Princeton Book Co.

Cratty, B. J. (1986). *Perceptual and Motor Development in Infants and Children*. Englewood Cliffs, NJ: Prentice-Hall.

Cratty, B. J., & Martin, M. (1969). *Perceptual-Motor Efficiency in Children*. Philadelphia: Lea & Febiger.

Deach, D. F. (1951). *Genetic development of motor skills in children two through six years of age*. Unpublished doctoral dissertation, University of Michigan.

DeOreo, K. L. (1971). *Dynamic and static balance in preschool children*. Unpublished doctoral dissertation, University of Illinois.

DeOreo, K. L. (1980). Performance of Fundamental Motor Tasks. In C. B. Corbin (Ed.), *A Textbook of Motor Development*. Dubuque, IA: Wm. C. Brown.

Eckert, H. (1987). *Motor Development*. Indianapolis: Benchmark Press.

Eckert, H. M., & Rarick, G. L. (1975). Stabliometer Performance of Educable Mentally Retarded and Normal Children. *Research Quarterly*, 47, 619–621.

Gad-Elmawla, E. K. G. (1980). *Kinematic and kinetic analysis of gain in children at different age levels in comparison with adults*. Unpublished doctoral dissertation, Indiana University.

Gallahue, D. L. (1993). *Developmental Physical Education for Today's Children*. Dubuque, IA: Brown & Benchmark.

Gallahue, D. L. (1993). Motor development and movement skill acquisition in early childhood education. In B. Spodek (Ed.), *Handbook on Research on the Education of Young Children*. New York: Macmillan.

Goetzinger, C. P. (1961). Re-evaluation of Heath Rail Walking 1951 to 1967. *Journal of Education Research*, 54, 187–191.

Grieve, D. W., & Gaer, R. J. (1966). The relationship between the length of stride, step, frequency, time of swing and speed of walking for children and adults. *Ergonomics*, 9, 379–399.

Guttridge, M. (1939). A study of motor achievements of young children. *Archives of Psychology*, 244, 1–178.

Halverson, L. E., & Roberton, M. A. (1966). *A study of motor pattern development in young children*. Paper presented at the Annual Convention of the AAHPER Conference, Chicago.

Halverson, L. E., & Roberton, M. A. (1979). *Motor Development Laboratory Manual*. Madison, WI: American Printing and Publishing.

Halverson, L. E., & Williams, K. (1985). Developmental sequences for hopping over distance: A prelongitudinal study. *Research Quarterly for Exercise and Sport*, 56, 37–44.

Haubenstricker, J. et al. (1983). *Preliminary validation of developmental sequences of throwing and catching*. Paper presented at the annual meeting of the North American Society for the Psychology of Sport and Physical Activity, East Lansing, MI.

Haubenstricker, J., & Seefeldt, V. (1986). Acquisition of motor skills during childhood. In V. Seefeldt (Ed.), *Physical Activity and Well-Being*. Reston, VA: AAHPERD.

Johnson, R. (1962). Measurement of achievement in fundamental skills of elementary school children. *Research Quarterly*, 33, 94–103.

Langendorfer, S. (1988). Goal of a motor task as a constraint on developmental status. In J. Clark, & J. Humphrey (Eds.), *Advances in Motor Development Research*. New York: AMS Press.

Leudke, G. C. (1980). *Range of motion as the focus of teaching the overhand throwing pattern to children*. Unpublished doctoral dissertation, Indiana University.

Martin, T. P., & Stull, G. A. (1969). Effects of various knee angle and foot spacing combinations on performance in the vertical jump. *Research Quarterly*, 40, 324.

McCaskill, C. L., & Wellman, B. L. (1938). A study of common motor achievements at the preschool ages. *Child Development*, 9, 141.

McClenaghan, B. A. (1976). *Development of an observational instrument to assess selected fundamental movement patterns of low motor functioning children*. Unpublished doctoral dissertation, Indiana University.

McClenaghan, B. A., & Gallahue, D. L. (1978). *Fundamental Movement: A Developmental and Remedial Approach*. Philadelphia: W. B. Saunders.

McClenaghan, B. A., & Gallahue, D. L. (1978). *Fundamental Movement: Observation and Assessment*. Philadelphia: W. B. Saunders.

Miller, S. (1978). *The facilitation of fundamental motor skill learning in young children*. Unpublished doctoral dissertation, Michigan State University.

Myers, C. B. et al. (1977). *Vertical jumping movement patterns of early childhood*. Unpublished paper, Indiana University, Physical Education Department.

Ozmun, J. C., & Robertson, L. D. (1992). *Motor skill characteristics of force production of young children*. Paper presented at the annual convention of the ACSM.

Pederson, E. J. (1973). *A study of ball catching abilities of first-, third-, and fifth-grade children on twelve selected ball catching tasks*. Unpublished doctoral dissertation, Indiana University.

Poe, A. (1976). Description of the movement characteristics of two-year-old children performing the jump and reach. *Research Quarterly*, 47, 200.

Roberton, M. A. (1978). Stability of stage categorization in motor development. In D. M. Landers, & R. W. Christina (Eds.), *Psychology in Motor Behavior and Sport—1977*. Champaign, IL: Human Kinetics.

Roberton, M. A. (1978). Stages in motor development. In M. Ridenour (Ed.), *Motor Development: Issues and Applications*. Princeton, NJ: Princeton.

Roberton, M. A. (1985). Changing motor patterns during childhood. In J. K. Thomas (Ed.), *Motor Development During Childhood and Adolescence*. Minneapolis: Burgess.

Roberton, M. A. (1987). Developmental level as a function of the immediate environment. In J. E. Clark, & J. H. Humphrey (Eds.), *Advances in Motor Development Research*. New York: AMS Press.

Roberton, M. A., & Halverson, L. E. (1984). *Developing Children: Their Changing Movement*. Philadelphia: Lea & Febiger.

Sapp, M. (1980). *Developmental sequence of galloping*. Unpublished materials, Michigan State University.

Saunders, J. E. et al. (1953). The major determinants in normal and pathological gait. *Journal of Bone and Joint Surgery*, 35, 543–558.

Seashore, H. G. (1949). The development of a beam walking test and its use in measuring development of balance in children. *Research Quarterly*, 18, 246–259.

Seefeldt, V. (1972). *Discussion of walking and running*. Unpublished research, Michigan State University.

Seefeldt, V., & Haubenstricker, J. (1976). *Developmental sequences of fundamental motor skills*. Unpublished research, Michigan State University.

Seefeldt, V., & Haubenstricker, J. (1981). *Developmental sequences of kicking: Second revision*. Paper presented at the Midwest AAHPERD Conference, Chicago.

Sinclair, C. (1973). *Movement of the Young Child*. Columbus, OH: Merrill.

Whiting, H. T. A. (1969). *Acquiring Ball Skill*. London: G. Bell and Sons.

Wickstrom, R. L. (1983). *Fundamental Motor Patterns*. Philadelphia: Lea & Febiger.

Wild, M. (1938). The behavioral pattern of throwing and some observations concerning its course of development in children. *Research Quarterly*, 3, 20.

Williams, H. (1970). *A study of perceptual-motor characteristics of children in kindergarten through sixth grade.* Unpublished paper, University of Toledo.

Williams, H. G. (1983). *Perceptual and Motor Development.* Englewood Cliffs, NJ: Prentice-Hall.

Williams, K. (1980). Developmental characteristics of a forward roll. *Research Quarterly for Exercise and Sport,* 51, 4, 703.

Chapter 12

AAHPERD (1980). *Health Related Physical Fitness Test, Manual.* Reston, VA: AAHPERD.

Amateur Athletic Union (1993). *The Chrysler Fund—Amateur Athletic Union Physical Fitness Program.* Bloomington, IN: Poplars Building.

American Academy of Pediatrics (1990). Strength training, weight and power lifting, and body building by children and adolescents. *Pediatrics,* 85, 801–803.

American Academy of Pediatrics Committee and Sports Medicine (1983). Weight training and weight lifting: Information for the pediatrician. *News and Comments,* 33, 7–8.

Andersen, K. L. et al. (1978). The rate of growth in maximal aerobic power of children in Norway. In J. Borms, & M. Hebbelinck (Eds.), *Medicine and Sport Science Series: Pediatric Work Psychology.* Basel, Belgium: S. Karger.

Andrish, J. T. (1984). Overuse syndromes of the lower extremities in youth sports. In R. A. Boileau (Ed.), *Advances in Pediatric Sport Sciences, Biological Issues.* Champaign, IL: Human Kinetics.

Armussen, E. (1973). Growth in muscular strength and power. In G. L. Rarick (Ed.), *Physical Activity: Human Growth and Development.* New York: Academic Press.

Astrand, P. O. (1952). *Experimental Studies of Working Capacity in Relation to Sex and Age.* Copenhagen, Denmark: Munksgaard.

Bailey, D. A. et al. (1978). Size dissociation of maximal aerobic power during growth in boys. In J. Borms, & M. Hebbelinck (Eds.), *Medicine and Sport Science Series, Pediatric Work Physiology.* Basel, Belgium: S. Karger.

Bandini, L. G. (1987). *Energy expenditure in obese and nonobese adolescents.* Unpublished doctoral dissertation. Cambridge, MA: Massachusetts Institute of Technology.

Baranowski, T. et al. (1992). Assessment, prevalence, and cardiovascular benefits of physical activity and fitness in youth. *Medicine and Science in Sports and Exercise,* 24, 6, 237–247.

Bar-Or, O. (1983). *Pediatric Sports Medicine for the Practitioner.* New York: Springer-Verlag.

Bar-Or, O. (1987). A commentary to children and fitness: A public health perspective. *Research Quarterly for Exercise and Sport,* 58, 4, 304–307.

Bar-Or, O. (1989). Trainability of the prepubescent child. *Physician and Sports Medicine,* 17, 5, 65–83.

Barrow, H. M., & McGee, R. (1978). *A Practical Approach to Measurement in Physical Education.* Philadelphia: Lea & Febiger.

Bergel, R. (1978). Motor performance and physical growth components of head start and non-head start pre-school children. In *Symposium Papers,* 1, 53–56. Reston, VA: AAHPERD Research Consortium.

Bernuth, G. A. et al. (1985). Age, exercise, and the endocrine system. In K. Fotherby, & S. B. Pal (Eds.), *Exercise Endocrinology.* New York: Walter de Gruyter.

Blair, S. N. (1992). Are American children and youth fit? The need for better data. *Research Quarterly for Exercise and Sport,* 63, 2, 120–123.

Blimkie, C. J. R. (1989). Age- and sex-associated variation in strength during childhood. *Perspectives in Exercise Science and Sports Medicine,* Vol. 2, Indianapolis, IN: Benchmark Press.

Blimkie, C. J. R., Ramsay, J., Sale, D., MacDougall, D., Smith, K., & Garner, S. (1989). Effects of 10 weeks of resistance training on strength development in prepubertal boys. In S. Oseid & K. H. Carlsen (Eds.), *International Series on Sport Sciences. Children and Exercise XIII.* Champaign, IL: Human Kinetics.

Borms, J. (1986). The child and exercise: An overview. *Journal of Sports Science,* 4, 1, 3–20.

Brown, C. H. et al. (1972). The effects of cross-country running on pre-adolescent girls. *Medicine and Science in Sports,* 4, 1–5.

CAHPER (1980).*Canadian Association of Health, Physical Education, and Recreation: Manitoba Physical Fitness Performance Test Manual and Fitness Objectives,* Ottawa, Canada, CAHPER.

Chausow, S. A. et al. (1984). Metabolic and cardiovascular responses of children during prolonged physical activity. *Research Quarterly for Exercise and Sport,* 55, 1, 1–7.

Clarke, D. (1975). Predicting Certified Weight of Young Wrestlers. *Medicine and Science in Sports,* 6, 52–57.

Clarke, H. H. (1971). *Physical Motor Tests in the Medbord Boys Growth Study.* Englewood Cliffs, NJ: Prentice-Hall.

Comalli, P. E. et al. (1959). Perception of verticality in middle and old age. *Journal of Psychology,* 47, 259–266.

Cooper, K. H. (1968). *Aerobics.* New York: Bantam.

Corbin, C. B. (Ed.) (1980). *A Textbook of Motor Development.* Dubuque, IA: Wm. C. Brown.

Corbin, C. B., & Pangrazi, R. P. (1992). Are American children and youth fit? *Research Quarterly for Exercise and Sport,* 63, 2, 96–106.

Cratty, B. J. (1986). *Perceptual and Motor Development in Infants and Children.* Englewood Cliffs, NJ: Prentice-Hall.

Cratty, B. J., & Martin, M. (1969). *Perceptual-Motor Efficiency in Children.* Philadelphia: Lea & Febiger.

Cumming, G. R. et al. (1969). Failure of school physical education to improve cardiorespiratory fitness. *Canadian Medical Association Journal,* 101, 69–73.

Cumming, G. R., & Friesen, W. (1967). Bicycle ergometer measurement of maximal oxygen uptake in children. *Canadian Journal of Physiology and Pharmacology,* 45, 937–946.

Cumming, G. R., & Hantiuk, A. (1980). Establishing of normal values for exercise capacity in a hospital clinic. In K. Berg, & B. Erickson (Eds.), *Children and Exercise IX.* Baltimore: Academic Press.

Daniels, J., & Oldridge, N. (1971). Changes in oxygen consumption of young boys during growth and training. *Medicine and Science in Sports,* 3, 161–165.

Delozier, M. G., Gutin, B., & Basch, C. E. (1988). Conducting treadmill tests on preschool children—Strategies and techniques. *Journal of Physical Education, Recreation and Dance,* October, 83–87.

DeOreo, K. L. (1971). *Dynamic and static balance in preschool children.* Unpublished doctoral dissertation, University of Illinois.

DeOreo, K. L. (1980). Performance of fundamental motor tasks. In C. B. Corbin (Ed.), *A Textbook of Motor Development.* Dubuque, IA: Wm. C. Brown.

DiNucci, J. M. (1976). Gross motor performance: A comprehensive analysis of age and sex differences between boys and girls ages six to nine years. In J. Browkhoff (Ed.), *Physical Education, Sports and the Sciences.* Eugene, OR: Microform Publications.

Duda, M. (1986). Prepubescent strength training gains support. *Physician and Sports Medicine,* 14, 2, 157–161.

Ekbolm, O. (1969). Effect of physical training on adolescent boys. *Journal of Applied Physiology,* 27, 350–355.

Errecart, M. T. et al. (1987). The national children and youth fitness study II: Sample design. *Journal of Physical Education, Recreation and Dance,* 58, 63–65.

Falls, H. B., & Pate, R. R. (1993). Status of physical fitness in U.S. children. In M. L. Leppo (Ed.), *Healthy from the Start: New Perspectives on Childhood Fitness.* Washington, DC: ERIC Clearinghouse on Teacher Education.

Frederick, S. D. (1977). *Performance of selected motor tasks by three, four, and five year old children.* Unpublished doctoral dissertation, Indiana University.

Gilliam, T. B. et al. (1981). Physical activity patterns determined by heart rate monitoring in 6–7 year old children. *Medicine and Science in Sports and Exercise,* 131, 65–67.

Gilliam, T. B., & Macconnie, S. E. (1984). Coronary heart disease risk in children and their physical activity patterns. In R. A. Boileau (Ed.), *Advances in Pediatric Sport Sciences: Volume One, Biological Issues.* Champaign, IL: Human Kinetics.

Glassow, R. L., & Kruse, P. (1960). Motor performance of girls age 6–14 years. *Research Quarterly,* 31, 426–431.

Goetzinger, C. P. (1961). Re-evaluation of heath rail walking 1951 to 1967. *Journal of Education Research,* 54, 187–191.

Gortmaker, S. L. et al. (1987). Increasing pediatric obesity in the U. S. *American Journal of Diseases in Children,* 14, 1, 535–540.

Gould, D. (1987). Understanding attrition in children's sports. In D. Gould, & M. R. Weiss (Eds.), *Advances in Pediatric Sport Sciences: Vol. 2, Behavioral Issues.* Champaign, IL: Human Kinetics.

Gumbs, V. L. et al. (1982). Bilateral distal radius and ulnar fractures in adolescent weight lifters. *The American Journal of Sports Medicine,* 10, 375–379.

Gutin, B., Manos, T., & Strong, W. (1992). Defining health and fitness: First steps toward establishing fitness standards. *Research Quarterly for Exercise and Sport,* 63, 2, 128–132.

Heath, S. R. (1949). The railwalking test: Preliminary motivational norm for boys and girls. *Motor Skills Research Exchange,* 1, 34.

Hejna, W. F. (1982). Prevention of sport injuries in high school students through strength training. *NSCA Journal,* 4, 1, 28–31.

Hupperich, F. L., & Sigerseth, P. (1950). The specificity of flexibility in girls. *Research Quarterly,* 21, 25–33.

Kallel, W. B., & Sorlie, P. (1979). Some health benefits of physical activity: The Framingham study. *Archives of Internal Medicine,* 139, 857–861.

Katch, V. L. (1983). Physical conditioning of children. *Journal of Adolescent Health Care,* 3, 241–246.

Keogh, J. F. (1965). *Motor Performance of Elementary School Children.* Los Angeles: University of California, Physical Education Department.

Krahenbuhl, G. S. et al. (1985). Developmental aspects of maximal aerobic power in children. In R. L. Terjung (Ed.), *Exercise Science and Sport Research.* New York: Macmillan.

Kraus, H., & Hirschland, R. P. (1954). Minimum muscular fitness tests in children. *Research Quarterly,* 25, 178.

Kuntzleman, C. T., & Reiff, G. G. (1992). The decline in American children's fitness levels. *Research Quarterly for Exercise and Sport,* 63, 2, 107–111.

Kuoppasaline, K., & Adlecreutz, H. (1985). Interaction between catabolic and anabolic steroid hormones in muscular exercise. In K. Fotherby, & S. B. Pas (Eds.), *Exercise Endocrinology.* New York: Walter de Gruyter.

Legwold, G. (1982). Does lifting weights harm a prepubescent athlete? *Physician and Sportsmedicine,* 10, 141–144.

Legwold, G. (1983). Preadolescents show dramatic strength gains. *Physician and Sportsmedicine,* 11, 25.

Leighton, J. R. (1956). Flexibility characteristics of males ten to eighteen years of age. *Archives of Physical Medicine and Rehabilitation,* 37, 494–499.

Lohman, T. G. (1986). Applicability of body composition techniques and constraints for children and youth. *Exercise and Sports Sciences Review,* 14, 325–357.

Luedke, G. C. (1980). *Range of motion as the focus of teaching the overhand throwing pattern to children.* Unpublished doctoral dissertation, Indiana University.

Malina, R. M. (1986). Physical growth and maturation. In V. Seefeldt (Ed.), *Physical Activity and Well-Being.* Reston, VA: AAHPERD.

Massicotte, L. R., & MacNab, B. J. (1974). Cardiorespiratory adaptations to training at specific intensities in children. *Medicine and Science in Sports,* 6, 242–246.

Mersch, F., and Stoboy, H. (1989). Strength training and muscle hypertrophy in children. In S. Oseid and K. H. Carlsen (Eds.), *International Series on Sport Sciences. Children and Exercise XIII* (pp. 165–182). Champaign, IL: Human Kinetics.

Micheli, L. J. (1983). Overuse injuries in children's sports: The growth factor. *Orthopedic Clinics of North America,* 14, 2, April.

Micheli, L. J. (1988). Strength training in the young athlete. In E. W. Brown, & C. E. Branta (Eds.), *Competitive Sports for Children and Youth.* Champaign, IL: Human Kinetics.

Micheli, L. J., & Melhonian, N. (1987). The child in sport. In *Proceedings of the Pan American Sports Medicine Congress XII.* Indiana University, Bloomington, IN.

Micheli, L. J., & Micheli, E. R. (1985). Children's running: Special risks? *Annals of Sports Medicine,* 2, 61–63.

Montoye, H. (1970). *Introduction to Measurement in Physical Education.* Indianapolis, IN: Phi Epsilon Kappa Fraternity.

Mrzena, B., & Macuek, M. (1978). Uses of treadmill and working capacity assessment in preschool children. In J. Borms, & M. Hebbelinck (Eds.), *Medicine and Sports Series, Vol. ii, Pediatric Work Physiology.* Basel, Belgium: S. Karger.

National Children's and Youth Fitness Study II (1987). *Journal of Physical Education, Recreation and Dance,* 58, 9, 49–96.

National Strength and Conditioning Association (1985). Position paper on prepubescent strength training. *National Strength and Conditioning Association Journal,* 7, 4, 27–31.

Ozmun, J. C., Mikesky, A. E., & Surburg, P. R. (in press). Neuromuscular adaptations following prepubescent strength training. *Medicine and Science in Sports and Exercise.*

Paffenbarger, R. S. et al. (1986). Physical activity, all-cause mortality, and longevity of college alumni. *New England Journal of Medicine,* 314, 605–613.

Parizkova, J. (1972). Somatic development and body composition changes in adolescent boys differing in physical activity and fitness: A longitudinal study. *Anthropologie,* 10, 3–36.

Parizkova, J. (1973). Body composition and exercise during growth and development. In G. L. Rarick (Ed.), *Physical Activity: Human Development.* New York: Academic Press.

Parizkova, J. (1977). *Body Fat and Physical Fitness.* The Hague, Netherlands: Martinus Nijkoff B. V. Medical Division.

Parker, D. E. (1980). The vestibular apparatus. *Scientific American,* 243, 118–135.

Pate, R. R., & Blair, S. N. (1978). Exercise and the prevention of atherosclerosis: Pediatric implications. In W. Strong (Ed.), *Pediatric Aspects of Atherosclerosis.* New York: Greene and Stratton.

Pate, R. R. et al. (1985). The new norms: A comparison with the 1980 AAHPERD norms. *Journal of Physical Education, Recreation and Dance,* 56, 1, 28–30.

Pate, R. R. et al. (1987). The national children and youth fitness study II: The modified pull-up test. *Journal of Physical Education, Recreation and Dance,* 58, 9, 71–73.

Pate, R. R., & Ward, D. S. (1990). Endurance exercise trainability in children and youth. In B. J. Sharkey (Ed.), *Advances in Sports Medicine and Fitness, Vol. 3.* Chicago: Yearbook Medical.

Payne, G. V., & Morrow, J. R. (1993). Exercise and VO_2 max in children: A meta-analysis, *Research Quarterly for Exercise and Sport,* 64, 305–313.

Peterson, K. L. et al. (1974). *Factor analyses of motor performance for kindergarten, first and second grade children: A tentative solution.* Paper presented at the Annual Convention of the AAHPER, Anaheim, CA.

Rarick, G. L., & Dobbins, A. (1975). Basic components in the motor performance of children six to nine years of age. *Medicine and Science in Sports,* 17, 105–110.

Research Quarterly for Exercise and Sport (1987). Review and Commentary: Children and Fitness, 58, 295–333.

Roberts, S. O. (1993). Trainability of prepubescent children: Current theories and training considerations. In M. L. Leppo (Ed.), *Healthy From the Start: New Perspectives on Childhood Fitness.* Washington, DC: ERIC Clearinghouse on Teacher Education.

Romanella, N. E. et al. (1990). Physical activity and attitudes in lean and obese children and their mothers. *International Journal of Obesity,* 15, 407–414.

Romanella, N. E. et al. (1991). Physical activity and attitudes in lean and obese children and their mothers. *International Journal of Obesity*, 15, 407–414.

Ross, J. G., & Gilbert, G. G. (1985). The national children and youth fitness study: A summary of findings. *Journal of Physical Education, Recreation and Dance*, 56, 45–50.

Ross, J. G., & Pate, R. R. (1987). The national children and youth fitness study II. *Journal of Physical Education, Recreation and Dance*, 58, 49–96.

Ross, J. G. et al. (1987). The national children and youth fitness study II: New health-related fitness norms. *Journal of Physical Education, Recreation and Dance*, 58, 66–70.

Rowland, T. W. (1991). Effects of obesity on aerobic fitness in adolescent females. *American Journal of Diseases of Children*, 145, 764–768.

Rowland, T. W. (Ed.) (1993). *Pediatric Laboratory Exercise Testing & Clinical Guidelines*. Champaign, IL: Human Kinetics.

Sale, D. G. (1989). Strength training in children. In C. V. Gisolfi, & D. R. Lamb (Eds.), *Perspectives in Exercise Science and Sports Medicine*, Vol. 2. Indianapolis, IN: Benchmark Press.

Savage, M. P. et al. (1986). Exercise training effects on serum lipids of prepubescent boys and adult men. *Medicine and Science on Sports Exercise*, 8, 97–204.

Seefeldt, V. (1980). Physical fitness guidelines for preschool children. In *Proceedings of the National Conference on Physical and Sports for All*. Washington, DC: President's Council on Physical Fitness and Sports, 5–19.

Seefeldt, V., & Voegel, P. (1989). Physical fitness testing of children: A thirty-year history of misguided efforts? *Pediatric Exercise Science*, 1, 4, 295–302.

Sewell, L., & Micheli, L. (1984). *Strength development in children*. Paper presented to the American College of Sports Medicine, San Diego.

Shepard, R. J. (1984). Physical activity and 'wellness' of the child. In R. A. Boilleau (Ed.), *Advances in Pediatric Sport Sciences, Volume 1*. Champaign, IL: Human Kinetics.

Simons-Morton, B. G. et al. (1987). Children and fitness: A public health perspective. *Research Quarterly for Exercise and Sport*, 58, 4, 295–303.

Tanner, J. M. (1978). *Foetus into Man*. Cambridge, MA: Harvard University Press.

Updyke, W. (1992). In search of relevant and credible physical fitness standards for children. *Research Quarterly for Exercise and Sport*, 63, 2, 112–119.

Vaccaro, P., & Mahon, A. (1987). Cardiorespiratory responses to endurance training in children. *Sports Medicine*, 4, 352–363.

Van Slooten, P. H. (1973). *Performance of selected motor-coordination tasks by young boys and girls in six socioeconomic groups*. Unpublished doctoral dissertation, Indiana University.

Vrijens, J. (1978). Muscle strength development in pre- and postpubescent age. In J. Borms, & M. Hebbelinck (Eds.), *Pediatric Work Physiology*. New York: Karjer.

Wapner, S., & Werner, H. (1957). *Perceptual Development: An Investigation Within the Sensory Tonic Field Theory*. Worchester, MA: Clark University Press.

Ward, D. S. et al. (1987). Effects of a multicomponent intervention program and reducing health risk in obese children. *The Physical Educator*, 45, 44–49.

Ward, D. S., & Bar-Or, O. (1986). Role of the physician and the physical education teacher in the treatment of obesity. *Pediatrician*, 13, 44–51.

Weltman, A., Janney, C., Rians, C. B., Strand, K., Berg, B., Tippitt, S., Wise, J., Cahill, B. R., & Katch, F. I. (1986). The effects of hydraulic resistance strength training in pre-pubertal males. *Medicine and Science in Sports and Exercise*, 18, 629–638.

Williams, M. (1993). *Lifetime Fitness and Wellness: A Personal Choice*. Dubuque, IA: Brown & Benchmark.

Wilmore, J. H., and Costill, D. L. (1988). *Training for Sport and Activity*. Dubuque, IA: Wm. C. Brown.

Chapter 13

Barsch, R. (1965). *Achieving Perceptual-Motor Efficiency*. Seattle: Special Child Publications.

Bower, T. G. R. (1977). *The Perceptual World of the Child*. Cambridge, MA: Harvard University Press.

Cooper, J. M. et al. (1982). *Kinesiology*. St. Louis: Mosby.

Cooper, J. M., & Andrews, W. (1975). Rhythm as a linguistic art. *Quest*, 65, 61–67.

Council on Learning Disabilities. (1987). The CLD position statements: Measurement and training of perceptual and perceptual-motor functions. *Journal of Learning Disabilities*, 20, 6, 347–350.

Delacato, C. (1959). *Treatment and Prevention of Reading Problems*. Springfield, IL: Charles C. Thomas.

Dorfman, P. W. (1977). Timing and anticipation: A developmental perspective. *Journal of Motor Behavior*, 9, 67–79.

Frostig, M. (1969). *Move Grow and Learn*. Chicago: Follett.

Frostig, M. et al. (1966). *Administration and Scoring Manual: Frostig Developmental Test of Visual Perception*. Palo Alto, CA: Consulting Psychologists Press.

Gallahue, D. L. (1968). The relationship between perceptual and motor abilities. *Research Quarterly*, 39, 948–952.

Gallahue, D. L. (1982). *Developmental Movement Experiences for Children*. New York: Wiley.

Getman, G. N. (1952). *How to Develop Your Child's Intelligence (a research publication)*. Lucerne, MN: G. N. Getman.

Hebb, D. O. (1949). *The Organization of Behavior*. New York: Wiley.

Held, R. (1965). Plasticity of sensory-motor systems. *Scientific American*, 213, 84–94.

Held, R., & Blossom, J. (1961). Neonatal deprivation and adult rearrangement: Complementary techniques for analyzing plastic sensory-motor coordinations. *Journal of Comparative Physiological Psychology*, 54, 33–37.

Held, R., & Hein, A. (1963). Movement-produced stimulation in the development of visually guided behavior. *Journal of Comparative Physiological Psychology*, 56, 872–876.

Held, R., & Mikaelian, H. (1964). Motor sensory feedback versus need in adaptation to rearrangement. *Perceptual Motor Skills*, 18, 685–688.

Hoepner, B. J. (1967). Comparison of motor ability, new motor skill learning and adjustment to a rearranged visual field. *Research Quarterly*, 38, 605–614.

Isaacs, L. D. (1980). Effects of ball size, ball color, and preferred color on catching by young children. *Perceptual and Motor Skills*, 51, 583–586.

Kavale, K., & Mattson, P. D. (1983). One jumped off the balance beam: Meta-analysis of perceptual-motor training. *Journal of Learning Disabilities*, 16, 165–173.

Kephart, N. C. (1971). *The Slow Learner in the Classroom*. Columbus, OH: Merrill.

Marsh, H. W. et al. (1991). Self-concepts of young children 5 to 8 years of age: Measurement and multidimensional structure. *Journal of Educational Psychology*, 83, 377–392.

Marsh, H. W., & Peart, N. (1988). Competitive and cooperative physical fitness training programs for girls: Effects of physical fitness and multidimensional self-concepts. *Journal of Sport and Exercise Psychology*, 10, 390–407.

Morris, G. S. (1977). Dynamic visual acuity: Implications for the physical educator and coach. *Motor Skills: Theory into Practice*, 2, 5–10.

Morris, G. S. (1980). *Elementary Physical Education: Toward Inclusion*. Salt Lake City: Brighton Publishing.

Myers, P.I., & Hammill, D. D. (1982). *Learning Disabilities: Basic Concepts, Assessment Practices and Instructional Strategies*. Austin, TX: Pro-Ed.

Payne, V. G. (1985). *The effects of object size, experimental design and distance of projection of object reception by children in the first grade*. Unpublished doctoral dissertation, Indiana University.

Payne, V. G., & Isaacs, L. D. (1987). *Human Motor Development: A Lifespan Approach.* Mountain View, CA: Mayfield.

Payne, V. G., & Isaacs, L. D. (1991). *Human Motor Development: A Lifespan Approach* (2nd Ed.). Mountain View, CA: Mayfield.

Piaget, J. (1952). *The Origins of Intelligence in Children.* New York: International Universities Press.

Piaget, J. (1954). *The Construction of Reality and the Child.* New York: Basic Books.

Riesen, A. H., & Aarons, L. (1959). Visual movement and intensity discrimination of pattern vision. *Journal of Comparative Physiological Psychology,* 52, 142–149.

Sage, G. H. (1984). *Motor Learning and Control: A Neuropsychological Approach.* Dubuque, IA: Wm. C. Brown.

Smith, H. (1970). Implications for movement education experience drawn from perceptual motor research. *Journal of Health, Physical Education and Recreation,* 4, 30–33.

Smith, O. W., & Smith, P. C. (1966). Developmental studies of spatial judgements by children and adults. *Perceptual Motor Skills,* (Monograph Supplement), 22, 3–73.

Whiting, H. T. A. (1974). Dynamic visual acuity and performance of a catching task. *Journal of Motor Behavior,* 6, 87–94.

Williams, H. G. (1983). *Perceptual and Motor Development.* Englewood Cliffs, NJ: Prentice-Hall.

Zeki, S. (1992). The visual image in mind and brain. *Scientific American,* 264, 69–76.

Chapter 14

Bandura, A. (1982). Self efficacy: Toward a unifying theory of behavioral change. In M. Rosenberg, & H. B. Kaplan (Eds.), *Social Psychology of the Self-Concept.* Arlington Heights, IL: Harlan Davidson.

Bigge, M. L., & Shermis, S. S. (1992). *Learning Theories for Teachers.* New York: Harper Collins.

Brookover, W. B. et al. (1967). *Self Concept of Ability and School Achievement.* U.S. Office of Education, Cooperative Research Project, No. 2831. East Lansing: Michigan State University.

Combs, A. W., & Snygg, D. (1959). *Individual Behavior.* New York: Harper & Row.

Connell, J. P. (1985). A new multidimensional measure of children's perceptions of control. *Child Development,* 56, 1018–1041.

Coopersmith, S. (1967). *The Antecedents of Self-Esteem.* San Francisco: W. H. Freeman.

Coopersmith, S. (1977). A method of determining types of self-esteem. *Journal of Abnormal and Social Psychology,* 59, 87–94.

Crawford, T. A. (1989). *A developmental analysis of competitive orientation in team sports and individual sports.* Unpublished doctoral dissertation, Indiana University.

Damon, W., & Hart, D. (1986). Stability and change in children's self-understanding. *Social Cognition,* 4, 2, 102–118.

Dickstein, E. (1977). Self and self-esteem: Theoretical foundations and their implications for research. *Human Development,* 20, 129–140.

Duda, J. (1986). Towards a developmental theory of children's motivation in sport. *Journal of Sport and Exercise Psychology,* 9, 130–145.

Erikson, E. (1963). *Childhood and Society.* New York: Norton.

Erikson, E. (1980). *Identity and the Life Cycle.* New York: Norton.

Feltz, D. L., & Petlichkoff, D. (1983). Perceived competence among interscholastic sport participants and dropouts. *Canadian Journal of Applied Sport Science,* 8, 231–235.

Fox, K., Corbin, C. B., & Couldry, W. H. (1985). Female physical estimation and attraction to physical activity. *Journal of Sport Psychology,* 7, 125–136.

Gallahue, D. L. (1993). *Developmental Physical Education for Today's Children.* Dubuque, IA: Brown & Benchmark.

Gould, D. (1987). Understanding attrition in children's sports. In D. Gould, & M. R. Weiss (Eds.), *Advances in Pediatric Sport Sciences: Vol. 2, Behavioral Issues.* Champaign, IL: Human Kinetics.

Gould, D., & Horn, T. (1984). Participation motivation in young athletes. In J. M. Silva, & R. S. Weinberg (Eds.), *Psychological Foundations of Sport.* Champaign, IL: Human Kinetics.

Granleese, J., Trew, K., & Turner, I. (1988). Sex differences in perceived competence. *British Journal of Sport Psychology,* 27, 181–184.

Harter, S. (1978). Effectance motivation reconsidered: Toward a developmental model. *Human Development,* 21, 34–64.

Harter, S. (1981). The development of competence motivation in the mastery of cognitive and physical skills: Is there still a place for joy? In G. C. Roberts, & D. M. Landers (Eds.), *Psychology of Motor Behavior and Sport.* Champaign, IL: Human Kinetics.

Harter, S. (1982a). Development perspectives on self-esteem. In E. M. Hetherinton (Ed.), *Handbook of Child Psychology, Volume IV: Socialization, Personality, and Social Developments.* New York: Wiley.

Harter, S. (1982b). The perceived competence scale for children. *Child Development,* 53, 87–97.

Harter, S. (1983). Developmental Perspectives on the Self System. In P. H. Mussen (Ed.), *Handbook of Child Psychology.* New York: Wiley.

Harter, S. (1984). A model of the relationship among children's academic achievement and children's perceptions of competence, control, and motivational orientation. In J. Nicholls (Ed.), *The Development of Achievement-Related Cognitions and Behaviors.* Greenwich, CT.

Harter, S. (1985). *Manual for the Self-Perception Profile for Children.* (Revision of the perceived competence scale for children). Denver: University of Denver.

Harter, S., & Connell, J. P. (1984). A model of the relationship among children's academic achievement and children's perceptions of competence, control and motivational orientation. In J. Nicholls (Ed.), *The Development of Achievement-Related Cognitions and Behaviors.* Greenwich, CT: J. A. I. Press.

Harter, S., & Pike, R. (1984). The pictorial scale of perceived competence and social acceptance for young children. *Child Development,* 55, 1967–1982.

James, W. (1890). *Psychology.* New York: Fawcett.

Knoppers, A. (1992). Personal and social skills. In V. Seefeldt, and E. W. Brown (Eds.), *Program for Athletic Coaches Education.* Dubuque, IA: Brown & Benchmark.

Marsh, H. W. (1985). Age and sex effects in multiple dimensions of preadolescent self-concept: A replication and extension. *Australian Journal of Psychology,* 37, 197–204.

Marsh, H. W. (1990). A multidimensional, hierarchical model of self-concept: Theoretical and empirical justification. *Educational Psychology Review,* 2, 77–172.

Marsh, H. W. et al. (1991). Self-concepts of young children 5 to 8 years of age: Measurement and multidimensional structure. *Journal of Educational Psychology,* 83, 3, 377–392.

Marsh, H. W., & Peart, N. D. (1988). Competitive and cooperative physical fitness training programs for girls: Effects on physical fitness and multidimensional self-concepts. *Journal of Sport and Exercise Psychology,* 10, 390–407.

Martinek, T., & Zaichkowsky, L. D. (1977). *The Martinek-Zaichkowsky Self-Concept Scale for Children.* Jacksonville, IL: Psychologists and Educators.

Maynard, R. (1973). *Guiding Your Child to a More Creative Life.* New York: Doubleday.

McCandless, B. R. (1976). *Children—Behavior and Development.* New York: Holt, Rinehart and Winston.

Roberts, G. C., Kleiber, D. A., & Duda, J. L. (1981). An analysis of motivation in children's sport: The role of perceived competence in motivation. *Journal of Sport Psychology,* 3, 206–216.

Rosenberg, M. (1979). *Conceiving the Self.* New York: Basic Books.

Rosenberg, M. (1982). Psychological selectivity in self-esteem formation. In M. Rosenberg, & H. B. Kaplan (Eds.), *Social Psychology of the Self-Concept.* Arlington Heights, IL: Harlan Davidson.

Schempp, P. G. et al. (1983). Influence of decision-making on attitudes, creativity, motor skills and self-concept in elementary children. *Research Quarterly*, 540, 2, 183–189.

Taylor, B. J. (1980). Pathways to a healthy self-concept. In T. D. Yaroke (Ed.), *The Self Concept of the Young Child*. Salt Lake City: Brigham Young Press.

Tuddenham, R. S. (1951). Studies in reputation III, Correlates of popularity among elementary school children. *Journal of Educational Psychology*, 42, 1–12.

Ulrich, B. (1987). Perceptions of physical competence, motor competence and participation in organized sports: Their interrelations in young children. *Research Quarterly for Exercise and Sport*, 58, 57–67.

van Wersch, A., Trew, K., & Turner, I. (1990). Pupils' perceived physical competence and its implications for the new PE curriculum. *Research Supplement of the Physical Education Association of Great Britain and Northern Ireland*, 7, 1–5.

Weiss, M. R. (1987). Self-esteem and achievement in children's sport and physical activity. In D. Gould, & M. R. Weiss (Eds.), *Advances in Pediatric Sport Science: Vol. 2, Behavior Issues*, Champaign, IL: Human Kinetics.

Weiss, M. R., & Horn, T. S. (1990). The relation between children's accuracy estimates of their physical competence and achievement-related characteristics. *Research Quarterly for Exercise and Sport*, 61, 3, 250–258.

Werner, E. E. (1989a). Children of the garden island. *Scientific American*, 264, 106–111.

Werner, E. E. (1989b). High risk children in young adulthood: A longitudinal study from birth to 32 years. *American Journal of Orthopsychiatry*, 59, 1, 72–81.

White, R. (1959). Motivation reconsidered. The concept of competence. *Psychological Review*, 66, 297–323.

Wylie, R. (1979). *The Self-Concept*. Lincoln: University of Nebraska Press.

Yamamoto, K. (1972). *The Child and His Image*. Boston: Houghton Mifflin.

Zaharopoulos, E., & Hodge, K. (1991). Self-concept and sport participation. *New Zealand Journal of Psychology*, 20, 12–16.

Zaichkowsky, L. B. et al. (1975). Self-concept and attitudinal differences in elementary age children after participating in a physical activity program. *Movement*, 243–245.

Zaichkowsky, L. D. et al. (1980). *Growth and Development: The Child and Physical Activity*. St. Louis, MO: C. V. Mosby.

Chapter 15

American College of Sports Medicine Position Statement of the Use and Abuse of Anabolic-Androgenic Steroids in Sports. (1987). *Medicine and Science in Sports*, 9, 11–13.

Cain, E. D. J., & Broekhoff, J. (1987). Maturity assessment: A viable preventive measure against physical and psychological insult to the young athlete? *The Physician and Sportsmedicine*, 15, 67–69.

Conger, J. J., & Peterson, A. C. (1984). *Adolescence and Youth*. New York: Harper & Row.

Duke, R. M. et al. (1980). Adolescence' self-assessment of sexual maturation. *Pediatrics*, 66, 918–920.

Heald, F. P., & Hung, W. (Eds.) (1970). *Adolescent Endocrinology*. Englewood Cliffs, NJ: Appleton-Century-Crofts.

Katchadourian, H. (1977). *The Biology of Adolescence*. San Francisco: W. H. Freeman.

Kreipe, R. E., & Gewanter, H. L. (1983). Physical maturity screening for participation in sports. *Pediatrics*, 75, 1076–1080.

Krogman, W. M. (1980). *Child Growth*. Ann Arbor, MI: University of Michigan Press.

Malina, R. M. (1986). Physical growth and maturation. In V. Seefeldt (Ed.), *Physical Acitivity and Well-Being*. Reston, VA: AAHPERD.

Malina, R. M., & Bouchard, C. (1991). *Growth, Maturation, and Physical Activity*. Champaign, IL: Human Kinetics.

Masters, W. H., & Johnson, V. E. (1970). *Human Sexual Inadequacy*. Boston: Little Brown.

National Children and Youth Fitness Study I. (1985). *Journal of Physical Education, Recreation and Dance*, 56, 1, 43–90.

National Children and Youth Fitness Study II. (1987). *Journal of Physical Education, Recreation and Dance*, 58, 9, 49–96.

Prior, J. C. (1990). Reproduction: Exercise-related adaptations and the health of women and men. In C. Bouchard et al. (Eds.), *Exercise Fitness and Health: A Concensus Of Current Knowledge*. Champaign, IL: Human Kinetics.

Tanner, J. M. (1962). *Growth at Adolescence*. Oxford, England: Blackwell Scientific Publications.

Tanner, J. M. (1989). *Fetus into Man* (Revised and expanded). Cambridge, MA: Harvard University Press.

Tanner, J. M. et al. (1975). *Assessment of Skeletal Maturity and Prediction of Adult Height*. New York: Academic Press.

Taylor, W. N. (1987). Synthetic anabolic-androgenic steroids: A plea for controlled substance status. *Physician and Sportsmedicine*, 15, 5, 140–147.

Updyke, W. (1993). *Chrysler–AAU Physical Fitness Program*. Bloomington, IN: Indiana University.

Wieczorek, R. R., & Natapoff, J. N. (1981). *A Conceptual Approach to the Nursing of Children*. Philadelphia: J. B. Lippincott.

Wierman, M. E., & Crowley, W. F., Jr. (1986). Neutroendocrine control of the onset of puberty. In F. Falkner, and J. M. Tanner (Eds.), *Human growth, volume 2: Postnatal growth*, revised edition. New York: Plenum.

Chapter 16

American Coaching Effectiveness Program: ACEP. (1993). Champaign, IL: Human Kinetics.

Christina, R. W., & Corcos, D. M. (1988). *Coaches Guide to Teaching Sport Skills*. Champaign, IL: Human Kinetics.

Fitts, P. M. (1962). Factors in complex skill learning. In R. Glasser (Ed.), *Training research and education*. Pittsburgh: University of Pittsburgh Press.

Fitts, P. M., & Posner, M. I. (1967). *Human performance*. Belmont, CA: Brooks/ Cole.

Gentile, A. (1972). A working model for skill acquisition with application to teaching. *Quest*, 17, 3–23.

Haubenstricker, J., & Seefeldt, V. (1986). Acquisition of motor skills during childhood. In V. Seefeldt (Ed.), *Physical Activity and Well-Being*. Reston, VA: AAHPERD.

Lawther, J. D. (1977). *The Learning and Performance of Physical Skills*. Englewood Cliffs, NJ: Prentice-Hall.

Magill, R. (1993). *Motor Learning: Concepts and Application*. Dubuque, IA: Wm. C. Brown.

Martens, R. (1990). *Successful Coaching*. Champaign, IL: Human Kinetics.

Program for Athletic Coaches Education: PACE. (1992). Youth Sports Institute, Michigan State University. Dubuque, IA: Brown & Benchmark.

Sage, G. H. (1984). *Motor Learning and Control: A Neurophyschological Approach*. Dubuque, IA: Wm. C. Brown.

Sawyer, T. (Ed.). (1992). Coaching education in North America. *Journal of Physical Education, Recreation and Dance*, 63, 33–64.

Seefeldt, V. (1980). Physical fitness guidelines for preschool children. In *Proceedings of the National Conference on Physical Fitness and Sports for All*. Washington, DC: President's Council on Physical Fitness and Sports, 5–19.

Seefeldt, V. et al. (1992). *Overview of Youth Sport Programs in the United States*. New York: Carnegie Council on Adolescent Development.

Seefeldt, V., & Brown, E. W. (Eds.) (1992). *Program for Athletic Coaches' Education*. Dubuque, IA: Brown & Benchmark.

Seefeldt, V., & Gould, D. (1980). Physical and psychological effects of athletic competition on children and youth. Washington, DC, ERIC Clearinghouse on Teacher Education.

Wickstrom, R. (1983). *Fundamental Motor Patterns*. Philadelphia: Lea & Febiger.

Chapter 17

Bandini, L. G. et al. (1990). Validity of reported energy intake in obese and nonobese adolescents. *American Journal of Clinical Nutrition*, 52, 421–425.

Bar-Or, O. (1983). *Pediatric Sports Medicine for the Practitioner*. New York: Springer-Verlag.

CAPHER (1980). Canadian Association for Health, Physical Education, and Recreation: *Manitoba Physical Fitness Performance Test Manual and Fitness Objectives*. Ottawa, Canada: CAHPER.

Corbin, C. B., & Pangrazi, R. P. (1992). Are American children and youth fit? *Research Quarterly for Exercise and Sport*, 63, 96–106.

Errecart, M. T. (1985). The National Children and Youth Fitness Study II: Sampling procedures. *Journal of Physical Education, Recreation and Dance*, 56, 54–56.

Gutin, B. et al. (1992). Defining health and fitness. *Research Quarterly for Exercise and Sport*, 63, 128–131.

Haubenstricker, J., & Seefeldt, V. (1986). Acquisition of motor skills during childhood. In V. Seefeldt (Ed.), *Physical Activity and Well-Being*. Reston, VA: AAHPERD.

Hunsicker, P., & Reiff, G. (1977). Youth fitness report, 1958–1965–1975. *Journal of Physical Education and Recreation*, 48, 32–36.

Kuntzleman, C. T., & Reiff, G. G. (1992). The decline in American children's fitness levels. *Research Quarterly for Exercise and Sport*, 63, 107–111.

Meredith, C. N., & Dwyer, J. T. (1991). Nutrition and exercise: Effects on adolescent health. *Annual Review of Public Health 1991*, 12: 309–333.

Moore, J. M. et al. (1991). Energy need in childhood and adult-onset obese women before and after a nine-month nutrition education and walking program. *International Journal of Obesity*, 15, 337–344.

National Children and Youth Fitness Study I. (1985). *Journal of Physical Education, Recreation and Dance*, 56, 43–90.

National Children and Youth Fitness Study II. (1987). *Journal of Physical Education, Recreation and Dance*, 58, 49–96.

Parizkova, J. (1982). Physical training in weight reduction of obese adolescents. *Annals of Clinical Research*, 34, 69–73.

Pate, R. R. et al. (1985). The new norms: A comparison with the 1980 AAHPERD norms. *Journal of Physical Education, Recreation and Dance*, 56, 70–72.

Reuschlein, P., & Haubenstricker, J. (Eds.) (1985). Physical education interpretive report: Grades 4, 7, and 10. Michigan Educational Assessment Program. State Board of Education, Michigan Department of Education, Lansing.

Romanella, N. E. et al. (1991). Physical activity and attitudes in lean and obese children and their mothers. *International Journal of Obesity*, 15, 407–414.

Ross, J. G. et al. (1987). Changes in the body composition of children. *Journal of Physical Education, Recreation and Dance*, 58, 9, 74–77.

Updyke, W. (1992). In search of relevant and credible physical fitness standards for children. *Research Quarterly for Exercise and Sport*, 63, 112–119.

Updyke, W., & Willett, M. (1989). Physical fitness trends in American youth: 1980–1989. Chrysler Fund–Amateur Athletic Union Physical Fitness Program. Bloomington, IN: Poplars Research Center.

Williams, H. G. (1983). *Perceptual and Motor Development*. Englewood Cliffs, NJ: Prentice-Hall.

Chapter 18

Bredemeier, B. J. & Shields, D. L. (1987). Moral growth through physical activity: A structural/developmental approach. In D. Gould, & M. R. Weiss, (Eds.), *Advances in Pediatric Sport Sciences, Vol. 2: Behavioral Issues*. Champaign, IL: Human Kinetics.

Campbell, R. M. (1984). *The New Science: Self-Esteem Psychology*. San Diego: University Press of America.

Carnegie Report (1987). *Preparing for Life: The Critical Transition of Adolescence*. Carnegie Corporation of New York.

Coakley, J. J. (1983). Play, games, and sports: Developmental implications for young people. In J. C. Harris, & R. J. Park (Eds.), *Play, Games, and Sports in Cultural Contexts*. Champaign, IL: Human Kinetics.

Coakley, J. J. (1987). Children and the sport socialization process. in D. Gould, & M. R. Weiss, (Eds.), *Advances in Pediatric Sport Sciences, Vol. 2: Behavioral Issues*. Champaign, IL: Human Kinetics.

Coakley, J. J. (1990). *Sport in Society: Issues and Controversies*. Boston, MA: Times Mirror/ Mosby.

Conger, J. J., & Peterson, A. C. (1984) *Adolescence and Youth*. New York: Harper & Row.

Gould, D. (1987). Understanding attrition in children's sports. In D. Gould, & M. R. Weiss (Eds.), *Advances in Pediatric Sport Sciences: Vol. 2. Behavioral Issues*. Champaign, IL: Human Kinetics.

Greendorfer, S. L. (1977). Role of socializing agents in female sports involvement. *Research Quarterly*, 48, 304–310.

Greendorfer, S. L. (1987). Psycho-social correlates of organized physical activity. *Journal of Physical Education, Recreation and Dance*, 58, 69–74.

Greendorfer, S. L., & Lewko, J. H. (1978). Role of family members in sport socialization of children. *Research Quarterly*, 49, 149–152.

Greenspan, (1983). *Little Winners: Inside the World of the Child Sports Star*. Boston: Little Brown.

Harter, S. (1982). Developmental perspectives on self-esteem. In E. M. Hetherinton (Ed.), *Handbook of Child Psychology: Vol. IV: Socialization, Personality and Social Developments*. New York: Wiley.

Kellman, H. C. (1968). Compliance, identification, and internalization: Three processes of attitude change. *Journal of Conflict Resolution*, 2, 51–60.

Kenyon, G. S. (1968). Six scales for assessing attitude toward physical activity. *Research Quarterly*, 39, 566–574.

Kohlberg, L. (1981). *The Philosophy of Moral Development: Moral Stages and Idea of Justice*. San Francisco: Harper & Row.

Kohlberg, L. (1984). *Essays of Moral Development: Vol. 2. The Psychology of Moral Development*. San Francisco: Harper & Row.

Martens, R. (1986). Youth sport in the USA. In M. R. Weiss, & D. Gould (Eds.), *Sport for children and youth*. Champaign, IL: Human Kinetics.

Piaget, J. (1932). *The Moral Judgement of the Child*. New York: Harcourt and Brace.

Sage, G. H. (1984). *Motor Learning and Control a Neurophyschological Approach*. Dubuque, IA: Wm. C. Brown.

Sage, G. H. (1986). Social development: In V. Seefeldt (Ed.), *Physical Activity and Well-Being*. Reston, VA: AAHPERD.

Seefeldt, V. (Ed.) (1987). Selling the potential rather than the record. *Journal of Physical Education, Recreation and Dance*, 58, 42–43.

Seefeldt, V., et al. (1992). *Overview of Youth Sports Programs in the United States*. New York: Carnegie Council of Adolescent Development.

U.S. Department of Commerce, Bureau of the Census (1987). *Statistical Abstract of the United States*. Washington, DC: U.S. Government Printing Office.

Vogel, P. G. (1986). Effects of physical education programs on children. In V. Seefeldt (Ed.), *Physical Activity and Well-Being*. Reston, VA: AAHPERD.

Weiss, M. R. (1987). Self esteem and achievement in children's sport and physical activity. In D. Gould, & M. R. Weiss (Eds.), *Advances in Pediatric Sport Sciences, Vol. 2: Behavioral Issues*. Champaign, IL: Human Kinetics.

Weiss, M. R., & Bredemeier, B. J. (1986). Moral development. In V. Seefeldt (Ed.), *Physical Activity and Well-Being*. Reston, VA: AAHPERD.

Wylie, R. (1979). *The Self Concept*. Lincoln: University of Nebraska Press.

Chapter 19

Dacey, J., & Travers, J. (1991). *Human Development Across the Lifespan*. Dubuque, IA: Wm. C. Brown.

Drinkwater, B. (1992). *Osteoporosis: The 'silent thief' of the golden years*. Presented at the American Alliance for Health, Physical Education, Recreation and Dance National Convention, Indianapolis, IN.

Dummer, G. M., Vaccaro, P., & Clarke, D. H. (1985). Muscular strength and flexibility of two female masters swimmers in the eighth decade of life. *Journal of Orthopaedic and Sports Physical Therapy*, 6, 235–237.

Fiatarone, M. A., Marks, E. C., Ryan, N. D., Meredith, C. N., Lipsitz, L. A., & Evans, W. J. (1990). High-intensity strength training in nonagenarians. *Journal of the American Medical Association*, 263, 3029–3034.

Gabbard, C. (1992). *Lifelong Motor Development*. Dubuque, IA: Wm. C. Brown.

Guyton, A. C. (1991). *Textbook of Medical Physiology* (8th ed.). Philadelphia: W. B. Saunders.

Hayflick, L. (1980). The cell biology of human aging. *Scientific American*, 242, 58–65.

Hazzard, W. R., Andres, R., Bierman, E. L., & Blass, J. P. (Eds.) (1990). *Principles of Geriatric Medicine and Gerontology*. New York: McGraw-Hill.

Heath, G., Hagberg, J., Ehsani, A., & Holloszy, J. (1981). A physiological comparison of young and older endurance athletes. *Journal of Applied Physiology*, 51, 634–640.

Mathiowetz, V., Kashman, N., Volland, G., Weber, K., Dowe, M., & Rogers, S. (1985). Grip and pinch strength: Normative data for adults. *Archives of Physical Medicine and Rehabilitation*, 66, 69–72.

Rybash, J. M., Roodin, P. A., & Santrock, J. W. (1991). *Adult Development and Aging* (2nd ed.). Dubuque, IA: Wm. C. Brown.

Saxon, S. V., & Etten, M. J. (1987). *Physical Change and Aging* (2nd ed.). New York: Tiresias Press.

Spirduso, W. W. (1986). Physical activity and the prevention of premature aging. In V. Seefeldt (Ed.), *Physical Activity & Well-Being* (pp. 142–160). Reston, VA: American Alliance for Health, Physical Education, Recreation, and Dance.

Spirduso, W. W., & MacRae, P. G. (1990). Motor performance and aging. In J. E. Birren & K. W. Schaie (Eds.), *Handbook of the Psychology of Aging* (3rd ed.) (pp. 183–200). San Diego: Academic Press.

Chapter 20

Baylor, A. M., & Spirduso, W. W. (1988). Systematic aerobic exercise and components of reaction time in older women. *Journal of Gerontology*, 43, 121–126.

Burley, L. R. (1944). A study of the reaction time of physically trained men. *Research Quarterly*, 15, 232–239.

Chen, H. C., Ashton-Miller, J. A., Alexander, N. B., & Schultz, A. B. (1991). Stepping over obstacles: Gait patterns of healthy young and old adults. *Journal of Gerontology*, 46, 196–203.

Crilly, R. G., Willems, D. A., Trenholm, K. J., Hayes, K. C., Delaquerriere-Richardson, L. F. (1989). Effect of exercise on postural sway in the elderly. *Gerontology*, 35, 137–143.

Dacey, J., & Travers, J. (1991). *Human Development Across the Lifespan*. Dubuque, IA: Wm. C. Brown.

Dummer, G. M., Vaccaro, P., & Clarke, D. H. (1985). Muscular strength and flexibility of two female masters swimmers in the eighth decade of life. *Journal of Orthopaedic and Sports Physical Therapy*, 6, 235–237.

Dunn, J. E., Rudberg, M. A., Furner, S. E., & Cassel, C. K. (1992). Mortality, disability, and falls in older persons: The role of underlying disease and disability. *American Journal of Public Health*, 82, 395–400.

Elble, R. J., Hughes, L., & Higgins, C. (1992). The syndrome of senile gait. *Journal of Neurology*, 239, 71–75.

Ferrandez, A. M., Pailhous, J., & Durup, M. (1990). Slowness in elderly gait. *Experimental Aging Research*, 16, 79–89.

Fiatarone, M. A., Marks, E. C., Ryan, N. D., Meredith, C. N., Lipsitz, L. A., & Evans, W. J. (1990). High-intensity strength training in nonagenarians. *Journal of the American Medical Association*, 263, 3029–3034.

Forssberg, H., & Nashner, L. (1982). Ontogenetic development of posture control in man: Adaptation to altered support and visual conditions during stance. *Journal of Neuroscience*, 2, 545–552.

Gabbard, C. (1992). *Lifelong Motor Development*. Dubuque, IA: Wm. C. Brown.

Hart, D., Bowling, A., Ellis, M., & Silman, A. (1990). Locomotor disability in very elderly people: Value of a programme for screening and provision of aids for daily living. *British Medical Journal*, 301, 216–220.

Hodgkins, J. (1963). Reaction time and speed of movement in males and females of various ages. *Research Quarterly*, 34, 335–343.

Jackson, T. W., & Lyles, K. W. (1990). Hip fractures. In W. R. Hazzard, R. Andres, E. L. Bierman, & J. P. Blass (Eds.), *Principles of Geriatric Medicine and Gerontology* (2nd ed.) (pp. 1200–1203). New York: McGraw-Hill.

Koller, W. C., & Glatt, S. L. (1990). Gait disorders. In W. R. Hazzard, R. Andres, E. L. Bierman, & J. P. Blass (Eds.), *Principles of Geriatric Medicine and Gerontology* (2nd ed.) (pp. 1183–1191). New York: McGraw-Hill.

Kroll, W., & Clarkson, P. M. (May, 1977). *Fractionated reflex time, resisted and unresisted fractionated reaction time under normal and fatigued conditions*. Paper presented at the Annual Conference of the North American Society for the Psychology of Sport and Physical Activity, Ithaca College, Ithaca, NY.

Manchester, D., Woollacott, M., Zederbauer-Hylton, N., & Marin, O. (1989). Visual, vestibular and somatosensory contributions to balance control in the older adult. *Journal of Gerontology*, 44, 118–127.

Mundle, P., Dietderich, S., & Harvey, R. (1992). *Masters Age Records for 1991*. North Hollywood, CA: National Masters News.

Payne, G. V., & Isaacs, L. D. (1991). *Human Motor Development: A Lifespan Approach*. Mountain View, CA: Mayfield.

Pierson, W. R., & Montoye, H. J. (1958). Movement time, reaction time, and age. *Journal of Gerontology*, 13, 418–421.

Rikli, R. E., & Edwards, D. J. (1991). Effects of a three-year exercise program on motor function and cognitive processing speed in older women. *Research Quarterly for Exercise and Sport*, 62, 61–67.

Rybash, J. M., Roodin, P. A., & Santrock, J. W. (1991). *Adult Development and Aging* (2nd ed.). Dubuque, IA: Wm. C. Brown.

Salthouse, T. A. (1976). Speed and age: Multiple rates of age decline. *Experimental Aging Research*, 2, 349–359.

Schmidt, R. A. (1988). *Motor Control and Learning: A Behavioral Emphasis*. Champaign, IL: Human Kinetics.

Shephard, R. J., Berridge, M., & Montelpare, W. (1990). On the generality of the 'sit and reach' test: An analysis of flexibility data for an aging population. *Research Quarterly for Exercise and Sport*, 61, 326–330.

Spirduso, W. W. (1975). Reaction and movement time as a function of age and physical activity level. *Journal of Gerontology*, 30, 435–440.

Spirduso, W. W. (1986). Physical activity and the prevention of premature aging. In V. Seefeldt (Ed.), *Physical Activity & Well-Being* (pp. 141–160). Reston, VA: American Alliance for Health, Physical Education, Recreation, and Dance.

Spirduso, W. W., & Clifford, P. (1978). Replication of age and physical activity effects on reaction and movement time. *Journal of Gerontology*, 33, 26–30.

Spirduso, W. W., & MacRae, P. G. (1990). Motor performance and aging. In J. E. Birren & K. W. Schaie (Eds.), *Handbook of the Psychology of Aging* (3rd ed.) (pp. 183–200). San Diego: Academic Press.

Stones, M. J., & Kozma, A. (1980). Adult age trends in record running performances. *Experimental Aging Research*, 6, 407–416.

Stones, M. J., & Kozma, A. (1981). Adult age trends in athletic performance. *Experimental Aging Research, 7*, 269–280.

Stones, M. J., & Kozma, A. (1982). Cross-sectional, longitudinal, and secular age trends in athletic performances. *Experimental Aging Research, 8*, 185–188.

Stones, M. J., & Kozma, A. (1986). Age by distance effects in running and swimming records: A note on methodology. *Experimental Aging Research, 12*, 203–206.

Tacstats/USA. (1992, October). National long distance running records and bests. *TacTimes, 6*, 6–10.

Teasdale, N., Stelmach, G. E., & Breunig, A. (1991). Postural sway characteristics of the elderly under normal and altered visual and support surface conditions. *Journal of Gerontology, 46*, 238–244.

Tinetti, M. E. (1990). Falls. In W. R. Hazzard, R. Andres, E. L. Bierman, & J. P. Blass (Eds.), *Principles of Geriatric Medicine and Gerontology* (2nd ed.) (pp. 1192–1199). New York: McGraw-Hill.

VanSant, A. F. (1990). Life-span development in functional tasks. *Physical Therapy, 70*, 788–798.

Wall, J. C., Hogan, D. B., Turnbull, G. I., & Fox, R. A. (1991). The kinematics of idiopathic gait disorder: A comparison with healthy young and elderly females. *Scandinavian Journal of Rehabilitation Medicine, 23*, 159–164.

Whipple, R. H., Wolfson, L. I., & Amerman, P. M. (1987). The relationship of knee and ankle weakness to falls in nursing home residents: An isokinetic study. *Journal of the American Geriatrics Society, 35*, 13–20.

Woollacott, M., Inglin, B., & Manchester, D. (1988). Response preparation and posture control: Neuromuscular changes in the older adult. *Annals of the New York Academy of Sciences, 515*, 42–53.

Woollacott, M. H., & Shumway-Cook, A. (1990). Changes in posture control across the life span: A systems approach. *Physical Therapy, 70*, 799–807.

Woollacott, M. H., Shumway-Cook, A., & Nashner, L. M. (1986). Aging and posture control: Changes in sensory organization and muscular coordination. *International Journal of Aging and Human Development, 23*, 97–114.

Chapter 21

Atchley, R. C. (1976). *The Sociology of Retirement*. Cambridge, MA: Schenkman.

Berryman-Miller, S. (1988). Dance/movement: Effects on elderly self-concept. *Journal of Physical Education, Recreation, and Dance, 59*, 42–46.

Dacey, J., & Travers, J. (1991). *Human Development Across the Lifespan*. Dubuque, IA: Wm. C. Brown.

Hird, J. S., & Williams, J. M. (1989). The psychological effects of chronic exercise in the elderly. In A. C. Ostrow (Ed.), *Aging and Motor Behavior* (pp. 173–200). Indianapolis, IN: Benchmark Press.

Levinson, D. (1978). *The Seasons of Man's Life*. New York: Knopf.

Levinson, D. J. (1986). A conception of adult development. *American Psychologist, 41*, 3–13.

Loomis, R. A., & Thomas, C. D. (1991). Elderly women in nursing home and independent residence: Health, body attitudes, self-esteem and life satisfaction. *Canadian Journal on Aging, 10*, 224–231.

Palmore, E. (1979). Predictors of successful aging. *The Gerontologist, 19*, 427–431.

Palmore, E. (1982). Predictors of the longevity difference: A 25-year follow-up. *The Gerontologist, 22*, 513–518.

Perri, S., & Templer, D. (1985). The effects of an aerobic exercise program on psychological variables in older adults. *International Journal of Aging and Human Development, 20*, 167–172.

Rybash, J. M., Roodin, P. A., & Santrock, J. W. (1991). *Adult Development and Aging* (2nd ed.). Dubuque, IA: Wm. C. Brown.

Shock, N. W. (1985). Longitudinal studies of aging in humans. In C. E. Finch & E. L. Schneider (Eds.), *Handbook of the Biology of Aging* (2nd ed.) (pp. 721–743). New York: Van Nostrand Reinhold.

Thomas, C. L. (Ed.) (1989). *Taber's Cyclopedic Medical Dictionary*. Philadelphia: F. A. Davis.

Valliant, P. M., & Asu, M. E. (1985). Exercise and its effects on cognition and physiology in older adults. *Perceptual and Motor Skills, 51*, 499–505.

Williamson, J. B., Munley, A., & Evans, L. (1980). *Aging and Society: An Introduction to Social Gerontology*. New York: Holt, Rinehart & Winston.

Chapter 22

Balan, C. M., & Davis, W. E. (1993). Ecological task analysis—An approach to teaching physical education. *Journal of Physical Education, Recreation and Dance, 64*, 9, 54–61.

Carlisle, C., & Cole, S. (1994). *Skillful Movers*. Dubuque, IA: Brown & Benchmark.

Fitts, P. M., & Posner, M. I. (1967). *Human Performance*. Belmont, CA: Brooks/Cole.

Gallahue, D. L. (1993). *Developmental Physical Education for Today's Children*. Dubuque, IA: Brown & Benchmark.

Gentile, A. (1972). A working model of skill acquisition with application to teaching. *Quest, 17*, 2–23.

Gilliom, B. C. (1970). *Basic Movement Education for Children*. Reading, MA: Addison-Wesley.

Keough, J., & Sugden, D. (1985). *Movement Skill Development*. New York: Macmillan.

Laban, R., & Lawrence, F. (1947). *Effort*. London: Unwin Brothers.

Lawther, J. D. (1977). *The Learning and Performance of Physical Skills*. Englewood Cliffs, NJ: Prentice-Hall.

Magill, R. A. (1993). *Motor Learning: Concepts and Applications*. Dubuque, IA: Brown & Benchmark.

Mooston, M., & Ainsworth, S. (1991). *Teaching Physical Education*. Columbus, OH: Charles E. Merrill.

Piaget, J. (1952). *The Origins of Intelligence in Children*. New York: International Universities Press.

Piaget, J. (1969). *The Psychology of the Child*. New York: Basic Books.

Riggs, M. L. (1980). *Jump to Joy*. Englewood Cliffs, NJ: Prentice-Hall.

Sage, G. H. (1984). *Motor Learning and Control*. Dubuque, IA: Wm. C. Brown.

Smith, K. V., & Smith, W. M. (1962). *Perception and Motion: An Analysis of Space-Structured Behavior*. Philadelphia: W. B. Saunders.

Chapter 23

Apgar, V. (1953). A proposal for a new method of evaluation of the newborn infant. *Current Research in Anesthesia and Analgesia, 32*, 260–267.

Apgar, V., & James, L. S. (1962). Further observations on the newborn scoring system. *American Journal of the Diseases of Children, 104*, 419–428.

Arnheim, D. D., & Sinclair, W. A. (1979). *The Clumsy Child*. St. Louis: C. V. Mosby.

Bayley, N. (1935). The development of motor abilities during the first three years. *Monograph of the Society for Research on Child Development, 1*, 1–26.

Bayley, N. (1969). *Manual for the Bayley Scales of Infant Development*. New York: Harper & Row.

Bayley Scales of Infant Development. New York, NY: The Psychological Corp.

Bruininks, R. H. (1978). *Bruininks-Oseretsky Test of Motor Proficiency*. Circle Pines, MN: American Guidance Service.

Buros, O. K. (Ed.) (1971). *The Seventh Mental Measurement Yearbook*. Highland Park, NJ: Gryphon Press.

Davis, W. E. (1984). Motor ability assessment of populations with handicapping conditions: Challenging basic assumptions. *Adapted Physical Activity Quarterly, 1,* 125–140.

Davis, W. E., & Burton, A. W. (1991). Ecological task analysis: Translating movement behavior theory into practice. *Adapted Physical Activity Quarterly, 8,* 154–177.

Denver Developmental Screening Test. Denver, CO: DDM, Inc.

Frankenburg, W. K., & Dodds, J. B. (1967). The Denver developmental screening test. *Journal of Pediatrics, 71,* 181–191.

Frankenburg, W. K. et al. (1990). *Denver II Technical Manual*. Denver, CO: Denver Developmental Materials, Inc.

Frankenburg, W. K. et al. (1992). The Denver II: A major revision and restandardization of the Denver Developmental Screening Test. *Pediatrics, 89,1,* 91–97.

Functional Fitness Assessment for Adults Over 60 Years. Reston, VA: American Alliance for Health, Physical Education, Recreation and Dance.

Gallahue, D. L. (1983). Assessing motor development in young children. *Studies in Educational Evaluation, 8,* 247–252.

Gallahue, D. L. (1993). *Developmental Physical Education for Today's Children* (2nd ed.). Dubuque, IA: Brown & Benchmark.

Haubenstricker, J. (1978). A critical review of selected perceptual-motor tests and scales currently used in the assessment of motor behavior. In D. M. Landers, and R. W. Christina (Eds.), *Psychology in Motor Behavior and Sport* (pp. 536–543). Champaign, IL: Human Kinetics.

Haubenstricker, J. et al. (1981, April). *The efficiency of the Bruininks-Oseretsky Test of Motor Proficiency in discriminating between normal children and those with gross motor dysfunction*. Paper presented at the Motor Development Academy at the AAHPERD Convention, Boston, MA.

Herkowitz, J. (1978). Assessing the motor development of children: Presentation and critique of tests. In M. V. Ridenour (Ed.), *Motor Development—Issues and Applications* (pp. 175–187). Princeton, NJ: Princeton.

Herkowitz, J. (1978). Instruments which assess the efficiency/maturity of children's motor pattern performance. In D. M. Landers, and R. W. Christina (Eds.), *Psychology in Motor Behavior and Sport*. Champaign, IL: Human Kinetics.

Ignico, A. (1994). *Assessment of Fundamental Motor Skills Videotapes*. Dubuque, IA: Brown & Benchmark.

Law, M., & Letts, L. (1989). A critical review of scales of activities of daily living. *The American Journal of Occupational Therapy, 43,* 522–528.

Linder, T. W. (1990). *Transdisciplinary Play-Based Assessment: A Functional Approach to Working with Young Children*. Baltimore: P. H. Brookes.

McClenaghan, B. A. (1976). *Development of an observational instrument to assess selected fundamental movement patterns of low motor functioning children*. Unpublished doctoral dissertation, Indiana University.

McClenaghan, B. A., & Gallahue, D. L. (1978). *Fundamental Movement: Observation and Assessment*. Philadelphia: W. B. Saunders.

Ohio State University Scale of Intra Gross Motor Assessment. Loundonville, OH: Mohican Publishing Co.

Paget, K. D., & Bracken, B. A. (1983). *The Psychoeducational Assessment of Preschool Children*. New York: Greene & Stratton.

Payne, V. G., & Isaacs, L. D. (1991). *Human Motor Development: A Lifespan Approach* (2nd ed.). Mountain View, CA: Mayfield.

Peabody Developmental Motor Scales. Allen, TX: DLM Teaching Resources Corp.

Riggen, K. J., Ulrich, D. A., & Ozmun, J. C. (1990). Reliability and concurrent validity of the Test of Motor Impairment-Henderson Revision. *Adapted Physical Activity Quarterly, 7,* 249–258.

Roach, E. G., & Kephart, N. C. (1966). *The Purdue Perceptual Motor Survey*. Columbus, OH: Merrill.

Seefeldt, V., & Haubenstricker, J. (1976). *Developmental sequences of fundamental motor skills*. Unpublished research, Michigan State University.

Self, P. A., & Horwitz, F. D. (1979). The behavioral assessment of the neonate: An overview. In J. D. Osofsky (Ed.), *The Handbook of Infant Development*, New York: Wiley.

Test of Motor Impairment-Henderson Revision. San Antonio, TX: The Psychological Corp.

Ulrich, D. A. (1985). *Test of Gross Motor Development*. Austin, TX: Pro-ED.

Ulrich, D. A. (1988). Children with special needs: Assessing the quality of movement competence. *Journal of Physical Education, Recreation & Dance, 59,* 43–47.

Verderber, J. M. S., & Payne, V. G. (1987). A comparison of the long and short forms of the Bruininks-Oseretsky Test of Motor Proficiency. *Adapted Physical Activity Quarterly, 4,* 51–59.

Index